CompTIA Network+: Exam N10

M000250834

OBJECTIVE		CHAPTER
1.0	**NETWORK CONCEPTS (21 PERCENT)**	
1.1	Compare the layers of the OSI and TCP/IP models: OSI model (Layer 1 – Physical, Layer 2 – Data link, Layer 3 – Network, Layer 4 – Transport, Layer 5 – Session, Layer 6 – Presentation, Layer 7 – Application); TCP/IP model (Network Interface Layer, Internet Layer, Transport Layer, Application Layer [Also described as: Link Layer, Internet Layer, Transport Layer, Application Layer])	1
1.2	Classify how applications, devices, and protocols relate to the OSI model layers: MAC address; IP address; EUI-64; Frames; Packets; Switch; Router; Multilayer switch; Hub; Encryption devices; Cable; NIC; Bridge	1, 3, 6, 7
1.3	Explain the purpose and properties of IP addressing: Classes of addresses (A, B, C and D, Public vs. Private); Classless (CIDR); IPv4 vs. IPv6 (formatting); MAC address format; Subnetting; Multicast vs. unicast vs. broadcast; APIPA	6
1.4	Explain the purpose and properties of routing and switching: EIGRP; OSPF; RIP; Link state vs. distance vector vs. hybrid; Static vs. dynamic; Routing metrics (Hop counts, MTU, bandwidth, Costs, Latency); Next hop; Spanning-Tree Protocol; VLAN (802.1q); Port mirroring; Broadcast domain vs. collision domain; IGP vs. EGP; Routing tables; Convergence (steady state)	7
1.5	Identify common TCP and UDP default ports: SMTP – 25; HTTP – 80; HTTPS – 443; FTP – 20, 21; TELNET – 23; IMAP – 143; RDP – 3389; SSH – 22; DNS – 53; DHCP – 67, 68	8
1.6	Explain the function of common networking protocols: TCP; FTP; UDP; TCP/IP suite; DHCP; TFTP; DNS; HTTPS; HTTP; ARP; SIP (VoIP); RTP (VoIP); SSH; POP3; NTP; IMAP4; Telnet; SMTP; SNMP2/3; ICMP; IGMP; TLS	4, 6, 8, 9, 12
1.7	Summarize DNS concepts and its components: DNS servers; DNS records (A, MX, AAAA, CNAME, PTR); Dynamic DNS	9
1.8	Given a scenario, implement the following network troubleshooting methodology: Identify the problem (Information gathering, Identify symptoms, Question users, Determine if anything has changed); Establish a theory of probable cause (Question the obvious); Test the theory to determine cause (Once theory is confirmed determine next steps to resolve problem; If theory is not confirmed, re-establish new theory or escalate); Establish a plan of action to resolve the problem and identify potential effects; Implement the solution or escalate as necessary; Verify full system functionality and if applicable implement preventative measures; Document findings, actions and outcomes	13
1.9	Identify virtual network components: Virtual switches; Virtual desktops; Virtual servers; Virtual PBX; Onsite vs. offsite; Network as a Service (NaaS)	12
2.0	**NETWORK INSTALLATION AND CONFIGURATION (23 PERCENT)**	
2.1	Given a scenario, install and configure routers and switches: Routing tables; NAT; PAT; VLAN (trunking); Managed vs. unmanaged; Interface configurations (Full duplex, Half duplex, Port speeds, IP addressing, MAC filtering); PoE; Traffic filtering; Diagnostics; VTP configuration; QoS; Port mirroring	7
2.2	Given a scenario, install and configure a wireless network: WAP placement; Antenna types; Interference; Frequencies; Channels; Wireless standards; SSID (enable/disable); Compatibility (802.11 a/b/g/n)	5
2.3	Explain the purpose and properties of DHCP: Static vs. dynamic IP addressing; Reservations; Scopes; Leases; Options (DNS servers, suffixes)	9
2.4	Given a scenario, troubleshoot common wireless problems: Interference; Signal strength; Configurations; Incompatibilities; Incorrect channel; Latency; Encryption type; Bounce; SSID mismatch; Incorrect switch placement	13
2.5	Given a scenario, troubleshoot common router and switch problems: Switching loop; Bad cables/improper cable types; Port configuration; VLAN assignment; Mismatched MTU/MTU black hole; Power failure; Bad/missing routes; Bad modules (SFPs, GBICs); Wrong subnet mask; Wrong gateway; Duplicate IP address; Wrong DNS	13
2.6	Given a set of requirements, plan and implement a basic SOHO network: List of requirements; Cable length; Device types/requirements; Environment limitations; Equipment limitations; Compatibility requirements	3, 4

Exam Objectives   The exam objectives listed here are current as of this book's publication date. Exam objectives are subject to change at any time without prior notice and at CompTIA's sole discretion. Please visit the CompTIA Certifications webpage for the most current listing of exam objectives: *http://certification.comptia.org/getCertified/ certifications.aspx.*

CompTIA Network+
Exam N10-005
Training Kit

Craig Zacker

Published with the authorization of Microsoft Corporation by:

O'Reilly Media, Inc.
1005 Gravenstein Highway North
Sebastopol, California 95472

ISBN: 978-0-7356-6275-9

1 2 3 4 5 6 7 8 9 QG 7 6 5 4 3 2

Printed and bound in the United States of America.

Microsoft Press books are available through booksellers and distributors worldwide. If you need support related to this book, email Microsoft Press Book Support at mspinput@microsoft.com. Please tell us what you think of this book at *http://www.microsoft.com/learning/booksurvey*.

Acquisitions and Developmental Editors: Ken Jones, Kenyon Brown
Production Editor: Holly Bauer
Editorial Production: Online Training Solutions, Inc.
Technical Reviewers: Dan Tuuri, Brian Blum
Copyeditor: Kathy Krause, Online Training Solutions, Inc.
Indexer: Angela Howard
Cover Design: Twist Creative • Seattle
Cover Composition: Karen Montgomery
Illustrator: Rebecca Demarest

Contents at a Glance

Contents

What do you think of this book? We want to hear from you!

Microsoft is interested in hearing your feedback so we can continually improve our books and learning resources for you. To participate in a brief online survey, please visit:

www.microsoft.com/learning/booksurvey/

Chapter 9   The Application Layer   369

What do you think of this book? We want to hear from you!

Microsoft is interested in hearing your feedback so we can continually improve our books and learning resources for you. To participate in a brief online survey, please visit:

www.microsoft.com/learning/booksurvey/

Introduction

This training kit is designed for information technology (IT) professionals who support or plan to support networks and who also plan to take the CompTIA Network+ exam. It is assumed that before you begin using this kit, you have a CompTIA A+ certification or the equivalent knowledge, as well as 9 to 12 months of work experience in IT networking.

The material covered in this training kit and on the Network+ exam relates to the technologies in a network that support distributed access to web content, media, operating systems, and applications. The topics in this training kit cover what you need to know for the exam as described on the Certification Exam Objectives document for the exam, which is available at:

http://certification.comptia.org/getCertified/certifications/network.aspx

By using this training kit, you will learn how to do the following:

- Use the Open Systems Interconnection (OSI) reference model to understand network processes.
- Install and maintain the various cables and other media used to build networks.
- Understand the protocols that networked computers use to communicate.
- Understand how routers and switches connect network devices to each other and to other networks.
- Connect to distant networks by using wide area network (WAN) technologies.
- Secure a network by using firewalls and other tools.
- Use network monitoring and diagnostic tools.
- Troubleshoot network problems in a systematic and logical manner.

Refer to the objective mapping page in the front of this book to see where in the book each exam objective is covered.

System Requirements

CompTIA suggests you have access to various hardware and software to help you prepare for the Network+ exam. The items include equipment, spare hardware, spare parts, tools, software, and other items you might need. You'll find a list of items at the back of the CompTIA Network+ Certification Exam Objectives: N10-005 guide, which you can download from the CompTIA website. Please visit *http://certification.comptia.org/getCertified/certifications/network.aspx* for more information.

Using the Companion CD

A companion CD is included with this training kit. The companion CD contains the following:

- **Practice tests**   You can reinforce your understanding of the topics covered in this training kit by using electronic practice tests that you customize to meet your needs. You can practice for the Network+ certification exam by using tests created from a pool of 200 realistic exam questions, which give you many practice exams to ensure that you are prepared.

- **An eBook**   An electronic version (eBook) of this book is included for when you do not want to carry the printed book with you.

> **NOTE COMPANION CONTENT FOR DIGITAL BOOK READERS**
>
> If you bought a digital-only edition of this book, you can enjoy select content from the print edition's companion CD. Visit *http://go.microsoft.com/FWLink/?Linkid=248373* to get your downloadable content.

How to Install the Practice Tests

To install the practice test software from the companion CD to your hard disk, perform the following steps:

1. Insert the companion CD into your CD drive and accept the license agreement. A CD menu appears.

> **NOTE IF THE CD MENU DOES NOT APPEAR**
>
> If the CD menu or the license agreement does not appear, AutoRun might be disabled on your computer. Refer to the Readme.txt file on the CD for alternate installation instructions.

2. Click Practice Tests and follow the instructions on the screen.

How to Use the Practice Tests

To start the practice test software, follow these steps:

1. Click Start, All Programs, and then select Microsoft Press Training Kit Exam Prep.

2. A window appears that shows all the Microsoft Press training kit exam prep suites installed on your computer.

3. Double-click the practice test you want to use.

When you start a practice test, you choose whether to take the test in Certification Mode, Study Mode, or Custom Mode:

- **Certification Mode**   Closely resembles the experience of taking a certification exam. The test has a set number of questions. It is timed, and you cannot pause and restart the timer.

- **Study Mode**   Creates an untimed test during which you can review the correct answers and the explanations after you answer each question.

- **Custom Mode**   Gives you full control over the test options so that you can customize them as you like.

In all modes, the user interface when you are taking the test is basically the same but with different options enabled or disabled depending on the mode.

When you review your answer to an individual practice test question, a "References" section is provided that lists where in the training kit you can find the information that relates to that question. After you click Test Results to score your entire practice test, you can click the Learning Plan tab to see a list of references for every objective.

How to Uninstall the Practice Tests

To uninstall the practice test software for a training kit, use the Programs And Features option in Control Panel.

Support & Feedback

The following sections provide information on errata, book support, feedback, and contact information.

Errata & Book Support

We've made every effort to ensure the accuracy of this book and its companion content. Any errors that have been reported since this book was published are listed on our Microsoft Press site at oreilly.com:

http://go.microsoft.com/FWLink/?Linkid=248372

If you find an error that is not already listed, you can report it to us through the same page.

If you need additional support, email Microsoft Press Book Support at:

mspinput@microsoft.com

Please note that product support for Microsoft software is not offered through the addresses above.

We Want to Hear from You

At Microsoft Press, your satisfaction is our top priority, and your feedback is our most valuable asset. Please tell us what you think of this book at:

http://www.microsoft.com/learning/booksurvey

The survey is short, and we read every one of your comments and ideas. Thanks in advance for your input!

Stay in Touch

Let's keep the conversation going! We are on Twitter: *http://twitter.com/MicrosoftPress*.

Preparing for the Exam

CompTIA certification exams are a great way to build your resume and let the world know about your level of expertise. Certification exams validate your on-the-job experience and product knowledge. Although there is no substitute for on-the-job experience, preparation through study and hands-on practice can help you prepare for the exam. We recommend that you augment your exam preparation plan by using a combination of available study materials and courses. For example, you might use the Training Kit and another study guide for your "at home" preparation, and take a CompTIA professional certification course for the classroom experience. Choose the combination that you think works best for you.

CHAPTER 1

Networking Basics

This chapter introduces the fundamental computer networking concepts that form the basis for all of the questions on the CompTIA Network+ examination. You might be inclined to skip around in this book during your exam preparation regimen, but you should make sure that you understand the principles in this chapter before you do so. Otherwise, you might find yourself struggling later, both in the exam room and on the job.

> **IMPORTANT**
>
> ### *Have you read page xxii?*
>
> It contains valuable information regarding the skills you need to pass the exam.

Exam objectives in this chapter:

Objective 1.1: Compare the layers of the OSI and TCP/IP models.

- OSI model:
  - Layer 1 – Physical
  - Layer 2 – Data link
  - Layer 3 – Network
  - Layer 4 – Transport
  - Layer 5 – Session
  - Layer 6 – Presentation
  - Layer 7 – Application

- TCP/IP model:
  - Network Interface Layer
  - Internet Layer
  - Transport Layer
  - Application Layer
    - (Also described as: Link Layer, Internet Layer, Transport Layer, Application Layer)

Objective 1.2: Classify how applications, devices, and protocols relate to the OSI model layers.

- MAC address
- IP address
- EUI-64
- Frames
- Packets
- Switch
- Router

- Multilayer switch
- Hub
- Encryption devices
- Cable
- NIC
- Bridge

Anyone familiar with the earlier incarnations of the CompTIA Network+ examination might notice that there are some rather profound differences between the objectives tested by the N10-004 version of 2009 and those in the N10-005 version released in late 2011. Some of these changes are representative of the latest developments in networking technology, and others demonstrate a definite change in the focus of the exam.

First, and most obvious, is the elimination of many technologies that have lapsed into obsolescence. With Ethernet now unquestionably the dominant data-link layer protocol on the desktop, older protocols such as Token Ring and Fiber Distributed Data Interface (FDDI), which were included in the 2005 edition of the objectives, are now gone. Conversely, the 802.11 wireless LAN standards that barely rated a mention in 2005 and received two objectives in 2009 now have four, making them a major part of the exam.

At the network and transport layers, TCP/IP is now ubiquitous, displacing older alternatives such as IPX/SPX, NetBEUI, and AppleTalk. This is not to say that you will never encounter any of these protocols in the field ever again, but they are now considered rare, if not actually endangered, species.

Whereas the 2005 objectives specified the need for basic knowledge of various server operating systems, the 2009 and 2011 objectives place far more concentration on specific areas of network support, such as configuration management, performance optimization, and troubleshooting methodologies. The operating system names no longer appear in the objectives at all.

The 2011 objectives also clarify the examination's emphasis on infrastructure management. New objectives single out services such as DNS and DHCP for particular concentration and deemphasize hardware and software technologies that are fading from general use.

Network Communications

What is a data network? Simply put, a data network is an array of computers and other devices connected together by a common medium that enables them to communicate with each other. That common medium can be wired, using copper or fiber optic cables; wireless, using infrared or radio signals; or connected to a service provider, such as a telephone or cable television network. A data network can be as simple as two home computers connected together, or as complex as the Internet, joining millions of computers together around the world.

Why connect computers together? The two primary reasons to create data networks are to:

- Share hardware
- Share data

In the early days of the PC, the only way to print a document was to connect a printer directly to a computer. As more and more companies adopted the PC as a business tool, it became impractical to buy a printer for every computer or to move a single printer from computer to computer as needed. By connecting computers to a network, they could share a single printer.

In the same way, networking made it possible for computers to share data. Rather than save a document file to a removable disk and walk it to another computer—a process colloquially known as the *sneakernet*—users could store files on a common server, enabling anyone to access them. As networks grew larger and more complex, so did the applications that made use of them. Today, in addition to document files and printer jobs, networks carry data in the form of email messages, webpages, video streams, and many other types.

LANs and WANs

The earliest PC networks used copper-based cables as the network medium, and many still do. A *local area network (LAN)* is a group of computers or other devices that share a common location, such as a room, a floor, or a building; and a common network medium, such as a particular type of cable. The medium interconnects the computers so that they are capable of sharing data with each other. LANs can include network connection devices, such as switches and routers, and are also characterized by their relatively high data transmission rates and their ability to function without the need for outside service providers.

A typical small LAN is shown in Figure 1-1. LANs are wholly owned by an organization and require no licensing or registration. Anyone can purchase the hardware required and assemble a LAN in his or her home or office.

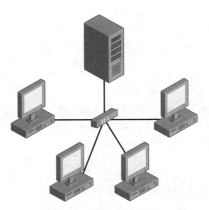

FIGURE 1-1 A typical small LAN.

Devices connected to a LAN, such as computers or printers, are generically referred to as *nodes*. A 50-node network is therefore a single network medium with 50 computers or other devices connected to it.

EXAM TIP

Virtually all of the wired LANs installed today use a technology known as Ethernet or, more precisely, IEEE 802.3. There are several other antiquated LAN technologies, including Token Ring and FDDI, that are no longer covered by the Network+ exam, and for which products are no longer available on the market, but that you might conceivably encounter in older installations.

 LANs are expandable within certain limits imposed by the protocols they use to communicate, but in large installations, it is often necessary to connect multiple LANs together. To do this, you use a device called a router, as shown in Figure 1-2. A *router* is simply a device that connects networks together, forming what is known as a "network of networks" or, more commonly, an "internetwork."

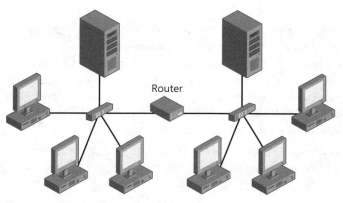

FIGURE 1-2 Two LANs connected by a router.

NOTE Internet or internet?

Do not confuse the terms "internetwork" or "internet" (with a lowercase "i") with the Internet (with a capital "I"). The term "Internet" describes a specific example of that for which "internetwork" is the generic designation. In other words, the Internet is a specific type of internetwork, but not every use of the term "internetwork" refers to the Internet.

 A *wide area network (WAN)* is a group of computers connected by a longer distance communication technology provided by a third-party service provider, such as a telephone company. Internet connections for LANs or individual computers, whether they use dial-up modems and telephone lines or broadband technologies, are all WAN links. Corporate networks also use WAN technologies to connect offices at remote sites together. Most WAN connections are point-to-point links joining two sites together; a company with multiple branch offices in different cities might have separate WAN links connecting each branch to the main office. As with LANs, WANs are connected together by routers, as shown in Figure 1-3.

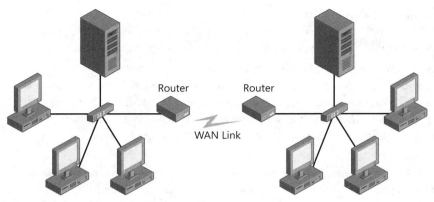

FIGURE 1-3 Two LANs connected by a WAN link.

MORE INFO   **WAN TECHNOLOGIES**

For more information on the various types of WAN technologies currently in use, see Chapter 10, "Wide Area Networking."

WAN connections can take many forms and use many different communications technologies. Subscribers, whether private individuals or large companies, can choose from among a variety of WAN providers offering connections with different speeds and services. Generally speaking, WAN connections are much slower than LAN connections and are far more expensive. Most LANs today run at 100 or 1,000 megabits per second (Mbps), and the only costs involved are for the required hardware components. WAN connections typically run at speeds of up to 4 Mbps for residential Internet connections, and up to 25 Mbps for business connections. Very few even approach the speed of a modest LAN. Subscription prices vary depending on the speed of the connection and the other services provided.

Signals and Protocols

All of the computers connected to a network communicate by exchanging signals with each other. The nature of the signals depends on the network medium. The three most common types of signals used for network communications are as follows:

- **Electrical**   Networks that use copper-based cables as a medium communicate by using electrical signals, voltages generated by the transceiver in each node.
- **Light**   Fiber optic cables carry signals in the form of pulses of light, and some wireless networks use infrared light as a signaling medium.
- **Radio**   Most wireless networks communicate by using radio signals.

In each of these cases, the signals form a simple code that enables the computers to transmit data over the network. At the signaling level, network communications are extremely simple, consisting only of positive or negative voltages, the presence or absence of light, or specific radio frequency variations. The process by which complex data structures, such as print jobs, email messages, and video streams, get reduced to simple signals is the responsibility of software components called protocols, which run on each computer.

Protocols are essentially languages that operate at various levels of the networking software on each computer or other device. Just as two people must speak the same language to be able to talk to each other, two computers on the same network must use the same protocols to communicate. Unlike human speech, however, which uses a single language, a networked computer uses multiple protocols in layers, forming a construction known as a *protocol stack*.

The signals that the computer transmits over the network medium are at the bottom of the stack, and the applications that handle the data are at the top, as shown in Figure 1-4. One of the primary functions of the protocol stack is to reduce the data generated by the applications running on the computer down to the simple signals suitable for the network medium. When the signals arrive at their destination, the protocol stack performs the same process in reverse, interpreting the incoming signals and restoring them to their original form.

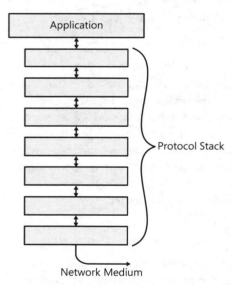

FIGURE 1-4 The protocol stack on a networked computer.

Ethernet, TCP, IP, and SMTP are all protocols operating at various layers of a typical networked computer's protocol stack. A large part of the Network+ exam is devoted to testing your knowledge and understanding of these various protocols.

Networking protocols can provide many different functions to the data structures on which they operate. The protocols protect the data as the computers transmit it over the network and see to it that the data arrives at its intended destination. Some of the most important protocol functions are described in the following list.

- **Addressing** A system for assigning a unique designation to each computer on a network and using those designations to transmit data to specific computers
- **Acknowledgment** The transmission of a return message by the receiving system to verify the receipt of data
- **Segmentation** The division of a large block of data into segments sufficiently small for transmission over the network
- **Flow control** The generation of messages by a receiving system that instruct the sending system to speed up or slow down its rate of transmission
- **Error detection** The inclusion of special codes in a data transmission that the receiving system uses to verify that the data was not damaged in transit
- **Error correction** The retransmission of data that has been corrupted or lost on the way to its destination
- **Encryption** The encoding of data with a cryptographic key to protect it during transmission over the network
- **Compression** The removal of redundant information from data blocks to minimize the amount of data transmitted over the network

Most of the networking protocols in use today are based on open standards so that different manufacturers can produce implementations that are fully compatible. Some of the organizations that are responsible for designing the networking protocol standards are as follows:

- **Institute of Electrical and Electronics Engineers (IEEE)** The US-based society responsible for the publication of the IEEE 802.3 working group, which includes the standards that define the protocol commonly known as Ethernet, as well as many others.
- **International Organization for Standardization (ISO)** A worldwide federation of standards bodies from more than 100 countries, responsible for the publication of the Open Systems Interconnection (OSI) reference model document.
- **Internet Engineering Task Force (IETF)** An ad hoc group of contributors and consultants that collaborates to develop and publish standards for Internet technologies, including the Transmission Control Protocol/Internet Protocol (TCP/IP) protocols.
- **American National Standards Institute (ANSI)** A private, nonprofit organization that administers and coordinates the United States' voluntary standardization and conformity assessment system. ANSI is the official US representative to the ISO, as well as to several other international bodies.
- **Telecommunications Industry Association/Electronic Industries Alliance (TIA/EIA)** Two organizations that have joined together to develop and publish the Commercial Building Telecommunications Wiring Standards, which define how the cables for data networks should be installed.
- **Telecommunication Standardization Sector of the International Telecommunication Union (ITU-T)** An international organization within which governments and the private sector work together to coordinate the operation of telecommunication networks and services, and to advance the development of communications technology.

Packet Switching and Circuit Switching

LANs typically use a shared network medium, meaning that all of the computers are connected to a medium that can only carry one signal, and they must take turns using it. A network that can only carry one signal at a time is called a *baseband network*.

When multiple computers have to share a single baseband network medium, they must transmit their data in the form of small, discrete units called *packets*. Otherwise, one computer might monopolize the network for long periods of time as it transmits large files. Instead of transmitting an entire file all at once, the protocols running on the computer break it down into packets and transmit them to the destination individually. This way, many computers can gain access to the network and take turns transmitting packets. If you were to imagine the network cable as a hose that has been cut with a knife, you would see packets originating from many different computers squirt out onto the floor, as shown in Figure 1-5.

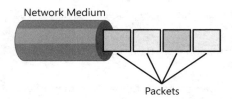
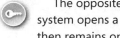

FIGURE 1-5 Packets transmitted over a baseband network.

Because computers on a baseband network have to break up their transmissions into separate packets, it is conceivable that the packets that compose a single file might take different routes to their destination, and might even arrive at the destination out of order. The destination system must therefore identify the incoming packets and reassemble them in the proper order to recreate the original data forms transmitted by the sender. This type of arrangement is known as a *packet-switching* network.

The opposite of a packet-switching network is a *circuit-switching* network, in which one system opens a circuit (or path) to another system prior to transmitting any data. The circuit then remains open for the duration of the data transaction.

Circuit-switching is not suitable for LANs, because it would monopolize the network medium for long periods. An example of circuit-switching is the Public Switched Telephone Network (PSTN) through which you receive all of your land-line telephone calls. When you pick up the ringing phone, it establishes a circuit to the caller's phone, and that circuit remains open—even when nobody is talking—until one of you hangs up the receiver.

To make circuit switching practical, some networks use an alternative to baseband communications called *broadband*. In recent years, the term "broadband" has come to refer to any high-speed Internet connection, but the actual definition of a broadband network is one that can carry multiple signals on a single network medium. Broadband networks use a technique called *multiplexing* to divide the bandwidth into separate channels, each of which can carry a different signal.

One of the most common types of broadband networks is the cable television (CATV) network connection found in many homes. The CATV service enters the home as a single cable, but if you have multiple television sets, each one can be tuned to a different channel. This means that the single cable is carrying the signals for dozens (or hundreds) of different channels simultaneously. That same cable can supply the home with other services as well, including Internet access and video on demand.

Client/Server and Peer-to-Peer Networks

The basic functions of a network typically involve one computer or other device providing some kind of service to other computers. This relationship is typically referred to as *client/server networking*. The server side of the partnership can be a computer that provides storage, access to a printer, email services, webpages, or any number of other services. The client is a computer running a program that accesses the services provided by servers.

In the early days of PC networking, these client and server roles were more clearly defined than they are today. Servers were computers dedicated exclusively to server functions; they could not function as clients.

Today, virtually all of the computers on a network are capable of functioning as both clients and servers simultaneously, and their roles are more a matter of the administrator's choice than the software running on the computer. This relationship is known as *peer-to-peer networking*. On a peer-to-peer network, for example, a computer can share its drives with the rest of the network and can also access shared drives on other computers, regardless of whether the system is running a server or a client operating system.

> **NOTE CLIENT/SERVER OPERATING SYSTEMS**
>
> One of the few successful network operating system products that operated on a strictly client/server model was Novell NetWare. All Windows, UNIX, and Linux operating systems are capable of using the peer-to-peer model.

Manufacturers of operating systems still tend to market separate server and client versions of their products, but a computer running a server operating system can still function as a client, and many home or small business networks consist solely of computers running client operating systems, which can also function as servers at the same time.

This might seem confusing, but suffice it to say that in today's computing world, the terms "client" and "server" refer not so much to machines or operating systems as they do to the roles or applications running on those machines or operating systems.

The OSI Reference Model

As mentioned earlier in this chapter, networked computers use protocols to communicate with each other, and the combination of protocols running at the same time in a network implementation is called the stack. The *Open Systems Interconnection (OSI) reference model* is a theoretical example of a network protocol stack, which networking students and administrators use to categorize and define a computer's various networking functions.

The OSI reference model consists of seven layers, which are as follows, from top to bottom:

- 7 - Application
- 6 - Presentation
- 5 - Session
- 4 - Transport
- 3 - Network
- 2 - Data-link
- 1 - Physical

> **NOTE OSI LAYER NUMBERS**
>
> The upper layers of the OSI model are seldom referenced by number. The most common use for the layer numbers is in discussions of routing and switching technologies. Switches operate primarily at Layer 2, the data-link layer, and routers at Layer 3, the network layer. However, these devices often have capabilities that span to other layers, resulting in references to technologies such as Layer 3 switching. For more information, see Chapter 7, "Routing and Switching."

The top of the model interacts with the applications running on the computer, which might at times require the services of the network. The bottom of the model connects to the network medium over which the system transmits its signals, as shown in Figure 1-6. There are different protocols operating at the various layers of the model, each of which provides functions needed to compete the network communication process.

When an application on a computer requests a network service, such as access to a file on a server or the transmission of an email message, it generates a network access request and passes it to a protocol operating at the application layer. For example, to access a file on a server, a Windows-based computer uses the Server Message Blocks (SMB) protocol; to send an email over the Internet, it uses the Simple Mail Transfer Protocol (SMTP).

After processing the request, the application layer protocol then passes the request down to the layer just below it. Each successive layer processes the request in some way, finally resulting in the conversion to appropriate signals at the bottom, or physical, layer. The network interface adapter in the computer then transmits the signals over the network medium.

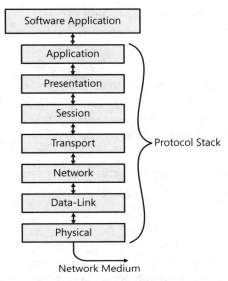

FIGURE 1-6 The seven layers of the OSI reference model.

When the signals arrive at their destination, they start at the bottom of the protocol stack and work their way up through the layers. The process is exactly the same, but reversed, as shown in Figure 1-7. Eventually, the message arrives at the corresponding application running on the destination computer.

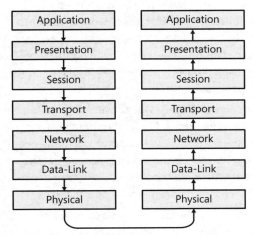

FIGURE 1-7 Protocols provide services to other protocols at adjacent layers, creating a path downward and upward through the stack.

The OSI reference model is defined in a standard document published in 1983 by the ISO called "The Basic Reference Model for Open Systems Interconnection." The same document was also published by the ITU-T as X.200. The standard divides the functions of the data networking process into the seven layers that form the protocol stack. The standard was originally intended to be the model for an actual implementation of a new protocol stack, but this never materialized. Instead, the OSI model has come to be used with the existing network protocols as a teaching and reference tool.

It is important to understand that the actual protocols running in most network implementations do not conform exactly to the architecture of the OSI reference model. For example, the protocol stack in most computers does not consist of precisely seven protocols, with one operating at each of the seven defined layers. Some of the most commonly used protocols have functions that span multiple layers, whereas other layers might require two or more protocols to fulfill their functions.

Despite this lack of an exact correlation between the OSI model and actual networks, however, the IT industry often uses OSI terminology to describe networking functions.

EXAM TIP

Remembering the names of the OSI reference model layers, in the correct order, is an important part of your exam preparation. There are many mnemonics that students use to recall the layer names, ranging from the standard "All People Seem To Need Data Processing" to the silly "Programmers Do Not Throw Sausage Pizza Away" to the obscene, which you will have to discover for yourself.

Protocol Interaction

The protocols that make up the stack on a particular computer, despite being defined by different standards bodies and possibly created by different manufacturers, work together to provide all of the networking services required by the computer's applications and operating system. From a functional perspective, the stack usually is not redundant, meaning that when a protocol at one layer provides a particular service, the protocols at the other layers do not provide the exact same service, even if they are capable of doing so.

Protocols at adjacent layers of the stack provide services for the layer above and request services from the layer below, enabling data to make its way down (or up) through the layers. For example, when there is a choice of protocols at the transport layer, the protocol at the network layer below specifies which of the transport layer protocols the data it is passing upward should use. There is always, therefore, a definitive path that data should take upward or downward through the stack, depending on the services needed to transmit or receive the data.

Protocols operating at the same layer on different computers also provide complementary functions to each other. For example, if a protocol at a particular layer is responsible for encrypting data, the equivalent protocol at the same layer on the destination system must be responsible for decrypting it. In this way, the protocols at equivalent layers can be said to provide services to each other, as shown in Figure 1-8.

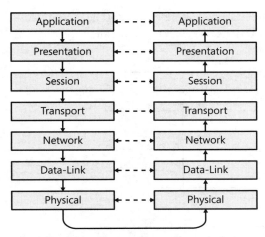

FIGURE 1-8 Protocols operating at the same layer on different computers provide complementary services to each other.

Data Encapsulation

The processing that occurs at each layer of the OSI reference model in most cases involves the application (or removal) of an additional block of data called a header to the *protocol data unit (PDU)* received from the adjacent layer. This process is called *data encapsulation*.

The process begins when an application creates a PDU containing a network access request at the application layer, as shown in Figure 1-9.

Application	Application Request
Presentation	
Session	
Transport	
Network	
Data-Link	
Physical	

FIGURE 1-9 Data encapsulation: the application layer.

The application layer protocol then passes the PDU down to the transport layer. The transport layer protocol adds a header, creating a PDU of its own with the application layer data as the payload, as shown in Figure 1-10.

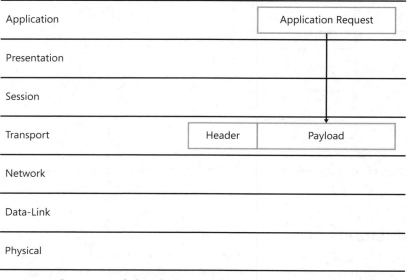

FIGURE 1-10 Data encapsulation: the transport layer.

The transport layer protocol header consists of fields containing information that implements the protocol's various functions. The application layer PDU becomes the data field of the transport layer PDU.

When the transport layer protocol passes the PDU down to the network layer, the network layer protocol adds its own header in exactly the same way, as shown in Figure 1-11. Headers vary in size, depending on the number and nature of the functions implemented by the protocol.

The process is varied slightly at the data-link layer, which adds both a header and a footer to the network layer PDU, as shown in Figure 1-12.

The packet is now complete and ready for transmission over the network. All that remains is to convert the data into signals appropriate for transmission over the network medium.

The following sections examine, in general terms, the functions that occur at each layer of the OSI reference model. For more detailed studies of the various protocols running on today's computers, see the subsequent chapters in this book, as referenced at the end of each section.

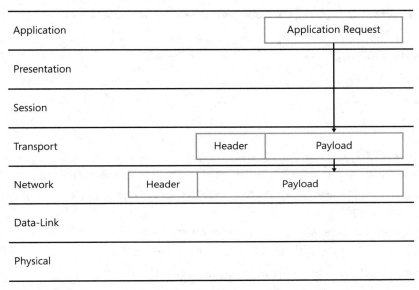

FIGURE 1-11 Data encapsulation: the network layer.

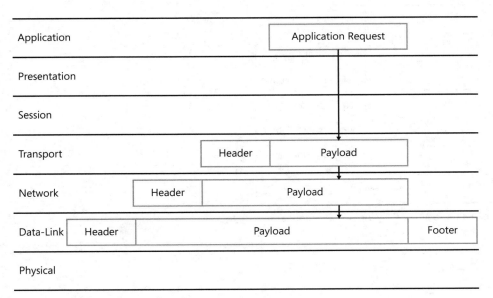

FIGURE 1-12 Data encapsulation: the data-link layer.

The Physical Layer

The physical layer, as shown in Figure 1-13, is at the bottom of the OSI reference model.

As the name implies, the physical layer is the layer that defines the hardware elements of the network, including the following:

- The network interface found in each computer or other device
- The nature of the signals used to transmit data over the network
- The characteristics of the network medium that carries the signals
- The physical topology of the network

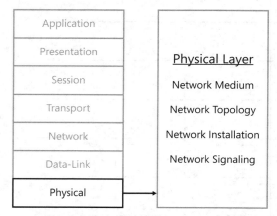

FIGURE 1-13 The physical layer of the OSI model.

Physical Layer Specifications for LANs

On a LAN, the physical layer specifications for the network are directly related to the selection of a data-link layer protocol. For example, if you elect to use Ethernet at the data-link layer, you must choose from among an assortment of physical layer specifications included in the Ethernet standards. These specifications dictate the types of cable you can use, the maximum lengths of the cables, and the number of devices you can connect to the LAN, among other things.

The data-link layer protocol standards do not necessarily contain all of the physical layer specifications needed to install a network, however. Some elements are defined in other standards.

One of the most commonly used physical layer specifications is the "Commercial Building Telecommunications Cabling Standard," published jointly by ANSI and the TIA/EIA as document 568-C. This document includes detailed specifications for installing cables for data networks in a commercial environment, including the required distances for cables from sources of electromagnetic interference and the pinouts for the cable connectors.

In most cases, organizations outsource large LAN cabling jobs to specialized cabling contractors, often the same ones responsible for wiring phone systems and other office infrastructure services. Any contractor you consider for a LAN cabling job should be very familiar with TIA/EIA 568-C and other such documents, including your local building codes.

Physical Layer Specifications for WANs

The physical and data-link specifications for LANs are closely associated because the LAN protocol is largely devoted to the sharing of the network medium among many computers. WAN links, however, are usually point-to-point connections between two—and only two—systems. As a result, WAN technologies typically use a relatively simple protocol at the data-link layer called the Point-to-Point Protocol (PPP), which does not contain any physical layer specifications. The WAN protocol can therefore have a completely independent hardware implementation at the physical layer.

Physical Layer Signaling

The final element found at the physical layer is the signaling method that systems use to transmit data over the network medium. The basic nature of the signals is, of course, determined by the network medium. Copper cables use electrical voltages, fiber optic cables use light pulses, and wireless networks can use several different radio and infrared signaling methods.

By the time data reaches the bottom of the protocol stack, it is a simple binary sequence—zeros and ones—and the signaling method is just a mechanism for encoding those binary digits. The actual signaling scheme that a network uses is not controllable by the network administrator; it is specified by the data-link layer protocol in the case of a LAN, or by the WAN technology. Therefore, although it might be interesting for a network administrator to know that Ethernet networks use a signaling scheme called Differential Manchester and how it works, it is not a subject that comes up in daily practice.

MORE INFO **LEARNING MORE ABOUT PHYSICAL LAYER PROTOCOLS**

For more detailed information about the physical layer specifications of specific types of networks, see the chapters listed in Table 1-1.

TABLE 1-1 Physical Layer Protocol Cross-References

Physical Layer Protocols	Chapter Coverage
EIA/TIA 568B	Chapter 2, "The Physical Layer"
IEEE 802.11a/b/g/n	Chapter 5, "Wireless Networking"
10Base-T / 100Base-TX / 1000Base-T, and others	Chapter 4, "The Data-Link Layer"
WAN Protocols	Chapter 10, "Wide Area Networking"

The Data-Link Layer

The data-link layer, as shown in Figure 1-14, is the second layer—or layer 2—of the OSI reference model.

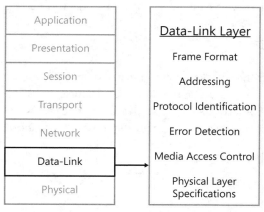

FIGURE 1-14 The data-link layer of the OSI model.

The protocol you elect to use at this layer is the primary factor that determines what networking hardware you purchase and how you install it. To implement a data-link layer protocol, you need the following hardware and software:

- **Network interface adapter**   The hardware device that provides the computer with the actual connection to the network and implements some of the data-link layer protocol functions. Network adapters can be integrated into the computer's motherboard or take the form of internal expansion cards or external USB devices.

- **Network adapter driver**   A software device driver that enables the computer to utilize the functions of the network interface adapter hardware.

- **Network cables (or other media) and other connecting hardware**

- **Network switches, hubs, or access points**

> **NOTE** **NETWORKING WITHOUT A HUB**
>
> Although it is possible to connect computers together without a switch, hub, or access point—by using a crossover cable or an ad hoc wireless network—these are in most cases temporary solutions not suitable for a permanent installation.

Most of these components are designed specifically for a certain data-link layer protocol, and more specifically, for a protocol running at a certain speed. For example, you might decide to use Ethernet at the data-link layer, but when purchasing hardware, you must be careful to distinguish between products supporting regular Ethernet, Fast Ethernet, and Gigabit Ethernet. Most of the newer products on the market are backward compatible with older, slower devices, but each branch of your network will only be as fast as its slowest link.

It is the network interface adapter in each computer, in combination with the network adapter driver, that actually implements the data-link layer protocol. Some of the data-link layer protocol functions are performed by the adapter independently, before incoming data is passed to the computer and before outgoing data leaves it. Other functions are performed by the driver after the adapter passes incoming data to the computer and before the computer passes outgoing data to the adapter. Generally speaking, higher-end—and higher-priced—adapters contain processors that perform more of the networking functions on board, rather than leaving them to the system processor.

Data-Link Layer Standards for LANs

In the case of LANs, the data-link layer protocols in most common use today are Ethernet (IEEE 802.3) and Wi-Fi (IEEE 802.11). The standards for these protocols consist of the following elements:

- A frame format
- A media access control mechanism
- Physical layer specifications

These components are discussed in the following sections.

FRAME FORMAT

Data-link layer LAN protocols use the term *frame* to refer to the protocol data unit they create by using the information they receive from the network layer. This is largely because the data-link layer protocol adds both a header and a footer to the network layer PDU.

The data-link layer frame typically performs the following functions:

- **Addressing** The header and footer that the data-link layer protocol applies functions as the outermost envelope in the figurative mailing of a packet. The header contains addresses identifying the packet's sending and receiving systems. These addresses—known as "hardware addresses" or "media access control (MAC) addresses"—are 6-byte hexadecimal strings hard-coded into the computers' network interface adapters.

IMPORTANT **PROTOCOL DATA UNITS**

The protocols operating at the different layers of the OSI reference model use different terms to refer to the PDUs they create. The terms most often found in the networking literature are listed in Table 1-2.

TABLE 1-2 PDU Terminology

OSI Model Layer	Protocol	PDU Terminology
Data-Link	Ethernet	Frame
Network	Internet Protocol	Datagram
Transport	User Datagram Protocol	Datagram
Transport	Transmission Control Protocol	Segment
Application	Various	Message

The term "packet" is generic and can refer to the PDU at any stage of the data encapsulation process.

NOTE **DATA-LINK LAYER COMMUNICATIONS**

It is important to understand that data-link layer protocols are limited to communication with systems on the same subnet. A computer might transmit a packet to a destination on another LAN, but the data-link layer protocol is only involved in local subnet communications. The hardware address in a data-link layer protocol header always refers to a system on the same subnet. This typically means that the data-link layer protocol carries the packet only as far as the nearest router. Inside the router, a network layer protocol assumes responsibility for delivering the packet to its final dsestination, as discussed later in this chapter.

- **Network layer protocol identification**   The data-link layer protocol header contains a code that specifies which network layer protocol is encapsulated within the frame. This way, when the packet works its way up the protocol stack on the receiving system, the data-link layer protocol can determine where to pass the encapsulated data.

- **Error detection**   The transmitting system performs a *cyclical redundancy check (CRC)* calculation on the data in the frame and appends the result to the packet as a footer. When the packet arrives at the destination, the receiving system performs the same calculation. If the results do not match, the receiving system assumes that a transmission error has occurred and discards the packet.

MEDIA ACCESS CONTROL

When computers are connected to a shared baseband medium, as on a typical LAN, it is possible for two systems to transmit packets at exactly the same time. This results in a *collision*, causing the corruption and loss of both packets. One of the primary functions of a data-link layer protocol on a LAN is to prevent, minimize, or handle collisions. To do this, the protocol includes a *media access control (MAC)* mechanism. The MAC mechanism provides each of the computers on the LAN with regular opportunities to transmit its data.

On modern switched Ethernet networks, the switches provide each pair of devices with a dedicated channel, eliminating the need for computers to share the network medium, and consequently reducing the need for a MAC mechanism. Media access control is also not so elaborate a function on WANs because there are only two systems involved, and they can simply take turns transmitting.

PHYSICAL LAYER SPECIFICATIONS

One of the main reasons why LAN data-link layer protocol standards include physical layer specifications is to support the protocol's MAC mechanism. If, for example, the cables are too long on an Ethernet network, the systems will be unable to detect packet collisions when they occur, and collision detection is one of the critical elements of the Ethernet MAC mechanism. Excessively long cables can also result in signal degradation and the increased likelihood of signal interference.

MORE INFO   **LEARNING MORE ABOUT DATA-LINK LAYER PROTOCOLS**

For more detailed information about the data-link layer specifications of specific types of networks, see the chapters listed in Table 1-3.

TABLE 1-3 Data-Link Layer Protocol Cross-References

Data-Link Layer Protocols	Chapter Coverage
Ethernet	Chapter 4, "The Data-Link Layer"
IEEE 802.11	Chapter 5, "Wireless Networking"
Point-to-Point Protocol (PPP)	Chapter 4, "The Data-Link Layer"

The Network Layer

The network layer, as shown in Figure 1-15, is the third layer—or layer 3—of the OSI reference model.

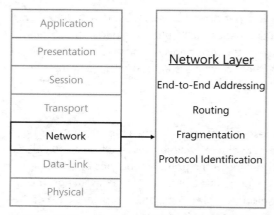

| Application |
| Presentation |
| Session |
| Transport |
| Network |
| Data-Link |
| Physical |

Network Layer

End-to-End Addressing

Routing

Fragmentation

Protocol Identification

FIGURE 1-15 The network layer of the OSI model.

Just as the data-link layer protocol is responsible for communications within a LAN or WAN, the network layer protocol is primarily responsible for end-to-end communications between a packet's source and its ultimate destination.

For example, when a workstation on a corporate network accesses a webpage on the Internet, the stack's data-link protocol is only responsible for getting the packets to the router on the local network. The network layer protocol, however, is responsible for getting the packets to the web server on the Internet, which might involve transmission through dozens of different networks. Those intermediate networks might use different data-link layer protocols, but they all use the same network layer protocols.

At one time, there were several different end-to-end protocols that systems could use at the network layer. Today, however, the TCP/IP protocol suite is nearly ubiquitous, due to its role as the backbone of the Internet, and the end-to-end network layer protocol in that suite is the *Internet Protocol (IP)*.

EXAM TIP

Obsolete protocols at the network layer include Internetwork Packet Exchange (IPX), an end-to-end protocol developed for use with Novell NetWare networks, and NetBEUI, a non-routable file and printer sharing protocol used in early versions of the Windows operating system. These protocols were formerly part of the Network+ curriculum, but the latest version of the exam covers only IP.

As noted earlier in this chapter, the network layer protocol encapsulates data it receives from the layer above by applying a header. The functions performed by the IP header are described in the following sections.

Addressing

A network layer protocol header contains a source address and a destination address—just as a data-link layer protocol header does. However, the difference between the two is that the network layer destination address identifies the final recipient of the packet, whether it is on the local network or another network thousands of miles away.

Although some of the obsolete network layer protocols used the same hardware addresses as Ethernet and other data-link layer protocols, IP has its own independent addressing system that uses 32-bit or 128-bit numerical strings. IP addresses identify both the system itself and the network on which the system is located.

> **NOTE IP VERSIONS**
>
> The IP protocol is currently in the midst of a lengthy transition from version 4 (IPv4) to version 6 (IPv6). IPv4 uses 32-bit addresses, but in IPv6, the address space is expanded to 128 bits. For more details, see Chapter 6, "The Network Layer."

Fragmentation

When a network layer protocol encapsulates the data it receives from the layer above, it creates a datagram that will remain intact as a PDU until it reaches its final destination. However, that datagram might have to pass through dozens of different data-link layer networks on its journey. These networks might have different properties, including various maximum frame sizes. When a computer has to transmit a datagram that is too large for the data-link layer network, it splits the datagram into fragments and transmits each one in a separate data-link layer frame.

Depending on the nature of the intervening networks, individual fragments might be fragmented again before they complete their journey. It is not until the fragments reach their final destination—that is, the system identified by the destination address in the network layer protocol header—that the network layer protocol reassembles them into the original datagram.

Routing

As noted earlier in this chapter, routers are the devices that connect LANs and WANs together, forming an internetwork. A router has a minimum of two network interfaces, enabling it to communicate on two networks simultaneously. Routing is the process of directing a network layer datagram from its source to its final destination, while attempting to use the most efficient possible path through the internetwork.

There are two types of systems in internetwork communications: end systems and intermediate systems. *End systems* are the sources or destinations of individual packets, that is, the systems whose addresses appear in the network layer protocol header. *Intermediate systems* are the routers that pass datagrams from one network to another.

When an end system processes a packet, all seven layers of the OSI reference model are involved. When a packet passes through an intermediate system, it enters through one network interface, travels up through the stack only as high as the network layer, and then travels down again to the other network interface and out over the second network, as shown in Figure 1-16. In this way, the routers pass the datagram from network to network until it reaches the destination network—that is, the network on which the destination system is located.

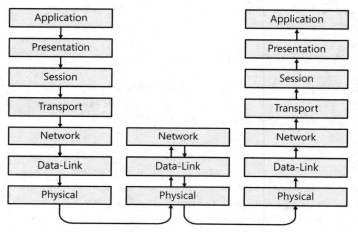

FIGURE 1-16 The network layer protocol in a router accepts incoming packets and transmits them to the next stop on their journey.

To direct packets to their destinations, routers maintain information about the networks around them in a routing table, which they store in memory. It is possible for administrators to manually create entries in a routing table, but it is more common for the systems to compile the routing information themselves by using specialized routing protocols. An intermediate system only has direct knowledge of the networks to which it is directly connected, but by using a routing protocol, it can share that information with other routers and receive information about distant networks in return.

By sharing this information, each router creates entries in its routing table. Each entry contains the address of another network, the address of an intermediate system providing access to that network, and a value called a metric that rates the comparative efficiency of that particular route. When a router receives an incoming datagram, it reads the destination address from the network layer protocol header, and checks that address against its routing table. If the router has information about the destination network, it forwards the datagram to the next router in its path.

Each journey from one router to another is referred to as a *hop*. In many cases, the efficiency of a route is measured by the number of hops—that is, intervening routers—between the source and the destination. On a corporate internetwork, the routing process is often very simple, but on the Internet, the path of a datagram from source to destination can consist of dozens of hops.

Network Layer Error Detection

Data-link layer protocols for LANs typically have an error detection mechanism, as described earlier in this chapter. However, this mechanism only provides protection from transmission errors on the LAN; it does not provide end-to-end protection for the datagram's entire journey from source to destination.

Network layer protocols might therefore have their own error detection mechanisms, but this can also be the province of the transport layer. In the case of IP, the network layer protocol does have end-to-end error protection, but only for the contents of the IP header, not for the payload carried inside the datagram.

Transport Layer Protocol Identification

The network layer protocol header contains a code that identifies the transport layer protocol encapsulated in the packet, just as the data-link layer header identifies the network layer protocol. This ensures that the datagram arriving at the network layer is passed to the appropriate protocol at the transport layer.

When IP is the network layer protocol, the protocol identification code in the header typically references either the User Datagram Protocol (UDP) or the Transmission Control Protocol (TCP).

> **MORE INFO** **LEARNING MORE ABOUT NETWORK LAYER PROTOCOLS**
>
> For more detailed information about the network layer specifications of specific types of networks, see the chapters listed in Table 1-4.
>
> **TABLE 1-4** Network Layer Protocol Cross-References
>
> | Network Layer Protocols | Chapter Coverage |
> | --- | --- |
> | Internet Protocol | Chapter 6, "The Network Layer"
 Chapter 7, "Routing and Switching" |

The Transport Layer

The protocols at the transport layer of the OSI reference model, as shown in Figure 1-17, work in conjunction with the network layer protocol to provide a unified quality of service required by the application that is making use of the network.

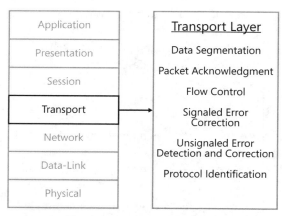

| Application |
| Presentation |
| Session |
| **Transport** |
| Network |
| Data-Link |
| Physical |

Transport Layer

Data Segmentation

Packet Acknowledgment

Flow Control

Signaled Error Correction

Unsignaled Error Detection and Correction

Protocol Identification

FIGURE 1-17 The transport layer of the OSI model.

Because they work together providing the services that the application needs, the network and transport layer protocols are nearly always created by the same team of standards-makers and are specifically designed to complement each other.

The protocol combinations at the network and transport layers are so intimately linked that the protocol suites they come from are frequently named for them. The TCP/IP suite takes its name from the combination of the *Transmission Control Protocol (TCP)*, one of its transport layer protocols, and IP, at the network layer. In the same way, the once-dominant protocol suite for the Novell NetWare operating system was called IPX/SPX, for the Inter-network Packet Exchange and Sequenced Packet Exchange protocols, at the network and transport layers, respectively.

The TCP/IP suite also provides a second protocol at the transport layer, called the *User Datagram Protocol (UDP)*. Generally speaking, the TCP protocol provides a wide range of services, at the cost of a great deal of data transmission overhead. UDP provides a minimal service, with much less overhead.

Connection-Oriented and Connectionless Protocols

There are two basic types of protocols at the transport layer—and at the network layer, for that matter—connection-oriented and connectionless. A *connection-oriented protocol* is one in which the two communicating systems establish a connection between themselves before they begin transmitting any data. The connection establishment process ensures that the two systems are operational and ready to communicate.

TCP is a connection-oriented protocol, and the procedure it uses to establish a connection with the destination system is called a three-way handshake. When the systems have finished exchanging data, they perform another handshake to terminate the connection.

TCP also provides other services to the applications that are running in the upper layers, including data segmentation, packet acknowledgment, flow control, and end-to-end error detection and correction. To implement all of these services, TCP needs a large header, and the handshakes force the systems to transmit additional packets. This is all in addition to the actual application layer data they have to transmit.

The transmission overhead for a connection-oriented protocol is therefore quite high, making it suitable only for applications that require its extensive services. In most cases, applications that use TCP are those that require bit-perfect data transmission, such as the transfer of a program file. If even one bit of a program is incorrect, it won't run properly.

Some applications do not require bit-perfect transmission, however. For example, when a system is streaming video over a network, the loss of a few bits might cause a momentary degradation of the picture quality, but it will not cause the application to fail. This type of data exchange can use a *connectionless protocol* instead, one that does not require a connection establishment process and one that provides a minimum of additional services. Because connectionless protocols do not provide additional services, their headers are smaller, and their transmission overhead is much lower than that of a connection-oriented protocol. For example, though the TCP header is typically 20 bytes, the header of the connectionless UDP protocol is only 8 bytes.

> **NOTE CONNECTIONLESS PROTOCOLS**
>
> The network layer IP protocol is also considered to be connectionless. Because nearly all data packets use IP at the network layer, it is sensible to use a connectionless protocol at that layer, and reserve the optional connection-oriented services for the transport layer.

A typical UDP transaction consists of only two messages: a request and a reply. In this type of transaction, the reply functions as a tacit acknowledgment, so there is no need for a connection establishment process or an elaborate packet acknowledgment mechanism.

Transport layer protocols can provide a variety of services to applications. In the TCP/IP suite, UDP provides minimal service, and TCP is considered to be the full-service protocol. In addition to connection orientation, TCP also provides the services described in the following sections.

Packet Segmentation

Applications generate data without considering the nature of the network at all, so one of the primary functions of the transport layer is to split the application layer data into segments of a size suitable for transmission. The protocol assigns numbers to the segments, which the receiving system uses to identify specific packets for acknowledgment, retransmission, and reassembly.

> **NOTE SEGMENTATION**
>
> Transport layer segmentation is a completely separate process from the fragmentation that occurs at the network layer. Data might end up being both segmented and fragmented during the course of its transmission to a specific destination.

Packet Acknowledgment

TCP is often referred to as a "reliable" protocol because it provides guaranteed delivery, a service that takes the form of acknowledgment messages transmitted by the receiving system back to the sender. Although there have at times been protocols that generated a separate acknowledgment message for each individual transmitted packet, TCP is able to acknowledge multiple segments with one acknowledgment, which helps to reduce the protocol's overhead.

> **NOTE   RELIABLE PROTOCOLS**
>
> In this case, "reliable" is a technical term referring to the fact that each packet transmitted by using the TCP protocol has been acknowledged by the recipient, and has been verified as having been transmitted without error. It is not an indication that other protocols—such as UDP—cannot be trusted to deliver their data.

Flow Control

Flow control is a mechanism that enables a receiving system to regulate the rate at which the sending system transmits data. If the sender transmits too many packets in a specified period of time, the buffer on the receiving system might fill up, preventing it from receiving any more packets until the buffer empties.

When this occurs, the only alternative is for the receiving system to discard some of the packets. The transmitting system will eventually have to resend the missing packets, but the error detection and correction processes reduce the efficiency of the connection.

To prevent this condition from continuing, the receiving system sends a series of flow control messages to the sender, ordering it to reduce its transmission rate. When the buffer empties, the receiver can order the sender to speed up again.

Error Detection and Correction

In TCP/IP, the transport layer protocol is the only protocol that provides complete end-to-end error detection and correction for the entire packet, including the data passed down from the application layer. The data-link layer protocol can detect errors, but it cannot correct them by retransmitting packets. Instead, the data-link layer protocol passes the error information up the stack—such messages are called signaled errors—and the transport layer protocol takes responsibility for the error correction process.

The transport layer protocol also performs its own CRC check on the entire packet. Errors that the protocol discovers itself are called unsignaled errors. The protocol corrects the errors by manipulating the packet acknowledgment messages it transmits back to the sender. When the sender does not receive an acknowledgment for each packet within a certain period of time, the retransmission process is automatic.

Application Layer Protocol Identification

To maintain the integrity of the protocol stack, the transport layer protocol must include codes in its header identifying the applications responsible for the data on the source and destination computers. These codes are called port numbers, and they identify specific protocols running at the application layer.

MORE INFO   **LEARNING MORE ABOUT TRANSPORT LAYER PROTOCOLS**

For more detailed information about transport layer protocols, see the chapters listed in Table 1-5.

TABLE 1-5 Transport Layer Protocol Cross-References

Transport Layer Protocols	Chapter Coverage
Transmission Control Protocol (TCP)	Chapter 8, "The Transport Layer"
User Datagram Protocol (UDP)	Chapter 8, "The Transport Layer"

The Session Layer

The boundary between the transport layer and the session layer, as shown in Figure 1-18, is a major division in the protocol stack.

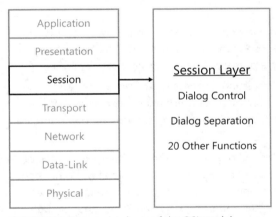

FIGURE 1-18 The session layer of the OSI model.

It is common for administrators to refer to the session, presentation, and application layers collectively as "the upper layers," because this is where the real-world protocol implementations start to bear less of a resemblance to the OSI model.

For example, it is common for an application layer protocol to provide services associated with the session and/or presentation layers, as well as the application layer. Although session layer protocols do exist, they are typically not independent entities like the protocols you find at the lower layers. Instead, they are integrated into larger networking components.

REAL WORLD **NETBIOS AND THE SESSION LAYER**

NetBIOS (network basic input/output system) provides session layer services to Windows workgroup (that is, non-Active Directory) networks. For example, the 16-character computer names assigned to all workgroup computers are actually NetBIOS names. Even computers that are connected to an Active Directory Domain Services (AD DS) network have NetBIOS equivalents to their AD DS names.

However, in the current versions of Windows, NetBIOS takes the form of an application programming interface (API), not a networking protocol. Workgroup networks use a hybrid protocol called NetBIOS Over TCP/IP (NetBT) to transmit data by using the standard TCP/IP network and transport layer protocols. Therefore, you can think of components such as NetBIOS as session layer services, but they are distinctly different from the lower layer protocols in their implementations.

The session layer is also the dividing line where computers leave behind all concerns for efficient transmission of data across the network. Protocols at the session layer and above do not provide any of the services—such as addressing, routing, and error correction—needed to get data from point A to point B. These functions are strictly relegated to the lower-layer protocols.

Because of its name, many people associate the session layer exclusively with security functions, such as the network logon process that establishes a "session" between two computers. In fact, the session layer does not have a single primary function, unlike the lower layers.

The session layer is more of a "toolbox" containing a variety of functions. The OSI model standard defines 22 services for the session layer, many of which are concerned with the ways in which networked systems exchange information. Many of these services are quite obscure to everyone except application developers.

Some of the most important session layer functions are concerned with the exchange of data by the two end systems involved in a connection. However, the session layer is not concerned with the nature of the data being exchanged, but rather with the exchange process itself, which is called a *dialog*. Maintaining an efficient dialog between connected computers is more difficult than it might appear, because requests and replies can cross each other in transit, leaving the computers in an unknown state. The session layer functions include mechanisms that help the systems maintain an efficient dialog. The most important of these services are dialog control and dialog separation.

Dialog Control

The exchange of information between two systems on the network is a dialog, and dialog control is the selection of a mode that the systems will use to exchange messages. When the dialog begins, the systems can choose one of two modes: two-way alternate (TWA) mode or two-way simultaneous (TWS) mode. In TWA mode, the two systems exchange a data token, and only the computer in possession of the token is permitted to transmit data. This eliminates problems caused by messages that cross in transit. TWS mode is more complex, because there is no token and both systems can transmit at any time, even simultaneously.

Dialog Separation

Dialog separation is the process of creating checkpoints in a data stream that enable communicating systems to synchronize their functions. The difficulty of checkpointing depends on whether the dialog is using TWA or TWS mode. Systems involved in a TWA dialog perform minor synchronizations that require only a single exchange of checkpointing messages, but systems using a TWS dialog perform a major synchronization using a major/activity token.

> **MORE INFO** **LEARNING MORE ABOUT SESSION LAYER PROTOCOLS**
>
> For more detailed information about session layer protocols, see the chapters listed in Table 1-6.

TABLE 1-6 Session Layer Protocol Cross-References

Session Layer Protocols	Chapter Coverage
Layer 2 Tunneling Protocol (L2TP)	Chapter 10, "Wide Area Networking"
Point-to-Point Tunneling Protocol (PPTP)	Chapter 10, "Wide Area Networking"

The Presentation Layer

The presentation layer, as shown in Figure 1-19, is the simplest of the seven in the OSI model.

For the most part, the presentation layer functions as a simple pass-through connecting the application layer to the session layer. For each of the 22 session layer functions defined in the OSI model standard, there is a corresponding pass-through function defined at the presentation layer. This is so that an application layer protocol can access any of the session layer services by sending a request to the presentation layer, which passes it down to the correct session layer function.

In addition to the pass-through services, the presentation layer also provides a syntax translation service that enables two computers to communicate, despite their use of different bit-encoding methods. This translation service also enables systems using compressed or encrypted data to communicate with each other.

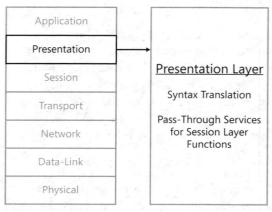

FIGURE 1-19 The presentation layer of the OSI model.

Here again, as in the session layer, the presentation layer standards do not take the form of networking protocols. For example, two of the most prominent bit-encoding methods, ASCII (American Standard Code for Information Interchange) and EBCDIC (Extended Binary Coded Decimal Interchange Code), are simply tables of binary codes equivalent to the standard US English character set.

The translation occurs in two stages. The presentation layer on the sending system translates the message from its native form, which is called an *abstract syntax*, to a *transfer syntax*, which is a common syntax agreed upon by the two connected end systems. After it receives the message, the destination system translates the message from the transfer syntax to that computer's own abstract syntax.

The Application Layer

The application layer, at the top of the protocol stack, as shown in Figure 1-20, is the entrance point that programs running on a computer use to access the network protocol stack.

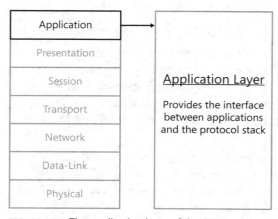

FIGURE 1-20 The application layer of the OSI model.

TABLE 1-7 Application Layer Protocol Cross-References

Application Layer Protocols	Chapter Coverage
Dynamic Host Configuration Protocol (DHCP)	Chapter 6, "The Network Layer"
Domain Name System (DNS)	Chapter 6, "The Network Layer"
File Transfer Protocol (FTP)	Chapter 9, "The Application Layer"
Hypertext Transfer Protocol (HTTP)	Chapter 9, "The Application Layer"
Internet Message Access Protocol (IMAP)	Chapter 9, "The Application Layer"
Network File System (NFS)	Chapter 9, "The Application Layer"
Network Time Protocol (NTP)	Chapter 9, "The Application Layer"
Open Shortest Path First (OSPF)	Chapter 7, "Routing and Switching"
Post Office Protocol version 3 (POP3)	Chapter 9, "The Application Layer"
Real-time Transport Protocol (RTP)	Chapter 9, "The Application Layer"
Routing Information Protocol (RIP)	Chapter 7, "Routing and Switching"
Secure Shell (SSH)	Chapter 11, "Understanding Network Security"
Session Initiation Protocol (SIP)	Chapter 9, "The Application Layer"
Simple Network Management Protocol (SNMP)	Chapter 12, "Network Management"
Simple Mail Transfer Protocol (SMTP)	Chapter 9, "The Application Layer"
Telnet	Chapter 9, "The Application Layer"
Trivial File Transfer Protocol (TFTP)	Chapter 9, "The Application Layer"

In nearly all cases, the application layer protocol is not the actual application that the user sees; it is rather an application programming interface (API) call or protocol that provides a service to the application. All of the processes operating at the other OSI model layers are triggered when a program calls for the services of an application layer protocol. For example, an email client application provides users with tools to create a message, but it does not have actual networking capabilities built into it. When the client is ready to send the email message, it calls a function of the Simple Mail Transfer Protocol (SMTP), which is the application layer protocol that most email programs use. SMTP then generates an appropriately format-ted message and starts it on its way down through the layers of the protocol stack.

Application layer protocols often include session and presentation layer functions, which is why there are few dedicated presentation or session layer protocols. As a result, a typical packet is encapsulated four times before being transmitted over the network, by protocols running at the application, transport, network, and data-link layers.

Applications and application layer protocols are integrated to varying degrees. In the case of the email client mentioned earlier, the client program is a separate application, and SMTP is implemented as part of the TCP/IP protocol suite. However, in other cases, the application layer protocol is indistinguishable from the application. For example, FTP and Telnet imple-mentations contain both user interface and application layer interface components.

The TCP/IP Model

The development of the TCP/IP protocols began years before the documents defining the OSI reference model were published, but the protocols conform to a layered model in much the same way. Instead of the seven layers used by the OSI model, the TCP/IP model—sometimes called the Department of Defense (DoD) model—has four layers, which are defined in RFC 1122, "Requirements for Internet Hosts – Communication Layers." The TCP/IP model layers, in comparison with those of the OSI model, are shown in Figure 1-21.

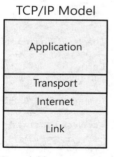

FIGURE 1-21 The four TCP/IP model layers, compared with the seven-layer OSI reference model.

EXAM TIP

The N10-005 revision of the Network+ exam objectives released in 2011 adds the TCP/IP model and specifically requires students to compare its layers with those of the OSI model. Be careful to distinguish between the two models, and familiarize yourself with the differ-ences between the corresponding layers.

The TCP/IP model layers—even those with the same names—are not exactly analogous to the OSI model layers, nor are the purposes of the models the same. The OSI model is intended to be a guide for the creation of networking protocols, whereas the TCP/IP model is a representation of protocols that already exist.

The four TCP/IP layers, from bottom to top, are discussed in the following sections.

> **NOTE THE TCP/IP MODEL**
>
> Although the functionality defined in the four layers of the TCP/IP protocol stack can encompass the OSI model from data-link to application layer, the TCP/IP protocol stack is hardware-independent by design and therefore does not include physical layer specifications.

The Link Layer

The link layer, like the data-link layer of the OSI model, defines the mechanism for moving packets between two devices on the same local subnet, referred to as a *link* in TCP/IP terminology. The TCP/IP protocol suite includes two link layer protocols: Serial Line Internet Protocol (SLIP) and Point-to-Point Protocol (PPP). SLIP is now all but obsolete in PC networking, and PPP is used for direct connections between nodes, as in most WAN technologies.

Despite being roughly analogous to the OSI data-link layer, the TCP/IP link layer does not include physical specifications of any kind, nor does it include complex LAN protocols such as Ethernet. Therefore, on many TCP/IP networks, the protocol operating at the link layer might not be part of the TCP/IP suite.

> **NOTE IETF STANDARDS**
>
> The IETF develops the TCP/IP specifications using a philosophy different from that of the other organizations responsible for networking standards, such as the ISO and the IEEE. Unlike the OSI reference model document, for example, the specification describing the TCP/IP model is informal, and deliberately omits certain aspects of the protocol stack, enabling implementers to exercise greater freedom in their designs. The omission of any specific functionality of the link is an excellent example of this philosophy.

When a TCP/IP system uses PPP at the link layer, the protocol stack assumes the presence of a network medium providing the physical connection, because PPP also does not include physical layer specifications. When the link layer functionality is provided by a non-TCP/IP protocol, as on a LAN, TCP/IP assumes the presence of both a valid network medium and a protocol that provides an interface to that medium.

Although the TCP/IP standards do not define the link layer protocol itself on a LAN, there are TCP/IP standards that define the interaction between the internet layer protocol (IP) and the protocol that provides the link layer functionality. For example, to reconcile the MAC addresses of network interface adapters with the IP addresses used at the internet layer, systems use a protocol in the TCP/IP suite called the Address Resolution Protocol (ARP). In addition, the use of Ethernet with TCP/IP is governed by the following standards:

- **RFC 826** "Ethernet Address Resolution Protocol: Or Converting Network Protocol Addresses to 48-bit Ethernet Address [sic] for Transmission on Ethernet Hardware"
- **RFC 894** "A Standard for the Transmission of IP Datagrams over Ethernet Networks"

The Internet Layer

The TCP/IP internet layer is exactly equivalent to the network layer of the OSI reference model. As in the OSI model, the Internet Protocol (IP) is the primary protocol operating at this layer. IPv4 and IPv6 provide connectionless services to the protocols operating at the transport layer above, including data encapsulation, routing, and addressing. Two additional protocols, the Internet Control Message Protocol (ICMP) and the Internet Group Management Protocol (IGMP), also operate at the internet layer, as do some specialized dynamic routing protocols.

EXAM TIP

In this context, the term "internet" is a generic reference to an internetwork and uses a lowercase "i," as opposed to the public, packet-switching Internet, with an uppercase "I." Be careful not to confuse the two.

The Transport Layer

The TCP/IP transport layer is roughly equivalent to the transport layer in the OSI model, in that it contains the same two protocols: the Transmission Control Protocol (TCP) and the User Datagram Protocol (UDP). TCP and UDP provide connection-oriented and connectionless data transfer services, respectively, to application layer protocols.

The TCP/IP transport layer can in some ways be said to encompass some of the functionality attributed to the OSI session layer as well as the transport layer in the OSI model, but not in every case. Windows systems, for example, use TCP/IP to carry the session layer NetBIOS messages they use for their file and printer sharing activities.

This is one illustration of how the layers of the TCP/IP model are roughly equivalent to those of the OSI model, but not precisely so. Administrators now use these models more as pedagogical and diagnostic tools than as guidelines for protocol development and deployment; they sometimes do not hold up to strict comparisons of the various layers' functions with the actual working protocols.

The Application Layer

The TCP/IP application layer is analogous to the application, presentation, and session layers of the OSI model. However, the TCP/IP standards do not require application layer protocols to implement the functions of all three layers. In some cases, two or three separate protocols can provide these functions, whereas other application layer protocols are monolithic in their design.

The TCP/IP protocols at the application layer take two distinct forms, as follows:

- **User protocols**   Provide services directly to users, as in the case of the File Transfer Protocol (FTP) and Telnet protocols
- **Support protocols**   Provide common system functions, as in the case of the Dynamic Host Configuration Protocol (DHCP) and Domain Name System (DNS) protocols

As in the OSI model, application layer protocols are not concerned with transport; they assume the existence of a functional transport mechanism at the layers below, without duplicating any of the lower-layer services.

 Quick Check

1. Which layer of the OSI reference model does not have a corresponding layer in the TCP/IP model?
2. What two TCP/IP protocols operate at the link layer of the TCP/IP model?

Quick Check Answer

1. The physical layer
2. SLIP and PPP

Exercise

The answers for this exercise are located in the "Answers" section at the end of this chapter.

Match the following terms to the OSI model layers with which they are most commonly associated.

1. frame
2. port
3. fragment
4. end-to-end addressing
5. segment
6. footer

7. message

8. media access control

9. flow control

10. LAN addressing

11. dialog separation

12. physical topology

13. abstract syntax

14. routing

15. packet acknowledgment

Chapter Summary

- A local area network (LAN) is a group of computers or other devices that share a common medium, such as a particular type of cable or wireless technology. A wide area network (WAN) is a group of computers connected by a longer distance communication technology provided by a third-party service provider, such as a telephone company.

- Protocols are languages that operate at various levels of the networking software on each computer. Two computers on the same network must use the same protocols to communicate.

- The combination of protocols running at the same time in a network implementation is called the network protocol stack. The Open Systems Interconnection (OSI) reference model is a theoretical example of a networking stack, which networking students and administrators use to categorize and define a computer's various networking functions.

- Protocols at adjacent layers of the networking stack provide services for the layer above and request services from the layer below, enabling data to make its way down (or up) through the layers.

- The processing that occurs at each layer of the OSI reference model in most cases involves the addition (or corresponding removal) of an extra block of data called a header. This process is called data encapsulation.

- The physical layer is the layer that defines the hardware elements of the network.

- The protocol you elect to use at the data-link layer is the primary factor that determines what networking hardware you will need to purchase and how you install it.

- The network layer protocol is primarily responsible for end-to-end communications between a packet's source and its ultimate destination.

- The protocols at the transport layer of the OSI model work in conjunction with the network layer protocol to provide a unified quality of service required by the application making use of the network.

- The application layer, at the top of the protocol stack, is the entrance point that programs running on a computer use to access the network protocol stack.

Chapter Review

Test your knowledge of the information in Chapter 1 by answering these questions. The answers to these questions, and the explanations of why each answer choice is correct or incorrect, are located in the "Answers" section at the end of this chapter.

1. Which of the following OSI model layers provides end-to-end error detection and correction for the entire packet?

    A. Data-link

    B. Network

    C. Transport

    D. Application

2. Which of the following OSI model layers includes pass-through services for the session layer functions?

    A. Data-link

    B. Application

    C. Network

    D. Presentation

3. Which of the following is an example of a circuit-switching network?

    A. A local area network running Ethernet

    B. The PSTN

    C. A wireless local area network

    D. A cable television network

4. Which of the following operating system kernels is unable to operate using the peer-to-peer model?

    A. Windows

    B. UNIX

    C. Linux

    D. Novell NetWare

Answers

This section contains the answers to the questions for the Exercise and Chapter Review in this chapter.

Exercise

1. Data-link
2. Transport
3. Network
4. Network
5. Transport
6. Data-link
7. Application
8. Data-link
9. Transport
10. Data-link
11. Session
12. Physical
13. Presentation
14. Network
15. Transport

Chapter Review

1. **Correct Answer:** C

    A. **Incorrect:** The data-link layer protocol provides error detection, but not error correction.

    B. **Incorrect:** The network layer protocol provides error correction, but only of the network layer protocol header.

    C. **Correct:** The transport layer protocol can provide end-to-end error correction for the entire packet.

    D. **Incorrect:** The application layer protocols do not provide error detection or correction.

2. **Correct Answer:** D

   A. **Incorrect:** Data-link layer protocols do not interact directly with session layer services.

   B. **Incorrect:** The application layer does not require pass-through services, because there are no layers above it.

   C. **Incorrect:** Network layer protocols do not interact directly with session layer services.

   D. **Correct:** The presentation layer includes pass-through services for the 22 functions performed by the session layer, so that application layer protocols can issue calls for session layer services.

3. **Correct Answer:** B

   A. **Incorrect:** All local area networks are packet-switching networks.

   B. **Correct:** The PSTN is a circuit-switching network because the system establishes a connection between two nodes before any user data is transmitted.

   C. **Incorrect:** All local area networks are packet-switching networks.

   D. **Incorrect:** A cable television network is an example of a packet-switching network.

4. **Correct Answer:** D

   A. **Incorrect:** Windows is capable of running in peer-to-peer mode.

   B. **Incorrect:** UNIX operating systems are capable of running in peer-to-peer mode.

   C. **Incorrect:** Linux operating systems are capable of running in peer-to-peer mode.

   D. **Correct:** Novell NetWare can only operate in client/server mode.

CHAPTER 2

The Physical Layer

The physical layer of the OSI reference model defines the characteristics of the hardware that connects the network interfaces in computers and other network devices together. In the case of a typical local area network (LAN), this hardware consists of a series of cables, as well as the connectors and other components needed to install them. This chapter describes the types of cables that data networks use, the procedures for installing and maintaining them, and the types of cabling issues that network administrators often have to address while on the job.

> **NOTE WIRELESS LANS**
>
> Wireless LANs are an increasingly popular physical layer option in homes, in offices, and in public businesses. This chapter is devoted to cabled networks. For wireless network coverage, see Chapter 5, "Wireless Networking."

Exam objectives in this chapter:

Objective 3.1: Categorize standard media types and associated properties.

- Fiber:
  - Multimode
  - Singlemode
- Copper:
  - UTP
  - STP
  - CAT3
  - CAT5
  - CAT5e
  - CAT6
  - CAT6a
  - Coaxial
  - Crossover
  - T1 Crossover
  - Straight-through
- Plenum vs. non-plenum
- Media converters:
  - Singlemode fiber to Ethernet
  - Multimode fiber to Ethernet
  - Fiber to Coaxial
  - Singlemode to multimode fiber
- Distance limitations and speed limitations
- Broadband over powerline

Objective 3.2: Categorize standard connector types based on network media.

- Fiber:
  - ST
  - SC
  - LC
  - MTRJ

- Copper:
  - RJ-45
  - RJ-11
  - BNC
  - F-connector
  - DB-9 (RS-232)
  - Patch panel
  - 110 block (T568A, T568B)

Objective 3.5: Describe different network topologies.

- MPLS
- Point to point
- Point to multipoint
- Ring
- Star

- Mesh
- Bus
- Peer-to-peer
- Client-server
- Hybrid

Objective 3.6: Given a scenario, troubleshoot common physical connectivity problems.

- Cable problems:
  - Bad connectors
  - Bad wiring
  - Open, short
  - Split cables
  - DB loss

  - TXRX reversed
  - Cable placement
  - EMI/Interference
  - Distance
  - Cross-talk

Objective 3.8: Identify components of wiring distribution.

- IDF
- MDF
- Demarc

- Demarc extension
- Smart jack
- CSU/DSU

Objective 4.2: Given a scenario, use appropriate hardware tools to troubleshoot connectivity issues.

- Cable tester
- Cable certifier
- Crimper
- Butt set
- Toner probe
- Punch down tool

- Protocol analyzer
- Loop back plug
- TDR
- OTDR
- Multimeter
- Environmental monitor

For home networks, small businesses, or installations in which portability is more important than invisibility, the first option is inexpensive and easy to install without special tools or
skills. For large networks, those involving many rooms or floors, or those requiring a nearly
invisible installation, the bulk cable method is preferable.

Installing bulk cable is a specialized skill that network administrators typically outsource
to a wiring contractor who has the appropriate tools and experience, often the same one
who handles the office's telephone wiring. Depending on the local building and fire codes,
a licensed electrician and official inspection might be required. It is relatively rare for the
average network administrator to perform large cable installations, but he or she might be
expected to troubleshoot cabling problems and use basic cable testing tools as part of the
troubleshooting process.

Cables and Connectors

As noted in Chapter 1, "Networking Basics," a data network must have a network medium
that connects the computers and other devices together. Until relatively recently, that network medium was a cable of some sort. Most of the cables used throughout the history of
data networks have been copper-based. One or more strands of electrically conductive copper are encased within a non-conductive sheath. The computers transmit signals by applying
electric voltages to the copper conductors in a pattern that the receiving systems interpret as
binary data.

Although copper cables are relatively efficient transmitters of signals, they are prone to a
few shortcomings that have occasionally made them troublesome in certain network situations.
The first problem is that signals transmitted over copper cables are prone to *attenuation*; that
is, the gradual weakening of the signal over distance. The longer the cable is, the weaker the
signal gets, until it eventually becomes unviable. There are, therefore, always length limitations
to copper-based network segments.

Signals traveling over copper cables are also prone to disruption by noise and *electromagnetic interference (EMI)*, such as that caused by other electrical equipment. When installing
copper cables, contractors must be careful to avoid sources of EMI.

To avoid these problems, it is also possible to build a network by using another type of cable, called fiber optic cable. A *fiber optic* cable consists of a glass or plastic core surrounded by a reflective sheath. The signals on a fiber optic network are not electrical; they are beams of light generated by a laser. Fiber optic networks are much less affected by attenuation than copper networks, so they can span much greater distances. Fiber optic networks are often utilized in connecting LANs or remote networks. They are also completely resistant to EMI, making them a viable medium in environments where copper networks cannot function.

Fiber optic is—and has always been—a marginal networking technology for LAN installations, due its much greater cost when compared to copper, and the special skills and tools required to install and maintain it. Copper-based LAN cable installations have always vastly outnumbered fiber optic ones, not least because the copper cables used today are similar to those used for telephone systems.

However, fiber optic is the dominant cable technology for wide area network (WAN) infrastructures, such as those used to connect LANs together and deliver broadband services to residential and business customers. It is estimated by the Telecommunications Industry Association that the amount of installed fiber optic cable has more than doubled in the last seven years.

EXAM TIP

The average Network+ exam candidate has probably seen and worked with twisted pair cabling, but might not have experience with fiber optic cable. Be sure not to neglect this critical part of the exam objectives.

Copper Cable Types

For the most part, the history of copper-based data networks mirrors the history of the Ethernet LAN protocol. As Ethernet has evolved in the nearly four decades of its existence, it has increased in speed and changed the types of copper cables defined in its physical layer specifications. The following sections describe the various types of copper cables that Ethernet has supported over the years.

Twisted Pair Cable

A twisted pair cable is a cluster of thin copper wires, with each wire having its own sheath of insulation. Individual pairs of insulated wires are twisted together, usually gathered in groups of four pairs, for a total of eight wires, and encased in another insulating sheath, as shown in Figure 2-1. The individual wire pairs in the sheath are twisted at differing rates of twists per foot, which is crucial to making the wires in the same cable resistant to *crosstalk*—that is, the bleeding of signals from one wire pair to another in the same cable.

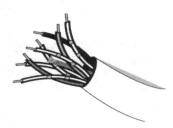

FIGURE 2-1 A twisted pair cable.

There are many different types of twisted pair cables, designed to accommodate various environmental, legal, and performance requirements. In addition to the conductive wires, some types of twisted pair cable have an extra piece of fabric or other material to help strengthen the cable and to aid in removing the outer cover. These cable types are described in the following sections.

UNSHIELDED TWISTED PAIR

Unshielded twisted pair (UTP) cable is the standard medium for copper-based Ethernet LANs these days. A typical UTP cable contains four wire pairs within a sheath approximately 0.21 to 0.24 inches in outside diameter. UTP grew to replace coaxial cable for Ethernet networks for two main reasons: first, the eight separate wires in a UTP cable make it much more flexible and easy to install within walls and ceilings. Second, voice telephone systems also tend to use UTP, which means that the same contractors who install telephone cables can often install data networking cables as well.

> **NOTE UNUSED WIRE PAIRS**
>
> Most UTP cables for Ethernet networks have four pairs (eight wires) in a single sheath, but in some cases, the network nodes use only two of the four pairs for actual communication. Despite the fact that the other two pairs are left unused, the standard does not permit the use of them for other traffic, such as voice telephone communications. Leaving these additional wire pairs unused can also provide an avenue for a future upgrade to a four-pair technology.

Voice telephone networks do not have performance requirements as strict as those for data networks, so they are less liable to suffer from crosstalk and other types of interference. As a result, installers often use larger UTP cables for telephone connections. UTP cables are available in configurations containing 25 wire pairs and 100 wire pairs in a single sheath, which enables installers to service multiple users with a single cable. Telephone company cable installers also have their own specialized tools, such as the ubiquitous *butt set*, a one-piece telephone with alligator clips that enables its operator to connect to a line anywhere that the cables are accessible.

SHIELDED TWISTED PAIR

For environments with greater levels of EMI, there are also various types of *shielded twisted pair (STP)* cables. Some STP variants have metal shielding around each pair of wires, which provides greater protection against crosstalk. Some STP cables have shielding inside the sheath surrounding all of the pairs. This type of shielding is called screening and protects against outside EMI sources. Some cable types have both shielding and screening.

Some now-obsolete data-link layer protocols, such as Token Ring, had physical layer specifications that called for STP cables. Today, however, Ethernet networks only use them in special situations that require additional protection from EMI.

STRANDED VS. SOLID CONDUCTORS

As mentioned earlier, copper-based cables are subject to attenuation, and one of the factors affecting that subjectivity is the composition of the copper conductors within the individual wires. A twisted pair cable that has stranded conductors uses seven separate copper filaments within each of its eight wires. These separate filaments make the cable more flexible, and therefore easier to install and move without damage, but they also make it more expensive and more subject to attenuation, limiting its maximum length.

For cable segments 50 feet or longer, it is more common to see UTP cables with solid conductors; that is, with a single, thicker copper filament within each wire. The solid conductors make the cables stiffer, more prone to breakage, and more difficult to install, but they are also more resistant to attenuation.

PLENUM VS. NON-PLENUM

A *plenum* is an enclosed air space within a building, a passage through which HVAC equipment circulates breathable air, such as the space above a dropped ceiling or below a raised floor. When cables are to be installed in an existing building, using the plenums is often the most expedient way to run a cable from one location to another. The only problem with this is that in the event of a fire, the polyvinyl chloride (PVC) outer sheath of many cables can outgas toxic vapors when it burns. Releasing these vapors into an air space can obviously be hazardous to the people in the building. A plenum-grade cable is a cable with a sheath that produces less toxic smoke when it burns. Plenum-grade cables are typically much more expensive than non-plenum cables, but building codes in many cities require them when you install data network cable in air spaces.

ENVIRONMENTAL COMPENSATION

Some manufacturers create UTP cables with special qualities that are designed to enable their
use in special environments. For example, cables with UV-rated sheaths can survive exposure
to direct sunlight without degradation.

A UTP cable also has an air space inside the sheath, where condensation can gather when
the cable runs between indoor and outdoor environments or is buried directly in the ground.
In these environments, installers might want to seal the ends of the cable or fill them with gel
to eliminate the air space.

UTP CATEGORIES

UTP cable comes in a variety of different grades, called *categories* in the cabling standards
published by the Telecommunications Industry Association/Electronic Industries Alliance
(TIA/EIA). The categories define the signal frequencies that the various cable types support,
along with other characteristics, such as resistance to certain types of interference. The higher
the category number, the higher the cable quality and, not surprisingly, the price. The cable
categories that administrators are likely to encounter are as follows:

- **Category 3 (CAT3)**   Long the standard for telephone communications, CAT3 cables
  were used by the first UTP-based Ethernet networks (called 10Base-T). CAT3 cables
  supported frequencies up to 16 megahertz (MHz). Insufficient for any of the faster
  Ethernet types, CAT3 is no longer supported for new installations.

- **Category 5 (CAT5)**   Designed for 100Base-TX Fast Ethernet networks and supporting
  frequencies up to 100 MHz, CAT5 cabling was dropped from the latest version of the
  TIA/EIA cabling standards.

- **Category 5e (CAT5e)**   Still rated for frequencies up to 100 MHz, CAT5e cable is de-
  signed to support full duplex transmissions over all four wire pairs, as on 1000Base-T
  Gigabit Ethernet networks. The standard calls for increased resistance to Near-End
  Crosstalk (NEXT) and Return Loss (RL) and also adds testing requirements for Power
  Sum Near-End Crosstalk (PS-NEXT), Equal-Level Far-End Crosstalk (EL-FEXT), and
  Power Sum Equal-Level Far-End Crosstalk (PS-ELFEXT).

- **Category 6 (CAT6)**   Designed to support frequencies of up to 250 MHz, CAT6 cables easily handle 1000Base-T Gigabit Ethernet traffic and, with special installation considerations, 10Gbase-T.

- **Augmented Category 6 (CAT6a)**   Created for 10Gbase-T installations with cable segments up to 100 meters long, CAT6a supports frequencies up to 500 MHz and includes an Alien Crosstalk (AXT) testing requirement. CAT6a cables use larger conductors and leave more space between the wire pairs, meaning that the outside diameter of the sheath is larger than a CAT6 cable, about 0.29 to 0.35 inches. CAT6a was added to the most recent version of the TIA/EIA standards in 2008.

- **Category 7 (CAT7)**   Not officially ratified by the TIA/EIA, the CAT7 standard calls for a fully shielded and screened cable design, supporting frequencies up to 600 MHz. At the current time, this cable is recommended for high-bandwidth applications such as broadband video, environments with high levels of EMI, or as a lower-cost substitute for fiber optic segments.

- **Category 7a (CAT7a)**   CAT7a, also not ratified by the TIA/EIA, is a fully shielded and screened cable that extends the frequency range to 1000 MHz. With full support for 10Gbase-T, CAT7a is expected to have a lifespan of 15 years or more, including the next iteration of Ethernet, running at 40 gigabytes (GB) per second.

Although CAT3 and CAT5 cables have been dropped from the official standards, this does not mean that administrators no longer encounter them. There are many CAT5 installations still in operation, and CAT5 cables are still available to maintain them.

IMPORTANT   **CABLE STANDARDS**

If you are working in a CAT5 environment and you have no plans to install a higher grade of cable in the near future, it makes little sense to pay extra money for CAT5e or CAT6 patch cables. Like a chain, a network is only as strong as its weakest link, so CAT5 products are likely to remain available for a while.

EXAM TIP

CAT3 cable is still included in the Network+ objectives, but in today's networks it is decidedly less prevalent in the installed base because most CAT3 networks have long since been upgraded to at least Fast Ethernet (at 100 megabits per second), which requires a minimum of CAT5 cable.

At the time of this writing, the data networking cable marketplace is in a period of transition from CAT5e to CAT6 as the dominant cable type. Sales of CAT5 cable still dominate the market, but forward-thinking network designers and administrators who consider 10Gbase-T part of their future, or who run high-bandwidth applications such as streaming video, would be well advised to consider installing CAT6 or higher.

TWISTED PAIR CONNECTORS

Twisted pair cables use modular connectors that are most commonly referred to by the telephone networking designation *RJ45*, but which should properly be called *8P8C*. Network interface adapters, wall plates, patch panels, and other networking components, such as switches and hubs, all have female connectors. The patch cables used to connect everything together have male connectors, as shown in Figure 2-2.

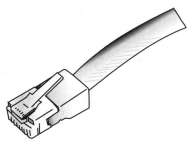

FIGURE 2-2 A UTP patch cable with an 8P8C (often incorrectly referred to as RJ45) connector.

Although designed for telephones, the RJ45 connector was actually seldom used for that purpose. The smaller, four-pin *RJ11* connector became the standard for telephone connections, and remains so to this day. When UTP came into use for data networks, the connectors were so similar in appearance to the RJ45 telephone company connector that network administrators adopted the designation for their own use.

> *NOTE* **CATEGORIZING CONNECTORS**
>
> Connectors for UTP cables are categorized, just as the cables are. When purchasing components for a modular cable installation, be sure that you select connectors of the same category rating as your cable. A cable installation must be rated according to its lowest-rated component. You might use all CAT6 cable for your network, but if you use CAT5 connectors, it is a CAT5 installation.

The actual name for the UTP connector that Ethernet networks use is *8P8C*, indicating that there are eight positions in the connector and eight electrical contacts in place in those positions. The RJ45 for telephone use is also known as an 8P2C, because though it has the same eight positions, there are only two conductors connected.

EXAM TIP

Although a network administrator might be technically correct in referring to an Ethernet cable as having 8P8C connectors, few (if any) other people will know what he or she is talking about. RJ45 is the colloquial term that the Network+ exam and much of the networking literature (as well as the rest of this book) uses to refer to this connector.

Coxial Cable

Prior to the introduction of UTP cables, Ethernet networks called for *coaxial cable* of various types. A coaxial cable consists of a central copper conductor—which carries the signals—surrounded by a layer of insulation. Surrounding the insulation is a shielding, typically made of copper mesh—which functions as a ground—and the whole assembly is encased in a sheath, as shown in Figure 2-3. The mesh shielding in coaxial cables makes them quite resistant to EMI.

FIGURE 2-3 A coaxial cable.

ETHERNET OVER COAXIAL CABLE

All of the coaxial cable types have been removed from the TIA/EIA network cabling standards, and you are unlikely to encounter any coaxial Ethernet networks in the field, but they are an important part of the history of data networking.

The physical layer specifications for the first Ethernet networks—referred to as thick Ethernet, thicknet, or 10Base5—called for a type of coaxial cable similar to RG-8, but with extra braided shielding. RG-8 is a 50-ohm cable, 0.405 inches in diameter. The large conductors, thick insulation, and frequently yellow sheath make the cable relatively inflexible, resulting in the nickname "frozen yellow garden hose."

> **NOTE COAXIAL CORES**
>
> Coaxial cable designations appended with a /U suffix indicate that the cable has a solid core. Designations with an A/U suffix indicate that the core is stranded.

Thick Ethernet cable was so inflexible that it had to be installed in a relatively straight run, usually along the floor. To connect it to computers and other devices, installers used thinner drop cables that connected to the coaxial by using external transceivers with metal teeth that pierced the insulation and made contact with the conductors. These connectors were called

vampire taps. The other end of the transceiver cables had AUI connectors that plugged into an external transceiver or a network interface adapter.

Later iterations of Ethernet—called thin Ethernet, thinnet, or 10Base2—required RG-58 coaxial cable, still 50-ohm but much thinner than RG-8 (0.195 inches in diameter) and relatively flexible. This type of coaxial cable could run all the way to the individual computers, using a T configuration with three *BNC connectors*, as shown in Figure 2-4.

The Network+ objectives do not include a spellout for the acronym BNC, so you do not have to be concerned about remembering the correct one. Various sources cite several different meanings, including "British Naval Connector" and "Bayonet Nut Connector." In fact, the Bayonet Neill-Concelman connector was invented by and named after two engineers, Paul Neill and Carl Concelman—neither of whom was British—who developed the connector in the late 1940s.

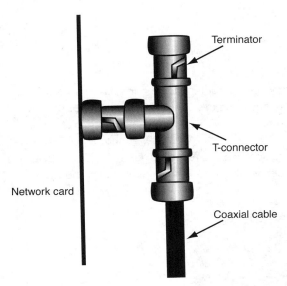

FIGURE 2-4 A coaxial cable with BNC connectors.

CABLE TV OVER COAXIAL CABLE

Although coaxial cable is no longer used for Ethernet networks, it still has applications in the networking industry. Perhaps the application most familiar to people is cable television (CATV) networking. CATV networks often use fiber optic cables for the trunk lines, but in most cases, the service enters the subscribers' homes by using 75-ohm coaxial cable.

Early CATV networks used *RG-59* coaxial, a cable with relatively light shielding that was sufficient for short runs. Today, this cable's primary use is for closed-circuit television. With digital cable and Internet access nearly ubiquitous on cable systems, CATV providers switched to *RG-6* coaxial, which has more shielding and is therefore slightly larger in diameter (0.27 inches versus 0.242 inches for RG-59).

 LANs that use a CATV provider for Internet access have a modem to which you connect the incoming RG-6 cable, using a screw-on *F connector*, as shown in Figure 2-5. The modem also usually has RJ45 and USB connectors, which you use to attach it to a router or a computer.

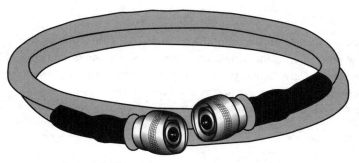

FIGURE 2-5 A coaxial cable with F connectors.

Serial Cable

Although they are not even present on many new computers, serial ports have also provided an avenue for connecting a system to a network in the past. The original design for the IBM PC called for the inclusion of one or more serial ports with a 9-pin male D-subminiature connector (also known as a DE9, although incorrectly referred to as a DB9), as shown in Figure 2-6. The serial connection is based on the Electronic Industries Alliance's (EIA's) RS-232 standard, which predates the PC by many years and defines the functions of the nine pins and the speed of the interface.

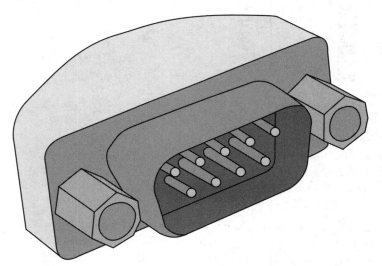

FIGURE 2-6 The 9-pin D-subminiature connector of a computer's serial port.

The most common use for the serial port has traditionally been to connect a computer to an external modem, enabling it to establish a connection to another modem at a remote location. The modem cable was a short, copper-based cable with D-shell connectors at both ends. You could also use the serial port to connect a printer, the advantage over the traditional parallel port being that the cable could be longer.

Although the practice was extremely rare, it is also possible to network computers together by using serial port connections. The RS-232 interface is extremely slow by any standard—only 56,000 bits per second—and supports only point-to-point connections, but some custom applications have used serial port connections to build ad hoc client/server networks.

Fiber Optic Cable

Fiber optic cable is a form of network medium that is completely different from copper and that avoids nearly all of copper's shortcomings. However, it does have a few shortcomings of its own.

Instead of transmitting electrical voltages over copper conductors, fiber optic cables transmit pulses of light through a filament of plastic or glass. The core filament is surrounded by a reflective layer called the *cladding*. The cladding is surrounded by a protective layer of woven fibers, a plastic spacer, and an outer sheath, as shown in Figure 2-7.

FIGURE 2-7 Fiber optic cables.

It is the reflective nature of the cladding that enables the light pulses to travel through the filament, even when the cable bends around corners. The light impulses bounce back and forth off of the reflective cladding walls as they move forward through the cable.

Unlike electrical voltages, light pulses are completely unaffected by EMI, which means that you can install fiber optic cables near light fixtures, heavy machinery, or other environments in which copper would be problematic. Fiber optic cable is also much less prone to attenuation than any copper cable.

Most of the twisted pair media used for networking today are limited to cable segments no longer than 100 meters. Older copper media, such as thick Ethernet, could span distances as long as 500 meters. Fiber optic cables can span distances as long as 120 kilometers and are also immune to outdoor conditions, which makes them ideal for installations that span long distances or connect campus buildings together.

Fiber optic cables are also inherently more secure than copper, because it is extremely difficult to tap into the cable and intercept the signals it carries without disturbing them.

Fiber optic cables have been available as an alternative to copper for decades. Even the early 10-Mbps Ethernet standards included a fiber optic specification. However, for local area networking, fiber optic has never been more than a marginal solution, used only in situations where copper cables were untenable. The primary reasons for this are that fiber optic cables are much more expensive than copper, and that their installation is much more difficult, requiring a completely different skill set (and tool set).

Fiber Optic Cable Types

There are two primary types of fiber optic cable: singlemode and multimode, which differ in size and in the means used to generate the light pulses they carry. Fiber optic cable sizes are measured in microns (millionths of a meter, represented by the symbol μm) and consist of two numbers that refer to the diameter of the core filament followed by the diameter of the cladding surrounding it. The characteristics of the two main fiber optic cable types used in data networking are shown in Table 2-1.

TABLE 2-1 Fiber Optic Cable Characteristics

Cable Type	Core/Cladding Diameter	Light Source
Singlemode	8.3/125 μm	Laser
Multimode	62.5/125 μm	Light emitting diode (LED)

Fiber optic cables do not require a ground, as copper cables carrying electrical signals do, so there is no need for a second, ground conductor for each signal-carrying conductor, as with copper cables. However, nearly all networking technologies with fiber optic specifications at the physical layer call for the cables to be installed in pairs, with one filament dedicated to sending data and one to receiving it. Some manufacturers make dual fiber optic cables, with two complete cable assemblies joined side by side, like a large lamp cord, but most cables are single and require the installer to use two separate lengths for each run.

Multimode fiber optic is more common than singlemode, largely because the cable is less expensive and has a smaller bend radius, which means that you can bend it more sharply around corners. Multimode fiber typically uses an LED light source with an 850 or 1,300 nanometer (nm) wavelength.

Singlemode cables use a laser light source at a wavelength of 1,310 or 1,550 nm. Because of its expense and relative inflexibility, administrators rarely choose singlemode fiber for LANs, preferring it for long, straight runs instead.

EXAM TIP

The primary advantages of fiber optic cable over copper-based twisted pair are its resistance to electromagnetic interference and its ability to span longer distances.

Fiber Optic Connectors

Unlike twisted pair and coaxial cables, which give you no choice, fiber optic cables offer a large number of different connectors. The type of connector you elect to use is a matter of compatibility with your existing equipment and personal preference. All fiber optic connectors perform basically the same function, to precisely join two ends of core filament together, face to face, so that light pulses can pass from one cable segment to another. Most are spring loaded so that the faces of the cores are pressed together under pressure.

There are literally dozens of fiber optic connectors on the market, the most common of which are identified in Table 2-2.

TABLE 2-2 Fiber Optic Connectors

Connector Type	Image
ST (Straight Tip)	
SC (Subscriber Connector)	
LC (Local Connector or Lucent Connector)	
MT-RJ (Mechanical Transfer – Registered Jack)	

EXAM TIP

Although ST and SC connectors are still common, connectors with smaller form factors, such as the LC and MT-RJ connectors, are increasingly popular because they allow administrators to fit more connections into the same space in data centers.

Power Line Networking

The technology for transmitting data over power lines has existed for many years. As a low-bandwidth home networking alternative, a power line technology called HomePlug eliminates the need for dedicated network cabling by running data signals through residential power lines. HomePlug networks typically run at slower speeds than wired Ethernet networks, however, and the increased popularity of wireless LANs has reduced their market share.

 Broadband over power lines (BPL) is a similar technology on a larger scale that is designed to supply homes with Internet access by using the public electric power grid, rather than a dedicated data network, like those of cable television and telephone providers. Although the principle is the same as the home networking products, BPL uses different frequencies to achieve higher communication speeds over longer distances.

The advantages of BPL in principle are obvious: the vast existing power grid infrastructure eliminates the need for the construction of new networks, particularly to remote locations. However, the physical characteristics of the electrical network are highly various, with some areas using cables that are nearly a century old. These variations make it very difficult to establish a standard for power line communication that would accommodate every instance.

In addition, transmitting broadband data over power lines generates a great deal of electromagnetic interference that compromises radio reception. A few pilot programs designed to provide citywide subscribers with broadband access have not been economically successful.

As an incentive to cable and DSL providers to provide service to remote locations, BPL might have had value, but as a practical alternative to traditional broadband technologies, it is essentially a failure as a concept.

Media Converters

Ethernet supports several physical layer specifications that call for different media, but the other basic elements of the protocol—the frame format and the media access control (MAC) mechanism—remain the same, no matter what medium they use. As a result, you can use a physical layer device called a media converter to connect Ethernet networks that use different media together.

 Like a repeater, a *media converter* is simply a box with two network connectors in it, the only difference being that the connectors are for two different network media. The most common configuration for an Ethernet media converter is one port for UTP cable and one for fiber optic. Thus, if you have a UTP network covering most of your systems, but there are still a few that require the extra-long segment length or EMI resistance that fiber optic provides, you can build a fiber optic network for those computers and connect it to your UTP network by using a media converter.

There are media converters available to connect a UTP segment to either a singlemode or multimode fiber optic cable. For cases where a network uses relatively short multimode segments, and a need for a longer length arises, there are singlemode to multimode media converters as well. Finally, for legacy networks, there are converters that can connect a coaxial cable segment to a fiber optic one.

Quick Check

1. Which of the cable types described in this section provides complete resistance to electromagnetic interference?
2. What is the term used to describe an air-handling duct through which network cables are often strung?

Quick Check Answers

1. Fiber optic
2. Plenum

Topologies and Tools

The physical layer of the OSI reference model defines not only the types of cables you can use for a data network, but how to install and configure them so that the network functions properly. This section examines the various ways you can design the cable infrastructure for your network, the standards that define how to install the cables, and the tools that installers and administrators frequently use.

Cable Topologies

Selecting the correct cable type is certainly an important factor in the network deployment process, but after you have the cables, it's not as though you can simply start connecting computers together with no thought to a pattern. The physical topology of a network is the pattern you use to connect the computers and other devices together.

When deploying a LAN, the topology you use is directly related to the type of cable you select. Each physical layer specification for data-link layer LAN protocol has installation requirements that you must observe if the network is to function properly, and the topology is one of those requirements.

A WAN solution for a large network with offices at multiple distant sites can use any one of several topologies, depending on the organization's communication requirements and of course its budget. The following sections describe the topologies most commonly used for LANs and WANs.

The Star Topology

The most common LAN topology in use today is the *star topology*, in which each computer or other device is connected by a separate cable run to a central cabling nexus, which can be either a switch or a hub, as shown in Figure 2-8. Compared to the other LAN topologies, the star affords a good deal of fault tolerance. The failure of a cable affects only the connection of one node to the network. The switch or hub does provide a central point of failure, however, which can bring down the entire network, but failure of these devices is comparatively rare.

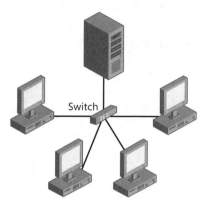

Switch

FIGURE 2-8 A local area network using a star topology.

All of the UTP-based Ethernet networks in use today call for the star topology, as do many fiber optic–based LAN protocols. In addition, many of the obsolete LAN protocols that called for ring topologies in theory actually used a physical star; the ring was implemented logically, inside a specially designed hub.

The hub or switch at the center of a star network provides a shared medium, just like a bus or ring topology does. When a computer transmits a broadcast message, the hub or switch receiving it over one port propagates the message out through all of its other ports to all of the other nodes on the network.

> **NOTE** **COMPARING HUBS WITH SWITCHES**
>
> Hubs and switches process broadcast messages in the same way. The difference between a hub and a switch is in how it processes unicast messages. A hub is a physical layer device that simply forwards all incoming data—broadcasts and unicasts—out through all of its other ports. A switch, in contrast, is a data-link layer device that reads the destination addresses of incoming unicasts and forwards them out only through the one port to which the destination node is connected, if the destination's port is known to it. For more information on hubs and switches, see Chapter 3, "Network Devices."

A basic star network can be as large as the number of ports available in the switch or hub. When a switch or hub is fully populated, it is possible to expand the network further by adding another switch or hub and connecting it to the first. This creates what is known as a *hierarchical star topology* (or sometimes a *branching tree topology*), as shown in Figure 2-9. You can continue to expand the network in this way, within certain limits specified in the Ethernet standards.

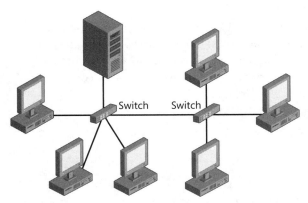

FIGURE 2-9 A local area network using a hierarchical star topology.

NOTE **ETHERNET STANDARDS**

For more information on Ethernet specifications, see Chapter 4, "The Data-Link Layer."

The Bus Topology

 A *bus topology* is one in which each computer is connected to the next one in a straight line. The first two Ethernet standards called for coaxial cable in a bus topology. The first, thick Ethernet, used a single length of cable up to 500 meters long, with individual transceiver cables connecting the computers to the main trunk. Thin Ethernet used the smaller RG-58 cable in lengths, attaching the T connectors on the computers' network interface adapters, forming a bus up to 200 meters long, as shown in Figure 2-10.

Thick Ethernet

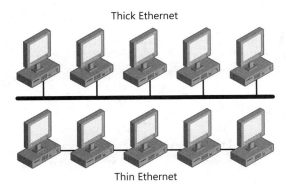

Thin Ethernet

FIGURE 2-10 A local area network using a bus topology.

On a bus network, when any computer transmits data, the signal travels down the cable in both directions. Both ends of the bus must be terminated with resistor packs that negate the signals arriving there. On a bus that is not properly terminated, signals reaching the end of the cable tend to echo back in the other direction and interfere with any newer signals that the computers transmit. This condition is called an *impedance mismatch*.

The inherent weakness of the bus topology is that a single cable failure can disrupt communications for the entire network. A broken cable splits the bus into two halves, preventing the nodes on one side from communicating with those on the other. In addition, both halves of the network are left with one end in an unterminated state, which prevents computers on the same side of the break from communicating effectively.

The only Ethernet networks that used the bus topology were those wired with coaxial cable. The decline of Ethernet on coaxial cable also meant the decline of the bus topology, which is no longer used today.

The Ring Topology

 A *ring topology* is essentially a bus with the two ends joined together, as shown in Figure 2-11, so that a signal transmitted by a computer in one direction circulates around a ring, eventually ending up back at its source. The data-link layer protocol traditionally associated with the ring topology is the now-obsolete Token Ring protocol.

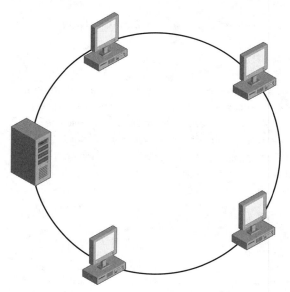

FIGURE 2-11 A local area network using a ring topology.

Token Ring networks use a MAC mechanism called token passing, which requires a special packet called a token to circulate endlessly around the network. Only the computer in possession of the token has permission to transmit data.

Early Token Ring networks were cabled together in an actual ring, with each computer connected to the next. However, Token Ring was also the origin of the *hybrid topology*, in which a single network contained the attributes of two different topologies.

In the majority of Token Ring networks, including nearly all of the few left in operation, the ring is a logical topology implemented in the wiring of the network. Physically, most Token Ring networks take the form of a star topology, with a cable running from each computer to a central cabling nexus called a multistation access unit (MAU). The MAU implements the logical ring by transmitting signals to each node in turn and waiting for the node to send them back before it transmits to the next node. Thus, although the cables are physically connected in a star, the data path takes the form of a ring, as shown in Figure 2-12. This is sometimes referred to as a star ring topology.

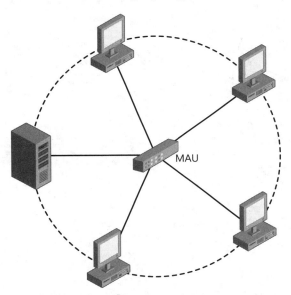

FIGURE 2-12 A local area network using a logical ring topology.

That the ring topology's physical design is that of a star makes it possible for the network to function even when a cable fails. The MAU contains circuitry that can remove a malfunctioning workstation from the ring but still preserve the logical topology. By comparison, a network that is literally cabled as a ring would have no MAU, so a cable break would cause the network to stop functioning completely.

> **NOTE HYBRID TOPOLOGIES**
> Another example of a hybrid topology is the star bus topology, in which you have multiple star networks, each of which is connected to a backbone network that uses a bus topology.

One protocol—also obsolete—that does allow for a physical ring topology is Fiber Distributed Data Interface (FDDI). FDDI is a 100-Mbps fiber optic solution that was fairly popular on backbone networks back in the days when Ethernet only ran at 10 Mbps. Because a ring is not fault tolerant—a cable break anywhere on the network prevents packets from circumnavigating the ring—FDDI calls for a double ring topology. Traffic on the double ring flows in opposite directions, and computers are connected to both rings, as shown in Figure 2-13. This way, the network can tolerate a cable break by diverting traffic to the other ring.

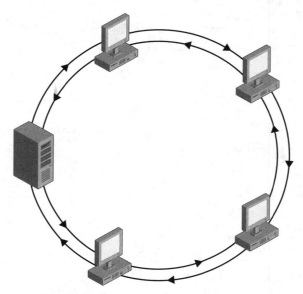

FIGURE 2-13 A local area network using a double ring topology.

The Mesh Topology

As mentioned earlier, data-link layer LAN protocols do not provide much flexibility when it comes to choosing a network topology. The characteristics of specific cable types impose exacting limitations on how you can install them. However, when you are designing an internetwork topology—such as when you are installing multiple LANs at one location, building a large enterprise infrastructure in a data center, or connecting remote networks with WAN links—you have a lot more freedom.

To connect networks together—forming an internetwork—you use routers, and the topology you create when linking networks together is not subject to the same restrictions as the creation of a LAN with a specific cable type.

For example, if your organization has several branch offices located around the country, you can install WAN links to connect them in any way you see fit. By connecting each branch office to the company headquarters, you are using point-to-point connections to build a star

WAN topology, as shown in Figure 2-14. In the same way, you could create a bus or a ring topology, although these models are rare in WAN implementations due to their lack of fault tolerance.

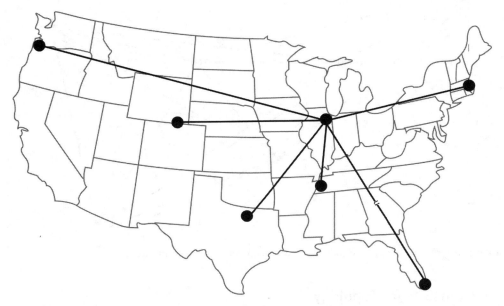

FIGURE 2-14 A star topology built by using WAN point-to-point connections.

Another option, in these circumstances, is to create some form of *mesh topology*, in which each office is connected to two or more other offices. This can be an expensive solution, but its redundancy enables the network to continue functioning even in the case of the failure of one or more links. There are two types of mesh topology: a partial mesh, in which each site has a point-to-point link to at least two other sites, and a full mesh, in which each site is connected to every other site, as shown in Figure 2-15.

In both types of mesh topologies, there are at least two routers on each network. In the event that a router is unable to send data to a specific destination, it can forward the data through another router for transmission by using a different pathway.

Mesh topologies—especially full mesh topologies—can be extremely expensive and difficult to install and maintain. The number of links required to establish the mesh rises precipitously with the addition of each node you have to connect.

The formula for calculating the number of point-to-point links required to establish a full mesh topology is as follows:

$n(n - 1)/2$

Thus, a business with a headquarters and nine branch offices would require 10(10-1)/2 or 45 separate WAN links to create a full mesh.

FIGURE 2-15 A full mesh topology built by using WAN point-to-point connections.

The Point-to-Point Topology

No topology is simpler than the *point-to-point topology*, in which one computer is directly connected to another, as shown in Figure 2-16. Obviously, this topology limits the network to two computers.

FIGURE 2-16 A point-to-point topology connecting two computers.

It is possible to connect two computers together by using a single Ethernet cable, creating the simplest possible LAN, but this can require a special cable called a crossover cable. In most cases, even two-node LANs connect by using a switch or a hub instead.

Point-to-point connections are also possible with wireless networks. In wireless LAN parlance, two computers connected directly together by using wireless network interface adapters form what is called an *ad hoc* network.

The point-to-point topology is more commonly found in wide area networking, which consists of all point-to-point links. For example, when you connect your home computer to the Internet, you are establishing a point-to-point WAN connection between your computer and your Internet service provider's (ISP's) network. Corporate networks also use point-to-point WAN links to connect LANs in remote offices together.

The Point-to-Multipoint Topology

As noted earlier, in a point-to-point topology, one node transmits and one node receives. The alternative to this model is the *point-to-multipoint topology*, in which a single node transmits and multiple nodes receive the data, as shown in Figure 2-17. All of the other topologies discussed in the previous sections are essentially variations on these two models.

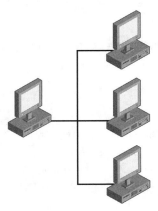

FIGURE 2-17 A point-to-multipoint topology.

The star, mesh, and logical ring topologies, with their variants, are all basically collections of point-to-point links. The only wired LAN topology that uses the point-to-multipoint model is the bus, because the network propagates the signals transmitted by each node to every other node, without any intervening switch, hub, MAU, or other device. The other main example of the point-to-multipoint topology on LANs is in wireless networking, where a single system can transmit to multiple destinations simultaneously. For more information on wireless LAN topologies, see Chapter 5.

EXAM TIP

By far, the most commonly used cable topology in local area networking is the star topology and its variant, the hierarchical star. The bus and ring topologies are practically obsolete in the LAN world.

Multiprotocol Label Switching

Multiprotocol label switching (MPLS) is a packet forwarding technology that is designed to lessen the burden on intermediate routers. On a typical internetwork, packets are forwarded from router to router and at each hop, the router must read the destination address, compare it to its routing table, and decide where to send it next. With MPLS, one router analyzes the packet and inserts a short label into the packet header. The label identifies a complete channel through the internetwork to the destination, so subsequent routers do not have to repeat the analysis. Reading the MPLS label is a far less labor-intensive process than reading the packet's destination address and looking it up in the routing table. Therefore, the increase in efficiency MPLS supplies is substantial.

MPLS is defined by some administrators as working at layer 2.5 of the OSI model, between the data-link and network layers. Therefore, the data carried in the packets can be generated by any protocol.

EXAM TIP

MPLS is more of a WAN technology than a physical topology, and does not rightly belong in this particular CompTIA Network+ exam objective.

Cabling Standards

Until 1991, there were no standards defining the nature of the cabling used for LANs, other than the physical layer specifications in the data-link layer protocol standards. This often resulted in hardware incompatibilities and confusion for cable installers. It was eventually recognized that the networking industry needed a standard defining a cabling system that could support a variety of different networking technologies.

To address this need, the American National Standards Institute (ANSI) and the Telecommunications Industry Association (TIA), a division of the Electronic Industries Alliance (EIA), along with a consortium of telecommunications companies, developed a set of documents that define the best practices for designing, installing, and maintaining networks that use twisted pair and fiber optic cabling.

 Originally called the *ANSI/TIA-568 Commercial Building Telecommunications Cabling Standard*, this document was revised in 1995, 2001, and 2009, and is now known as ANSI/TIA-568-C. The latest revision of the standard consists of four documents, as follows:

- **ANSI/TIA-568-C.0** "Generic Telecommunications Cabling for Customer Premises"
- **ANSI/TIA-568-C.1** "Commercial Building Telecommunications Cabling Standard"
- **ANSI/TIA-568-C.2** "Balanced Twisted-Pair Telecommunication Cabling and Components Standard"
- **ANSI/TIA-568-C.3** "Optical Fiber Cabling Components Standard"

NOTE OBTAINING STANDARDS

The standards listed here are available from the TIA at *http://www.tiaonline.org*. Unfortunately, unlike many of the other standards organizations mentioned in this book, the TIA does not distribute their standards for free.

The 568-C standard defines a structured cabling system for voice and data communications in office environments that has a usable life span of at least 10 years, supporting the products of multiple technology vendors and using twisted pair or fiber optic cable.

For each of the cable types, the standards define the following elements:

- Cable characteristics and technical criteria determining the cable's performance level
- Installation guidelines, including topology, segment length, pull tension, and bend radius specifications
- Connector specifications and pinouts

The standard also includes specifications for the installation of the cable within a building space. In doing this, the standard divides a building into the following subsystems:

- **Building entrance**   The location where the building's internal cabling interfaces with outside cabling.
- **Telecommunications rooms and enclosures**   Also known as the *intermediate distribution frames (IDF),* this is the location of localized telecommunications equipment such as the interface between the horizontal cabling and the backbone.
- **Equipment rooms**   The location of equipment providing the same functions as that in a telecommunications room, but which might be more complex.
- **Backbone cabling**   The cabling that connects the building's various equipment rooms, telecommunications closets, and the building entrance, as well as connections between buildings in a campus network environment.
- **Horizontal cabling**   The cabling and other hardware used to connect the telecommunications rooms to the work areas.
- **Work area**   The components used to connect the telecommunications outlet to the workstation.

Thus, a typical cable installation for a modern building might consist of the following elements:

- Cables for external telephone and other services enter through the building entrance and run to the equipment room, which contains the Private Branch Exchange (PBX) system, network servers, and other equipment.
- A backbone network connects the equipment room to various telecommunications rooms throughout the building, which contain network connection devices such as switches and routers.
- Horizontal cabling originates in the telecommunications rooms and runs out into the work areas, terminating at wall plates.
- The wall plates in the work area are connected to computers and other equipment by using patch cables.

In addition to the ANSI/TIA-568-C standard, there are other TIA/EIA standards that provide guidelines for specific types of cabling within and between the subsystems listed here. Any contractor that you hire to perform an office cable installation should be familiar with these standards and should be willing to certify that his work conforms to these standards.

NOTE **PHYSICAL LAYER SPECIFICATIONS**

The ANSI/TIA standards are not the only ones that installers must consult when deploying network equipment. See Chapter 4 for more information about the physical layer specifications included in the standards for Ethernet and other data-link layer protocols.

 Quick Check

1. Which of the cable topologies discussed in this section is designed to provide a network with fault tolerance?

2. Which of the topologies discussed in this section can be implemented physically, in the arrangement of its cables, or logically, in the wiring of a hub?

Quick Check Answers

1. The mesh topology

2. The ring topology

Installing Cables

The process of installing the cables for a network can be relatively simple or extremely complex. If your intention is to build a LAN in your home or in a small office, you can purchase everything you need at virtually any computer center or electronics store. For a larger office installation, or for one in which the cables must be hidden in the walls and ceilings, a professional contractor is probably in order. A qualified cable installer not only has the tools and experience to pull cable, but also knowledge of local codes and applicable wiring standards.

The following sections examine the process of performing an external cable installation by using off-the-shelf products and an internal, bulk cable installation.

Installing External Cables

An external cable installation is one in which you purchase prefabricated patch cables and a switch and install them yourself, without running them inside the room's walls. This type of installation is suitable for a small network with computers in one room or perhaps two adjacent rooms. If you feel more daring, you can consider drilling holes to run cable through walls or floors.

NOTE **REPLACING HUBS**

In most networking markets, switches have almost completely replaced hubs. For information on the differences between the two and the reasons for purchasing switches instead of hubs, see Chapter 3.

The advantage of an external installation is that you only have to buy a minimum number of components. You use patch cables with the connectors already attached, so you don't have to buy separate connectors or wall plates and patch panels. An external network is also portable. You can coil up the cables and move everything to a new location if necessary.

The main drawback of an external installation is its appearance. The cables remain visible after the installation is completed, which might or might not be important to you. An external installation can be neat; you can purchase cables in colors to match your walls, and secure them to baseboards or woodwork to keep the cables out of the way. However, an external installation will never be as neat or professional looking as an internal cable installation.

The basic steps of an external installation process are as follows.

1. Select locations for computers and other devices (such as printers) and your switch. The switch should be in a central location, relative to the computers, to keep cable lengths to a minimum.

2. Plan the exact route for each cable, from the computer (or other device) to the switch. Note any obstacles along each route, such as furniture, doorways, and walls, and plan how you will run your cables around or through them.

3. Measure the route from each computer to the switch, taking the entire path of the cable into account. Include vertical runs around doorways, paths through walls, and other obstacles. Leave at least a few extra yards of slack to compensate for unforeseen obstacles and adjustments in the location of the computer or the switch.

4. Select the data-link layer protocol you intend to use for your network, and an appropriate cable grade and switch suitable for that protocol. For example, if your computers are all equipped with integrated Gigabit Ethernet adapters, you will probably want to use CAT5e or CAT6 cables, and you must be sure to select a switch with a sufficient number of ports that supports Gigabit Ethernet.

5. Purchase UTP patch cables of appropriate lengths and, if necessary, colors, for each cable run. Make sure that all of the cables you buy are of the proper grade, and consider whether it is worth paying for additional features such as molded boots around the connectors, to protect them from being damaged.

6. Lay out the cable for each run loosely without connecting the cables to the equipment or securing them to the walls. Leave enough slack to reach around doorways or other obstacles, as well as at each end, so that the connectors can reach the computer and the switch comfortably.

7. Starting at one end of each cable run, secure the cable to the walls, floor, or woodwork, working your way to the other end, using staples, cable ties, or raceways. Make sure that none of the cable is compressed or kinked anywhere along its length and that all cables are protected from damage caused by foot traffic or furniture.

8. When the cables are secured, plug one end of each cable run into the switch and the other end into the computer or other device. When the switch is connected to a power source and the computer is turned on, the link pulse lights in the switch and the computer's network interface adapter (if one exists) should light up, indicating that a connection has been established.

The situation most clearly suitable for an external cable installation is one in which all of the computers and other devices are located in the same room. A one-room network eliminates the single biggest problem of external cable installations: running cables between rooms, or worse, between floors. For a small, one-room network, you can generally run the cables along the walls around the room, securing them to the baseboards or running them behind furniture, as shown in Figure 2-18. You can also purchase UTP patch cables in a variety of colors to match your décor and keep the installation as discreet as possible.

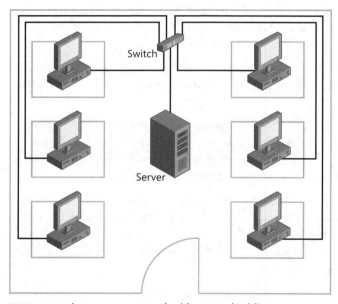

FIGURE 2-18 A one-room network with external cabling.

You can also buy rubber cable protectors that run across the floor. These provide a safe conduit for the cable and prevent people from tripping over them. You can also run patch cables through a dropped ceiling and then down through a ceiling tile to the appropriate location on the floor. Floor-to-ceiling service poles are available that provide a safe cable conduit and a neater appearance. When you begin thinking about running cables through the ceiling, however, you should consider whether an internal installation might be a better idea.

External cabling also becomes far more complicated when you have computers in more than one room or on more than one floor. To run patch cables to another room, you have to drill larger holes than with bulk cable, so that the connector can pass through. In such cases, consider an internal installation.

Installing Internal Cables

Almost anyone can perform a basic external cable installation, but installing cables internally requires specialized tools and skills borne of experience. In an external installation, you connect the computer to the switch with a single length of cable. An internal installation uses three cable lengths for each connection.

The primary—and usually the longest—piece of cable is a run connecting a wall plate in the vicinity of the computer to the telecommunications room in which the switch is located. This is the part of the installation that the ANSI/TIA-568-C standard describes as *horizontal cabling*. This part of the installation is also the internal part, because the cable is completely hidden inside the building's walls and ceilings.

The wall plate is a plastic or metal box, embedded in the wall, that contains one or more female RJ45 jacks. The outward appearance is like that of an electrical outlet, except with different connectors, as shown in Figure 2-19. The second of the three cable lengths is an ordinary patch cable with RJ45 connectors, which connects the computer to the wall plate. This is the *work area* cabling described in ANSI/TIA-568-C. You can purchase prefabricated patch cables for this part of the installation, but some installers make their own, attaching connectors to short lengths of bulk cable.

FIGURE 2-19 RJ45 jacks on a wall plate.

In the telecommunications room—which can be a data center, a server closet, or anything in between—the other end of the internal cable runs to a cabling nexus called a patch panel. A patch panel is just a framework of plastic or metal with rows of female RJ45 connectors in it, as shown in Figure 2-20. In large installations, patch panels are mounted in standard 19-inch racks, providing access to hundreds or thousands of internal cable runs.

FIGURE 2-20 An RJ45 patch panel.

As with the other end of the internal run, administrators use short patch cables to connect patch panel jacks to the ports of a switch. Switches too can be mounted in racks. Large data centers can have many aisles lined with racks with bundles of cables snaking all around the room.

Pulling Cable

The process of installing the cable runs inside the walls and ceilings is often referred to as *pulling cable*. Though not terribly difficult, this part of the installation requires careful planning and organization, or it could end up in a tangled mess of cable ends.

Bulk cable comes on spools (as shown in Figure 2-21), in boxes, or on spools within boxes, in lengths of 500 to 1,000 feet or more. Boxed cable frequently feeds out through a plastic nozzle. The installers, leaving the spool or bundle in the box for protection from tangles, can pull out as much as they need, enabling them to install runs of any length. The cable sold in bulk is rated by using the same categories as individual patch cables and usually has solid conductors. In addition to resisting attenuation, the solid conductors are much easier to attach to connectors.

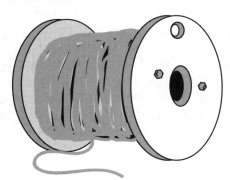

FIGURE 2-21 Bulk cable.

The basic steps involved in installing internal cable runs are as follows.

1. Select the locations for your computers and other network-connected devices and a central, protected location for your switches and patch panels. One end of each cable run will terminate at the patch panel, so be sure to select a location with sufficient access to the entire site, away from possible sources of EMI, and with room to work easily.

2. Using a floor plan or blueprint, plan the routes for your cables from the patch panel to the location of each wall plate, taking into account all obstacles, such as barrier walls, light fixtures, and plumbing stacks.

3. With your spool of bulk cable located at the patch panel site, label the lead end of the cable with the intended location of its wall plate.

4. Feed the lead end of the bulk cable into the ceiling or wall and pull the cable to the location of the wall plate. Do not cut the cable off the spool until you have pulled it all the way to the wall plate. Leave several yards of slack inside the ceiling or wall to avoid problems making the connections or locating the equipment.

5. Secure the cables in place along their routes so that they can't shift location or be damaged by other people working in the same area.

6. Label the end of the cable with the name of the wall plate location, and cut the cable from the spool. Never cut an unlabeled cable from the spool.

7. Proceed with the cable connection process, as detailed later in this chapter.

The process of actually pulling the cables is not technically difficult, but if you ever see an experienced installer do it, you will observe how methodical repetition enables him or her to proceed much more quickly than an amateur. The process naturally involves a lot of ladder climbing, and installers tend to develop their own techniques for moving the cables through the ceiling plenum.

 There are various snaking tools for pulling wire through hollow walls or across drop ceilings. Some people use a specialized tool called a *telepole*, as shown in Figure 2-22, which is a telescoping wand not unlike a fishing pole, which they use to push the cable along in the ceiling. Some people throw a ball of string across the ceiling space while holding on to the end. They can then tie the string to one or more cable ends and pull them from the destination. This is a particularly useful technique when you have multiple cable runs to install to the same destination. Other installers simply coil the cables and throw them, some with the accuracy of a rodeo cowboy.

FIGURE 2-22 A cable installer's telepole.

With the cables in place, the installer then secures them by using tape, zip ties, or some other means. The object is to hold the cables securely in place without exerting so much pressure that the conductors inside are damaged. The ANSI/TIA-568-C standards provide detailed installation specifications regarding distances from EMI sources, bend radii, and other factors. A professional installation begins with a carefully wrought plan detailing the location of every cable, and securing the cables in place ensures that they remain compliant with the standards.

A detailed cable plan should be a required deliverable in every cabling contract and should become a permanent part of the network documentation. The plan should specify the actual route and location of every cable run and be labeled with the names used on the wall plates and patch panels. This plan will be an essential tool for the network administrators responsible for maintaining and troubleshooting the cable plant after the installers are gone.

Installers must also be careful not to pull too hard on the cable, to avoid kinks, and to keep the cables away from sources of heat, electricity, and moisture. If these are unavoidable, then the installers should take special precautions to protect the cables, such as running them inside a dedicated conduit.

The ease or difficulty of an internal cabling job is often dependent on the age and construction of the building. New construction with dropped ceilings and plasterboard walls is usually ideal for cable installers, but older buildings can present any number of obstacles, including sources of EMI that can disturb data signals, fire breaks in the walls that prevent installers from running vertical cables, asbestos insulation, service components such as ventilation ducts and light fixtures, and structural components, such as concrete pilings and steel girders. Most of these obstructions should be detected during the network planning process, but cable installers are still accustomed to running into surprises.

Dropping Cables

With the cable deployed in the ceilings, the next step is to bring them down to floor level, where installers traditionally locate the wall plates. This tool is a process that can take some time to master. Some installers simply cut a hole in the wall, dangle the cable down inside the wall space, and grab the loose end through the hole. A wire coat hanger can be helpful when reaching through the hole to grab the cable.

 The official tool for this task is called a *fish tape*—a flexible band of steel or fiberglass wound on a spool, as shown in Figure 2-23, much like a tape measure or a plumber's snake. You push the tape up to the ceiling through the hole in the wall, attach the cable to the hook, and pull it down and out through the hole. You can also run the tape down and out through the hole to pull a cable up to the ceiling, or through the ceiling to the floor above.

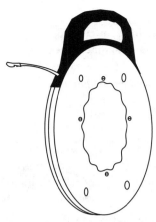

FIGURE 2-23 A cable installer's fish tape.

Depending on the location of your patch panel and how it is situated, you might have to drop the other end of the cable runs down through a wall as well. Smaller installations often use patch panels mounted on a wall, enabling you to drop the cables down to a hole located behind the mounted panel. Larger networks using rack-mounted equipment typically have cables that drop down from an open ceiling into the back of the rack assembly.

Making Connections

When the cables are in place, it is time to attach the RJ45 connectors that enable you to attach the cable runs to your computers and your switches. This is the most critical part of an internal installation because this is where errors can occur that prevent the network from functioning properly. If you connect the wires in a cable end to the wrong pins in the connector, or if you don't have adequate connections between the wires and the pins, or if the wires themselves are damaged, signals will be lost or garbled, and you might have a terrible time identifying the cause of the problem.

WIRING PATTERNS

The process of attaching a jack to a cable end is called *punching down*, and the process is essentially the same whether you are connecting the cable to a wall plate, a patch panel, or a patch cord connector. In each case, you must strip off the outer sheath to expose the individual wires inside the cable and punch down each wire into the correct pin on the jack.

Punching down the wires to the correct pins is an essential part of the process. UTP cable for local area networks is wired *straight through*, meaning that each pin at one end of the cable must be connected to the corresponding pin at the other end. A connection between two devices on a network must contain a signal crossover somewhere. The signal transmitted over the send pin at one end must somehow end up at the receive pin on the other end, but data networks rely on network devices such as switches, routers, and hubs to supply the crossover circuit.

Crossover cables—that is, cables in which the send and receive pinouts are reversed on one end—do exist. They have traditionally had two uses: to connect two computers together without a switch or hub, creating an ad hoc network; and to connect two hubs together that lack uplink ports or auto crossover.

Standard LAN crossover cables have pins 1 and 3 and pins 2 and 6 transposed. Another type of cable, called a T-1 crossover cable, is used to connect two CSU/DSU devices together for a leased line installation. This cable has pins 1 and 4 and pins 2 and 5 transposed instead.

> **NOTE   MDI AND MDIX PORTS**
>
> A medium dependent interface (MDI) port is one in which the transmit and receive pairs are arranged to be connected to a medium dependent interface crossover (MDIX) port, which has them reversed. Auto crossover (also known as Auto-MDIX) technology, which is common on most switches today, can sense whether the devices to which the switch is connected require MDI or MDIX ports, and arranges its ports accordingly.

A standard four-pair UTP cable has wires that are color coded, using the colors blue, orange, green, and brown. Each twisted pair in the cable consists of a solid color wire and a white wire with a stripe of the same color.

The ANSI/TIA-568-C standard (along with its predecessors) defines two wiring patterns— T568A and T568B—that specify the wire colors that should correspond to the numbered pins in the connectors. A cable run is wired straight through when it uses the same wiring pattern on both ends of the cable. Table 2-3 lists the pinouts for the T568A pattern, and Table 2-4 contains the T568B pattern.

TABLE 2-3 T568A Pinouts for UTP Cables

Pin Number	T568A Pair	T568A Color
1	3	Green stripe
2	3	Green solid
3	2	Orange stripe
4	1	Blue solid
5	1	Blue stripe
6	2	Orange solid
7	4	Brown stripe
8	4	Brown solid

TABLE 2-4 T568B Pinouts for UTP Cables

Pin Number	T568B Pair	T568B Color
1	2	Orange stripe
2	2	Orange solid
3	3	Green stripe
4	1	Blue solid
5	1	Blue stripe
6	3	Green solid
7	4	Brown stripe
8	4	Brown solid

> **NOTE   THE USOC PINOUT**
>
> There is a third pinout, the USOC pinout, which was the original standard for voice communication in the United States. You absolutely must not use this pinout for data networking, because it calls for pins 1 and 2 to be connected to separate wire pairs.

The wiring pattern you elect to use for your installation is irrelevant; there is no performance advantage to either one. What is critically important, however, is that all of the installers involved in the project use the same pinouts, so that every cable is wired identically on both ends.

PUNCHING DOWN

In a typical UTP installation, there are three types of RJ45 connectors that installers have to punch down. The *keystone connector*, shown in Figure 2-24, is the snap-in module that fits into a standard keystone wall plate. Keystone modules are available in a variety of configurations, enabling you to mix different types of cables in a single plate. Most of the connectors on the market today are color coded. Some are available in T568A and T678B versions; others have color codes for both pinouts.

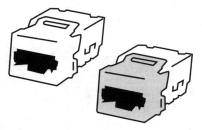

FIGURE 2-24 RJ45 keystone connectors.

Patch panels have connectors called punchdown blocks on the reverse side, as shown in Figure 2-25. The punchdown blocks for UTP data networks with RJ45 connectors are called *110 blocks*.

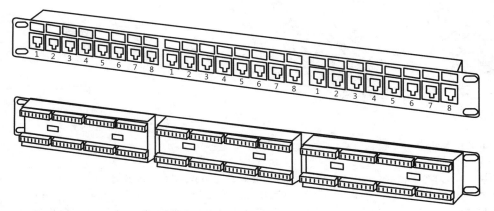

FIGURE 2-25 An 8P8C patch panel with 110 punchdown blocks.

The older standard for punchdown blocks is the *66 block*, as shown in Figure 2-26. Rarely used for data networking, 66 blocks are still found in many telephone service installations.

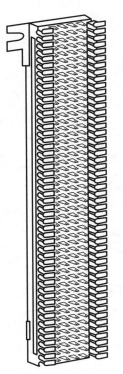

FIGURE 2-26 A 66 punchdown block.

Finally, if you intend to make your own patch cords, you can purchase male RJ45 connectors like those shown in Figure 2-27.

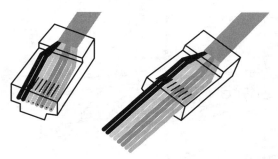

FIGURE 2-27 Male RJ45 connectors.

 The tools required for punching down are minimal. You need a pair of scissors (or specialized cable snips) for cutting off the cable sheath and for cutting the ends of the wires, and you need a specialized *punchdown tool*, like that shown in Figure 2-28. Punchdown tools are available with a variety of bits, to support different cable types. The elaborateness and expense of the tool you need depends on the types of cables you will be installing.

FIGURE 2-28 A punchdown tool.

The process of punching down a keystone connector or a patch panel connection consists of the following steps:

1. Strip a few inches of the insulating sheath off the cable end to expose the wires, being careful not to cut into the wires themselves.

2. Separate each of the four twisted wire pairs at the end.

3. Place each of the eight wires into the appropriately colored contact in the connector, as shown in Figure 2-29. Leave as little space as possible between each wire's connection and the beginning of the wire pair's twists. Also, leave as little space as possible between the wires and the beginning of the sheath.

4. Using your punchdown tool held vertically, punch each of the eight wires down into its receptacle.

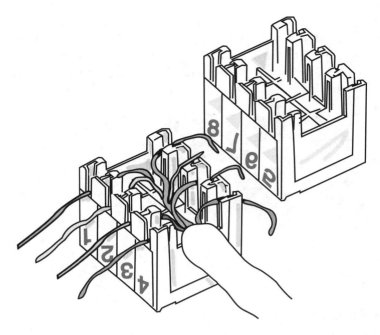

FIGURE 2-29 The punching down process.

Though stripping off the cable's sheath might seem to be the easiest part of this operation, it is also one of the most error-prone. It is important that you do not damage the insulation on the wires or the conductors in the wires in the process. Many cables include a string with the four wire pairs, running the full length of the cable. Pulling back hard on the string splits the cable sheath open without damaging the wires. There are also specialized wire stripper devices available, which some installers prefer.

The punchdown tool is critical to this operation. In one motion, the tool presses the wire down into place, allowing the connector to pierce its insulation to make electrical contact, and cuts off the excess at the end. Without this tool, the process of punching down would require you to strip the insulation off of each wire, press it into place, and trim off the end, which would be laborious.

> **NOTE   EXTRA WIRE PAIRS**
>
> Some of the data-link layer protocols, such as 10Base-T and 100Base-TX, utilize only two of the four wire pairs in a UTP cable. However, this does not mean that you should feel free to use those extra pairs for a second network connection or telephone wiring. The first reason for this is that the cable specifications for those protocols make them liable to experience crosstalk with the signals on the extra wire pairs. The second reason is that if you ever plan to run 1000Base-T over the network, you will need all four pairs to do so.

Attaching male connectors to make a patch cable is a slightly different process, requiring a different tool, called a *crimper*. After stripping off the cable sheath, as before, you line the conductors up in the proper order, insert them into the connector, and use the crimper, shown in Figure 2-30, to squeeze the connector closed around them, and to pierce the insulation with the eight pins of the connector, thereby making the electrical connection.

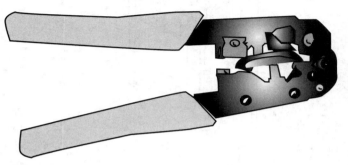

FIGURE 2-30 A crimper for attaching RJ45 connectors.

Working with Fiber Optic Cable

The internal cable installation described in this chapter uses UTP cable—the most common network medium—as an example. However, many networks use other media, or a combination of media, including fiber optic, wireless, and sometimes even legacy media left over from the past, such as coaxial cable.

All of the hardware components described in this chapter are available in various configurations that support other media. For example, if you use rack-mounted patch panels in your telecommunications rooms, you can purchase patch panels for fiber optic cables and mix them in a single rack.

Installing fiber optic cable—the most likely alternative to UTP—is roughly similar to the procedure described earlier, at least as far as the cable pulling part is concerned. Fiber optic supports longer runs, and you might have to use different bend radii when installing around corners, but you still have to get the cable through the ceiling from one location to another and drop it down inside the walls.

The big difference in a fiber optic installation is in the attachment of the connectors. Unlike the connectors used on copper cables, which completely contain the ends of the wires and provide their own conductors, fiber optic connectors are really just sleeves that fit around the end of the cable and let the central core protrude from the end. The connector's only function is to lock the signal-carrying core in place when it's plugged into the jack.

The process of attaching a connector to a multimode fiber optic cable basically consists of stripping the outer sheath off the end of the cable, gluing the connector in place with an epoxy adhesive, allowing the adhesive to cure, and then polishing the protruding core so that the pulses of light carried by the cable reach their terminus in the best possible condition. Installers terminate singlemode cables by permanently splicing a *pigtail* to them, which is a short length of cable with a connector already attached to it. This is necessary because the tolerances of singlemode fiber are much tighter than those of multimode.

Professional fiber optic cable installers typically use a tiny electric oven to cure the epoxy; otherwise, they must leave the adhesive to cure overnight. Applying the correct amount of epoxy and polishing the cable end are both processes that require a certain amount of skill and experience. In addition, the heat curing process takes some time—about 25 minutes per connection.

There are several alternative connector types on the market that are designed to speed up or simplify this process. Some have the epoxy pre-measured on the connector or polish the connector at the factory, which reduces the skill level required. There are also connectors that crimp onto the cable and require no adhesive at all. These connectors also go on much faster than the glue and polish type and require far less skill from the installer. Some professionals swear by these, but others prefer to stick with the traditional method.

Generally speaking, there is a trade-off between the time and skill needed to apply fiber optic connectors and the cost of the connectors themselves. The easier the connectors are to attach, the more expensive they are. For cable contractors, the choice often comes down to whether the amount of fiber optic cable they install balances with the cost of hiring or training skilled fiber optic installers.

 Quick Check

1. Which tool do you use to make patch cables by attaching RJ45 connectors to lengths of bulk cable?

2. Which tool does a telephony installer use to connect directly to a circuit and place calls?

Quick Check Answers

1. A crimper

2. A butt set

Testing Cable Runs

Installing internal cable runs is a complex and detailed process, and even the most seasoned professionals can make mistakes. It is therefore essential that the installers test each cable run to ensure that it functions properly.

Plugging the two ends of a cable run into a computer and a switch by using patch cables is not an adequate form of testing. There are many types of cabling errors that can cause intermittent performance problems that are not immediately evident. The computer can function normally at first, and only display the symptoms of a cabling problem later. Besides, in many cases, contractors install the cables before the switches, computers, and other equipment are in place, making it impossible to test them under real-world conditions. As an alternative to real-world testing, installers can use a variety of tools to perform offline tests of the cable runs.

As discussed earlier, the ANSI/TIA-568-C standard describes the performance levels required for each category of UTP cable. The higher-category cables are intended for faster networks, which in turn require higher levels of performance. Therefore, the tests that installers should perform on their cable runs are based on the intended speed of the network.

Not surprisingly, cable testing tools go up in price depending on the number and type of tests they can perform. Simple continuity testers are good to have around for basic troubleshooting and are within the financial means of most network administration departments. However, high-end cable certification devices that are able to test all of the performance levels specified by the ANSI/TIA-568-C standard can have prices from US $10,000 to US $20,000. Equivalent tools for fiber optic cables can cost double those amounts.

IDENTIFYING CABLES

The first tool needed for testing is called a *tone generator and locator*, as shown in Figure 2-31. The same device can also be called a toner probe or fox and hound tester. The tone generator is a device that you connect to one end of a cable run and which generates a signal over the cable. At the other end of the run, you touch the locator to the cable, and it produces an audible sound when it detects the signal. You can use this type of device to locate and identify the one cable you need in a bundle.

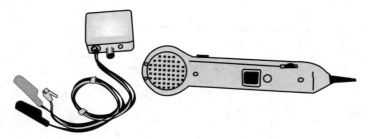

FIGURE 2-31 A tone generator and locator.

TESTING FOR CONTINUITY

After you've identified both ends of the cable to be tested, the first and most essential test that installers must perform on every cable run is a continuity test, which ensures that each wire on both ends of the cable is connected to the correct pin, and only the correct pin. A wire that is not connected to both ends of the cable—either because the connection itself is flawed or because the wire is broken somewhere in the cable—generates a condition called an *open circuit*. If a pin on one end of a cable run is connected to two or more pins on the other end, you have a *short circuit*.

It is possible to test cable continuity by using a standard electrical multimeter. By touching the meter's probes to opposite ends of the cable and setting the readout to ohms, you should see a result close to 0 ohms if you have a proper connection, and infinite ohms if you do not.

Identifying and testing each cable thoroughly by using a tone generator and locator or multimeter is a lengthy and arduous process; professional installers rarely use them. For a few dollars more, you can purchase a device called a *wiremap tester*, which functions on the same principles but connects to all eight wires at once on both ends and tests them at the same time. Wiremap testers, like most cable testers, consist of a main handheld unit that you connect to one end of the cable and a loopback device that you connect to the other end, as shown in Figure 2-32. A wiremap tester can detect opens and shorts, as well as transposed wires, also known as TX/RX reversals. However, it cannot detect split pairs. This usually requires a more sophisticated testing device.

> **NOTE LOOPBACK PLUGS**
>
> A *loopback plug* is a device that connects to the end of a cable and reflects all incoming signals back along the cable to the source.

A *split pair* is a connection in which two wires are incorrectly mapped in exactly the same way on both ends of the cable. In a properly wired connection, each twisted pair of wires should contain a signal and a ground. In a split pair, you can have two signal wires twisted together as a pair. This can generate excessive amounts of crosstalk, corrupting both of the signals involved.

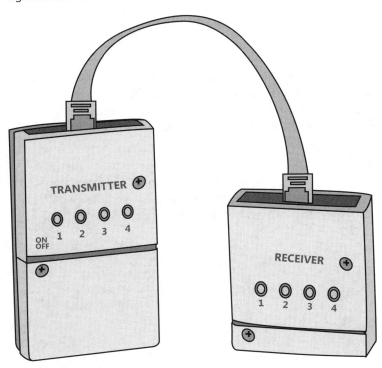

FIGURE 2-32 A wiremap tester.

TESTING CABLE LENGTH

UTP cables have length limitations because signals tend to lose strength (or attenuate) over distance. Installers should be conscious of their cable run lengths as they install them, but testing the actual length of the installed cable runs is always recommended.

> **NOTE ESTIMATING CABLE LENGTHS**
>
> When installing and testing internal cable runs, be sure to account for the length of your patch cables. Most of the Ethernet physical layer specifications for UTP cables limit the cable length from the computer to the switch to 100 meters. However, most installers observe a more modest limit for their internal runs—such as 90 meters—so that the patch cables do not put the total length over the 100-meter limit.

As you move upward in the cable tester market, you find units that have the ability to determine the length of a cable run, locate a break in any one of the wires, and specify the location of the break, in terms of the distance from the cable end. The technique that provides this capability is called *time domain reflectometry (TDR)*. The tester transmits a signal over the cable and measures how long it takes for a reflection of the signal to return from the other end. Using this information and the cable's *nominal velocity of propagation (NVP)*—a specification supplied by the cable manufacturer—the device can calculate the length of a cable run. If the result is not the same for all eight wires, then the device knows that there is a break somewhere.

TESTING PERFORMANCE CHARACTERISTICS

As described earlier, the ANSI/TIA-568-C standard rates UTP cables by specifying maximum acceptable levels of various types of interference. As you move up to the higher categories, there are more tests to conduct, and more stringent limitations to meet. Testing these characteristics in the field therefore requires more sophisticated (and more expensive) equipment.

Cable testing devices at this level of performance are typically called *cable certifiers*, scanners, or media testers. These are handheld devices of great sophistication, as shown in Figure 2-33, which fortunately make the testing process utterly foolproof. After connecting the main unit to one cable end and the remote unit to the other end, you select a battery of tests, and the certifier runs through them all in a matter of seconds.

FIGURE 2-33 A cable certifier.

Most of these devices are already configured with the appropriate tests and performance levels specified by the ANSI/TIA-568-C standards. You can usually also create your own battery of tests, enabling the device to retain its usefulness even when requirements change. Prices of cable certifiers can be very high, depending on the other features they provide. Higher-end units have faster testing speeds, can interface with a computer to maintain records of your tests, and might have support for add-on modules that enable you to test other cable types.

Some of the tests that cable certifiers can typically perform include the following:

- **Attenuation**   By comparing the strength of a signal at the far end of a cable to its strength when transmitted, the tester determines the cable's attenuation (measured in decibels).

- **Near-End Crosstalk (NEXT)**   Testing for NEXT is a matter of transmitting a signal over one of a cable's wires and then detecting the strength of the signal that bleeds over into the other wires near the end of the cable where the transmitter is located. Keeping the wire pair twists as close as possible to the connector pins helps to minimize NEXT.

- **Far-End Crosstalk (FEXT)**   Testing for FEXT involves transmitting a signal over one of a cable's wires and then detecting the strength of the signal that bleeds over into the other wires near the far end of the cable.

- **Power Sum NEXT (PS-NEXT)**   PS-NEXT measures the crosstalk that is generated when three of the four wire pairs are carrying signals at once. This test is intended for networks that use technologies such as Gigabit Ethernet that utilize all four wire pairs.

- **Equal-Level Far-End Crosstalk (EL-FEXT)**   EL-FEXT measures the crosstalk at the opposite end of the cable from the transmitter, corrected to account for the amount of attenuation in the connection.

- **Power Sum EL-FEXT (PS-ELFEXT)**   PS-ELFEXT measures the crosstalk that is generated at the far end of the cable by three signal-carrying wire pairs, corrected for attenuation.

- **Alien Crosstalk (AXT)**   Introduced for the CAT6a rating, Alien Crosstalk is the measurement of the signal bleedover from a wire pair in one cable to the same pair in an adjacent cable.

- **Propagation delay**   The propagation delay is the amount of time required for a signal to travel from one end of a cable to the other.

- **Delay skew**   Delay skew is the difference between the lowest and the highest propagation delay measurements for the wires in a cable. Because the wire pairs inside a UTP cable are twisted at different rates, their relative lengths can differ, and the delay skew measurement quantifies that difference.

- **Return Loss (RL)**   Return Loss measures the accumulated signal reflection caused by variations in the cable's impedance along its length. These impedance variations are typically caused by untwisting the wires when making connections.

> **NOTE   TESTING BULK CABLE**
>
> When you purchase bulk cable with a particular category rating, the manufacturer is certifying that the product meets certain levels of performance, including attenuation. However, it is always a good idea to test (or at least spot check) the cable before you install it, to make sure that the product itself isn't faulty, or that some mix-up hasn't occurred, resulting in the wrong category of cable being packed into the box.

TESTING FIBER OPTIC CABLES

Cable testing for fiber optic cables is—not surprisingly—a completely different world from copper cable testing, and a far more expensive one as well. Fiber optic cables are subject to different types of interference and have largely different performance level requirements. The ANSI/TIA-568-C standards include specifications for fiber optic as well as copper cables, however, and there are cable certifiers designed for testing fiber optic as well.

Fiber optic cables do not have multiple wire pairs, so wire mapping is not a concern, and neither is any type of crosstalk. However, cable length and cable breaks are as much of a concern in fiber optic as in copper cable installations. The fiber optic equivalent of a TDR is called an *optical time domain reflectometer (OTDR),* as shown in Figure 2-34, and it can determine cable lengths and locate cable breaks, just like the copper testing device.

FIGURE 2-34 An optical time domain reflectometer (OTDR).

Some of the other primary characteristics that fiber optic cable certifiers usually test include the following:

- **Attenuation**   Weakening of the light signal as it travels over long distances
- **Dispersion**   Spreading of the light signal as it travels over long distances
- **Light leakage**   Signal damage caused by exceeding the cable's bend radius during installation
- **Modal distortion**   Signal damage unique to multimode fiber optic cable caused by the various modes having different propagation velocities

 Quick Check

1. What is the term that describes the weakening of a signal as it travels through a cable's length?

2. Which two types of interference are measured on three of the four signal-carrying wire pairs?

Quick Check Answers

1. Attenuation

2. Power Sum NEXT and Power Sum EL-FEXT

Connecting to the Backbone

The components and processes described thus far in this chapter concern the installation of a single LAN. An enterprise network reaches well beyond a single LAN, however. Large corporate networks typically consist of multiple LANs that are joined together by another network, informally referred to as a *backbone*.

Picture an office building with multiple floors, each of which has its own LAN, consisting of a telecommunications room and horizontal cabling that leads out to the work areas. Picture then another network running vertically through the building, connecting all of the telecommunications rooms together, as shown in Figure 2-35. This is the backbone network.

The ANSI/TIA-568-C standards don't stop at the horizontal cabling and the telecommunications rooms for individual LANs. They also define the networking infrastructure for the entire enterprise, including backbone networks and services originating outside the building, such as telephone and Internet services.

As noted earlier, each telecommunications room contains a switch that actually connects the work area cable runs together. With the cable installation completed, you use patch cables to connect the ports in the patch panels to the ports in the switch. In the parlance of structured cabling, this switch is the *horizontal cross connect*; it joins all of the individual horizontal cable runs into a single LAN.

> **NOTE CONTRACTING CABLE INSTALLERS**
>
> When you hire a third-party contractor to install cables, their responsibility typically ends at the patch panels and the wall plates. The selection, installation, and configuration of switches and other components are the responsibility of the network's administrators.

At this point in the example, what you have is a series of individual LANs, one on each floor. The object, though, is to connect all of the LANs together, so that a computer on any LAN can communicate with a computer on any other LAN. You also want all of the computers on all of the LANs to be able to access a single connection to the Internet.

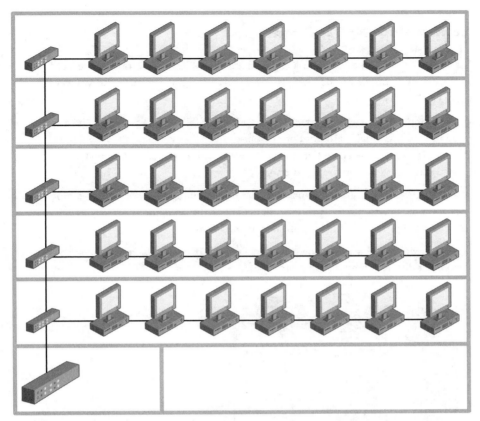

FIGURE 2-35 A backbone network connecting the horizontal cabling on multiple floors.

The backbone is another network, the primary function of which is to connect the LANs together. There are no workstations connected directly to the backbone. In some cases, you might connect servers to it, but many backbones carry nothing but intermediate traffic.

 Somewhere in the building, often on the ground floor or in the basement, there is an equipment room containing another patch panel. This patch panel, called the *vertical cross connect*, contains one end of the vertical cable runs leading to each of the other telecommunications rooms in the building. These vertical cable runs can use the same or a different type of cable as the horizontal runs on each floor.

Also in the equipment room is the backbone switch that connects all of the LANs together into one internetwork. As in the telecommunications rooms, you use patch cables to connect the ports in the vertical cross connect patch panel to the ports in the backbone switch.

Configuring the Backbone

Because the backbone network carries all of the internetwork traffic generated by the computers on the LANs, it should be as fast and as efficient as you can make it.

If, for example, you use Fast Ethernet on your horizontal networks, it would be a good idea to run Gigabit Ethernet on the backbone. However, now that Gigabit Ethernet is common, even on horizontal networks, you might consider moving up to 10 Gigabit Ethernet on the backbone.

Many networks also use a different medium for backbone networks. If, for example, your topmost horizontal network is 50 floors above the equipment room, you will need to use fiber optic cable to span such a long distance.

Modular switches such as the one shown in Figure 2-36 are available to enable you to connect different media to the same unit.

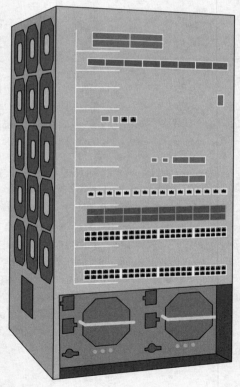

FIGURE 2-36 A modular switch.

You also use the backbone network to provide the LANs with access to services arriving from outside the building, such as telephone services and WAN connections. The place where an outside service enters the building is called a demarcation point—or *demarc*. The demarc is where the responsibility of the network administrator ends. If a problem occurs outside the demarc, it is up to the service provider to fix it. Inside the demarc, it is the network administrator's problem.

A demarc typically takes the form of a hardware device or interface furnished by the service provider, sometimes referred to as a network interface unit (NIU) or a network interface device (NID). On a home network that receives access to the Internet through a cable television company, the little box referred to as the cable modem is the NIU.

In the case of a large corporate installation, the NIUs for WAN connections are more than simple wiring devices; they can be much more complex. Most NIUs are equipped with *smartjacks*, like those shown in Figure 2-37, which enable them to perform additional functions, such as signal translation, signal regeneration, and remote diagnostics. A site with multiple WAN connections might have a modular cabinet with a smartjack on a separate expansion card for each service connection.

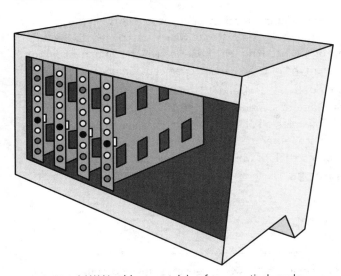

FIGURE 2-37 A WAN cabinet containing four smartjack cards.

A large enterprise network will—at minimum—have a demarc for telephone services and one for a connection to an ISP's network. There might also be connections for WAN links to other offices as well. In an ideal situation, these services will enter the building in the same equipment room that houses the backbone switch. This room is then called the *main distribution frame (MDF)*.

EXAM TIP

The Network+ objectives include the acronyms IDF and MDF without explanation. Candidates should be familiar with the concepts of the intermediate distribution frame and the main distribution frame for the exam; candidates are often familiar with the technology, but not with those particular terms.

NOTE PROTECTING EQUIPMENT

The MDF for a large network, like all of the telecommunications rooms in a building, contains a lot of critically important—and extremely expensive—equipment. To keep the equipment functional and safe, you must see to it that these rooms remain cool, dry, and secure. You must also ensure that all of the equipment has access to a high-quality source of power. Adequate locks, alarms, and HVAC equipment are essential. You might also want to install monitoring equipment to ensure that the conditions are maintained, even when the room is vacant. A voltage event recorder can monitor the power for interruptions, and a temperature monitor can ensure that climate conditions remain constant.

The next unit on the interior side of a demarc is called a *demarc extension*. In the case of an Internet connection, for example, the backbone switch to which you connect to the ISP's network is the demarc extension. For the incoming telephone service, the demarc extension might be a multiplexer or some other type of telephone company equipment.

Of course, situations rarely turn out to be ideal, and it is not unusual for the MDF equipment to be spread among several different locations. A single office building might house networks for dozens of different companies, all of whom also require telephone service as well. You might find that various services enter the building at different locations and must be routed to various equipment rooms, each of which is a maze of racks and cables. As with the cabling itself, labeling and organization is an essential part of maintaining a complex installation.

Exercise

The answers for this exercise are located in the "Answers" section at the end of this chapter. Fill in the missing word or phrase for each of the following sentences.

1. The unshielded twisted pair cable most commonly used for local area networks contains _____ wire pairs.

2. Fiber optic cable is completely resistant to _____ interference.

3. Ethernet networks that used coaxial cable were installed by using a _____ topology.

4. The more commonly used term for the 8P8C connector that unshielded twisted pair cables use is _____.

5. Unshielded twisted pair cables with longer lengths often use _____ conductors.

6. The technology that measures the length of a cable by transmitting a signal and measuring how long it takes for a reflection of the signal to return from the other end is called _____.

7. A horizontal cable run is typically attached to a wall plate at one end and a _____ at the other end.

8. Most of the wired local area networks installed today use the _____ topology.

9. The fiber optic cable type that uses a laser light source and spans longer distances is called _____ cable.

10. The place where an outside service, such as a telephone or WAN connection, enters a building is called a _____.

Chapter Summary

- A twisted pair cable is a collection of thin copper wires, with each wire having its own sheath of insulation. Individual pairs of insulated wires are twisted together, gathered in groups of four pairs (or more), and encased in another insulating sheath. Unshielded twisted pair (UTP) cable is the standard medium for copper-based Ethernet LANs.

- UTP cable comes in a variety of different categories that define the signal frequencies that the various cable types support, along with other characteristics, such as resistance to certain types of interference.

- Twisted pair cables use modular connectors that are most commonly referred to by the telephone networking designation RJ45, but which should properly be called 8P8C.

- A coaxial cable consists of a central copper conductor—which carries the signals—surrounded by a layer of insulation. Surrounding the insulation is a shielding conductor, typically made of copper mesh—which functions as the ground—and the whole assembly is encased in a sheath.

- Fiber optic cable transmits pulses of light through a filament of plastic or glass. The core filament is surrounded by a reflective layer called the *cladding*. The cladding is surrounded by a protective layer of woven fibers, a plastic spacer, and an outer sheath.

- The most common LAN topology in use today is the star topology, in which each computer or other device is connected by a separate cable run to a central cabling nexus, which can be either a switch or a hub.

- The process of attaching a jack to a cable end is called *punching down*, and the process is essentially the same whether you are connecting the cable to a wall plate, a patch panel, or a patch cord connector.

- Fiber optic connectors are sleeves that fit around the end of the cable and let the central core protrude from the end. The connector's only function is to lock the signal-carrying core in place when it's plugged into the jack.
- An enterprise network reaches well beyond a single LAN. Large corporate networks typically consist of multiple LANs that are joined together by another network, informally referred to as a backbone.

Chapter Review

Test your knowledge of the information in Chapter 2 by answering these questions. The answers to these questions, and the explanations of why each answer choice is correct or incorrect, are located in the "Answers" section at the end of this chapter.

1. Which of the following cable types is least susceptible to attenuation?
   - **A.** Shielded twisted pair
   - **B.** Unshielded twisted pair
   - **C.** Singlemode fiber optic
   - **D.** Multimode fiber optic

2. Which of the following data-link layer protocols is the only one that uses a physical double ring topology?
   - **A.** Fiber Distributed Data Interface
   - **B.** Token Ring
   - **C.** Coaxial-based Ethernet
   - **D.** Frame relay

3. In which of the following components do you find 110 blocks?
   - **A.** Demarcs
   - **B.** Patch panels
   - **C.** BNC connectors
   - **D.** Smartjacks

4. You have just finished installing the horizontal cabling for a LAN using UTP cable, and now you have to test your cable runs. However, the only tool you have is a basic wire-map tester. Which of the following connectivity issues will you be unable to detect by using your current equipment? (Choose all correct answers.)
   - **A.** Open circuits
   - **B.** Short circuits
   - **C.** Split pairs
   - **D.** Crosstalk

Answers

This section contains the answers to the questions for the Exercise and Chapter Review in this chapter.

Exercise

1. Eight

2. Electromagnetic

3. Bus

4. RJ45

5. Solid

6. Time domain reflectometry

7. Patch panel

8. Star

9. Singlemode

10. Demarcation point or demarc

Chapter Review

1. **Correct Answer:** C

   A. **Incorrect:** Twisted pair cables are more susceptible to attenuation than fiber optic cables.

   B. **Incorrect:** Shielding has no effect on a twisted pair cable's susceptibility to attenuation.

   C. **Correct:** Singlemode fiber optic cable is highly resistant to attenuation, enabling it to span long distances.

   D. **Incorrect:** Multimode fiber optic cable is more susceptible to attenuation than singlemode.

2. **Correct Answer:** A

   A. **Correct:** FDDI supports a physical double ring topology, with traffic flowing in opposite directions on the two rings, for fault tolerance.

   B. **Incorrect:** Token Ring uses a single ring topology, and it is in most cases a logical ring. The physical topology is a star.

   C. **Incorrect:** Coaxial Ethernet uses a bus topology, not a ring.

D. Incorrect: The Frame relay is a WAN protocol that uses a point-to-multipoint topology, not a ring.

3. **Correct Answer:** B

   A. Incorrect: Demarcation points are where outside services enter the building. They do not have 110 blocks.

   B. Correct: Patch panels containing RJ45 connectors have 110 blocks, to which you connect your internal cable runs.

   C. Incorrect: All keystone connectors are modular devices that snap into wall plates. They do not have 110 blocks.

   D. Incorrect: Smartjacks enable service providers to exercise control over the services running into a customer's site. They do not have 110 blocks.

4. **Correct Answer:** C and D

   A. Incorrect: A wiremap tester is capable of detecting open circuits.

   B. Incorrect: A wiremap tester is capable of detecting short circuits.

   C. Correct: A wiremap tester is not able to detect split pairs, because the signals still originate and terminate at the same pins.

   D. Correct: A wiremap tester is not able to measure crosstalk, because it can only detect the presence or absence of signals.

CHAPTER 3

Network Devices

Cables form the fabric of a local area network (LAN), but the sole function of a cable is to carry signals from one device to another. In Chapter 2, "The Physical Layer," you learned about the various types of cables used in networking, their properties, and how to install them. In this chapter, you will learn about the various types of networking devices that the cables link together.

Computers, printers, and other network nodes must have network interface adapters to connect to a LAN. On the infrastructure side of the network, you can find several other devices. Switches and routers are the most common, but other devices can include hubs, repeaters, and bridges.

> **NOTE WIRELESS LANS**
>
> As with Chapter 2, this chapter omits coverage of wireless LAN technologies, which are becoming increasingly prevalent in homes, offices, and public businesses. For wireless network coverage, see Chapter 5, "Wireless Networking."

Exam objectives in this chapter:

Objective 1.2: Classify how applications, devices, and protocols relate to the OSI model layers.

- MAC address
- IP address
- EUI-64
- Frames
- Packets
- Switch
- Router
- Multilayer switch
- Hub
- Encryption devices
- Cable
- NIC
- Bridge

Objective 2.6: Given a set of requirements, plan and implement a basic SOHO network.

- List of requirements
- Cable length
- Device types/requirements
- Environment limitations
- Equipment limitations
- Compatibility requirements

REAL WORLD   **THE ABSTRACT AND THE SPECIFIC**

It is difficult to discuss the subjects of this chapter in the abstract, because they are so closely associated with specific networking technologies. For example, when the chapter discusses a hub or a switch, it is almost always talking about an Ethernet device. When discussing a router, it is nearly always referring to a TCP/IP router. However, this was not always the case.

In the earlier days of PC networking—and in earlier versions of the Network+ exam—there were other technologies to which these terms applied. Other data-link layer protocols, such as Token Ring and ARCnet, had their own types of hubs that were most definitely not compatible with Ethernet devices. Today, those technologies are obsolete. The products are no longer available on the market, and CompTIA has removed the topics from the Network+ exam. Ethernet and TCP/IP are unquestionably the industry standards at the data-link and the network/transport layers.

The effect that these changes have on a study guide such as this are primarily organizational. It would be nice to have all of the information on Ethernet in one place, and all of the TCP/IP coverage in another. However, these two technologies are so pervasive in PC networking that it is difficult to talk about hubs and switches without bringing Ethernet into the picture. In the same way, it is difficult to talk about routers without introducing the Internet Protocol. As a result, this chapter inevitably contains some Ethernet and TCP/IP Content before those two subjects have been formally introduced (in Chapter 6, "The Network Layer," and Chapter 7, "Routing and Switching," respectively).

Network Interface Adapters

 A *network interface adapter* is the hardware implementation of a data-link layer LAN protocol. Virtually every computer sold today has an Ethernet adapter incorporated into its motherboard, but network adapters are also available in the form of expansion cards that plug into a computer's internal slot or external devices that plug into a Universal Serial Bus (USB) port.

 EXAM TIP

Network interface adapters built onto expansion cards are commonly known as network interface cards, or more frequently, NICs. In the early days of local area networking, before adapters were incorporated into motherboard designs, a card was the only way to add a network adapter to a computer, and the use of the term "NIC" became so common that many people still use it today, even when referring to an integrated adapter.

As with any interface, an adapter is a device that connects two systems together. An Ethernet adapter always has a cable connector, to which you attach a network cable, as shown in Figure 3-1, as well as some attachment to the computer itself. Most Ethernet adapters have a female RJ45 (more appropriately called an 8P8C) connector for an unshielded twisted pair (UTP) cable. However, there are fiber optic Ethernet adapters that can have any of the popular fiber optic connectors.

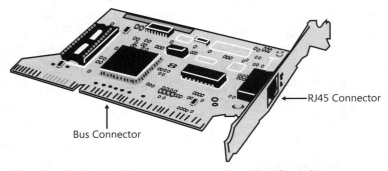

FIGURE 3-1 The RJ45 cable connector on a network interface adapter.

In the early days of Ethernet, it was common for network interface adapters to have multiple cable connectors on them, as shown in Figure 3-2. One typical configuration had an RJ45 connector for 10Base-T, a BNC connector for Thin Ethernet, and an AUI connector for a Thick Ethernet transceiver cable. This enabled administrators to purchase one adapter card for use on any of the three main 10-Mbps Ethernet network media. However, you could only use one of the cable connectors at a time. You could not connect two or three cables simultaneously.

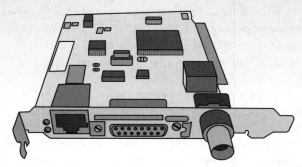

FIGURE 3-2 A 10-Mbps Ethernet adapter with connectors for three cable types.

Network interface cards (NICs) have connectors appropriate for a computer's expansion bus, such as Peripheral Component Interconnect (PCI), as shown in Figure 3-3, but there are still older models available that support other bus types. External adapters have USB 2.0 ports that you use to connect to a computer's USB port. Adapters that are incorporated into the motherboard have their own direct PCI connections to the system bus.

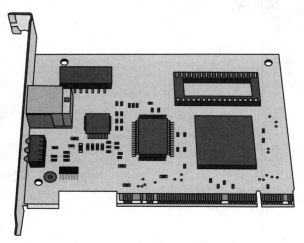

FIGURE 3-3 The bus connector on a network interface card.

In addition to the connectors, the other components of a network interface adapter that are useful to the network administrator are the light-emitting diodes (LEDs), usually located near the cable connectors. Depending on its capabilities, an adapter can have one or as many as four LEDs, as well as LEDs that can glow in different colors. The functions provided by the LEDs can include the following:

- **Link**   The link is a signal that network interface adapters exchange with other directly connected network devices, indicating each other's presence. When you connect the adapter to a switch or hub port, for example, the link LEDs on both devices glow continuously, indicating an active connection. As long as both devices are connected to a power source, the link LEDs might even work if the computer is not turned on.

- **Speed**   Many network interface adapters (as well as switches and hubs) support multiple transmission speeds, and devices often use LEDs to indicate which speed the device is currently using. There is no standard method for indicating speed by using LEDs. In some cases, an LED will glow in different colors to represent the different speeds. In other cases, the LED might be on for one speed and off for the other.

- **Activity**   Some network adapters have an LED that flickers when the unit is transmitting or receiving data. This can be a valuable troubleshooting tool. A link LED indicates that the two devices are correctly wired together, but an activity LED indicates that the devices are actually able to send and receive data.

- **Collisions**   Collisions occur when two nodes on an Ethernet network transmit at the same time. A certain number of collisions is normal, and some older network adapters have an LED that flashes when the system detects a collision on the network. Most modern adapters do not have this feature.

Most network interface adapters also have hardware addresses (also known as media access control or MAC addresses, and officially, by the IEEE, as EUI-48 identifiers) permanently assigned to them by their manufacturers. The address is a 6-byte (or 48-bit) hexadecimal value permanently stored in read-only memory. The first 3 bytes of the address consist of an *organizationally unique identifier (OUI)* that is assigned to the manufacturer by the Institute of Electrical and Electronics Engineers (IEEE). The second 3 bytes are a unique value generated by the manufacturer itself. Data-link layer protocols use these addresses to uniquely identify every node on a network.

EXAM TIP

Candidates for the Network+ exam should be familiar with the differences between the hardware address (or MAC address) built into a network adapter and the IP address assigned by the network administrator. Hardware addresses are 6 bytes long and are expressed as hexadecimals, whereas IPv4 addresses are 4 bytes (32 bits) long and expressed as decimals. Bear in mind, however, that IPv6 addresses are 16 bytes (128 bits) long and are hexadecimals that are often based on the computer's hardware address.

To display the hardware address of a computer's network interface adapter in Windows, you can run the System Information (Msinfo32.exe) utility, as shown in Figure 3-4, or execute the ipconfig /all command from the command prompt. On a Unix or Linux system, you can run the ifconfig command.

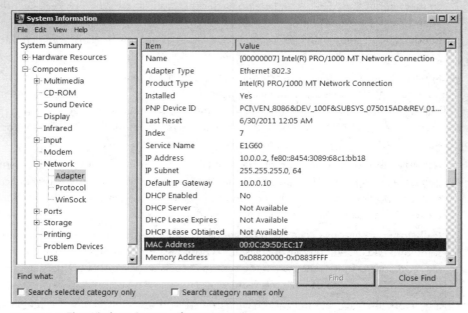

FIGURE 3-4 The Windows System Information utility.

The network interface adapter hardware, along with the device driver that enables the computer to access the adapter, implements the entirety of the data-link layer protocol that the computer uses to communicate with the LAN.

Computers are not the only devices that can have network interface adapters. It has become an increasingly common practice in recent years to connect printers, copiers, and multifunction devices directly to the network. This enables administrators to place the devices nearly anywhere, while providing all of the network users with ready access to them. There are many print devices available with built-in Ethernet or wireless network interface adapters, often of modular design, that plug into proprietary expansion slots. There are also external devices—print servers—that contain network interface adapters as well as connections for print devices.

The most recently developed application for network interface adapters is the storage area network (SAN), which is a specialized network of servers and storage devices, such as drive arrays and network attached storage (NAS) units. Devices on this type of network typically use protocols that are different from those of LANs, such as Fibre Channel or iSCSI, but the basic principles of the network adapters they use are the same.

 Quick Check

1. Name two of the functions that can be performed by the LEDs on a typical network interface adapter.
2. The majority of the network interface cards on the market support which two data-link layer protocols?

Quick Check Answers

1. They can indicate the presence of a connection to another system, activity on the network, the speed of the network, or the occurrence of a collision.
2. Ethernet and IEEE 802.11 wireless.

Network Interface Adapter Functions

Though it is obvious that the primary function of the network interface adapter is to provide a computer with access to the network medium, it also performs many other functions. The following sequence describes the basic functions of a network interface adapter when it is connecting a computer to a LAN. The functions occur in the order listed for an adapter transmitting data over the network. For incoming network data, the functions occur in reverse order.

1. **Data transfer**   The top of the protocol stack, from the application layer down to the network layer, exists only in the computer's memory. As the system passes data down from the network layer to the data-link layer, it transfers the data from system memory to the network interface adapter by using a technology such as polling, programmed input/output (I/O), interrupt I/O, or direct memory access (DMA).

2. **Data buffering**   Network interface adapters transmit and receive data a frame at a time, so they must have on-board memory to serve as a buffer space for partially formed frames. Adapters have separate buffers for incoming and outgoing data, the size of which depends on the adapter model. An Ethernet frame is 1,500 bytes, so the typical minimum amount of buffer memory is 4 kilobytes (KB), 2 for incoming data and 2 for outgoing. High-performance adapters, such as those used in servers, can have more buffer memory.

3. **Data encapsulation**   For outgoing traffic, the network interface adapter and its device driver are responsible for constructing the data-link layer frame around the information passed down to them from the network layer protocol. For incoming traffic, the adapter performs a cyclical redundancy check (CRC) calculation, by using the value in the frame footer, to confirm that the packet has arrived intact. Then the adapter strips off the data-link layer frame and passes the information it finds inside up to the appropriate network layer protocol.

4. **Media access control (MAC)**   The network interface adapter implements the MAC mechanism of the data-link layer protocol. On an Ethernet network, the MAC mechanism is called Carrier Sense Multiple Access with Collision Detection (CSMA/CD). The MAC mechanism ensures that nodes access the shared network medium in a controlled fashion, tries to prevent packet collisions from occurring, and detects collisions in a timely manner when they do occur.

5. **Parallel/serial conversion**   Network interface adapters connected to a computer's system bus often use parallel communication to access the system memory array, sending and receiving multiple bits at one time. (The exception to this is PCI Express, which is a multilane serial bus design.) Baseband LANs use serial communication, sending and receiving one bit at a time. To transmit the data it receives from system memory over the network, the adapter must convert each 16, 32, or 64 bits it receives in parallel into a stream of single bits. For incoming data from the network, the adapter performs the conversion in reverse, from serial to parallel.

6. **Signal encoding/decoding**   The network interface adapter takes the binary data of the data-link layer frame and converts it by using an encoding scheme appropriate to the network medium at the physical layer, using electrical voltages, light pulses, or radio frequencies. For copper-based Ethernet networks, for example, the adapter uses a scheme called Manchester encoding. For incoming signals, the adapter performs the same conversion in reverse, producing binary data that it passes to the network layer protocol.

7. **Data transmission/reception**   At the appropriate time, according to the MAC mechanism, and using signals of the appropriate amplitude, the network interface adapter transmits the data over the network medium. The adapter also stands ready to read incoming signals at any time.

MORE INFO   **THE DATA-LINK LAYER**

For more information on packet formation and media access control on Ethernet networks, see Chapter 4, "The Data-Link Layer."

Optional Network Adapter Functions

In addition to the basic functions listed in the previous section, some network interface adapters perform additional functions. In most cases, these adapters are high-end adapters intended for servers, high-performance workstations, or managed networks. Some of the most common optional adapter functions are described in the following sections.

Processor Offloading

Many of the expansion devices in the average computer require specialized processing tasks, and in the early days of the PC, the typical design practice was to make these devices as simple as possible and let the system processor handle all of these processing tasks. However, it has become an increasingly common practice in recent years for manufacturers to build adapters that have their own processors and that perform specialized tasks on board, thus lightening the burden on the system processor.

For example, most video display adapters on the market today include a graphics processor that is specifically designed to perform certain image manipulation tasks faster and more efficiently than the system processor. Some network interface adapters also have their own processors, enabling them to offload tasks from the system processor, using techniques such as bus mastering. Under normal circumstances, when a network interface adapter uses the system bus to communicate with the system memory array, the system processor functions as an intermediary, initiating the transactions as needed. Some adapters are capable of functioning as bus masters, which enables them to arbitrate access to the system bus without the intervention of the system processor.

Some of the tasks commonly offloaded to the adapter are as follows:

- **Error Detection**   The error detection mechanisms in the data-link, network, and transport layer protocols require transmitting computers to perform a Cyclic Redundancy Check (CRC) calculation and save the resulting value in a header or footer. On receiving computers, the system performs the same calculation and compares its results with those in the packet. Some network adapters can offload some or all of those CRC calculations and perform them using a processor on the adapter, instead of the system processor.

- **Large send processing**   When a computer on a Transmission Control Protocol/Internet Protocol (TCP/IP) network transmits a large amount of data in a single TCP transaction, the TCP protocol at the transport layer must split the data into segments of appropriate size and assign sequence numbers to each segment. Some network interface adapters can take on these processes themselves, rather than force the system processor to do them. The adapter does this by advertising a larger Maximum Segment Size (MSS) value to the TCP implementation and creating a buffer of the same size. TCP therefore creates segments that are artificially large, and the adapter is responsible for splitting them into smaller segments suitable for transmission.

- **IPsec processing**   IP security (IPsec) is a collection of security standards that enable computers on a TCP/IP network to encrypt and digitally sign their transmissions. This prevents anyone who intercepts the transmissions from deciphering their contents. The IPsec encryption and signature calculations can place a heavy burden on the system processor, depending on the amount of data being secured and the length of the encryption keys the system is configured to use. Offloading these processes to the network interface adapter can have a noticeable effect on system performance.

Network Management

Administrators of enterprise networks often use network management systems to track the performance of critical network components. A network management system consists of a central console and a series of programs called agents, which are incorporated into hardware and software components scattered around the network. An agent transmits information about the performance of a specific component back to the console on a regular schedule, using a specialized protocol such as *Simple Network Management Protocol (SNMP)*.

Some network interface adapters have agents built into them so that they can report information about the network performance of the computers into which they are installed. SNMP agents can also generate messages called traps, which they can send to the console immediately when a specific situation requiring attention occurs.

Wake-on-LAN

One of the most persistent irritants for system administrators who work on computers at remote locations during off hours is when users turn their systems off, contrary to instructions. In the past, the administrator either had to travel to the computer to turn it on again or work on the system at another time. Wake-on-LAN is a feature that enables an administrator to power up a computer remotely.

Wake-on-LAN lets a network interface adapter operate in a low power mode, even when the computer is turned off. When the adapter is in this mode, it continues to monitor the traffic arriving over the network, although it takes no action unless it receives a special "magic" packet from the administrator. When it receives an appropriate magic packet, the adapter sends an instruction to the computer's motherboard, which causes the motherboard to activate the power supply and start the system.

Implementation of Wake-on-LAN requires both the network interface adapter and the motherboard to support the standard. The Wake-on-LAN feature is incorporated into many current network interface adapters.

Network Fault Tolerance

Some network interface adapters intended for servers have a failover capability that enables a secondary adapter to take over all network communication tasks when the system's primary adapter fails. When the failed adapter returns to service, it resumes its role as the primary adapter for the computer. Installing multiple adapters in a single computer can also provide a performance advantage, as noted later in the discussion of link aggregation.

Multiple Ports

There are several applications that call for multiple network adapters in a single computer, including server virtualization, network segmentation, and bandwidth aggregation. However, it is often the case that a computer requiring multiple adapters does not have a sufficient number of expansion slots available to support two, three, or four NICs.

Some manufacturers, therefore, have marketed NICs with multiple adapters on a single expansion card, as shown in Figure 3-5. These devices have multiple RJ45 connectors and are the functional equivalent of installing multiple NICs in a single computer.

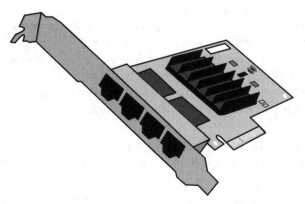

FIGURE 3-5 A multiport network interface adapter card.

The Preboot Execution Environment

The Preboot Execution Environment (PXE) is a feature that implements a limited TCP/IP client in the network adapter's memory. This enables a computer with no installed operating system to start, obtain an IP address from a Dynamic Host Configuration Protocol (DHCP) server, and locate a server from which it can download and execute a minimal operating system or boot file.

In cooperation with an application such as Windows Deployment Services, PXE enables administrators to perform unattended operating system deployments and updates to computers on the network.

Purchasing Network Interface Adapters

The first question a relatively inexperienced network administrator might ask when faced with the issue of purchasing network adapters is: why purchase them in the first place, when nearly every computer in the world has a motherboard with an adapter integrated into it? There are several possible reasons why it might be necessary to purchase new network adapters for computers that already have them, especially in a large enterprise environment. Some of these reasons are as follows:

- **To speed up the network** For older computers with relatively slow integrated adapters, you might want to purchase new, faster adapters, assuming that your cables, switches, and other components are capable of supporting the higher speed.

- **To use an alternative medium** Integrated network adapters are usually intended for unshielded twisted pair networks. If you want to connect your computers to a wireless or fiber optic network, you will have to purchase adapters supporting that medium.

- **To manage the network** Integrated network adapters rarely have network management agents. If you want to manage the network activity of your computers by using an SNMP-based product, you will most likely have to purchase new, manageable adapters.

- **To use link aggregation** Also called bonding, *link aggregation* is the ability to install multiple network adapters in a computer and combine their bandwidth. If, for example, you have a group of users that routinely accesses large image files on a server, and that traffic is having a negative effect on the performance of the entire network, installing a second network interface adapter in the server and in each of the workstations can, under certain circumstances, be a far less expensive solution than upgrading the entire network to a faster speed.

- **To add features** Although it seems a less likely reason than the others listed here, there might be other features that are important enough to you to be worth the expense and the trouble of purchasing and installing new network interface adapters. For example, support for PXE in your adapters might mean the difference between automating the installation of the operating system on 100 computers and performing those 100 installations manually.

- **To standardize a configuration**   Installing the same network interface adapter in all of an organization's computers can simplify administration by standardizing on the same drivers and maintenance tools.

When selecting network interface adapters for your computers, you must not only consider the additional features you require, you must also make sure that the adapters you choose are compatible with your computers and your network. Be sure to consider each of the following criteria before you make your purchases.

- **Data-link layer protocol**   Though in the past there were many other selections, nearly all of the network interface adapters on the market today are designed for the Ethernet or Wi-Fi protocols. However, be sure to look for the proper variant of the protocol you need. There are adapters supporting Ethernet, Fast Ethernet, Gigabit Ethernet, and 10 Gigabit Ethernet on the market, and Wi-Fi adapters come in IEEE 802.11a, b, g, and n variants.

- **Transmission speed**   In most cases, the newer, faster variants of the Ethernet and Wi-Fi protocols are backward compatible with the previous versions and can fall back to slower speeds by using an autonegotiation process. Buying the fastest adapters available might be slightly more expensive, but it generally ensures compatibility, and also provides a path for future network upgrades.

> **NOTE** **PRE-STANDARD PRODUCTS**
>
> It is common for the manufacturers of networking products to release network adapters and other components that use the latest, fastest technology, even before the standards for that technology have been officially ratified. When you purchase these products, there is a risk that there might be incompatibilities with other manufacturers' implementations, or that the technology might change before the standard is finally completed. Sometimes you can update pre-standard devices after the finalized standards are published, by flashing the device's ROM.

- **Network interface**   In the case of Ethernet network adapters, there are models available for UTP networks, which have the standard RJ45 (8P8C) connector, and those for fiber optic networks, which can have any of the connector types described in Chapter 2.

- **System bus type**   Before you even consider adding network interface adapter cards to your computers, you must be sure that the computers have expansion slots available. You must also determine what type of slot is available in each computer and purchase adapters with the correct interface. Most of the desktop PCs in use today have PCI or PCI Express slots. PCI Express devices come in various lane configurations, notated as x2 for two-lane, x4 for four-lane, and so on. You might run into older computers with obsolete bus types, such as Industry Standard Architecture (ISA) or VESA Local Bus. Network adapters for these buses might be difficult to locate. For laptops and other portable computers, adapters are available for the PC Card Cardbus standard (which provides performance comparable to PCI) or the MiniPCI bus. For computers without internal slots, USB adapters are available. However, you must be aware of the USB version of the slots in the computer. USB 1.1 is insufficient for network use; USB 2.0 can support Fast Ethernet but not Gigabit Ethernet. USB 3.0 slots can support Gigabit Ethernet but not 10 Gigabit Ethernet.

- **Driver availability**   All network interface adapters require a device driver for the operating system running on the computer. Make sure that the manufacturer of the adapters you select provides drivers for the operating system you plan to run on the computers. Older model adapters might not have drivers for the latest Windows versions, and driver support for Unix and Linux can be even more problematic.

- **Price**   Network interface adapters are available at a wide range of prices, from less than US $10 to several hundred dollars. Although you might be tempted to purchase the least expensive adapters that have the features you require, consider the advantages of the name brand. You generally receive advanced features, better and more frequent driver updates, and the ability to return products that don't perform well.

Installing a Network Interface Adapter

To install a network interface card into a computer's expansion slot, use the following procedure.

> **IMPORTANT   ELECTROSTATIC DISCHARGE**
>
> Before touching the internal components of the computer or removing the new network adapter from its protective bag, be sure to ground yourself by touching the metal frame of the computer's power supply, or use a wrist strap or antistatic mat to protect the equipment from damage done by electrostatic discharge.

1. Turn off the power to the computer and unplug the power cord.

   Inserting an expansion card into a slot while the computer is on can destroy the card and cause serious injuries. Accidentally dropping a screw or slot cover into the case can also cause serious damage if the computer is powered up.

2. Open the computer case.

   In older PCs, this can be the most difficult part of the installation process. You might have to remove several screws to loosen the case cover and wrestle with the computer a bit to get the cover off. Many newer systems, on the other hand, secure the case cover with thumbscrews that are much easier to open.

3. Locate a free slot.

   You must check to see what type of expansion slots are available in the computer before you select a card. Most adapters now use the PCI or PCI Express bus.

4. **Remove the slot cover.**

   Empty slots are protected by a slot cover that prevents them from being exposed through the back of the computer. These slots are secured by a screw or a latch mechanism. Loosen the screw or open the latch securing the slot cover in place, and remove the slot cover.

5. **Insert the card into the slot.**

   Line up the edge connector on the card with the slot and press the card down until it is fully seated in the slot, as shown in Figure 3-6.

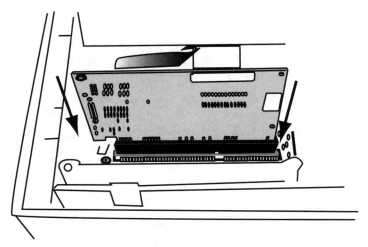

FIGURE 3-6 Inserting a network interface card.

6. **Secure the card by replacing the slot cover screw or closing the latch.**

   This seats the card firmly in the slot. Some network technicians omit this step and leave the screw off, but it is an important step, because a yank on the network cable can pull the card partially out of the slot and cause intermittent problems that are difficult to diagnose.

7. **Replace the cover on the computer case and secure it with the fasteners provided.**

> **NOTE TESTING ADAPTERS**
> It's a good idea to test the network interface adapter by connecting it to the LAN and running it before you close the case and return the computer to its original location. Newly installed components seem to be more likely to malfunction if you put the case cover on before testing them.

Troubleshooting a Network Interface Adapter

When a computer or other device fails to communicate with the network, the network interface adapter might be at fault, but it's far more likely that some other component is causing the problem.

Before addressing the network interface adapter itself, check for the following problems:

- Make sure the network cable is firmly seated into the connector on the network interface adapter. Check the cable connection on the hub or switch as well. Loose connections are a common cause of communications problems.

- Try using a different cable that you know is good. If you are using permanently installed cable runs, plug the computer into another jack that you know is functioning properly, and use a different patch cable. Also try replacing the patch cable between the distribution panel and the switch or hub. One of the cables could be causing the problem, even if there is no visible fault.

- Make sure the proper device driver is installed. Check the driver documentation and the website of the network interface adapter manufacturer for information on possible driver problems or driver updates for your operating system before you open up the computer.

- Check to see that all of the other software components required for network communications, such as clients and protocols, are properly installed and configured.

EXAM TIP

Integrated network interface adapters are far less likely to suffer from hardware faults than network interface cards. When troubleshooting integrated adapters, look to driver issues or cable faults before you assume that the adapter hardware itself is malfunctioning.

If you cannot find a problem with the driver, the cable, or the network configuration parameters, look at the network interface adapter itself. Before you open the computer case, check to see if the adapter's manufacturer has provided its own diagnostic software. In some cases, the manufacturer provides a utility that includes diagnostic features to test the functions of the card.

If the diagnostics program finds a problem with the card itself, you need to open up the computer and physically examine the adapter. If the adapter is damaged or defective, there is not much you can do except replace it. Before you do this, however, you should check to see that the card is fully seated in the slot, because this is a prime cause of communication problems. If the card is not secured with a screw, press it down firmly into the slot at both ends and secure it.

If the problem persists, remove the card from the slot, clean out the slot with a blast of compressed air, and install the card again. If there is still a problem, use another slot, if one is available. If the adapter still fails to function properly, install a different adapter in the computer. You can use either a new one or one from another computer that you know is working properly. If the replacement adapter functions, then you know that the original adapter itself is to blame, and you should replace it.

Quick Check

1. What are the two terms used to refer to the ability to install multiple network adapters in a computer and combine their bandwidth?

2. What is the term used to describe the first 3 bytes of a network interface adapter's hardware address?

Quick Check Answers

1. Link aggregation and bonding

2. Organizationally unique identifier

At the Other End of the Cable

Computers, printers, and other devices with network adapters in them sit at one end of your cables. So what do you find at the other end?

In the early days of local area networking, you would have found computers connected directly to each other in a bus topology using coaxial cables. Since the introduction of UTP-based networks, however, and up until today, you find network nodes connected to some sort of central cabling nexus, using a star topology. The history of the devices at the other end of the cable tracks the evolution of local area networking, as described in the following sections.

EXAM TIP

Some of the devices described in the following sections are rarely seen on today's networks, but for the Network+ exam, you should be familiar with their functions and the layers of the OSI reference model at which they operate.

Using Repeaters

Ethernet networks have always had limits to their cable segment lengths. Cables that are too long can cause signals to attenuate and prevent the Ethernet MAC mechanism from functioning properly. In the days of coaxial Ethernet, if you had a cable segment that exceeded the maximum length—185 meters for Thin Ethernet and 500 meters for Thick Ethernet—you could extend it by inserting a repeater somewhere along its length.

A *repeater* is simply a box with two cable connectors on it that amplifies any signals arriving through one connector and transmits them out through the other. Although designed for use on a specific type of network, such as Ethernet, the repeater is simply an electrical device, operating at the physical layer.

EXAM TIP

Stand-alone two-port repeaters are unheard of on today's Ethernet networks because these networks no longer use coaxial cable. The repeating function on modern UTP and fiber optic networks—if it is necessary—is handled by a hub or switch.

Using Hubs

The earliest Ethernet physical layer specification calling for UTP cable is called 10Base-T, and it requires the computers and other nodes to be connected to a device called a hub. To all appearances, a *hub*—sometimes called a concentrator—is simply a box with a power supply and a number of female RJ45 connectors in it, and usually an array of LEDs for each connector, as shown in Figure 3-7.

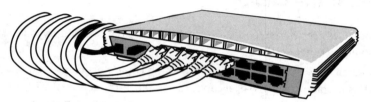

FIGURE 3-7 An Ethernet hub.

EXAM TIP

Although other—now obsolete—data-link layer protocols called for the use of hubs, the only such devices available now are those for Ethernet networks. However, Ethernet hubs are becoming increasingly rare as well, mainly because switches are available at comparable prices.

Hubs can have anywhere from 4 to 96 or more ports, usually in multiples of 8. Hubs can be small, stand-alone devices, such as those used for home and small office networks, or large, open-framed units that mount in the standard racks found in data centers.

Signal Repeating

Technically, a hub is a device called a *multiport repeater*. The hub takes all signals entering through any of its ports, amplifies them, and transmits them out through all of the other ports, as shown in Figure 3-8. As a result, the packets transmitted by any of the nodes on the network are forwarded to all of the other nodes on the network.

Because of the way the hub functions, computers on the network receive a great many packets that they do not need. These are packets destined for other systems, and the computers simply discard them. This is not a terrible thing, as long as the traffic levels on the network do not reach the saturation point.

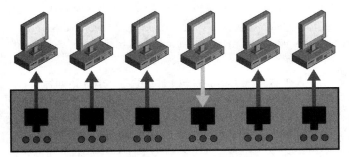

FIGURE 3-8 The signal propagation pattern of an Ethernet hub.

Because the hub functions as a repeater, the maximum distance between two network nodes is extended. The Ethernet specifications for UTP cable specify a maximum segment length of 100 meters, meaning that the cable connecting a computer to the hub can be 100 meters long. However, the distance between any two computers on the network can be as much as 200 meters—the distance from the first computer to the hub and from the hub to the second computer. The Ethernet media access control mechanism can still function at this distance because the hub repeats the signals.

Like two-port repeaters, most hubs are strictly physical layer devices, purely electrical in nature. They manipulate electrical signals; they do not read or interpret them as binary data. Hubs are therefore often referred to as "dumb," whereas switches and other devices that can interpret the signals are referred to as "intelligent" or "smart."

EXAM TIP

By amplifying signals, repeaters protect against signal loss caused by attenuation and enable cable segments to span longer distances.

Connecting devices together with a hub creates a shared network medium and therefore a single collision domain. A *collision domain* is a group of network devices connected in such a way that if two devices transmit at the same time, a collision occurs.

Signal Crossover

Another function provided by a hub is the signal crossover. As mentioned in Chapter 2, UTP networks are wired "straight through," meaning that the transmit pin at one end of each cable run is wired to the transmit pin at the other end. At some point, however, a crossover is needed, so that the data that one computer sends over the transmit pin arrives at the other computer on the receive pin. The hub provides that crossover.

A problem arises, however, when you have more than one hub on a network. If, for example, you have an eight-port hub that is completely populated, you can add another hub to the network to provide more ports. However, if you use a standard patch cable to connect a standard port in one hub to a standard port in another, you are introducing two crossovers into the circuit, which cancel each other out, leaving that transmit pin wired to the transmit pin.

To connect hubs together, therefore, you must use a special uplink port, which does not include a crossover circuit. Most hubs have an uplink port, but manufacturers can implement them in any one of three ways, as follows:

- **Dedicated** A dedicated uplink port is one that is permanently wired without a crossover circuit. The port might be labeled with the word "uplink," or with any one of several other names, and might or might not count as one of the ports advertised as the device's total. In some cases, a dedicated port is adjacent to a standard port, with markings relating the two, and in those cases, you can only use one of the two.

- **Toggled** On a toggled uplink port, you can enable or disable the signal crossover circuit as needed, by using a switch of some type. This enables you to use the port for a computer connection if you do not need it to function as an uplink port.

- **Automatic** An automatic port senses whether it is connected to a computer or another hub and activates the crossover circuit as needed. Hubs with this technology frequently offer it on every port, rather than just one, as in the cases of dedicated or toggled ports.

> *NOTE* **THE UPLINK PORT**
>
> When purchasing a hub, be sure to account for the uplink port when totaling up the ports available for computer connections. In some cases, an eight-port hub might actually have only seven ports available for computer connections, because one is an uplink port.

To connect two hubs together, you use a standard patch cable to connect the uplink port on one hub to a standard port on the other hub, as shown in Figure 3-9. Do not connect one uplink port to another uplink port, or you will end up having a circuit with no crossovers. Every path from computer to computer must have one—and only one—crossover.

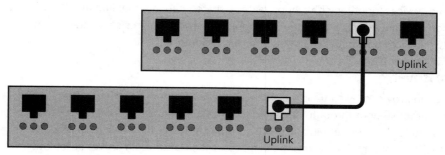

FIGURE 3-9 Two hubs linked by connecting an uplink port to a standard port.

 If you have two hubs, neither of which includes an uplink port, you can still link them together by using a crossover cable. A *crossover cable* has the transmit pins in each connector wired to the receive pins in the other connector. This creates the crossover circuit in the cable instead of the hub. You can also use a crossover cable to create a simple two-node network by connecting two computers together without a hub. The one thing you must not do is use a crossover cable to connect a computer to a standard hub port.

When you have more than two hubs that you want to connect together, you can daisy chain them, as shown in Figure 3-10. By connecting each hub to the next hub, you maintain the proper crossover configuration between any two computers on the network.

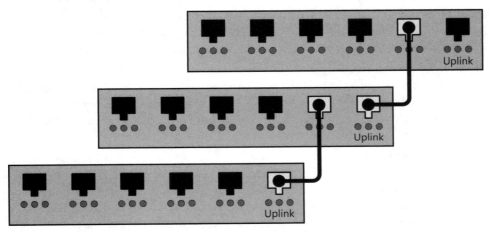

FIGURE 3-10 Hubs connected by using a daisy chain configuration.

NOTE **ETHERNET HUBS**

The Ethernet specifications limit the number of hubs you can connect together on a single network. For more information on these limitations, see Chapter 4. Some manufacturers also market *stackable hubs*, which are hubs that you can link together to expand their port density without Ethernet recognizing them as separate devices.

Choosing a Hub

Most of the Ethernet hubs on the market support the electrical specifications for various transmission speeds. When you purchase a hub, you must select one that supports the speed you are using on your network. If you have a mixture of speeds running on the same network, or if you are planning a gradual upgrade to the next higher speed, multispeed hubs can be worthwhile.

However, the biggest question that most administrators will face when purchasing hubs is whether to purchase them at all. In the market and on most networks, hubs have been re-placed by switches. Switches have more intelligence than hubs, and though they were at first more expensive, years of product maturation have brought prices down. For information on the differences between switches and hubs, see "Using Switches" later in this chapter.

Using Bridges

Early Ethernet networking technologies had growth potential, but that growth had limits. Bus networks and hub-based star networks both use a shared network medium, which means that every node on the network receives all of the packets transmitted by all of the other nodes. As you expand the network by adding more and more nodes, the amount of traffic increases, eventually resulting in a state approaching saturation.

A saturated network is one in which there are so many packets being transmitted that nodes trying to send data experience delays in gaining access to the network medium. These delays are known as *latency*. When a network reaches the point at which it can handle no more traffic, the only solution is to somehow split the traffic between two networks.

The first glimmer of intelligence in Ethernet networking equipment was in a device called a *bridge*, which was designed to address this type of traffic problem. Unlike repeaters and hubs, which are physical layer devices, bridges operate at the data-link layer, meaning that they are capable of opening packets and reading the data-link layer protocol header information they find there.

A bridge splits an Ethernet LAN in half, much like a repeater, except that a repeater always forwards every packet it receives, whereas bridges are selective about the packets they forward. When a packet arrives through one of the bridge's interfaces, the bridge reads the destination hardware address from the Ethernet header. If the packet is destined for a computer on the other side of the bridge, the bridge forwards the packet out through its other interface, as shown in Figure 3-11. If the packet is destined for a computer on the same side of the bridge from which it was received, the bridge simply discards the packet.

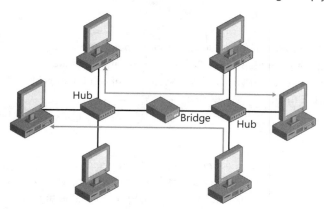

FIGURE 3-11 An Ethernet bridge in action.

The bridge therefore acts as a *packet filter*, allowing only packets destined for the other side of the network to get by. This reduces the amount of traffic on both sides of the bridge, enabling the network to function more efficiently.

Of course, for a bridge to function effectively, it has to know which computers are on either side of the network. The earliest bridges required administrators to manually configure the device with the hardware addresses of all the computers on the network, which was an onerous task. Later, manufacturers introduced a technique called *transparent bridging*, in which bridges compiled their own address tables from the information in the packets they read.

At first, before the bridge has compiled its tables, it does no filtering, and simply forwards all incoming packets to the other side. As it collects enough information to do so, the bridge begins filtering.

Bridges wait until they have received an entire packet before they forward it to the other side of the network. This means that the bridge effectively splits the LAN into two separate collision domains, because computers on opposite sides of the bridge transmitting simultaneously do not cause a collision. Fewer collisions means fewer retransmissions and a more efficient network.

A bridge splits one LAN into two collision domains, but it preserves a single broadcast domain. The *broadcast domain* of a network is the group of computers that will receive a broadcast message transmitted by any one of its members. Broadcasts are an essential element of Ethernet networking—as are collisions—but bridges always forward all broadcast messages to the other side of the network.

This is the fundamental difference between a bridge and a router. A router splits a LAN into two separate collision domains and two separate broadcast domains. A bridge creates two collision domains but a single broadcast domain, which enables many of the LAN protocols to continue functioning.

> **NOTE** **TRANSMISSION TYPES**
>
> Networking recognizes three basic types of transmissions: broadcasts, which are packets transmitted to every node on the network; unicasts, which are packets transmitted to just one node; and multicasts, which are packets transmitted to a group of nodes.

In the Ethernet world, bridges are all but obsolete, because the vast majority of networks today use switches rather than hubs, which eliminates the need for them. However, bridges are still used on wireless LANs.

 Quick Check

1. At which layer of the OSI model do repeaters and hubs operate?
2. Bridges and switches operate primarily at what layer of the OSI model?

Quick Check Answers

1. Physical
2. Data-link

Using Routers

Routers connect networks together, forming internetworks. As local area networking exploded in popularity, Ethernet networks began to grow too large even for bridges to make them manageable. Large organizations, therefore, began to build what are today known as enterprise networks, private internetworks consisting of multiple LANs connected together by routers.

Chapter 2 illustrated the basic enterprise network configuration: a series of horizontal LANs—such as those found on the individual floors of a building—with each LAN connected to a vertical backbone network. The backbone joins the individual LANs together, enabling any computer to communicate with any other computer, without having to traverse more than three LANs.

In the original form of enterprise network, administrators used routers to connect the horizontal networks to the backbone, as shown in Figure 3-12. The telecommunications room on each floor of the building had a router that was connected both to the backbone and to that floor's horizontal network.

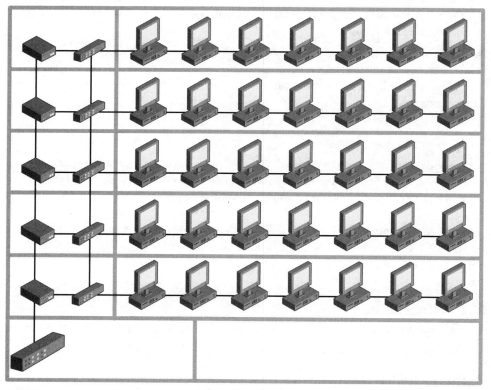

FIGURE 3-12 An enterprise network consisting of LANs connected by routers.

It is possible to connect LANs together by using a different configuration, such as a daisy chain in which a succession of routers connect each LAN to another, but this is a less efficient arrangement, because it can require packets to pass through more routers to get to a destination.

It is more common today to use Layer 3 switches rather than individual routers. Layer 3 switches provide a more efficient and economical routing method. See Chapter 7 for more information.

Packet Routing

A *router* is a network layer device with two network interfaces, which allow it to connect to two separate networks. It is crucial for you to understand that devices such as hubs, repeaters, and bridges are ways to expand a single LAN. When you connect two separate Ethernet networks together with a router, you still have two separate Ethernet networks with two separate collision domains and two separate broadcast domains.

When you have two computers on two separate Ethernet LANs, there is no way for them to communicate directly at the data-link layer. The computer on LAN A can't address a data-link layer frame to a computer on LAN B because it has no way of determining that computer's hardware address. The only way for computers on those two separate networks to communicate with each other is to transcend the data-link layer protocol, and this is the job of the router.

> **NOTE** **LOCATING COMPUTERS**
>
> On Ethernet networks, computers discover each other by using broadcast messages, essentially shouting "Is Computer X here?" to the whole room and waiting for X to answer. If Computer X is on a different Ethernet LAN, it is in a different broadcast domain and therefore cannot hear the shouts in the other room.

With its two network interfaces, a router can connect to two networks at the same time. Packets arriving on one of the interfaces travel up through the protocol stack as high as the network layer, as shown in Figure 3-13. Routers are sometimes called *intermediate systems* because their function is to relay packets to different networks on the way to their destinations. In its journey from source to destination, a packet might pass through several (or even dozens) of routers, but it never reaches higher than the network layer in any intermediate system. The actual application data inside the packet remains intact until the packet reaches its final destination system.

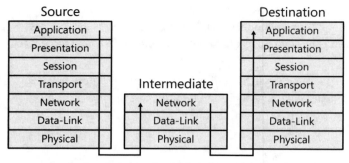

FIGURE 3-13 Packets only travel as high as the network layer on intermediate systems.

When a packet transcends the data-link layer, the system strips off the data-link layer frame, leaving only the network layer protocol data unit, called a datagram. As noted in Chapter 1, "Networking Basics," the network layer of the OSI reference model is the bottom-most layer concerned with end-to-end communications.

Data-link layer hardware addresses are only good for local communications on the same LAN, so the network layer protocol uses another identifier (usually an IP address) to determine the destination of the packet. If the destination system is on the other LAN to which the router is connected, the device passes the datagram down to the data-link layer again, this time using the other network interface adapter. The adapter packages the datagram in a new data-link layer protocol frame and transmits it out to the destination system on the other network, as shown in Figure 3-14.

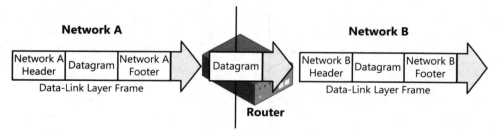

FIGURE 3-14 Routers receive packets from one network and transmit them out to another network.

Enterprise Routing

The example of packet routing described in the previous section is a relatively simple one, involving two systems on adjacent networks. In actual operation, a router might have to deal with packets destined for networks on the other side of the building or the other side of the planet.

Routers are more selective than hubs, bridges, and switches about the packets they forward to other networks. Because they operate at the boundaries of LANs, routers do not forward broadcast messages, except in certain specific cases. When a router forwards a packet based on the destination address in the network layer protocol header, it consults an internal table (called a *routing table*) that contains information about the local and adjacent networks. The router uses this table to determine where to send each packet. If the packet is addressed to a destination on one of the networks to which the router is connected, the router can transmit the packet directly to that system. If the packet is addressed to a system on a distant network, the router transmits the packet across one of the adjacent networks to another router.

Consider a typical corporate internetwork composed of a backbone and several horizontal networks that are connected to the backbone by means of routers. The computers on each horizontal network use the router connecting that network to the backbone as their default gateway. The computers transmit all of the packets they generate either to a specific system on the local network or to the default gateway.

EXAM TIP

In TCP/IP parlance, the term "gateway" is synonymous with the term "router," in that it refers to a network layer device. However, the term "gateway" is also used in other contexts to describe an application layer device that provides access to another network, such as a proxy server.

When a computer on one of the horizontal networks transmits a packet to a destination on another horizontal network, the following procedure occurs:

1. The source computer generates a packet containing the address of the final destination system in the network layer protocol header and the address of its default gateway router in the data-link layer protocol header and transmits the packet onto the horizontal network.

2. The default gateway router receives the packet, strips away its data-link layer frame, and reads the destination address from the network layer protocol header.

3. Using the information in its routing table, the gateway router determines which of the other routers on the backbone network it must use to access the horizontal network on which the destination system is located. The routing table also tells the router which of its two network interfaces it must use to access the backbone network.

4. The gateway router constructs a new data-link layer frame for the packet, using the backbone's data-link layer protocol (which might be different from the protocol used on the horizontal network) and specifying the router leading to the destination network as the data-link layer destination address. The gateway router then transmits the packet over the backbone network.

5. When the packet reaches the next router on the backbone network, the process repeats itself. The router again strips away the data-link layer frame and reads the destination address from the network layer protocol header. This time, however, the router's routing table indicates that the destination system is on the horizontal network to which the router is attached. The router can therefore construct a new data-link layer frame that transmits the packet directly to the destination system.

When a packet has to pass through multiple networks on the way to its final destination, each router that processes it is referred to as a *hop*, as shown in Figure 3-15. Routers often measure the efficiency of a given path through the network by the number of hops required to reach the destination. One of the primary functions of a router is to select the most efficient path to a destination based on the data in its routing tables.

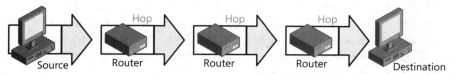

FIGURE 3-15 Router hops.

If this seems complicated, imagine what routing is like on the Internet, where packets must pass through dozens of routers to get to a destination. How routers gather information about other networks and compile that information into their routing tables is explained in Chapter 7.

Routers and WANs

Routers can connect any two network types together, not just LANs. Due to the increasing popularity of switches for LAN-to-LAN connections, the most common application for routers in today's networking industry is to connect LANs to wide area networks (WANs). If an enterprise network has offices in several cities, there might be multiple LANs at each site, but the sites are probably linked together by using WAN connections, such as leased telephone lines. This means that each WAN connection must have a router at each end, connecting it to the local network, as shown in Figure 3-16.

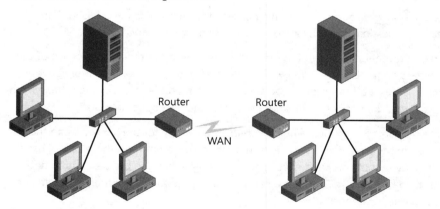

FIGURE 3-16 Routers connecting LANs to a WAN.

As with the other devices discussed in this chapter, the large, complex routers designed for use on enterprise networks often take the form of open framework devices that you can mount in standard data center racks. Some of these routers are large modular housings, into which you can plug modules that accommodate various WAN and LAN technologies. A rack-mountable router is shown in Figure 3-17.

FIGURE 3-17 A rack-mountable router.

Routers are also available as smaller, stand-alone devices in several formats. One of the most common applications for these devices is to connect a home or small business network to the Internet. Consider, for example, your own home or small business network. To create that connection, your Internet Service Provider (ISP) gives you a device that you probably call a modem. That device constitutes one end of a WAN connection that ultimately leads to the ISP's network.

To connect that device to your network, you need a router. You most likely will go to your local electronics store and purchase what is known as a broadband router, cable router, or DSL router. This device connects to both your ISP's modem and your network, and routes traffic between them.

EXAM TIP

Broadband routers often provide a variety of other functions, including wireless access points, switched ports, firewalls, and DHCP servers. As a result, the Network+ objectives also refer to them as multifunction devices.

However, you might also just connect the ISP's modem to one of your computers and use a software feature such as Microsoft's Internet Connection Sharing (ICS) to enable the other computers on your network to access the Internet. In this case, you are using a software router, and your computer is responsible for forwarding traffic between the two networks.

Using Switches

The discussion of repeaters, hubs, and bridges in this chapter contains important concepts, but it is largely a history lesson. Although you might encounter some of these devices in legacy network installations, you will not see them installed in new networks. Today's Ethernet networks use switches in place of all of these older components.

The *switch* is the next step in the evolution of network intelligence. Whereas bridges maintain a list of the hardware addresses found on each network segment, switches rely on more detailed information about which node is connected to which port.

A switch looks very much like a hub: a box with a row of female RJ45 connectors in it and an array of LEDs for each connector. In fact, some manufacturers have identical hub and switch product lines that are almost indistinguishable visually, except for their markings.

Installing your first switch is virtually the same as installing a hub. You simply plug the cables connected to your computers into the switch's ports. However, the internal operations of the switch are different from those of the hub, and the result is a great leap forward in Ethernet performance and efficiency.

Like a bridge, a switch can read the headers of incoming data-link layer protocol frames. The first thing a switch does when you connect a computer to it is read the incoming packets from the computer and add that computer's hardware address to a table associating it with a particular switch port. When the switch knows which computer is connected to each of its ports, it can begin processing incoming packets.

NOTE **SWITCHES**

When they first come online, switches behave just like hubs, forwarding all traffic out through all of their ports, until they compile a table of hardware addresses and port assignments. Only then do they begin forwarding selectively.

The switch reads the destination hardware address in each packet it receives and, instead of forwarding it out through all of its ports as a hub does, or splitting the network in two as a bridge does, it forwards the packet out through the port associated with the destination address (if known), and only that port, as shown in Figure 3-18.

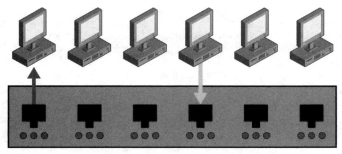

FIGURE 3-18 The signal propagation pattern of an Ethernet switch.

This might seem like a simple thing, but switching actually signifies a monumental change in the operation of Ethernet networks in several ways:

- **No shared medium**   Because the unicast packets transmitted by each computer only go to their destinations and nowhere else, the network is no longer using a shared medium for those transmissions. Computers no longer receive, process, and discard unicast packets they do not need. Broadcast transmissions, however, still reach every device on the subnet, and switches still forward packets with unknown addresses to every port to see which one responds.

- **No media access control**   The defining characteristic of Ethernet, the CSMA/CD media access control mechanism, is no longer needed because computers no longer have to vie for access to a shared medium.

- **No bandwidth contention**   Computers are no longer vying for the same limited bandwidth (except in the case of broadcast transmissions). Each pair of computers has a dedicated connection running at the full speed of the network.

- **No collisions**   Because each computer has what amounts to a dedicated connection to every other computer on the network, collisions are all but eliminated. Each pair of computers forms its own collision domain.

> *NOTE* **COLLISIONS**
> Although switches minimize on-cable collisions, or eliminate them entirely, every transmission that would have been a cable collision handled by the MAC mechanism of the data-link layer protocol now needs to be handled by the switch, queued, and forwarded to destination devices as their paths becomes available. This introduces a new networking problem when the switch's buffer is exceeded. Switches go a long way toward reducing the bandwidth limitations of unswitched networks, but they can also introduce their own new communication problems.

Switch Types

There are two basic types of switches, based on when they forward arriving packets, as follows:

- **Cut-through**   A cut-through switch begins forwarding an incoming packet as soon as it has read the destination hardware address. Usually, the first bits of the packet are leaving the switch through the outgoing port before the last few bits have arrived at the incoming port. This type of switch uses a technique called matrix switching or crossbar switching, in which a grid of input/output circuits enables data to enter and leave the switch through any port. Cut-through switches are relatively inexpensive and minimize the latency incurred as the switch processes packets.

- **Store-and-forward**   A store-and-forward switch is one that waits until an entire incoming packet arrives before it begins forwarding any data out to the destination. This type of switch contains buffer memory in which it stores the incoming data, either in the form of a common buffer shared by all the ports, or individual buffers for each port, connected by a bus. Many switches of this type take advantage of the time that the complete packet is stored in memory to perform cyclical redundancy check (CRC) calculations and other tests for problems peculiar to the data-link layer protocol. As a result, store-and-forward switches maintain a higher quality of service, but they are generally more expensive than cut-through switches and are also slower, in that they introduce an additional degree of latency to the switching process.

Expanding Switched Networks

As with hubs, you can expand a switched network by connecting multiple switches together to add more ports. Switches have an advantage over hubs, however, in that you can connect switches together however you like, in a daisy chain or a star topology, as needed. Because switching eliminates the need for media access control and collision detection, you can connect switches together using any configuration you want.

In fact, many administrators who originally designed their networks along the structured cabling model—with a separate backbone network connecting multiple horizontal networks—have upgraded their installations by simply replacing all of the hubs and routers with switches, as shown in Figure 3-19.

The result is one big, switched network. However, because of the nature of switching, administrators need to be less concerned about the excessive amounts of traffic or the large number of collisions such a big network could generate if it was connected by using hubs.

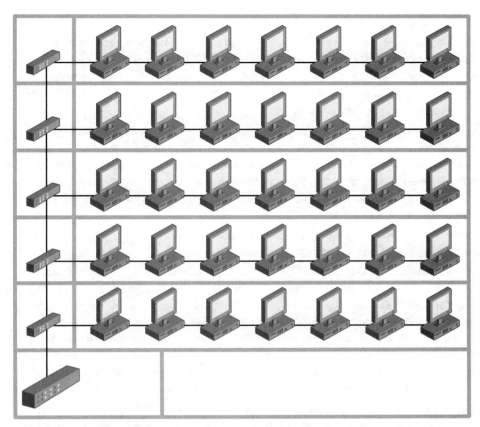

FIGURE 3-19 An enterprise network using switches instead of routers and hubs.

Bridge Loops

One of the potential problems administrators can encounter when replacing hubs and routers with switches occurs when there are multiple paths through the switches to a given destination. Installing multiple switches on a network can provide fault tolerance if a switch fails. However, it is also possible for the switches to begin forwarding traffic in an endless cycle, a condition called a *bridge loop* (because it can also occur with bridges).

To address the problem of bridge looping, switches (and bridges) use a technique called the *spanning tree protocol (STP)*. STP is a data-link layer protocol that selects a non-redundant subset of switches to form the spanning tree, deactivating the others. Data circulating throughout the network uses only the switches in the tree unless a switch fails, in which case the protocol activates one of the inactive switches to replace it.

Switches and Broadcasts

As noted earlier, switching causes each pair of computers on the network to function as a separate collision domain. Switching does not eliminate collisions entirely. A pair of computers can still transmit at exactly the same time. However, those two computers will never suffer from excess traffic generated by other systems' collisions, or the retransmissions that are the result of those collisions.

There is another concern resulting from the creation of a large switched network, though. Each pair of computers might form a separate collision domain, but the network still functions as one huge broadcast domain. Routers do not forward broadcast messages, but switches do. Therefore, when any computer on the network generates a broadcast message, all of the other computers receive it and process it. On a network with hundreds of computers, a great deal of broadcast traffic can result

There are several technologies that switch manufacturers have introduced into their products to address this problem, including the following:

- **Virtual LANs (VLANs)**   With a VLAN, you can create subnets on a switched network that exist only in the switches themselves. The physical network is still switched, but you can specify the addresses of the systems that belong to a specific subnet. These systems can be located anywhere because the subnet is virtual and is not constrained by the physical layout of the network. When a computer on a particular subnet transmits a broadcast message, the packet goes only to the computers in that subnet, rather than being propagated throughout the entire network. Communication between subnets can be either routed or switched, but all traffic within a VLAN is switched.

- **Layer 3 switching**   Layer 3 switching is a variation on the VLAN concept that minimizes the amount of routing needed between the VLANs. When systems on different VLANs need to communicate, a router establishes a connection between the systems, and then the switches take over, a process sometimes called "route once, switch many." Routing occurs only when absolutely necessary. Unlike data-link layer switches, which can read only the contents of the data-link layer protocol header in the packets they process, layer 3 switches can read the addresses in the network layer protocol header as well.

Technologies such as these bring switches out of the exclusive province of the data-link layer. These multilayer switches can provide a variety of additional functions. For more information, see Chapter 7.

Using Multifunction Devices

 The so-called broadband routers that many people use to connect home or small business networks to the Internet are usually much more than just routers. More correctly called *multifunction devices*, as shown in Figure 3-20, these products can include any or all of the following functions:

- **Router**   The primary function of a multifunction device of this type is to provide a WAN interface to an ISP's network and to route traffic between a LAN and that ISP network. This enables the device to function as a default gateway for all of the computers and other devices on the LAN, providing them access to the Internet.

- **WAN connection or modem**   A multifunction device typically contains a port for a connection to a cable or DSL modem. However, some models have the modem integrated into the unit.

- **Switch**   Most multifunction devices have an array of switch (or hub) ports that enable you to connect multiple computers or other devices directly to the LAN. This prevents you from having to purchase a separate switch or hub, unless you need additional ports.

- **Wireless Access Point (WAP)**   Many multifunction devices also function as wireless access points, enabling clients with IEEE 802.11 network adapters to connect to the network. These WAPs might even be routed separately from any wired LAN ports on the device. For more information on wireless access points, see Chapter 5.

- **DHCP server**   Many multifunction devices include a DHCP server, which enables computers on the network to request and receive IP addresses and other TCP/IP configuration parameters. For more information on DHCP, see Chapter 6.

- **NAT router** Network address translation (NAT) is a network layer technology that enables all of the computers on a network to share a single registered IP address, thus protecting them from direct intrusion from the Internet. For more information on NAT, see Chapter 6.

- **Firewall** Multifunction devices often include a variety of firewall features, such as port forwarding and packet filtering.

- **Web server** Multifunction devices typically have web servers, but not for hosting their own websites. The device uses the web server to provide a configuration interface that users can access from a web browser.

FIGURE 3-20 A multifunction device.

Exercise

The answers for this exercise are located in the "Answers" section at the end of this chapter. For each of the following descriptions, specify to which of the following devices it can apply: network interface adapter, repeater, hub, bridge, router, and/or switch.

1. Connects networks together

2. Builds its own table of MAC addresses and their equivalent ports

3. Can function as a bus master

4. Forwards incoming packets out through all of its ports at all times

5. Contains two ports only and operates at the physical layer of the OSI model

6. Creates two collision domains and two broadcast domains

7. Forwards unicasts to one port and broadcasts to every port

8. Spans the physical layer and the data-link layer

9. Extends the maximum length of a network segment

10. Also known as a multiport repeater

Chapter Summary

- A network interface adapter is the hardware implementation of a data-link layer LAN protocol. Virtually every computer sold today has an Ethernet adapter incorporated into its motherboard, but network adapters are also available in the form of expansion cards that plug into a computer's internal slot or external devices that plug into a Universal Serial Bus (USB) port.

- A repeater is simply a box with two cable connectors on it that amplifies any signals arriving through one connector and transmits them out through the other.

- A hub—sometimes called a concentrator—is simply a box with a power supply and several female RJ45 connectors in it, and usually an array of LEDs for each connector. Any signals arriving at the hub through one connector are transmitted out through all of the others.

- A bridge splits an Ethernet LAN in half, much like a repeater, except that a repeater always forwards every packet it receives, whereas bridges are selective about the packets they forward.

- A router is a network layer device with two network interfaces so that it can connect to two separate networks.

- A switch looks very much like a hub: a box with a row of female RJ45 connectors in it and an array of LEDs for each connector. However, instead of forwarding traffic out through all of its ports, a switch only forwards data to its destination (if known).

Chapter Review

Test your knowledge of the information in Chapter 3 by answering these questions. The answers to these questions, and the explanations of why each answer choice is correct or incorrect, are located in the "Answers" section at the end of this chapter.

1. Which of the following devices would create a separate collision domain and a separate broadcast domain if you were to use it to join two separate LANs together?

   A. A repeater

   B. A bridge

   C. A switch

   D. A router

2. Which of the following devices is capable of constructing new data-link layer frames for the packets it processes?

   A. A transparent bridge

   B. A broadband router

   C. A store-and-forward switch

   D. A cut-through switch

3. To add another hub to an existing LAN, which of the following should you do?

   A. Connect the uplink port on the new hub to the uplink port on an existing hub by using a patch cable.

   B. Connect the uplink port on the new hub to a standard port on an existing hub by using a crossover cable.

   C. Connect a standard port on the new hub to the uplink port on an existing hub by using a patch cable.

   D. Connect a standard port on the new hub to a standard port on an existing hub by using a patch cable.

4. Which of the following terms describe the ability to combine the bandwidth of multiple network interface adapters? (Choose all correct answers.)

   A. Media access control

   B. Link aggregation

   C. Bonding

   D. Large send processing

Answers

This section contains the answers to the questions for the Exercise and Chapter Review in this chapter.

Exercise

1. Router or switch

2. Bridge or switch

3. Network interface adapter

4. Hub

5. Repeater

6. Router

7. Switch

8. Network interface adapter

9. Repeater or hub

10. Hub

Chapter Review

1. **Correct Answer:** D

   A. **Incorrect:** Installing a repeater does not affect the configuration of the network's broadcast or collision domains.

   B. **Incorrect:** Installing a bridge affects the configuration of the network's collision domains, but not its broadcast domains.

   C. **Incorrect:** Installing a switch affects the configuration of the network's collision domains, but not its broadcast domains.

   D. **Correct:** Installing a router creates two separate collision domains and two separate broadcast domains.

2. **Correct Answer:** B

   A. **Incorrect:** A transparent bridge is a data-link layer device that filters frames, but does not construct them.

   B. **Correct:** A broadband router strips the frame from incoming packets and constructs a new frame for the outgoing network.

C. **Incorrect:** A store-and-forward switch is a data-link layer device that filters frames, but does not construct them.

D. **Incorrect:** A cut-through switch is a data-link layer device that filters frames, but does not construct them.

3. **Correct Answer:** C

A. **Incorrect:** Connecting the uplink ports together would eliminate the crossover circuit.

B. **Incorrect:** Connecting an uplink port to a standard port with a crossover cable would result in two crossovers canceling each other out.

C. **Correct:** Connecting a standard port to an uplink port results in a circuit that is properly crossed over.

D. **Incorrect:** Connecting a standard port to a standard port with a patch cable would result in two crossovers canceling each other out.

4. **Correct Answers:** B and C

A. **Incorrect:** Media access control regulates access to a shared network medium. It has nothing to do with combining bandwidth of multiple adapters.

B. **Correct:** Link aggregation is the ability to combine the bandwidth of multiple network adapters.

C. **Correct:** Bonding is another term for link aggregation, which is the ability to combine the bandwidth of multiple network adapters.

D. **Incorrect:** Large send processing has nothing to do with combining bandwidth of multiple adapters.

CHAPTER 4

The Data-Link Layer

The second layer of the Open Systems Interconnection (OSI) reference model—the data-link layer—is where the physical manifestation of the network meets with the logical one, which is implemented in the software running on the computer. In Chapter 2, "The Physical Layer," you learned about the various types of physical media that connect computers together, and in Chapter 3, "Network Devices," you learned about the various hardware components used to construct a local area network (LAN). As noted in those chapters, most of these hardware elements are part of the data-link layer protocol implementation.

This chapter examines the rest of the data-link layer LAN protocol, the logical elements that enable the hardware components to function properly. It also discusses the data-link layer protocols used in wide area network (WAN) implementations.

Exam objectives in this chapter:

Objective 1.6: Explain the function of common networking protocols.

- TCP
- FTP
- UDP
- TCP/IP suite
- DHCP
- TFTP
- DNS
- HTTPS
- HTTP
- ARP
- SIP (VoIP)
- RTP (VoIP)
- SSH
- POP3
- NTP
- IMAP4
- Telnet
- SMTP
- SNMP2/3
- ICMP
- IGMP
- TLS

Objective 2.6: Given a set of requirements, plan and implement a basic SOHO network.

- List of requirements
- Cable length
- Device types/requirements
- Environment limitations
- Equipment limitations
- Compatibility requirements

Objective 3.7: Compare and contrast different LAN technologies.

- Types:
  - Ethernet
  - 10BaseT
  - 100BaseT
  - 1000BaseT
  - 100BaseTX
  - 100BaseFX
  - 1000BaseX
  - 10GBaseSR
  - 10GBaseLR
  - 10GBaseER
  - 10GBaseSW
  - 10GBaseLW
  - 10GBaseEW
  - 10GBaseT

- Properties:
  - CSMA/CD
  - CSMA/CA
  - Broadcast
  - Collision
  - Bonding
  - Speed
  - Distance

Objective 5.2: Explain the methods of network access security.

- ACL:
  - MAC filtering
  - IP filtering
  - Port filtering
- Tunneling and encryption:
  - SSL VPN
  - VPN
  - L2TP
  - PPTP
  - IPSec
  - ISAKMP
  - TLS
  - TLS2.0
  - Site-to-site and client-to-site

- Remote access:
  - RAS
  - RDP
  - PPPoE
  - PPP
  - ICA
  - SSH

Ethernet

Any discussion of the history of the local area network (LAN) is also a discussion of the history of Ethernet. Ethernet was the first LAN protocol, originally conceived in 1973, and it has been evolving steadily ever since. Other data-link layer protocols—such as Token Ring and ARCnet—have come and gone, but Ethernet has remained. Its only rival in the local area networking market today is the wireless LAN, which is covered in Chapter 5, "Wireless Networking."

The longevity of Ethernet is due primarily to its continuous evolution. The earliest commercial Ethernet networks ran at 10 Mbps (megabits per second), and successive iterations of the protocol increased the networks' transmission speeds to 100, 1,000, and now 10,000 Mbps. Despite these massive changes beneath the surface, however, many of the basic elements of an Ethernet network remain the same as they were in the old days.

Ethernet Standards

Xerox Corporation was responsible for the original development of the Ethernet networking system and, in 1980, joined with Digital Equipment Corporation (DEC) and Intel Corporation to publish the first Ethernet standard, called "The Ethernet, A Local Area Network: Data-Link Layer and Physical Layer Specifications." This standard, one of two upon which commercial Ethernet implementations were based, was known informally as *DIX Ethernet*.

DIX Ethernet

This first Ethernet standard described a network that used RG-8 coaxial cable in a bus topology up to 500 meters long, with a transmission speed of 10 Mbps. This was commonly known as Thick Ethernet or 10Base5. The consortium published a second version of the standard, called *DIX Ethernet II*, in 1982. This version added a second physical layer specification, calling for RG-58 coaxial cable. This came to be known as Thin Ethernet or 10Base2. RG-58 cable is thinner and less expensive than RG-8 but more susceptible to interference and attenuation, so the maximum segment length is restricted to 185 meters.

Development of the DIX Ethernet standard stopped after the publication of version II.

EXAM TIP

The terms that the CompTIA Network+ exam objectives use for the various Ethernet technologies, such as 10Base5 and 10Base2, are shorthand designations for Ethernet physical layer specifications. The number 10 refers to the speed of the network (10 Mbps); the word "Base" refers to the use of baseband signaling on the network; and the numbers 5 and 2 refer to the maximum length of a cable segment, which is 500 meters for Thick Ethernet and 200 (actually 185) meters for Thin Ethernet. Subsequent designations have used letters representing the cable type, rather than numbers indicating cable lengths. For example, the "T" in 10Base-T refers to the use of twisted pair cable. The designations beginning with 10Base-T also include a hyphen, to prevent people from pronouncing it "bassett." Candidates for the exam must be familiar with the designations for the various Fast Ethernet, Gigabit Ethernet, and 10 Gigabit Ethernet physical layer specifications.

IEEE 802.3

Also in 1980, the Institute of Electrical and Electronics Engineers (IEEE) began work on an international standard defining the Ethernet network, one a privately owned standard, as DIX Ethernet was. The result was a document called "*IEEE 802.3* Carrier Sense Multiple Access with Collision Detection (CSMA/CD) Access Method and Physical Layer Specifications," which the IEEE published in 1985.

The original 802.3 standard describes a network that is almost identical to DIX Ethernet, except for a minor change in the frame format (described later in this chapter). The main difference between IEEE 802.3 and DIX Ethernet is that the IEEE has continued to revise its standard in the years since the original publication.

The 802.3 working group updates its standards by publishing amendments that contain additional physical layer specifications and descriptions of other new technologies. They publish the amendments with a letter and a date. For example, the first amendment, 802.3a-1988, added the 10Base2 physical layer specification to the original standard.

At regular intervals, the working group incorporates the published amendments into the main 802.3 document. As of this writing, the current standard is called IEEE 802.3-2008, "IEEE Standard for Information technology-Specific requirements - Part 3: Carrier Sense Multiple Access with Collision Detection (CSMA/CD) Access Method and Physical Layer Specifications." This document, published in five sections and totaling nearly 3,000 pages, includes the specifications from dozens of amendments and defines physical layer specifications ranging from 10 Mbps to 10 Gigabit Ethernet, over a variety of physical media.

The latest amendment, IEEE 802.3bg-2011, which has yet to be incorporated into the standard, defines the next iteration of Ethernet networks and is called "Amendment 6: Physical Layer and Management Parameters for Serial 40 Gb/s Ethernet Operation Over Single Mode Fiber."

NOTE **OBTAINING STANDARDS**

The IEEE 802 standards are available as free downloads from the institute's website at *http://standards.ieee.org*.

REAL WORLD **AN ETHERNET BY ANY OTHER NAME**

Technically speaking, the only Ethernet networks worthy of the name are those running on coaxial cable using a bus topology. All of the physical layer specifications that define networks using twisted pair or fiber optic cable are part of the IEEE 802.3 standard and should actually be called by that name. However, the name "Ethernet" is still ubiquitous in the networking industry, both on product packaging and in common usage among network administrators. It is universally understood that an Ethernet network today actually refers to one that is compliant with the IEEE 802.3 standard.

Ethernet Components

The Ethernet standards—both DIX Ethernet and IEEE 802.3—include the following three components:

- **The Ethernet frame**   The packet format that Ethernet systems use to transmit data over the network

- **Carrier Sense Multiple Access with Collision Detection (CSMA/CD)**   The media access control (MAC) mechanism that early Ethernet systems use to regulate access to the network medium

- **Physical layer specifications**   Specifications that define the various types of network media that you can use to build Ethernet networks, as well as the topologies and signaling types they support

The Ethernet Frame

The Ethernet *frame* is essentially the mailing envelope that the protocol uses to transmit data to other systems on the local area network. The frame consists of a header and footer that surround the information that the data-link layer protocol receives from the network layer protocol operating at the layer above (which is usually the IP).

The frame is divided into sections of various lengths called fields, which perform different functions. The format of the Ethernet frame is shown in Figure 4-1, and the functions of the Ethernet frame fields are as follows:

- **Preamble (7 bytes)**   Contains 7 bytes of alternating 0s and 1s, which the communicating systems use to synchronize their clock signals.

- **Start of Frame Delimiter (1 byte)**   Contains 6 bits of alternating 0s and 1s, followed by two consecutive 1s, which is a signal to the receiver that the transmission of the actual frame is about to begin.

- **Destination Address (6 bytes)**   Contains the 6-byte hexadecimal MAC address of the network interface adapter on the local network to which the packet will be transmitted.

- **Source Address (6 bytes)**   Contains the 6-byte hexadecimal MAC address of the network interface adapter in the system generating the packet.

- **Ethertype/Length (2 bytes)**   In the DIX Ethernet frame, this field contains a code identifying the network layer protocol for which the data in the packet is intended. In the IEEE 802.3 frame, this field specifies the length of the data field (excluding the pad).

- **Data and Pad (46 to 1,500 bytes)**   Contains the data received from the network layer protocol on the transmitting system, which is sent to the same protocol on the destination system. Ethernet frames (including the header and footer, except for the Preamble and Start of Frame Delimiter) must be at least 64 bytes long; therefore, if the data received from the network layer protocol is less than 46 bytes, the system adds padding bytes to bring it up to its minimum length.

- **Frame Check Sequence (4 bytes)** The frame's footer is a single field that comes after the network layer protocol data and contains a 4-byte checksum value for the entire packet. The sending computer computes this value and places it into the field. The receiving system performs the same computation and compares it to the field to verify that the packet was transmitted without error.

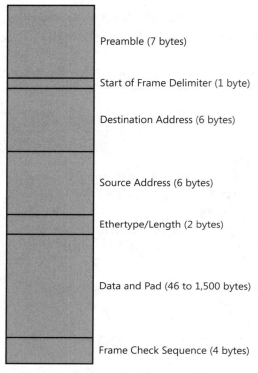

Preamble (7 bytes)

Start of Frame Delimiter (1 byte)

Destination Address (6 bytes)

Source Address (6 bytes)

Ethertype/Length (2 bytes)

Data and Pad (46 to 1,500 bytes)

Frame Check Sequence (4 bytes)

FIGURE 4-1 The Ethernet frame format.

ETHERNET ADDRESSING

The primary function of the Ethernet frame—as with a mailing envelope—is to identify the addressee of the packet. As noted in Chapter 3, Ethernet networks use the 6-byte hexadecimal values called *organizationally unique identifiers (OUIs)*, hardcoded into network interface adapters, to identify systems on the local network.

Data-link layer protocols are concerned only with communications on the local area network. Therefore, the values in the Destination Address and Source Address fields must identify systems on the local network. If a computer on the LAN is transmitting to another computer on the same LAN, then its packets contain the address of that target computer in their Destination Address fields. If a computer is transmitting to another computer on a different network, then the value in the Destination Address field must be the address of a router on the LAN. In this case, it is up to the network layer protocol to supply the address of the packet's final destination.

EXAM TIP

In TCP/IP terminology, a router is also known as a gateway, and many user interfaces still refer to the local router as the default gateway. Be prepared to see either term on the Network+ exam.

PROTOCOL IDENTIFICATION

The other main function of the data-link layer protocol is to identify the protocol at the network layer that is the destination of the data in the frame. This is so that the system receiving the frame can pass the data up through the protocol stack. The method by which the frame identifies the network layer protocol is the primary difference between the DIX Ethernet and the IEEE 802.3 standards.

The DIX Ethernet standard uses the 2 bytes immediately following the Source Address field to store an Ethertype value. An *Ethertype* is a hexadecimal value that identifies the protocol that generated the data in the packet. The only Ethertype values left in common use are 0800 for the IP and 0806 for the Address Resolution Protocol (ARP).

The Ethertype field is the last vestige of the DIX Ethernet standard still used on networks today. Because the TCP/IP protocols were developed in the 1970s, when DIX Ethernet was still the industry standard, most TCP/IP implementations still rely on the Ethertype value from the DIX Ethernet frame format for protocol identification.

In the IEEE 802.3 standard, those same 2 bytes following the Source Address field perform a different function; they indicate the length of the information in the Data field (excluding the Pad). Because the maximum length of data permissible in an Ethernet packet is 1,500 bytes, Ethernet systems assume that any value in this field larger than 0600 hexadecimal (1536 decimal) is an Ethertype.

For protocol identification, IEEE 802.3 relies on an outside protocol called IEEE 802.2 *Logical Link Control (LLC)*. LLC is a separate protocol that the IEEE 802 group developed to work with several data-link layer protocols they were developing at the same time. The LLC protocol adds two subheaders to the packet, which are carried in the Data field of the Ethernet frame. The format of the LLC subheader is shown in Figure 4-2 and contains three fields, as follows:

- Destination Service Access Point (DSAP) (1 byte)
- Source Service Access Point (SSAP) (1 byte)
- Control (1 or 2 bytes)

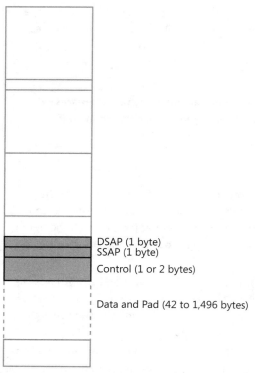

DSAP (1 byte)
SSAP (1 byte)
Control (1 or 2 bytes)

Data and Pad (42 to 1,496 bytes)

FIGURE 4-2 The Logical Link Control subheader format.

The format of the *Subnetwork Access Protocol (SNAP)* subheader is shown in Figure 4-3 and consists of the following two fields:

- OUI (3 bytes)
- Protocol ID (2 bytes)

LLC is designed to enable an 802.3 LAN to multiplex two or more network layer protocols, which is a relatively rare requirement today. To emulate the function of the Ethertype field, implementations typically insert a value of 170 in the DSAP field, which points the receiving system to the SNAP subheader. With a value of 0 in the OUI field, the Protocol ID field can then use standard Ethertype values.

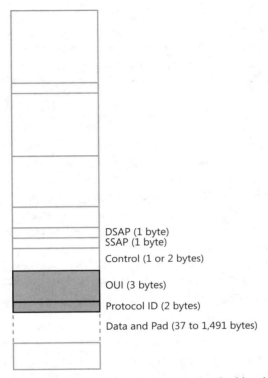

DSAP (1 byte)
SSAP (1 byte)
Control (1 or 2 bytes)
OUI (3 bytes)
Protocol ID (2 bytes)
Data and Pad (37 to 1,491 bytes)

FIGURE 4-3 The Subnetwork Access Protocol subheader format.

CSMA/CD

In the early implementations of Ethernet, its MAC mechanism, called *Carrier Sense Multiple Access with Collision Detection (CSMA/CD),* was the single most defining characteristic of the network. For multiple computers to share a single network medium, it is critical for there to be an orderly means to arbitrate network access. Each computer must have an equal chance to use the network, or the network performance will degrade.

Media access control is the main reason why Ethernet networks have such exacting physical layer specifications. If cable segment lengths are too long, or if there are too many repeaters on the network, the CSMA/CD mechanism does not function properly, causing access control to break down and systems to receive corrupt data.

CARRIER SENSE

The name "Carrier Sense Multiple Access with Collision Detection" describes the successive phases of the media access control process. When a computer on an Ethernet network has data to transmit, the computer begins by listening to the network to see if it is in use. This is the *carrier sense* phase of the process. If the network is busy, the system does nothing for a given period and then checks again.

MULTIPLE ACCESS

When the network is free, the computer transmits its data packet. This is called the *multiple access* phase, because all of the computers on the network are contending for access to the same network medium. Even though computers perform an initial check during the carrier sense phase, it is still possible for two systems on the LAN to transmit at the same time, resulting in a signal quality error (SQE) or, as it is more commonly known, a collision. For example, if Computer A performs its carrier sense and Computer B has already begun transmitting but its signal has not yet reached Computer A, a collision will occur if Computer A transmits. When a collision occurs, both systems must discard their packets and retransmit them. These collisions are a normal and expected part of Ethernet networking; they are not a problem unless there are too many of them or the computers cannot detect them.

COLLISION DETECTION

The *collision detection* phase of the transmission process is the most important part of the CSMA/CD process. If the systems cannot detect when their packets collide, corrupted data might reach a packet's destination system and be treated as valid. To avoid this, Ethernet networks are designed so that packets are large enough to fill the entire network cable with signals before the last bit leaves the transmitting computer. Ethernet packets must be at least 64 bytes long; systems pad out short packets to 64 bytes before transmission. The Ethernet physical layer specifications also impose strict limitations on the lengths of cable segments.

The amount of time it takes for a transmission to propagate to the farthest end of the network and back again is called the network's *round trip delay time.* A collision can occur only during this interval. After the signal arrives back at the transmitting system, that system is said to have "captured the network." No other computer will transmit on the network while it is captured because the source computer will detect the traffic during its carrier sense phase.

Ethernet computers on twisted pair or fiber optic networks assume that a collision has occurred if they detect signals on both their transmit and receive wires at the same time. If the network cable is too long, if the packet is too short (called a *runt*), or if there are too many hubs, a system might finish transmitting before the collision occurs and be unable to detect it.

When a computer detects a collision, it immediately stops transmitting data and starts sending a jam pattern instead. The jam pattern alerts the other systems on the network that a collision has taken place, that they should discard any partial packets they may have received, and that they should not attempt to transmit any data until the network has been cleared. After transmitting the jam pattern, the system waits a specified period of time before attempting to transmit again. This is called the *backoff period*. Both of the systems involved in a collision compute the length of their own backoff periods, by using a randomized algorithm called *truncated binary exponential backoff*. They do this to try to avoid causing another collision by backing off for the same period of time.

Because of the way CSMA/CD works, the more computers you have on a network segment or the more data the systems transmit over the network segment, the more collisions occur. Collisions are a normal part of Ethernet operation, but they cause delays because systems have to retransmit the damaged packets. When the number of collisions is minimal, the delays aren't noticeable, but when network traffic increases, the number of collisions increases and the accumulated delays can begin to have a noticeable effect on network performance. You can reduce the traffic on the LAN by installing a bridge or switch, or by splitting the LAN into two networks and connecting them with a router.

EXAM TIP

The description of an Ethernet collision makes it sound like a disastrous occurrence, but a modest number of regular collisions is normal on an Ethernet network and is no cause for concern. It is only massive numbers of collisions that are cause for alarm.

Quick Check

1. What prevents two systems that have already experienced a collision from colliding again?

2. What must you do to split an Ethernet network into two collision domains?

Quick Check Answers

1. A backoff period calculated by using a randomized algorithm called truncated binary exponential backoff.

2. Split the network by installing a router.

THE MODERN ETHERNET

The IEEE 802.3 standard still includes the term "Carrier Sense Multiple Access with Collision Detection" as part of the document name, but the fact is that very few Ethernet networks actually use CSMA/CD anymore. The need for a media access control mechanism hinges on the use of a shared network medium. The early networks that used coaxial cable connected all of the computers to a single cable segment in a bus topology, and the first twisted pair networks used hubs to create a star topology.

As noted in Chapter 3, a hub is essentially a multiport repeater. When a hub receives a signal through any of its ports, it transmits that signal out through all of the other ports, resulting in a shared network medium. These networks all required a MAC mechanism to arbitrate access to the network.

The big change came when switches began to replace hubs in the marketplace. As with most new technologies, the first switches were too expensive for all but large network installations, but prices soon dropped and before long, hubs were all but obsolete. On a switched network, unicast data arriving at a switch through one of its ports leaves through only one of its other ports, the one connected to the destination system. As a result, there is no shared network medium; each pair of computers has a dedicated connection and there is no need for further media access control.

Modern Ethernet variants also use full duplex connections between hosts, which means that computers can transmit and receive data at the same time. This also eliminates the need for media access control. Although the Ethernet standards still include CSMA/CD, for backward compatibility purposes, it is all but obsolete on today's networks.

 EXAM TIP

The Network+ exam objectives include technologies that are outdated and some that are all but obsolete, particularly in the area of Ethernet. Candidates must be familiar with these older technologies, even if they are rarely seen in the field anymore.

Physical Layer Specifications

Although the Ethernet frame format and the CSMA/CD MAC mechanism have remained relatively stable, the IEEE has revised the physical layer specifications for the protocol many times throughout its history. The primary motivation for this is the continual demand for more network transmission speed, which has led the 802.3 working group to increase the speed of Ethernet transmissions by tenfold no fewer than three times in a little more than 30 years. To support these greater speeds, other changes were required as well, both in the nature of the cable and in the signaling the systems use to transmit data.

The following sections examine the four primary iterations of Ethernet network, represented by their respective transmission speeds of 10, 100, 1,000, and 10,000 Mbps.

ETHERNET

The original IEEE 802.3 standard retained the RG-8 coaxial cable specification from the DIX Ethernet document, but by 1993, the IEEE had published several amendments adding unshielded twisted pair (UTP) and fiber optic cable specifications, also running at 10 Mbps. The 10 Mbps Ethernet physical layer specifications are listed in Table 4-1.

EXAM TIP

10Base5 and 10Base2, also known as Thick Ethernet and Thin Ethernet, are the only LAN protocols covered on the Network+ exam that use a bus topology.

TABLE 4-1 10 Mbps Ethernet Physical Layer Specifications

Designation	Cable Type	Topology	Maximum Segment Length
10Base5	RG-8 coaxial	Bus	500 meters
10Base2	RG-58 coaxial	Bus	185 meters
10Base-T	CAT3 UTP	Star	100 meters
FOIRL	62.5/125 multimode fiber optic	Star	1,000 meters
10Base-FL	62.5/125 multimode fiber optic	Star	2,000 meters

EXAM TIP

10Base-T Ethernet uses only two of the four wire pairs in the UTP cable, one pair for transmitting data and one for receiving it. The other two wire pairs are unused and must remain unused for the network to function properly. According to the ANSI/TIA-568-C cabling standard, you must not use the remaining pairs for telephony or any other application.

The Ethernet fiber optic specifications offered longer segment lengths and resistance to electromagnetic interference, but relatively few networks used them, mainly because another data-link layer protocol—Fiber Distributed Data Interface (FDDI)—was available at the same time and uses the same type of fiber optic cable at 100 Mbps, 10 times the speed of Ethernet. The *Fiber Optic Inter-Repeater Link (FOIRL)* specification was designed to provide long-distance links between repeaters, and *10Base-FL* expanded that capability to include fiber optic links from repeaters to computers as well.

EXAM TIP

The Network+ exam objectives contain some, but not all, of the physical layer specifications in the Ethernet standard. The IEEE 802.3 document includes several other physical layer specifications that were either never implemented or never caught on in the marketplace. These specifications are not included in the tables in this chapter, and knowledge of them is not necessary for the exam.

THE 5-4-3 RULE

In addition to cable types and segment lengths, the Ethernet physical layer specifications also limit the number of repeaters that are permitted in a network configuration. As explained in Chapter 3, a repeater is a physical layer device that enables you to extend the length of a network segment by amplifying the signals. The *5-4-3 rule* states that an Ethernet network can have as many as five cable segments, connected by four repeaters, of which three segments are mixing segments.

This rule was originally intended for coaxial networks, on which a *mixing segment* is defined as a length of cable with more than two devices connected to it. A length of cable with only two devices—that is, a cable connecting two repeaters together—is called a link segment. Therefore, a coaxial Ethernet network of the maximum possible size would appear as shown in Figure 4-4. Using Thin Ethernet, such a network could span as long as 925 meters, and Thick Ethernet could span as long as 2,500 meters.

Despite the presence of repeaters, two computers anywhere on this network that transmit at exactly the same time will cause a collision. This network is therefore said to consist of a single *collision domain*. If you were to connect the segments with bridges, switches, or routers instead, there would be multiple collision domains.

On networks that use a star topology, such as 10Base-T networks, there are no mixing segments, because all of the cables connect only two devices, but the 5-4-3 rule still applies. A 10Base-T hub functions as a multiport repeater, so a 10Base-T network of the maximum possible size would consist of four connected hubs, as shown in Figure 4-5. The longest possible distance between two computers would therefore be 500 meters.

The 10Base-FL specification includes some modifications to the 5-4-3 rule. When there are five cable segments present on a 10Base-FL network connected by four repeaters, the segments can be no more than 500 meters long. When four cable segments are connected by three repeaters, 10Base-FL segments can be no more than 1,000 meters long. Cable segments connecting a computer to a hub can also be no more than 400 meters for 10Base-FL.

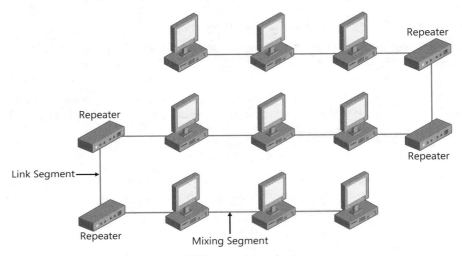

FIGURE 4-4 The 5-4-3 rule on a coaxial Ethernet network.

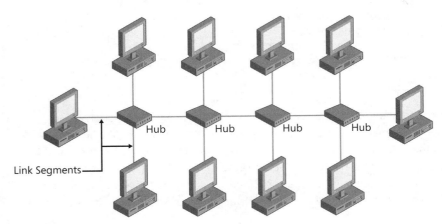

FIGURE 4-5 The 5-4-3 rule on a 10Base-T Ethernet network.

CALCULATING ETHERNET CABLING SPECIFICATIONS

The 5-4-3 rule is a basic rule of thumb that has enabled most Ethernet administrators to design properly functioning networks. However, the Ethernet standards also define a more mathematically precise method for determining whether a network is physically compliant. In most cases, these calculations are not necessary, but you might have to resort to them if you are designing a network that pushes the limits in terms of cable length or number of hubs, or if you are troubleshooting a persistent late collision problem.

To precisely determine Ethernet timing, you must calculate the round trip delay time for the worst case path through the network. The *worst case path* is the route between the two most distant systems on the network, in terms of cable length and number of hubs. To calculate the round trip delay time, you multiply the length of each cable segment (in meters) by a constant round trip delay per meter factor for the particular cable type and add a base value for each segment, using the following formula:

segment delay = (segment length x round trip delay per meter) + segment base

For example, on a 10Base-T network with four cable segments connected by three hubs, as shown in Figure 4-6, the constant for 10Base-T is 0.113, so the calculation would proceed as follows:

75 x 0.113	Segment 1 length x constant
15.25	Left end base
82 x 0.113	Segment 2 length x constant
42	Middle segment base
28 x 0.113	Segment 3 length x constant
42	Middle segment base
47 x 0.113	Segment 4 length x constant
65	Right end base
_____	
190.46	Total

As long as the total for all of your segments is less than 575, your network is compliant with the specification. The value of 575 is derived from the 64 bytes (512 bits minus 1) required to fill the entire length of cable in the collision domain, plus the 64 bits that form the Preamble and Start of Frame Delimiter in the Ethernet frame. If the delay time is less than 575 bit times, this means the node at one end of the worst case path will be unable to send more than 511 bits of the frame plus the Preamble and Start of Frame Delimiter before it is notified of a collision.

Another calculation, for the *interframe gap shrinkage*, ensures that there is a sufficient delay between packet transmissions to make certain that network interfaces have sufficient time to cycle between transmit and receive modes. If the variable timing delays in the network components and the signal reconstruction delays in the repeaters cause this gap to become too small, the frames might arrive too quickly and overwhelm the interface of the receiving node.

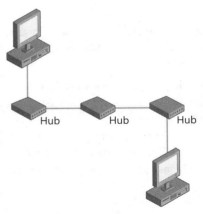

FIGURE 4-6 Sample calculation of round trip delay time.

NORMAL LINK PULSE SIGNALS

Standard Ethernet networks use *normal link pulse (NLP)* signals to verify the integrity of a link between two devices. Most Ethernet hubs and network interface adapters have a link pulse LED that lights when the device is connected to another active device. For example, when you take a UTP cable that is connected to a hub and plug it into a computer's network adapter and turn the computer on, the LEDs on both the adapter and the hub port to which it's connected should light. This is the result of the two devices transmitting NLP signals to each other. When each device receives the NLP signals from the other device, it lights the link pulse LED. If the network is wired incorrectly, because of a cable fault or improper use of a crossover cable or hub uplink port, the LEDs will not light. These signals do not interfere with data communications, because the devices transmit them only when the network is idle.

> ***NOTE*** **LINK PULSE TESTING**
>
> The link pulse LED indicates only that the network is wired correctly, not that it's capable of carrying data. If you use the wrong cable for the protocol, you will still experience network communications problems, even though the devices might pass the link integrity test.

FAST ETHERNET

The *100Base-TX* specification retains the 100-meter maximum segment length from 10Base-T, as well as the use of two wire pairs. However, to support the higher transmission speeds, the standard calls for a higher grade of cable: CAT5 instead of CAT3.

To provide a direct upgrade path to Fast Ethernet on existing CAT3 cable installations, the IEEE also published a specification called *100Base-T4*. This network did not require a cable upgrade, but to compensate, it made use of all four wire pairs instead of just two and used a different signaling scheme. Together, the two UTP Fast Ethernet specifications are known as *100Base-T*. However, for whatever reason, 100Base-T4 never caught on in the marketplace, and CAT5 quickly became the industry standard for UTP cable installations. Table 4-2 provides the Fast Ethernet physical layer specifications.

TABLE 4-2 100 Mbps Fast Ethernet Physical Layer Specifications

Designation	Cable Type	Maximum Segment Length
100Base-TX	CAT5 UTP	100 meters
100Base-FX	62.5/125 multimode fiber optic	412 meters (half duplex)/ 2,000 meters (full duplex)

EXAM TIP

Although 100Base-T4 never succeeded in the marketplace, it is part of the 100Base-T specification, which is included in the Network+ exam objectives.

On the fiber optic side, 100Base-FX uses the same 4B/5B signaling method as 100Base-TX, and as a result, the two specifications are known collectively as *100Base-X*. The maximum segment length on a 100Base-FX network depends both on the cable type and on the use of full duplex communications. Using standard multimode fiber optic cable and full duplex communication, a segment can be as long as 2,000 meters. Half-duplex signaling reduces the length to 412 meters. Using singlemode cable, a full-duplex segment can be 20 kilometers (km) long or more.

It has long been a standard practice in local area networking to connect multiple LANs together with a backbone network. Because the backbone must carry internetwork traffic from all of the LANs, many administrators run it at a higher speed than the horizontal LANs. Before the introduction of Fast Ethernet, FDDI (or its copper alternative, CDDI) was the most common high-speed backbone solution. Fast Ethernet enabled administrators to build backbones by using roughly the same technology as their horizontal networks.

When Fast Ethernet first appeared, its speed seemed wondrous, and most administrators assumed that it would be used only on backbones and other networks requiring higher performance levels. However, the prices for Fast Ethernet network interface cards, hubs, and switches began to drop precipitously, and hardware manufactures began making dual-speed equipment that could automatically sense the speed of the network and adjust itself accordingly. Before long, administrators began to realize the advantages of running Fast Ethernet to the desktop, and it quickly became the standard for the industry.

The introduction and acceptance of Gigabit Ethernet followed the same pattern. What seemed at first to be a backbone-only technology has been rapidly accepted for use on the desktop. Most new computers sold today include an integrated network interface adapter that can connect to an Ethernet network running at 10, 100, or 1,000 Mbps.

As of this writing, 10 Gigabit Ethernet is still in the early stages of its product deployment, and it remains to be seen whether the pattern will hold true for this next iteration of Ethernet technology.

FAST ETHERNET CABLING LIMITATIONS

The 5-4-3 rule does not apply to Fast Ethernet networks. Fast Ethernet hubs are available in two classes:

- **Class I**   Connects different types of Fast Ethernet cable segments together, such as fiber optic to UTP or 100Base-TX to 100Base-T4
- **Class II**   Connects Fast Ethernet cable segments of the same type together

Each Fast Ethernet hub must be identified by the appropriate Roman numeral in a circle. You can have as many as two Class II hubs on a single LAN, with a total cable length (for all three segments) of 205 meters for UTP cable and 228 meters for fiber optic cable, as shown in Figure 4-7.

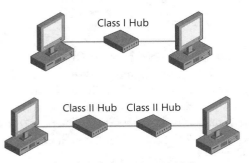

FIGURE 4-7 Fast Ethernet cabling guidelines.

Because Class I hubs must perform an additional signal translation, which slows down the transmission process, you can have only one hub on the network, with maximum cable lengths of 200 and 272 meters for UTP and fiber optic, respectively.

CALCULATING FAST ETHERNET CABLING SPECIFICATIONS

Fast Ethernet uses the same CSMA/CD media access control mechanism as 10 Mbps Ethernet; the signals just travel 10 times faster. Therefore, you can precisely calculate the compliance of your Fast Ethernet cable installation by using a formula similar to that for standard Ethernet.

For Fast Ethernet, you only have to calculate the round trip delay time; there is no inter-frame gap shrinkage calculation. The round trip delay time consists of a delay per meter measurement for the specific type of cable your network uses, plus an additional delay constant for each node and repeater on the path.

Thus, the formula for a typical 100Base-TX network that uses CAT5 UTP cable would be as follows:

round trip delay time = (segment lengths x 1.112) + (number of nodes x 50) + 140/Class I hub + 92/Class II hub

If the resulting value is less than 512, then the network is compliant with the Fast Ethernet specification.

> ### *NOTE* NVPS
>
> The constants for specific cable types included in the Fast Ethernet specification are general estimates that apply to most cable. However, it is possible to perform your calculations with even greater precision by determining the delay value for your specific cable product. Cable manufacturers usually supply a specification called the cable's *nominal velocity of propagation*. This is the cable's transmission speed, relative to the speed of light. By looking up this value in a table that provides alternative round trip delay per meter values, you can determine the exact value you should use when multiplying by the segment lengths.

FULL-DUPLEX ETHERNET

The CSMA/CD media access control mechanism is the defining element of the Ethernet protocol, but it is also the source of many of its limitations. The fundamental shortcoming of the Ethernet protocol is that data can travel only in one direction at a time. This is known as *half-duplex* operation. With special hardware, it is also possible to run Ethernet connections in *full-duplex* mode, meaning that the device can transmit and receive data simultaneously. This effectively doubles the bandwidth of the network. Full-duplex capability for Ethernet networks was standardized in the 802.3x amendment to the 802.3 standard in 1997.

When operating in full-duplex mode, Ethernet systems ignore the CSMA/CD MAC mechanism. Computers do not listen to the network before transmitting; they simply send their data whenever they want to. Because both of the systems in a full-duplex link can transmit and receive data at the same time, there is no possibility of collisions occurring. Because no collisions occur, the cabling restrictions designed to support the collision detection mechanism are unnecessary. This means that, in many cases, you can have longer cable segments on a full-duplex network. The only limitation is the signal transmitting capabilities (that is, the resistance to attenuation) of the network medium itself.

This is a particularly important point on a Fast Ethernet network that uses fiber optic cable, because the collision detection mechanism is responsible for its relatively short maximum segment lengths. Although a half-duplex 100Base-FX link between two devices can only be a maximum of 412 meters long, the same link operating in full-duplex mode can be up to 2,000 meters (2 km) long, because it is restricted only by the strength of the signal. A 100Base-FX link that uses singlemode fiber optic cable can span distances of 20 km or more. The signal attenuation on twisted pair networks, however, makes 10Base-T, 100Base-TX, and 1000Base-T networks still subject to the 100-meter segment length restriction.

There are three requirements for full-duplex Ethernet operation:

■ A network medium that supports separate transmit and receive signals

■ A dedicated link between every two systems

■ Network interface adapters and switches that support full-duplex operation

Full-duplex Ethernet is possible only on link segments that have separate channels for the communications in each direction. This means that twisted pair and fiber optic networks can support full-duplex communications by using regular, Fast, and Gigabit Ethernet, but coaxial cable cannot.

Full-duplex Ethernet also requires that every two computers have a dedicated link between them. This means that you can't use repeating hubs on a full-duplex network, because these devices operate in half-duplex mode by definition and create a shared network medium. Instead, you must use switches, which effectively isolate each pair of communicating computers on their own network segment and provide the packet-buffering capabilities needed to support bidirectional communications.

Finally, each of the devices on a full-duplex Ethernet network must support full-duplex communications and be configured to use it. Switches that support full-duplex are readily available, as are network interface adapters. Full-duplex operation is an essential component of 1000Base-T Gigabit Ethernet, and many 1000Base-X Gigabit Ethernet adapters support full-duplex as well.

> **MORE INFO** **GIGABIT ETHERNET**
> For more information on 1000Base-T and 1000Base-X, see "Gigabit Ethernet," later in this chapter.

Ensuring that your full-duplex equipment is actually operating in full-duplex mode can sometimes be tricky. Autonegotiation is definitely the easiest way of doing this; full-duplex operation always takes priority over half-duplex at the same speed during connection negotiations. Ethernet devices that support multiple speeds all include support for autonegotiation, which means that simply connecting a full-duplex network adapter to a full-duplex switch will enable full-duplex communications. Ethernet network adapters that use fiber optic cables, however, are sometimes single-speed devices, and might or might not include autonegotiation capability. You might have to manually configure the adapter before it will use full-duplex communications.

The switching hubs on full-duplex Ethernet networks have to be able to buffer packets as they read the destination address in each one and perform the internal switching needed to send it on its way. The amount of buffer memory in a switch is, of course, finite, and as a result, it's possible for a switch to be overwhelmed by the constant input of data from freely transmitting full-duplex systems. Therefore, the 802.3x supplement defines an optional flow control mechanism that full-duplex systems can use to make the system at the other end of a link pause its transmissions temporarily, enabling the other device to catch up.

Full-duplex Ethernet capabilities are most often provided in Fast Ethernet and Gigabit Ethernet adapters and switches. It's possible to run standard Ethernet networks, such as 10Base-T, in full-duplex mode also, but it generally is not worth upgrading a 10Base-T network to full duplex when you can upgrade it to Fast Ethernet at the same time, without spending a lot more money.

Though full-duplex operation theoretically doubles the bandwidth of a network, the actual performance improvement realized depends on the nature of the communications involved. Upgrading a desktop workstation to full duplex will probably not provide a dramatic improvement in performance. This is because desktop communications typically consist of request/response transactions that are themselves half-duplex in nature, and providing a full-duplex medium won't change that. Full-duplex operation is better suited to the communications between switches on a backbone, which are continually carrying large amounts of traffic generated by computers all over the network.

GIGABIT ETHERNET

The physical layer specifications for Gigabit Ethernet, running at 1,000 Mbps, appeared in 1998 and 1999. The fiber optic specifications, known collectively as 1000Base-X, were published as IEEE 802.3z, and the 1000Base-T UTP specification as IEEE 802.3ab. These specifications are listed in Table 4-3.

TABLE 4-3 1,000 Mbps Gigabit Ethernet Physical Layer Specifications

Designation	Cable Type	Maximum Segment Length
1000Base-T	CAT5, CAT5e, or CAT6 UTP	100 meters
1000Base-LX	9/125 singlemode fiber optic	5,000 meters
1000Base-LX	50/125 or 62.5/125 multimode fiber optic	550 meters
1000Base-SX	50/125 or 62.5/125 multimode fiber optic	500 meters / 220 meters
1000Base-CX	150-ohm shielded, balanced twinaxial copper cable	25 meters

Gigabit Ethernet once again increased network speeds tenfold, while retaining the same basic UTP configuration and segment length, making upgrades possible in many cases without the need for new cable installations. As with each previous Ethernet speed increase, Gigabit Ethernet increased the requirements for the UTP cables. *1000Base-T* uses all four wire pairs, unlike 100Base-TX, and is more susceptible to certain types of crosstalk. To address this issue, the Telecommunications Industry Association/Electronic Industries Alliance (TIA/EIA) created the CAT5e and CAT6 cable grades, which are designed to support Gigabit Ethernet communications.

> **MORE INFO**   **UTP CABLE GRADES**
>
> For more information on UTP cable grades and their specifications, see Chapter 2.

> **NOTE**   **1000BASE-TX**
>
> The TIA also created an alternative Gigabit Ethernet physical layer specification called 1000Base-TX. Like 100Base-TX, 1000Base-TX uses only two of the four wire pairs in a UTP cable. However, to compensate for that lack of two wire pairs, the 1000Base-TX specification requires CAT6 UTP cabling. Due perhaps to the cost of the cables, this specification has not been popular in the marketplace.

The *1000Base-X* specifications include two fiber optic configurations, essentially long-distance and short-distance options, plus a unique, short-run copper alternative. *1000Base-LX* is intended to be the long-distance option, supporting segment lengths up to 5 kilometers with singlemode fiber, and up to 10 kilometers with high-quality optics in a variant called 1000Base-LX10. Some specialized installations also use repeating equipment to create much longer links.

1000Base-LX is designed to be used by large carriers as a long-distance Ethernet backbone, so it is not likely that the average network administrator will ever work with it, nor will you find 1000Base-LX network interface adapters on the shelf at your local computer store.

The 1000Base-LX specification also allows for the use of multimode fiber optic cable at shorter distances, but *1000Base-SX* is the shorter-distance specification designed for virtually any type of multimode cable. As with most fiber optic alternatives, 1000Base-SX works well as a link between buildings and on campus networks.

1000Base-CX is a copper specification calling for a *twinaxial cable*, which is a special shielded 150-ohm cable with two copper cores that uses either 9-pin D-shell or 8-pin Fibre Channel connectors. The maximum segment length is only 25 meters, making the specification good for links within data centers, such as equipment connections within server clusters, and little else. At the time the IEEE published the 802.3z document, 1000Base-CX was the only copper cable specification available, but the 1000Base-T specification appeared a year later, leaving 1000Base-CX as a marginalized technology.

GIGABIT BACKBONES

Gigabit Ethernet is virtually assured of a place in the networking market because, like Fast Ethernet before it, it uses the same frame format, frame size, and MAC mechanism as standard 10 Mbps Ethernet. Fast Ethernet quickly replaced FDDI as the dominant 100 Mbps solution because it allowed network administrators to avoid having to use a different protocol on the backbone. In the same way, Gigabit Ethernet can allow administrators to avoid having to use a different protocol such as Asynchronous Transfer Mode (ATM) for their backbones.

Connecting an ATM or FDDI network to an Ethernet network requires the intervening router to convert the data at the network layer from one frame format to another. Connecting two Ethernet networks together, even when they're running at different speeds, is a data link layer operation because the frames remain unchanged. In addition, using Ethernet throughout your network eliminates the need to train administrators to work with a new protocol and purchase new testing and diagnostic equipment. The bottom line is that in most cases, it is possible to upgrade a Fast Ethernet backbone to Gigabit Ethernet without completely replacing hubs, switches, and cables.

This is not to say, however, that some hardware upgrades will not be necessary. Modular hubs and switches will need modules that support the new protocol, and networking monitoring and testing products might also have to be upgraded to support the higher speed.

As with Fast Ethernet, Gigabit Ethernet emerged as a backbone technology, but it wasn't long before triple-speed 10/100/1000 network interface adapters and switches were cheap and plentiful. Administrators who at one time scoffed at the idea of running 1,000 Mbps connections to the desktop were soon doing just that. At the time of this writing, virtually every new personal computer sold includes a Gigabit Ethernet network interface adapter.

GIGABIT REFINEMENTS

Gigabit Ethernet is designed to operate in full-duplex mode on switched networks. As discussed earlier, full-duplex communication eliminates the need for the CSMA/CD MAC mechanism. For backward compatibility purposes, though, Gigabit Ethernet continues to support hub-based networks and half-duplex communication.

For systems on a Gigabit Ethernet network to operate in half-duplex mode, it was necessary for the specifications to modify the CSMA/CD mechanism. Ethernet's collision-detection mechanism only works properly when collisions are detected while a packet is still being transmitted. After the source system finishes transmitting a packet, the data is purged from its buffers, and it is no longer possible to retransmit that packet in the event of a collision.

When the speed at which systems transmit data increases, the round trip signal delay time during which systems can detect a collision decreases. When Fast Ethernet increased the speed of an Ethernet network by 10 times, the specification compensated by reducing the maximum diameter of the network. This enabled the protocol to use the same 64-byte minimum packet size as the original Ethernet standard and still be able to detect collisions effectively.

Gigabit Ethernet increases the transmission speed another 10 times, but reducing the maximum diameter of the network again was impractical because it would result in networks no longer than 20 meters or so. As a result, the 802.3z supplement increases the size of the CSMA/CD carrier signal from 64 bytes to 512 bytes. This means that although the 64-byte minimum packet size is retained, the MAC sublayer of a half-duplex Gigabit Ethernet system appends a carrier extension signal to small packets that pads them out to 512 bytes. This ensures that the minimum time required to transmit each packet is sufficient for the collision detection mechanism to operate properly, even on a network with the same diameter as Fast Ethernet.

AUTONEGOTIATION

Backward compatibility has always been a major priority with the designers of the IEEE 802.3 standards. Most of the Ethernet networking hardware on the market today enables a computer to connect to the network at Gigabit Ethernet speed or negotiate a slower speed connection, if that is all the network supports.

The Fast Ethernet specifications define an optional *autonegotiation* system that enables a dual-speed device to sense the capabilities of the network to which it is connected and to adjust its speed and duplex status accordingly. The Gigabit Ethernet specifications expand the capabilities of the autonegotiation system, enabling devices to also communicate their port type and clocking parameters. In Gigabit Ethernet that uses copper cable, support for autonegotiation is mandatory.

The Ethernet autonegotiation mechanism is based on *fast link pulse (FLP)* signals, which are themselves a variation on the NLP signals used by 10Base-T and 10Base-FL networks. An Ethernet device capable of transmitting at multiple speeds transmits an FLP signal, which includes a 16-bit data packet within a burst of link pulses, producing what is called an *FLP burst*. The data packet contains a *link code word (LCW)* with two fields: the selector field and the technology ability field. Together, these fields identify the capabilities of the transmitting device, such as its maximum speed and whether it is capable of full-duplex communications.

Because the FLP burst has the same duration (2 nanoseconds) and interval (16.8 nanoseconds) as an NLP burst, a standard Ethernet system can simply ignore the LCW and treat the transmission as a normal link integrity test. The multiple-speed system attempting the negotiation then sets itself to operate at 10Base-T speed, by using a technique called *parallel detection*. This same method applies also to Ethernet devices incapable of multiple speeds, or those intentionally configured to use only a single speed.

When two Ethernet devices capable of operating at multiple speeds autonegotiate, they exchange FLP packets to determine the best performance level they have in common and configure themselves accordingly. The systems use the following list of priorities when comparing their capabilities, with full-duplex 1000Base-T providing the best performance and half-duplex 10Base-T providing the worst.

1. 1000Base-T (full-duplex)
2. 1000Base-T (half-duplex)

3. 100Base-TX (full-duplex)

4. 100Base-T4

5. 100Base-TX (half-duplex)

6. 10Base-T (full-duplex)

7. 10Base-T (half-duplex)

NOTE FLP SIGNALS

FLP signals account only for the capabilities of the devices generating them, not the connecting cable. If you connect a multispeed 1000Base-T computer to a 1000Base-T hub by using a CAT3 cable network, autonegotiation will still configure the devices to operate at 1000 Mbps, even though the cable can't reliably support transmissions at this speed.

The benefit of autonegotiation is that it permits administrators to upgrade a network gradually with a minimum of reconfiguration. If, for example, you have 10/100/1000 multi-speed network adapters in all your workstations, you can run the network at 100 Mbps using 100Base-TX switches. Later, you can simply replace the switches with models supporting Gigabit Ethernet, and the network adapters will automatically reconfigure themselves to operate at the higher speed during the next system reboot. No manual configuration at the workstation is necessary.

AUTOMATIC MDI/MDIX CONFIGURATION

The term *medium dependent interface (MDI)* refers to the connection between a network device, such as a network interface adapter or a switch, and the network medium. On a typical Ethernet LAN, the MDIs take the form of the connectors on the adapters and switches. The Ethernet specifications also define a *medium dependent interface crossover (MDIX)* connection, which usually takes the form of an uplink port in a hub or switch.

As discussed in Chapter 3, hubs and switches often include a dedicated uplink port, or a port that you can switch between normal and uplink wiring. This enables you to connect two switches together without using a crossover cable.

The 1000Base-T specification defines an optional feature called *automatic MDI/MDIX configuration (Auto-MDIX)*, which eliminates the need even to switch uplink ports or procure crossover cables. When you connect an Auto-MDIX port to another device, whether the other device is Auto-MDIX or not, the system determines which type of connection is required—MDI or MDIX—and configures itself accordingly. Although support for Auto-MDIX is optional, virtually all of the Gigabit Ethernet and 10 Gigabit Ethernet switches, hubs, and routers manufactured today support it.

10 GIGABIT ETHERNET

Once again, the call went out for more Ethernet bandwidth, and the IEEE 802.3 working group responded in 2002 with the first standards defining an Ethernet network running at 10 gigabits per second (Gbps), which is 10,000 Mbps. With 10 Gigabit Ethernet, the developers appear to have reached a turning point, because they have abandoned their previous devotion to backward compatibility. 10 Gigabit Ethernet networks support only four-pair, full-duplex communication on switched networks. Gone is the support for half-duplex communication, hubs, and CSMA/CD. However, the standard Ethernet frame format remains, and as with all of the previous Ethernet standards, there is a copper-based UTP solution that uses 8P8C connectors and a 100-meter maximum segment length.

As with each of the previous Ethernet speed iterations, the 10 Gigabit Ethernet standards include a variety of physical layer specifications. Some of them have already fallen by the wayside, but the technology is still young enough that the marketplace hasn't yet completed the process of winnowing out the unsuccessful ones. Table 4-4 lists the most prominent of the 10 Gigabit Ethernet physical layer specifications defined by the IEEE standards.

TABLE 4-4 10 Gigabit Ethernet Physical Layer Specifications

Designation	Cable Type	Wavelength	Maximum Segment Length
10Gbase-T	CAT6/CAT6a	N/A	55 meters/100 meters
10Gbase-SR	Multimode fiber optic	850 nm	26–400 meters
10Gbase-LR	Singlemode fiber optic	1310 nm	10 kilometers
10Gbase-ER	Singlemode fiber optic	1550 nm	40 kilometers
10Gbase-SW	Multimode fiber optic	850 nm	26–400 meters
10Gbase-LW	Singlemode fiber optic	1310 nm	10 kilometers
10Gbase-EW	Singlemode fiber optic	1550 nm	40 kilometers

The designers of 10 Gigabit Ethernet intended it to be both a LAN and a WAN solution, and for many administrators, LAN means copper-based UTP cables with a 100-meter maximum segment length. It was not until 2006 that the IEEE published the 802.3an amendment, which defined the *10Gbase-T* specification, but they knew it had to be done.

Unfortunately, to support transmissions at such high speeds with copper cables, it was necessary to define a new set of cable performance standards. To support 100-meter segments, 10Gbase-T requires CAT6a cable, which has an increased resistance to alien crosstalk (interference from signals on other, nearby cables). With standard CAT6 cable, 10Gbase-T only supports cable segments up to 55 meters long. The standard does not support UTP cables below CAT6 at all.

The 10 Gigabit Ethernet specifications for fiber optic cable predate the copper and provide a wide variety of options for both LAN and WAN implementations. The possibilities of 10 Gigabit Ethernet as a WAN solution led the developers to create a separate set of specifications that utilize the existing Synchronous Optical Network (SONET) infrastructure to carry Ethernet signals.

As shown in Table 4-4, there are three pairs of fiber optic specifications that all begin with the "10Gbase" abbreviation. The first letter of the two-letter code that follows specifies the type and wavelength of the fiber optic cable. The second letter indicates whether the specification is intended for LAN use ("R") or WAN use ("W").

The "S" in the *10Gbase-SR* and *10Gbase-SW* specifications describes the short wavelength (850 nanometers) of the lasers used to generate the signals on the cable. As with most short-range fiber optic solutions, these specifications call for multimode cable. The maximum segment length depends on the exact cable the network uses. For example, the 62.5-micron multimode fiber commonly used on FDDI networks (OM1) can only support segments up to 26 meters long. With the newly ratified OM4 cable, 10Gbase-SR segments can be as long as 400 meters.

The *10Gbase-LR* and *10Gbase-LW* specifications use a long wavelength laser (1,310 nm) and singlemode cables to achieve segment lengths of 10 kilometers. The extra-long wavelength of the *10Gbase-ER* and *10Gbase-EW* specifications can support segments up to 40 kilometers long.

None of the 10 Gigabit Ethernet physical layer specifications indicate the types of connectors the cables should use. The actual implementation is left up to the equipment manufacturers.

10 GIGABIT ETHERNET PHYSICAL IMPLEMENTATIONS

Because the 10 Gigabit Ethernet standard has many supported cable types and no standard connector specifications, designing, marketing, and manufacturing 10 Gigabit Ethernet equipment might seem to be a daunting task. To address this problem, networking equipment manufacturers have devised a new solution. Instead of building a specific physical layer interface into a networking device, thus requiring multiple versions to support many different media, manufacturers have started building devices with a standard socket, into which consumers can

plug a *physical layer (PHY) module* that contains a transceiver and supports their cable and connector, as shown in Figure 4-8.

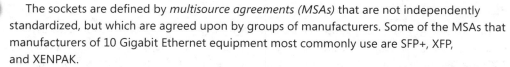

The sockets are defined by *multisource agreements (MSAs)* that are not independently standardized, but which are agreed upon by groups of manufacturers. Some of the MSAs that manufacturers of 10 Gigabit Ethernet equipment most commonly use are SFP+, XFP, and XENPAK.

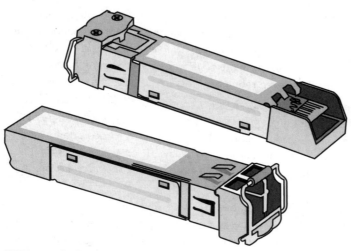

FIGURE 4-8 An SFP+ physical layer module.

Point-to-Point Protocol (PPP)

 The other major protocol operating at the data-link layer of the OSI reference model is the *Point-to-Point Protocol (PPP)*. PPP is much simpler than Ethernet because it is designed for use by WAN connections that consist of only two systems. Because there are only two devices involved, there is no need for the protocol to support complex procedures such as node addressing or media access control. However, PPP does include support for a variety of ancillary protocols that provide authentication and other services.

PPP is part of the TCP/IP protocol suite. PPP and the Serial Line Internet Protocol (SLIP) are the only TCP/IP protocols that provide full data-link layer functionality. Systems connected to a LAN rely on one of the standard data link layer protocols, such as Ethernet, to control the actual connection to the network. This is because the systems might be sharing a common medium and must have a MAC mechanism to regulate access to it.

PPP is designed for use with modems and other direct connections in which there is no need for media access control. Because it connects only two systems, PPP is called a *point-to-point* or *end-to-end protocol*. On a system that uses PPP, the TCP/IP protocols define the workings of the entire protocol stack, except for the physical layer itself, which relies on a hardware standard such as that for the RS-232 serial port interface that provides a computer with a connection to a modem.

In most cases, systems use PPP to provide Internet or WAN connectivity, whether or not the system is connected to a LAN. Virtually every stand-alone PC that ever used a modem to connect to an Internet service provider (ISP) for Internet access did so by using a PPP connection. LANs also use PPP connections in their routers to connect to an ISP to provide Internet access to the entire network or to connect to another LAN, forming a WAN connection. Although PPP is commonly associated with modem connections, other physical layer technologies can also use PPP, including leased lines and various forms of broadband connections.

PPP is a connection-oriented protocol that provides a data link between two systems in the simplest sense of the term. It encapsulates IP datagrams for transport between computers, just as Ethernet does, but the frame it uses is far simpler. This is because the protocol is not subject to the same problems as the LAN protocols.

PPP was created as an alternative to SLIP that provides greater functionality, such as the capability for multiplexing different network layer protocols and support for various authentication protocols. Naturally, the cost of these additional features is a larger header, but PPP still only adds a maximum of 8 bytes to a packet (compared to the 16 bytes needed for an Ethernet frame). Many connections to ISPs, whether by stand-alone systems or routers, use PPP in some form because it enables the ISP to implement access control measures that protect their networks from intrusion by unauthorized users.

PPP Standards

A typical PPP session consists of several connection establishment and termination procedures, using other protocols in addition to PPP itself. These procedures can include the following:

- **Connection establishment** The system initiating the connection uses the *Link Control Protocol (LCP)* to negotiate communication parameters that the two machines have in common.

- **Authentication** Although this is not required, the system might use an authentication protocol such as PAP (the Password Authentication Protocol) or CHAP (the Challenge Handshake Authentication Protocol) to negotiate access to the other system.

- **Network layer protocol connection establishment** For each network layer protocol that the systems use during the session, they perform a separate connection establishment procedure by using a Network Control Protocol (NCP) such as IPCP (the Internet Protocol Control Protocol).

Like other TCP/IP protocols, PPP is standardized, but the specifications are divided among several different Requests for Comments (RFCs). The documents for each of the protocols are as follows:

- **RFC 1661** The Point-to-Point Protocol (PPP)
- **RFC 1662** PPP in HDLC-like Framing
- **RFC 1663** PPP Reliable Transmission
- **RFC 1332** The PPP Internet Protocol Control Protocol (IPCP)
- **RFC 1552** The PPP Internetworking Packet Exchange Control Protocol (IPXCP)
- **RFC 1334** PPP Authentication Protocols
- **RFC 1994** PPP Challenge Handshake Authentication Protocol (CHAP)
- **RFC 1989** PPP Link Quality Monitoring

The PPP Frame

RFC 1661 defines the basic frame used by the PPP protocol to encapsulate other protocols and transmit them to the destination. The frame is small, only 8 (or sometimes 10) bytes, and is illustrated in Figure 4-9.

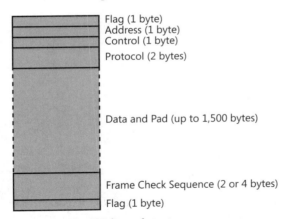

Flag (1 byte)
Address (1 byte)
Control (1 byte)
Protocol (2 bytes)

Data and Pad (up to 1,500 bytes)

Frame Check Sequence (2 or 4 bytes)
Flag (1 byte)

FIGURE 4-9 The PPP frame format.

The functions of the fields in the frame are as follows:

- **Flag (1 byte)** Contains a hexadecimal value of *7e* and functions as a packet delimiter.
- **Address (1 byte)** Contains a hexadecimal value of *ff*, indicating that the packet is addressed to all stations.
- **Control (1 byte)** Contains a hexadecimal value of *03*, identifying the packet as containing a High-Level Data-Link Control (HDLC) unnumbered information message.
- **Protocol (2 bytes)** Contains a code identifying the protocol that generated the information in the data field. Code values in the *0xxx* to *3xxx* range are used to identify network layer protocols; values from *4xxx* to *7xxx* identify low-volume network layer protocols with no corresponding NCP; values from *8xxx* to *bxxx* identify network layer protocols with corresponding NCPs; and values from *cxxx* to *fxxx* identify link layer control protocols such as LCP and the authentication protocols. The permitted codes, as designated by the Internet Assigned Numbers Authority (IANA), include the following:
  - **0021** Internet Protocol version 4
  - **0023** OSI Network Layer
  - **002d** Van Jacobson Compressed TCP/IP
  - **002f** Van Jacobson Uncompressed TCP/IP
  - **004f** IP6 Header Compression
  - **0057** Internet Protocol version 6
  - **0059** PPP Muxing
  - **8021** Internet Protocol Control Protocol (IPCP)
  - **8023** OSI Network Layer Control Protocol
  - **803d** Multi-Link Control Protocol
  - **804f** IP6 Header Compression Control Protocol
  - **8057** IPv6 Control Protocol
  - **c021** Link Control Protocol (LCP)
  - **c023** Password Authentication Protocol (PAP)
  - **c029** Callback Control Protocol (CBCP)
  - **c05b** Vendor-Specific Authentication Protocol (VSAP)
  - **c223** Challenge Handshake Authentication Protocol (CHAP)
  - **c227** Extensible Authentication Protocol
- **Data and Pad (variable, up to 1,500 bytes)** Contains the payload of the packet, up to a default maximum length (called the *maximum receive unit*, or *MRU*) of 1,500 bytes. The field might contain meaningless bytes to bring it up to the MRU size.

- **Frame Check Sequence (FCS) (2 or 4 bytes)**   Contains a cyclical redundancy check (CRC) value calculated on the entire frame, excluding the flag and frame check sequence fields, for error-detection purposes.
- **Flag (1 byte)**   Contains the same value as the flag field at the beginning of the frame. When a system transmits two packets consecutively, one of the flag fields is omitted because two would be mistaken as an empty frame.

Several of the fields in the PPP frame can be modified as a result of LCP negotiations between the two systems, such as the length of the protocol and FCS fields and the MRU for the data field. The systems can agree to use a 1-byte protocol field or a 4-byte FCS field.

The LCP Frame

PPP systems use LCP to negotiate their capabilities during the connection establishment process so that they can achieve the most efficient possible connection. LCP messages are carried within PPP frames and contain configuration options for the connection. When the two systems agree on a configuration they can both support, the link establishment process continues. By specifying the parameters for the connection during the link establishment process, the systems don't have to include redundant information in the header of every data packet.

The LCP message format is shown in Figure 4-10. The functions of the individual fields are as follows:

- **Code (1 byte)**   Specifies the LCP message type, by using the following codes:
    - **1**   Configure-Request
    - **2**   Configure-Ack
    - **3**   Configure-Nak
    - **4**   Configure-Reject
    - **5**   Terminate-Request
    - **6**   Terminate-Ack
    - **7**   Code Reject
    - **8**   Protocol-Reject
    - **9**   Echo-Request
    - **10**   Echo-Reply
    - **11**   Discard-Request
- **Identifier (1 byte)**   Contains a code used to associate the request and replies of a particular LCP transaction
- **Length (2 bytes)**   Specifies the length of the LCP message, including the code, identifier, length, and data fields
- **Data (variable)**   Contains multiple configuration options, each of which is composed of three subfields

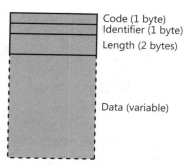

Code (1 byte)
Identifier (1 byte)
Length (2 bytes)

Data (variable)

FIGURE 4-10 The LCP message format.

Each of the options in the LCP message's data field consists of the subfields shown in Figure 4-11. The functions of the subfields are as follows:

- **Type (1 byte)**   Specifies the option to be configured, by using a code assigned by the IANA

- **Length (1 byte)**   Specifies the length of the LCP message, including the code, identifier, length, and data fields

- **Data (variable)**   Contains information pertinent to the specific LCP message type, as indicated by the code field

The LCP protocol is also designed to be extensible. By using a code value of 0, vendors can supply their own options without standardizing them with the IANA, as documented in RFC 2153, "PPP Vendor Extensions."

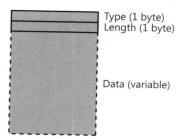

Type (1 byte)
Length (1 byte)

Data (variable)

FIGURE 4-11 The LCP option format.

Authentication Protocols

PPP connections can optionally require authentication to prevent unauthorized access, by using an external protocol agreed on during the exchange of LCP configuration messages and encapsulated within PPP frames. Two of the most popular authentication protocols—PAP and CHAP—are defined by TCP/IP specifications, but systems can also use other proprietary protocols developed by individual vendors.

The PAP Frame

PAP is inherently the weaker of the two main PPP authentication protocols because it uses only a two-way handshake and transmits account names and passwords over the link in clear text. Systems generally use PAP only when they have no other authentication protocols in common. PAP packets have a value of *c023* in the PPP header's protocol field and use a message format that is basically the same as LCP, except for the options. The functions of the message fields are as follows:

- **Code (1 byte)**   Specifies the type of PAP message, by using the following values:
  - **1**   Authenticate Request
  - **2**   Authenticate Ack
  - **3**   Authenticate Nak
- **Identifier (1 byte)**   Contains a code used to associate the request and replies of a particular PAP transaction
- **Length (2 bytes)**   Specifies the length of the PAP message, including the code, identifier, length, and data fields
- **Data (variable)**   Contains several subfields, depending on the value in the code field, as follows:
  - **Peer ID Length (1 byte)**   Specifies the length of the peer ID field (Authenticate Request messages only)
  - **Peer ID (variable)**   Specifies the account the destination computer will use to authenticate the source system (Authenticate Request messages only)
  - **Password Length (1 byte)**   Specifies the length of the password field (Authenticate Request messages only)
  - **Password (variable)**   Specifies the password associated with the account name in the peer ID field (Authenticate Request messages only)
  - **Message Length (1 byte)**   Specifies the length of the message field (Authenticate Ack and Authenticate Nak messages only)
  - **Message (variable)**   Contains a text message that will be displayed on the user interface describing the success or failure of the authentication procedure (Authenticate Ack and Authenticate Nak messages only)

The CHAP Frame

The CHAP protocol is considerably more secure than PAP because it uses a three-way hand-shake and never transmits account names and passwords in clear text. CHAP packets have a value of *c223* in the PPP header's protocol field and use a message format almost identical to PAP's. The functions of the message fields are as follows:

- **Code (1 byte)** Specifies the type of CHAP message, using the following values:
  - **1** Challenge
  - **2** Response
  - **3** Success
  - **4** Failure
- **Identifier (1 byte)** Contains a code used to associate the request and replies of a particular CHAP transaction
- **Length (2 bytes)** Specifies the length of the CHAP message, including the code, identifier, length, and data fields
- **Data (variable)** Contains several subfields, depending on the value of the code field, as follows:
  - **Value Size (1 byte)** Specifies the length of the value field (Challenge and Response messages only)
  - **Value (variable)** In a Challenge message, contains a unique byte string that the recipient uses along with the contents of the identifier field and an encryption "secret" to generate the value field for the Response message (Challenge and Response messages only)
  - **Name (variable)** Contains a string that identifies the transmitting system (Challenge and Response messages only)
  - **Message (variable)** Contains a text message to be displayed on the user interface describing the success or failure of the authentication procedure (Success and Failure messages only)

The IPCP Frame

PPP systems use *network control protocols (NCPs)* to negotiate connections for each of the network layer protocols they will use during a session. Before a system can multiplex the traffic generated by different protocols over a single PPP connection, it must establish a connection for each protocol by using the appropriate NCPs.

The *Internet Protocol Control Protocol (IPCP)*, which is the NCP for IP, is a good example of the protocol structure. The message format of the NCPs is nearly identical to that of LCP, except that it supports only values 1 through 7 for the code field (the link configuration, link termination, and code reject values) and uses different options in the data field. Like LCP, the messages are carried in PPP frames, but with a value of *8021* in the PPP header's protocol field.

The options that IPCP messages can carry in the data field use the following values in the type field:

- **2 – IP Compression Protocol**   Specifies the protocol the system should use to compress IP headers, for which the only valid option is Van Jacobson compression.

- **3 – IP Address**   Used by the transmitting system to request a particular IP address or, if the value is 0.0.0.0, to request that the receiving system supply an address (replaces the type 1 IP Addresses option, which is no longer used).

PPP Connection Establishment

When the physical layer connection between the two systems has been established (through a modem handshake or other procedure), the PPP connection establishment process begins. The two systems pass through several distinct phases during the course of the session, as illustrated in Figure 4-12 and discussed in the following sections.

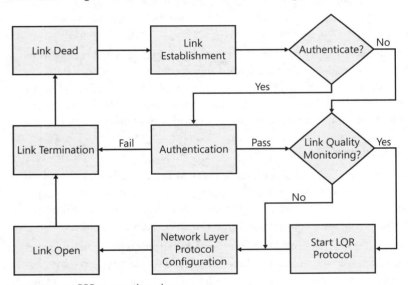

FIGURE 4-12 PPP connection phases.

The Link Dead Phase

Both systems begin and end the session in the Link Dead phase, which indicates that no physical layer connection exists between the two machines. In a typical session, an application or service on one system initiates the physical layer connection by dialing the modem or using some other means. After the hardware connection process is completed, the systems pass into the Link Establishment phase.

The Link Establishment Phase

In the Link Establishment phase, the system initiating the connection transmits an LCP Configure Request message to the destination containing the options it would like to enable, such as the use of specific authentication, link quality monitoring, and network layer protocols (if any), and whether the systems should modify standard features, such as the size of the FCS field or use of a different MRU value. If the receiving system can support all the specified options, it replies with a Configure Ack message containing the same option values, and this phase of the connection process is completed.

If the receiving system recognizes the options in the request message but cannot support the values for those options supplied by the sender (for example, if the system supports authentication, but not with the protocol the sender has specified), it replies with a Configure Nak message containing the options with values it cannot support. Along with these options, the replying system supplies all the values it does support and also might include other options it would like to see enabled. Using this information, the connecting system generates another Configure Request message containing options it knows are supported, to which the receiver replies with a Configure Ack message.

If the receiving system fails to recognize any of the options in the request, it replies with a Configure Reject message containing only the unrecognized options. The sender then generates a new Configure Request message that does not contain the rejected options, and the procedure continues as previously outlined. Eventually, the systems perform a successful request/acknowledgment exchange and the connection process moves on to the next phase.

The Authentication Phase

The Authentication phase of the connection process is optional and is triggered by the inclusion of the Authentication Protocol option in the LCP Configure Request message. During the LCP link establishment process, the two systems agree on an authentication protocol to use. Use of the PAP and CHAP protocols is common, but other protocols are available.

The message format and exchange procedures for the Authentication phase are dictated by the selected protocol. In a PAP authentication, for example, the sending system transmits an Authenticate Request message containing an account name and password, and the receiver replies with either an Authenticate Ack or Authenticate Nak message.

CHAP is inherently more secure than PAP and requires a more complex message exchange. The sending system transmits a Challenge message containing data that the receiver uses with its encryption key to compute a value that it returns to the sender in a Response message. Depending on whether the value in the response matches the sender's own computations, it transmits a Success or Failure message.

A successful transaction causes the connection procedure to proceed to the next phase, but the effect of a failure is dictated by the implementation of the protocol. Some systems proceed directly to the Link Termination phase in the event of an authentication failure, whereas others might permit retries or limited network access to a help subsystem.

Link Quality Monitoring

The use of a link quality monitoring protocol is also an optional element of the connection process and is triggered by the inclusion of the Quality Protocol option in the LCP Configure Request message. Although the option enables the sending system to specify any protocol for this purpose, only one has been standardized, the Link Quality Report protocol. The negotiation process that occurs at this phase enables the systems to agree on an interval at which they should transmit messages containing link traffic and error statistics throughout the session.

Network layer Protocol Configuration

PPP supports the multiplexing of network layer protocols over a single connection, and during this phase, the systems perform a separate network layer connection establishment procedure for each of the network layer protocols that they have agreed to use during the Link Establishment phase. Each network layer protocol has its own Network Control Protocol (NCP) for this purpose, such as the Internet Protocol Control Protocol (IPCP). The structure of an NCP message exchange is similar to that of LCP, except that the options carried in the Configure Request message are unique to the requirements of the protocol. During an IPCP exchange, for example, the systems inform each other of their IP addresses and agree on whether or not to use Van Jacobson header compression. Other protocols have their own individual needs that the systems negotiate as needed. NCP initialization and termination procedures can also occur at any other time during the connection.

The Link Open Phase

When the individual NCP exchanges are completed, the connection is fully established and the systems enter the Link Open phase. Network layer protocol data can now travel over the link in either direction.

The Link Termination Phase

When one of the systems ends the session or when the session is ended as a result of other conditions such as a physical layer disconnection, an authentication failure, or an inactivity timeout, the systems enter the Link Termination phase. To sever the link, one system transmits an LCP Terminate Request message, to which the other system replies with a Terminate Ack. Both systems then return to the Link Dead phase.

NCPs also support the Terminate Request and Terminate Ack messages, but they are intended for use while the PPP connection remains intact. In fact, the PPP connection can remain active even if all of the network layer protocol connections have been terminated. It is unnecessary for systems to terminate the network layer protocol connections before terminating the PPP connection.

EXAM TIP

The Network+ objectives refer to PPP primarily as a network access security mechanism. Candidates should be particularly aware of how PPP integrates various authentication protocols into its connection establishment sequence.

 Quick Check

1. Why is PAP considered a weak authentication protocol?

2. What protocol does PPP use to negotiate the communication parameters that the two connecting machines have in common?

Quick Check Answers

1. Because it transmits user names and passwords in clear text

2. Link Control Protocol

Address Resolution Protocol (ARP)

The *Address Resolution Protocol (ARP)* occupies an unusual place at the data-link layer and in the TCP/IP suite because it defies all attempts at categorization. Unlike the other data-link layer protocols, ARP does not carry application data packets across the network, and unlike most other TCP/IP protocols, ARP messages are not carried within IP datagrams. The IANA has defined a separate protocol identifier that data-link layer protocols use to indicate that they contain ARP messages.

Because of this confusion, there is some difference of opinion about the layer of the protocol stack to which ARP belongs. Some say ARP is a data-link layer protocol because it provides a service to IP, whereas others associate it with the network layer because its messages are carried within data-link layer frames.

The function of the ARP protocol, as defined in RFC 826, "An Ethernet Address Resolution Protocol," is to reconcile the IP addresses used to identify systems at the upper layers of the protocol stack with the hardware addresses at the data-link layer. When a TCP/IP application requests network resources, it supplies the destination IP address used in the IP protocol header. The system might discover the IP address by using a Domain Name System (DNS) or NetBIOS name resolution process, or it might use an address supplied by an operating system or application configuration parameter.

Data-link layer protocols such as Ethernet, however, have no use for IP addresses and cannot read the contents of the IP datagram anyway. To transmit the packet to its destination, the data-link layer protocol must have the hardware address coded into the destination system's network interface adapter. ARP converts an IP address into a hardware address by broadcasting a request packet containing the IP address on the local network and waiting for the holder of that IP address to respond with a reply containing the equivalent hardware address.

> **NOTE** **ARP ORIGINS**
>
> ARP was originally developed for use with DIX Ethernet networks but has been generalized to allow its use with other data-link layer protocols.

The biggest difference between IP addresses and hardware addresses is that IP is responsible for the delivery of the packet to its ultimate destination, whereas an Ethernet implementation is only concerned with delivery to the next stop on the journey. If the packet's destination is on the same network segment as the source, then the IP protocol uses ARP to resolve the IP address of the ultimate destination into a hardware address. If, however, the destination is located on another network, the IP protocol will not use ARP to resolve the ultimate destination address (that is, the destination address in the IP header). Instead, it will pass the IP address of the default gateway to the ARP protocol for address resolution.

This is because the data-link layer protocol header must contain the hardware address of the next intermediate stop as its destination, which might well be a router. It is up to that router to forward the packet on the next leg of its journey. Thus, in the course of a single internetwork transmission, many different machines might perform ARP resolutions on the same packet with different results.

ARP Message Format

ARP messages are carried directly within data-link layer frames, using *0806* as the Ethertype or SNAP Local Code value to identify the protocol being carried in the packet. There is one format for all of the ARP message types, which is illustrated in Figure 4-13.

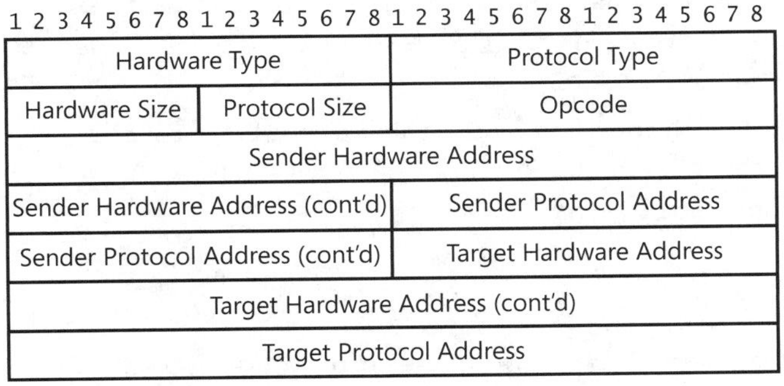

```
1 2 3 4 5 6 7 8 1 2 3 4 5 6 7 8 1 2 3 4 5 6 7 8 1 2 3 4 5 6 7 8
```

Hardware Type		Protocol Type	
Hardware Size	Protocol Size	Opcode	
Sender Hardware Address			
Sender Hardware Address (cont'd)		Sender Protocol Address	
Sender Protocol Address (cont'd)		Target Hardware Address	
Target Hardware Address (cont'd)			
Target Protocol Address			

FIGURE 4-13 The ARP message format.

The functions of the fields in an ARP message are as follows:

- **Hardware Type (2 bytes)**   Specifies the type of hardware addresses found in the Sender Hardware Address and Target Hardware Address fields. The hexadecimal value for Ethernet is *0001*.

- **Protocol Type (2 bytes)**   Specifies the type of protocol addresses found in the Sender Protocol Address and Target Protocol Address fields. The hexadecimal value for IP addresses is *0800* (the same as the Ethertype value for IP).

- **Hardware Size (1 byte)**   Specifies the size (in bytes) of the hardware addresses found in the Sender Hardware Address and Target Hardware Address fields. The value for Ethernet hardware addresses is 6.

- **Protocol Size (1 byte)**   Specifies the size (in bytes) of the protocol addresses found in the Sender Protocol Address and Target Protocol Address fields. The value for IP addresses is 4.

- **Opcode (2 bytes)**   Specifies the type of message contained in the packet, by using the following values:
  - **1**   ARP Request
  - **2**   ARP Reply
  - **3**   RARP Request
  - **4**   RARP Reply

- **Sender Hardware Address (length specified by the value of the Hardware Size field)**   Specifies the hardware (for example, Ethernet) address of the system sending the message, in both requests and replies.

- **Sender Protocol Address (length specified by the value of the Protocol Size field)**   Specifies the protocol (for example, IP) address of the system sending the message, in both requests and replies.

- **Target Hardware Address (length specified by the value of the Hardware Size field)**   Left blank in request messages; in replies, contains the value of the Sender Hardware Address field in the associated request.

- **Target Protocol Address (length specified by the value of the Protocol Size field)**   Specifies the protocol (for example, IP) address of the system to which the message is being sent, in both requests and replies.

NOTE **USING RARP**

The RARP Request and RARP Reply message types are not used in the course of standard TCP/IP network traffic. However, they were used at one time for IP address assignment. For more information on the Reverse Address Resolution Protocol (RARP), see Chapter 9, "The Application Layer."

ARP Transactions

An ARP transaction occurs when the IP protocol in a TCP/IP system is ready to transmit a datagram over the network. The system knows its own hardware and IP addresses, as well as the IP address of the packet's intended destination. All it lacks is the hardware address of the system on the local network that is to receive the packet. The ARP message exchange proceeds according to the following steps:

1. The transmitting system generates an ARP Request packet containing its own addresses in the Sender Hardware Address and Sender Protocol Address fields (see the captured packet shown in Figure 4-14). The Target Protocol Address field contains the IP address of the system on the local network that is to receive the datagram, and the Target Hardware Address field is left blank. Some implementations insert a broadcast address or other value into the Target Hardware Address field of the ARP Request message, but this value is ignored by the recipient because this is the address the protocol is trying to ascertain.

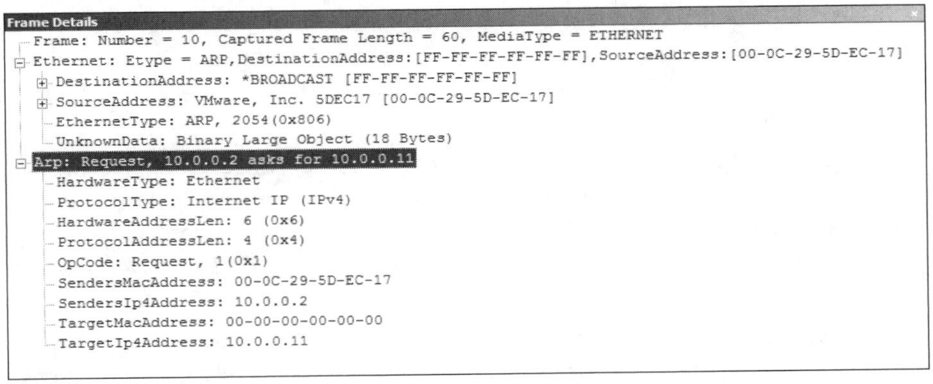

```
Frame Details
  ┌─Frame: Number = 10, Captured Frame Length = 60, MediaType = ETHERNET
  ├─Ethernet: Etype = ARP,DestinationAddress:[FF-FF-FF-FF-FF-FF],SourceAddress:[00-0C-29-5D-EC-17]
  │ ├─DestinationAddress: *BROADCAST [FF-FF-FF-FF-FF-FF]
  │ ├─SourceAddress: VMware, Inc. 5DEC17 [00-0C-29-5D-EC-17]
  │ ├─EthernetType: ARP, 2054(0x806)
  │ └─UnknownData: Binary Large Object (18 Bytes)
  └─Arp: Request, 10.0.0.2 asks for 10.0.0.11
      ├─HardwareType: Ethernet
      ├─ProtocolType: Internet IP (IPv4)
      ├─HardwareAddressLen: 6 (0x6)
      ├─ProtocolAddressLen: 4 (0x4)
      ├─OpCode: Request, 1(0x1)
      ├─SendersMacAddress: 00-0C-29-5D-EC-17
      ├─SendersIp4Address: 10.0.0.2
      ├─TargetMacAddress: 00-00-00-00-00-00
      └─TargetIp4Address: 10.0.0.11
```

FIGURE 4-14 The ARP Request message.

2. The system transmits the ARP Request message as a broadcast to the local network, asking, in effect, "Who is using this IP address, and what is your hardware address?"

3. Each TCP/IP system on the local network receives the ARP Request broadcast and examines the contents of the Target Protocol Address field. If the system does not use that address on one of its network interfaces, it silently discards the packet. If the system does use the address, it generates an ARP Reply message in response. The system uses the contents of the Request message's Sender Hardware Address and Sender Protocol Address fields as the values for its reply message's Target Hardware Address and Target Protocol Address fields. The system then inserts its own hardware address and IP address into the Sender Hardware Address and Sender Protocol Address fields, respectively (see Figure 4-15).

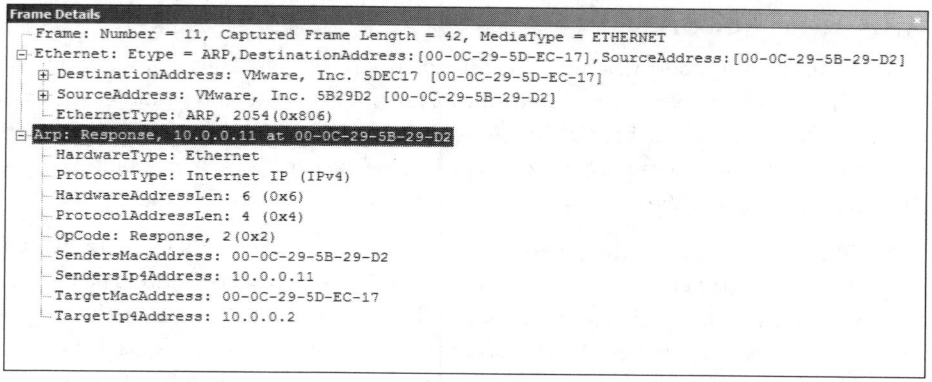

```
Frame Details                                                                              x
    ┌ Frame: Number = 11, Captured Frame Length = 42, MediaType = ETHERNET
    ⊟ Ethernet: Etype = ARP,DestinationAddress:[00-0C-29-5D-EC-17],SourceAddress:[00-0C-29-5B-29-D2]
      ⊞ DestinationAddress: VMware, Inc. 5DEC17 [00-0C-29-5D-EC-17]
      ⊞ SourceAddress: VMware, Inc. 5B29D2 [00-0C-29-5B-29-D2]
       └ EthernetType: ARP, 2054(0x806)
    ⊟ Arp: Response, 10.0.0.11 at 00-0C-29-5B-29-D2
      ├ HardwareType: Ethernet
      ├ ProtocolType: Internet IP (IPv4)
      ├ HardwareAddressLen: 6 (0x6)
      ├ ProtocolAddressLen: 4 (0x4)
      ├ OpCode: Response, 2(0x2)
      ├ SendersMacAddress: 00-0C-29-5B-29-D2
      ├ SendersIp4Address: 10.0.0.11
      ├ TargetMacAddress: 00-0C-29-5D-EC-17
      └ TargetIp4Address: 10.0.0.2
```

FIGURE 4-15 The ARP Response message.

4. The system using the requested IP address transmits the reply message as a unicast back to the original sender. On receipt of the reply, the system that initiated the ARP exchange uses the contents of the Sender Hardware Address field as the Destination Address for the data link layer transmission of the IP datagram.

ARP Caching

Because of its reliance on broadcast transmissions, ARP can generate a significant amount of network traffic. To lessen the burden of the protocol on the network, TCP/IP systems cache the hardware addresses discovered through ARP transactions in memory for a designated period of time. This way, a system transmitting a large string of datagrams to the same host doesn't have to generate individual ARP requests for each packet.

This is particularly helpful in an internetwork environment in which systems routinely transmit the majority of their packets to destinations on other networks. When a network segment has only a single router, all IP datagrams destined for other networks are sent through that router. When systems have the hardware address for that router in the ARP cache, they can transmit the majority of their datagrams without using ARP broadcasts.

The amount of time that entries remain in the ARP cache varies with different TCP/IP implementations. Windows systems purge entries after two minutes when they are not used to transmit additional datagrams.

EXAM TIP

The Windows operating systems include a command-line utility called Arp.exe, which you can use to create entries manually in the ARP cache. The Network+ objectives require candidates to be familiar with this tool. Unlike dynamically created entries, manual ARP cache entries are permanent. If you have a stable network, you can reduce network traffic by adding ARP cache entries for the routers that provide access to other networks (and particularly to the Internet). Client applications (such as web browsers) are then able to access systems on other networks without generating repeated ARP Request broadcasts. For more information on using the Arp.exe utility, see Chapter 13, "Network Troubleshooting."

 Quick Check

1. ARP relies on what type of transmissions to locate the system with a particular hardware address?
2. Why is there some confusion about the OSI model layer at which ARP operates?

Quick Check Answers

1. Broadcast transmissions.
2. Because ARP messages are carried directly within data-link frames, not IP datagrams.

Exercise

The answers for this exercise are located in the "Answers" section at the end of this chapter.

Using the information in Chapters 2, 3, and 4, design a network for a small graphic design firm with a total of five employees. The company is located in a single 20-by-15-foot room with cubicles for the workers, as shown in Figure 4-16. The president of the company and the four employees are all designers who will require powerful graphics workstations to run the software they need. The computers they have purchased do not have integrated network adapters. All will need high-speed access to the Internet, and to a printer as well. The users routinely work with very large files, which they will store on an in-house server. Some of the designs the firm creates are highly confidential, so security is an important consideration.

To complete the exercise, create a list of all the hardware components the firm will need to build their network. Then modify the diagram by drawing in the components in appropriate locations. Finally, write a description of your network, explaining how your design satisfied all of the firm's requirements.

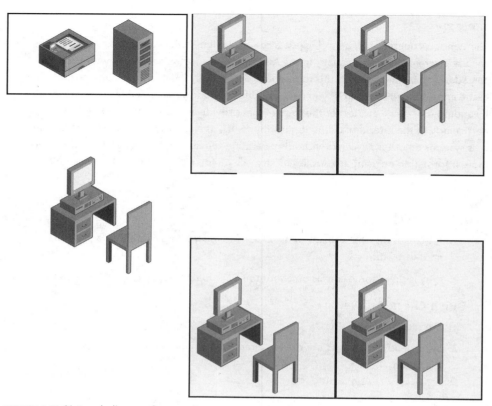

FIGURE 4-16 Network diagram for exercise.

Chapter Summary

- The second layer of the Open Systems Interconnection (OSI) reference model—the data-link layer—is where the physical manifestation of the network meets with the logical one, implemented in the software running on the computer.

- Ethernet was the first LAN protocol, originally conceived in 1973, and it has been evolving steadily ever since. The first Ethernet standard described a network that used RG-8 coaxial cable in a bus topology up to 500 meters long, with a transmission speed of 10 Mbps. This was commonly known as Thick Ethernet or 10Base5.

- The second version of the standard, called DIX Ethernet II, added a second physical layer specification, calling for RG-58 coaxial cable. This came to be known as Thin Ethernet or 10Base2. Development of the DIX Ethernet standard stopped after the publication of version II.

- The original 802.3 standard describes a network that is almost identical to DIX Ethernet, except for a minor change in the frame format. The main difference between IEEE 802.3 and DIX Ethernet is that the IEEE has continued to revise its standard in the years since the original publication.

- The Ethernet standards—both DIX Ethernet and IEEE 802.3—include the following three components: the Ethernet frame, CSMA/CD, and several physical layer specifications.

- The primary function of the Ethernet frame—as with a mailing envelope—is to identify the addressee of the packet. Ethernet networks use the 6-byte hexadecimal values called organizationally unique identifiers (OUIs), hardcoded into network interface adapters, to identify systems on the local network.

- In the early implementations of Ethernet, its media access control (MAC) mechanism, called Carrier Sense Multiple Access with Collision Detection (CSMA/CD), was the defining characteristic of the network.

- The original IEEE 802.3 standard retained the coaxial cable specifications from the DIX Ethernet document, but by 1993, the IEEE had published several amendments adding unshielded twisted pair (UTP) and fiber optic cable specifications, also running at 10 Mbps.

- The physical layer specifications for Gigabit Ethernet, running at 1,000 Mbps, appeared in 1998 and 1999. The fiber optic specifications, known collectively as 1000Base-X, were published as IEEE 802.3z, and the 1000Base-T UTP specification was published as IEEE 802.3ab.

- In 2002, the IEEE 802.3 working group published the first standards defining an Ethernet network running at 10 Gbps (or 10,000 Mbps).

- The other major protocol operating at the data-link layer of the OSI reference model is the Point-to-Point Protocol (PPP). PPP is much simpler than Ethernet, because it is designed for use by WAN connections that consist of only two systems. Because there are only two devices involved, there is no need for the protocol to support complex procedures such as node addressing or media access control.

- The Address Resolution Protocol (ARP) occupies an unusual place at the data-link layer and in the TCP/IP suite because it defies all attempts at categorization. Unlike the other data-link layer protocols, ARP does not carry application data packets across the network, and unlike most other TCP/IP protocols, ARP messages are not carried within IP datagrams.

Chapter Review

Test your knowledge of the information in Chapter 4 by answering these questions. The answers to these questions, and the explanations of why each answer choice is correct or incorrect, are located in the "Answers" section at the end of this chapter.

1. Which of the following fields in an IEEE 802.3 frame contains the same values as the Ethertype field in the DIX Ethernet frame?

   A. The Preamble field

   B. The Control field in the LLC subheader

   C. The Length header

   D. The Protocol ID field in the SNAP subheader

2. Which of the following Ethernet physical layer specifications call for copper cables?

   A. 1000Base-X

   B. 10Gbase-LW

   C. 1000Base-CX

   D. 100Base-TX

3. The Point-to-Point Protocol maintains network security by using which of the following methods?

   A. By adding authentication credentials to the PPP header in each frame.

   B. By encrypting all of the data transmitted within PPP frames.

   C. By authenticating the user with a separate protocol handshake during the PPP connection establishment process.

   D. By requiring the user to log on after the PPP connection establishment process is completed.

4. Which of the following is the reason why ARP can be described as a data-link layer protocol?

   A. Because there is a protocol identifier that data-link layer protocols use to indicate that a packet contains an ARP message.

   B. Because ARP carries application information in its data field.

   C. Because ARP messages are carried within IP datagrams.

   D. Because ARP provides a service to IP.

Answers

This section contains the answers to the questions for the Exercise and Chapter Review in this chapter.

Exercise

- Six 1000Base-T network interface cards
- One eight-port 1000Base-T switch
- Nine CAT6 UTP patch cables (10-50 feet)
- One cable modem
- One cable router

A wired network is preferable to a wireless one in this case because of the security concerns. Because the computers are all located in a single room, UTP patch cables provide a simple, portable, and inexpensive alternative to an internal cable installation. Ethernet cable runs can be as long as 100 meters, which presents no problem for this installation. Installing a network interface card in each of the computers and connecting them to the switch enables all of the workstations to access the server and each other. Connecting the printer to the switch provides all network users with access. Connecting a cable modem to a cable router and the router to the switch provides the entire network with Internet access.

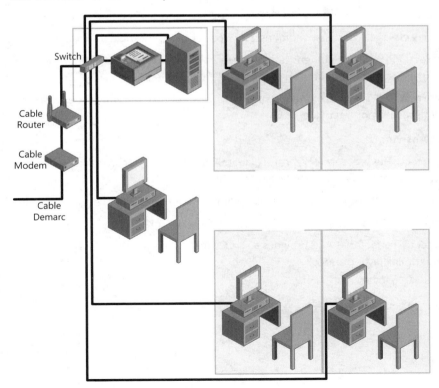

Chapter Review

1. **Correct Answer:** D

    A. **Incorrect:** The Preamble field does not contain Ethertype values.

    B. **Incorrect:** The Control field does not contain Ethertype values.

    C. **Incorrect:** The Length field contains values that are deliberately different from the Ethertype values in the DIX Ethernet frame.

    D. **Correct:** The SNAP subheader identifies the protocol represented in the Data field, by using the same values as the Ethertype field.

2. **Correct Answers:** C and D

    A. **Incorrect:** The 1000Base-X designation refers to the various fiber optic Gigabit Ethernet solutions.

    B. **Incorrect:** The 10Gbase-LW designation is a fiber optic WAN specification.

    C. **Correct:** 1000Base-CX is a Gigabit Ethernet designation that calls for twinaxial copper cable over short distances.

    D. **Correct:** 100Base-TX is a Fast Ethernet specification that calls for standard copper cables.

3. **Correct Answer:** C

    A. **Incorrect:** PPP does not use the PPP frame to authenticate the user.

    B. **Incorrect:** Under normal conditions, PPP does not encrypt the data it transmits.

    C. **Correct:** PPP adds an authentication sequence to the link establishment process by using a separate authentication protocol.

    D. **Incorrect:** PPP's support for authentication occurs only during the link establishment process, not afterward.

4. **Correct Answer:** D

    A. **Incorrect:** The presence of a protocol identifier is more of a reason to call ARP a network layer than a data-link layer protocol.

    B. **Incorrect:** ARP does not carry application information in its data field.

    C. **Incorrect:** ARP messages are not carried within IP datagrams.

    D. **Correct:** The fact that ARP provides a service to IP is a legitimate reason for calling it a data-link layer protocol.

CHAPTER 5

Wireless Networking

Wireless networking technologies have existed for decades, but it is only in recent years that wireless local area networks (LANs) have been available in the consumer networking market. For many home and small business users, until recently the primary factor preventing them from installing a network was the cabling.

Given a choice between an unsightly external cable installation and a costly and elaborate internal installation, many chose no network at all, or relied instead on stopgap technologies, such as dial-up connections or the "sneakernet." The advent of inexpensive wireless LANs offers a compromise between cost and performance that is attractive to many people, and wireless LANs are now all but ubiquitous features of homes, offices, restaurants, and coffee shops.

In Chapter 2, "The Physical Layer," you learned about the various types of cables used in data networking, including the properties of those cables and how to install them. In Chapter 3, "Network Devices," you learned about the various components that administrators use to build wired networks. In this chapter, you will learn about the wireless equivalents of both of these subjects, including the radio signals that replace the cables and the devices used by wireless computers to communicate with a wired network.

Exam objectives in this chapter:

Objective 2.2: Given a scenario, install and configure a wireless network.

- WAP placement
- Antenna types
- Interference
- Frequencies
- Channels
- Wireless standards
- SSID (enable/disable)
- Compatibility (802.11 a/b/g/n)

Objective 3.3: Compare and contrast different wireless standards.

- 802.11 a/b/g/n standards
  - Distance
  - Speed
  - Latency
  - Frequency
  - Channels
  - MIMO
  - Channel bonding

Wireless networking technologies in the past were based on a variety of media, including infrared signals and microwaves. Today, the dominant medium for wireless networks is radio signals, mostly in the 2.4-gigahertz (GHz), 3.6-GHz, and 5-GHz frequency bands, using several different frequency modulation technologies. Wireless networking technologies are known collectively as unbounded media, because they have no natural restrictions to signal access. By contrast, wired networks are known as bounded media, because the signals are restricted to the cables.

Radio frequency-based (RF) networks have several advantages. For example, they are inexpensive to implement and they are not limited to line-of-sight transmissions. However, on the negative side, wireless networks offer huge security problems, and many of them operate using crowded frequencies and are prone to interference from devices such as microwave ovens and cordless phones. Radio frequencies are also prone to attenuation: the weakening of signals due to intervening walls and other obstructions. Although the process of setting up a wireless network might seem incredibly easy, achieving acceptable levels of security and performance can often be a challenge, especially for the enterprise administrator.

Wireless LAN Standards

The wireless LAN equipment on the market today is based on the 802.11 standards published by the Institute of Electrical and Electronics Engineers (IEEE), from the same LAN/MAN Standards Committee—IEEE 802—that publishes the 802.3 Ethernet standards. Because its standards are produced by the same standards body, the 802.11 wireless technology fits neatly into the same layered structure as the Ethernet specifications.

As discussed in Chapter 4, "The Data-Link Layer," the 802.3 standards divide the data-link layer of the Open Systems Interconnection (OSI) model in two, with the Logical Link Control (LLC) layer on top, and the media access control (MAC) layer on the bottom, as shown in Figure 5-1. The LLC layer is defined in a separate standard: IEEE 802.2. A wireless LAN uses the same LLC layer as an 802.3 Ethernet network, with the 802.11 documents defining the physical layer and MAC layer specifications.

IEEE 802.2 - Logical Link Control	
IEEE 802.3 – Media Access Control	IEEE 802.11 – Media Access Control
IEEE 802.3 Physical Layer Specifications	IEEE 802.11 Physical Layer Specifications

FIGURE 5-1 IEEE standards in the OSI model.

Building a Wireless Standard

Despite the inclusion of the 802.11 standards in the same company as 802.3, the use of wireless media calls for administrators to make certain fundamental changes in the way they think about a local area network and its use. Some of the most significant differences are as follows:

- **Unbounded media**   A wireless network does not have readily observable connections to the network or boundaries beyond which network communication ceases.

- **Dynamic topology**   Unlike cabled networks, in which the LAN topology is meticulously planned out before the installation and remains static until the administrator makes deliberate changes, the topology of a wireless LAN changes frequently, if not continuously.

- **Unprotected media**   The stations on a wireless network are not protected from outside signals as those on cabled networks are. On a cabled network, outside interference can affect signal quality, but there is no way for the signals from two separate but adjacent networks to be confused. On a wireless network, roving stations can conceivably wander into a different network's operational perimeter, compromising performance and security.

- **Unreliable media**   Unlike with a cabled network, on a wireless network, a protocol cannot work under the assumption that every station on the network receives every packet and can communicate with every other station.

- **Asymmetric media**   The propagation of data to all of the stations on a wireless network does not necessarily occur at the same rate. There can be differences in the transmission rates of individual stations that change as one of the devices moves or the environment in which it is operating changes.

Because of these differences, the traditional elements of a data-link layer LAN protocol—the MAC mechanism, the frame format, and the physical layer specifications—have to be designed with different operational criteria in mind. Therefore, in addition to the material required in any physical/data-link layer standard, such as media specifications, signaling techniques, and frame formats, the 802.11 standard includes a list of wireless-specific functions that the document is intended to provide, including the following:

- The means by which devices compliant with the standard can participate in a network with other wireless equipment or with wired devices
- Procedures for the operation of a compliant device in an environment with multiple overlapping wireless networks
- Procedures to support applications with quality of service (QoS) requirements, such as streaming video
- Procedures to support asynchronous delivery services
- Requirements for authenticating devices and ensuring data confidentiality
- Mechanisms by which the wireless networking equipment can satisfy government regulatory standards

IEEE 802.11 Standards

As with the 802.3 Ethernet standard, the IEEE has updated and expanded on the 802.11 specification several times over the years, increasing the maximum transmission speed of the network and altering the frequencies and modulation techniques. The standard publications and their basic specifications are listed in Table 5-1.

TABLE 5-1 IEEE 802.11 Standards

Standard	Frequency (GHz)	Transmission Rate (Mbps)	Modulation Type	Range (Indoor/Outdoor) (meters)
802.11 – 1997	2.4	1, 2	DSSS, FHSS	20/100
802.11a – 1999	5	6 to 54	OFDM	35/120
802.11b – 1999	2.4	5.5 to 11	DSSS	38/140
802.11g – 2003	2.4	6 to 54	OFDM, DSSS	38/140
802.11 – 2007	Republication of the base standard with eight amendments			
802.11n – 2009	2.4 and 5	7.2 to 288 (at 20 MHz) 15 to 600 (at 40 MHz)	OFDM	70/250
802.11y – 2008	3.7	6 to 54	OFDM	5000+
802.11ac (Draft)	5	433 to 867 (at 80 MHz) 867 Mbps to 6.93 Gbps (at 160 MHz)	QAM	Undetermined

These standards are described in greater detail in the following sections.

IEEE 802.11

The first version of the *IEEE 802.11* standard, published in 1997, defined the specifications for a wireless networking protocol that would meet the following requirements:

- The protocol would provide wireless connectivity to automatic machinery, equipment, or stations that require rapid deployment—that is, rapid establishment of communications.

- The protocol would be deployable on a global basis.

- The protocol would support stations that are fixed, portable, or mobile, within a local area.

> ***NOTE*** **PORTABLE AND MOBILE STATIONS**
>
> The difference between a portable station and one that is mobile is that a portable station can access the network from various fixed locations, whereas a mobile station can access the network while it is actually in motion.

This document, in its original form, was known as IEEE 802.11, 1999 Edition, "Wireless LAN Medium Access Control (MAC) and Physical Layer (PHY) Specifications." This original standard, which was not widely implemented, defined three physical layer specifications: an infrared medium running at 1 Mbps and two types of radio signal modulation using the 2.4-GHz band: Direct-Sequence Spread Spectrum (DSSS) and Frequency-Hopping Spread Spectrum (FHSS), both running at 1 or 2 Mbps.

Despite its continued inclusion in the standard, no one has ever marketed an implementation of the infrared option, and the slow transmission speeds of this early standard made it an unattractive solution, even for users of the original 10-Mbps Ethernet network.

IEEE 802.11b

Despite its later designation, the *IEEE 802.11b* standard represents the next step in the evolution of the original document. All of the lettered publications are amendments to the original 802.11 standard, containing only revisions and additions.

> ***NOTE*** **IEEE STANDARDS**
>
> Unlike the Internet Engineering Task Force (IETF), which typically releases new, complete versions of its Requests for Comments (RFCs), the IEEE publishes amendments that contain only the new or changed material. Understanding of an amendment therefore requires a familiarity with the original standard as well. Eventually, the IEEE incorporates the amendments into a new version of the standard document and publishes it using a modified designation containing the year.

The 802.11b document retains the 2.4-GHz frequency and the DSSS modulation from the original standard, but increases the transmission speed to as much as 11 Mbps. This was, for the first time, a wireless LAN that could run at an acceptable speed for the typical network user. For users of 10-Mbps Ethernet, it theoretically represented an improvement, and even Fast Ethernet users could accept that level of wireless performance. Adoption of the 802.11b standard was quick; many manufacturers released products, and prices fell rapidly.

> **NOTE WIRELESS TRANSFER RATES**
>
> As with all speed measurements in the networking business, the 11-Mbps figure touted by makers of 802.11b equipment had to be taken with a degree of dubiety. All wireless networking technologies, including the latest and greatest, are subject to variations in transfer speed caused by any number of factors, from physical obstructions to electromagnetic interference to weather conditions. The effect of these factors is multiplied when you are working with mobile wireless equipment. IEEE 802.11b defined a mechanism by which network devices could drop to a lower speed when conditions prevented peak performance. The 11-Mbps transfer rate could drop to 5.5 Mbps, or even stop entirely, and then resume when conditions returned to an acceptable level.

IEEE 802.11a

Although it might appear to be an interim step in the development of 802.11 networking, the *IEEE 802.11a* amendment actually represented a fundamental change in the technology. One of the ongoing problems with 802.11 networks is the heavy use of the 2.4-GHz band by a variety of consumer products, including cordless telephones and Bluetooth devices. Wireless LAN performance can degrade in such a crowded environment, causing speed reductions or even service interruptions.

The 802.11a amendment calls for the use of the relatively vacant 5-GHz band and a different form of modulation called *Orthogonal Frequency-Division Multiplexing (OFDM)*. The data transfer rate can be as high as 54 Mbps, with fallbacks to 48, 36, 24, 18, 12, 9, and 6 Mbps.

> **EXAM TIP**
>
> Wireless networking introduces several technologies that are frequently alien to the average network administrator. However, the differences between the various modulation systems and other technical aspects of radio frequency communications are not required knowledge for the CompTIA Network+ exam, nor, for that matter, are they required by the administrator responsible for installing and maintaining a typical wireless LAN.

Because of complications in manufacturing, 802.11a products arrived on the market after 802.11b devices had achieved a considerable popularity, and they cost significantly more. The 802.11a technology also developed a reputation—perhaps unfounded—for having a shorter range than 802.11b and for being more susceptible to signal loss from attenuation. Whatever the reason, dedicated 802.11a equipment did not sell well. Later devices supporting both the 802.11a and 802.11b standards eventually came to market, and cross-compatibility between standards soon became a major selling point.

> **NOTE ALLOCATING FREQUENCIES**
>
> One of the most difficult aspects of the 802.11 development process was adhering to the stated intention that the wireless LAN defined in the standard be able to run anywhere in the world. Each country/region maintains its own regulations regarding the allocation of radio frequencies, and the developers' desire to use other bands for wireless LAN communications is hampered by political problems as often as it is by technical ones.

IEEE 802.11g

The *IEEE 802.11g* amendment built on the 802.11b technology by adopting the OFDM modulation from 802.11a while retaining the 2.4-GHz frequency from 802.11b. The result was a new standard that was fully backward compatible with 802.11b equipment but that pushed the maximum transfer rate up to 54 Mbps.

Even before the 802.11g amendment was officially ratified by the IEEE, the public began buying new wireless LAN products at an unprecedented rate. Most of the new products on the market supported both the "draft" 802.11g and 802.11b standards, and some added support for the 802.11a standard as well.

IEEE 802.11 – 2007

As mentioned earlier, the lettered documents published by the 802.11 working group are amendments to the previously released standard. These amendments consist only of the new material and the sections that have been changed, and they frequently contain extensive strikeouts and rewrites. In addition, some of the amendments contain revisions to previous amendments. Understanding the changes made to the original standard requires a careful study or an intimate knowledge of the original document and all of the previously released amendments.

To simplify understanding and further development, the working group published a composite standard in 2007 that incorporated all of the amendments released up to that time. This document incorporates all the modifications and additions from the 802.11a, b, d, e, g, h, i, and j amendments into the original base standard and is published as "IEEE Standard 802.11 – 2007: IEEE Standard for Information technology – Telecommunications and information exchange between systems – Local and metropolitan area networks – Specific requirements – Part 11: Wireless LAN Medium Access Control (MAC) and Physical Layer (PHY) Specifications."

EXAM TIP

Most of the standards published by the IEEE are only available for purchase, at prices that would discourage most individual students. However, the IEEE makes the standards published by the 802 committee available for free download six months after their publication. The 802.11 standards are available at *http://standards.ieee.org/about/get/802/802.11.html*. It is worth noting, though, that unlike the RFCs published by the IETF, many of which are quite understandable by students and junior administrators, the IEEE standards are often highly technical in nature and are generally not recommended for study by Network+ exam candidates.

IEEE 802.11n

As with Ethernet, administrators and users of wireless LANs are constantly asking for faster networks. However, the development of 802.11b/802.11g technology had reached a point at which a fundamental change was needed to improve performance. The *IEEE 802.11n* amendment introduces several modifications to the technology, including the potential doubling of channel widths and the addition of the 5-GHz frequency band from 802.11a to the standard 2.4-GHz band from 802.11b/g. 802.11n also includes two innovations that, combined with these other improvements, can push network transmission speeds well beyond the 54 Mbps realized by 802.11g to levels as high as 600 Mbps. These two innovations—MIMO and frame aggregation—are described in the following sections.

MIMO

Multiple-Input Multiple-Output (MIMO) is a physical layer enhancement that enables wireless devices to multiplex signals over a single channel simultaneously, by using a technique called Spatial Division Multiplexing (SDM). Each 802.11n device has an array of transmit and receive antennae and a transceiver capable of sending and receiving separate signals by using separate frequencies.

802.11n designations describing the MIMO capabilities of each device use the format $a \times b{:}c$, where a is the number of transmit antennae in the device, b is the number of receive antennae, and c is the number of data streams that the radio in the device supports. The maximum configuration defined by the standard is $4 \times 4{:}4$, indicating that a device has four transmit and four receive antennae and can send or receive on four channels at once.

802.11n devices are available in various configurations from $2 \times 2{:}2$ up to the maximum. The more antennae and the larger the number of simultaneous signals, the greater the throughput the device can achieve, and of course, the higher its price. As with any networking technology, though, both of the devices involved in a transaction must have the same capabilities to achieve the best possible performance. MIMO therefore adds another compatibility factor to the process of implementing a wireless network. It makes no sense to purchase a $4 \times 4{:}4$ access point if all of your workstations are equipped with $2 \times 2{:}2$ network interface adapters.

In addition to MIMO, the 802.11n standard also enables devices to double their channel widths from 20 megahertz (MHz) to 40 MHz, nearly doubling the data transfer rate in the process. However, in the 2.4-GHz band, this practice only exacerbates the existing signal crowding problem. For more information, see "Frequencies and Channels," later in this chapter.

FRAME AGGREGATION

The second innovation defined in the 802.11n document is a MAC layer technique called frame aggregation. In wireless networking, physical layer improvements can only do so much, because the control overhead is so high. In addition to the data-link layer frame, there are acknowledgment messages, spaces between frames, and radio communication transmissions, which in some circumstances can add up to more data than is carried in the payload.

 Frame aggregation is a technique that combines the payload data from several frames into one large frame, thus reducing the amount of overhead and increasing the information throughput of the network.

TRANSFER RATES

The 802.11n standard retains the fallback capabilities of the previous documents. Depending on a multitude of conditions, devices operating at peak speeds of 600 Mbps (using 4×4:4 MIMO and a 40-MHz channel) can drop down to successively lower rates and then speed up again when environmental conditions change. In addition, most 802.11n devices also support 802.11g and 802.11b, with some adding 802.11a as well.

Transfer rates for 802.11n networks are dependent on the capabilities of the equipment, the configuration settings selected by the administrator, and the usual environmental conditions that affect all wireless LANs. To calculate transfer rates, the 802.11n standard defines lists containing dozens of *Modulation and Coding Schemes (MCSs)*, which are indexed combinations of factors including the following:

- **Modulation type**   The modulation scheme used for the subcarriers created by OFDM
- **Spatial streams**   The number of MIMO streams (1 to 4)
- **Channel width**   20 MHz or 40 MHz
- **Guard interval**   The space inserted between transmissions to prevent interference (400 or 800 nanoseconds)
- **Coding rate**   The proportion of the data stream that is useful

For example, to achieve the maximum possible transmission rate of 600 Mbps (MCS index 31), an 802.11 network must have all of the following attributes:

- **Modulation type**   64-Quadrature Amplitude Modulation (64-QAM)
- **Spatial streams**   4
- **Channel width**   40 MHz
- **Guard interval**   400 nanoseconds
- **Coding rate**   5/6

Modifying any of these factors will reduce the data transfer rate to some degree. For example, each spatial stream accounts for 25 percent of the data transfer rate, and dropping to a 20 MHz channel width will reduce the rate by a little more than half.

PRODUCTS

As with 802.11g, equipment manufacturers released "draft" 802.11n devices to market long before the standard was officially ratified. In 2009, though, the standard was officially ratified, and products conforming to its specifications should be interoperable. However, because many of the attributes defined in the standard are not required, administrators must carefully examine product specifications to ensure interoperability.

IEEE 802.11y

The IEEE 802.11y amendment defines a modification to the 802.11a standard that would enable licensed operators to construct high-powered wireless networks by using the 3.7-GHz band. By transmitting with up to 20 watts of power, 802.11y networks are expected to achieve ranges of 5 kilometers or more.

IEEE 802.11ac

IEEE 802.11ac is a draft of a standard currently under development that is expected to represent the next iteration in wireless LAN technology. Expanding on the technology of 802.11n, 802.11ac devices will be able to support up to eight MIMO streams (instead of four) and channels 80 or 160 MHz wide, for theoretical transfer rates as high as 6.93 gigabytes per second (Gbps). The standard also calls for a new type of modulation technology called 256-Quadrature Amplitude Modulation (256-QAM).

Wi-Fi

The term *Wi-Fi* has entered the daily lexicon of mobile computer users, as increasing numbers of businesses and public places provide wireless LANs for the use of their customers. Despite its interchangeability with the term "802.11" in common parlance, "Wi-Fi" is a privately owned trademark; it is not a name sanctioned by the IEEE for 802.11 networks or equipment.

The name "Wi-Fi" is owned by an organization of hardware and software manufacturers called the Wi-Fi Alliance. The group operates an interoperability certification program for wireless LAN equipment and allows certified products to carry a special logo indicating their participation. Not all manufacturers submit their products for testing, however, which does not necessarily mean that they are not compatible.

EXAM TIP

Candidates for the Network+ exam must be familiar with the characteristics of the four main standards upon which wireless LAN hardware devices are based: 802.11a, 802.11b, 802.11g, and 802.11n.

Quick Check

1. Which of the IEEE standards described in this section enable wireless clients to connect to the network at a data transfer rate of 50 Mbps or more?

2. How many spatial streams can an 802.11n 4×4:3 access point support?

Quick Check Answers

1. IEEE 802.11a, 802.11g, 802.11n, and 802.11ac

2. Three

Wireless LAN Architecture

The elements that define a wireless LAN implementation are roughly similar to those of a wired LAN. There are multiple physical layer specifications, data-link layer frame formats, and a media access control mechanism. These elements are discussed in the following sections.

The Physical Layer

The various amendments to the 802.11 standard define a large number of physical layer attributes, including wireless topologies, media types, frequency bands, physical layer frame formats, radio frequency modulation types, channel widths, operational speeds, and others. Some of these attributes are discussed in the following sections.

Physical Layer Topologies

As you learned in Chapter 2, the term "topology" usually refers to the way in which the computers on a network are connected together. In a bus topology, for example, each computer is connected to the next one, in daisy chain fashion, whereas in a star topology, each computer is connected to a central hub. These examples apply to cabled networks, however. Wireless networks don't have a concrete topology as cabled ones do. Unbounded media, by definition, enable wireless network devices to transmit signals to all of the other devices on the network simultaneously.

However, this does not equate to a mesh topology. Although each device theoretically can transmit signals to all of the other wireless devices on the network at any time, this does not necessarily mean that it will. Mobility is an integral part of the wireless network design, and a wireless LAN protocol must be able to compensate for systems that enter and leave the area in which the medium can operate. The result is that the topologies used by wireless networks are defined by the basic rules that they use to communicate, and not static arrangements of devices at specific locations. IEEE 802.11 supports two types of wireless network topology: the ad hoc topology and the infrastructure topology.

The fundamental building block of an 802.11 wireless LAN is the *basic service set (BSS)*. A BSS is a geographical area in which properly equipped wireless stations can communicate. The configuration and area of the BSS are dependent on the type of wireless medium in use and the nature of the environment in which it is running, among other things.

A network using a radio frequency–based medium might have a BSS that is roughly spherical, for example, whereas an infrared network works in straight lines. The boundaries of the BSS can be affected by environmental conditions, architectural elements of the site, and many other factors, but when a station moves within the basic service set's sphere of influence, it can communicate with other stations also in the same BSS. When it moves outside of the BSS, communication ceases.

The simplest type of BSS consists of two or more wireless computers or other devices that have come within transmission range of each other, as shown in Figure 5-2. The process by which the devices enter into a BSS is called *association*. Each wireless device has an operational range dictated by its equipment, and as the two devices approach each other, the area of overlap between their ranges becomes the BSS.

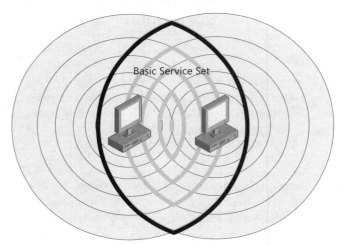

Basic Service Set

FIGURE 5-2 A basic service set with two wireless stations in range of each other.

NOTE **BSS CONFIGURATIONS**

Though this illustration depicts the BSS as roughly oval, and the convergence of the communicating devices as being caused by their physically approaching each other, the actual shape of the BSS is likely to be far less regular and much more ephemeral. The ranges of the devices can change instantaneously due to many different factors, and the BSS can grow, shrink, or even disappear entirely at a moment's notice.

This arrangement, in which all of the network devices in the BSS are mobile or portable, is called an *ad hoc topology* or an *independent BSS (IBSS)*. The term "ad hoc topology" refers to the fact that a network of this type might come together without prior planning and exist only as long as the devices need to communicate. This type of topology operates as a peer-to-peer network, because every device in the BSS can communicate with every other device.

> **NOTE AD HOC NETWORKING**
> Wireless networks using the ad hoc topology are relatively rare, particularly in the business world. Most wireless LAN devices are configured to use the infrastructure topology by default and require reconfiguration if they are to be used on an ad hoc network.

Although an ad hoc network uses basic service sets that are transient and constantly mutable, it is also possible to build a wireless network with BSSs that are somewhat more permanent. This is the basis of a network that uses an *infrastructure topology*. An infrastructure network consists of at least one *wireless access point (WAP)*, also referred to simply as an access point (AP), which is either a stand-alone device or a wireless-equipped computer that is also connected to a standard bounded network by using a cable. The access point has an operational range that is relatively fixed (when compared to an IBSS) and functions as the *base station* for a BSS.

Any mobile station that moves within the AP's sphere of influence is associated into the BSS and becomes able to communicate with the cabled network, as shown in Figure 5-3. Note that this is more of a client/server arrangement than a peer-to-peer one. The AP enables multiple wireless stations to communicate with the systems on the cabled network, but their ability to communicate with each other depends on the AP configuration. However, the use of an AP does not prevent mobile stations from communicating with each other independently of the AP.

It is because the AP is permanently connected to the cabled network and fixed in place that this type of network is said to use an infrastructure topology. This arrangement is typical in corporate installations that have a permanent cabled network and that also must support wireless devices that access resources on the cabled network.

An infrastructure network can have any number of access points, and therefore any number of basic service sets. The architectural element that connects BSSs together is called a *distribution system (DS)*. Multiple BSSs on a common DS might be configured with a common service set identifier (SSID), and if so configured, they and the DS that connects them are collectively called an *extended service set (ESS)*.

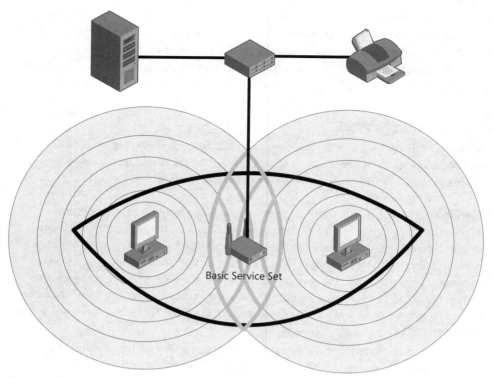

FIGURE 5-3 A basic service set with an access point and two wireless stations in range of it.

In practice, the DS is typically a cabled network that uses the IEEE 802.3 (Ethernet) protocol, but the network can conceivably use a *wireless distribution system (WDS)* also. A WDS is a device or group of devices that provides a wireless interconnection of access points, much as an Ethernet network provides such an interconnection in a wired DS. Technically, the WAP in a network of this type is also called a *portal*, because it provides access to a network using another data-link layer protocol. It's possible for the DS to function solely as a means of connecting APs together, and not provide access to resources on a cabled network, but this is relatively rare.

The configuration of the BSSs connected by a distribution system can take almost any physical form. The BSSs can be widely distant from each other, providing wireless network connectivity in specific remote areas, or they can overlap, providing a large area of contiguous wireless connectivity. It is also possible for an infrastructure BSS to be concurrent with an IBSS. The 802.11 standard makes no distinction between the two topologies, because both must present the exact same appearance to the LLC sublayer operating at the upper half of the data-link layer.

Infrastructure networks require some means of identification, so the 802.11 standard defines a means for creating addresses and names for them. Wireless devices have 6-byte MAC addresses (or hardware addresses), just as Ethernet devices do, so in a simple infrastructure network, the MAC address of the access point becomes the *basic service set identifier (BSSID)*

for the network. In the case of an ad hoc network, the BSSID is a randomly generated number, with the Universal/Local bit of the organizationally unique identifier (OUI) set to 1 (Local) and the Unicast/Multicast bit set to 0 (Unicast).

Because humans have trouble remembering long addresses, wireless networks have names as well. The *service set identifier (SSID)* is a 32-bit string that identifies a BSS and all of its members. The SSIDs are the names of the wireless LANs you see when you use a client to scan for a network to join. In an infrastructure network, the administrator typically assigns an SSID to the access point when configuring it. If not, the AP uses a default name set at the factory. In an ad hoc network, the first device joining the network sets the SSID.

> **NOTE   HIDING THE SSID**
>
> To connect a device to an access point, you select it by its SSID. In most cases, computers and other devices scan for wireless networks and display a list of the SSIDs they find, from which you can choose. This works because access points broadcast their SSIDs by default. However, some access points enable the administrator to suppress the SSID broadcasts, as a weak security measure. Clients can still connect to the AP, but they must know the SSID of the network to do so.

An extended service set must have all of its access points configured to use the same SSID. In this case, the name is technically referred to as an extended service set identifier (ESSID), although device interfaces often refer to it simply as the SSID.

> **EXAM TIP**
>
> The Network+ exam requires candidates to be familiar with the distinction between the ad hoc and infrastructure topologies, as well as with terms such as "access point," "service set," and "service set identifier."

Physical Layer Media

The IEEE 802.11 standard defines four basic types of physical layer media, three that use radio frequency signals and one that uses infrared light signals. A wireless LAN can use any one of these media, all of which interface with the same MAC layer. These four media types are as follows:

- Frequency-Hopping Spread Spectrum (FHSS)
- Direct-Sequence Spread Spectrum (DSSS)
- Orthogonal Frequency-Division Multiplexing (OFDM)
- Infrared

Two of the RF media use spread spectrum communications, which is a common form of radio transmission used in many wireless applications. Invented during the 1940s, spread spectrum technology takes an existing narrowband radio signal and spreads it among a range of frequencies in any one of several ways. Depending on the method employed, the result may be a signal that utilizes more bandwidth but that might be easier for a receiver to detect. At the same time, the signal might also be difficult to intercept, because attempts to locate it by scanning through the frequency bands turn up only isolated fragments, and it might be difficult to jam, because a wider range of frequencies would have to be blocked for the jamming to be effective.

The difference between the various types of spread spectrum communications lies in the method by which the signals are distributed among the frequencies. *Frequency-Hopping Spread Spectrum (FHSS)*, for example, uses a predetermined code or algorithm to dictate frequency shifts that occur continually, in discrete increments, over a wide band of frequencies. The 802.11 FHSS implementation calls for 79 channels of 1 MHz each, although some countries/regions impose smaller limits.

Obviously, the receiving device must be equipped with the same algorithm in order to read the signal properly. The rate at which the frequency changes (that is, the amount of time that the signal remains at each frequency before hopping to the next one) is independent of the bit rate of the data transmission. If the frequency hopping rate is faster than the signal's bit rate, the technology is called a *fast hop system*. If the frequency hopping rate is slower than the bit rate, you have a *slow hop system*. The 802.11 FHSS implementation runs at 1 Mbps, with an optional 2 Mbps rate. The use of FHSS was abandoned after the initial 802.11 standard.

In *Direct-Sequence Spread Spectrum (DSSS)* communications, the transmitting device modulates the signal by using a digital code called a *chip* or *chipping code*, which has a bit rate larger than that of the data signal. The chipping code is a redundant bit pattern that essentially turns each bit in the data signal into several bits that the device actually transmits. The longer the chipping code, the greater the enlargement of the original data signal. This enlargement of the signal makes it easier for the receiver to recover the transmitted data if some bits are damaged. The more the signal is enlarged, the smaller the significance is that is attributed to each bit. As with FHSS, a receiver that doesn't possess the chipping code used by the transmitter can't interpret the DSSS signal, seeing it as just noise.

The DSSS implementation in the original 802.11 document supports 1-Mbps and 2-Mbps transmission rates. IEEE 802.11b expands this capability by adding transmission rates of 5.5 and 11 Mbps. Of the spread spectrum media, only DSSS supports these faster rates, which is the primary reason why it was retained in 802.11b and FHSS was abandoned.

The third RF medium, *Orthogonal Frequency-Division Multiplexing (OFDM)*, uses a different type of signaling. Instead of using a single carrier, as the spread spectrum media do, OFDM uses multiple carriers running in parallel at low signal rates to provide a data transmission rate that is similar to those of single carrier modulation types. Each of the subcarriers uses a standard modulation technique, such as Quadrature Amplitude Modulation (QAM) or Binary Phase Shift Keying (BPSK). The advantage of OFDM over the single carrier media is in the fault tolerant nature of its signals. Factors such as attenuation and interference typically affect some of the OFDM subcarriers, but not all of them, leaving part of the transmission intact.

The original 802.11 standard also included an infrared specification for the physical layer, which uses frequencies in the 850 to 950 nanometer range, just below the visible light spectrum. This specification remains in the standard despite having never been implemented on wireless LANs, because of its limited range.

Unlike most infrared media, the IEEE 802.11 infrared implementation does not require direct line-of-sight communications; an infrared network can function using diffuse or reflected signals. However, the range of communications is limited to about 10 to 20 meters, and can only function properly in an indoor environment with surfaces that provide adequate signal diffusion or reflection. This makes infrared unsuitable for mobile devices and places more constraints on the physical location of the wireless device than any of the RF specifications. Like FHSS, the 802.11 infrared medium supports only a 1-Mbps transmission rate and an optional rate of 2 Mbps.

Frequencies and Channels

Most 802.11 networks in operation today are based on the 802.11b/g standards, using the 2.4-GHz frequency band that occupies the 83 MHz of bandwidth between 2.4000 and 2.4835 GHz. These frequencies are unlicensed in most countries/regions, although there are varying limitations on the signal strength imposed by different governments. As mentioned earlier, the 2.4-GHz band is comparatively crowded with signals from other wireless consumer devices.

The 802.11n standard reintroduces the use of the 5-GHz band from 802.11a, but implementations that support the 5-GHz band are relatively rare and are found at the high end of the price range. The 802.11ac standard, in its current form, will use only the 5-GHz band.

The wireless LAN standards divide the frequency band that a given technology uses into *channels*, so that multiple networks can coexist in the same area by using different parts of the available bandwidth. The channels defined by the standards up to and including 802.11g are 20 to 22 MHz in width (depending on the type of modulation).

For example, in implementations using DSSS modulation, the channels are 22 MHz wide, and the 2.4-GHz band contains channels that are 5 MHz apart. This enables the standard to define 13 channels in that band, as shown in Figure 5-4. (A fourteenth channel, located 12 MHz away from channel 13, was added by Japanese manufacturers and is not supported in all implementations.)

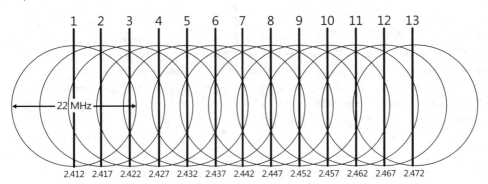

FIGURE 5-4 The 22-MHz channels in the 2.4-GHz band.

Of course, spacing 22-MHz channels 5 MHz apart means that the channels are going to overlap, making it possible for networks using different channels to interfere with each other. This can result in the need for retransmissions at the data-link layer, reducing network throughput and increasing latency. Therefore, in the 2.4-GHz band, it has become a common practice to favor channels 1, 6, and 11, because they do not overlap and do not interfere with each other, as shown in Figure 5-5. Administrators of large wireless LANs often create a *multiple channel architecture* that uses only those three channels for that reason.

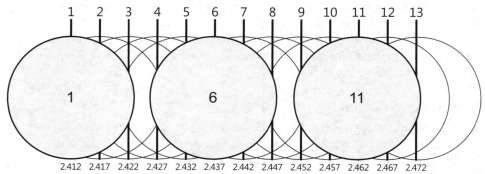

FIGURE 5-5 Non-overlapping 22-MHz channels in the 2.4-GHz band.

This practice has persisted even on 802.11g networks, which is unfortunate, because the OFDM modulation that 802.11g uses creates channels that are 20 MHz wide, not 22 MHz. With 20-MHz widths, the non-overlapping channels are 1, 5, 9, and 13, as shown in Figure 5-6.

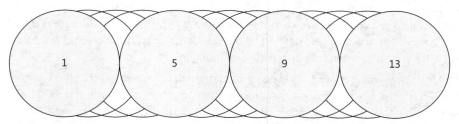

FIGURE 5-6 Non-overlapping 20-MHz channels on an 802.11g network.

> **NOTE FCC RESTRICTIONS**
>
> The use of channels 12 and 13 under low-power conditions is technically legal in the United States according to Federal Communications Commission (FCC) regulations. However, some implementations block them to avoid any possibility of interference with the adjacent 2.4835-GHz to 2.5000-GHz band, which is heavily restricted. The use of channel 14, allowed in Japan, is illegal in the United States.

802.11n networks support both 20-MHz and 40-MHz channels. When you select the 40-MHz option, the device allocates two adjacent 20-MHz channels and combines them, a process called *channel bonding*. Devices that do not have support for 40-MHz channels use only the 20-MHz primary channel; devices with 40-MHz channel support use both. This can effectively double the data transfer rate of the network, but there are complications to this practice.

In the 2.4-GHz band, there is no way to deploy a multiple channel architecture using 40-MHz channels without overlapping, as shown in Figure 5-7. The Wi-Fi Alliance recommends not using 40-MHz channels in the 2.4-GHz band for this reason.

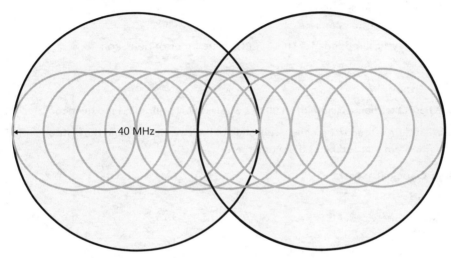

FIGURE 5-7 Overlapping 40-MHz channels in the 2.4-GHz band.

Fortunately, the 802.11n standard also supports the use of the 5-GHz band, which provides much more room for non-overlapping channels, as well as other advantages. Support for the 5-GHz band is not a requirement of the standard, however. Many 802.11n devices can use only the 2.4-GHz band. Those that do support the 5-GHz band are usually dual-band devices, so that they can connect with 802.11b/g equipment that uses only 2.4 GHz.

> **NOTE   USING THE STANDARD**
>
> The nature of the 802.11 standard's development process has resulted in a document that treats these physical media in a somewhat disjointed manner. Rather than grouping all of the DSSS material together, for example, the standard contains separate sections that represent the different applications of that modulation technique in the various amendments. Section 15 contains the original 1-Mbps and 2-Mbps DSSS specification. Section 18 contains the 802.11b material, which is called High Rate DSSS (HR/DSSS). Section 19 contains the 802.11g material, which it calls the Extended Rate PHY (ERP). It can sometimes be difficult to put the various elements of this 1,200-page document together in one's mind.

Physical Layer Frames

Instead of a relatively simple signaling scheme such as the Manchester encoding technique used by Ethernet, the media operating at the 802.11 physical layer have their own frame formats that encapsulate the frames generated at the data-link layer. This is necessary to support the complex nature of the media.

Each of the media that the 802.11 standard supports has its own physical layer frame format, but all of the frames perform the same basic functions, such as the following:

- Signaling the start of the frame
- Specifying the length of the data field
- Specifying the transmission rate
- Providing a cyclical redundancy check (CRC) value for error detection

 Quick Check

1. What is the channel width of an 802.11 wireless LAN using DSSS modulation?
2. What term is used to describe a collection of basic service sets and the distribution system that combines them together?

Quick Check Answers

1. 20 MHz
2. Extended service set

The Data-Link Layer

Like the IEEE 802.3 (Ethernet) standard, the 802.11 document defines only half of the functionality found at the data-link layer. As in the other IEEE 802 protocols, the LLC sublayer forms the upper half of the data-link layer and is defined in the IEEE 802.2 standard. The 802.11 document defines the MAC sublayer functionality, which consists of a connectionless transport service that carries LLC data to a destination on the network in the form of *MAC service data units (MSDUs)*. And as in other data-link layer protocols, this service is defined by a frame format (actually several frame formats, in this case) and a media access control mechanism. The MAC sublayer also provides security services, such as authentication and encryption, and reordering of MSDUs.

Data-Link Layer Frames

The 802.11 standard defines three basic types of frames at the MAC layer, which are as follows:

- **Data frames**   Used to transmit upper-layer data between stations
- **Control frames**   Used to regulate access to the network medium and to acknowledge transmitted data frames
- **Management frames**   Used to exchange network management information to perform network functions such as association and authentication

The general MAC frame format is shown in Figure 5-8.

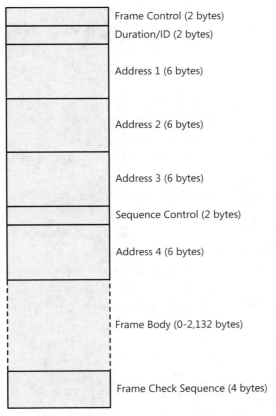

Frame Control (2 bytes)

Duration/ID (2 bytes)

Address 1 (6 bytes)

Address 2 (6 bytes)

Address 3 (6 bytes)

Sequence Control (2 bytes)

Address 4 (6 bytes)

Frame Body (0-2,132 bytes)

Frame Check Sequence (4 bytes)

FIGURE 5-8 The IEEE 802.11 MAC sublayer frame format.

The functions of the frame fields are as follows:

- **Frame Control (2 bytes)**   Contains 11 subfields that enable various protocol functions, including the version of the 802.11 standard, the MAC frame type, and the frame function.

- **Duration/ID (2 bytes)**   In control frames used for power-save polling, this field contains the association identity (AID) of the station transmitting the frame. In all other frame types, the field indicates the amount of time (in microseconds) needed to transmit a frame and its short interframe space (SIFS) interval.

- **Address 1 (6 bytes)**   Contains an address that identifies the recipient of the frame, using one of the five addresses used in 802.11 MAC sublayer communications.

- **Address 2 (6 bytes)**   Contains one of the five addresses used in 802.11 MAC sublayer communications.

- **Address 3 (6 bytes)**   Contains one of the five addresses used in 802.11 MAC sublayer communications.

- **Sequence Control (2 bytes)**   Contains two fields used to associate the fragments of a particular sequence and assemble them into the right order at the destination system.

- **Address 4 (6 bytes)**   Contains one of the five addresses used in 802.11 MAC sublayer communications. Not present in control and management frames and some data frames.

- **Frame Body (0 to 2,312 bytes)**   Contains the actual information being transmitted to the receiving station.

- **Frame Check Sequence (4 bytes)**   Contains a CRC value used by the receiving system to verify that the frame was transmitted without errors.

The four address fields in the MAC frame identify different types of systems depending on the type of frame being transmitted and its destination in relation to the DS. You can determine the systems whose addresses are contained in the four address fields by using the information in Table 5-2.

TABLE 5-2 MAC Sublayer Address Types

Function	Address 1 Value	Address 2 Value	Address 3 Value	Address 4 Value
Data frames exchanged by stations in the same IBSS, and all control and management frames	DA	SA	BSSID	Not Used
Data frames transmitted to the DS	DA	BSSID	SA	Not Used
Data frames exiting the DS	BSSID	SA	DA	Not Used
Wireless distribution system (WDS) frames exchanged by APs in a DS	RA	TA	DA	SA

The five different types of addresses referenced in the table are as follows:

- **Source Address (SA)**   A MAC individual address that identifies the system that generated the information carried in the Frame Body field.

- **Destination Address (DA)**   A MAC individual or group address that identifies the final recipient of an MSDU.

- **Transmitter Address (TA)**   A MAC individual address that identifies the system that transmitted the information in the Frame Body field onto the current wireless medium (typically an AP).

- **Receiver Address (RA)**   A MAC individual or group address that identifies the immediate recipient of the information in the Frame Body field on the current wireless medium (typically an AP).

- **Basic Service Set ID (BSSID)**   A MAC address that identifies a particular BSS. On an infrastructure network, the BSSID is the MAC address of the station functioning as the AP of the BSS. On an ad hoc network (IBSS), the BSSID is a randomly generated value generated during the creation of the IBSS.

Media Access Control

 As with all data-link layer protocols that use a shared network medium, the media access control (MAC) mechanism is one of the 802.11 protocol's primary defining elements. The standard defines the use of a MAC mechanism called *Carrier Sense Multiple Access with Collision Avoidance (CSMA/CA)*, which is a variation of the Carrier Sense Multiple Access with Collision Detection (CSMA/CD) mechanism used by Ethernet.

The basic functional characteristics of wireless networks limit which MAC mechanisms these networks can use. For example, the Ethernet CSMA/CD mechanism requires every device on the network to receive every transmitted packet. An Ethernet system that doesn't receive every packet can't reliably detect collisions. In addition, Ethernet systems detect collisions through signal voltage variances or the simultaneous transmission and receipt of signals, both of which are impractical in a wireless environment.

One of the characteristics of the wireless networks defined in 802.11 is that stations can repeatedly enter and leave the BSS because of their mobility and the vagaries of the wireless medium. Therefore, the MAC mechanism on a wireless network must be able to accommodate this behavior.

The carrier sense and multiple access parts of the CSMA/CA mechanism are the same as those of an Ethernet network. A computer with data to transmit listens to the network medium and, if the medium is available, begins transmitting its data. If the network is busy, the computer backs off for a specified interval and begins the listening process again.

As with Ethernet, the CSMA part of the process can result in collisions. The difference in CSMA/CA is that systems attempt to avoid collisions in the first place by reserving bandwidth in advance, by specifying a value in the Duration/ID field of the MAC frame, or by using specialized control messages called request-to-send (RTS) and clear-to-send (CTS) messages.

The carrier sense part of the transmission process occurs on two levels, the physical and the virtual. The physical carrier sense mechanism is specific to the physical layer medium the network is using and is equivalent to the carrier sense performed by Ethernet systems. The virtual carrier sense mechanism, called a *network allocation vector (NAV)*, involves the transmission of an RTS frame by the system with data to transmit, and a response from the intended recipient in the form of a CTS frame.

Both of these frames have a value in the Duration/ID field that specifies the amount of time needed for the sender to transmit the forthcoming data frame and receive an acknowledgment (ACK) frame in return. This message exchange essentially reserves the network medium for the life of this particular transaction, which is where the collision avoidance part of the mechanism comes in. Because both the RTS and CTS messages contain the Duration/ID value, any other system on the network receiving either one of the two messages observes the reservation and refrains from trying to transmit its own data during that time interval. This way, a station that is capable of receiving transmissions from one computer but not the other can still observe the CSMA/CA process.

In addition, the RTS/CTS exchange also enables a station to determine whether communication with the intended recipient is possible. If the sender of an RTS frame fails to receive a CTS frame from the recipient in return, it retransmits the RTS frame repeatedly, until a preestablished timeout is reached. Retransmitting the brief RTS message is much quicker than retransmitting large data frames, which shortens the entire process.

To detect collisions, IEEE 802.11 uses a positive acknowledgment system at the MAC sublayer. Each data frame that a station transmits must be followed by an ACK frame from the recipient, which is generated after a CRC check of the incoming data. If the frame's CRC check fails, the recipient considers the packet to have been corrupted by a collision (or other phenomenon) and silently discards it. The station that transmitted the original data frame then retransmits it as many times as needed to receive an ACK, up to a predetermined limit.

Note that the failure of the sender to receive an ACK frame could be due to the corruption or nondelivery of the original data frame or the nondelivery of an ACK frame that the recipient did send in return. The 802.11 protocol does not distinguish between the two.

Installing a Wireless LAN

After all of this explanation, you might be surprised to discover that setting up a wireless LAN is not all that difficult. For the home or small business user, it can be extremely simple, because many of the wireless products are designed to use default configurations that are suitable to that environment. In an enterprise environment, the situation is more complicated, and administrators might have to spend more time examining the site and evaluating products before they buy.

Examining the Site

In most cases, people consider installing a wireless network because a wired one is not practical for some reason. The installation of the cables might be too difficult or too expensive, or there is something preventing them from using a traditional Ethernet LAN. However, before you settle on 802.11 wireless as your solution, you should consider the possible complications of that as well.

A site survey is the first step in a wireless LAN deployment. Even though you might have already examined the location before rejecting a wired network as a possible solution, you should take another look when considering wireless—the criteria governing a wireless installation can be different. Distances are still a concern, because wireless devices have limited range, but the measurements you take will have different implications. For a wired network, you try to estimate the length of cable routes inside walls and ceilings, whereas wireless distances are direct routes through walls and other obstructions. You must have some idea of the maximum distances your devices will have to transmit. If those distances are well beyond the estimated ranges of the equipment you are considering, then you might have to add some form of range enhancement, such as a larger antenna. You might also consider building an ESS with multiple access points or installing multiple separate LANs.

Wireless transmission distances are also subject to interference from obstructions. The more walls there are between two wireless stations, the shorter the distance across which those stations can transmit successfully. You must also consider the composition of the walls. A typical office with drywall dividers will generate much less interference than a school building with cinderblock walls.

You must consider other potential sources of interference as well. Refrigerators, microwave ovens, and other electrical equipment can all interfere with wireless signals, some of them in maddeningly intermittent ways. A microwave oven, for example, might block all wireless traffic in the vicinity, but only when it's running. This is the sort of situation that drives technical support people insane.

Another factor to consider is interference from other wireless networks in the area. Most wireless devices are capable of scanning for other networks and displaying information about them, including their SSIDs, the channels they use, and their strengths. This will tell you what channels to avoid, and help you to make sure you don't duplicate a local SSID. You might also discover that the band you are scanning is so crowded that you should consider another one. Most of the 802.11 equipment on the market uses the 2.4-GHz band, and if you detect dozens of other networks in the area, the additional expense for equipment using the 5-GHz band might be worthwhile.

Using the information from your site survey, you should be able to determine approximate locations for your access points. Obviously, your first priority is to provide network access to all of your clients, but there are also security considerations involved in access point place-ment. Placing an access point too near an outside wall could enable outside users to gain access to your network.

Most access points come equipped with dipole antennas, which are omnidirectional. There-fore, placing access points near the center of the space you want to service is the usual pro-cedure. However, some access points permit you to connect an external antenna, as shown in Figure 5-9, and there are a variety of other antenna designs that can provide greater or more directional coverage.

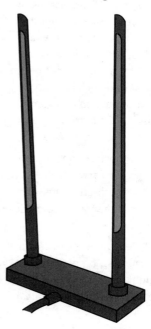

FIGURE 5-9 An external wireless LAN antenna.

Selecting Hardware

One of the nice things about constructing a wireless LAN when compared to a wired network is that there are far fewer bits and pieces to buy. Every computer you want to connect will need a wireless network interface adapter and, if you are building an infrastructure network, you will need at least one access point. Barring exceptional circumstances, that's it. You don't need cable components or wall plates or patch panels, and there are no special tools required for the installation.

Selecting Network Interface Adapters

Nearly all desktop computers have integrated Ethernet ports on their motherboards, but very few come with wireless LAN adapters. Virtually all of the mobile computing devices sold today, including laptops, netbooks, and tablets, come equipped with 802.11 network interface adapters, but the actual configuration of those adapters can vary widely.

Some new devices have 802.11b/g adapters, and others have 802.11b/g/n. Older devices might have only 802.11b. In addition, administrators often find that they can retrofit some of the mobile devices with different adapters, but others are not upgradable.

When you are equipping new computers with adapters, it is easy to standardize on one configuration or one device, but enterprise administrators often have to accommodate a variety of devices of varying ages. This is why access points often need to be as compatible as possible with every standard on the market.

With a highly compatible access point, administrators are free to purchase wireless network adapters to suit the needs of their various users. An adapter for a desktop computer usually takes the form of a standard expansion card with an antenna protruding through the slot cover, as shown in Figure 5-10. Adapters for mobile computers can take various forms, some with external antennae and some with internal.

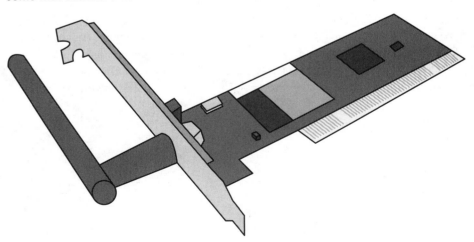

FIGURE 5-10 An internal 802.11 wireless network interface adapter.

Selecting Access Points

Wireless access points are available as stand-alone devices—most commonly used in enterprise settings—or integrated into multifunction devices, which are more popular for home and small business networks.

A stand-alone access point is a simple-looking device with a single port for a wired network connection, usually an RJ45, and one or more antennas, as shown in Figure 5-11. The physical installation of an AP is as simple as plugging it into a power source and connecting it to your Ethernet network. Then, any wireless device that connects to the AP can access the wired network, and wired devices can access the wireless ones.

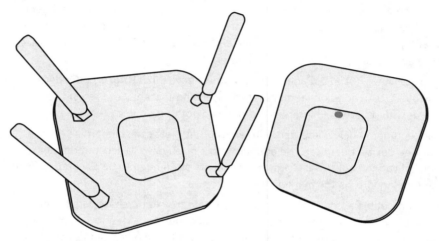

FIGURE 5-11 A stand-alone 802.11 wireless access point.

Multifunction devices that contain wireless access ports are usually designed as broadband routers that connect home or small office networks to the Internet. A typical multifunction device configuration will have an RJ45 port for a WAN connection—usually to a cable or DSL modem—and a number of switched RJ45 ports for Ethernet connections, as shown in Figure 5-12. The device might also contain additional internal functions, such as a firewall, a Dynamic Host Configuration Protocol (DHCP) server, and a Network Address Translation (NAT) router.

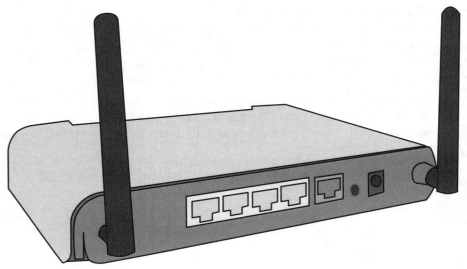

FIGURE 5-12 A multifunction device containing an 802.11 wireless access point.

Device Compatibility

The biggest concern when selecting hardware for a wireless LAN is compatibility. You must make sure that your devices can connect to each other, and do so with the appropriate levels of performance and security you need.

The following sections examine the compatibility factors you might have to consider when evaluating 802.11 wireless equipment.

STANDARDS

The vast majority of 802.11 wireless products on the market support a variety of standards. IEEE 802.11b/g devices are probably the most prevalent, and there are now many 802.11b/g/n devices as well. Some higher-end devices add support for 802.11a also, which means they can use the 5-GHz frequency band, probably with the 802.11n standard also.

It is also common practice for manufacturers to begin releasing equipment supporting the latest standard before the standard has actually been ratified by the IEEE. There will, no doubt, be 802.11ac devices arriving before long, but it is always a gamble to purchase equipment before the standard is finalized and ratified.

One of the trickiest aspects of the wireless standard development process has always been backward compatibility with the previous standards. There is little doubt that if you purchase a device based on a draft standard, it will work with other devices also based on that standard, but whether it will work with your older equipment is another question that you should explore carefully before you invest in a new technology.

If you are building a brand-new network, buying all new computers and access points, interoperability is easy to achieve. Problems arise, though, when you have existing computers that must work with your new equipment. When it comes to purchasing multistandard products for an infrastructure network, remember that the computers must be compatible with your access point, but they don't have to be compatible with each other.

Therefore, the safest course of action is to purchase access points that support all of the standards you are likely to find in your computers, as shown in Figure 5-13. 802.11a/b/g/n access points are readily available, and the technology has matured to the point that they are affordable for most administrators' budgets.

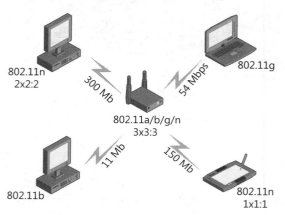

FIGURE 5-13 A multistandard access point connected to devices using various standards.

> **NOTE MIXING STANDARDS**
>
> Mixing wireless standards on a single network is convenient, but it can have a negative effect on performance. For example, on an 802.11b/g network, the presence of one 802.11b system on a network otherwise populated with 802.11g devices can reduce the performance of the entire network.

SECURITY PROTOCOLS

A wireless LAN is a massive security hole for several reasons, and protecting your network by encrypting your transmissions is no longer optional; you must do it. To ensure complete protection and complete connectivity, all of the devices on your network must support the exact permutation of the security protocols you plan to use. After you configure the security on your access point, any devices that do not support those protocols will not be able to connect.

MORE INFO WIRELESS LAN SECURITY

For more information on the security protocols supported on 802.11 networks, see Chapter 11, "Network Security."

DEVICE INTERFACES

Network interface adapters can connect to computers in many ways, and before you purchase wireless equipment, you must consider your alternatives. USB adapters are easy to install, and most computers have an extra USB port available, but the USB interface might prevent your systems from realizing their maximum performance levels.

Internal adapters are preferable, but before you purchase them, you must determine three things:

- What type of slots are in your computers
- Whether a slot is free
- Whether a slot is accessible

NOTE ACCESSING SLOTS

In many of today's computers, expansion slots might be free, but not necessarily available for use. Many of the video adapters on the market today have large heat sinks or fan assemblies that not only occupy a slot, but also block access to adjacent free slots. Unless you have a detailed inventory of your computers, you might have to open the cases to determine definitely whether slots are available.

FREQUENCY BAND

Most 802.11 wireless LAN equipment uses the 2.4-GHz frequency band, but as discussed earlier, there are reasons why you might not want to or be able to use that band for your network. If you want to take advantage of the 40-MHz channel width in 802.11n, or if the 2.4-GHz band is simply too crowded in your area, then you might want to use the 5-GHz band supported by 802.11a and 802.11n.

Be aware, however, that a device that complies with the 802.11n standard does not have to support the 5-GHz band. You must look for devices marketed as dual band or that explicitly say they support the 5-GHz band in 802.11n.

802.11N OPTIONS

IEEE 802.11n devices are a popular choice among users and administrators, due to their potential for high performance. However, the 802.11n standard presents compatibility issues other than the frequency band. As discussed earlier in this chapter, an 802.11n device can have from one to four MIMO spatial streams and can conceivably support 20-MHz and 40-MHz channel widths.

Here again, you must consider that the compatibility you need is between your access points and your computers, not between individual computers. Therefore, the access points you select should have the highest level of performance that you want to achieve. Then you can purchase 802.11n network interface adapters at various price points, depending on the performance level you need for each computer.

Installing and Configuring Wireless Hardware

Wireless access points have built-in web servers that provide their configuration interfaces, so after connecting the device to the network, you only have to use a browser to connect to its IP address and authenticate by using a default password supplied with the product documentation. After that, the first order of business is to change the password and configure the device with an appropriate IP address and TCP/IP configuration settings for your network.

The first step in configuring the wireless attributes of an access point is to specify an SSID other than the default and select the band and channel you want the device to use. Most products use standard web-based controls for this purpose, as shown in Figure 5-14. On other pages, you can select the security protocols the device will use and specify any additional information, such as pre-shared keys and other parameters.

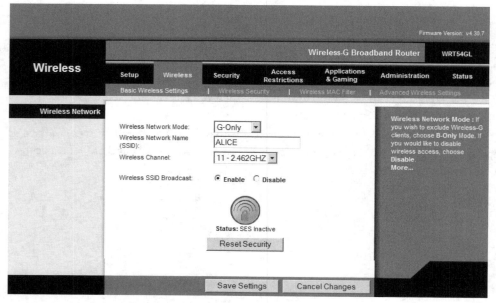

FIGURE 5-14 A web-based interface for a wireless access point.

If you are using multiple access points for your network, you must configure them with the same SSID, but use different channels so that they do not interfere with each other. This is the type of situation in which administrators often apply a multiple-channel architecture, using nonconflicting channels for adjacent access points, as shown in Figure 5-15. This enables the network to cover a large area without having the access points interfere with each other. Clients can wander into the area of a different access point, and the wireless adapter will compensate by changing to the appropriate channel.

FIGURE 5-15 A multiple-channel architecture.

When the access point is operational, the next step is to configure the network adapters in the computers and other devices to use the same settings. In some cases, the operating system provides a configuration interface for the wireless device settings, whereas in others you must use a configuration utility supplied by the manufacturer of the adapter. In either case, the settings you specify for the adapter must match those of the access point, or the two will not be able to communicate.

Exercise

The answers for this exercise are located in the "Answers" section at the end of this chapter. For each of the following descriptive phrases, specify which of the following standards it applies to: 802.11a, 802.11b, 802.11g, and/or 802.11n.

1. Uses multiple spatial streams to increase transmission rates

2. Supports a maximum transfer rate of 11 Mbps

3. Supports a channel width of 20 MHz

4. Supports a maximum transfer rate of 54 Mbps

5. Uses Direct-Sequence Spread Spectrum modulation

Chapter Summary

- The wireless LAN equipment on the market today is based on the 802.11 standards published by the Institute of Electrical and Electronics Engineers (IEEE). Because the protocols are produced by the same standards body, the 802.11 wireless technology fits neatly into the same layered structure as the Ethernet specifications.

- The IEEE 802.11a amendment fundamentally changed the technology by adding the 5-GHz band.

- The 802.11b document increases the transmission speed to as much as 11 Mbps.

- The IEEE 802.11g amendment built on the 802.11b technology by adopting the OFDM modulation from 802.11a while retaining the 2.4-GHz frequency from 802.11b.

- The IEEE 802.11n amendment introduces a number of modifications to the technology, including the potential doubling of channel widths and the addition of the 5-GHz frequency band from 802.11a to the standard 2.4-GHz band from 802.11b/g.

- Multiple-Input Multiple-Output (MIMO) is a physical layer enhancement that enables wireless devices to multiplex signals over a single channel simultaneously.

- Frame aggregation is a technique that combines the payload data from several smaller frames into one larger frame.

- The fundamental building block of an 802.11 wireless LAN is the basic service set (BSS). A BSS is a geographical area in which properly equipped wireless stations can communicate.

- An arrangement in which all of the network devices in the BSS are mobile or portable is called an ad hoc topology.

- The service set identifier (SSID) is a 32-bit string that identifies a BSS and all its members.

- The 802.11 standard defines the use of a MAC mechanism called Carrier Sense Multiple Access with Collision Avoidance (CSMA/CA), which is a variation of the Carrier Sense Multiple Access with Collision Detection (CSMA/CD) mechanism used by Ethernet.

Chapter Review

Test your knowledge of the information in Chapter 5 by answering these questions. The answers to these questions, and the explanations of why each answer choice is correct or incorrect, are located in the "Answers" section at the end of this chapter.

1. Which of the following wireless LAN standards are capable of using the 5-GHz frequency band?

    A. IEEE 802.11a

    B. IEEE 802.11b

    C. IEEE 802.11g

    D. IEEE 802.11n

2. What is the maximum transfer rate achievable on an 802.11n 4x4:4 network?

    A. 54 Mbps

    B. 150 Mbps

    C. 300 Mbps

    D. 600 Mbps

3. How is the BSSID of an infrastructure network determined?

    A. The administrator specifies the BSSID while configuring the access point.

    B. The BSSID is the MAC address of the access point.

    C. The BSSID is the IP address of the access point.

    D. The BSSID is assigned in part by the IEEE and in part by the administrator.

4. What is the advantage of configuring the access points on an 802.11g extended service set to use channels 1, 6, and 11?

    A. Channels 1, 6, and 11 operate at 5 GHz instead of 2.4 GHz.

    B. Channels 1, 6, and 11 have longer ranges than the other channels.

    C. Channels 1, 6, and 11 use frequencies that do not overlap.

    D. Channels 1, 6, and 11 are the only three channels that can be legally used on the same network in the United States.

Answers

This section contains the answers to the questions for the Exercise and Chapter Review in this chapter.

Exercise

1. IEEE 802.11n

2. IEEE 802.11b

3. IEEE 802.11a, IEEE 802.11g, IEEE 802.11n

4. IEEE 802.11a and IEEE 802.11g

5. IEEE 802.11b and IEEE 802.11g

Chapter Review

1. **Correct Answers:** A and D

   A. **Correct:** The IEEE 802.11a standard calls for the use of the 5-GHz band exclusively.

   B. **Incorrect:** The IEEE 802.11b standard calls for the use of the 2.4-GHz band exclusively.

   C. **Incorrect:** The IEEE 802.11g standard calls for the use of the 2.4-GHz band exclusively.

   D. **Correct:** The IEEE 802.11n standard calls for the use of either the 2.4-GHz or the 5-GHz band.

2. **Correct Answer:** D

   A. **Incorrect:** The IEEE 802.11a and 802.11g standards define a maximum transfer rate of 54 Mbps.

   B. **Incorrect:** An IEEE 802.11n network with one spatial stream can transmit at up to 150 Mbps.

   C. **Incorrect:** An IEEE 802.11n network with two spatial streams can transmit at up to 300 Mbps.

   D. **Correct:** An IEEE 802.11n network with four spatial streams can transmit at up to 600 Mbps.

3. **Correct Answer:** B

   A. **Incorrect:** The administrator does not configure the basic service set identifier.

   B. **Correct:** The basic service set identifier is the 6-byte MAC address assigned to the access point by the manufacturer.

   C. **Incorrect:** The basic service set identifier is a data-link layer element. It has nothing to do with IP addressing.

   D. **Incorrect:** Because it is a MAC address, the basic service set identifier is assigned in part by the IEEE, but the other part is assigned by the device manufacturer, not by the administrator.

4. **Correct Answer:** C

   A. **Incorrect:** Channels 1, 6, and 11 do not operate at 5 GHz.

   B. **Incorrect:** Channels 1, 6, and 11 do not have longer ranges than the other channels.

   C. **Correct:** Channels 1, 6, and 11 use frequencies that do not overlap. Therefore, there is no interference between the networks.

   D. **Incorrect:** There are no legal restrictions to using any combination of channels 1 through 11 in the United States.

CHAPTER 6

The Network Layer

As discussed in Chapter 4, "The Data-Link Layer," the data-link layer of the Open Systems Interconnection (OSI) reference model is about getting packets to their next destination. Data-link layer protocols are responsible for sending packets to another system on the same local area network (LAN), to a router on the LAN, or to a system at the other end of a wide area network (WAN) link. The network layer, by contrast, is responsible for the delivery of data to its ultimate destination, whether that is on the same network or another network, across the hall or halfway around the planet.

This is why it might seem as though network layer protocols have some redundant functions. For example, why should the *Internet Protocol (IP)* have its own addressing scheme, when Ethernet already has addresses? The answer is because Ethernet addresses are only good for local delivery. They tell computers where the local post office is, something IP cannot know. IP addresses tell computers the final destination of a packet. Therefore, a packet might have addresses at the data-link and network layers that identify two different systems.

EXAM TIP

In today's networking industry, IP is the only end-to-end network layer protocol in common use. At one time, the Network+ exam included coverage of the Novell NetWare protocols, including Internetwork Packet Exchange (IPX) at the network layer, and the AppleTalk protocols, including the Datagram Delivery Protocol (DDP). However, because these protocols have been deprecated from the industry, they have been removed from the exam.

Exam objectives in this chapter:

Objective 1.2: Classify how applications, devices, and protocols relate to the OSI model layers.

- MAC address
- IP address
- EUI-64
- Frames
- Packets
- Switch
- Router
- Multilayer switch
- Hub
- Encryption devices
- Cable
- NIC
- Bridge

Objective 1.3: Explain the purpose and properties of IP addressing.

- Classes of addresses
  - A, B, C and D
  - Public vs. Private
- Classless (CIDR)
- IPv4 vs. IPv6 (formatting)
- MAC address format
- Subnetting
- Multicast vs. unicast vs. broadcast
- APIPA

Objective 1.6: Explain the function of common networking protocols.

- TCP
- FTP
- UDP
- TCP/IP suite
- DHCP
- TFTP
- DNS
- HTTPS
- HTTP
- ARP
- SIP (VoIP)
- RTP (VoIP)
- SSH
- POP3
- NTP
- IMAP4
- Telnet
- SMTP
- SNMP2/3
- ICMP
- IGMP
- TLS

Since its inception in the 1970s, the TCP/IP protocol suite has evolved into the industry standard for data transfer protocols at the network and transport layers of the OSI model. In addition, the suite includes myriad other protocols that operate on layers as low as the data link layer and as high as the application layer.

Generally, a discussion of a network layer protocol or its functions is referring to IP. The TCP/IP suite is named for a combination of two protocols—IP at the network layer, and the Transmission Control Protocol (TCP) at the transport layer; together, these two protocols provide one of the most frequently used network transport services. TCP data is encapsulated within IP, as are most of the other protocols in the TCP/IP suite. IP essentially functions as the envelope that delivers TCP/IP data to its destination.

There are other protocols that operate at the network layer, such as the Internet Control Message Protocol (ICMP) and the Internet Group Management Protocol (IGMP), but these provide relatively limited services to other protocols. IP is the cornerstone of the network layer and of the TCP/IP protocol suite.

Internet Protocol (IP)

IP is the primary end-to-end protocol in the TCP/IP protocol stack. At the data-link layer, data might use Ethernet or a WAN protocol to reach its destination. At the transport layer, data might use TCP or User Datagram Protocol (UDP). However, at the network layer, all data uses the services provided by the IP protocol. There is no alternative.

IP Standards

The TCP/IP protocols are standardized in documents called *Requests for Comments (RFCs)*, which are published by an organization called the *Internet Engineering Task Force (IETF)*. These documents wend their way through a lengthy ratification process that eventually results in their publication as Internet standards. Unlike most networking standards, TCP/IP specifications are released to the public domain and are freely available on the Internet at many sites, including the IETF home page at *www.ietf.org*.

The IP specification was published in September 1981 as RFC 791, "Internet Protocol: DARPA Internet Program Protocol Specification," and was later ratified as Internet Standard 5. RFC 791 is a relatively brief document that concentrates primarily on IP's addressing and fragmentation functions. Other important functions of the IP protocol are defined in other RFC documents, including the following:

- RFC 894, "Standard for the Transmission of IP Datagrams over Ethernet Networks," April 1984

- RFC 950, "Internet Standard Subnetting Procedure," August 1985

- RFC 1042, "A Standard for the Transmission of IP Datagrams over IEEE 802 Networks," February 1988

- RFC 1812, "Requirements for IP Version 4 Routers," June 1995

NOTE **PUBLISHING RFCS**

When the IETF publishes an RFC and assigns it a number, that document never changes. If an RFC requires updating or augmentation, the IETF publishes a new document with a different number, containing either a revised version of the old RFC or just the new information. The official RFC database, maintained by the IETF, is fully cross-referenced, indicating which RFCs are rendered obsolete by new documents and where to look for the latest information on a particular topic. This index is available online at *http://www.rfc-editor.org/rfc.html*.

The IP protocol is also in the midst of a migration to an upgraded standard from version 4 (IPv4) to version 6 (IPv6). These upgrades are defined in many additional RFCs, such as the following:

- RFC 1881, "IPv6 Address Allocation Management," December 1995
- RFC 1887, "An Architecture for IPv6 Unicast Address Allocation," December 1995
- RFC 2460, "Internet Protocol Version 6 (IPv6) Specification"
- RFC 3596, "DNS Extensions to Support IP Version 6," October 2003
- RFC 4291, "IP Version 6 Addressing Architecture," February 2006
- RFC 6145, "IP/ICMP Translation Algorithm," April 2011
- RFC 6296, "IPv6-to-IPv6 Network Prefix Translation," June 2011

IP Versions

At the time the IP protocol was designed, the network we now know as the Internet was an experimental network called the ARPAnet that a few hundred scientists and engineers used to keep in touch with each other. Nobody at that time could have predicted that in less than 40 years, millions of people would have computers running IP in their homes, not to mention IP-equipped telephones in their pockets.

The IP protocol defined in RFC 791 is version 4, which is the version still used on most of the Internet. IPv4 includes a 32-bit address space, which means that the protocol can support approximately 4.29 billion addresses. This might seem like a lot, but there was a time when the IPv4 address seemed to be in danger of being depleted. The increased and prudent use of alternative address assignment strategies such as network address translation (NAT) circumvented the immediate danger.

However, work began on a new version of IP that would alleviate any potential address shortage. IP version 6 (*IPv6*) has a 128-bit address space that provides an enormous number of addresses.

> **NOTE** **CALCULATING AN ADDRESS SPACE**
>
> To calculate the number of possible addresses provided by a given address space, raise 2 to the power of n (that is, 2^n), where n equals the number of bits in the address space. Thus, the IPv4 address space consists of 2^{32}, or 4,294,967,296, possible addresses. By contrast, the IPv6 address space consists of 2^{128}, or 340,282,366,920,938,463,463,374,607,431,770,000,000 (340 undecillion) possible addresses. This number is sufficiently large to allocate 48,611,766,702,991,209,066,196,372,490 addresses to each of the approximately 7 billion people living today.

In addition to providing more addresses, IPv6 will also reduce the size of the routing tables in the routers scattered around the Internet. This is because the size of the addresses provides for more than the two levels of subnetting currently possible with IPv4.

Virtually all of the commercial operating systems now include support for IPv6, but deploying the protocol on the Internet is a much more complicated undertaking. Despite the fact that IPv6 has spent more than 12 years as a Standards Track protocol, the total number of IPv6 systems deployed on the Internet is still miniscule—less than 1 percent.

NAT and the like were effective stopgap measures, but as of this writing, the need for IPv6 is asserting itself again. In February 2011, the *Internet Assigned Numbers Authority (IANA)* issued the last of its blocks of free IPv4 addresses to the regional Internet registries (RIRs). The RIRs themselves still have addresses left to assign, but the exhaustion of the IPv4 address space is now clearly in sight.

In the meantime, there are many transition mechanisms available—such as Teredo and 6to4—that are essentially tunneling solutions that encapsulate IPv6 packets inside IPv4 packets for transmission over the Internet. Therefore, although network administrators must be familiar with the IPv6 standards and technologies, IPv4 will not be going away anytime soon.

IP Functions

On a TCP/IP internetwork, IP is the protocol responsible for transmitting data from its source to its final destination. IP is a connectionless protocol, meaning that it transmits messages to a destination without first establishing a connection to the receiving system. IP is also considered to be an unreliable protocol, because it does not require the receiving system to respond with acknowledgments.

> **NOTE RELIABLE NETWORKS**
>
> Networking literature frequently uses the term "unreliable" to describe a protocol that does not require acknowledgment of its transmissions. However, this does not necessarily mean that these protocols are unreliable in the traditional sense of the word. On a properly designed and maintained network, a vast number of IP datagrams reach their destinations successfully and intact. The protocol might therefore be technically unreliable, but hardly untrustworthy.

The IP service is connectionless and unreliable because it carries data generated by other protocols, only some of which require connection-oriented service. The TCP/IP suite includes both connection-oriented and connectionless services at the transport layer, making it possible for applications to select one or the other, depending on the quality of service they need. Because TCP provides connection-oriented service at the transport layer, there is no need to implement a connection-oriented service at the network layer. The network layer can therefore remain connectionless, thus reducing the amount of control overhead generated by the protocol stack.

IP performs several functions that are essential to the internetworking process, including the following:

- **Data encapsulation** The packaging of the transport layer data into an IP datagram
- **IP addressing** The identification of systems on the network by using unique addresses
- **IP routing** The selection of the most efficient path through the internetwork to the destination system
- **Fragmentation** The division of data into fragments of an appropriate size for transmission over the network
- **Protocol identification** The specification of the transport layer protocol that generated the data in the datagram

These functions—in both IPv4 and IPv6 iterations, where appropriate—are discussed in the following sections.

IPv4 Addressing

The self-contained *IP addressing* system is one of the most important elements of the TCP/IP protocol suite. IP addresses enable computers running any operating system on any platform to communicate by providing unique identifiers for the computer itself and for the network on which it is located. Understanding how IP addresses are constructed and how they should be assigned is an essential part of TCP/IP network administration.

An IPv4 address is a 32-bit value that contains both a network identifier portion and a host identifier portion. The address is notated by using four decimal numbers ranging from 0 to 255, separated by periods, as in 192.168.1.44. This is known as *dotted decimal notation*. Each of the four values is the decimal equivalent of an 8-bit binary value. For example, the binary value 10101010 is equal to the decimal value 170. To properly understand some of the concepts of IP addressing, you must remember that the familiar decimal numbers are only convenient equivalents of binary values.

EXAM TIP

In TCP/IP terminology, each of the 8-bit values that make up an IP address is called an "octet," and the combination of four octets is called a "word." The developers of the TCP/IP protocols deliberately avoided the more traditional term, "byte" because at the time, some computing platforms used a 7-bit rather than an 8-bit byte. Today, however, the terms "octet," "byte," and "quad" are all appropriate, and you should be prepared to see any or all of them on the Network+ exam.

As mentioned earlier, IP addresses represent network interfaces, and a computer can have more than one network interface. A computer with two interfaces is sometimes referred to as being "multihomed." A router, for example, has interfaces to at least two networks and must therefore have an IP address for each of those interfaces. Workstations on a LAN typically have only a single interface, but in some cases they use a modem to connect to another network, such as the Internet. In this case, the modem interface has its own separate IP address (usually assigned by the server at the other end of the modem connection) in addition to that of the LAN connection. If other systems on the LAN access the Internet through that computer's modem, such as via the Internet Connection Sharing (ICS) feature of the Windows operating system, that system is actually functioning as a router.

IPv4 Address Assignments

The hardware addresses that data-link layer protocols use to identify systems are hard-coded into network interface adapters at the factory, but network administrators must assign IP addresses to the systems on their networks, either by manually configuring the TCP/IP client or dynamically by using the Dynamic Host Configuration Protocol (DHCP). It is essential for each network interface to have its own unique IP address; when two systems have the same IP address, they can't communicate with the network properly.

As mentioned earlier, IP addresses consist of two logical parts: a network identifier and a host identifier. All of the network interface adapters on a particular subnet must have the same network identifier but different host identifiers. For systems on the Internet, the IANA assigns network identifiers to ensure that there is no address duplication. When an organization registers its network, it is assigned a network identifier. It is then up to the network administrators to assign unique host identifiers to each of the systems on that network. This two-tiered system of administration is one of the basic organizational principles of the Internet. Domain names are assigned in the same way.

> **NOTE   OBTAINING ADDRESSES**
>
> Although the IANA is ultimately responsible for the assignment of all Internet network addresses, network administrators seldom if ever deal with them directly. The IANA is managed by the Internet Corporation for Assigned Names and Numbers (ICANN), which allocates blocks of addresses to regional Internet registries (RIRs), which allocate smaller blocks in turn to Internet service providers (ISPs). Sometimes, large ISPs allocate blocks of addresses to smaller ISPs as well. An organization that wants to host a server on the Internet typically obtains a registered address from an ISP. Internet addresses often pass through several layers of service providers in this way before they get to the organization that actually uses them.

IPv4 Address Classes

The fact that an IPv4 address contains both a network identifier and a host identifier means that some of the 32 bits in the address specify the network on which the host is located and the rest of the bits identify the specific host on that network. The most complicated aspect of an IPv4 address is that the division between the network identifier bits and the host identifier bits is not always in the same place.

In a network interface adapter's hardware media access control (MAC) address, for example, the first three bytes are always the organizationally unique identifier (OUI) assigned to the manufacturer of the network adapter, and the last three bytes are the value that the manufacturer itself assigns to the adapter. However, IP addresses can have various numbers of bits assigned to the network identifier, depending on the size and organization of the network.

RFC 791 defines three classes of IP addresses, which provide support for networks of different sizes, as shown in Figure 6-1.

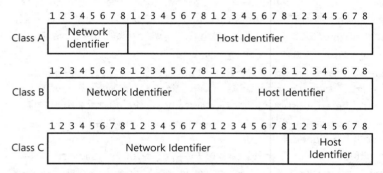

FIGURE 6-1 The three classes of IPv4 addresses.

The characteristics of these three address classes are listed in Table 6-1.

TABLE 6-1 IPv4 Address Classes

IP Address Class	Class A	Class B	Class C
First bit values (binary)	0	10	110
First byte value (decimal)	0–127	128–191	192–223
Number of network identifier bits	8	16	24
Number of host identifier bits	24	16	8
Number of possible networks	126	16,384	2,097,152
Number of possible hosts	16,777,214	65,534	254

The "First bit values" row in Table 6-1 specifies the values that the first one, two, or three bits of an address in each class must have. Some early TCP/IP implementations used these bit values to determine the class of an address. The binary values of the first bits of each address class limit the possible decimal values for the first byte of the address. For example, because the first bit of Class A addresses must be 0, the possible binary values of the first byte in a Class A address range from 00000000 to 01111111, which in decimal form are values ranging from 1 to 127. Thus, when you see an IP address in which the first byte is a number from 1 to 127, you know that this is a Class A address.

In a Class A address, the network identifier is the first 8 bits of the address, and the host identifier is the remaining 24 bits. Thus, there are only 126 possible Class A networks (network identifier 127 is reserved for diagnostic purposes), but each network can have up to 16,777,214 network interface adapters on it. Class B and Class C addresses devote more bits to the network identifier, which means that they support a greater number of networks, but at the cost of having fewer host identifier bits. This tradeoff reduces the number of hosts that can be created on each network.

The values in Table 6-1 for the number of hosts supported by each address class might appear low. For example, an 8-bit binary number can have 256 (that is, 2^8) possible values, not 254, as shown in the table for the number of hosts on a Class C address. The value 254 is used because the original IP addressing standard states that you can't assign the "all 0s" or "all 1s" addresses to individual hosts. The "all 0s" address identifies the network, not a specific host, and the "all 1s" identifier always signifies a broadcast address. You cannot assign either value to an individual host. Therefore, to calculate the number of possible network or host addresses you can create with a given number of bits, you use the formula $2^n - 2$, where n is the number of bits.

EXAM TIP

Classful IP addressing was superseded by Classless Inter-Domain Routing in 1993, but it remains part of the Network+ objectives.

IPv4 Address Types

IPv4 supports three basic types of addresses, as follows:

- **Unicast** A one-to-one transmission sent to an IP address with a specific host identifier, anywhere on the internetwork.

- **Broadcast** A one-to-many transmission sent to an IP address with a host identifier that consists of all 1s. Broadcast transmissions are received and processed by all of the hosts on the local network.

- **Multicast** A one-to-many transmission sent to a specially allocated multicast IP address. Multicast addresses are targeted at specific groups of hosts, which can be scattered around the internetwork.

Subnet Masking

It might at first seem odd that the IP address classes are defined as they are. After all, there aren't any private networks that have 16 million hosts on them, so it makes little sense even to have Class A addresses. In the early days of IP, no one worried about the depletion of the IP address space, so the wastefulness of the classful addressing system was not an issue.

Eventually, this wastefulness was recognized, and the designers of the protocol developed a system for subdividing network addresses by creating subnets on them. A *subnet* is simply a subdivision of a network address that administrators can use to represent a part of a larger network, such as one LAN on an internetwork or the client of an ISP. Thus, a large ISP might have a Class A address registered to it, and it might allocate sections of that network address to its clients in the form of subnets. In many cases, a large ISP's clients are smaller ISPs, which in turn supply addresses to their own clients.

To understand the process of creating subnets, you must understand the function of the *subnet mask*. As noted earlier, TCP/IP systems at one time recognized the class of an address simply by examining the values of the first three bits. Today, however, when you configure the TCP/IP client on a computer, you assign it an IPv4 address and a subnet mask. Simply put, the subnet mask specifies which bits of the IP address are the network identifier and which bits are the host identifier. For a Class A address, for example, the default subnet mask value is 255.0.0.0. When expressed as a binary number, a subnet mask's 1 bits indicate the network identifier, and its 0 bits indicate the host identifier. A mask of 255.0.0.0 in binary form is as follows:

```
11111111 00000000 00000000 00000000
```

This mask indicates that the first 8 bits of a Class A IP address are the network identifier bits and the remaining 24 bits are the host identifier. The default subnet masks for the three main address classes are as follows:

- **Class A** 255.0.0.0
- **Class B** 255.255.0.0
- **Class C** 255.255.255.0

Subnetting a Network Address

If all the IP addresses in a particular class used the same number of bits for the network and host identifiers, there would be no need for a subnet mask. The value of the first byte of the address would indicate its class. However, you can create multiple subnets, using a single address of a given class, by applying a different subnet mask. If, for example, you have a Class B address, the default subnet mask of 255.255.0.0 would allocate the first 16 bits for the network identifier and the last 16 bits for the host identifier. However, if you use a mask of 255.255.255.0 with a Class B address, you allocate an additional 8 bits to the network identifier, which you are borrowing from the host identifier. The third byte of the address thus becomes a subnet identifier, as shown in Figure 6-2.

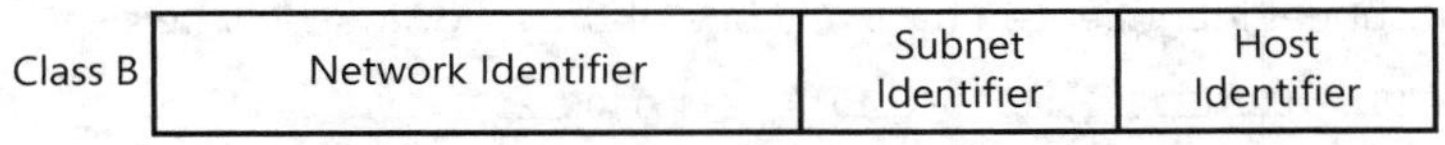

Class B	Network Identifier	Subnet Identifier	Host Identifier

FIGURE 6-2 Changing the subnet mask to create multiple subnets out of one network address.

> **NOTE** **SUBNET BITS**
> The term "subnet identifier" is not an official part of the IP addressing lexicon; it is just a conceptual aid for network planners. TCP/IP hosts can only distinguish between network bits and host bits; they do not recognize subnet bits as being different from the rest of the network bits.

By subnetting in this way, you can create up to 256 subnets by using that one Class B address, with up to 254 network interface adapters on each subnet. An IP address of 131.107.67.98 would therefore indicate that the network is using the Class B address 131.107.0.0, and that the interface is host number 98 on subnet 67. A large corporate network might use this scheme to create a separate subnet for each of its LANs.

Subnetting Between Bytes

To complicate matters further, the boundary between the network identifier and the host identifier does not have to fall between two bytes. An IP address can use any number of bits for its network address, and more complex subnet masks are required in this type of environment. Suppose, for example, that you have a Class C network address of 192.168.65.0 that you want to subnet. There are already 24 bits devoted to the network address, and you obviously can't allocate the entire fourth byte as a subnet identifier, or there would be no bits left for the host identifier. You can, however, allocate part of the fourth byte. If you use 4 bits of the last byte for the subnet identifier, you have 4 bits left for your host identifier. To do this, the binary form of your subnet mask must appear as follows:

11111111 11111111 11111111 11110000

The decimal equivalent of this binary value is 255.255.255.240, because 240 is the decimal equivalent of 11110000. This leaves a 4-bit subnet identifier and a 4-bit host identifier, which means that you can create up to 16 subnets with 14 hosts on each one. Figuring out the correct subnet mask for this type of configuration is relatively easy. Figuring out the IP addresses you must assign to your workstations is harder. To do this, you have to increment the subnet bits separately from the 4 host bits. Once again, this is easier to understand when you look at the binary values. The 4-bit subnet identifier can have any one of the following 16 values:

0000 0001 0010 0011 0100 0101 0110 0111 1000 1001 1010 1011 1100 1101 1110 1111

Each one of these subnets can have up to 14 workstations, with each host identifier having any one of the same values except for 0000 and 1111. Thus, to calculate the value of the IP address' fourth byte, you must combine the binary values of the subnet and host identifiers and convert them to decimal form. For example, the first host (0001) on the second subnet (0001) would have a fourth-byte binary value of 00010001, which in decimal form is 17. Thus, the IP address for this system would be 192.168.65.17, and its subnet mask would be 255.255.255.240.

The last host on the second subnet would use 1110 as its host identifier, making the value of the fourth byte 00011110 in binary form, or 30 in decimal form, for an IP address of 192.168.65.30. Then, to proceed to the next subnet, you would increment the subnet identifier to 0010 and decrement the host identifier back to 0001, for a binary value of 00100001, or 33 in decimal form. As you can see, the IP addresses you use on a network like this do not increment normally. You can't use the numbers 31 and 32, because they represent the broadcast address of the second subnet and the network address of the third subnet, respectively. You must compute the addresses carefully to create the correct values.

As an example of subnetting in the field, consider an organization with a network that spans two buildings, with only a low-speed connection between them. If the computers in both buildings are on the same subnet, then they are in the same broadcast domain as well, and the low-speed connection will be inundated by the broadcast traffic generated by computers in both buildings.

To address this traffic problem, the network administrator can separate the buildings by creating two subnets. Borrowing one bit from the host identifier would be sufficient in this case. Connecting the two subnets with routers will then create two separate broadcast domains. As a result, only the packets destined for the other network will pass over the connection between the buildings. This will reduce the traffic on the low-speed connection and increase the overall efficiency of the network.

Converting Binaries and Decimals

Part of the difficulty in calculating IP addresses and subnet masks is converting between decimal and binary numbers. The easiest way to do this, of course, is to use a calculator. Most scientific calculators are able to work with binary as well as decimal numbers and can usually convert between the two. However, it is also useful to be able to perform the conversions manually.

To convert a binary number to a decimal, you assign a numerical value to each bit, starting at the right with 1 and proceeding to the left, doubling the value each time. The values for an 8-bit number are therefore as follows:

```
128   64   32   16   8   4   2   1
```

You then line up the values of your 8-bit binary number with the eight conversion values as follows:

```
1     1    1    0    0   0   0   0
128   64   32   16   8   4   2   1
```

Finally, you add together the conversion values for the 1 bits only:

```
1     1    1    0    0    0    0    0
128   +64  +32  +0   +0   +0   +0   +0   =224
```

Therefore, the decimal equivalent of the binary value 11100000 is 224.

At times it might be necessary to convert decimal numbers into binaries. To do this, you use the same basic process in reverse, by subtracting the conversion values from the decimal you want to convert, working from left to right. For example, to convert the decimal number 202 into binary form, you subtract the conversion value 128 from 202, leaving a remainder of 74. Because you were able to subtract 128 from 202, you put a value of 1 in the first binary bit as follows:

1							
128	64	32	16	8	4	2	1

You then subtract 64 from the remaining 74, leaving 10, so the second binary bit has a value of 1 also:

1	1						
128	64	32	16	8	4	2	1

You can't subtract 32 or 16 from the remaining 10, so the third and fourth binary bits are 0:

1	1	0	0				
128	64	32	16	8	4	2	1

You can subtract 8 from 10, leaving 2, so the fifth binary bit is a 1:

1	1	0	0	1			
128	64	32	16	8	4	2	1

You can't subtract 4 from 2, so the sixth binary bit is a 0, but you can subtract 2 from 2, so the seventh bit is a 1. There is now no remainder left, so the eighth bit is a 0, completing the calculation as follows:

1	1	0	0	1	0	1	0
128	64	32	16	8	4	2	1

Therefore, the binary value of the decimal number 202 is 11001010.

EXAM TIP

Many software tools are available that can simplify the process of calculating IP addresses and subnet masks for complex subnetted networks. However, you should be aware that tools like these are not permitted when you are taking the Network+ exam, so you must be capable of performing the calculations yourself. You can, however, use the Windows Calculator, which in its Scientific mode or Programmer mode is capable of converting between digital, binary, and hexadecimal numbers.

Calculating IP Addresses by Using the Subtraction Method

Manually calculating IP addresses by using binary values can be a slow and tedious task, especially if you are going to have hundreds or thousands of computers on your network. However, when you have the subnet mask for the network and you understand the relationship between subnet and host identifier values, you can calculate IP addresses without having to convert them to binary values.

The first subnet uses the network address itself. To calculate the network address of the second subnet, begin by taking the decimal value of the octet in the subnet mask that contains both subnet and host identifier bits, and subtracting it from 256. For example, with a network address of 192.168.42.0 and a subnet mask of 255.255.255.224, the result of 256 minus 224 is 32. The network address of the first subnet is therefore 192.168.42.0 and the address of the second subnet is 192.168.42.32. To calculate the network addresses of the other subnets, you repeatedly increment the result of your previous subtraction by itself. For example, if the network address of the second subnet is 192.168.42.32, the addresses of the remaining five subnets are as follows.

```
192.168.42.64
192.168.42.96
192.168.42.128
192.168.42.160
192.168.42.192
```

To calculate the IP addresses in each subnet, you repeatedly increment the host identifier by one. The IP addresses in the first subnet are therefore 192.168.42.33 to 192.168.42.62. The 192.168.42.63 address is omitted because this address has a binary host identifier value of 11111, which is a broadcast address. The IP address ranges for the subsequent subnets are as follows.

```
192.168.42.65 to 192.168.42.94
192.168.42.97 to 192.168.42.126
192.168.42.129 to 192.168.42.158
192.168.42.161 to 192.168.42.190
192.168.42.193 to 192.168.42.222
```

Classless Inter-Domain Routing

Because of its wastefulness, classful addressing was gradually obsolesced by a series of sub-netting methods, including variable length subnet masking (VLSM) and eventually *Classless Inter-Domain Routing (CIDR)*. CIDR, as defined in RFC 4632, "Classless Inter-domain Routing (CIDR): The Internet Address Assignment and Aggregation Plan," is a subnetting method that enables administrators to place the division between the network bits and the host bits anywhere in the address, not just between octets. This makes it possible to create networks of almost any size.

ꓛꓲDR Notation

ꓛꓲDR also introduced a new notation for network addresses. A standard dotted-decimal address representing the network is followed by a forward slash and a numeral specifying the size of the network-identifying prefix. For example, 192.168.43.0/24 represents an address that uses a 24-bit network identifier, leaving the other 8 bits for up to 254 host identifiers, which would formerly be known as a Class C address. Each of those 254 hosts would receive an address from 192.168.43.1 to 192.168.43.254, using the subnet mask 255.255.255.0.

However, by using CIDR, an administrator can subnet this address further, by allocating some of the host bits to create subnets. To create subnets for four branch offices, for example, the administrator can take two of the host identifier bits, changing the network address in CIDR notation to 192.168.43.0/26. Because the network identifier is now 26 bits, the subnet masks for all four networks will now be 11111111.11111111.11111111.11000000, in binary form, or 255.255.255.192 in standard decimal form. Each of the four networks will have up to 62 hosts, using the IP address ranges shown in Table 6-2.

TABLE 6-2 Sample CIDR 192.168.43.0/26 Networks

Network Address	Starting IP Address	Ending IP Address	Subnet Mask
192.168.43.0	192.168.43.1	192.168.43.62	255.255.255.192
192.168.43.64	192.168.43.65	192.168.43.126	255.255.255.192
192.168.43.128	192.168.43.129	192.168.43.190	255.255.255.192
192.168.43.192	192.168.43.193	192.168.43.254	255.255.255.192

If the administrator needs more than four subnets, changing the address to 192.168.43.0/28 adds two more bits to the network address, for a maximum of 16 subnets, each of which can support up to 14 hosts. The subnet mask for these networks would therefore be 255.255.255.240.

Supernetting

In addition to simplifying network notation, CIDR also makes a technique called *IP address aggregation* or *supernetting* possible, which can help to reduce the size of Internet routing tables. A *supernet* is a combination of contiguous networks that all contain a common CIDR prefix. When an organization possesses multiple contiguous networks that can be expressed as a supernet, it becomes possible to list those networks in a routing table using only one entry instead of many.

For example, if an organization has the following subnets, standard practice would be to create a separate routing table entry for each one.

```
172.16.40.0/24
172.16.41.0/24
172.16.42.0/24
172.16.43.0/24
172.16.44.0/24
```

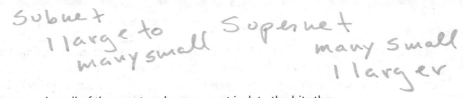

172.16.45.0/24
172.16.46.0/24
172.16.47.0/24

To create a supernet encompassing all of these networks, you must isolate the bits they have in common. When you convert the network addresses from decimal to binary, you get the following values.

172.16.40.0	**10101100**.**00010000**.**00101**000.00000000
172.16.41.0	**10101100**.**00010000**.**00101**001.00000000
172.16.42.0	**10101100**.**00010000**.**00101**010.00000000
172.16.43.0	**10101100**.**00010000**.**00101**011.00000000
172.16.44.0	**10101100**.**00010000**.**00101**100.00000000
172.16.45.0	**10101100**.**00010000**.**00101**101.00000000
172.16.46.0	**10101100**.**00010000**.**00101**110.00000000
172.16.47.0	**10101100**.**00010000**.**00101**111.00000000

In binary form, you can see that all of the addresses have the same first 21 bits. Those 21 bits become the network identifier of the supernet address, as follows.

10101100.00010000.00101

After zeroing out the host bits to form the network address and converting the binary number back to decimal form, as follows, the resulting supernet address is 172.16.40.0/21.

10101100.00010000.00101000.00000000   172.16.40.0/21

This one network address can replace the original eight in routing tables duplicated throughout the Internet. Obviously, this is just an example of a technique that administrators can use to combine dozens or even hundreds of subnets into single routing table entries.

Registered and Unregistered Addresses

For a computer to be accessible from the Internet, it must have a public IP address that is registered with the IANA. However, not every computer that can access the Internet has to be accessible from the Internet, so a registered address is not necessary for the average workstation. If organizations used registered addresses for all of their workstations, the IPv4 address space would have been depleted long ago.

The computers on a private network typically use unregistered, private IP addresses, which the network administrator can freely assign without registering them with an ISP or the IANA. RFC 1918, "Address Allocation for Private Internets," defines a range of network addresses for each class that are intended for use on private networks and are not registered to anyone. When building a private network, you should use these addresses rather than simply choosing an address at random.

The unregistered addresses for each class are as follows:

- **Class A**   10.0.0.0 through 10.255.255.255
- **Class B**   172.16.0.0 through 172.31.255.255
- **Class C**   192.168.0.0 through 192.168.255.255

For security reasons, networks typically use a firewall of some type to protect their private networks from intrusion by outside computers. These firewalls use various techniques to provide workstations with access to Internet resources without making them accessible to other systems on the Internet. Some of these techniques are described in the following sections.

EXAM TIP

The Network+ objectives refer to registered and unregistered IPv4 addresses as *public* and *private addresses*. Candidates should be familiar with both sets of terms.

Using Network Address Translation

The issue of how workstations with unregistered private addresses communicate with registered servers on the Internet presents an interesting problem. A browser running on an unregistered workstation can conceivably send messages to an Internet web server, but how can the web server respond when the workstation is using an address that is not visible from the Internet, and also might be shared by dozens of other computers throughout the Internet? The answer is by using a technology called *network address translation (NAT)* or a slightly different mechanism called a *proxy server*.

NAT is a network layer routing technology that enables a group of workstations to share a single registered address. A NAT router is a device with two network interfaces, one connected to a private network and one to the Internet. When a workstation on the private network wants to access an Internet resource, it sends a request to the NAT router.

Normally, a router passes traffic from one network to another without modifying the packets. However, in this case, the NAT router substitutes its own registered IP address for the workstation's private address, and sends the request on to the Internet server. The server responds to the NAT router, thinking that the router generated the original request. The router then performs the same substitution in reverse and forwards the response back to the original unregistered workstation. The router therefore functions as an intermediary between the client and the server.

A single NAT router can perform this same service for hundreds of private workstations, by maintaining a table of the address substitutions it has performed. In addition to conserving the IPv4 address space, NAT also provides a certain amount of protection to the network workstations. Because the workstations are functionally invisible to the Internet, attackers cannot readily probe them for open ports and other common exploits.

MORE INFO   **NETWORK ADDRESS TRANSLATION**

For more information on NAT, see Chapter 7, "Routing and Switching."

Using a Proxy Server

Because NAT routers function at the network layer of the protocol stack, they can handle any kind of traffic, regardless of the application that generated it. A proxy server is another type of intermediary—functioning at the application layer—that is designed to forward specific types of traffic to destinations on the Internet. In most cases, the primary function of a proxy server is to provide workstations with web access through a browser, such as Windows Internet Explorer.

Like a NAT router, a proxy server receives requests from clients on a private network and forwards those requests to the destination on the Internet, by using its own registered address to identify itself. The primary difference between a proxy server and a NAT router is that the proxy server interposes additional functions into the forwarding process. These functions can include the following:

- **Filtering** Administrators can configure proxy servers to limit user access to the Internet by filtering out requests sent to undesirable sites.
- **Logging** A proxy server can maintain logs of user Internet activity for later evaluation and reporting.
- **Caching** A proxy server can store frequently accessed Internet data in a local cache, which it can then use to satisfy subsequent requests for the same data at higher speeds.
- **Scanning** A proxy server can scan incoming data from the Internet for various types of malware and outgoing data for confidential company information.

Unlike a NAT router, which is invisible to the workstation, a proxy server requires applications to be configured to use it, a process that can be manual or automatic.

 Quick Check

1. What is the primary reason for supernetting?
2. What is the primary function of network address translation?

Quick Check Answers

1. To reduce the size of routing tables on the Internet
2. To conserve the IPv4 address space

Obtaining IP Addresses

If you need only a few registered IP addresses for your network, you can usually obtain them individually from your ISP, although you might have to pay an extra monthly fee for them. If the computers requiring the registered address are all on the same LAN and must communicate with one another, be sure that you obtain addresses on the same subnet. If you need a large number of registered IP addresses, you can obtain a network address from the ISP and use it to create as many host addresses as you need.

A network address is the network identifier portion of an IP address. For example, if your ISP assigns you the network address 131.107.118.0, with a subnet mask of 255.255.255.0, you could assign IP addresses ranging from 131.107.118.1 to 131.107.118.254 to your computers. The network address you receive from the ISP depends on the class of the address and on the number of computers you have that require registered addresses.

Assigning IPv4 Addresses

In addition to understanding how IP addressing works, a network administrator must be familiar with the methods for deploying IP addresses to the computers on a network. To assign IPv4 addresses, there are three basic alternatives:

- Manual configuration
- Automatic Private IP Addressing (APIPA)
- Dynamic Host Configuration Protocol (DHCP)

The advantages and disadvantages of these methods are discussed in the following sections.

Manual IPv4 Address Configuration

Configuring a TCP/IP client manually is not terribly difficult, nor is it very time consuming. Most operating systems provide a graphical interface that enables you to enter an IPv4 address, a subnet mask, and various other TCP/IP configuration parameters, as shown in Figure 6-3.

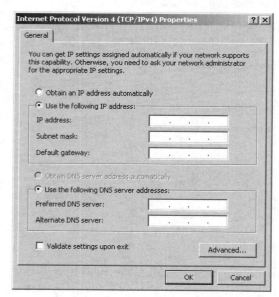

FIGURE 6-3 The Internet Protocol Version 4 (TCP/IPv4) Properties sheet.

The big problem with manual configuration, of course, is that a task that requires two min-utes for one workstation requires several hours for 100 workstations. Manually configuring all but the smallest networks is highly impractical, and not just for reasons of time. There is also the matter of tracking the IPv4 addresses you assign and making sure each system has an address that is unique. This can end up being a logistical nightmare, which is why few network administrators choose this option.

Dynamic Host Configuration Protocol

The *Dynamic Host Configuration Protocol (DHCP)* is an application and an application-layer protocol, and these together enable administrators to dynamically allocate IP addresses from a pool. Computers equipped with DHCP clients automatically contact a DHCP server when they start, and the server assigns them unique addresses and all of the other configuration parameters the TCP/IP client requires.

The DHCP server provides addresses to clients on a leased basis, and after a predetermined interval, each client either renews its address or releases it back to the server for reallocation. DHCP not only automates the address assignment process; it also keeps track of the addresses it assigns, preventing any address duplication on the network.

> **MORE INFO**   **DYNAMIC HOST CONFIGURATION PROTOCOL**
>
> For more information about DHCP, see Chapter 9, "The Application Layer."

Automatic Private IP Addressing (APIPA)

Automatic Private IP Addressing is the name assigned by Microsoft to a DHCP failover mech-anism used by all of the current Windows operating systems. On computers running the Windows operating system, the DHCP client is enabled by default. If, after several attempts, a system fails to locate a DHCP server on the network, APIPA takes over and automatically assigns an address on the 169.254.0.0/16 network to the computer. The system then uses the Address Resolution Protocol (ARP) to ensure that no other computer on the local network is using the same address.

For a small network that consists of only a single unrouted LAN, APIPA is a simple and ef-fective alternative to installing a DHCP server. However, for installations consisting of multiple LANs, with routers connecting them, administrators must take more positive control over the IP address assignment process. This usually means deploying one or more DHCP servers in some form.

IPv6 Addressing

As most administrators know, IPv6 is designed to increase the size of the IP address space, thus providing addresses for many more devices than IPv4. However, IPv6 addresses are different from IPv4 addresses in many ways other than length. Instead of the four 8-bit decimal numbers separated by periods that IPv4 uses, IPv6 addresses use a notation called *colon-hexadecimal format*, which consists of eight 16-bit hexadecimal numbers, separated by colons, as follows:

XX:XX:XX:XX:XX:XX:XX:XX

Each X represents 8 bits (or 1 byte), which in hexadecimal notation is represented by two characters, as in the following example:

21cd:0053:0000:0000:e8bb:04f2:003c:c394

> **NOTE HEXADECIMALS**
>
> Hexadecimal notation is another name for base 16, which means that each digit can have 16 possible values. To express hexadecimal numbers, you use the numerals 0 through 9 and the letters A through F to represent those 16 values. In binary (base 2) notation, an 8-bit (1-byte) number can have 256 possible values, but to express those 256 possible values in hexadecimal form, two characters are required. This is why some of the 2-byte XX values in the sample IPv6 address require four digits in hexadecimal notation.

When an IPv6 address has two or more consecutive 8-bit blocks of 0s, you can replace them with a double colon, as follows (but you can only use one double colon in any IPv6 address).

21cd:0053::e8bb:04f2:003c:c394

You can also remove the leading 0s in any block where they appear, as follows.

21cd:53::e8bb:4f2:3c:c394

There are no subnet masks in IPv6. Network addresses use the same slash notation as CIDR to identify the network bits. In the example specified here, the network address is notated as follows.

21cd:53::/64

This is the contracted form for the following network address.

21cd:0053:0000:0000/64

EXAM TIP
Network+ candidates must be familiar with the rules for contracting IPv6 addresses.

IPv6 Address Types

There are no broadcast transmissions in IPv6, and therefore no broadcast addresses, as there are in IPv4. IPv6 supports three address types, as follows:

- **Unicast** Provides one-to-one transmission service to individual interfaces, including server farms that share a single address. IPv6 supports several types of unicast addresses, including global, link-local, and unique local, which are terms that identify the scope of the address. Each type of unicast has a different format prefix (FP), a sequence of bits that identifies the type, just as an IPv4 address used a sequence of bits to identify its class.

- **Multicast** Provides one-to-many transmission service to groups of interfaces identified by a single multicast address.

- **Anycast** Provides one-to-one-of-many transmission service to groups of interfaces, only the nearest of which (measured by the number of intermediate routers) receives the transmission.

EXAM TIP

In IPv6, the *scope* of an address refers to the size of its functional area. For example, the scope of a global unicast is unlimited; it is the entire Internet. The scope of a link-local unicast is the immediate link; that is, the local network. The scope of a unique local unicast consists of all the subnets within an organization. Do not confuse this use of the term "scope" with that of DHCP, which uses the word to refer to a range of IP addresses.

Global Unicast Addresses

A *global unicast address* is the equivalent of a registered IPv4 address, routable worldwide and unique on the Internet. The original format of the address, as shown in Figure 6-4, consists of the following elements:

- **Format prefix (FP)** An FP value of 001, identifying the address as a global unicast
- **Top Level Aggregator (TLA)** A 13-bit globally unique identifier allocated to regional Internet registries by the IANA
- **Reserved** An 8-bit field that is currently unused
- **Next Level Aggregator (NLA)** A 24-bit field that the TLA organization uses to create a multilevel hierarchy for allocating blocks of addresses to its customers
- **Site Level Aggregator (SLA)** A 16-bit field that organizations can use to create an internal hierarchy of sites or subnets
- **Extended Unique Identifier (EUI-64)** A 64-bit field, derived from the network interface adapter's MAC address, identifying a specific interface on the network

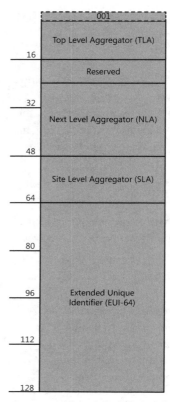

	001
	Top Level Aggregator (TLA)
16	Reserved
32	Next Level Aggregator (NLA)
48	Site Level Aggregator (SLA)
64	
80	
96	Extended Unique Identifier (EUI-64)
112	
128	

FIGURE 6-4 The original IPv6 global unicast address format.

These original field descriptions still appear in many IPv6 descriptions, but the standard was actually modified in 2003 to eliminate the separate TLA and NLA fields and rename the SLA field. The current official format for global unicast addresses, as shown in Figure 6-5, consists of the following elements:

- **Global routing prefix**   A 48-bit field beginning with the 001 FP value, the hierarchical structure of which is left up to the RIR

- **Subnet ID**   Formerly known as the SLA, a 16-bit field that organizations can use to create an internal hierarchy of sites or subnets

- **Interface ID**   A 64-bit field identifying a specific interface on the network

Theoretically, the global routing prefix and subnet ID fields can be any size. They are represented in the IPv6 standard by the letters "n" and "m," with the size of the interface ID specified as "128–n–m." In practice, however, organizations obtaining an address from an RIR or ISP are usually supplied with a 48-bit prefix, known colloquially as a "/48."

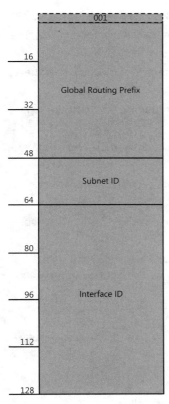

FIGURE 6-5 The current IPv6 global unicast address format.

NOTE **IPV6 ADDRESS REGISTRATION**

As with IPv4 addresses, there are three hierarchical levels involved in IPv6 global unicast address registration. At the top of the hierarchy is ICANN, which manages assignments for the IANA. At the second level are RIRs, which receive blocks of addresses from ICANN and allocate them in smaller blocks to ISPs.

The organization then has the 16-bit subnet ID with which to create an internal subnet hierarchy if they so choose. Some of the possible subnetting options are as follows:

- **One-level subnet**   By setting all of the subnet ID bits to 0, you can make all of the computers in the organization part of a single subnet. This option is only suitable for smaller organizations.

- **Two-level subnet**   By creating a series of 16-bit values, you can split the network into as many as 65,536 subnets. This is the functional equivalent of IPv4 subnetting, but with a much larger subnet address space.

- **Multilevel subnet** By allocating specific numbers of subnet ID bits, you can create multiple levels of subnets, sub-subnets, and sub-sub-subnets, suitable for an enterprise of almost any size.

In one example, designed to support a large international enterprise, you could split the subnet ID as follows:

- **Country (4 bits)** Creates up to 16 subnets representing countries in which the organization has offices
- **State (6 bits)** Creates up to 64 sub-subnets within each country, representing states, provinces, or other geographical divisions
- **Office (2 bits)** Creates up to four sub-sub-subnets within each state or province, representing offices located in various cities
- **Department (4 bits)** Creates up to 16 sub-sub-sub-subnets within each office, representing the various departments or divisions

To create a subnet ID for a particular office, it is up to the enterprise administrators to assign values for each of the fields. To use the value 1 for the United States, the Country bits would be as follows.

0001------------

To create a subnet for an office in Alaska, you can use a value of 49 in the State field, which in binary form would appear as follows.

----110001------

For the second office in Alaska, use the value 2 for Office bits, as follows.

----------10----

For the Sales department in the office, use the value 9 for the Department bits, as follows.

------------1001

The resulting value for the subnet ID, in binary form, would therefore be as follows.

0001110001101001

In hexadecimal form, that would be 1c69.

Because the subnet ID is wholly controlled by the organization that owns the prefix, enterprise administrators can adjust the number of levels in the hierarchy and the number of bits dedicated to each level as needed.

Finally, the last field, the interface ID, contains a unique identifier for a specific interface on the network. The Institute of Electrical and Electronics Engineers (IEEE) defines the format for the 48-bit MAC address assigned to each network adapter by the manufacturer, as well as the EUI-64 identifier format derived from it.

A MAC address consists of two 24-bit values, which are usually already expressed in hexadecimal notation. The first 24 bits, an organizationally unique identifier (OUI), identifies the company that made the adapter. The second 24 bits is a unique value for each individual device.

To derive the 64-bit interface ID for an interface, an IPv6 implementation takes the two 24-bit values and adds a 16-bit value between them: *11111111 11111110* in binary or *ff fe* in hexadecimal. Then it changes the seventh bit in the OUI—called the universal/local bit—from a 0 to a 1. This changes the hexadecimal value of the first byte in the address from 00 to 02.

Therefore, as shown in Figure 6-6, a computer with a network adapter that has a MAC address of *00-1a-6b-3c-ba-1f* would have an IPv6 global unicast address with the following interface ID.

`021a:6bff:fe3c:ba1f`

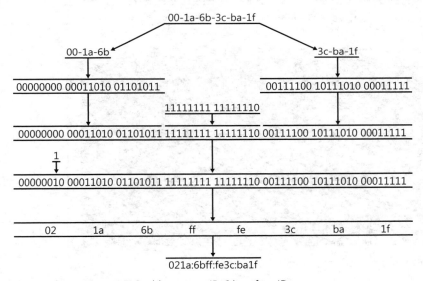

FIGURE 6-6 Converting a MAC address to an IPv6 interface ID.

One perceived problem with this method of deriving interface IDs from the computer's hardware is that the location of a mobile computer might be tracked based on its IPv6 address. Another involves the possible identification of vulnerabilities. This raises privacy and security concerns. Instead of using MAC addresses, Windows operating systems generate random interface IDs by default. Figure 6-7 demonstrates this, by showing a system with a randomly generated IPv6 address that does not match the Physical Address value.

To modify this default behavior, you can type the following at an elevated command prompt.

`netsh interface ipv6 set global randomizeidentifiers=disabled`

With this feature disabled, the system reverts to the standard practice of creating an interface ID from the MAC address, as shown in Figure 6-8.

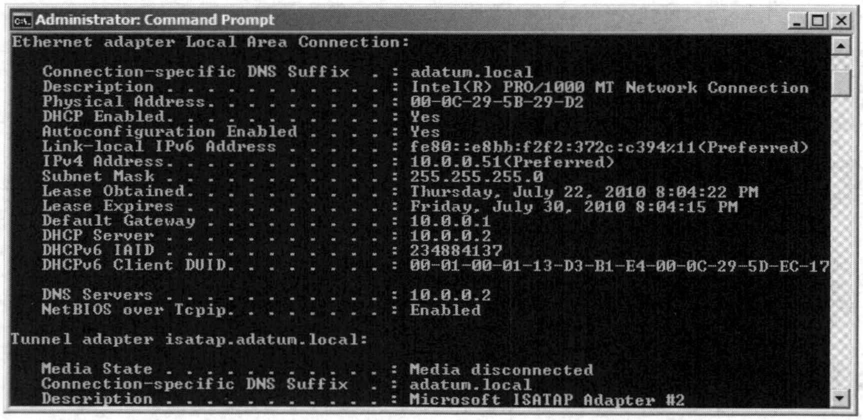

FIGURE 6-7 A randomly generated IPv6 address.

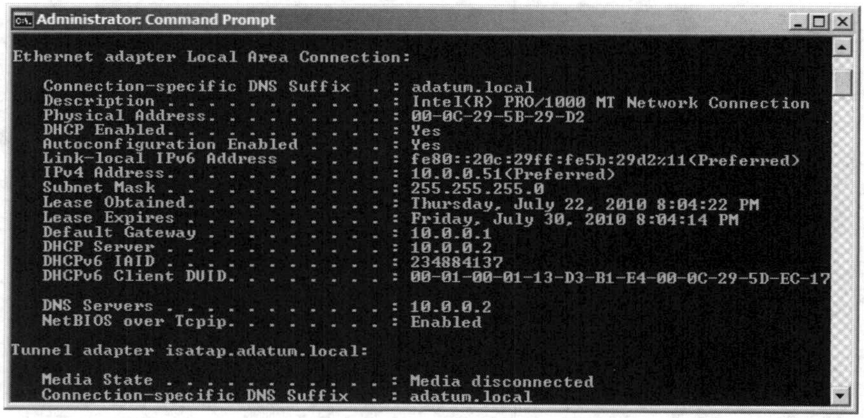

FIGURE 6-8 An IPv6 address generated from the MAC address.

Link-Local Unicast Addresses

In IPv6, systems that assign themselves an address automatically create a *link-local unicast address*, which is essentially the equivalent of an Automatic Private IP Addressing (APIPA) address in IPv4.

All link-local addresses have the same network identifier: a 10-bit FP of 11111110 10 followed by 54 zeroes, resulting in the following network address.

`fe80:0000:0000:0000/64`

In its more compact form, the link-local network address is as follows.

`fe80::/64`

Because all link-local addresses are on the same network, they are not routable, and systems possessing them can only communicate with other systems on the same link.

Unique Local Unicast Addresses

Unique local unicast addresses are the IPv6 equivalent of the 10.0.0.0/8, 172.16.0.0/12, and 192.168.0.0/16 private network addresses in IPv4. Like the IPv4 private addresses, unique local addresses are routable within an organization. Administrators can also subnet them as needed to support an organization of any size.

The format of a unique local unicast address, as shown in Figure 6-9, is as follows:

- **Global ID** A 48-bit field beginning with an 8-bit FP of 11111101 in binary, or fd00::/8 in hexadecimal. The remaining 40 bits of the global ID are randomly generated.

- **Subnet ID** A 16-bit field that organizations can use to create an internal hierarchy of sites or subnets.

- **Interface ID** A 64-bit field identifying a specific interface on the network.

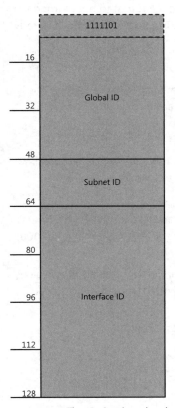

FIGURE 6-9 The IPv6 unique local unicast address format.

Because unique local addresses are not routable outside the organization, it is in most cases not essential for the global ID to be unique. In fact, because part of the global ID value is randomly generated, there is a remote possibility that two organizations might end up using the same value. However, the IPv6 standards make every attempt short of creating a central registrar to keep these identifiers unique. This is so that there are not likely to be addressing conflicts when organizations merge, when virtual private network (VPN) address spaces overlap, or when mobile computers connect to different enterprise networks.

> **NOTE SITE-LOCAL UNICASTS**
>
> Many sources of IPv6 information continue to list site-local unicast addresses as a valid type of unicast, with a function similar to that of the private IPv4 network addresses. Site-local addresses have an FP of 11111110 11 in binary, or fec0::/10 in hexadecimal. For various reasons, site-local unicast addresses have been deprecated, and although their use is not forbidden, their functionality has been replaced by unique local unicast addresses.

Special Addresses

There are two other IPv6 unicast addresses with special purposes, which correspond to equivalents in IPv4. The "loopback address" causes any messages sent to it to be returned to the sending system. In IPv6, the loopback address is 0:0:0:0:0:0:0:1, more commonly notated as follows.

`::1`

The other special address is 0:0:0:0:0:0:0:0, also known as the "unspecified address." This is the address a system uses while requesting an address assignment from a DHCP server.

Multicast Addresses

Multicast addresses always begin with an FP value of 11111111 in binary, or ff in hexadecimal. The entire multicast address format, as shown in Figure 6-10, is as follows:

- **FP** An 8-bit field that identifies the message as a multicast.
- **Flags** A 4-bit field that specifies whether the multicast address contains the address of a rendezvous point (0111), is based on a network prefix (0010), is permanent (0000), or is transient (0001).
- **Scope** A 4-bit field that specifies how widely routers can forward the address. Values include interface-local (0001), link-local (0010), site-local (0101), organization-local (1000), and global (1110).
- **Group ID** A 112-bit field uniquely identifying a multicast group.

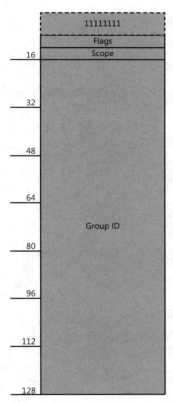

FIGURE 6-10 The IPv6 multicast address format.

Anycast Addresses

The function of an anycast address is to identify the routers within a given address scope and send traffic to the nearest router, as determined by the local routing protocols. Organizations can use anycast addresses to identify a particular set of routers in the enterprise, such as those that provide access to the Internet. To use anycasts, the routers must be configured to recognize the anycast addresses as such.

Anycast addresses do not have a special network identifier format; they are derived from any of the standard unicast formats and consist of the entire subnet identifier and an interface identifier set to all 0s. Thus, the scope of an anycast address is the same as that of the unicast address from which it is derived.

As an example, the anycast address for the sample network used earlier in this chapter would be as follows, with the first 64 bits serving as the subnet ID.

```
21cd:0053:0000:0000:0000:0000:0000:0000
```

IPv6 Address Assignment

As with IPv4, a computer can obtain an IPv6 address by three possible methods:

- **Manual allocation** A user or administrator manually types an address and other TCP/IP information into a configuration interface, such as the one from Windows Server 2008 R2 shown in Figure 6-11.

- **Self-allocation** The computer creates its own address using a process called stateless address autoconfiguration.

- **Dynamic allocation** The computer solicits and receives an address from a DHCPv6 server on the network.

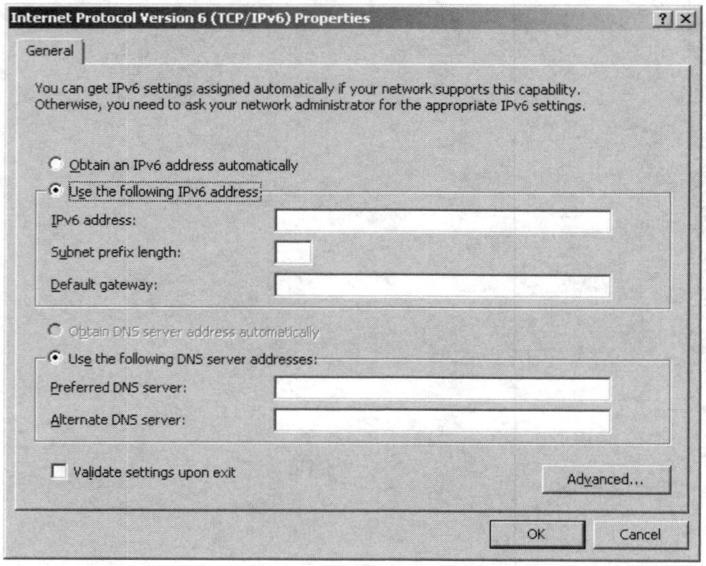

FIGURE 6-11 The Internet Protocol Version 6 (TCP/IPv6) Properties sheet.

For the enterprise administrator, manual address allocation is even more impractical than in IPv4 because of the length of the addresses involved. Therefore, the other two options are more prevalent.

Stateless Address Autoconfiguration

In most cases, when a computer supporting IPv6 starts, it initiates the *stateless address auto-configuration* process, during which it assigns each interface a link-local unicast address. This assignment always occurs, even when the interface is to receive a global unicast address later. The link-local address enables the system to communicate with the router on the link, which provides additional instructions.

The steps of the stateless address autoconfiguration process are as follows.

1. **Link-local address creation** The IPv6 implementation on the system creates a link-local address for each interface by using the fe80::/64 network address and generating an interface ID, either by using the interface's MAC address or a pseudorandom generator.

2. **Duplicate address detection** By using the IPv6 Neighbor Discovery (ND) protocol, the system transmits a Neighbor Solicitation message to determine if any other computer on the link is using the same address, and listens for a Neighbor Advertisement message sent in reply. If there is no reply, then the system considers the address to be unique on the link. If there is a reply, the system must generate a new address and repeat the procedure.

3. **Link-local address assignment** When the system determines that the link-local address is unique, it configures the interface to use that address. On a small network consisting of a single segment or link, this may be the interface's permanent address assignment. On a network with multiple subnets, the primary function of the link-local address assignment is to enable the system to communicate with a router on the link.

4. **Router advertisement solicitation** The system uses the ND protocol to transmit Router Solicitation messages to the All Routers multicast address. These messages compel routers to transmit the Router Advertisement messages more frequently.

5. **Router advertisement** The router on the link uses the ND protocol to transmit Router Advertisement messages to the system; these messages contain information on how the autoconfiguration process should proceed. The Router Advertisement messages typically supply a network prefix, which the system will use with its existing interface ID to create a global or unique local unicast address. The messages might also instruct the system to initiate a stateful autoconfiguration process by contacting a specific DHCPv6 server. If there is no router on the link, as determined by the system's failure to receive Router Advertisement messages, then the system must attempt to initiate a stateful autoconfiguration process.

6. **Global or unique local address configuration** Using the information it receives from the router, the system generates a suitable address—one that is routable, either globally or within the enterprise—and configures the interface to use it. If so instructed, the system might also initiate a stateful autoconfiguration process by contacting the DHCPv6 server specified by the router and obtaining a global or unique local address from that server, along with other configuration settings.

Using Stateful Autoconfiguration (DHCPv6)

For the enterprise administrator with a multisegment network, it will be necessary to use unique local or global addresses for internetwork communication, so either routers that advertise the appropriate network prefixes or DHCPv6 servers that can supply addresses with the correct prefixes will be required. DHCPv6 is the stateful counterpart to stateless address autoconfiguration and is widely implemented as part of existing DHCPv4 servers.

> **MORE INFO** **DYNAMIC HOST CONFIGURATION PROTOCOL**
>
> For more information about DHCPv6, see Chapter 9.

  Quick Check

1. Which type of IPv6 address do computers assign themselves during the stateless address autoconfiguration process?
2. What application/protocol provides clients with stateful IPv6 address allocation services?

Quick Check Answers

1. A link-local unicast address
2. DHCPv6

Data Encapsulation

Just as Ethernet packages network layer data for transmission over a LAN, IP encapsulates data that it receives from the transport layer protocols, such as Transmission Control Protocol (TCP) and User Datagram Protocol (UDP), for transmission to a destination. At the network layer, IP encapsulates data by adding a header, thus creating a *datagram* (also known as a packet), as shown in Figure 6-12.

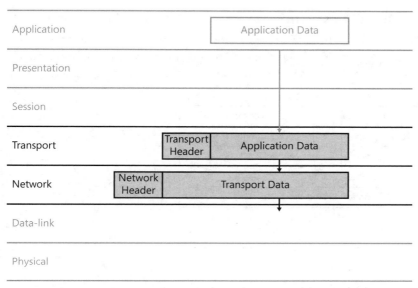

FIGURE 6-12 Transport layer data encapsulated in an IP datagram.

The IP datagram is addressed to the computer that will ultimately use the data, whether that computer is located on the local network or on another network far away. Except for a few minor modifications, the datagram remains intact throughout the packet's journey to its destination. After IP has created the datagram, it passes it down to a data-link layer protocol for transmission over the network.

> **NOTE PROTOCOL DATA UNITS**
>
> Protocols operating at different layers of the OSI reference model use different terms for the protocol data units (PDUs) they create. For example, network layer protocols create datagrams or packets, while data-link layer protocols create frames. The term "PDU" is layer-agnostic and can refer to the data structure created by any protocol.

During the transportation process, various routers might encapsulate a datagram in different data-link layer protocol frames, but the datagram itself remains intact. The process is similar to the delivery of a letter by the post office, with IP functioning as the envelope. The letter might be placed into different mailbags and transported by various trucks and planes during the course of its journey, but the envelope remains sealed. Only the addressee is permitted to open it and use the contents.

The IPv4 Datagram Format

The header that IPv4 applies to the data it receives from the transport layer protocol is typically 20 bytes long and contains information needed to send the datagram to its destination, just like an address on an envelope. The IPv4 datagram format is shown in Figure 6-13.

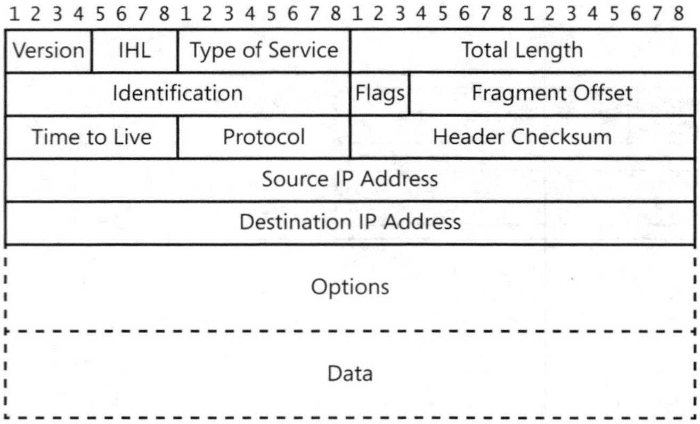

```
1 2 3 4 5 6 7 8 1 2 3 4 5 6 7 8 1 2 3 4 5 6 7 8 1 2 3 4 5 6 7 8
┌─────────┬───────┬──────────────┬──────────────────────────────┐
│ Version │  IHL  │Type of Service│         Total Length         │
├─────────┴───────┴──────┬───────┼──────────────────────────────┤
│     Identification      │ Flags │       Fragment Offset        │
├──────────────┬──────────┴───────┼──────────────────────────────┤
│ Time to Live │     Protocol     │       Header Checksum        │
├──────────────┴──────────────────┴──────────────────────────────┤
│                      Source IP Address                         │
├────────────────────────────────────────────────────────────────┤
│                    Destination IP Address                      │
├────────────────────────────────────────────────────────────────┤
┆                          Options                               ┆
├╌╌╌╌╌╌╌╌╌╌╌╌╌╌╌╌╌╌╌╌╌╌╌╌╌╌╌╌╌╌╌╌╌╌╌╌╌╌╌╌╌╌╌╌╌╌╌╌╌╌╌╌╌╌╌╌╌╌╌╌╌╌┤
┆                           Data                                 ┆
└╌╌╌╌╌╌╌╌╌╌╌╌╌╌╌╌╌╌╌╌╌╌╌╌╌╌╌╌╌╌╌╌╌╌╌╌╌╌╌╌╌╌╌╌╌╌╌╌╌╌╌╌╌╌╌╌╌╌╌╌╌╌┘
```

FIGURE 6-13 The IPv4 datagram format.

The IPv4 datagram fields perform the following functions:

- **Version (4 bits)** Specifies the version of the IP protocol used to create the datagram. The version currently in use on most networks is IPv4, but IPv6 is in the process of being deployed.

- **Internet Header Length (IHL, 4 bits)** Specifies the length of the datagram's header (exclusive of the Data field), in 32-bit (4-byte) words. The typical length of a datagram header is five words (20 bytes), but if the datagram includes additional options, it can be longer, which is the reason for the existence of this field.

- **Type of Service (1 byte)** Contains a code that specifies the service priority for the datagram. This is a feature that enables a system to assign a priority to a datagram that routers observe while forwarding it through an internetwork.

- **Total Length (2 bytes)** Specifies the length of the entire datagram, including the Data field and all of the header fields, in bytes.

- **Identification (2 bytes)** Contains a value that uniquely identifies the datagram. The destination system uses this value, along with the contents of the Flags and Fragment Offset fields, to reassemble datagrams that have been fragmented during transmission.

- **Flags (3 bits)** Contains bits used to regulate the datagram fragmentation process, as follows:
  - **Bit 1** Unused.
  - **Bit 2** Don't fragment. When this bit has a value of 1, systems receiving the datagram are instructed never to fragment it.

- **Bit 3**   More fragments. A value of 0 for this bit notifies the receiving system that the last fragment of the datagram has been transmitted. A value of 1 for this bit indicates that there are still more fragments to be transmitted.

- **Fragment Offset (13 bits)**   When a datagram is fragmented, this field contains a value (in 8-byte units) that identifies the fragment's place in the datagram.

- **Time to Live (TTL, 1 byte)**   Specifies the number of networks that the datagram should be permitted to travel through on the way to its destination. Each router that forwards the datagram reduces the value of this field by 1. If the value reaches 0, the datagram is discarded. This mechanism prevents packets from circulating endlessly due to routing errors. The value currently recommended by the IANA for the Time To Live field is 64, but many IP implementations use larger values.

- **Protocol (1 byte)**   Contains a code identifying the protocol that generated the information found in the Data field, as follows:

  - **1**   Internet Control Message Protocol (ICMP)

  - **2**   Internet Group Management Protocol (IGMP)

  - **6**   Transmission Control Protocol (TCP)

  - **17**   User Datagram Protocol (UDP)

- **Header Checksum (2 bytes)**   Contains a checksum value computed on the IP header fields only (not on the contents of the Data field) for the purpose of error detection.

- **Source IP Address (4 bytes)**   Specifies the IP address of the system that generated the datagram.

- **Destination IP Address (4 bytes)**   Specifies the IP address of the system for which the datagram is destined.

- **Options (variable)**   Present only when the datagram contains one or more of the 16 available IP options (discussed in the next section). The size and content of the field depend on the number and the nature of the options.

- **Data (variable)**   Contains the information generated by the protocol specified in the Protocol field, which is usually a transport layer protocol. The size of the field depends on the data-link layer protocol used by the network over which the system will transmit the datagram.

IPv4 Options

IPv4 options are additional header fields that enable datagrams to carry extra information and, in some cases, to accumulate information as they travel through an internetwork on the way to their destinations. To include options, the datagram contains an additional subheader, as shown in Figure 6-14.

```
1 2 3 4 5 6 7 8 1 2 3 4 5 6 7 8 1 2 3 4 5 6 7 8 1 2 3 4 5 6 7 8
```

Option Type	Option Length	Option Data

FIGURE 6-14 The IP option subheader.

The functions of the fields in the IP option subheader are as follows:

- **Option Type (1 byte)**   Contains three subfields that specify the function of the option, as follows:

  - **Copied Flag (1 bit)**   When the datagram is fragmented, this flag specifies whether the option should be copied to each fragment.

  - **Option Class (2 bits)**   Specifies the basic function of the option. A value of 0 indicates a control option, and a value of 2 indicates a debugging and measurement option.

  - **Option Number (5 bits)**   Contains a number uniquely identifying the option, assigned and published by the IANA.

- **Option Length (1 byte)**   Specifies the total length of the option subheader, including the Option Type, Option Length, and Option Data fields.

- **Option Data (Option Length value minus 2)**   Contains option-specific information to be delivered to the destination system.

> **MORE INFO   IP OPTIONS**
>
> The current list of IP options is available at *http://www.iana.org/assignments/ip-parameters*.

Table 6-3 contains some of the most commonly used IP options, along with the values for their Option Type subfields and an option value that is often used to identify the option. All the options listed in this table are defined in RFC 791, but other options are defined in various other RFCs.

TABLE 6-3 Commonly Used IP Options

Copied Flag	Option Class	Option Number	Option Value	Option Name	Designation
0	0	0	0	End of Options List	EOOL
0	0	1	1	No Operation	NOP
1	0	3	131	Loose Source Routing	LSR
0	2	4	68	Internet Timestamp	TS
0	0	7	7	Record Route	RR
1	0	9	137	Strict Source Routing	SSR

The functions of the options listed in the table are as follows:

- **End of Options List (EOOL)**   Functions as a delimiter that indicates the end of the Options field in a datagram. When a datagram includes multiple options, there is only one EOOL option included, not one for each option. EOOL is one of two options that consists only of an Option Type field. There is no Option Length or Option Data field in this option.

- **No Operation (NOP)**   Functions as a padding byte between options to align the beginning of the subsequent option on the boundary of a 32-bit word. As with EOOL, the NOP option consists only of an Option Type field.

- **Loose Source Routing (LSR)**   Provides a means for a sending system to include routing information in a datagram. In the LSR option, the Option Data field contains a pointer plus the IP addresses of selected gateways on the internetwork that the datagram must pass through on the way to its destination. The pointer contains a value (in number of bytes relative to the beginning of the option) that indicates which IP address in the option field should be processed next. In loose source routing the datagram must be processed by the specified gateways, but it can also pass through other gateways. For security reasons, many Internet routers on the Internet block packets containing the loose source routing option.

- **Internet Timestamp (TS)**   Provides a means for gateways to add time stamps indicating when they processed the datagram. In the TS option the Option Data field contains the following subfields:

    - **Pointer (1 byte)**   Specifies the location (in number of bytes relative to the beginning of the option) where the next time stamp should be recorded.

    - **Overflow (4 bits)**   Specifies the number of gateways that can't record their time stamps because the Option Data field is full. The size of the Option Data field for the TS option specified by the sending system must be sufficient to hold all of the expected time stamp information, because this field can't be expanded while the datagram is en route.

    - **Flag (4 bits)**   Specifies the nature of the information stored in the rest of the Option Data field. A value of 0 indicates that the field contains 32-bit time stamps only. A value of 1 indicates that each time stamp is preceded by the IP address of the gateway that added it. A value of 3 indicates that the IP addresses of the gateways that are to record their time stamps are already specified in the Option Data field.

    - **IP Addresses/Timestamps**   Contains the time stamp information (or IP address and time stamp information, depending on the value of the Flag field) recorded by the gateways processing the datagram.

- **Record Route (RR)**   Provides a means for a datagram to record the IP addresses of the gateways processing the packet on the way to its destination. In the RR option, the Option Data field initially contains a pointer specifying the location (in number of bytes relative to the beginning of the option) where the next gateway address should be written. As the datagram travels through the internetwork, each gateway system adds its IP address to the Option Data field and increments the value of the pointer by 4.

- **Strict Source Routing (SSR)**   Provides a means for a sending system to include routing information in a datagram. In the SSR option, the Option Data field contains a pointer, and the field also must contain the IP addresses of all gateways on the internetwork that the datagram must pass through on the way to its destination. The pointer contains a value (in number of bytes relative to the beginning of the option) that indicates which IP address in the option field should be processed next. In strict source routing, the datagram must include a complete route to the destination, because no gateways other than those specified in the datagram are permitted to process the packet.

EXAM TIP

Although knowledge of specific IP options is not required for the Network+ exam, it is important to understand how IPv4 expands its capabilities by using options, especially as compared with IPv6. The appearance of options in IP packets is also useful in network monitoring and protocol analysis, as discussed later in Chapter 12, "Network Management."

The IPv6 Datagram Format

In version 6 of IP, the header is necessarily different, to accommodate the larger addresses. A typical IPv6 header is 40 bytes long, as opposed to the 20 bytes of an IPv4 header. There are also some changes to the functions the header performs. For example, in IPv6, intermediate systems—that is, routers—no longer perform fragmentation on IP datagrams while they are en route. All fragmentation is performed by end systems, so the datagram no longer includes the header fields used in the fragmentation process.

The IPv6 datagram format is shown in Figure 6-15.

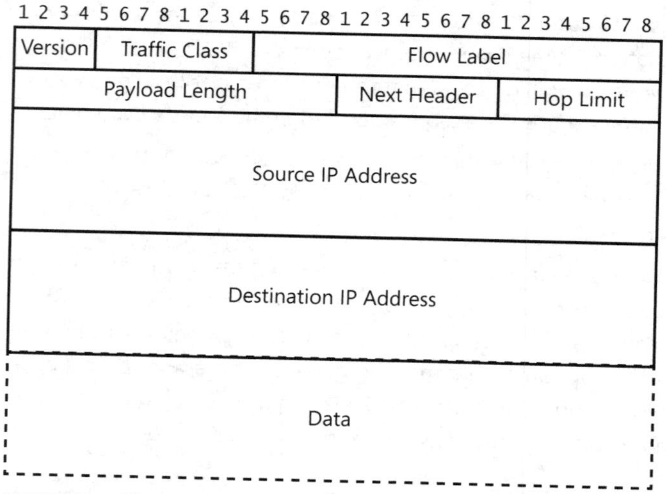

1 2 3 4 5 6 7 8 1 2 3 4 5 6 7 8 1 2 3 4 5 6 7 8 1 2 3 4 5 6 7 8

Version	Traffic Class		Flow Label	
Payload Length			Next Header	Hop Limit
Source IP Address				
Destination IP Address				
Data				

FIGURE 6-15 The IPv6 datagram format.

The functions of the IPv6 datagram fields are as follows:

- **Version (4 bits)**   Specifies the version of the IP protocol used to create the datagram. The version currently in use on most networks is IPv4, but IPv6 is in the process of being deployed.

- **Traffic Class (1 byte)**   The first 6 bits contain a Differentiated Services Codepoint (DSCP) value that specifies the per-hop behavior (PHB) for the packet at each network node along its path. This field replaces the Type Of Services value in the IPv4 header. The remaining two bits are reserved for an optional feature called explicit congestion notification (ECN).

- **Flow Label (20 bits)**   Used to contain a value that identifies the packet as part of a flow—that is, a real-time sequence of packets sent from a particular source to a particular destination. Labeling a flow enables an IPv6 implementation to provide it with special services complementing its real-time nature. Specific applications for the field are currently emerging.

- **Payload Length (2 bytes)**   Specifies the size of the payload in the packet in bytes, including any extension headers.

- **Next Header (1 byte)**   Identifies the protocol that generated the next header in the packet after the IPv6 header. In most circumstances, this will be the transport layer protocol that generated the data in the packet. However, if there are extension headers in the packet, this value will identify the source of the first extension header. The values are the same as those used for the Protocol field in the IPv4 packet.

- **Hop Limit (1 byte)**   Just like the Time To Live field in the IPv4 header, specifies the number of networks that the datagram should be permitted to travel through on the way to its destination. Each router that forwards the datagram reduces the value of this field by 1. If the value reaches 0, the datagram is discarded. This mechanism prevents packets from circulating endlessly due to routing errors.

- **Source IP Address (128 bits)**   Specifies the IPv6 address of the system that generated the datagram.

- **Destination IP Address (128 bits)**   Specifies the IPv6 address of the system for which the datagram is destined.

- **Data (variable)**   Contains the information generated by the protocol specified in the Next Header field, usually a transport layer protocol. The size of the field depends on the data-link layer protocol used by the network over which the system will transmit the datagram.

IPv6 Extension Headers

As with IPv4, IPv6 provides a means of extending the functionality of the protocol by adding subheaders that implement options or external protocols. IPv6 recognizes the presence of additional headers by using a chain of references that begins in the IPv6 Next Header field.

Unlike the IPv4 Protocol field, which specifies the protocol that generated the data in the packet, the Next Header field identifies the program or protocol that generated the header immediately following the IPv6 header. In a packet without any additional options, the Next Header value identifies the protocol in the Data field, which is usually TCP or UDP. When a packet does contain options, the Next Header field identifies the protocol that generated the subheader immediately following the IPv6 header. Each of the permitted subheaders has a Next Header field of its own, which it uses to identify the next subheader. A packet can carry multiple extension headers, the last of which must eventually identify the TCP or UDP header for the packet's original payload.

The extension headers supported by IPv6 are listed in Table 6-4.

TABLE 6-4 Extension Headers for IPv6 Datagrams

Next Header Value	Extension Header	Description
0	Hop-by-hop Options	Contains one or more IPv6 options that must be examined by the end nodes and every intermediate node on the path to the packet's destination
43	Routing	Contains a list of one or more intermediate nodes that must process the packet on the way to its destination
44	Fragment	Used by end nodes to transmit a packet larger than would fit in the path maximum transmission unit (MTU) to its destination
50	Encapsulating Security Payload (ESP)	IPsec protocol that secures upper-layer protocol information by using encryption
51	Authentication Header (AH)	IPsec protocol that secures upper-layer protocol data by using digital signatures and authentication
59	No Next Header	Indicates that the packet contains nothing at all beyond the current header, not even an upper-layer protocol header
60	Destination Options	Contains one or more IPv6 options that must be examined only by the destination node on the packet's path

The formats of the extension headers themselves vary depending on their functions. All extension headers must be a multiple of 8 bytes in size and are padded to reach the required length.

The two extension headers designed to carry IPv6 options—Hop-by-hop Options and Destination Options—themselves contain one or more option headers similar to those used by IPv4. Each option has 8-bit Option Type and Option Data Length fields, and a variable-length Option Data field.

The result of this arrangement is a far more flexible and extensible packet format than was defined in IPv6.

IPv4 Fragmentation

The size of the IP datagrams used to transmit the transport-layer data depends on the data-link layer protocol in use. Ethernet networks, for example, can carry datagrams up to 1,500 bytes in size. The system transmitting the datagram uses the *maximum transmission unit (MTU)* of the connected network—that is, the largest possible frame that the data-link layer protocol is capable of transmitting—as one factor in determining how large each datagram should be.

During the course of its journey from the source to the destination, an IPv4 packet might encounter networks with different MTUs. As long as the MTU of each network is larger than the packet, intermediate IPv4 routers will transmit the datagram without a problem. If a packet is larger than the MTU of a network, however, an IPv4 router cannot transmit the packet in its current form. When this occurs, the IPv4 protocol in the router providing access to the network is responsible for splitting the datagram into fragments smaller than the MTU. The router then transmits each fragment in a separate packet with its own header.

Depending on the number and nature of the networks it passes through, a datagram may be fragmented more than once before it reaches the destination. A router might split a datagram into fragments that are themselves too large for networks further along in the path. Another router, therefore, will split the fragments into still smaller fragments. Reassembly of a fragmented datagram takes place only at the destination system after it has received all of the packets containing the fragments, not at the intermediate routers.

When a router receives a datagram that it must fragment, it creates a series of new packets by using the same value for the IP header's Identification field as the original datagram. The other fields of the header are the same as well, with three important exceptions, as follows:

- The router changes the value of the Total Length field to reflect the size of the fragment, instead of the size of the entire datagram.
- The router changes bit 3 of the Flags field, the More Fragments bit, to a value of 1 to indicate that further fragments are to be transmitted, except in the case of the datagram's last fragment, in which this bit is set to a value of 0.
- The router changes the value of the Fragment Offset field to reflect each fragment's place in the datagram, based on the size of the fragments (which is, in turn, based on the MTU of the network across which the fragments are to be transmitted). The value for the first fragment is 0; the next is incremented by the size of the fragment, in bytes.

> **NOTE DATAGRAMS AND FRAGMENTS**
>
> Technically speaking, an IPv4 datagram is defined as the unit of data, packaged by the source system, containing a specific value in the IPv4 header's Identification field. When a router fragments a datagram, it uses the same Identification value for each new packet it creates, meaning that the individual fragments are collectively known as a datagram. Referring to a single fragment as a datagram (although a common practice) is an incorrect use of the term.

These changes to the IPv4 header are necessary for the destination system to properly reassemble the fragments. The router transmits the fragments like any other packets, and because IP is a connectionless protocol, the individual fragments might take different routes to the destination and arrive in a different order. The receiving system uses the More Fragments bit to determine when it should begin the reassembly process, and the Fragment Offset field to assemble the fragments in the proper order.

Selecting the size of the fragments is left up to individual IPv4 implementations. Typically, the size of each fragment is the MTU of the network over which it must be transmitted, minus the size of the data-link and IPv4 protocol headers, and rounded down to the nearest 8 bytes. Some systems, however, automatically create 576-byte fragments, because this is the default path MTU used by many routers.

Fragmentation is not desirable, but it is a necessary evil. Obviously, because fragmenting a datagram creates many packets out of one packet, it increases the control overhead incurred by the transmission process. Also, if one fragment of a datagram is lost or damaged, all of the datagram fragments must be retransmitted. No means of reproducing and retransmitting a single fragment exists, because the source system has no knowledge of the fragmentation performed by the intermediate routers. The IPv4 implementation on the destination system does not pass the incoming data up to the transport layer until all the fragments have arrived and have been reassembled. The transport-layer protocol must therefore detect the missing data and arrange for the retransmission of the datagram.

IPv6 Fragmentation

IPv6 requires that all of the individual networks on the Internet have a maximum transmission unit value of at least 1,280 bytes. For networks with a configurable MTU, such as Point-to-Point Protocol links, IPv6 recommends an MTU of 1,500 bytes or more. The object of these increased packet size requirements is to allow as many packets as possible to pass through an internetwork path without resorting to fragmentation at the network layer.

IPv6 does not support hop-by-hop datagram fragmentation as IPv4 does. Any fragmentation required must be performed by the source end node, and reassembly must be done by the destination end node. For this to occur, the nodes on the network must support a technique called Path MTU Discovery (as defined in RFC 1981), which enables an end system to determine the path MTU for a particular route.

When necessary, IPv6 fragmentation is implemented as an extension header with a Next Header value of 44. The Fragment extension header contains values similar to those that IPv4 uses for fragmentation, including a Fragment Offset, an Identification value, and a Last Fragment flag. This is the information that the destination node will need to reassemble the fragments.

IP Routing

Routing is a critical function of the Internet Protocol. It is the means by which packets find their way around the vastness of the Internet and locate a single destination system among millions. For more information on routing and routing protocols, see Chapter 7.

 Quick Check

1. How does IPv6 minimize the amount of fragmentation that occurs on a network?

2. The function of the Protocol field in the IPv4 header is replaced by what field in the IPv6 header?

Quick Check Answers

1. By requiring that all of the individual networks on the Internet have a maximum transmission unit value of at least 1,280 bytes

2. The Next Header field

Internet Control Message Protocol (ICMP)

 The *Internet Control Message Protocol (ICMP)* is a network layer protocol that does not carry user data, although its messages are encapsulated in IP datagrams. ICMP fills two roles in the TCP/IP suite; it provides error reporting functions, informing the sending system when a transmission cannot reach its destination, for example, and it carries query and response messages for diagnostic programs. The Ping utility, for instance, which is included in every TCP/IP implementation, uses ICMP echo messages to determine if another system on the network is able to receive and send data.

 EXAM TIP

ICMP, apart from appearing in the Network+ objectives, is also the basis for some of the most essential TCP/IP troubleshooting tools, including Ping and Traceroute. Candidates for the exam should be familiar with these, as well as other functions of ICMP.

ICMPv4

The ICMP protocol, as defined in RFC 792, consists of messages that are carried in IPv4 datagrams, with a value of 1 in the IPv4 header's Protocol field and 0 in the Type of Service field. Since the introduction of ICMPv6, a new version of the protocol designed for use with IPv6 traffic, the original version of ICMP has unofficially become known as ICMPv4.

ICMPv4 Message Format

The ICMPv4 message format is illustrated in Figure 6-16 and consists of the following fields:

- **Type (1 byte)** Contains a code identifying the basic function of the message
- **Code (1 byte)** Contains a secondary code identifying the function of the message within a specific type
- **Checksum (2 bytes)** Contains the results of a checksum computation on the entire ICMP message, including the Type, Code, Checksum, and Data fields (with a value of 0 in the Checksum field for computation purposes)
- **Data (variable)** Contains information specific to the function of the message

```
1 2 3 4 5 6 7 8 1 2 3 4 5 6 7 8 1 2 3 4 5 6 7 8 1 2 3 4 5 6 7 8
┌───────────────┬───────────────┬───────────────────────────────┐
│     Type      │     Code      │           Checksum            │
├───────────────┴───────────────┴───────────────────────────────┤
┆                            Data                                ┆
└────────────────────────────────────────────────────────────────┘
```

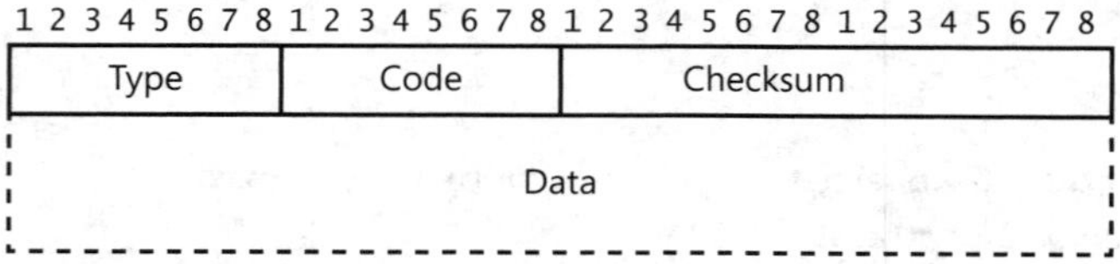

FIGURE 6-16 The ICMPv4 message format.

The ICMPv4 message types are listed in Table 6-5.

TABLE 6-5 ICMPv4 Message Types

Type	Code	Query/ Error	Function
0	0	Q	Echo Reply
3	0	E	Net Unreachable
3	1	E	Host Unreachable
3	2	E	Protocol Unreachable
3	3	E	Port Unreachable
3	4	E	Fragmentation Needed and Don't Fragment Was Set
3	5	E	Source Route Failed
3	6	E	Destination Network Unknown
3	7	E	Destination Host Unknown
3	8	E	Source Host Isolated
3	9	E	Communication with Destination Network is Administratively Prohibited
3	10	E	Communication with Destination Host is Administratively Prohibited
3	11	E	Destination Network Unreachable for Type of Service

Type	Code	Query/Error	Function
3	12	E	Destination Host Unreachable for Type of Service
4	0	E	Source Quench
5	0	E	Redirect Datagram for the Network (or Subnet)
5	1	E	Redirect Datagram for the Host
5	2	E	Redirect Datagram for the Type of Service and Network
5	3	E	Redirect Datagram for the Type of Service and Host
8	0	Q	Echo Request
9	0	Q	Router Advertisement
10	0	Q	Router Solicitation
11	0	E	Time to Live Exceeded in Transit
11	1	E	Fragment Reassembly Time Exceeded
12	0	E	Pointer Indicates the Error
12	1	E	Missing a Required Option
12	2	E	Bad Length
13	0	Q	Timestamp
14	0	Q	Timestamp Reply
15	0	Q	Information Request
16	0	Q	Information Reply
17	0	Q	Address Mask Request
18	0	Q	Address Mask Reply
30	0	Q	Traceroute
31	0	E	Datagram Conversion Error
32	0	E	Mobile Host Redirect
33	0	Q	IPv6 Where-are-you
34	0	Q	IPv6 I-am-here
35	0	Q	Mobile Registration Request
36	0	Q	Mobile Registration Reply

ICMPv4 Error Messages

Because of the way that TCP/IP networks distribute routing chores among various systems, there is no way for either of the end systems involved in a transmission to know what has happened during a packet's journey. IP is a connectionless protocol, so there are no acknowledgment messages returned to the sender at that level. When using a connection-oriented protocol at the transport layer, such as TCP, the destination system acknowledges transmissions, but only for the packets that it receives. If something happens during the transmission process that prevents the packet from reaching the destination, there is no way for IP or TCP to inform the sender what happened.

ICMP error messages are designed to fill this void. When an intermediate system such as a router has trouble processing a packet, it typically discards it, leaving it to the upper-layer protocols to detect its absence and arrange for a retransmission. ICMP messages enable the router to inform the sender of the exact nature of the problem. Destination systems can also generate ICMP messages when a packet arrives successfully but cannot be processed.

The Data field of an ICMPv4 error message always contains the IPv4 header of the datagram that the system could not process, plus the first 8 bytes of the datagram's own Data field. In most cases, these 8 bytes will contain a UDP header or the beginning of a TCP header, including the source and destination ports and the sequence number (in the case of TCP). This enables the system receiving the error message to isolate the exact time that the error occurred and the transmission that caused it.

However, ICMPv4 error messages are informational only. The system receiving them does not respond, nor does it necessarily take any action to correct the situation. It might be left up to the user or administrator to address the problem that is causing the failure.

In general, all TCP/IP systems are free to transmit ICMPv4 error messages, except in certain specific situations. These exceptions are intended to prevent ICMPv4 from generating too much traffic on the network by transmitting large numbers of identical messages. These exceptional situations are as follows:

- TCP/IP systems do not generate ICMPv4 error messages in response to other ICMPv4 error messages. Without this exception, it would be possible for two systems to bounce error messages back and forth between them endlessly. Systems can generate ICMPv4 errors in response to ICMPv4 queries, however.

- In the case of a fragmented datagram, a system only generates an ICMPv4 error message for the first fragment.

- TCP/IP systems never generate ICMPv4 error messages in response to broadcast or multicast transmissions, transmissions with a source IP address of 0.0.0.0, or transmissions addressed to the loopback address.

The following sections examine the most common types of ICMPv4 error messages and their functions.

DESTINATION UNREACHABLE MESSAGES

ICMPv4 Destination Unreachable messages have a value of 3 in the Type field and any one of 13 values in the Code field. As the name implies, these messages indicate that a packet or the information in a packet could not be transmitted to its destination. The various messages specify exactly which component was unreachable and, in some cases, why. This type of message can be generated by a router when it cannot forward a packet to a certain network or to the destination system on one of its connected networks. Destination systems themselves can also generate these messages when they cannot deliver the contents of the packet to a specific protocol or host.

In most cases, the error is a result of some type of failure, either temporary or permanent, in a computer or the network medium. However, it is also possible for these errors to occur as a result of IPv4 options that prevent the transmission of the packet, such as when datagrams must be fragmented for transmission over a specific network and the Don't Fragment flag in the IPv4 header is set.

THE SOURCE QUENCH MESSAGE

The source quench message, with a Type value of 4 and a Code value of 0, functions as an elementary form of flow control by informing a transmitting system that it is sending packets too fast. When the receiver's buffers are in danger of being overfilled, the system can transmit a source quench message to the sender, which slows down its transmission rate as a result. The sender should continue to reduce the rate until it is no longer receiving the messages from the receiver.

This is a very basic form of flow control that is reasonably effective for use between systems on the same network, but which generates too much additional traffic on routed internetworks. In most cases, it is not needed, because TCP provides its own flow control mechanism.

REDIRECT MESSAGES

Redirect messages are generated only by routers, to inform hosts or other routers of better routes to a particular destination. In the network diagram shown in Figure 6-17, a host on Network A transmits a packet to another host on Network B and uses Router 1 as the destination of its first hop. After consulting its routing table, Router 1 determines that the packet should be sent to Router 2, but also realizes that Router 2 is located on the same network as the original transmitting host.

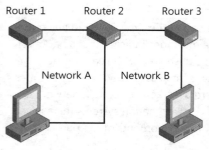

FIGURE 6-17 Packets transmitted to a host on another network can often take any one of multiple routes to the destination.

Because it would be more efficient for the host to send the packets intended for that destination directly to Router 2, Router 1 sends a Redirect Datagram for the Network message (type 5, code 0) to the transmitting host after it forwards the original packet to Router 2. The redirect message contains the usual IPv4 header and partial data information, as well as the IPv4 address of the router that the host should use for its future transmissions to that network.

In this example, the redirect message indicates that the host should use the other router for the packets it will transmit to all hosts on Network B in the future. The other redirect messages (with codes 1 through 3) enable the router to specify an alternative router for transmissions to the specific host, to the specific host with the same Type of Service value, and to the entire network with the same Type of Service value.

TIME EXCEEDED MESSAGES

Time exceeded messages are used to inform a transmitting system that a packet has been discarded because a timeout has elapsed. The Time to Live Exceeded in Transit message (Type 11, Code 0) indicates that The Time-to-Live value in a packet's IPv4 header has reached 0 before arriving at the destination, forcing the router to discard it.

It is this message that enables the TCP/IP Traceroute program to display the route through the network that packets take to a given destination. By transmitting a series of packets with incremented values in the Time To Live field, each successive router on the path to the destination discards a packet and returns an ICMPv4 time exceeded message to the source.

> ***MORE INFO*** **TRACEROUTE**
>
> For more information on Traceroute, see Chapter 13, "Network Troubleshooting."

The Fragment Reassembly Time Exceeded message (Code 1) indicates that a destination system has not received all of the fragments of a specific datagram within the time limit specified by the host. As a result, the system must discard all of the fragments that it has received and return the error message to the sender.

ICMPv4 Query Messages

ICMPv4 query messages are not generated in response to other activities, as are the error messages. Systems use them for self-contained request/reply transactions in which one computer requests information from another, which responds with a reply containing that information.

Because they are not associated with other IP transmissions, ICMPv4 queries do not contain datagram information in their Data fields. The data they do carry is specific to the function of the message. The following sections examine some of the most common ICMPv4 query messages and their functions.

ECHO REQUESTS AND REPLIES

Echo Request and Echo Reply messages are the basis for the TCP/IP Ping utility, which sends test messages to another host on the network to determine if it is capable of receiving and responding to messages. Each ping consists of an ICMPv4 Echo Request message (Type 8, Code 0) that, in addition to the standard ICMPv4 Type, Code, and Checksum fields, adds Identifier and Sequence Number fields that the systems use to associate requests and replies. Packet captures of a typical request and reply exchange are shown in Figure 6-18 and Figure 6-19.

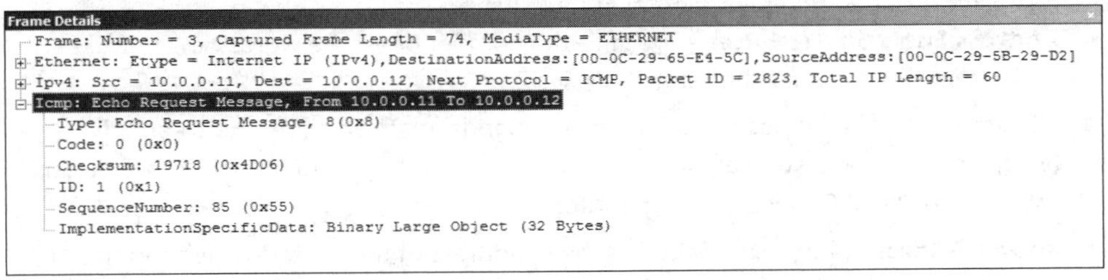

```
Frame Details                                                                                    ×
 ─ Frame: Number = 3, Captured Frame Length = 74, MediaType = ETHERNET
 ⊞ Ethernet: Etype = Internet IP (IPv4),DestinationAddress:[00-0C-29-65-E4-5C],SourceAddress:[00-0C-29-5B-29-D2]
 ⊞ Ipv4: Src = 10.0.0.11, Dest = 10.0.0.12, Next Protocol = ICMP, Packet ID = 2823, Total IP Length = 60
 ⊟ Icmp: Echo Request Message, From 10.0.0.11 To 10.0.0.12
    ─ Type: Echo Request Message, 8(0x8)
    ─ Code: 0 (0x0)
    ─ Checksum: 19718 (0x4D06)
    ─ ID: 1 (0x1)
    ─ SequenceNumber: 85 (0x55)
    ─ ImplementationSpecificData: Binary Large Object (32 Bytes)
```

FIGURE 6-18 An ICMPv4 Echo Request message.

```
Frame Details                                                                                    ×
 ─ Frame: Number = 4, Captured Frame Length = 74, MediaType = ETHERNET
 ⊞ Ethernet: Etype = Internet IP (IPv4),DestinationAddress:[00-0C-29-5B-29-D2],SourceAddress:[00-0C-29-65-E4-5C]
 ⊞ Ipv4: Src = 10.0.0.12, Dest = 10.0.0.11, Next Protocol = ICMP, Packet ID = 464, Total IP Length = 60
 ⊟ Icmp: Echo Reply Message, From 10.0.0.12 To 10.0.0.11
    ─ Type: Echo Reply Message, 0(0)
    ─ Code: 0 (0x0)
    ─ Checksum: 21766 (0x5506)
    ─ ID: 1 (0x1)
    ─ SequenceNumber: 85 (0x55)
    ─ ImplementationSpecificData: Binary Large Object (32 Bytes)
```

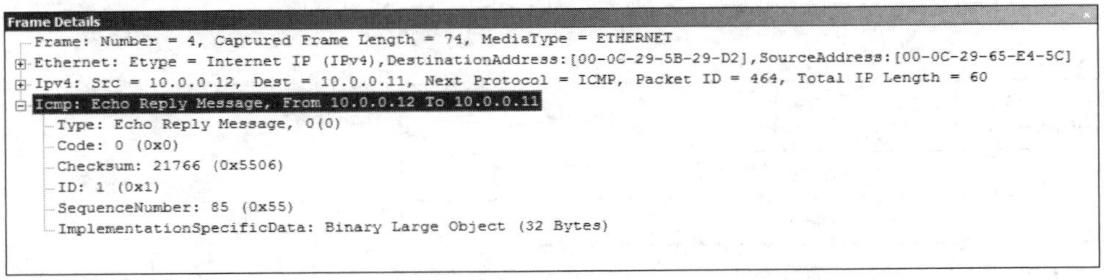

FIGURE 6-19 An ICMPv4 Echo Reply message.

If the system receiving the message is functioning normally, it reverses the source and destination IP address fields in the IP header, changes the value of the Type field to 8 (Echo Reply), and recomputes the checksum before transmitting it back to the sender.

MORE INFO PING

For more information on Ping, see Chapter 13.

ROUTER SOLICITATIONS AND ADVERTISEMENTS

These messages make it possible for a host system to discover the addresses of the routers connected to the local network. Systems can use this information to configure the default gateway entry in their routing tables. When a host broadcasts or multicasts a Router Solicitation message (Type 10, Code 0), the routers on the network respond with Router Advertisement messages (Type 9, Code 0). Routers continue to advertise their availability at regular intervals (typically 7 to 10 minutes). A host might stop using a router as its default gateway if it fails to receive continued advertisements.

The Router Solicitation message consists only of the standard Type, Code, and Checksum fields, plus a 4-byte pad in the Data field. The Router Advertisement message format is shown in Figure 6-20 and contains the following additional fields:

- **Number of Addresses (1 byte)**   Specifies the number of router addresses contained in the message. The format can support multiple addresses, each of which will have its own Router Address and Preference Level fields.

- **Address Entry Size (1 byte)**   Specifies the number of 4-byte words devoted to each address in the message. The value is always 2.

- **Lifetime (2 bytes)**   Specifies the time, in seconds, that can elapse between advertisements before a system assumes that a router is no longer functioning. The default value is usually 1,800 seconds (30 minutes).

- **Router Address (4 bytes)**   Specifies the IP address of the router generating the advertisement message.

- **Preference Level (4 bytes)**   Contains a value specified by the network administrator that host systems can use to select one router over another.

1 2 3 4 5 6 7 8	1 2 3 4 5 6 7 8	1 2 3 4 5 6 7 8 1 2 3 4 5 6 7 8
Number of Addresses	Address Entry Size	Lifetime
Router Address		
Preference Level		

FIGURE 6-20 The Router Advertisement message format.

ICMPv6

IPv6 has its own version of ICMP, which is defined in RFC 4443, "Internet Control Message Protocol (*ICMPv6*) for the Internet Protocol Version 6 (IPv6) Specification." The newer version of the protocol uses the same message format, and functions in much the same way. The primary difference is in the Type and Code values for the various messages. There are also some important new message types.

As with ICMPv4, ICMPv6 messages are carried within IP datagrams. A datagram carrying an ICMPv6 message must have the value 58 in the IPv6 Next Header field. The Type and Code values for the standard ICMPv6 messages are listed in Table 6-6.

TABLE 6-6 ICMPv6 Message Types

Type	Code	Info/Error	Function
1	0	E	No route to destination
1	1	E	Communication with destination administratively prohibited
1	2	E	Beyond scope of source address
1	3	E	Address unreachable
1	4	E	Port unreachable
1	5	E	Source address failed ingress/egress policy
1	6	E	Reject route to destination
1	7	E	Error in source routing header
2	0	E	Packet too big
3	0	E	Hop limit exceeded in transit
3	1	E	Fragment reassembly time exceeded
4	0	E	Erroneous header field encountered
4	1	E	Unrecognized next header type encountered
5	2	E	Unrecognized IPv6 option encountered
128	0	I	Echo Request
129	0	I	Echo Reply
130	0	I	Multicast Listener Query
131	0	I	Multicast Listener Report
132	0	I	Multicast Listener Done
133	0	I	Router Solicitation (NDP)
134	0	I	Router Advertisement (NDP)
135	0	I	Neighbor Solicitation (NDP)
136	0	I	Neighbor Advertisement (NDP)

Type	Code	Info/Error	Function
137	1	I	Redirect Message (NDP)
138	0	I	Router Renumbering Command
138	1	I	Router Renumbering Result
138	255	I	Sequence Number Reset
139	0	I	ICMP Node Information Query - The Data field contains an IPv6 address which is the Subject of this Query
139	1	I	ICMP Node Information Query - The Data field contains a name which is the Subject of this Query, or is empty, as in the case of a NOOP.
139	2	I	ICMP Node Information Query - The Data field contains an IPv4 address which is the Subject of this Query.
140	0	I	ICMP Node Information Response - A successful reply. The Reply Data field may or may not be empty.
140	1	I	ICMP Node Information Response - The Responder refuses to supply the answer. The Reply Data field will be empty.
140	2	I	ICMP Node Information Response - The Qtype of the Query is unknown to the Responder. The Reply Data field will be empty.
141	0	I	Inverse Neighbor Discovery Solicitation Message
142	0	I	Inverse Neighbor Discovery Advertisement Message
144	0	I	Home Agent Address Discovery Request Message
145	0	I	Home Agent Address Discovery Reply Message
146	0	I	Mobile Prefix Solicitation
147	0	I	Mobile Prefix Advertisement

Chief among the additions in ICMPv6 is the *Neighbor Discovery (ND) protocol,* a new data-link layer protocol that performs multiple functions, including the following:

- Local network system discovery
- Hardware address resolution
- Duplicate address detection
- Router discovery
- Domain Name System (DNS) server discovery
- Address prefix discovery
- Neighbor unreachability detection

In these roles, NDP replaces the Address Resolution Protocol (ARP) and the ICMPv4 Router Advertisement and Router Redirect messages.

> ✔ **Quick Check**
>
> 1. Which ICMPv4 message types are generated by the Ping utility?
> 2. What protocol implemented in ICMPv6 replaces the Address Resolution Protocol used by IPv4?
>
> **Quick Check Answers**
>
> 1. Echo Request and Echo Reply
> 2. Neighbor Discovery Protocol

Internet Group Management Protocol (IGMP)

As mentioned earlier in this chapter, TCP/IP systems can transmit packets to all of the systems on a network (as broadcasts), to specific individual systems on a network (as unicasts), to the nearest system on the network (as an anycast), or to groups of systems (as multicasts). Broadcasts, unicasts, and anycasts are relatively simple to implement, because the TCP/IP system simply sends its packets to an address with the appropriate format. Multicasting is more complicated, however.

EXAM TIP

IGMP is critical to the multicasting process that is a particularly important aspect of IPv6, which is designed to reduce broadcast traffic on the network. Network+ candidates should be familiar with the protocol itself and its role in multicast addressing, both of which are included in the exam objectives.

As discussed earlier, Class D IP addresses ranging from 224.0.1.0 to 238.255.255.255 are reserved for multicasting purposes. A multicast transmission is simply a packet transmitted to one of those Class D addresses. However, determining which systems are part of the multicast group that recognizes that address is a complex process that involves the use of a specialized protocol called the *Internet Group Management Protocol (IGMP)*.

Unicasts are one-to-one transmissions, involving only a single source and a single destination. Broadcasts are one-to-many transmissions, with a single source and multiple destinations. Anycasts are one-to-one-of-many transmissions that target a single router. A multicast is another form of one-to-many transmission that is designed to be more efficient than a broadcast, because it targets a specific group of systems, as shown in Figure 6-21.

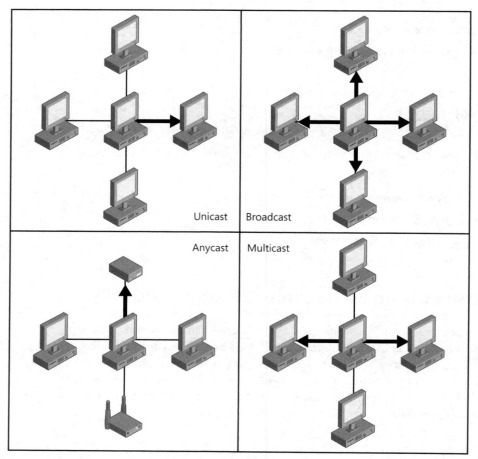

FIGURE 6-21 Unicast, broadcast, anycast, and multicast transmissions.

For example, if an application wants to transmit a message to all of the routers on a network, it could conceivably use a broadcast, but this would cause two problems. First, the broadcast would have to be processed by all of the workstations on the network unnecessarily, and second, the broadcast would be limited to the local network only.

Multicasts overcome both of these problems, because only systems that recognize themselves as part of the host group represented by the multicast address process the message, and because routers can propagate multicast messages throughout an internetwork. However, for multicasting to function properly, the appropriate systems must be added to each host group and the routers on the network must know which systems are in each host group. To become a member of a host group, a TCP/IP system uses the IGMP protocol to register itself with the routers on the local network.

Routers can also use IGMP to report their host group membership information to other routers. A router can therefore use IGMP for two purposes: to register its own group memberships and to exchange its group membership information with other routers. In addition to IGMP, there are also other protocols that routers can use to exchange group membership information, including Distance Vector Multicast Routing Protocol (DVMRP), the Multicast Open Shortest Path First (MOSPF) protocol, and the Protocol Independent Multicast (PIM) protocol.

For a network to support multicasting, the following elements are required:

- All host group members and all of the routers that provide internetwork access to the host group members must support IGMP.

- All of the routers that provide internetwork access to the host group members must have a means of sharing their host group membership information, by using IGMP or another protocol.

- All of the network interfaces in the routers must support multicast promiscuous mode, a special mode that causes the network interface adapter to process all incoming packets that have the multicast bit (that is, the last bit of the first byte of the destination hardware address) set to a value of 1.

Exercises

The answers for these exercises are located in the "Answers" section at the end of this chapter.

Scenario #1

Wingtip Toys is a company with 30 small sales offices scattered around the country, each having no more than five computers. As the network consultant for the company, you have obtained the 172.16.61.0/24 network address for them, which you want to use to network all of the offices. To create a separate subnet for each office, what is the minimum number of bits you would have to allocate from the address for a subnet identifier? Explain your answer.

Scenario #2

You work for a large corporation that owns the 172.16.128.0/17 network address, which they have further subnetted by allocating 6 bits to a subnet address. This enables the corporation to use a different subnet for each of its 50 offices around the world. What subnet mask value would you use when configuring the computers on one of these subnets? Explain your answer.

Chapter Summary

- IP is the primary end-to-end protocol in the TCP/IP protocol stack. At the network layer, all data uses the services provided by the IP protocol. There is no alternative.

- The IP protocol defined in RFC 791 is version 4, which is the version still used on most of the Internet. IPv4 includes a 32-bit address space, which means that the protocol can support approximately 4.29 billion addresses. IP version 6 (IPv6) has a 128-bit address space that provides an enormous number of addresses.

- IP performs several functions that are essential to the internetworking process, including data encapsulation, IP addressing, IP routing, fragmentation, and protocol identification.

- The self-contained IP addressing system is one of the most important elements of the TCP/IP protocol suite. IP addresses enable any computer running any operating system on any platform to communicate by providing a unique identifier for the computer itself and for the network on which it is located.

- An IPv4 address is a 32-bit value that contains both a network identifier and a host identifier. The address is notated by using four decimal numbers ranging from 0 to 255, separated by periods, as in 192.168.1.44.

- RFC 791 defines three classes of IP addresses, which provide support for networks of different sizes.

- A *subnet* is a subdivision of a network address that administrators can use to represent a part of a larger network, such as one LAN on an internetwork or the client of an ISP.

- Classful addressing was gradually obsolesced by a series of subnetting methods, including Classless Inter-Domain Routing (CIDR).

- IPv6 addresses use a notation called colon-hexadecimal format, which consists of eight 16-bit hexadecimal numbers, separated by colons.

- When a computer supporting IPv6 starts, it initiates the stateless address autoconfiguration process, during which it assigns each interface a link-local unicast address.

- DHCPv6 is the stateful counterpart to stateless address autoconfiguration and is widely implemented as part of existing DHCPv4 servers.

- IP encapsulates data that it receives from the transport layer protocols, such as Transmission Control Protocol (TCP) and User Datagram Protocol (UDP), for transmission to a destination. At the network layer, IP encapsulates data by adding a header, thus creating a datagram.

- In version 6 of IP, the header is necessarily different, to accommodate the larger addresses. A typical IPv6 header is 40 bytes long, as opposed to the 20 bytes of an IPv4 header.

- The Internet Control Message Protocol (ICMP) is a network layer protocol that provides error reporting functions and carries query and response messages for diagnostic programs.

- Chief among the additions in ICMPv6 is the Neighbor Discovery Protocol (NDP), a new data-link layer protocol that performs multiple functions, including the following: local network system discovery, hardware address resolution, duplicate address detection, and router discovery.

- As discussed earlier, Class D IP addresses are reserved for multicasting purposes. However, determining which systems are part of the multicast group that recognizes that address is a complex process that involves the use of a specialized protocol called the *Internet Group Management Protocol (IGMP)*.

Chapter Review

Test your knowledge of the information in Chapter 6 by answering these questions. The answers to these questions, and the explanations of why each answer choice is correct or incorrect, are located in the "Answers" section at the end of this chapter.

1. Which of the IPv4 address classes provides for the largest number of hosts?

   A. Class A

   B. Class B

   C. Class C

   D. All of the classes provide the same number of hosts

2. What kind of IP address must a system have to be visible from the Internet?

   A. Subnetted

   B. Registered

   C. Binary

   D. Class A

3. Which of the following subnet mask values would you use when configuring a TCP/IP client with an IPv4 address on the 172.16.32.0/19 network?

   A. 255.224.0.0

   B. 255.240.0.0

   C. 255.255.224.0

   D. 255.255.240.0

   E. 255.255.255.240

4. Which of the following statements about ICMP is/are true?

   A. ICMP messages are carried directly within IP datagrams.

   B. ICMP messages are carried directly within Ethernet frames.

   C. ICMP provides services to data-link layer protocols.

   D. ICMP provides services to IP.

Answers

This section contains the answers to the questions for the Exercises and Chapter Review in this chapter.

Exercises

- **Scenario #1:** The answer is 5. Allocating 5 of the 8 host bits in the network address enables you to create a maximum of 32 (that is, 2^5) subnets with six (2^3-2) hosts on each subnet.

- **Scenario #2:** The answer is 255.255.254.0. Adding a 6-bit subnet identifier to the existing 17 brings the total number of network bits to 23. The binary value of the subnet mask would therefore be 11111111 11111111 11111110 00000000, which converts to 255.255.254.0 in decimal form.

Chapter Review

1. **Correct Answer:** A

    A. **Correct:** Class A addresses provide more than 16 million hosts.

    B. **Incorrect:** Class B addresses provide 65,534 hosts.

    C. **Incorrect:** Class C addresses provide 254 hosts.

    D. **Incorrect:** Each of the address classes provides a different number of hosts.

2. **Correct Answer:** B

    A. **Incorrect:** Subnetted addresses can be visible or invisible to the Internet.

    B. **Correct:** For an address to be visible from the Internet, it must be registered with the IANA.

    C. **Incorrect:** Binary is a system of numbering that can be used to express any IP address.

    D. **Incorrect:** All address classes can be visible or invisible to the Internet.

3. **Correct Answer:** C

    A. **Incorrect:** In binary form, the mask 255.224.0.0 is as follows:
       11111111.11100000.00000000.00000000
       This contains only 11 network identifier bits.

    B. **Incorrect:** In binary form, the mask 255.240.0.0 is as follows:
       11111111.11110000.00000000.00000000
       This contains only 12 network identifier bits.

C. Correct: In binary form, the mask 255.255.224.0 is as follows:
11111111.11111111.11100000.00000000
This contains 19 network identifier bits.

D. Incorrect: In binary form, the mask 255.255.240.0 is as follows:
11111111.11111111.11110000.00000000
This contains 20 network identifier bits.

E. Incorrect: In binary form, the mask 255.255.255.240 is as follows:
11111111.11111111.11111111.11110000
This contains 28 network identifier bits.

4. **Correct Answers:** A and D

A. Correct: ICMP messages are carried in IP datagrams.

B. Incorrect: ICMP messages are carried directly within IP datagrams, not Ethernet frames.

C. Incorrect: ICMP does not provide services to data-link layer protocols.

D. Correct: ICMP messages are typically generated in response to IP-related events.

CHAPTER 7

Routing and Switching

Chapter 6, "The Network Layer," describes the functionality of the Internet Protocol (IP), the primary end-to-end protocol of the TCP/IP suite, but it omits the discussion of one of IP's primary functions: routing. Routing is the process of forwarding data packets—that is, IP datagrams—from one network to another, until they reach their final destinations. Routing is so crucial to the functionality of internetworks, including the Internet, that it appears here, in its own chapter.

Discussed here alongside routing, which is one of the oldest TCP/IP functions, is one of the newest: switching. In the last decade, administrators have replaced virtually all of their hubs and bridges with switches, and inside the enterprise, switches have replaced many routers as well.

Both routing and switching are complex processes that require the additional functionality of many other specialized TCP/IP processes and protocols. This chapter examines some of the most common ones, but there are many more that are well beyond the scope of the Network+ examination.

Exam objectives in this chapter:

Objective 1.2: Classify how applications, devices, and protocols relate to the OSI model layers.

- MAC address
- IP address
- EUI-64
- Frames
- Packets
- Switch
- Router
- Multilayer switch
- Hub
- Encryption devices
- Cable
- NIC
- Bridge

Objective 1.4: Explain the purpose and properties of routing and switching.

- EIGRP
- OSPF
- RIP
- Link state vs. distance vector vs. hybrid
- Static vs. dynamic
- Routing metrics
  - Hop counts
  - MTU, bandwidth
  - Costs
  - Latency

- Next hop
- Spanning-Tree Protocol
- VLAN (802.1q)
- Port mirroring
- Broadcast domain vs. collision domain
- IGP vs. EGP
- Routing tables
- Convergence (steady state)

Objective 2.1: Given a scenario, install and configure routers and switches.

- Routing tables
- NAT
- PAT
- VLAN (trunking)
- Managed vs. unmanaged
- Interface configurations
  - Full duplex
  - Half duplex
  - Port speeds
  - IP addressing
  - MAC filtering

- PoE
- Traffic filtering
- Diagnostics
- VTP configuration
- QoS
- Port mirroring

REAL WORLD **ROUTERS AND GATEWAYS**

In traditional TCP/IP terminology, the term "gateway" is synonymous with the term "router." However, this is not the case in other networking disciplines, where a gateway can refer to a different type of device that connects networks at the application layer instead of at the network layer.

Though many of the older TCP/IP standards freely use "gateway" when referring to a router, the only two places that the average network administrator is likely to encounter it in the field are in routing tables and in the Default Gateway setting found in Windows' and some other TCP/IP clients.

Routing

In Chapter 3, "Network Devices," you learned what a router does. Simply stated, a router connects two networks together by receiving packets through one interface and transmitting them out through the other one. As a network layer device, the router extracts the payload from a data-link layer protocol frame, reads the contents of the IP header fields, and uses that information to forward the data to the next stop on its journey to its final destination. That next stop might be another router, or it might be the destination computer itself.

EXAM TIP

Routing is always associated with the network layer, layer 3, of the Open Systems Interconnection (OSI) model, and the internet layer of the TCP/IP model. When you see the terms "router" or "layer 3" associated with a device from another layer, such as a switch, it is because the manufacturer has built routing capabilities into a layer 2 device, forming a multifunction product.

What Is Routing?

Many questions about routing still remain, however. Chapter 3 might explain what a router does, but exactly how does the router do it? How does it know whether to send a packet to a computer or another router? How does it determine what each packet's next stop should be—especially on the Internet, when the destination might be thousands of miles and dozens of networks away?

On a small internetwork, a router's job can be quite simple. For example, when two Ethernet LANs are connected by one router, the router simply receives packets from one network and forwards those destined for the other network. There is no question of where the router should forward the packets because there are no other routers to which it can send them. The only issue is whether the router should forward the packet or not.

It is critical to remember that routers do not forward all of the packets they receive. Like any system on an Ethernet network, a router receives all of the packets transmitted on the LAN. However, the router only forwards the packets that are destined for another network; it discards all of the others. Routers also do not forward broadcast transmissions, which is an important concern for applications that rely on broadcasts, such as the Dynamic Host Configuration Protocol (DHCP). Before the advent of switches, splitting one LAN into two by adding a router was a simple way of reducing traffic congestion.

On a large internetwork, however, the router's role is more complicated. A router might have to forward packets to several different networks, and in some cases, the networks might have more than one router connected to them, as shown in Figure 7-1. This redundant router arrangement enables packets to take different paths to a given destination. If one router should fail, packets can bypass it and still reach their destinations.

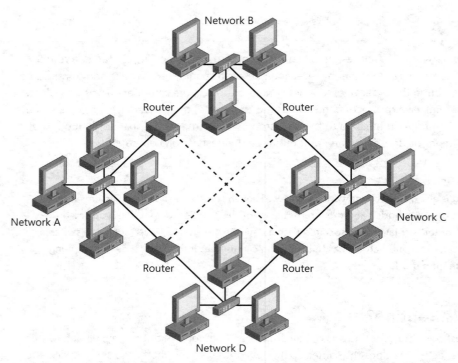

FIGURE 7-1 Internetworks with redundant routers provide multiple paths between two end systems.

On a complex internetwork such as this, selecting the most efficient route to a packet's destination is an important part of a router's job. Usually, the most efficient route is the path that gets a packet to its destination using the fewest hops (that is, by passing through the smallest number of routers). Routers share information about the networks to which they are attached with other routers in the immediate vicinity. As a result, each router eventually develops a composite picture of the networks around it, but on a large internetwork such as the Internet, no single router has the entire picture. Instead, the routers work together sequentially by passing each packet from router to router, one hop at a time. As long as each router has enough information to get the packets to their next hop, the system works.

> **MORE INFO** ROUTING
>
> To review the forwarding process a router performs when it receives a packet over one of its interfaces, see the "Enterprise Routing" section in Chapter 3.

Router Functions

Although the primary function of a router is to connect networks together and pass traffic between them, routers can fulfill several different roles in a network design. The type of router used for a specific function determines its size, cost, and capabilities. The simplest type of routing architecture is when a LAN must be connected to another LAN some distance away, by using a wide area network (WAN) connection, as shown in Figure 7-2. A branch office for a large corporation, for example, might have a WAN connection to the corporate headquarters in another city.

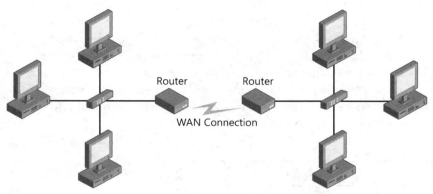

FIGURE 7-2 Routers connecting LANs to a WAN.

To enable the networks in the two offices to communicate, each must connect its LAN to a router, and the two routers are linked by the WAN connection. The WAN connection might take the form of a leased telephone line, an ISDN or DSL connection, or even a dial-up modem connection—any of the technologies described in Chapter 10, "Wide Area Networking." The technology used to connect the two networks is irrelevant, as long as the routers in both offices are connected.

Routers are required in this example because the LAN and WAN technologies are designed for distinctly different purposes. You generally would neither run an Ethernet connection between two cities nor use leased telephone lines to connect each workstation to the file server in the next room.

As discussed earlier, in the past, LAN internetworks also used routers to connect horizontal networks to a backbone. Routers were needed for this purpose for several possible reasons:

- To support a larger number of workstations than a single LAN could handle
- To create multiple broadcast and/or collision domains
- To connect LANs located in other parts of a building or in separate buildings on the same campus
- To connect LANs that used different network media

In the days before switching became popular, these two examples of router use were often combined. A large corporate internetwork using a backbone to connect multiple LANs almost certainly needed to be connected to the Internet. This meant that another router was required to support some type of WAN connection to an Internet Service Provider (ISP). This would allow users anywhere on the corporate network to access Internet services.

NOTE SWITCHING

NOTE SWITCHING

Today, it is more common for switches to connect horizontal networks to backbones, forming a single large network. For more information, see the "Switching" section later in this chapter.

Both of these scenarios use routers to connect a relatively small number of networks, but they are both dwarfed by the Internet, which is a routed internetwork composed of thousands of networks all over the world. To make it possible for packets to travel across this maze of routers with reasonable efficiency, a hierarchy of routers leads from smaller, local points of presence (POPs) to company backbones or regional providers, which in turn connect to network access points (NAPs), as shown in Figure 7-3.

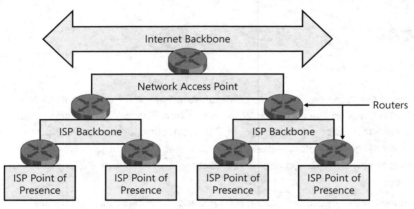

FIGURE 7-3 The Internet's hierarchy of routers.

Internet traffic originating from a system connected to a local ISP travels up from router to router through this virtual tree to one of the NAPs, from which it can access the main backbones of the Internet. The data travels across the Internet backbones, and then wends its way back down through the hierarchy via another NAP, back down through the router hierarchy to the destination.

EXAM TIP

One of the tools mentioned in the Network+ objectives that can help you to see the route that packets take from your computer through the Internet to a specific destination is the traceroute utility. For more information on traceroute, see Chapter 13, "Network Troubleshooting."

Discarding Packets

In many cases, the goal of a router is to transmit packets to their destinations by using the path that incurs the smallest number of hops, but routers also track the number of hops that packets take on the way to their destinations for another reason. When a malfunction or mis-configuration occurs in one or more routers, it is possible for packets to get caught in a router loop and be passed endlessly from one router to another.

To prevent this, the IPv4 header contains a Time to Live (TTL) field (and the IPv6 header contains a Hop Limit field), to which the source system assigns a certain numerical value when it creates a packet. (On Windows-based systems, the value is 128, by default.) As a packet travels through the network, each router that processes it decrements the value of these fields by 1.

If, for any reason, the packet passes through a sufficient number of routers to bring the value of this field down to 0, the last router removes the packet from the network and discards it. The router then returns an Internet Control Message Protocol (ICMP) Time to Live Exceeded in Transit message to the source system to inform it of the problem.

Router Products

A router can be a stand-alone hardware device or a regular computer. Server operating systems such as Windows Server and many UNIX and Linux distributions can route IP traffic. Creating a router from a computer running one of these operating systems is simply a matter of installing two network interface adapters, connecting the computer to two different networks, and configuring the system to route traffic between those networks. In TCP/IP terminology, a computer with two or more network interfaces is called a *multihomed* system.

Many of the workstation versions of Windows also include a feature called Internet Connection Sharing (ICS), which enables other computers on the same LAN to access the Internet through one system's broadband or dial-up connection to an ISP.

There are also third-party software products that provide Internet connection sharing. In essence, these products are software routers that enable your computer to forward packets between the local network and the network run by your ISP. By using these products, all of the computers on a LAN installed in a home or a small business can share a single computer's connection to the Internet, no matter what type of connection it is.

All routers must have two network interfaces, each of which must have a unique IP address appropriate for the network to which it is connected. When you use a computer as an IP router, this means you must have two network interface adapters (or possibly one adapter and one dial-up modem) installed. (This is why IP addresses are associated with network interfaces, not with computers.) When one of the two networks is an ISP connection, the ISP's server typically supplies the address for that interface. The other IP address is the one that you assign to your network interface adapter when you install it.

A stand-alone router is a hardware device that is essentially a special-purpose computer. The device has multiple built-in network interface adapters, a processor, and memory for storing its routing information and temporary packet buffers. Routers are available at a wide range of prices and with a variety of capabilities. Home users can purchase inexpensive stand-alone routers that let them share an Internet connection with a small network for less than US $100, whereas large corporations use enormously expensive rack-mounted models that connect the LANs of a large internetwork or provide wide area connectivity to remote offices or ISPs.

EXAM TIP

In addition to their basic packet-forwarding function, many of the devices marketed as "routers" have other features as well, such as firewalls, switches, DHCP servers, Wi-Fi transceivers, web servers, print servers, and Network Address Translation (NAT). The range of products is immense, with prices that reflect the devices' capabilities. The Network+ objectives also refer to these products as "multifunction devices."

Understanding Routing Tables

The *routing table* is the heart of any router; without it, all that's left is the mechanics of packet forwarding. The routing table holds the information that the router uses to forward packets to the proper destinations. However, routers are not the only devices that have routing tables; every TCP/IP system has a routing table, which it uses to determine where to send its packets.

On a LAN, routing is essentially the process of determining what data-link layer protocol address the system should use to reach a particular IP address. In the case of an Ethernet LAN, IP must determine what MAC address the system should use in its Ethernet frames. If a computer wants to transmit a packet to a destination on the local network, for example, the routing table instructs it to address the packet directly to that system. This is called a *direct route*. In this case, the Destination IP Address field in the IP header and the Destination Address field in the Ethernet header refer to the same computer, as shown in Figure 7-4.

If a packet's destination is on another network, the routing table supplies the address of the router that the system should use to reach that destination. In this case, the Destination IP Address and Ethernet Destination Address fields specify different systems. Remember that data-link layer protocols such as Ethernet can only send frames to the local network. Because the final destination of the packet is on a distant network, the Ethernet destination on the lo- cal network must be a router, as shown in Figure 7-5. This is called an *indirect route*.

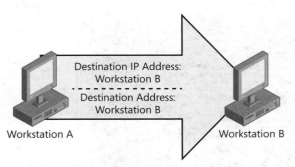

FIGURE 7-4 Routing packets to a local network destination.

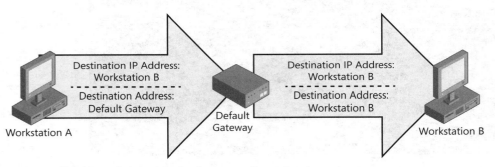

FIGURE 7-5 Routing packets to a destination on another network.

The Windows Routing Table Format

A routing table is essentially a list of network (and possibly host) addresses, plus the addresses of routers that the system can use to reach them. Although different operating systems display the routing table in various formats, the information in them is generally the same. In addition, if an operating system supports IPv6 as well as IPv4, it will maintain two sets of routing table entries, also possibly in different formats.

The routing table for a Windows Server 2008 R2 workstation is shown in Figure 7-6.

> **NOTE** **ROUTING TABLE UTILITIES**
>
> The utilities that display the routing table in a particular operating system can have different defaults and different operational syntaxes. For example, the Route.exe program in Windows displays both the IPv4 and IPv6 routing table entries by default. By contrast, the route program in the Linux distribution shown in Figure 7-7, later in this chapter, displays only the IPv4 entries by default. You must modify the command line to add the IPv6 entries as well.

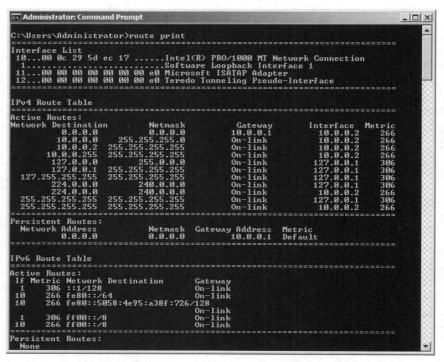

FIGURE 7-6 IPv4 and IPv6 entries in a Windows Server 2008 R2 routing table.

The data in the columns of a Windows routing table's IPv4 entries have the following functions:

- **Network Destination** Specifies the IP address of the network or host for which the table is providing routing information.

- **Netmask** Specifies the subnet mask for the value in the Network Destination column. As with any subnet mask, the system uses the Netmask value to determine which parts of the Network Destination value are the network identifier, the subnet identifier (if any), and the host identifier.

- **Gateway** Specifies the IP address of the router that the system should use to send packets to the network or host identified in the Network Destination column. On an Ethernet LAN, the MAC address for the system identified by the Gateway value will become the Destination Address value in the packet's Ethernet header.

- **Interface** Specifies the IP address of the network interface that the computer should use to transmit packets to the system identified in the Gateway column.

- **Metric** Contains a value that specifies the efficiency of the route. Metric values are relative; a lower value indicates a more efficient route than a higher value. When a routing table contains multiple routes to the same destination, the system always uses the table entry with the lower Metric value.

The Windows IPv6 routing table is arranged differently but contains the same information. The Interface column is abbreviated "If" and uses numbers assigned to the computer's interfaces, rather than the addresses of the interfaces themselves. An Interface List appears at the top of the routing table display, which in this case assigns the number 10 to the computer's network interface adapter and the number 1 to the system's loopback interface. The Metric, Network Destination, and Gateway columns perform the same functions as their IPv4 counterparts, using IPv6 addresses. The Netmask column is omitted, of course, because IPv6 does not use subnet masks.

Default Windows IPv4 Routing Table Entries

The sample Windows routing table shown earlier in Figure 7-6 contains the typical entries for a workstation that is not functioning as a router. The functions of each entry in the sample routing table are explained in the following sections.

ENTRY 1

```
Network Destination        Netmask       Gateway      Interface    Metric
          0.0.0.0          0.0.0.0       10.0.0.1      10.0.0.2      266
```

The value 0.0.0.0 in the Network Destination column, found in the first entry in the table, identifies the default gateway entry. The default gateway is the router on the LAN that the system uses when there are no routing table entries that match the Destination IP Address of an outgoing packet. Even if multiple routers are available on the local network, a routing table can have only one functional default gateway entry, which the system creates by using the computer's TCP/IP configuration settings.

On a typical workstation that is not a router, the majority of packets go to the default gateway; the only packets that do not use it are those destined for systems on the local network. The Gateway column contains the IP address of a router on the local network, and the Interface column contains the IP address of the network interface adapter in the computer that connects it to the network.

ENTRY 2

```
Network Destination        Netmask       Gateway      Interface    Metric
         10.0.0.0      255.255.255.0     On-link       10.0.0.2      266
```

The IP address of the network interface adapter in the computer to which this routing table belongs is 10.0.0.2. Therefore, the second entry in the sample routing table contains the address of the local network on which the computer is located. The Network Destination and Netmask values indicate that it is a Class A address, subnetted to a Class C, which would be notated as 10.0.0.0/24.

This is the entry that the computer uses for direct routes when it transmits packets to other systems on the local network. The "On-link" value in the Gateway column indicates that the destination is local and that a gateway (or router) is not needed to reach it. Earlier versions of Windows placed the computer's own IP address in the Gateway column, implying that the system is functioning as its own gateway, which is not exactly true.

The Interface column contains the IP address of the computer's network interface adapter, indicating that the computer should use that adapter to transmit the packets to the destination. In the case of a single-homed workstation such as this, the Interface column is superfluous because there is only one interface, but on a router, there is more than one from which to choose.

ENTRY 3

Network Destination	Netmask	Gateway	Interface	Metric
10.0.0.2	255.255.255.255	On-link	10.0.0.2	266

The third entry in the sample routing table contains the host address of the computer itself, as identified by the 255.255.255.255 Netmask value. Routing tables can contain host address entries, as well as network address entries. This entry instructs the system to transmit data addressed to itself to its own address on the local network. Some implementations use the loopback address (127.0.0.1) in the Interface field for this purpose instead.

IP always searches the routing table for host address entries before it searches for network address entries; therefore, when processing any packets addressed to the computer's own address (10.0.0.2), IP would select this entry before the entry above it, which specifies the system's network address.

ENTRY 4

Network Destination	Netmask	Gateway	Interface	Metric
10.0.0.255	255.255.255.255	On-link	10.0.0.2	266

The fourth entry in the sample routing table contains the first of several broadcast addresses, as identified by the 255 value of the last quad, which is the result of having all 1 bits in the address's host identifier. In this case, the entry contains the local network's broadcast address (10.0.0.255). As with the entry for the computer's own host address, no gateway is needed, and the system will send the packets out through the interface by using the data-link layer protocol's broadcast address (which in Ethernet is FFFFFFFFFFFF).

ENTRIES 5, 6, AND 7

Network Destination	Netmask	Gateway	Interface	Metric
127.0.0.0	255.0.0.0	On-link	127.0.0.1	306
127.0.0.1	255.255.255.255	On-link	127.0.0.1	306
127.255.255.255	255.255.255.255	On-link	127.0.0.1	306

In the fifth entry, the address in the Network Destination column, 127.0.0.0, is designated by the IP standard as a TCP/IP loopback address. IP automatically routes all packets destined for any address on the 127.0.0.0 network back to the incoming packet queue on the same computer. The packets never reach the data-link layer or leave the computer. This entry ensures the loopback functionality by specifying that the system should use its own loopback address (127.0.0.1) for the interface to the destination.

The sixth entry contains the loopback host address (127.0.0.1), and performs the same function for packets addressed specifically to that address. The seventh entry contains the loopback broadcast address, which enables the system to handle generic local network broadcasts.

Notice also that the values in the Metric column for the three loopback entries are higher (306) than those for the entries on the 10.0.0.0/24 network (266). In the case of a single-homed workstation, the Metric values themselves represent no actual measurement; they are just relative values indicating that IP should use the network adapter's host address (10.0.0.2) rather than the loopback address whenever possible.

ENTRIES 8 AND 9

Network Destination	Netmask	Gateway	Interface	Metric
224.0.0.0	240.0.0.0	On-link	127.0.0.1	306
224.0.0.0	240.0.0.0	On-link	10.0.0.2	266

The eighth and ninth entries in the sample routing table contain the network address for the multicast addresses designated by the Internet Assigned Numbers Authority (IANA). The eighth entry references the interface that uses the loopback address, and the ninth entry uses the computer's host address. As in the previous entries, the Metric values instruct the system to favor the host over the loopback address.

ENTRIES 10 AND 11

Network Destination	Netmask	Gateway	Interface	Metric
255.255.255.255	255.255.255.255	On-link	127.0.0.1	306
255.255.255.255	255.255.255.255	On-link	10.0.0.2	266

The tenth and eleventh entries in the routing table contain the generic IP host broadcast address, once again providing the option to use either the computer's host address or the loopback address as the interface.

All of the entries in the routing table, other than the first one, account for all of the possible types of traffic that the system might have to transmit directly to destinations on the local network. The first entry handles all other traffic, by sending it to the default gateway address.

ROUTER ENTRIES

The routing table on a router is often considerably longer and more complex than this sample because it contains entries for all of the networks to which it is attached, as well as entries for more distant networks, provided either manually by administrators or dynamically by routing protocols.

A router also makes greater use of the values in the Interface and Metric columns. On a multihomed system, the value in the Interface column is a crucial part of transmitting a packet correctly. Each entry must specify which interface the system should use when transmitting packets to that specific destination.

It is also possible for a router to have multiple entries for a specific network address. On a complex internetwork with many interconnected routers, there might be multiple paths to the same destination network, so the system uses the Metric value to choose the most efficient one. The type and significance of the Metric values depends on the administrator or routing protocol that created them.

Default Windows IPv6 Routing Table Entries

The IPv6 routing table in Windows is substantially different in appearance from the IPv4 version, but it works in basically the same way.

```
If Metric    Network Destination                    Gateway
 1    306    ::1/128                                On-link
10    266    fe80::/64                              On-link
10    266    fe80::5058:4e95:a38f:726/128           On-link
 1    306    ff00::/8                               On-link
10    266    ff00::/8                               On-link
```

The routing table in the sample is from a computer with a self-assigned link-local unicast address. The first entry in the table contains the IPv6 loopback address (::1) in the Network Destination field and directs the system to use the Software Loopback Interface for any packets containing that address.

The second entry contains the standard link-local unicast network address (fe80::/64), enabling the system to transmit packets to other link-local addresses on the same network.

The third entry contains the computer's own link-local unicast host address, thus performing the same function as the host address entry (10.0.0.2) in the IPv4 table.

The fourth and fifth entries contain the IPv6 multicast network addresses, with the Metric values causing the network interface adapter entry to take precedence over the loopback interface entry.

This IPv6 routing table is simpler than the IPv4 table, because the computer that generated it is located on an isolated LAN, and also because the Internet does not as yet have native support for IPv6 communications. However, the Interface List included with the table also includes entries for ISATAP and Teredo, two transition technologies that enable systems to encapsulate IPv6 datagrams within IPv4 packets for transmission over IPv4-only networks.

The Linux Routing Table Format

The routing table for a Linux system with one network interface is shown in Figure 7-7. Here again, the columns are slightly different from those shown in the Windows tables, but the basic functionality is the same.

```
⊗ ⊜ ⊜    mlee@Wkstn1: ~
mlee@Wkstn1:~$ route -n --inet --inet6
Kernel IP routing table
Destination      Gateway          Genmask          Flags Metric Ref    Use Iface
0.0.0.0          192.168.2.99     0.0.0.0          UG    0      0        0 eth0
169.254.0.0      0.0.0.0          255.255.0.0      U     1000   0        0 eth0
192.168.2.0      0.0.0.0          255.255.255.0    U     1      0        0 eth0
Kernel IPv6 routing table
Destination                        Next Hop                Flag Met Ref Use If
fe80::/64                          ::                      U    256 0     0 eth0
::/0                               ::                      !n   -1  1     1 lo
::1/128                            ::                      Un   0   1     1 lo
fe80::20c:29ff:fe86:857a/128       ::                      Un   0   1     0 lo
ff00::/8                           ::                      U    256 0     0 eth0
::/0                               ::                      !n   -1  1     1 lo
mlee@Wkstn1:~$ ▮
```

FIGURE 7-7 IPv4 and IPv6 entries in a Linux routing table.

The functions of the columns in this sample Linux IPv4 routing table are as follows:

- **Destination** Specifies the IP address of the network or host for which the table is providing routing information

- **Gateway** Specifies the IP address of the router that the system should use to send packets to the network or host identified in the Destination column

- **Genmask** Specifies the subnet mask for the value in the Destination column

- **Flags** Contains a series of flags that supply source or status information about the entry, including the following:

  - **U** Route is up

  - **H** Target is a host

  - **G** Use gateway

  - **R** Reinstate route for dynamic routing

  - **D** Dynamically installed by daemon or redirect

  - **M** Modified from routing daemon or redirect

  - **A** Installed by addrconf

  - **C** Cache entry

  - **!** Reject route

- **Metric** Contains a value that specifies the efficiency of the route

- **Ref** Specifies the number of references to this route

- **Use** Count of lookups for the route

- **Iface** Identifies the network interface that the computer should use to transmit packets to the system identified in the Gateway column

Quick Check

1. How do you identify the routing table entry that represents the computer's default gateway?

2. When there is more than one routing table entry for a particular network, how does the system decide which one to use?

Quick Check Answers

1. The default gateway entry is the one with a network address of 0.0.0.0.

2. The system uses the entry with the lower Metric value.

Selecting a Routing Table Entry

When a TCP/IP system has data to transmit, the IP protocol selects a route for each packet, using the procedure shown in Figure 7-8.

The steps of the procedure, using the Windows routing table format, are as follows:

1. After packaging the transport layer information into a datagram, IP compares the Destination IP Address value from the IP header with the routing table, looking for a host address with the same value. A host address entry in the table has a full IP address in the Network Destination column and the value 255.255.255.255 in the Netmask column.

2. If there is no host address entry that exactly matches the Destination IP Address value, the system then scans the routing table's Network Destination and Netmask columns for an entry that matches the address's network and subnet identifiers. If there is more than one entry in the routing table that contains the desired network and subnet identifiers, IP selects the entry with the lower value in the Metric column.

3. If there are no table entries that match the network and subnet identifiers of the Destination IP Address value, the system searches for a default gateway entry that has a value of 0.0.0.0 in the Network Destination and Netmask columns.

4. If there is no default gateway entry, the system generates an error message. If the system transmitting the datagram is a router, it transmits an ICMP Destination Unreachable message back to the end system that originated the datagram. If the system transmitting the datagram is itself an end system, the error message gets passed back up to the application that generated the data.

5. When the system locates a viable routing table entry, IP prepares to transmit the datagram to the router identified in the Gateway column. The system obtains the hardware address of the router by accessing the ARP cache or by performing an ARP procedure.

6. After the system has discovered the router's hardware address, IP passes that address and the datagram down to the data-link layer protocol associated with the address specified in the Interface column. The data-link layer protocol constructs a frame, using the router's hardware address in its Destination Address field, and transmits the frame out over the designated interface.

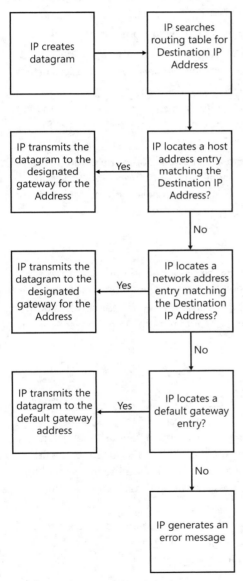

FIGURE 7-8 The IP routing procedure.

Routing in IPv6

Because IPv6 addresses are larger than IPv4 addresses, IPv6 headers are larger, and IPv6 routing table entries must be larger than those for IPv4. However, although these two factors might seem to increase the router processing burden, IPv6 is actually designed to improve router efficiency.

IPv6 adheres more closely to one of the guiding principles of network design, the *end-to-end principle*, which states that it is inherently more efficient to implement application functions in end systems, rather than in intermediate systems (routers). Some examples of this in IPv6 include the following:

- The simplification of the IP header, achieved by moving fields formerly found in every header to options included only when needed
- The removal of the checksum from the IP header, which in IPv4 had to be recalculated by routers when they modified IP header values
- The elimination of fragmentation in IPv6 routers, forcing end systems to perform path maximum transmission unit (MTU) discovery or use packets no larger than the IPv6 default minimum

However, the IPv6 feature with the most profound effect on routing is the nature of its subnetting procedure, which enables routers to aggregate subnet prefixes more efficiently, resulting in smaller routing tables throughout the internetwork. Smaller routing tables means faster router packet processing and improved performance throughout the network.

Routing and ICMP

The Internet Control Message Protocol (ICMP) provides several important functions to routers and the systems that use them. Chief among these is the capability of routers to use ICMP messages to provide routing information to other routers. Routers send ICMP Redirect messages to source systems when they know of a better route than the one the system is currently using.

> ***NOTE* ICMP REDIRECT**
>
> For more information on ICMP Redirect messages, see Chapter 6.

Routers also generate ICMP Destination Unreachable messages of various types when they are unable to forward packets. If a router receives a packet that is destined for a workstation on a locally attached network, and it can't deliver the packet because the workstation is offline, the router generates a Host Unreachable message and transmits it to the system that originated the packet.

If the router is unable to forward the packet to another router that provides access to the destination, it generates a Network Unreachable message instead. Network layer protocols provide end-to-end communications, meaning that it is usually the end systems that are involved in a dialog. ICMP is a mechanism that enables intermediate systems (routers) to communicate with a source end system (the transmitter) in the event that the packets can't reach the destination end system.

Other ICMP packets, called Router Solicitation and Advertisement messages, can enable workstations to discover the routers on the local network. A host system generates a Router Solicitation message and transmits it either as a broadcast or a multicast to the All Routers on This Subnet address (224.0.0.2). Routers receiving the message respond with Router Advertisement messages that the host system uses to update its routing table. The routers then generate periodic updates to inform the host of their continued operational status. In ICMPv6, Router Solicitation and Router Advertisement messages are an essential element of the stateless address autoconfiguration process.

Routing and Network Address Translation

Network Address Translation (NAT) is a routing technique that enables computers with private (or unregistered) IP addresses to access the Internet. If you connect a network to the Internet without firewall protection of any kind, you must use registered IP addresses for your computers so that they can communicate with other systems. However, registered IP addresses are visible from the Internet. This means that any user on the Internet can access your network's computers and, with a little ingenuity, wreak havoc on your network. NAT prevents this from happening by enabling you to assign unregistered IP addresses to your computers.

As you learned in Chapter 6, the Internet Assigned Numbers Authority (IANA) has designated three address ranges for use on private networks. These address ranges are not registered to any Internet user and are not visible from the Internet. You can safely deploy them on your computers without the danger of exposing them to Internet intruders.

However, this also means that Internet servers, when they receive requests from the private network computers, cannot send replies to them, because they do not have viable addresses. NAT solves this problem by functioning as an intermediary between the Internet and a client computer on an unregistered network. For each packet generated by a client, the NAT router substitutes a registered address for the client's unregistered address.

NAT Communications

Under normal conditions, routers do not modify datagrams any more than the postal service modifies envelopes. A NAT router, however, modifies each outgoing datagram it receives from an unregistered client computer by changing the value of the Source IP Address field in its IP header. The following steps explain this process:

1. When a client sends a request message to an Internet server, the datagram containing the request first goes to a NAT router.

2. NAT substitutes a registered IP address for the client computer's unregistered IP address in the datagram and then forwards it to the destination server on the Internet.

The NAT router also maintains a table of those unregistered addresses and the public address assigned to them, in order to keep track of the datagrams it has processed.

3. When the destination server on the Internet receives the request, it processes it in the normal manner and generates its reply. However, because the Source IP Address value in the request datagram is the NAT router's registered address, the destination server addresses its reply to the NAT router, not to the original client.

4. When the NAT router receives the reply from the Internet server, it modifies the datagram again, substituting the client's original, unregistered address for the Destination IP Address in the datagram's IP header, and forwards the packet to the client on the private network.

The NAT router's processes are invisible both to the client on the private network and to the server on the Internet. The client generates a request and sends it to a server, and the client eventually receives a reply from that server. The server receives a request from the NAT router and transmits its reply to the same router. Both the client and the server function normally, unaware of the NAT router's intervention. More importantly, the client computer remains invisible to the Internet and is protected from most types of unauthorized access originating from outside the private network.

Because NAT functions at the network layer of the OSI model, it works with any application that communicates by using IP. Client computers on the private network can run Internet email clients, web browsers, FTP clients, or any other Internet application, and NAT provides protection against intruders.

NAT Types

There are several different types of NAT, some of which share the same acronyms, as follows:

-   **Static NAT**   Static NAT (SNAT) translates multiple unregistered IP addresses to an equal number of registered addresses, as shown in Figure 7-9. This enables each client to always use the same registered address. This type of NAT does not conserve IP address space, because you need the same number of registered addresses as unregistered addresses. Static NAT is also not as secure as the other NAT types because each computer is permanently associated with a particular registered address. This makes it possible for Internet intruders to direct traffic to a particular computer on your network by using that registered address.

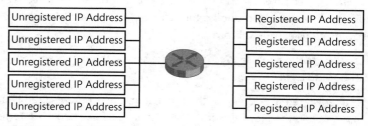

FIGURE 7-9 Static NAT.

- **Dynamic NAT** Dynamic NAT is for situations when you have fewer registered IP addresses than unregistered computers, as shown in Figure 7-10. Dynamic NAT translates each unregistered address to one of the available registered addresses. Because the registered address assigned to each client changes frequently, it is more difficult for intruders on the Internet to associate a registered address with a particular computer, as in static NAT. The main drawback of dynamic NAT is that it can support only the same number of simultaneous users as the number of available registered IP addresses. If all the registered addresses are in use, a client attempting to access the Internet receives an error message.

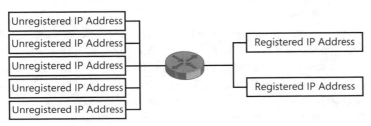

FIGURE 7-10 Dynamic NAT.

- **Port address translation (PAT)** Also known as masquerading, this method translates all the unregistered IP addresses on a network by using a single registered IP address, as shown in Figure 7-11. The NAT router uses port numbers to differentiate between packets generated by and destined for different computers, so that multiple clients can access the Internet simultaneously. Masquerading provides the best security of the NAT types because the association between the unregistered client and the registered IP address/port number combination in the NAT router lasts only for a single connection.

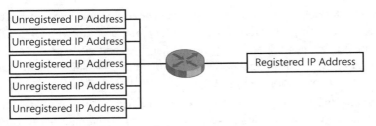

FIGURE 7-11 Port address translation.

EXAM TIP
There are several NAT product manufacturers who use the acronym SNAT to refer to different technologies, including secure NAT and stateful NAT. However, static NAT, referring to the use of one registered address for each unregistered address, is the most common spellout for SNAT.

NAT Security

Most NAT implementations today rely on masquerading because it minimizes the number of registered IP addresses needed, and because it maximizes the security provided by NAT. However, NAT by itself, even if it uses masquerading, is not a true firewall, and it does not provide ironclad security for high-risk environments. NAT effectively blocks unsolicited requests and other probes from the Internet, meaning that it prevents intruders from searching for unprotected file shares, open ports, and private web or FTP servers on the private network. However, NAT does not prevent users on the Internet from launching directed denial of service (DoS) attacks against specific computers or from using other more complex tactics to compromise your network security.

 NAT also does not prevent users from inadvertently running dangerous programs that initiate contact with servers on the Internet. A *Trojan horse* is an application disguised as an innocuous file that functions as a client, enabling intruders on the Internet to establish contact with a computer, even if it has an unregistered IP address. Remember, NAT can only prevent unsolicited communication from the Internet to an unregistered computer. If the unregistered computer initiates the communication, intentionally or not, the system is vulnerable. Using private addresses provides a distinct advantage over using public addresses, but it is not a perfect solution.

Port Forwarding

Because the NAT router functions are invisible to unregistered computers, users can access the Internet with any client application. However, the one thing you can't do with a standard NAT implementation is run an application that provides Internet server functions, such as a web or game server. The client must initiate the client/server transaction, and a client computer on the Internet has no way to contact a server running on an unregistered computer first.

 However, you can host a web server or other Internet server application on an unregistered system by using a technique called *port forwarding*. Port forwarding occurs when the NAT router creates a mapping between a specific registered IP address and port number and a specific unregistered address on the private network. This mapping enables traffic that the NAT router would ordinarily block to pass through to its destination.

Another benefit of port forwarding is that the router can manipulate the translation to provide additional functionality, such as load balancing. A NAT server with advanced capabilities can receive requests destined for one particular registered address and distribute them among several unregistered addresses. If your website receives a lot of traffic, you can deploy multiple, identical web servers and split the incoming traffic load among them.

NAT Implementations

NAT is implemented in a variety of products, both hardware and software. Most of the hardware routers that provide shared Internet access support NAT, particularly the low-end devices intended for home or small business use.

Many operating systems support NAT as well. The Windows operating systems have two different NAT implementations. In the Windows Server operating systems, including Windows Server 2008 R2, NAT is integrated into the Routing and Remote Access Service (RRAS), enabling a computer that is functioning as a router to translate IP addresses between any two network interfaces. The workstation operating systems, including Windows 7, have a feature called Internet Connection Sharing (ICS), which is similar to the NAT/ DHCP implementations in stand-alone router products. With ICS, a computer can share a network connection to an ISP with other computers on the LAN, allowing them to access the Internet by using the ISP-connected computer as a router.

UNIX and Linux typically implement NAT as part of the operating system kernel. In Linux, NAT is integrated into the same netfilter component that provides packet filtering capabilities. You use the same iptables tool to configure both the NAT process and packet filtering.

Static and Dynamic Routing

Now that you have learned how TCP/IP systems use the routing table to determine the next destination for each packet they transmit, the next thing to consider is how the information gets into the routing table. The sample routing tables shown earlier in this chapter contain only the default entries created automatically by a workstation. This is known as *minimal routing*. Routers can have many more entries, depending on the size of the internetwork and the method used to create the table.

 There are two techniques for updating the routing table: static routing and dynamic routing. In *static routing*, a network administrator manually creates routing table entries, using a program designed for this purpose. In *dynamic routing*, routers use specialized protocols to create routing table entries automatically. Two examples of these dynamic protocols are the Routing Information Protocol (RIP) and the Open Shortest Path First (OSPF) protocol, both of which are discussed later in this chapter. Routers use these protocols to exchange messages containing routing information with other nearby routers. Each router is essentially sharing its routing table with other routers.

It should be obvious that although static routing can be an effective routing solution on a small internetwork, it isn't a viable option for a large installation. However, if you have a network with a configuration that never changes, or one with only one possible route to each destination, running a routing protocol can be a waste of time, energy, and bandwidth.

The advantage of dynamic routing, in addition to reducing the network administrator's workload, is that it automatically compensates for changes in the network infrastructure. For example, if a particular router goes down, its failure to communicate with the other routers nearby means that it will eventually be deleted from their routing tables, and packets will take different routes to their destinations. When that router comes back online, it will resume communications with the other routers and will be again added to their tables. On an internetwork as large as the Internet, for which the IP routing system was designed, dynamic routing is essential; it would be impossible for administrators to keep up with the constant changes occurring on the network without dynamic routing.

Managing Static Routes

To manage static routes, administrators use a utility supplied with the TCP/IP protocol stack that can create, modify, or delete entries in the routing table. In most cases, TCP/IP implementations include a command-line utility for router table management, but there are some graphical utilities available as well. Stand-alone routers run their own proprietary software that uses a command set created by the manufacturer. The utilities for various operating systems capable of static routing are described in the following sections.

MANAGING STATIC ROUTES IN WINDOWS

All Windows-based operating systems include a command-line program called Route.exe, which you can use to modify the contents of the system's routing table. The syntax for Route.exe is as follows.

```
ROUTE [-f] [-p] [command [destination] [MASK netmask]
  [gateway] [METRIC metric] [IF interface]
```

- **-f** Deletes all entries from the routing table. When used with the ADD command, deletes the entire table before adding the new entry.

- **-p** When used with the ADD command, creates a persistent entry in the routing table. A *persistent route* is one that remains in the table permanently, even after the system is restarted. When -p is used with the PRINT keyword, the system displays only the persistent routes in the table.

- *command* Contains one of the following keywords that specifies the function of the command:

  - **PRINT** Displays the contents of the routing table. When used with the -p parameter, displays only the persistent routes in the routing table.

  - **ADD** Creates a new entry in the routing table.

  - **DELETE** Deletes an existing entry from the routing table.

  - **CHANGE** Modifies the parameters of an existing entry in the routing table.

- *destination* Specifies the network or host address of the table entry being managed.

- **MASK** *netmask* Specifies the subnet mask to be applied to the address indicated by the *destination* variable.

- *gateway* Specifies the IP address of the router that the system should use to reach the host or network indicated by the *destination* variable.

- **METRIC** *metric* Specifies a value that indicates the relative efficiency of the route in the table entry.

- **IF** *interface* Specifies the number of the network interface that the system should use to reach the router specified by the *gateway* variable.

For example, if you were using the network configuration shown in Figure 7-12 to create an entry that informs Router A of the existence of network 192.168.3.0, which is accessible through Router B, you would execute a Route.exe command like the following at the Router A system's command line:

```
ROUTE ADD 192.168.3.0 MASK 255.255.255.0 192.168.2.7 IF 1 METRIC 1
```

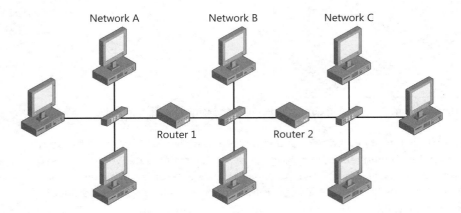

FIGURE 7-12 When the administrator adds a static route to the routing table in the Router A system, Router A can forward packets to the 192.168.3.0 network through Router B.

The functions of the Route.exe parameters in this particular command are as follows:

- **ADD** Indicates that the program should create a new entry in the existing routing table
- **192.168.3.0** The address of the network to be added to the Router A routing table
- **MASK 255.255.255.0** The subnet mask to be applied to the destination address
- **192.168.2.7** The local address of the gateway (Router B) that provides access to the destination network
- **IF 1** The number of the interface in Router A that provides access to the network containing the specified gateway (Router B)
- **METRIC 1** Indicates that the destination network is one hop away

This new routing table entry essentially tells Router A that when it has traffic to send to any address on the 192.168.3.0 network, it should send the traffic to the router with the address 192.168.2.7, using the Router A network interface adapter designated by the system as interface 1.

On a computer running one of the Windows Server operating systems that is configured to function as a router, you can also use the Routing And Remote Access console to create static routing table entries, using the interface shown in Figure 7-13.

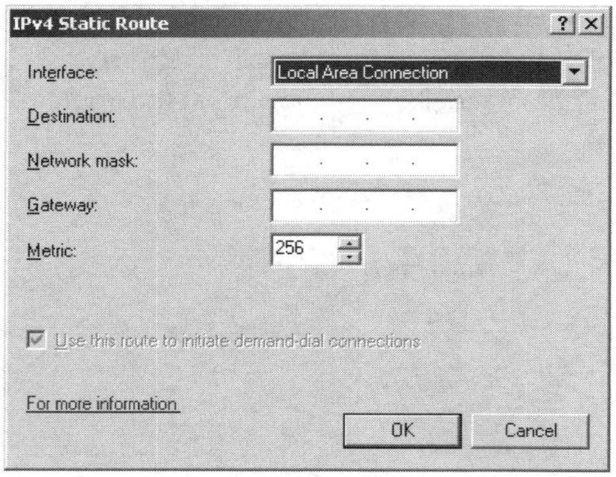

FIGURE 7-13 The IPv4 Static Route dialog box in the Routing And Remote Access console.

However, the functionality for editing routing tables in this console is limited. You can create new entries in the routing table and manage or delete the static routes you have already created by using the console, but you cannot manage the default routing table entries or static routes created with Route.exe. Route.exe is the more comprehensive tool, because it can manage all of the routing table's entries, whatever their source.

MANAGING STATIC ROUTES IN UNIX/LINUX

Most UNIX and Linux distributions use a daemon called *routed* (pronounced *route-dee*) to route IP traffic. To modify the contents of the routed routing table, you use a tool called *route*, which uses the following syntax.

```
route command [-net|-host] destination [netmask netmask]
  [gw gateway] [metric metric] [mss bytes] [dev interface]
```

- *command*   Contains one of the following keywords that specifies the function of the command:
  - **Add**   Creates a new entry in the routing table
  - **Del**   Deletes an existing entry from the routing table
- **-net|-host**   Specifies whether the value of the *destination* variable is a network or host address.
- *destination*   Specifies the network or host address value of the table entry the program is creating or managing.
- **netmask *netmask***   Specifies the subnet mask to be applied to the address indicated by the *destination* variable.
- **gw *gateway***   Specifies the IP address of the router that the system should use to reach the host or network specified by the *destination* variable.
- **metric *metric***   Specifies a value that indicates the relative efficiency of the route in the table entry.

- **mss *bytes*** Specifies the maximum segment size (mss) for packets using this route.
- **dev *interface*** Specifies the device name of the network interface the system should use to reach the router specified by the *gateway* variable. When this is the final parameter in the command line, the word *dev* is optional.

Therefore, the UNIX/Linux route command for creating the same static route specified in the Windows Route.exe example provided earlier would be as follows.

```
route add -net 192.168.3.0 mask 255.255.255.0 gw 192.168.2.7 metric 1 eth0
```

Dynamic Routing

A router only has direct knowledge of the networks to which it is connected. When an internetwork has two or more routers connected to it, dynamic routing enables each of the routers to know about the others and create routing table entries that identify the networks to which the other routers are connected. Dynamic routing uses special application layer protocols that are designed specifically for router-to-router communications.

Consider the following points for the example network shown in Figure 7-14:

- Router 1 has direct knowledge of Networks A and B because the router is connected to both networks.
- Router 2 has direct knowledge of Networks B and C because the router is connected to both networks.
- Router 1 has no direct knowledge of Network C because it is not connected to that network.
- By using a dynamic routing protocol, Router 2 can share its knowledge of Network C with Router 1.
- After Router 2 shares its routing table entry for Network C with Router 1, Router 1 can add an entry for the distant Network C to its routing table.

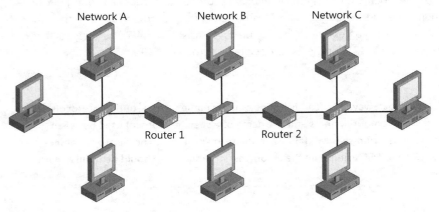

FIGURE 7-14 A dynamic routing example.

On a larger internetwork, the process is repeated throughout the enterprise. Routers compile information about the networks to which they are connected and share it with other routers, by using a routing protocol. By sharing their information in this way, routers can obtain information about distant networks and can route packets more efficiently as a result.

There are many different routing protocols in the TCP/IP suite. On a private internetwork, a single routing protocol such as RIP is usually sufficient to keep all of the routers updated with the latest network information. On the Internet, however, routers use various protocols, depending on their place in the network hierarchy.

Routing protocols are generally divided into two categories: *interior gateway protocols (IGPs)* and *exterior gateway protocols (EGPs)*. On the Internet, a collection of networks that fall within the same administrative domain is called an *autonomous system (AS)*. Autonomous systems are the largest and highest-level administrative units on the Internet. Autonomous systems have unique identifiers called autonomous system numbers (ASNs), consisting of two 16-bit decimal numbers, separated by a period.

> **NOTE AUTONOMOUS SYSTEM NUMBERS**
>
> Autonomous system numbering began as a single 16-bit space until 2007, when it was expanded to its present size. The original 16-bit addresses are now notated with all zeroes in the first 16-bit field.

The AS designation was originally intended to describe systems owned by large private internetworks administered by a single authority, such as a corporation, educational institution, or government agency. The current definition of an AS defines a multilevel structure in which multiple networks using private AS numbers communicate through a single ISP that has a registered AS number.

The routers within an AS use an interior gateway protocol, such as the Routing Information Protocol (RIP) or the Open Shortest Path First (OSPF) protocol, to exchange routing information among themselves. At the edges of an AS are routers that communicate with the other ASes on the Internet, using an exterior gateway protocol (as shown in Figure 7-15) such as the Border Gateway Protocol (BGP) or the Exterior Gateway Protocol (EGP).

> **EXAM TIP**
>
> The term "exterior gateway protocol" is both a generic name for the routing protocols used between autonomous systems and the name of a specific protocol used between ASes. In the latter, the phrase is capitalized, in the former it is not. The Network+ objectives refer to IGP and EGP using only the acronyms, so candidates should be familiar with both usages.

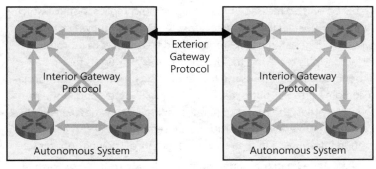

FIGURE 7-15 IGPs and EGPs within and between autonomous systems.

Because the routing chores are split into a two-level hierarchy, packets traveling across the Internet pass through routers that contain only the information needed to get them to the right AS. When the packets arrive at the edge of the AS in which the destination system is located, the routers they access there contain more specific information about the networks within the AS.

The concept is much like the way IP addresses and domain names are assigned on the Internet. Outside entities track only the various network addresses or domains; the individual administrators of each network are responsible for maintaining the host addresses and host names within the network or domain.

EXAM TIP

Because routing protocols operate at the application layer of the OSI model, there is some argument about whether routing is a network layer or an application layer process. However, because the only function of the routing protocols is to populate routing tables, it is only logical to consider the process that makes use of the information in the table to be the primary function of a router, and that is a network layer process.

The following sections examine some of the most common dynamic routing protocols.

ROUTING INFORMATION PROTOCOL (RIP)

The *Routing Information Protocol (RIP)* is one of the most commonly used interior gateway protocols in the TCP/IP suite and on networks around the world, largely because it is supported by many operating systems and is easy to set up and use. In fact, RIP often requires no configuration at all.

Originally designed for UNIX systems, RIP was eventually ported to many other platforms and was standardized in RFC 1058, "Routing Information Protocol," in 1988. Later, RIP was updated to a version 2, which was published in 1998 as RFC 2453.

Most RIP exchanges are based on two message types, requests and replies, both of which are packaged in User Datagram Protocol (UDP) packets addressed to well-known port number 520. When a RIP router starts, it generates a RIP request and transmits it as a broadcast over all of its network interfaces. Upon receiving the broadcast, every other router on any network that supports RIP generates a reply message that contains its routing table information. A reply message can contain up to 25 routes, each of which is 20 bytes long. If the routing table contains more than 25 entries, the router generates multiple reply messages until it has transmitted its entire routing table. When the router that sent the request receives the replies, it integrates the routing information in the reply messages into its own routing table.

RIPv1 messages consist of a 4-byte header and one or more 20-byte routes, as shown in Figure 7-16. A single message can contain up to 25 routes, for a total UDP datagram size of 512 bytes (including the 8-byte UDP header).

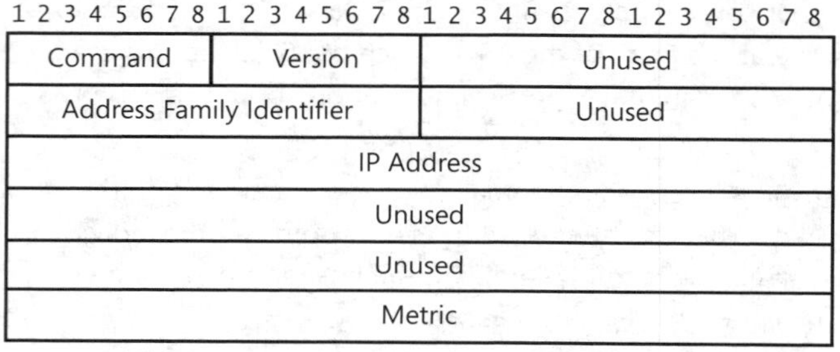

```
1 2 3 4 5 6 7 8 1 2 3 4 5 6 7 8 1 2 3 4 5 6 7 8 1 2 3 4 5 6 7 8
```

Command	Version	Unused	
Address Family Identifier		Unused	
IP Address			
Unused			
Unused			
Metric			

FIGURE 7-16 A RIP version 1 reply message.

The functions of the fields in RIPv1 message are as follows:

- **Command (1 byte)**   Specifies the function of the message, using the following values:
  - **1 – Request**   Requests transmission of the entire routing table or a specific route from all routers on the local network
  - **2 – Reply**   Transmits routing table entries
- **Version (1 byte)**   Specifies the version of RIP running on the system that generated the packet. Possible values are 1 and 2.
- **Address Family Identifier (2 bytes)**   Identifies the network layer protocol for which the message is carrying routing information. The value for IP is 2.
- **IP Address (4 bytes)**   Specifies the address of a network or a host that is accessible through the router generating the message.
- **Metric (4 bytes)**   Specifies the number of hops between the system generating the message and the network or host identified by the IP Address field value.

The metric value included with each RIP route determines the efficiency of the route, based on the number of hops required to reach the destination. When routers receive routing table entries from other routers using RIP, they increment the value of the metric for each route to reflect the additional hop required to reach the destination. The maximum value for a metric in a RIP message is 15. Networks or hosts more than 15 hops away are considered to be un-reachable. This demonstrates that the protocol was designed for use on private internetworks and not the Internet, because Internet routes often require more than 15 hops. A routing protocol that uses metrics based on the number of hops to the destination is called a *distance vector protocol*.

RIP PROBLEMS

In a distance vector routing protocol, every router on the network advertises its routing table to its neighboring routers. Each router then examines the information supplied by the other routers, chooses the best route to each destination network, and adds it to its own routing table.

After their initial exchange of RIP messages, the routers transmit updates every 30 seconds to ensure that all of the other routers on the networks to which they are connected have cur-rent information. If a RIP-supplied routing table entry is not refreshed every three minutes, the router assumes that the entry is no longer viable, increases its metric value to 16 (an illegal value), and eventually removes the entry from the table completely.

The process of updating the routing tables on all of a network's routers in response to a change in the network (such as the failure or addition of a router) is called *convergence*. Dis-tance vector routing is relatively simple and reasonably efficient in terms of locating the best route to a specific network, but it has some fundamental problems.

Distance vector protocols such as RIP have a rather slow convergence rate because updates are generated by each router asynchronously—that is, without synchronization or acknowledgment. They are, therefore, prone to a condition known as the *count-to-infinity problem*.

The count-to-infinity problem occurs when a router detects a failure in the network, modi-fies the appropriate entry in its routing table accordingly, and then has that entry updated by an advertisement from another router before it can broadcast it in its own advertisements. The routers then proceed to bounce their updates back and forth, increasing the metric for the same entry each time until it reaches infinity (16). The process eventually corrects itself, but the delay incurred each time a change occurs in the network slows down the entire rout-ing process.

RIP is also widely criticized for the amount of broadcast traffic it produces. Every RIP router on an internetwork broadcasts its entire routing table every 30 seconds. Depending on the size of the network, this may involve several RIP messages per server. One advantage of the use of broadcasts, however, is that it is possible for systems to process the advertisement messages without advertising their own routing tables. This is called *silent RIP*, and it is more likely to be implemented in host systems that are not routers.

RIP also does not include a subnet mask with each route in an advertisement message. The protocol is designed for use with network addresses that conform to the standard IP address classes, which can be identified by the first three bits of the address.

If the network address for a routing table entry fits the address classes, the protocol uses the subnet mask associated with its class. When this is not possible, the protocol uses the subnet mask of the network interface over which the RIP message was received. If this mask does not fit, the protocol assumes that the table entry contains a host route and uses a subnet mask of 255.255.255.255. These assumptions can cause routers on certain types of networks, such as those that use variable-length subnets or disjointed subnets, to forward traffic incorrectly.

RIP also does not support any form of authentication for participating routers. A RIP router accepts and processes messages from any source, making it possible for the entire network's routing tables to be corrupted with incorrect information supplied (either accidentally or deliberately) by a rogue router.

RIP version 2 (RIPv2) addresses all of these problems.

RIPV2

The primary difference between RIPv1 and RIPv2 is the format of the routes included in the reply messages. The RIPv2 reply message is no larger than that of RIPv1 and uses the same header, but it employs the unused fields from the RIPv1 format to include additional information about each route. The format of a RIPv2 route is shown in Figure 7-17.

1 2 3 4 5 6 7 8 1 2 3 4 5 6 7 8 1 2 3 4 5 6 7 8 1 2 3 4 5 6 7 8

Address Family Identifier	Route Tag
IP Address	
Subnet Mask	
Next Hop	
Metric	

FIGURE 7-17 A RIPv2 route.

The functions of the RIPv2 route fields are as follows:

- **Address Family Identifier (2 bytes)** Contains a code that identifies the protocol for which routing information is being provided. The code for IP is 2. (RIP supports other protocols besides IP.)
- **Route Tag (2 bytes)** Contains an AS number that enables RIP to communicate with EGPs.
- **IP Address (4 bytes)** Specifies the address of the network or host for which the protocol is providing routing information.
- **Subnet Mask (4 bytes)** Contains the subnet mask that the router should apply to the IP Address value.
- **Next Hop (4 bytes)** Specifies the address of the gateway that the router should use to forward traffic to the network or host specified in the IP Address field.
- **Metric (4 bytes)** Contains a value that specifies the relative efficiency of the route.

The other main differences between RIPv1 and RIPv2 are that RIPv2 supports the use of multicast transmissions and can authenticate routes.

The multicast address that RIPv2 uses is 224.0.0.9. Transmissions sent to that address are processed only by the routers and do not affect other systems. By using a multicast address instead of broadcasts, RIPv2 can significantly reduce the amount of extraneous traffic to be processed by the other computers.

The use of multicasts is optional on all RIPv2 routers; broadcasts are still supported. The only possible drawback to the use of multicasts is that if the network contains systems that are using silent RIP, those systems cannot monitor the multicast address for RIP traffic.

RIPv2 also supports the use of authentication, to ensure that incoming RIP messages originate from authorized routers. To authenticate itself to other routers, a RIPv2 router uses the hexadecimal value FFFF for the Address Family Identifier value in the first routing table entry of a reply message. This causes the system to repurpose the entry to contain authentication instead of routing information. The format for the authentication entry is shown in Figure 7-18.

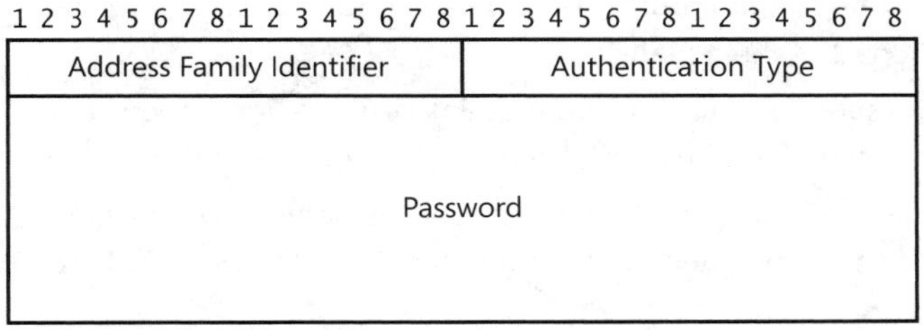

FIGURE 7-18 A RIPv2 authentication entry.

The functions of the fields in an authentication entry are as follows:

- **Address Family Identifier (2 bytes)** Contains the value FFFF, indicating that the entry contains authentication information.

- **Authentication Type (2 bytes)** Specifies the type of authentication information provided in the entry. The only available option is type 2, indicating a simple password.

- **Password (16 bytes)** Contains a plain text password up to 16 bytes long.

OPEN SHORTEST PATH FIRST (OSPF)

Distance vector routing has a fundamental flaw: it bases its routing metrics solely on the number of hops between two networks, and judging routes by the number of hops required to reach a destination is not always efficient. When an internetwork consists of multiple LANs in the same location, all connected by using the same data-link layer protocol, the hop count is a valid indicator. However, when WAN links are involved, a single hop can refer to anything from a high-speed leased line to a standard dial-up modem connection. It is therefore possible for traffic moving over a route with a smaller number of hops to take longer than one with more hops.

The alternative to distance vector routing is called *link state routing,* most commonly used in the *Open Shortest Path First (OSPF)* protocol. A link state routing protocol works by flooding the network with messages called link state advertisements. Each router receiving such a message propagates it to its neighbors, incrementing a sequence number value for each entry that indicates its distance from the source. Using these advertisements, each router compiles a map of the network and uses it to construct its own routing table.

OSPF is an interior gateway protocol that was documented by the Internet Engineering Task Force (IETF) in 1989 and published as RFC 1131. The current specification, which is for OSPF version 2, has been ratified as an IETF standard and was published in April 1998 as RFC 2328.

Unlike with RIP and most other TCP/IP protocols, OSPF messages are not carried within a transport protocol such as UDP or TCP. The OSPF messages are encapsulated directly in IP datagrams and addressed to other routers by using port 89.

Link state routing, as implemented in OSPF, uses a formula called the Dijkstra algorithm to judge the efficiency of a route based on several criteria, including the following:

- **Hop count**   Though link state routing protocols still use the hop count to judge a route's efficiency, it is only part of the equation.
- **Transmission speed**   The speed at which the various links operate is an important part of a route's efficiency. Faster links obviously take precedence over slow ones.
- **Congestion delays**   Link state routing protocols consider the network congestion caused by the current traffic pattern when evaluating a route, and bypass links that are overly congested.
- **Route cost**   The route cost is a metric assigned by the network administrator used to rate the relative usability of various routes. The cost can refer to the literal financial expense incurred by the link, or any other pertinent factor.

Link state routing is more complex than RIP and requires more processing by the router, but it judges the relative efficiency of routes more precisely and has a better convergence rate than RIP. OSPF also reduces the amount of bandwidth used by the routing protocol because it transmits updates to other routers only when changes in the network configuration take place, unlike RIP, which continually transmits the entire routing table.

Several of the advantages of OSPF are clearly the inspiration for the improvements made in the RIP version 2 specification. For example, all OSPF routes include a subnet mask, and OSPF messages are all authenticated by the receiving router before they are processed. The protocol can also use routing information obtained from outside sources, such as exterior gateway protocols. In addition, OSPF provides the capability for creating discrete *areas* within an autonomous system that exchange routing information among themselves. Only certain routers, called *area border routers,* exchange information with other areas. This further reduces the amount of network traffic generated by the routing protocol.

Unlike RIP, OSPF can maintain multiple routes to a specific destination. When two routes to a single network address have the same metric, OSPF balances the traffic load between them.

Version 2 of RIP, therefore, is comparable to OSPF in its features and is definitely the preferable alternative on a relatively small internetwork that does not have severe traffic problems. However, on an internetwork that relies heavily on WAN connections or that has many routers with large routing tables that would generate a lot of network traffic, OSPF is the preferable alternative.

EXAM TIP

Network+ exam candidates must be conscious of which routing protocols are distance vector protocols, which are link state protocols, and which are those they call hybrids. They must also know the differences between these types of routing protocols.

INTERMEDIATE SYSTEM TO INTERMEDIATE SYSTEM (IS-IS)

Intermediate System to Intermediate System (IS-IS) is another link state routing protocol, developed at approximately the same time as OSPF. Like OSPF, IS-IS is an interior gateway protocol that uses the Dijkstra algorithm to calculate route metrics. Though OSPF was specifically designed for use on TCP/IP networks, Digital Equipment Corporation (DEC) designed IS-IS for the Open Systems Interconnection (OSI) protocol stack. It was only later that DEC extended the protocol to route IP traffic, resulting in the RFC 1195 document, "Use of OSI IS-IS for Routing in TCP/IP and Dual Environments."

Like OSPF, IS-IS is capable of subdividing an autonomous system into areas, to reduce the network traffic generated by the routing protocol. Each IS-IS router can be configured to exchange routes within a specific area (called Level 1), between areas (Level 2), or both (Level 1-2). Level 1 and Level 2 routers are only capable of exchanging information with other routers of the same type.

The differences between OSPF and IS-IS are subtle, and mostly involve the way in which each protocol defines and interacts with areas. The ultimate result is that IS-IS is better suited to larger networks, because it generates slightly lower traffic levels.

ENHANCED INTERIOR GATEWAY ROUTING PROTOCOL (EIGRP)

Before OSPF became available, the outcry against RIP grew so loud that Cisco Systems, a prominent manufacturer of router products, came out with the Interior Gateway Routing Protocol (IGRP), and eventually the *Enhanced Interior Gateway Routing Protocol (EIGRP)*. Unlike all of the other routing protocols discussed in this chapter, these protocols are proprietary. EIGRP is something of a hybrid between a distance vector and a link state protocol, relying on six vector metrics to compare the value of the routes in the table. These vector metrics are as follows:

- **Bandwidth**   The bandwidth of the link between the router and the destination network

- **Load**   The relative traffic saturation of the link between the router and the destination network

- **Delay**   The total transmission delay between the router and the destination network

- **Reliability**   The relative reliability of the link between the router and the destination network
- **MTU**   The path maximum transfer unit (MTU) value of the link between the router and the destination network
- **Hop count**   The number of intermediate systems between the router and the destination network

BORDER GATEWAY PROTOCOL (BGP)

RIP, OSPF, and IS-IS are all interior gateway protocols. Administrators of enterprise networks can decide for themselves which of these protocols they want to use. Exterior gateway protocols facilitate the exchange of routing information between autonomous systems. The routers in the ASes that communicate by using an EGP are called border routers or edge routers.

The original exterior gateway protocol was actually called Exterior Gateway Protocol (notice the capitalization). This was a relatively simple protocol that maintained information about the continued reachability of neighboring routers. Conceived when the Internet was young, the Exterior Gateway Protocol became obsolete, but the concept of the exterior gateway protocol (again, notice the capitalization) did not. Today, the operative exterior gateway protocol on the Internet is the *Border Gateway Protocol (BGP),* now in version 4.

Internet Service Providers rely on BGP for communication between the border routers of autonomous systems. Therefore, the typical server or LAN administrator might never work directly with the BGP protocol in his or her entire career. However, as a core underlying protocol of the Internet, BGP provides benefits to virtually all computer users and administrators as they use the Internet to access distant resources around the world.

Unlike the routers connecting LANs together, or connecting LANs to WAN connections, the border routers of autonomous systems are relatively stable, and their routing information does not change frequently. For this reason, administrators actually create the peer relationships between BGP routers manually, after which the routers establish connections to each other by using TCP port 179.

> *NOTE* **INTERIOR BGP**
>
> It is entirely possible to use BGP for communication between routers within an autonomous system. In this case, the protocol is referred to as Interior BGP. When border routers in different autonomous systems communicate, the protocol is called Exterior BGP.

Strictly speaking, BGP is not a distance vector protocol; it is a path vector protocol because it exchanges path information with its neighboring routers, not the hop counts used by RIP and the like. BGP update messages include the AS number of each route's origin, and other information not typically found in IGP messages. BGP routers also have elaborate rules that they use to assess the relative value of the routes they receive from neighbors.

EXAM TIP

BGP does not rely solely on hop counts when comparing routes, so it is technically not a distance vector routing protocol. However, the Network+ exam objectives refer to it as such, and you might see this terminology used on the actual exam.

 Quick Check

1. Distance vector routing protocols rely on what metric when evaluating the relative efficiency of routing table entries?

2. Which link state IGP was developed for use with the OSI protocol stack?

Quick Check Answers

1. Hop counts

2. IS-IS

Switching

The original internetwork configuration used multiple LANs connected by routers to form a network that was larger than was possible with a single LAN. This was necessary because LANs are based on a shared network medium, and there is a limit to the number of systems that can share the medium before the network is overwhelmed by traffic. Routers segregate the traffic on the individual LANs, forwarding only those packets addressed to systems on other LANs.

Routers have been around for decades, but switches are a relatively new type of device. Switches have revolutionized network design and made it possible to create LANs of almost unlimited size. As discussed in Chapter 3, a *switch* is a multiport bridging device in which each port forms a separate network segment. Similar in appearance to a hub, a switch receives incoming traffic through any of its ports and forwards the traffic out to the single port needed to reach the destination.

For example, in a small workgroup network with each computer connected to a port in the same switch, each system has a dedicated, full-bandwidth connection to the switch. Except for the switch itself, there is no shared network medium, and consequently, there are no collisions. In addition, the computers realize increased security because, without a shared medium, an unauthorized workstation cannot monitor and capture the traffic not intended for it.

Switches operate at layer 2 of the OSI reference model, the data-link layer, creating what is essentially a single large network, instead of a series of smaller networks connected by routers. This also means that the switches can support any network layer protocol. Like transparent bridges, switches can learn the topology of a network and perform functions such as forwarding and packet filtering. Some switches are also capable of full-duplex communications and automatic speed adjustment.

In the traditional arrangement for a larger internetwork, multiple LANs are connected to a backbone network with routers. The backbone network is a shared-medium LAN like all of the others, however, and must therefore carry all of the internetwork traffic generated by the horizontal networks. This is why the backbone network traditionally uses a faster protocol. On a switched network, workstations are connected to individual workgroup switches, which in turn are connected to a single, high-performance switch, thus enabling any system on the network to open a dedicated connection to any other system. This arrangement can be expanded further to include an intermediate layer of departmental switches as well. You can then connect servers required by all users directly to a departmental switch or to the top-level switch, for better performance.

Replacing hubs and routers with switches is an excellent way to improve the performance of a network without changing protocols or modifying individual workstations. A Fast Ethernet network exhibits a dramatic improvement when each workstation is given a full 100 Mbps of bandwidth, rather than sharing it with 20 or 30 other systems. Full-duplex switches can double the effective bandwidth to 200 Mbps, providing a full 100 Mbps in each direction. Gigabit and 10-gigabit switches offer 10 and 100 times more bandwidth, respectively.

Routing vs. Switching

As mentioned in Chapter 3, switching is faster and cheaper than routing, but it raises some problems in most network configurations. By using switches, you eliminate subnets and create a single flat network segment that hosts all of your computers. Any two systems can communicate by using a dedicated link that is essentially a temporary two-node network. This is a brilliant solution for small to medium-sized networks, but when the network reaches a certain size, there are problems with this model.

The problems arise when workstations generate broadcast messages. Because a switched network forms a single broadcast domain, all broadcast messages are propagated throughout the whole network and every system must process them, which can waste enormous amounts of bandwidth and processor time.

One of the advantages of creating multiple LANs and connecting them with routers is that broadcasts are limited to the individual networks. Routers also provide security by limiting transmissions to a single subnet. To avoid the wasted bandwidth caused by broadcasts, it has become necessary to implement certain routing concepts on switched networks. This has led to several new technologies that integrate routing and switching to varying degrees. This combination of functions has resulted in a class of network connection devices that span levels 2 and 3 of the OSI model. Not surprisingly, these are often referred to as *multilevel devices*.

Multilevel Devices

The type of broadband router that many residential and small business users have in their homes and offices connects a private network to an ISP's network, making it a level 3, or network layer, device. However, the same device typically includes a wireless access point or multiple switched Ethernet ports (or both), making it a level 2, or data-link layer device, as well. This is one type of multilevel device.

The switches that administrators use to create larger network infrastructures are multilevel devices as well, but in a different way. Starting off with a simple level 2 switch, manufacturers add level 3 routing capabilities that address the issue of broadcast management.

Virtual LANs

A *virtual LAN* or VLAN is a group of systems on a switched network that functions as a logical network segment. The systems on a VLAN can communicate locally with each other, but not with systems on other VLANs. The physical network is still switched, however; the VLANs exist as a logical overlay to the switching fabric, as shown in Figure 7-19.

The standard that defines the use of virtual LANs on an Ethernet network is 802.1Q, published by the Institute of Electrical and Electronics Engineers (IEEE). This standard defines a method by which switches add a 32-bit subheader into Ethernet frames. The subheader is called a *VLAN tag*, and it identifies the LAN to which the frame belongs. When a frame is transmitted from one VLAN to another, the tag identifies the VLAN of its origin. For transmissions between computers on the same VLAN, the switches remove the tags.

The ability to create and manage VLANs is a feature built into some switch products. Network administrators create VLANs by using a web-based configuration utility built into the switch. With this utility, administrators can specify the MAC addresses or switch ports of the systems that are to be part of each VLAN. Because VLANs are independent of the physical network, their members can be located anywhere, and a single system can even be a member of more than one VLAN.

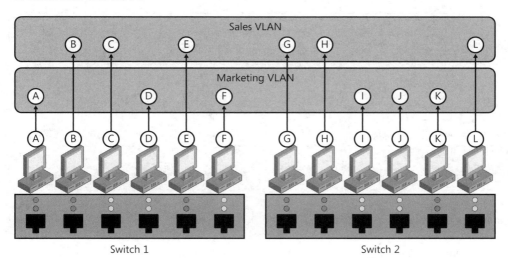

FIGURE 7-19 VLANs on a switched network.

VLAN Memberships

Both of these methods of designating VLAN memberships have advantages. When you define the members of a VLAN by supplying their MAC addresses, then it doesn't matter what switch you connect the computers to or which port in the switch you use. You can physically move computers to any location and they will remain in the same VLANs. This is useful when you base your VLAN design on job types or departmental boundaries that are independent of physical locations.

If you base your VLANs on switch ports, then any computer you plug into a particular port becomes a member of the designated VLAN. This is the preferred solution if you base your VLANs on geographic boundaries.

Trunking

A large network typically has multiple switches, and as you have seen, configuring VLANs results in switch ports being dedicated to specific VLANs. You can create VLANs that span multiple switches, but to do so, there must be a means for the switches to exchange traffic outside of the VLAN substructure.

To make this possible, you designate a port on each switch as a trunk port and use it to connect that switch to the others on your network, as shown in Figure 7-20. *Trunking* enables the members of a VLAN on one switch to communicate with members of the same VLAN on another switch, just as if you connected them to the same device.

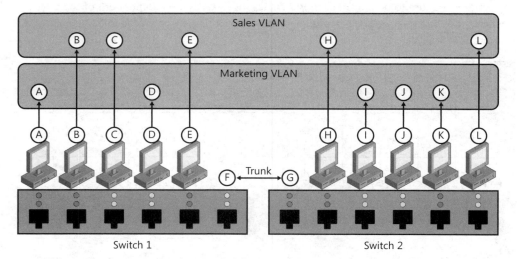

FIGURE 7-20 Trunking between VLAN switches.

Trunk ports are basically switch ports that can forward and receive frames that are tagged or untagged. When a trunk port receives an untagged frame, it forwards it to the port's default VLAN. If an incoming frame is tagged, the port forwards it to the VLAN specified in the tag.

Routing VLANs

After VLANs are in place on your network switches, broadcast messages generated by any of the computers are limited to the VLAN where they originated, just as on a routed network. VLANs therefore address the broadcast problem by creating isolated broadcast domains. However, there is still the problem of communication between VLANs. Even though your network segments are virtual, and all of the computers on the network are connected by switches, you still need a router to enable a computer on one VLAN to communicate with a computer on another.

LAYER 2 SWITCHING

Most early switches and lower-end models are limited to layer 2 functionality, which prevents them from routing traffic between VLANs themselves. With these devices, the only way to enable interworking between VLANs is to physically connect a router to two ports on different VLANs, as shown in Figure 7-21. With this model, traffic flows just as it would if you used physical, and not virtual, LANs. All traffic within the VLAN is switched, and all inter-VLAN traffic is routed. This method is sometimes called "switch where you can; route where you must."

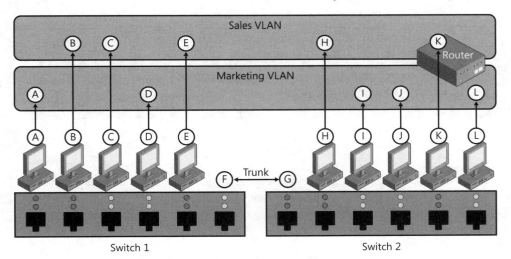

FIGURE 7-21 Connecting VLANs with a physical router.

The efficiency of this arrangement depends on how much of your network traffic remains within the VLANs and how much must be routed between VLANs. Routing is inherently slower than switching, because there is more processing involved. The more inter-VLAN traffic there is on your network, the more the additional speed of your switches is squandered.

LAYER 3 SWITCHING

Today's advanced switches are capable of resolving this problem another way. Instead of using physical routers to connect VLANs, some switches can create logical routers that connect VLANs within the virtual infrastructure. This is sometimes called *layer 3 switching*, which is really a contradiction in terms, although hardware manufacturers have given it a variety of other names, including interVLAN routing, IP switching, and multilayer routing.

A layer 3 switch enables you to create a virtual router between two VLANs, as shown in Figure 7-22, that can forward traffic between them, just as a physical router does. The advantage of this method, apart from saving you the expense of purchasing routers, is that the switch uses the virtual routers to establish a connection between the two VLANs, after which the underlying switching infrastructure takes over. This technique is called "route once, switch afterward," because the amount of routed traffic is minimized, even when systems on different VLANs are communicating.

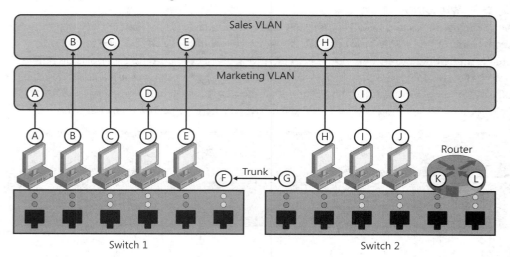

FIGURE 7-22 Connecting VLANs with virtual routers.

Layer 3 switches are true multilevel devices because their functions encompass both bridging and routing. These capabilities add significantly to the cost of the device, but compared to the cost of the additional hardware you would need otherwise, they can be the most economical solution for many organizations.

Configuring VLAN Trunking Protocol (VTP)

In an enterprise network environment, it is common to have multiple switches at various locations, with virtual LANs (VLANs) that are spread among the switches. Configuring the VLANs involves selecting the ports (or conceivably the addresses) that belong to each subnet. It is possible to configure the switches manually, but this can be time-consuming, and like all manual configuration processes, is prone to input error.

Cisco Systems has developed a proprietary switch configuration mechanism called the VLAN Trunking Protocol (VTP). VTP enables administrators to configure one switch and automatically replicate the settings to the other switches on the enterprise network.

While VTP can only configure switches made by Cisco Systems, there are also open standards defining configuration protocols for switches, including the Multiple VLAN Registration Protocol (MVRP).

> ✔ **Quick Check**
>
> 1. To create a VLAN that spans two switches, you must enable communication between the switches by using a process called _____.
>
> 2. The "route once, switch afterward" technique is a property of a device called a _____ switch.
>
> **Quick Check Answers**
>
> 1. Trunking
>
> 2. Layer 3

Power Over Ethernet (PoE)

Power over Ethernet (PoE) is a technology for delivering electrical power to network devices over standard Ethernet cables, along with regular data signals. The advantages of this are several: supplying power through the network eliminates the need for an electrical socket at every network device location.

PoE also enables administrators to centralize power conditioning and monitoring services. Rather than supply each device with its own surge protector or uninterrupted power supply, the administrator can protect one single power source, and use it to supply power to devices all over the network.

The capabilities of PoE are limited. PoE cannot deliver anywhere near the amount of power that a computer requires to run, for example. The current standard defining PoE calls for a maximum of 25.5 watts, while a typical desktop computer has at least a 250 watt power supply. Devices that can receive power using PoE include wireless access points, remote switches, VoIP telephones, and video cameras. PoE also cannot deliver power over fiber optic cables (which do not carry electrical signals at all), and cannot deliver high power over any twist pair cable lower than Cat 5.

EXAM TIP

While the Network+ exam objectives associate PoE with routers and switches, the technology is not always implemented by these devices. There are also standalone devices that can inject power into an existing cable.

Exercises

The answers for these exercises are located in the "Answers" section at the end of this chapter.

Scenario #1

On your corporate internetwork, there are two computers running Windows Server 2008 R2 that have been configured to function as routers, called Server A and Server B. Both servers have two network interface adapters installed in them, and neither is running any routing protocols. The network interface adapters in Server A have been assigned the IP addresses 192.168.42.1 and 192.168.65.1. Server B is configured to use IP addresses 192.168.65.8 and 192.168.12.1. All four addresses use the same subnet mask, 255.255.255.0. What Route.exe command should you execute on Server A to enable it to route traffic to both of the networks to which Server B is connected? What Route.exe command should you execute on Server B to enable it to route traffic to both of the networks to which Server A is connected?

Scenario #2

Two small businesses, Adventure Works and Blue Yonder Airlines, have decided to merge. Both companies have made substantial investments in their networking equipment, and Blue Yonder intends to move its entire headquarters operation to Adventure Works's office building.

Adventure Works has an internetwork that consists of 12 subnets, all located in the one office building and all connected to a single backbone. These subnets have network addresses ranging from 172.16.0.0 through 172.27.0.0, with a subnet mask of 255.255.0.0.

Blue Yonder has an internetwork that consists of three subnets at their headquarters and 15 others located in branch offices around the country, which are connected to the headquarters by means of routers and WAN links of various types, ranging from dial-up modem VPN connections to high-speed leased lines. The Blue Yonder networks have network addresses ranging from 192.168.1.0 through 192.168.18.0, with a subnet mask of 255.255.255.0.

The newly merged company has plans to open several other offices during the next year. After moving Blue Yonder's headquarters network to the new location, the owners intend to connect it to the Adventure Works network, using a computer running Windows Server 2008 R2 configured to function as a router. Which of the following router configuration solutions would best suit this network environment? Explain your answer.

A. Use static routing.

B. Install RIPv1 on all of the network's routers.

C. Install RIPv2 on all of the network's routers.

D. Install OSPF on all of the network's routers.

Chapter Summary

- The simplest type of routing architecture is used when a LAN must be connected to another LAN some distance away, by using a wide area network (WAN) connection.

- A router can be a stand-alone hardware device or a regular computer. Server operating systems such as Windows Server and many UNIX and Linux distributions can route IP traffic.

- The routing table is the heart of any router. It holds the information that the router uses to forward packets to the proper destinations.

- Because IPv6 addresses are larger than IPv4 addresses, IPv6 headers are larger, and IPv6 routing table entries must be larger than those for IPv4. However, although these two factors might seem to increase the router processing burden, IPv6 is actually designed to improve router efficiency.

- The Internet Control Message Protocol (ICMP) provides several important functions to routers and the systems that use them.

- Network Address Translation (NAT) is a routing technique that enables computers with private (or unregistered) IP addresses to access the Internet.

- There are two techniques for updating the routing table: static routing and dynamic routing. In static routing, a network administrator manually creates routing table entries. In dynamic routing, routers use specialized protocols to create routing table entries automatically.

- The Routing Information Protocol (RIP) is one of the most commonly used interior gateway protocols in the TCP/IP suite and on networks around the world, largely because it is supported by many operating systems and is easy to set up and use. In fact, RIP often requires no configuration at all.

- The primary difference between RIPv1 and RIPv2 is the format of the routes included in the reply messages.

- A switch is a multiport bridging device in which each port forms a separate network segment. Similar in appearance to a hub, a switch receives incoming traffic through any of its ports and forwards the traffic out to the single port needed to reach the destination.

- A virtual LAN (also called a VLAN) is a group of systems on a switched network that functions as a logical network segment.

- Trunking enables the members of a VLAN on one switch to communicate with members of the same VLAN on another switch, just as if you connected them to the same device.

- Some switches can create logical routers that connect VLANs within the virtual infrastructure. This is sometimes called layer 3 switching.

Chapter Review

Test your knowledge of the information in Chapter 7 by answering these questions. The answers to these questions, and the explanations of why each answer choice is correct or incorrect, are located in the "Answers" section at the end of this chapter.

1. The address in the Next Hop field of a RIPv2 route ends up in which column of a Windows routing table?

    A. Network Destination

    B. Netmask

    C. Gateway

    D. Metric

2. Which of the following standards defines the formation of VLANs and the trunking protocol?

    A. IEEE 802.1Q

    B. IEEE 802.11n

    C. IEEE 802.3ab

    D. IEEE 802.1X

3. Which of the following are link state routing protocols?

    A. RIPv1

    B. RIPv2

    C. OSPF

    D. BGP

    E. IS-IS

4. What switching technique makes it possible to host a VLAN on multiple switches at the same time?

    A. Layer 3 switching

    B. Trunking

    C. Silent RIP

    D. Convergence

Answers

This section contains the answers to the questions for the exercises and Chapter Review in this chapter.

Exercises

- **Scenario #1:**

```
route add 192.168.12.0 mask 255.255.255.0 192.168.65.8 if 1 metric 1

route add 192.168.42.0 mask 255.255.255.0 192.168.65.1 if 1 metric 1
```

- **Scenario #2:** Answer D is correct because OSPF is best suited to a network with a large number of WAN links of different types. OSPF rates the efficiency of a route by measuring the actual properties of each network connection, as opposed to simply counting the number of hops.

Chapter Review

1. **Correct Answer:** C

    A. **Incorrect:** The value from the IP Address field goes in the Network Destination column.

    B. **Incorrect:** The value from the Subnet Mask field goes in the Netmask column.

    C. **Correct:** The value from the Next Hop field goes in the Gateway column.

    D. **Incorrect:** The value from the Metric field goes in the Metric column.

2. **Correct Answer:** A

    A. **Correct:** The IEEE 802.1Q standard defines the creation of VLANs on Ethernet networks.

    B. **Incorrect:** The 802.11n document is a wireless networking standard.

    C. **Incorrect:** The 802.3ab document is a Gigabit Ethernet standard.

    D. **Incorrect:** The 802.1X document defines the EAP network authentication mechanism.

3. **Correct Answers:** C and D

    A. **Incorrect:** RIPv1 is a distance vector routing protocol.

    B. **Incorrect:** RIPv2 is a distance vector routing protocol.

    C. **Correct:** OSPF is a link state routing protocol.

    D. **Correct:** IS-IS is a link state routing protocol.

E. **Incorrect:** BGP is a path vector protocol that the Network+ objectives refer to as a distance vector protocol, but in no case is it a link state protocol.

4. **Correct Answer:** B

A. **Incorrect:** Layer 3 switching is a technique that enables administrators to create virtual routers that connect VLANs together at the network layer.

B. **Correct:** Trunking is a technique that connects switches together and enables them to exchange all types of traffic.

C. **Incorrect:** Silent RIP is a routing technique, not a switching technique.

D. **Incorrect:** Convergence is the process by which routers modify their routing tables to accommodate changes in the network infrastructure.

The Transport Layer

As discussed in Chapter 6, "The Network Layer," the Internet Protocol (IP) is the primary end-to-end protocol in the TCP/IP suite. However, as you might guess from the name *TCP/IP*, TCP—a transport layer protocol—plays a prominent role as well. In TCP/IP communications, the network layer and the transport layer actually work together to provide the end-to-end services that an application needs.

To clarify the individual functions of the network and transport layers, you could say that IP at the network layer provides the essential services for end-to-end transmission through the internetwork, whereas the transport layer provides the optional functions that enable the protocols to achieve a required quality of service. The only essential function of the transport layer is protocol identification, which specifies the source and destination applications that generated and that will receive the data in the packet.

Exam objectives in this chapter:

Objective 1.5: Identify common TCP and UDP default ports.

- SMTP – 25
- HTTP – 80
- HTTPS – 443
- FTP – 20, 21

- TELNET – 23
- IMAP – 143
- RDP – 3389
- SSH – 22

- DNS – 53
- DHCP – 67, 68

Objective 1.6: Explain the function of common networking protocols.

- TCP
- FTP
- UDP
- TCP/IP suite
- DHCP
- TFTP
- DNS
- HTTPS
- HTTP

- ARP
- SIP (VoIP)
- RTP (VoIP)
- SSH
- POP3
- NTP
- IMAP4
- Telnet
- SMTP

- SNMP2/3
- ICMP
- IGMP
- TLS

The TCP/IP suite uses two protocols at the transport layer to provide different levels of service for applications: the *Transmission Control Protocol (TCP)* and the *User Datagram Protocol (UDP)*. Both TCP and UDP generate protocol data units (PDUs) that are carried inside IP datagrams. TCP is a connection-oriented protocol that provides reliable service with guaranteed delivery, packet acknowledgment, flow control, and error correction and detection. UDP is a connectionless protocol that provides unreliable service with a minimum of overhead.

TCP is designed for transmitting data that requires perfect bit accuracy, such as program and data files. Many applications use UDP for short transactions that consist only of a single request and reply; others use it for data transmissions that can survive the loss of a few bits, such as audio and video streams. Not surprisingly, TCP generates much more control traffic than UDP does because it provides all of these services, whereas the UDP overhead is quite low.

Transmission Control Protocol (TCP)

TCP/IP gets its name from the combination of the TCP and IP protocols, which together provide the service that accounts for the majority of traffic on a TCP/IP network. Internet applications such as web browsers and email clients depend on the TCP protocol to retrieve large amounts of data from servers, without error. TCP is defined in Request for Comments (RFC) 793, "Transmission Control Protocol: DARPA Internet Program Protocol Specification," published in 1981 by the Internet Engineering Task Force (IETF) and ratified as Internet Standard 7.

The TCP Header

Transport layer protocols encapsulate data that they receive from the application layer protocols operating above them in the OSI model by applying a header, just as the protocols at the lower layers do. The TCP header, in its default configuration, is 20 bytes long, the same size as the IP header.

In many cases, an application layer protocol will pass more data to TCP than can fit into a single packet, so TCP splits the data into smaller pieces. Each piece is called a segment, and the segments that compose a single transaction are known collectively as a sequence. TCP applies a separate header to each segment, as illustrated in Figure 8-1, and passes the segment down to the network layer for transmission in a separate datagram.

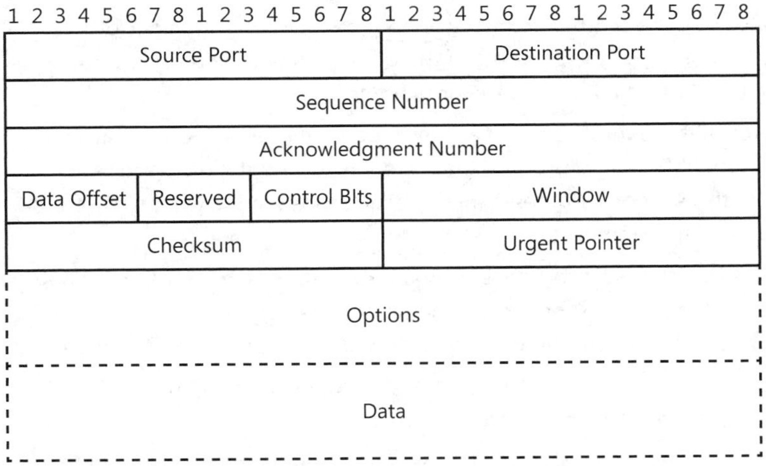

FIGURE 8-1 The TCP message format.

The TCP header on each segment contains information specifying where it belongs in the sequence. When all of the segments arrive at the destination system, the receiving computer uses the header information to reassemble the segments back into their original order. At the same time, the header carries information that enables the destination system to acknowledge packets received intact, check packets for errors, order the retransmission of lost packets, and regulate the transmission rate of the sender.

The functions of the TCP message fields are as follows:

- **Source Port (2 bytes)**   Identifies the process or application on the transmitting system that generated the information carried in the Data field.

- **Destination Port (2 bytes)**   Identifies the process on the receiving system for which the information in the Data field is intended.

- **Sequence Number (4 bytes)**   Identifies the location of the data in this segment in relation to the entire sequence.

- **Acknowledgment Number (4 bytes)**   In acknowledgment (ACK) messages, specifies the sequence number of the next segment expected by the receiving system.

- **Data Offset (4 bits)**   Specifies the number of 4-byte words in the TCP header.

- **Reserved (6 bits)**   Unused.

- **Control Bits (6 bits)**   Contains six flag bits that identify the functions of the message, as follows:

  - **URG**   Indicates that the segment contains urgent data. When this flag is present, the receiving system reads the contents of the Urgent Pointer field to determine which part of the Data field contains the urgent information.

  - **ACK**   Indicates that the message is an acknowledgment of a previously transmitted segment. When this flag is present, the system receiving the message reads the contents of the Acknowledgment Number field to determine what part of the sequence it should transmit next.

  - **PSH**   Indicates that the receiving system should push (that is, forward) the data it has received in the current sequence to the process identified in the Destination Port field immediately, rather than waiting for the rest of the sequence to arrive.

  - **RST**   Causes the receiving system to reset the TCP connection and discard all of the segments of the sequence it has received thus far.

  - **SYN**   Synchronizes the systems' respective Sequence Number values during the establishment of a TCP connection.

  - **FIN**   Terminates a TCP connection.

- **Window (2 bytes)**   Specifies how many bytes the computer can accept from the connected system.

- **Checksum (2 bytes)** Contains the results of a cyclical redundancy check (CRC) performed by the transmitting system. These results are used by the receiving system to detect errors in the TCP header, data, and parts of the IP header.

- **Urgent Pointer (2 bytes)** When the urgent (URG) control bit is present, indicates which part of the data in the segment the receiver should treat as urgent.

- **Options (variable)** Contains information related to optional TCP connection configuration features.

- **Data (variable)** Contains one segment of an information sequence generated by an application layer protocol.

MORE INFO   **MORE ON PORTS**

For more information on the values used for the Source Port and Destination Port fields, see the "Ports and Sockets" section later in this chapter.

It is possible for some TCP implementations to use a slightly modified format of the TCP header, depending on their support for other RFCs published since the ratification of the TCP protocol. For example, there is an improved technique for detecting network congestion called Explicit Congestion Notification (ECN), as defined in RFC 3168, which requires two additional control bits in the TCP header, which it takes from the Reserved field immediately preceding the Control Bits field.

TCP Options

TCP has an Options field that can carry additional information that performs a variety of extra functions. The Options field contains a subheader, as shown in Figure 8-2.

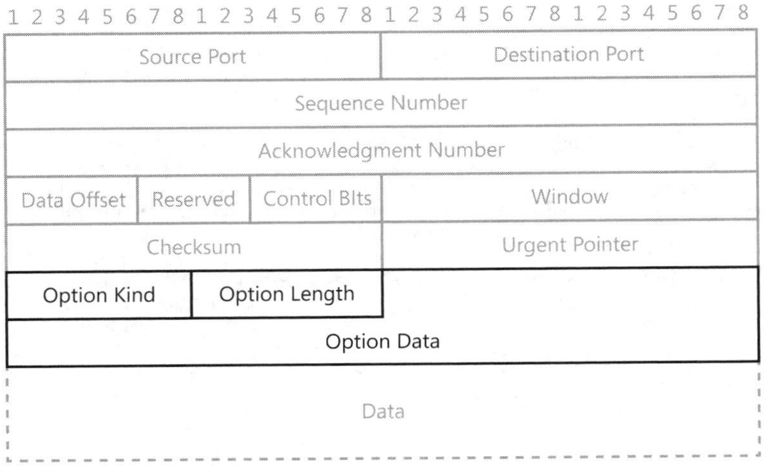

FIGURE 8-2 The TCP Options subheader.

The Options subheader consists of the following three fields:

- **Option Kind (1 byte)** Specifies the function of the option
- **Option Length (1 byte)** Specifies the length of the Options field, including all three subfields
- **Option Data (variable)** Contains information specific to the option's function

> **NOTE TCP RFCS**
>
> As with the Options field in the IP header, there are several RFCs that expand the functionality of the protocol by defining new options for specific purposes. The current list of TCP options is available at *http://www.iana.org/assignments/tcp-parameters/tcp-parameters.xml*.

Some of the most commonly used TCP options are listed in Table 8-1, along with their Option Kind and Option Length values.

TABLE 8-1 Commonly Used TCP Options

Option Kind	Option Length (in Bytes)	Option Name	Description
0	N/A	End Of Options List	Indicates the end of the Options field in a datagram. When a datagram includes multiple options, the End Of Options List option appears after the last one.
1	N/A	No Operation (NOOP)	Functions as a padding byte between options to align the beginning of the subsequent option on the boundary of a 32-bit word.
2	4	Maximum Segment Size	In segments containing the SYN control bit, specifies the size of the largest segment the system can receive.
3	3	WSOPT – Window Scale	Enables the systems involved in a TCP connection to expand the functionality of the Window field from 16 to 32 bits.
4	2	SACK Permitted	Enables a TCP system receiving data to acknowledge individual segments that have arrived successfully so that specific segments that have been dropped can be retransmitted individually.
5	Variable	SACK	
8	10	TSOPT – Timestamp	Enables systems receiving TCP data packets to include time stamps in their acknowledgments, enabling the sender to measure the round trip time for the two systems.

TCP Communications

As noted in Chapter 1, "Networking Basics," TCP is a connection-oriented protocol, which means that before two systems can exchange application layer data, they must first establish a connection. This connection ensures that both computers are present, operating properly, and ready to send and receive data. The systems also exchange information about their capabilities, which determines how subsequent communications will proceed. The TCP connection remains active during the entire exchange of data, after which the systems close it in an orderly manner.

In most cases, a TCP connection exists for the duration of a single file transmission. For example, when a web browser connects to a server on the Internet, it first establishes a connection with the server, then it transmits a Hypertext Transfer Protocol (HTTP) request message specifying the file it wants to download, and finally it receives the file from the server. After the file is transferred, the systems terminate the connection. As the browser processes the downloaded file, it might detect links to graphic images, audio clips, or other files needed to display the webpage. The browser then establishes a separate connection to the server for each of the linked files, retrieves them, and displays them as part of the downloaded page. Thus, downloading a single webpage might require the browser to create many separate TCP connections to the server to download the individual files.

Establishing a Connection

The process that TCP uses to establish a connection is known as a *three-way handshake*. This process consists of an exchange of three messages (as shown in Figure 8-3), none of which contain any application layer data. The purpose of these messages, apart from determining that the other computer actually exists and is ready to receive data, is to exchange the sequence numbers that the computers will use to number the messages they transmit. At the start of the handshake, each computer selects an *initial sequence number (ISN)* for the first TCP message it transmits. The computers then increment the sequence numbers for each subsequent message. The computers select an ISN by using an incrementing algorithm that makes it highly unlikely for connections between the same two computers to use identical sequence numbers at the same time. Each computer maintains its own sequence numbers, and, during the handshake, each informs the other of the numbers it will use.

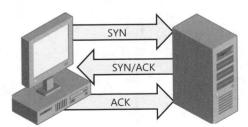

FIGURE 8-3 The TCP three-way handshake.

TCP Connectivity

The connection established by two TCP systems is only a logical connection, not a permanent channel between the two, as is the case on a circuit-switching network. The systems still transmit the individual TCP messages within IP datagrams, using IP's connectionless service. The messages might take different routes to the destination and might even arrive in a different order from that in which they were transmitted. TCP accounts for all of these possibilities. The sequence numbers in each segment enable the receiving system to rearrange the data segments into the proper order.

THE FIRST MESSAGE

The messages that contain the ISN for each computer have the SYN flag set in the Control Bits field. In a typical TCP transaction, a client computer transmits a SYN message, as shown in Figure 8-4, with its ISN (891949873, in this case) in the Sequence Number field. The client then enters the SYN-SENT state, indicating that it is waiting to receive an acknowledgment from the server. The server is initially in the LISTEN state as it waits for a connection from a client.

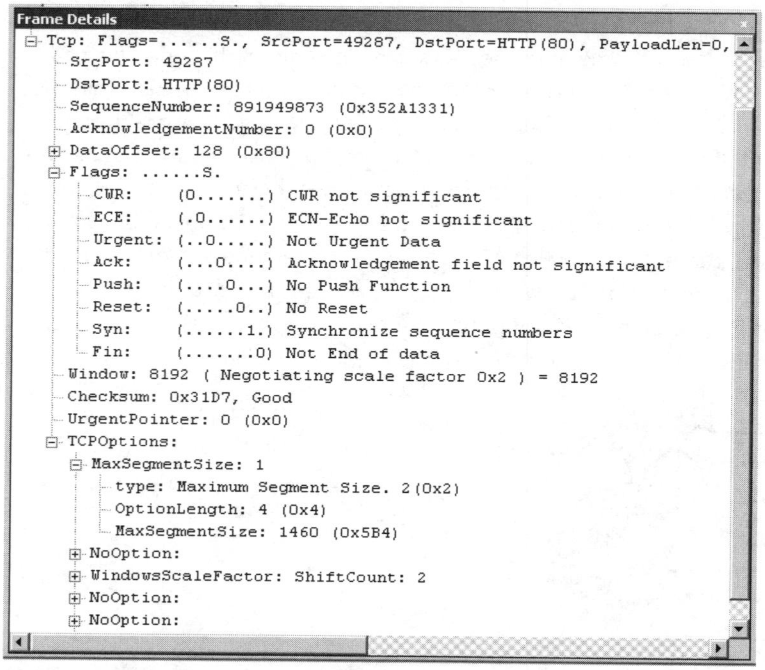

```
Frame Details                                                        x
├ Tcp: Flags=......S., SrcPort=49287, DstPort=HTTP(80), PayloadLen=0,
│   ├ SrcPort: 49287
│   ├ DstPort: HTTP(80)
│   ├ SequenceNumber: 891949873 (0x352A1331)
│   ├ AcknowledgementNumber: 0 (0x0)
│   ├ DataOffset: 128 (0x80)
│   ├ Flags: ......S.
│   │   ├ CWR:    (0.......) CWR not significant
│   │   ├ ECE:    (.0......) ECN-Echo not significant
│   │   ├ Urgent: (..0.....) Not Urgent Data
│   │   ├ Ack:    (...0....) Acknowledgement field not significant
│   │   ├ Push:   (....0...) No Push Function
│   │   ├ Reset:  (.....0..) No Reset
│   │   ├ Syn:    (......1.) Synchronize sequence numbers
│   │   └ Fin:    (.......0) Not End of data
│   ├ Window: 8192 ( Negotiating scale factor 0x2 ) = 8192
│   ├ Checksum: 0x31D7, Good
│   ├ UrgentPointer: 0 (0x0)
│   ├ TCPOptions:
│   │   ├ MaxSegmentSize: 1
│   │   │   ├ type: Maximum Segment Size. 2(0x2)
│   │   │   ├ OptionLength: 4 (0x4)
│   │   │   └ MaxSegmentSize: 1460 (0x5B4)
│   │   ├ NoOption:
│   │   ├ WindowsScaleFactor: ShiftCount: 2
│   │   ├ NoOption:
│   │   └ NoOption:
```

FIGURE 8-4 The first message in the TCP three-way handshake.

Another function of the SYN messages generated by two computers during the three-way handshake is for each system to inform the other of its *maximum segment size (MSS)*. Each system uses the other system's MSS to determine how much data it should include in each segment it transmits. The MSS value for each system depends on which data-link layer protocol the network on which each system resides is using. The MSS is included as a TCP option in the two SYN packets. In this example, the client advertises its MSS value as 1,460 bytes, which is the standard 1,500-byte size for an Ethernet network, minus 40 bytes for the IP and TCP headers.

THE SECOND MESSAGE

When the server receives the client's SYN message, it generates a response that performs two functions, as shown in Figure 8-5. First, the ACK flag is set so that the message functions as an acknowledgment of the client's SYN message. Second, in addition to the ACK control bit, the server's response message also has the SYN flag set and includes its own ISN in the Sequence Number field, as well as the MSS option. After transmitting this message, the server enters the SYN-RECEIVED state.

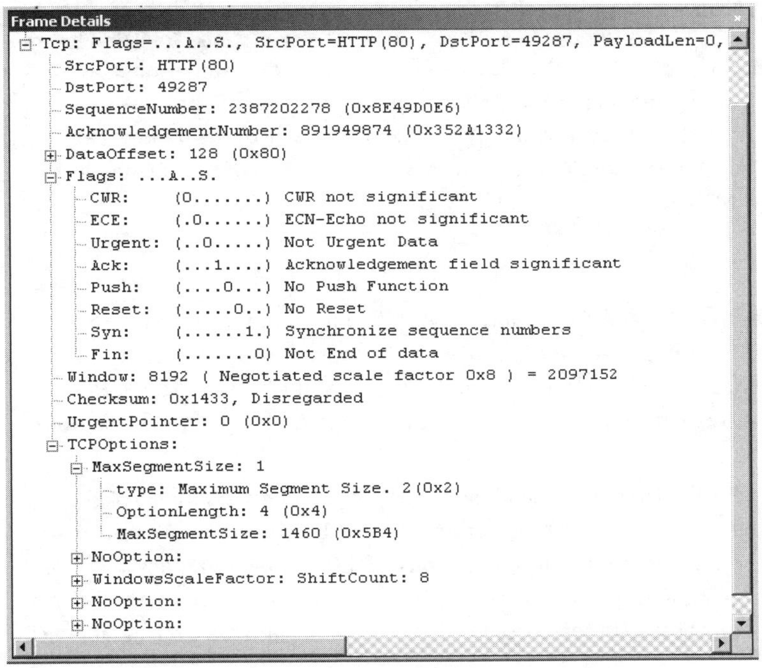

```
Frame Details                                                          ×
⊟ Tcp: Flags=...A..S., SrcPort=HTTP(80), DstPort=49287, PayloadLen=0, ▲
   ├ SrcPort: HTTP(80)
   ├ DstPort: 49287
   ├ SequenceNumber: 2387202278 (0x8E49D0E6)
   ├ AcknowledgementNumber: 891949874 (0x352A1332)
   ⊞ DataOffset: 128 (0x80)
   ⊟ Flags: ...A..S.
   │  ├ CWR:     (0.......) CWR not significant
   │  ├ ECE:     (.0......) ECN-Echo not significant
   │  ├ Urgent:  (..0.....) Not Urgent Data
   │  ├ Ack:     (...1....) Acknowledgement field significant
   │  ├ Push:    (....0...) No Push Function
   │  ├ Reset:   (.....0..) No Reset
   │  ├ Syn:     (......1.) Synchronize sequence numbers
   │  └ Fin:     (.......0) Not End of data
   ├ Window: 8192 ( Negotiated scale factor 0x8 ) = 2097152
   ├ Checksum: 0x1433, Disregarded
   ├ UrgentPointer: 0 (0x0)
   ⊟ TCPOptions:
   │  ⊟ MaxSegmentSize: 1
   │  │  ├ type: Maximum Segment Size. 2(0x2)
   │  │  ├ OptionLength: 4 (0x4)
   │  │  └ MaxSegmentSize: 1460 (0x5B4)
   │  ⊞ NoOption:
   │  ⊞ WindowsScaleFactor: ShiftCount: 8
   │  ⊞ NoOption:
   │  ⊞ NoOption:                                                       ▼
```

FIGURE 8-5 The second message in the TCP three-way handshake.

In this case, the server's MSS value is the same as that of the client, so the systems agree on the segment size they will use for their data transmissions. If the two systems have different MSS values, the TCP standard leaves the process of selecting an appropriate segment size up to the individual TCP implementations. In some cases, the systems use the smaller of the two MSS values, whereas others default to 536 bytes. According to the IP standard, 536 bytes is the minimum datagram size that all TCP/IP systems must support (576 bytes minus 40 bytes for the headers).

Some TCP implementations also use a special technique to determine the *path maximum transmission unit (MTU)* for the connection. The path MTU is the largest packet size permitted on any network connecting the two systems. For example, if both end systems are on Ethernet networks, as in this case, they both support the same 1,460-byte MSS value. However, if the two Ethernet networks are connected by the Internet, some or all of the intermediate networks are probably limited to the 576-byte minimum datagram size. Therefore, the path MTU for this connection would be 536 bytes. Determining the path MTU before the systems begin sending data prevents IP routers from having to fragment packets during their journey.

> ***NOTE*** **MSS VS. MTU**
>
> Do not confuse the maximum segment size parameter with the maximum transmission unit. The MSS is a TCP option that imposes a limit on the size of the segments that TCP can create. The MTU is a data-link layer parameter that limits the size of the frames that a system can transmit over a network. Typically, the MSS plus the sizes of the TCP and IP headers add up to the MTU.

THE THIRD MESSAGE

When the client receives the message containing the ACK flag from the server, the client enters the ESTABLISHED state because the client-to-server connection is now active. However, because the client has also received the server's SYN flag at the same time, it generates a response of its own, as shown in Figure 8-6, which contains the ACK flag in response to the server's SYN.

 After the server receives the client's acknowledgment, the server enters the ESTABLISHED state because the server-to-client connection is active. Both systems are now ready to exchange messages containing application data. Thus, a TCP connection is actually two separate connections running in opposite directions. TCP is therefore known as a *full-duplex protocol* because the systems establish each connection separately and later terminate each one separately.

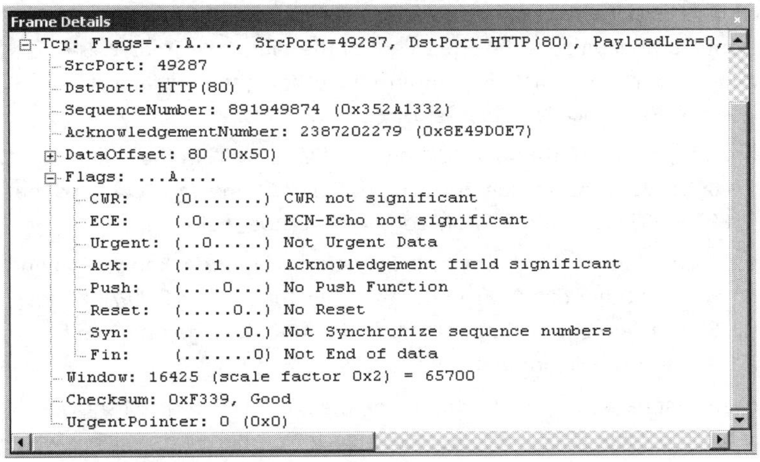

```
Frame Details                                                                    x
Tcp: Flags=...A...., SrcPort=49287, DstPort=HTTP(80), PayloadLen=0,
    SrcPort: 49287
    DstPort: HTTP(80)
    SequenceNumber: 891949874 (0x352A1332)
    AcknowledgementNumber: 2387202279 (0x8E49D0E7)
    DataOffset: 80 (0x50)
    Flags: ...A....
        CWR:      (0.......) CWR not significant
        ECE:      (.0......) ECN-Echo not significant
        Urgent:   (..0.....) Not Urgent Data
        Ack:      (...1....) Acknowledgement field significant
        Push:     (....0...) No Push Function
        Reset:    (.....0..) No Reset
        Syn:      (......0.) Not Synchronize sequence numbers
        Fin:      (.......0) Not End of data
    Window: 16425 (scale factor 0x2) = 65700
    Checksum: 0xF339, Good
    UrgentPointer: 0 (0x0)
```

FIGURE 8-6 The third message in the TCP three-way handshake.

Transmitting Data

After the two systems have completed the three-way handshake and established connections, each computer has all of the following information, which it needs for TCP to begin transmitting application data:

- **Port number**   The client is already aware of the well-known port number for the server, which it needed to initiate the connection establishment process. The messages from the client to the server contain an ephemeral port number (in the Source Port field) that the server must use in its replies.

- **Sequence number**   Each system uses the other system's sequence numbers in the Acknowledgment Number field of its own messages.

- **MSS**   Using the information in the MSS option, the systems know how large to make the segments of each sequence.

The application determines whether the client or the server transmits its data first. A transaction between a web browser client and a web server begins with the client sending a request to a server, typically requesting a site's home page. Other client/server transactions might begin with the server sending data to the client.

PACKET ACKNOWLEDGMENT

The Sequence Number and Acknowledgment Number fields are the keys to TCP's packet acknowledgment and error correction systems. During the three-way handshake, when the server replies to the client's SYN message, the server's SYN/ACK message contains its own ISN in the Sequence Number field, and it also contains a value in its Acknowledgment Number field. This Acknowledgment Number value is the equivalent of the client's ISN plus 1. The function of the Acknowledgment Number field is to inform the other system what value is expected in the next message's Sequence Number field.

For example, in the first of the handshake packets shown earlier, the ISN in the client's Sequence Number field is 891949873. As a result, the server's SYN/ACK message contains the value 891949874 (that is, 891949873+1) in its Acknowledgment Number field.

Because the TCP connection is bidirectional, the same Sequence Number/Acknowledgment Number process also occurs in the other direction. In this example, the server's SYN/ACK message contained 2387202278 in its Sequence Number field, so the ACK message returned by the client had 2387202279 as its Acknowledgment Number value.

When the client sends its first data message to the server, the HTTP GET request shown in Figure 8-7, that message has the value 891949874 in its Sequence Number field, which is what the server expects.

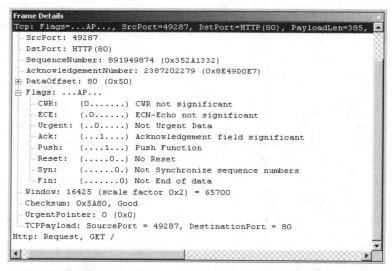

FIGURE 8-7 The client's first data message after the three-way handshake.

NOTE **SEQUENCE NUMBERS**

You might wonder why the client's first data message has the Sequence Number value 891949874 when the client previously had to send an ACK message in response to the server's SYN. It may seem as though the ACK message should have used Sequence Number 891949874, but in fact, messages that function solely as acknowledgments do not increment the sequence number counter. The server's SYN/ACK message does increment the counter because it includes the SYN flag.

When the systems begin to send data, they increment their Sequence Number values for each byte of data they transmit. Therefore, when the server acknowledges the client's GET request, the ACK message it sends to the client has the value 891950259 in the Acknowledgment Number field, as shown in Figure 8-8.

Because the number 891950259 is 385 larger than 891949874, the server is informing the client that it has successfully received 385 bytes in the GET message and that it expects the client's next message to have 891950259 in its Sequence Number field.

At this point, the server has transmitted no data yet, except for its SYN/ACK message, so the ACK message generated by the server in response to the client's GET request still contains 2387202279 (the server's ISN+1) in its Sequence Number field. When the server replies to the GET request with an HTTP Response, its first message will contain that same Sequence Number.

```
Frame Details                                                              ✕
Tcp: Flags=...A...., SrcPort=HTTP(80), DstPort=49287, PayloadLen=0, Se ▲
  ─SrcPort: HTTP(80)
  ─DstPort: 49287
  ─SequenceNumber: 2387202279 (0x8E49D0E7)
  ─AcknowledgementNumber: 891950259 (0x352A14B3)
 ⊞─DataOffset: 80 (0x50)
 ⊟─Flags: ...A....
     ─CWR:     (0.......) CWR not significant
     ─ECE:     (.0......) ECN-Echo not significant
     ─Urgent:  (..0.....) Not Urgent Data
     ─Ack:     (...1....) Acknowledgement field significant
     ─Push:    (....0...) No Push Function
     ─Reset:   (.....0..) No Reset
     ─Syn:     (......0.) Not Synchronize sequence numbers
     ─Fin:     (.......0) Not End of data
  ─Window: 256 (scale factor 0x8) = 65536
  ─Checksum: 0x1427, Disregarded
  ─UrgentPointer: 0 (0x0)                                            ▼
◄ ░                                            ░░░░░░░░░░            ►
```

FIGURE 8-8 The server's acknowledgment of the client's first data message.

In this example, the client's GET request is small and requires only one TCP message, but in a typical transaction, the server responds by transmitting a Hypertext Markup Language (HTML) file containing a webpage, which will likely be large enough to require a sequence of TCP messages consisting of multiple segments. The server first divides the HTML file into segments no larger than the client's MSS value. When the server begins to transmit the segments, it increments its Sequence Number value according to the amount of data in each message. So, if the server's ISN is 2387202278, the Sequence Number of its first data message will be 2387202279 . If the client's MSS is 1460, the server's second data message will have a Sequence Number of 2387203739, the third will be 2382705199, and so on.

DELAYED ACKNOWLEDGMENTS

When the TCP systems involved in a connection begin receiving data from each other, they are both responsible for acknowledging each other's data. TCP uses a system called *delayed acknowledgments*, which means that the systems do not have to generate a separate acknowledgment message for every data message they receive. The intervals at which the systems generate their acknowledgments are determined by the individual TCP implementations. Each acknowledgment message that a receiving system sends in response to another system's data messages has the ACK flag, and the value of its Acknowledgment Number field reflects the number of bytes in the entire sequence that the system has successfully received.

If a TCP system receives messages that fail the CRC check, or if the system fails to receive messages containing some of the segments in a sequence, it notifies the sender, using the Acknowledgment Number field in its ACK messages. The Acknowledgment Number value reflects the number of bytes from the beginning of the sequence that the destination system has received correctly.

For example, if a sequence consists of 10 segments and all are received correctly except the seventh segment, the recipient's acknowledgment message will contain an Acknowledgment Number value that reflects the number of bytes in the first 6 segments only. The system will discard segments 8 through 10, even though it received them correctly, and call for the sender to retransmit them along with segment 7. This is called *positive acknowledgment with retransmission*, because the destination system acknowledges only the messages that it received correctly. A protocol that uses negative acknowledgment would assume that all messages were received correctly except for those that the destination system explicitly listed as having errors.

> **NOTE** **SELECTIVE ACKNOWLEDGMENT**
>
> The selective acknowledgment TCP option, as defined in RFC 2018, prevents systems from having to retransmit segments that were actually received without error, as described in the previous example. In a TCP connection using selective acknowledgment, the recipient would acknowledge the successful receipt of segments 1 through 6 and 8 through 10, leaving the sender to retransmit only segment 7.

Each TCP system maintains a queue of the messages that it has transmitted and deletes those messages for which acknowledgments have arrived. Messages that remain in a system's queue for a predetermined period of time without being acknowledged are assumed to be lost or discarded, and the system automatically retransmits them.

After the sending system transmits all of the segments in a sequence and the receiving system acknowledges that it has received all of the segments correctly, the systems terminate the connection. This termination procedure is described in the "Connection Termination" section later in this chapter. If the segments arrive at their destination out of sequence, the receiving system uses the Sequence Number values to reassemble them in the proper order.

In the case of the web client/server exchange described earlier, the TCP connection the systems established for the initial GET/RESPONSE transaction is only one of many that they will need for the client to request and receive an entire webpage. On a typical website, the HTML file that the client requests initially contains some text, which the browser displays, but it also contains references to graphics, multimedia files, and other sites. To display this additional content, the client must establish, use, and eventually terminate separate TCP connections for each content file. Thus, in the few seconds that it takes to render a single webpage, the client system might have to enter into literally dozens of TCP transactions.

However, other types of applications might maintain a single TCP connection for a much longer period of time and perform repeated exchanges of data in both directions. In a case like this, both systems can exchange data messages and acknowledgments, with the error detection and correction processes occurring on both sides.

DETECTING ERRORS

Two things can go wrong during a TCP transaction: messages can arrive at their destination in a corrupted state, or they can fail to arrive at all. When messages fail to arrive, the lack of acknowledgments from the destination system causes the sender to retransmit the missing messages. If a serious network problem prevents the systems from exchanging any messages, the TCP connection eventually times out, and the entire process must start again.

When messages arrive at their destination, the receiving system checks them for accuracy by performing the same checksum computation that the sender performed before transmitting the data. The receiving system then compares the results with the value in the Checksum field. If the values don't match, the system discards the message. This is a crucial element of the TCP protocol because it is the only end-to-end checksum performed on the actual application layer data.

IP includes an end-to-end checksum, but only on its header. Data-link layer protocols contain a checksum, but only for one hop at a time. If the packets pass through a network that doesn't provide a checksum, such as a Point-to-Point Protocol (PPP) link, there is a potential for errors to be introduced that the systems can't detect at the data-link or network layer.

As the only end-to-end error detection mechanism in the TCP/IP stack, TCP is often required to compensate for packet loss or damage incurred at other layers of the OSI model. For example, collisions on an Ethernet network that are not detectable by the CSMA/CD mechanism can be detected and retransmitted at the transport layer.

The checksum that TCP performs is unusual because it is calculated not only on the entire TCP header and the application data but also on a *pseudo-header*. The pseudo-header in an IPv4 environment consists of the IP header's Source IP Address, Destination IP Address, Protocol, and Length fields, plus 1 byte of padding, to bring the total number of bytes to an even 12 (three 4-byte words), as shown in Figure 8-9. Including the pseudo-header ensures that the datagrams are delivered to the correct computer and to the correct transport layer protocol on that computer.

In an IPv6 environment, the format of the pseudo-header must be modified to accommodate the 128-bit IPv6 addresses. The format of the TCP pseudo-header in an IPv6 datagram, as shown in Figure 8-10, is defined in RFC 2460.

```
1 2 3 4 5 6 7 8 1 2 3 4 5 6 7 8 1 2 3 4 5 6 7 8 1 2 3 4 5 6 7 8
┌───────────────────────────────────────────────────────────┐  ⎫
│                    Source IP Address                        │  │  IPv4
├───────────────────────────────────────────────────────────┤  ⎬  Pseudo-
│                  Destination IP Address                     │  │  Header
├─────────────────┬─────────────────┬───────────────────────┤  │
│     Unused      │    Protocol     │         Length         │  ⎭
├─────────────────┴─────────────────┼───────────────────────┤
│          Source Port              │    Destination Port    │
├───────────────────────────────────┴───────────────────────┤
│                    Sequence Number                         │
├───────────────────────────────────────────────────────────┤
│                 Acknowledgment Number                      │
├───────────┬──────────┬────────────┬───────────────────────┤
│Data Offset│ Reserved │Control Bits│        Window          │
├───────────┴──────────┴────────────┼───────────────────────┤
│            Checksum               │    Urgent Pointer      │
├───────────────────────────────────┴───────────────────────┤
┆                       Options                              ┆
├────────────────────────────────────────────────────────────┤
┆                         Data                               ┆
└────────────────────────────────────────────────────────────┘
```

FIGURE 8-9 The fields TCP uses to calculate its checksum, including a pseudo-header derived from the IPv4 header.

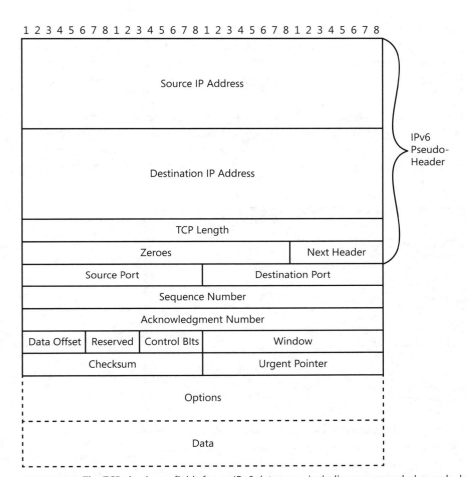

FIGURE 8-10 The TCP checksum fields for an IPv6 datagram, including an expanded pseudo-header.

FLOW CONTROL

Flow control is the process by which the destination system in a TCP connection provides information to the source system that enables that source system to regulate the speed at which it transmits data. Each system has a limited amount of buffer space to store incoming data. The data remains in the buffer until the receiving system generates messages acknowledging that data. If the system transmitting the data sends too much information too quickly, the receiver's buffers could fill up, forcing it to discard data messages.

The lack of acknowledgments for the dropped messages would eventually cause the source system to resend them, but the error detection and correction processes take time and waste bandwidth that could better be saved by slowing down the transmission.

The system receiving the data uses the Window field in its acknowledgment messages to let the sender know how much buffer space it has available at the time of each message's transmission. The transmitting system uses that Window value along with the Acknowledgment Number value to determine how much data from the sequence it is permitted to transmit.

To continue the earlier example of the web client/server transaction, assume that the server began transmitting an image file to the client in a sequence that required several segments. After receiving the first segment, the client sent an ACK message to the server that contained an Acknowledgment Number value of 2387206134 and a Window value of 65700, as shown in Figure 8-11.

```
Frame Details                                                                    x
⊟ Tcp: Flags=...A...., SrcPort=49287, DstPort=HTTP(80), PayloadLen=0, ▲
    SrcPort: 49287
    DstPort: HTTP(80)
    SequenceNumber: 891950567 (0x352A15E7)
    AcknowledgementNumber: 2387206134 (0x8E49DFF6)
  ⊞ DataOffset: 80 (0x50)
  ⊟ Flags: ...A....
      CWR:     (0.......) CWR not significant
      ECE:     (.0......) ECN-Echo not significant
      Urgent:  (..0.....) Not Urgent Data
      Ack:     (...1....) Acknowledgement field significant
      Push:    (....0...) No Push Function
      Reset:   (.....0..) No Reset
      Syn:     (......0.) Not Synchronize sequence numbers
      Fin:     (.......0) Not End of data
    Window: 16425 (scale factor 0x2) = 65700
    Checksum: 0xE175, Good
    UrgentPointer: 0 (0x0)
◄                                                                              ►
```

FIGURE 8-11 Acknowledgment of the first data transmission in a sequence.

With this acknowledgment, the client is informing the server that it has received all of the data in the sequence through byte 2387206134, and that the server may now transmit another 65700 bytes, which would be bytes 2387206135 through 2387271835. If the server receives no additional acknowledgments by the time it transmits those 65700 bytes, it must stop transmitting until the next acknowledgment arrives.

IMPORTANT **TCP WINDOW SCALE OPTION**

You might notice that the Window value in the figure contains a scale factor of 0x2. This is a result of the TCP Window Scale Option, as defined in RFC 1323, "TCP Extensions for High Performance." The Window Scale option is a factor specified in a system's SYN packet that enables the Window field to contain a value larger than will fit into the 16-bit space allotted to it. Using the scale specified in the computer's SYN message, the system shifts the Window value (in binary) by the appropriate number of places. So the original Window value of 16425 (10000000010100, in binary) becomes 65700 (1000000001010000).

In this particular sequence, the client's ACK messages all have the same Window value, because the two computers are on the same network and there is no traffic congestion. If, however, the Window value decreased in subsequent ACK messages, the server might be required to throttle down its transmissions until the Window values come up again.

This type of flow control is called a *sliding window* technique. The offered window (shown in Figure 8-12) is the series of bytes that the receiving system has permitted the transmitting system to send. As the receiving system acknowledges the incoming bytes, the left side of the window moves to the right. As the system passes the acknowledged bytes up to the application layer process indicated by the Destination Port number, the right side of the window moves to the right. Thus the window can be said to be sliding along the incoming byte stream, from left to right.

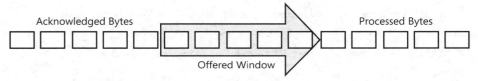

FIGURE 8-12 The sliding window flow control technique.

TERMINATING THE CONNECTION

When the systems in a TCP connection have finished exchanging data, they terminate the connection by using control messages, much like those used in the three-way handshake. As with the establishment of the connection, the application generating the data determines which system initiates the termination sequence. In the case of the web client/server transaction used as an example earlier, the server begins the termination process by setting the FIN flag in the Control Bits field of its last data message. In other cases, the system initiating the termination process might use a separate message containing the FIN flag and no data. The system then enters the FIN-WAIT-1 state, indicating that it is waiting for a FIN message from the other system or an acknowledgment of its own FIN message.

The system that receives the first FIN flag transmits an acknowledgment message and then generates its own message containing a FIN flag, after which it enters the CLOSING state. The other system then must respond with its own ACK message, and then enters the CLOSED state.

This double acknowledgment is necessary because the connection runs in both directions, so both systems must terminate their respective connections, using a total of four messages, as shown in Figure 8-13.

Unlike in the connection establishment procedure, the computers can't combine the FIN and ACK flags in the same message, which is why four messages are needed instead of three. When the final ACK message arrives, both systems enter the CLOSED state, which is actually a null condition, because the connection no longer exists.

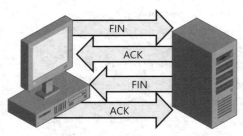

FIGURE 8-13 The TCP connection termination process.

 Quick Check

1. What is the term used to refer to the process of regulating the transmission speed of a system involved in a TCP connection?

2. What is the term for the IP header fields included in the TCP checksum calculation?

Quick Check Answers

1. Flow control

2. Pseudo-header

User Datagram Protocol (UDP)

UDP is defined in RFC 768, "User Datagram Protocol." Unlike TCP, UDP is a connectionless protocol, so it provides no segmentation, no packet acknowledgment, no flow control, and no guaranteed delivery. As a result, UDP is far simpler than TCP and generates much less control overhead. The UDP header is much smaller than that of a TCP header—8 bytes as opposed to 20 bytes or more—and there are no separate control messages, such as those used to establish and terminate connections.

UDP is designed for transactions that consist of only two messages: a request and a reply, with the reply functioning as a tacit acknowledgment. For this reason, many of the applications that use UDP transport only amounts of data small enough to fit into a single message. Domain Name System (DNS) and Dynamic Host Configuration Protocol (DHCP) are two of the most common application layer protocols that use UDP.

The format of a UDP message is shown in Figure 8-14.

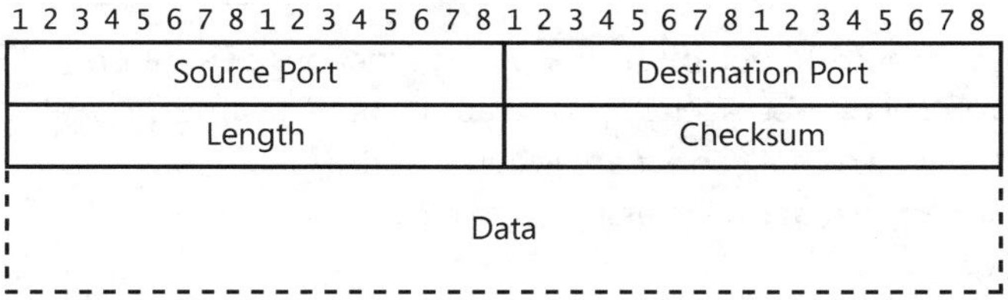

```
1 2 3 4 5 6 7 8 1 2 3 4 5 6 7 8 1 2 3 4 5 6 7 8 1 2 3 4 5 6 7 8
```

Source Port	Destination Port
Length	Checksum
Data	

FIGURE 8-14 The UDP message format.

The functions of the UDP message fields are as follows:

- **Source Port (2 bytes)** Identifies the process on the transmitting system that generated the information carried in the Data field. This field performs the same function as in the TCP header.

- **Destination Port (2 bytes)** Identifies the process on the receiving system for which the information in the Data field is intended. This field performs the same function as in the TCP header.

- **Length (2 bytes)** Specifies the length of the UDP header and data in bytes. By subtracting the known length of the header, this field specifies how much data is included in the message.

- **Checksum (2 bytes)** Contains the results of a CRC performed by the transmitting system, which the receiving system can use to detect errors in the packet. The systems calculate the Checksum value by using the message header, the data, and the IPv4 or IPv6 pseudo-header, just as in TCP.

- **Data (variable)** Contains the information generated by the application layer process specified in the Source Port field.

NOTE **UDP CHECKSUMS**

The UDP standard specifies that the use of the checksum is optional. The transmitting system fills the Checksum field with zeroes if it is unused. There has been a great deal of debate about whether UDP messages should include checksums. RFC 768 requires all UDP systems to be capable of using checksums to check for errors, and most current implementations include the checksum computations.

Ports and Sockets

As with data-link and network layer protocols, one of the important functions of a transport layer protocol is to identify the protocol or process that generated the data it carries so that the receiving system can deliver the data to the correct application. Both TCP and UDP do this by specifying the number of a port that has been assigned to a particular process by the Internet Assigned Numbers Authority (IANA).

> **MORE INFO** **IANA PORT NUMBERS**
>
> These port numbers are published at the following website: *http://www.iana.org/assignments/service-names-port-numbers/service-names-port-numbers.xml.* A list of the most common ports is included with every TCP/IP client in a text file called Services.

When a TCP/IP packet arrives at its destination, the transport layer protocol receiving the IP datagram from the network layer reads the value in the Destination Port field and delivers the information in the Data field to the program or protocol associated with that port.

All of the common Internet applications have particular port numbers associated with them, called *well-known ports*. The IANA has designated all of the port numbers less than 1024 as well-known ports, but not all of them are assigned to applications. Table 8-2 lists the most commonly used well-known ports. For example, web servers use port 80, and DNS servers use port 53. TCP and UDP both maintain their own separate lists of well-known port numbers. For example, the File Transfer Protocol (FTP) uses TCP ports 20 and 21. Because FTP uses only TCP (and not UDP) at the transport layer, a different application layer protocol can use the same ports (20 and 21) with the UDP protocol. However, in some cases, a protocol can use either one of the transport layer protocols. DNS, for example, is associated with both TCP port 53 and UDP port 53.

TABLE 8-2 Well-Known Port Numbers

Service Name	Port Number	Protocol	Function
ftp-data	20	TCP	FTP data channel; used for transmitting files between systems
ftp	21	TCP	FTP control channel; used by FTP-connected systems for exchanging commands and responses
ssh	22	TCP and UDP	SSH (Secure Shell) Remote Login Protocol; used to securely log on to a computer from another computer on the same network and execute commands
telnet	23	TCP	Telnet; used to execute commands on network-connected systems

Service Name	Port Number	Protocol	Function
smtp	25	TCP	Simple Mail Transfer Protocol (SMTP); used to send email messages
domain	53	TCP and UDP	DNS; used to receive host name resolution requests from clients
bootps	67	TCP and UDP	Bootstrap Protocol (BOOTP) and DHCP servers; used to receive TCP/IP configuration requests from clients
bootpc	68	TCP and UDP	BOOTP and DHCP clients; used to send TCP/IP configuration requests to servers
tftp	69	TCP and UDP	Trivial File Transfer Protocol; a simplified form of the File Transfer Protocol (FTP) with no security capabilities that is typically used by diskless workstations to download executable files from network servers
http	80	TCP	HTTP; used by web servers to receive requests from client browsers
pop3	110	TCP	Post Office Protocol version 3 (POP3); used by email client programs to retrieve email requests from servers
nntp	119	TCP and UDP	Network News Transfer Protocol; used to post and distribute messages to, and retrieve them from, Usenet servers on the Internet
ntp	123	TCP and UDP	Network Time Protocol; used to exchange time signals for the purpose of synchronizing the clocks in network computers
imap	143	TCP and UDP	Internet Message Access Protocol version 4; used by email client programs to retrieve messages from a mail server
snmp	161	TCP and UDP	Simple Network Management Protocol (SNMP); used by SNMP agents to transmit status information to a network management console
https	443	TCP and UDP	Hypertext Transfer Protocol Over TLS/SSL

EXAM TIP

Familiarity with the port numbers associated with the most commonly used application layer protocols is essential for candidates for the Network+ certification exam.

When one TCP/IP system addresses traffic to another, it uses a combination of an IP address and a port number. The combination of an IP address and a port is called a *socket*. To specify a socket in a Uniform Resource Locator (URL), you enter the IP address first and then follow it with a colon and the port number.

For example, the socket 192.168.2.10:21 addresses port 21 on the system with the address 192.168.2.10. Because the port number for the FTP control port is 21, this socket addresses the FTP server running on that computer. In most cases, however, URLs contain DNS names, not IP addresses; the format remains the same, but with the DNS name replacing the IP address (for example, ftp.adatum.com:21).

You usually don't have to specify the port number when you're typing a URL because most programs assume that you want to connect to the well-known port. Your web browser, for example, addresses all the URLs you enter to port 80, the HTTP web server port, unless you specify otherwise.

The IANA port numbers are recommendations, not ironclad rules, however. You can configure a web server to use a port number other than 80; in fact, many web servers assign alternate ports to their administrative configuration pages so that only users who know the correct port number can access them.

For example, you can create a semi-secret website of your own by configuring your server to use port 81 instead of 80. Users would then have to type a URL such as *http://www.myserver.com:81* into their browsers instead of just *http://www.myserver.com* to access your site.

In other cases, firewalls might prevent access to the well-known port, forcing administrators to use an alternative. Mail servers in particular tend not to use the well-known ports anymore, due to abuse by unauthorized users on the Internet.

The well-known ports published by the IANA refer mostly to servers. Because it is usually the client that initiates communication with the server, rather than the other way around, clients don't need permanently assigned port numbers. Instead, a client program typically selects a port number at random to use while communicating with a particular server. This randomly selected port is called an *ephemeral port number*. The IANA only manages port numbers from 1 to 1,023, so ephemeral port numbers always have values of 1,024 or higher. A server receiving a packet from a client uses the value in the TCP header's Source Port field to address its reply to the correct ephemeral port in the client system.

✔ **Quick Check**

1. Which application layer protocol uses two separate port numbers at the same time?

2. Web browsers append what port number to URLs with the http:// prefix by default?

Quick Check Answers

1. FTP

2. 80

Exercise

The answers for this exercise are located in the "Answers" section at the end of this chapter.

Match the following terms with the appropriate phrases.

1. Pseudo-header
2. Ephemeral port
3. Three-way handshake
4. Sliding window
5. Socket

A. A random number selected by a client
B. Network layer information used in a transport layer process
C. Identifies an application running on a particular computer
D. Controls the flow control process
E. Precedes every TCP data transmission

Chapter Summary

- The TCP/IP suite uses two protocols at the transport layer to provide different levels of service for applications: the Transmission Control Protocol (TCP) and the User Datagram Protocol (UDP).

- Internet applications such as web browsers and email clients depend on the TCP protocol to retrieve large amounts of data from servers, without error.

- In many cases, an application layer protocol will pass more data to TCP than can fit into a single packet, so TCP splits the data into smaller pieces. Each piece is called a segment, and the segments that compose a single transaction are known collectively as a sequence.

- The process that TCP uses to establish a connection is known as a three-way handshake. This process consists of an exchange of three messages. The purpose of these messages, apart from determining that the other computer actually exists and is ready to receive data, is to exchange the sequence numbers that the computers will use to number the messages they transmit.

- The Sequence Number and Acknowledgment Number fields are the keys to TCP's packet acknowledgment and error correction systems.

- When the TCP systems involved in a connection begin receiving data from each other, they are both responsible for acknowledging each other's data. TCP uses a system called delayed acknowledgments, which means that the systems do not have to generate a separate acknowledgment message for every data message they receive.

- The checksum that TCP performs is unusual because it is calculated not only on the entire TCP header and the application data but also on a pseudo-header.

- Flow control is the process by which the destination system in a TCP connection provides information to the source system that enables that source system to regulate the speed at which it transmits data.

- Unlike TCP, UDP is a connectionless protocol, so it provides no segmentation, no packet acknowledgment, no flow control, and no guaranteed delivery. As a result, UDP is far simpler than TCP and generates much less control overhead.

- One of the important functions of a transport layer protocol is to identify the protocol or process that generated the data it carries so that the receiving system can deliver the data to the correct application.

- All of the common Internet applications have particular port numbers called well-known ports associated with them.

- When one TCP/IP system addresses traffic to another, it uses a combination of an IP address and a port number. The combination of an IP address and a port is called a socket.

Chapter Review

Test your knowledge of the information in Chapter 8 by answering these questions. The answers to these questions, and the explanations of why each answer choice is correct or incorrect, are located in the "Answers" section at the end of this chapter.

1. Which of the following is the correct URL for an administrative website configured to use TCP port 1056?

   A. http://admin.adatum.com/1056

   B. http://admin.adatum.com:1056

   C. http://1056.admin.adatum.com

   D. http:1056//admin.adatum.com

2. Which of the control bits must be set in the TCP connection establishment message that includes a system's Initial Sequence Number?

A. SYN

B. ACK

C. FIN

D. PSH

3. A client computer receiving a data file from a server generates an acknowledgment message for one of the incoming segments that contains the following values:

- Control Bits: ACK
- Sequence Number: 432565432
- Acknowledgment Number: 1109847
- Window: 1460

What will the Sequence Number be in the next segment that the server transmits?

A. 1111307

B. 423565423

C. 1109847

D. 432566892

4. Which of the following TCP header fields implements the protocol's flow control capability?

A. Window

B. The URG control bit

C. Data Offset

D. Urgent Pointer

Answers

This section contains the answers to the questions for the Exercise and Chapter Review in this chapter.

Exercise

1. B

2. A

3. E

4. D

5. C

Chapter Review

1. **Correct Answer:** B

   A. **Incorrect:** This would be the format for a subdirectory, not a port.

   B. **Correct:** The proper format for including a port number in a URL is to follow the server name with a colon and the port number.

   C. **Incorrect:** This would be the format for a subdomain, not a port.

   D. **Incorrect:** The proper format for including a port number in a URL is to follow the server name with a colon and the port number.

2. **Correct Answer:** A

   A. **Correct:** The message containing the ISN must have the SYN control bit set.

   B. **Incorrect:** The ACK bit can be set in a message that includes an ISN, but it is not required.

   C. **Incorrect:** The FIN bit is used to terminate a connection, whereas the ISN is included in a connection establishment message.

   D. **Incorrect:** The PSH bit is used to expedite data processing in the receiving system, not to supply the ISN.

3. **Correct Answer:** C

   A. **Incorrect:** The Sequence Number value should not be the sum of the Acknowledgment Number and Sequence Number fields.

   B. **Incorrect:** The Sequence Number of the next segment should not be the other system's Sequence Number value.

   C. **Correct:** The function of the Acknowledgment Number field is to inform the other system what value is expected in the next message's Sequence Number field.

   D. **Incorrect:** The Sequence Number of the next segment should not be derived from the other system's Sequence Number value.

4. **Correct Answer:** A

   A. **Correct:** The Window field specifies the number of bytes the system is capable of receiving in the next message.

   B. **Incorrect:** The URG control bit has no part in the TCP flow control mechanism.

   C. **Incorrect:** The Data Offset field has no part in the TCP flow control mechanism.

   D. **Incorrect:** The Urgent Pointer field has no part in the TCP flow control mechanism.

CHAPTER 9

The Application Layer

The protocols that operate at the application layer of the Open Systems Interconnection (OSI) reference model are not concerned with the network communication issues addressed by the data-link, network, and transport layer protocols. An application layer protocol is concerned solely with the communication between a client program on one computer and a server program on another. The application layer protocol assumes that a connection between the two systems that provides an appropriate quality of service already exists.

Application layer protocols use different combinations of protocols at the lower layers to achieve the level of service they require. For example, when servers use Hypertext Transfer Protocol (HTTP) or File Transfer Protocol (FTP) to transmit entire files to client systems, the files must arrive at their destinations without error. These protocols, therefore, use a combination of TCP and IP at the transport and network layers to achieve connection-oriented, reliable communications. On the other hand, Dynamic Host Configuration Protocol (DHCP) and Domain Name System (DNS) servers exchange small messages between clients and servers that they can easily retransmit if necessary, so they use the connectionless service provided by User Datagram Protocol (UDP) and IP.

Exam objectives in this chapter:

Objective 1.6: Explain the function of common networking protocols.

- TCP
- FTP
- UDP
- TCP/IP suite
- DHCP
- TFTP
- DNS
- HTTPS
- HTTP
- ARP
- SIP (VoIP)

- RTP (VoIP)
- SSH
- POP3
- NTP
- IMAP4
- Telnet
- SMTP
- SNMP2/3
- ICMP
- IGMP
- TLS

Objective 1.7: Summarize DNS concepts and its components.

- DNS servers
- DNS records (A, MX, AAAA, CNAME, PTR)
- Dynamic DNS

Objective 2.3: Explain the purpose and properties of DHCP.

- Static vs. dynamic IP addressing
- Reservations
- Scopes
- Leases
- Options (DNS servers, suffixes)

Application Layer Communications

Many application layer protocols use a communication method that differs from that of the protocols in the TCP/IP suite discussed thus far. The protocols at the lower layers of the OSI model use a message format based on header fields containing codes that perform specific functions. For example, the function of an ICMP message is indicated by the values of its Type and Code fields. By contrast, many application layer protocols use text commands rather than function codes. When you use a client program to log on to an FTP server, for example, the client sends the following commands in clear text:

```
USER username
PASS password
```

The *username* and *password* variables contain the name of the account the client will use to access the server and the password associated with that account. In response, the FTP server sends text-based reply codes that indicate whether the client's commands succeeded or failed. As the FTP session proceeds, the client can send commands requesting the server to perform file management and transfer operations.

The following sections examine some of the most commonly used application layer protocols and the functions they perform for the applications running on client and server computers.

DHCP

The chief administrative problem with deploying and maintaining a TCP/IP network is the need to assign a unique IP address to each node and configure the various other TCP/IP parameters with appropriate values. On a large network deployment, performing these tasks manually on individual workstations is not only labor intensive, it also requires careful planning to ensure that no IP addresses are duplicated.

The *Dynamic Host Configuration Protocol (DHCP)* is designed to address this problem. DHCP takes the form of a service that network administrators configure with ranges of IP addresses and other settings. Computers and other devices configured to run as DHCP clients contact a DHCP server at boot time, and the server assigns each one a set of appropriate TCP/IP parameters, including a unique IP address. The computer uses these parameters to configure its TCP/IP client, and network communication commences with no manual configuration necessary.

DHCP is a platform-independent service that can configure the TCP/IP parameters of any operating system with DHCP client capabilities. DHCP server software is available for many platforms, including Windows and various UNIX and Linux distributions.

DHCP Origins

DHCP was developed in the early 1990s as a workstation configuration solution for large enterprise networks. As large organizations began to adopt TCP/IP for their networks, administrators realized that the task of manually assigning IP addresses to thousands of machines located at various sites around the world was enormous, as was the continued tracking of those addresses as they added computers to and removed them from the network.

The concept of server-based IP address assignment was not a new one, however. DHCP is based on two earlier protocols called RARP and BOOTP.

RARP

The *Reverse Address Resolution Protocol (RARP)* does the opposite of ARP, the Address Resolution Protocol used on every TCP/IP system. Whereas ARP converts network layer IP addresses into data-link layer hardware addresses, RARP works by broadcasting a system's hardware address and receiving an IP address in return from a RARP server. The two protocols use the same message format, as described in Chapter 4, "The Data-Link Layer."

Designed for use with diskless workstations that have no means to store their own TCP/IP configuration information, RARP allows servers to supply IP addresses to all of the systems on a segment. However, RARP was not sufficient for a large enterprise's needs, for the following reasons:

- Clients must locate RARP servers by using broadcast messages, because there is no way for a diskless workstation to store the address of the RARP server. Because broadcasts are limited to the local subnet, there must be a RARP server on every network segment to service the clients on that segment.

- RARP is only capable of supplying client systems with IP addresses. To be useful on today's networks, a protocol must provide values for other configuration parameters as well, such as DNS servers and default gateways.

- RARP is only a mechanism for the storage and delivery of IP addresses. Administrators must still manually assign addresses to clients by creating a lookup table on the RARP server.

EXAM TIP

When taking the Network+ exam, be sure not to confuse ARP with RARP. ARP is used on every TCP/IP computer to resolve IP addresses into hardware (or MAC) addresses. RARP is an antiquated protocol that administrators once used to assign IP addresses to diskless workstations; they now use DHCP instead.

BOOTP

The *Bootstrap Protocol (BOOTP)* is an improvement over RARP and is still in use today on some networks. DHCP takes much of its functionality from the BOOTP standards (published by the Internet Engineering Task Force [IETF] as RFC 951, "Bootstrap Protocol," with extensions in RFC 1533 and RFC 1542). BOOTP was also designed for use with diskless workstations and is capable of delivering more than just IP addresses; it uses standard UDP/IP datagrams instead of a specialized data-link layer protocol such as RARP.

In addition to supplying IP addresses and other TCP/IP parameters, BOOTP servers can use the Trivial File Transfer Protocol (TFTP) to deliver an executable boot file to a diskless client system. Like RARP, BOOTP clients use broadcast transmissions to contact a server, but the standard calls for the use of BOOTP relay agents to make it possible for one BOOTP server to service clients on multiple network segments.

The primary shortcoming of BOOTP is that, like RARP, administrators must manually create a lookup table on the server containing the IP addresses and other configuration parameters to be assigned to the clients. This makes the system subject to many of the same errors and administrative problems encountered with RARP and, for that matter, with manual client configuration.

DHCP Objectives

BOOTP eliminates the need for administrators to travel to every workstation to configure the TCP/IP client manually, but the possibility still exists for systems to be assigned duplicate IP addresses because of typographical errors in the lookup table. What administrators needed for their large networks was a service that would automatically allocate addresses to systems on demand and keep track of which addresses have been assigned and which are available for use.

DHCP improves on the BOOTP concept by enabling administrators to create a pool of IP addresses. As a client system boots, it requests an address from the DHCP server. The server then assigns one from the pool, along with the other static configuration parameters the client needs.

There are problems inherent in this concept, however. One problem is the possibility of a shortage of IP addresses in the pool. After a client system receives an address for use on a particular subnet, what happens to that address if someone moves the machine to another department on a different subnet? DHCP can assign the system a different address on the new subnet, but a mechanism must exist to reclaim the old address.

The solution to this problem lies in DHCP's mechanism for leasing IP addresses to client systems. Each time the server assigns an address, it starts a clock that will eventually run out if the system does not renew the lease. Each time the client system restarts, it renews the lease. If the lease runs out, the server releases the assigned IP address and returns it to the pool for reassignment.

The other problem with automatic address assignment is the possibility that a client's IP address might change periodically, which can affect the association between the host's IP address and its DNS name. Administrators can address this problem in two ways: by creating permanent DHCP address assignments for computers with names that must not change, such as web servers, or by using Dynamic DNS to update name server resource records whenever DHCP assigns a new address to a computer.

MORE INFO **DYNAMIC DNS**

For more information on Dynamic DNS, see the "DNS" section later in this chapter.

The overall objectives the designers of DHCP used when creating the service are as follows:

- The DHCP server should be able to provide a workstation with all the settings needed to configure the TCP/IP client so that no manual configuration is needed.
- The DHCP server should be able to function as a repository for the TCP/IP configuration parameters for all of a network's clients.
- The DHCP server should assign IP addresses in such a way as to prevent the duplication of addresses on the network.
- The DHCP server should be able to configure clients on other subnets through the use of relay agents.
- The DHCP server should support the assignment of specific IP addresses to specific client systems.
- DHCP clients should be able to retain their TCP/IP configuration parameters despite a reboot of either the client or the server system.

To achieve these objectives, the designers created a DHCP system that consists of two basic elements:

- A service that assigns TCP/IP configuration settings to client systems
- A protocol used for communications between DHCP clients and servers

The architecture of the DHCP system is defined by a public standard published by the IETF as RFC 2131, "Dynamic Host Configuration Protocol." The document defines the message format for the protocol and the sequence of message exchanges that take place between the DHCP client and server.

IP Address Assignment

The primary function of DHCP is to assign IP addresses and to accommodate the needs of all types of client systems. The standard defines three types of address assignments:

- **Manual allocation** The administrator configures the DHCP server to assign a specific IP address to a given system; the IP address will never change unless it is manually modified. This is equivalent in functionality to RARP and BOOTP.

- **Automatic allocation** The DHCP server assigns permanent IP addresses allocated from a pool; the addresses do not change unless they are manually modified by the user or the administrator.

- **Dynamic allocation** The DHCP server assigns IP addresses from a pool by using a limited-time lease so that an address can be reassigned if the client system doesn't periodically renew it.

EXAM TIP

The terms *manual*, *automatic*, and *dynamic allocation* are those used by the DHCP standards. Most DHCP server implementations support all three types of address allocation, but they generally do not allow you to select them by using these exact names. The Network+ exam objectives use the term *static addressing* to refer to a manually configured TCP/IP client and *dynamic addressing* to refer to one configured by using DHCP.

In the Microsoft DHCP Server service, dynamic allocation is the default. If you want to use automatic allocation, you must change the Lease Duration setting to unlimited. For manual allocation, you create what the Microsoft server and the Network+ objectives call an *address reservation*.

Manual allocation—also known as reservation—is suitable for Internet servers and other machines that require IP addresses that do not change because they rely on DNS name resolution for user access. This form of address allocation is nothing more than a remote configuration solution because the end result is no different than if the administrator manually configured the TCP/IP client.

There are two advantages to manually allocating addresses, however. First, you can deliver additional TCP/IP configuration settings along with the address, changing them as needed. Second, manual allocation is also an organizational aid that enables you to keep track of all the addresses used on your network. Keeping all the address assignments in one database makes it easier to track the assignments and reduces the likelihood of accidental address duplication.

Automatic allocation is useful on stable single-segment networks or multisegment networks where machines are not routinely moved to other segments. This method reduces the network traffic generated by DHCP by eliminating the address lease renewal procedures. In most cases, the savings are minimal, however. Automatic allocation is also not recommended if your organization is working with a limited supply of registered IP addresses.

Once configured, dynamic allocation provides the greatest amount of flexibility with the least amount of administrative intervention. The DHCP server assigns IP addresses to systems on any subnet and automatically reclaims the addresses no longer in use for reassignment. Also, there is no possibility of duplicate addresses on the network (as long as DHCP manages all of the network's addresses).

Creating Scopes

In DHCP terminology, a *scope* is a range of IP addresses on a particular subnet that a DHCP server uses as a pool for its lease assignments. When a client requests an address, the server selects the first available one from an appropriate scope and creates a lease for it. If the lease expires, the client must stop using the address and the server returns it to the pool for reassignment. This enables the server to utilize all available addresses and keep track of all the address assignments on the network.

EXAM TIP

The word "scope" is not an official term used in the DHCP standards, but the Network+ objectives mention it specifically, as well as "reservation," another term from the Microsoft DHCP implementation.

TCP/IP Client Configuration

In addition to IP addresses, DHCP can also provide clients with values for the other parameters needed to configure a TCP/IP client, including the subnet mask, default gateway, and name server addresses. In DHCP terminology, these are called options. The object is to eliminate the need for any manual TCP/IP configuration on a client system. For example, the Microsoft DHCP server includes dozens of configuration options that it can deliver along with the IP address, even though Windows clients can only use a few of those parameters.

The RFC 2132 document, "DHCP Options and BOOTP Vendor Extensions," defines an extensive list of parameters that compliant servers should support, and most of the major DHCP server implementations adhere closely to this list. Many of these parameters are designed for use by specific system configurations and are submitted by vendors for inclusion in the standard document.

DHCP servers typically support two types of options: scope and server. A scope option is a setting that is associated with a specific pool of addresses and is only supplied to clients receiving an address from that pool. For example, a default gateway setting—referred to as the Router option by DHCP—is usually a scope option, because you are likely to have a different gateway address for each scope.

A server option is one delivered with all of the server's address assignments, regardless of scope. For example, DNS server addresses are usually server options, because the clients on all scopes typically use the same DNS servers.

DHCP Packet Structure

DHCP communications use eight different types of messages, all of which use the same basic packet format. DHCP traffic is carried within standard UDP/IP datagrams, using well-known port 67 at the server and port 68 at the client. These are the same ports used by BOOTP.

The packet format is shown in Figure 9-1.

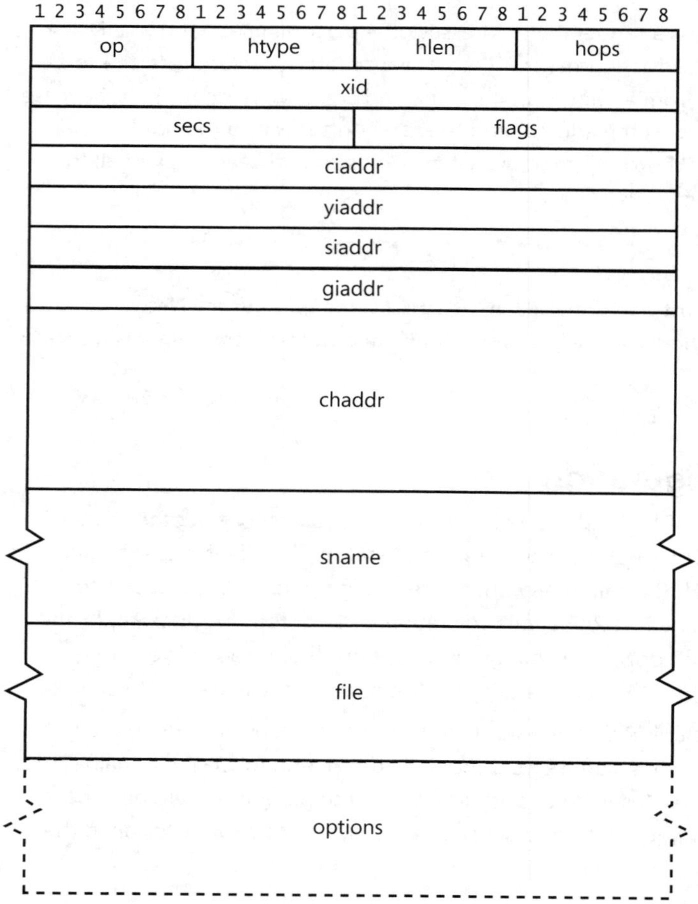

FIGURE 9-1 The DHCP message format.

The following fields make up the DHCP packet:

- **op (Op Code), 1 byte**   Specifies whether the message is a request or a reply, using the following codes:
    - **1**   BOOTREQUEST
    - **2**   BOOTREPLY

- **htype (Hardware Type), 1 byte**   Specifies the type of hardware address used in the chaddr field, using codes from the ARP section of the IETF "Assigned Numbers" list. The value for Ethernet hardware addresses is 1.

- **hlen (Hardware Address Length), 1 byte**   Specifies the length (in bytes) of the hardware address found in the chaddr field, according to the value of the htype field (for example, if htype is 1, indicating an Ethernet hardware address, the value of hlen will be 6 bytes).

- **hops, 1 byte**   Specifies the number of network segments between the client and the server. The client sets the value to 0, and each DHCP relay system increments it by 1 during the journey to the server.

- **xid (Transaction ID), 4 bytes**   Contains a transaction identifier that systems use to associate the request and response messages of a single DHCP transaction.

- **secs (Seconds), 2 bytes**   Specifies the number of seconds elapsed since the IP address was assigned or the lease was last renewed. This enables the systems to distinguish between messages of the same type generated during a single DHCP transaction.

- **flags, 2 bytes**   Contains the broadcast flag as the first bit, which, when set to a value of 1, specifies that DHCP servers and relay agents should use broadcasts, not unicasts, to transmit to the client. The remaining bits in the field are unused and must have a value of 0.

- **ciaddr (Client IP Address), 4 bytes**   Specifies the client's IP address in DHCPREQUEST messages transmitted while in the bound, renewal, or rebinding state. At all other times, the value must be 0.

- **yiaddr (Your IP Address), 4 bytes**   Specifies the IP address being offered or as-signed by a server in DHCPOFFER or DHCPACK messages. At all other times, the value must be 0.

- **siaddr (Server IP Address), 4 bytes**   Specifies the IP address of the next server in a bootstrap sequence. Servers include this information in DHCPOFFER and DHCPACK messages only when DHCP is configured to supply an executable boot file to clients and the boot files for various client platforms are stored on different servers.

- **giaddr (Gateway IP Address), 4 bytes**   Specifies the IP address of the DHCP relay agent to which a server should send its replies when the client and server are located on different subnets. When the client and server are on the same segment, the value must be 0.

- **chaddr (Client Hardware Address), 16 bytes**   Specifies the hardware address of the client system in DHCPDISCOVER and DHCPREQUEST messages, which the server uses to address its unicast responses to the client. The format of the hardware address is specified by the values of the htype and hlen fields.

- **sname (Server Host Name), 64 bytes**   Specifies the (optional) host name of the DHCP server. This field is more commonly used to hold overflow data from the options field.

- **file (Boot File Name), 128 bytes**   Specifies the name of an executable boot file for diskless client workstations in DHCPDISCOVER messages (in which case a generic file name is supplied) or DHCPOFFER messages (in which the field contains a full path and file name. This field is more commonly used to hold overflow data from the options field.

- **options, variable size, minimum 312 bytes**   Contains the magic cookie that specifies how the rest of the field should be interpreted and the DHCP Message Type option that defines the function of the message, as well as other options, defined in RFC 2132, that contain configuration data for other TCP/IP client parameters.

DHCP Options

The DHCP message format is almost identical to the BOOTP message defined in RFC 951. The primary difference is the options field, which in a DHCP message is a catchall area designed to carry the various parameters (other than the IP address) used to configure the client system's TCP/IP stack. Because you can configure a DHCP server to deliver many options to clients, defining separate fields for each one would be impractical.

The Magic Cookie

The options field always begins with the so-called *magic cookie*, which informs the server about what is contained in the rest of the field. The magic cookie is a 4-byte subfield containing the dotted decimal value 99.130.83.99.

The Option Field Format

The individual options in the options field contain various types and amounts of data, but most of them use the same basic structure, which consists of three subfields, as shown in Figure 9-2.

```
1 2 3 4 5 6 7 8 1 2 3 4 5 6 7 8 1 2 3 4 5 6 7 8 1 2 3 4 5 6 7 8
```
code	length	data

FIGURE 9-2 The DHCP option field format.

The functions of the subfields are as follows:

- **code (1 byte)**   Contains a code specifying the function of the option, as defined in RFC 2132
- **length (1 byte)**   Specifies the length of the data field associated with the option, making it possible for systems that do not support a particular option to skip directly to the next one
- **data (variable)**   Contains information used by the client in various ways depending on the code value and the message type

For example, in the Subnet Mask option, the code subfield has a value of 1, the length subfield has a value of 4, and the data field contains the 4-byte mask associated with the IP address assigned to the client.

DHCP options must fall within 4-byte word boundaries. If they do not, the server uses a Pad option as a filler so that option boundaries fall between 4-byte words. Unlike most other options, the Pad option has no length or data field and consists only of a 1-byte code field with a value of 0.

Because DHCP messages are carried within UDP datagrams, the packets are limited to a maximum size of 576 bytes, and the inclusion of a large number of options can test this limit. Because the DHCP message's sname and file fields are carryovers from the BOOTP protocol that are rarely used today, the DHCP standard allows these fields to be used to contain options that do not fit in the standard options field.

The DHCP Message Type Option

The DHCP Message Type option identifies the overall function of the DHCP message and is required in all DHCP packets. The code subfield for the option is 53 and the length is 1. The data subfield contains one of the following codes:

- **1   DHCPDISCOVER**   Used by a client system to locate DHCP servers and request an IP address
- **2   DHCPOFFER**   Used by a server to offer an IP address to a client
- **3   DHCPREQUEST**   Used by a client to request a specific IP address assignment or to renew a lease
- **4   DHCPDECLINE**   Used by a client to reject an IP address offered by a server
- **5   DHCPACK**   Used by a server to acknowledge a client's acceptance of an offered IP address
- **6   DHCPNACK**   Used by a server to reject a client's acceptance of an offered IP address
- **7   DHCPRELEASE**   Used by a client to terminate a lease
- **8   DHCPINFORM**   Used by a client that has already been assigned an IP address to request additional configuration parameters

TCP/IP Configuration Options

The DHCP options defined in RFC 2132 fall into several functional categories. The most commonly used options are included in the DHCP standard exactly as defined in RFC 1497 for use with BOOTP and contain the basic TCP/IP configuration parameters used by most client systems, such as the following:

- **Subnet Mask (code 1)**   Specifies which bits of the IP address identify the host system and which bits identify the network where the host system resides
- **Router (code 3)**   Specifies the IP address of the router (or default gateway) on the local network segment that the client should use to transmit to systems on other network segments
- **Domain Name Server (code 6)**   Specifies the IP addresses of the servers that the client will use for DNS name resolution
- **Host Name (code 12)**   Specifies the DNS host name that the client system will use
- **Domain Name (code 15)**   Specifies the name of the DNS domain on which the system will reside

The RFC 2132 document defines a great many other options that administrators can use to identify other servers on the network and configure the behavior of the TCP/IP client, the DHCP client, and the data-link layer interface. DHCP also includes the ability to support vendor-specific options provided in custom implementations.

The End Option

The End option signifies the end of the option field. Any bytes in the option field coming after the End option must contain nothing but 0 (Pad option) bytes. Like the Pad option, the End option consists only of a 1-byte code, with no length or data fields. The code has a value of 255.

DHCP Communications

When you configure a workstation to be a DHCP client, the system initiates an exchange of messages with a DHCP server. Whether you are using dynamic, automatic, or manual address allocation, the first exchange of messages, resulting in an IP address assignment for the client, is the same.

IP Address Allocation

The entire IP address negotiation process is illustrated in Figure 9-3. Before the initial client/server exchange can begin, however, a question arises: How is the client to find the server and communicate with it when its TCP/IP stack has not yet been configured? A DHCP client that does not yet have an IP address is said to be in the *init state*. In this state, even though the workstation has no information about the servers on the network and no IP address of its own, it is still capable of sending broadcast transmissions.

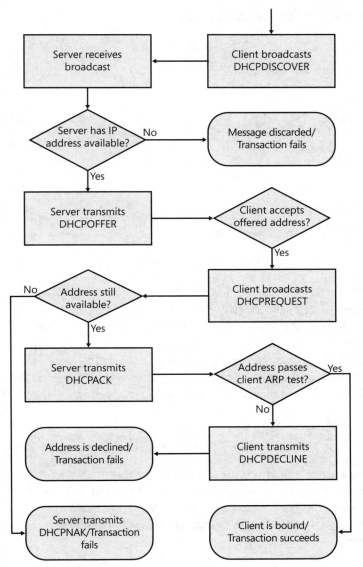

FIGURE 9-3 The DHCP IP address negotiation procedure.

The client begins the exchange by broadcasting a series of DHCPDISCOVER messages. In this packet, the DHCP Message Type option has a value of 1 in its data field, and the hardware address of the client is included in the chaddr (Client Hardware Address) field, as shown in Figure 9-4. In most cases, the client hardware address will be the MAC address hardcoded into the network interface adapter, as identified by the values of the htype and hlen fields. Because the client has no IP address of its own yet, the source address field in the IP header contains the value 0.0.0.0.

```
Dhcp: Request, MsgType = DISCOVER, TransactionID = 0x1B02DAD1
  OpCode: Request, 1(0x01)
  Hardwaretype: Ethernet
  HardwareAddressLength: 6 (0x6)
  HopCount: 0 (0x0)
  TransactionID: 453171921 (0x1B02DAD1)
  Seconds: 0 (0x0)
  Flags: 0 (0x0)
  ClientIP: 0.0.0.0
  YourIP: 0.0.0.0
  ServerIP: 0.0.0.0
  RelayAgentIP: 0.0.0.0
  ClientHardwareAddress: 00-0C-29-5B-29-D2
  ServerHostName:
  BootFileName:
  MagicCookie: 99.130.83.99
  MessageType: DISCOVER - Type 53
  clientID: (Type 1) - Type 61
  DHCPEOptionsHostName:
  DHCPEOptionsVendorClassIdentifier:
  ParameterRequestList:  - Type 55
  End:
  Padding: Binary Large Object (17 Bytes)
```

FIGURE 9-4 The DHCPDISCOVER message.

Each of the servers receiving the DHCPDISCOVER packet responds to the client with a DHCPOFFER message that contains an IP address in the yiaddr (Your IP Address) field. This is the address the server is offering for the client's use. The message also contains options specifying values for the other TCP/IP parameters that the server is configured to deliver, as well as the DHCP extension options, as shown in Figure 9-5. Because each DHCP server on the network operates independently, the client may receive several offers, each with a different IP address.

> *NOTE* **RELAY AGENTS**
>
> If there are any systems that are functioning as DHCP (or BOOTP) relay agents on the same network segment as the client, the agent systems will propagate the broadcasts to other segments, resulting in additional DHCPOFFER messages from remote servers being transmitted back to the client through the agent. See the "Relay Agents" section later in this chapter for more information.

After a predetermined interval, the client stops broadcasting DHCPDISCOVER messages and selects one of the offers it has received. If the client receives no DHCPOFFER messages, it retries its broadcasts and eventually times out with an error message. No other TCP/IP communications are possible while the machine is in this state.

```
⊟ Dhcp: Reply, MsgType = OFFER, TransactionID = 0x1B02DAD1
    OpCode: Reply, 2(0x02)
    Hardwaretype: Ethernet
    HardwareAddressLength: 6 (0x6)
    HopCount: 0 (0x0)
    TransactionID: 453171921 (0x1B02DAD1)
    Seconds: 0 (0x0)
  ⊞ Flags: 0 (0x0)
    ClientIP: 0.0.0.0
    YourIP: 10.0.0.11
    ServerIP: 10.0.0.2
    RelayAgentIP: 0.0.0.0
  ⊞ ClientHardwareAddress: 00-0C-29-5B-29-D2
    ServerHostName:
    BootFileName:
    MagicCookie: 99.130.83.99
  ⊞ MessageType: OFFER - Type 53
  ⊞ SubnetMask: 255.255.255.0 - Type 1
  ⊞ RenewTimeValue: Subnet Mask: 4 day(s),0 hour(s) 0 minute(s) 0 second(s) - Type 58
  ⊞ RebindingTimeValue: Subnet Mask: 7 day(s),0 hour(s) 0 minute(s) 0 second(s) - Type 59
  ⊞ IPAddressLeaseTime: Subnet Mask: 8 day(s),0 hour(s) 0 minute(s) 0 second(s) - Type 51
  ⊞ ServerIdentifier: 10.0.0.2 - Type 54
  ⊞ DomainName: adatum.local - Type 15
  ⊞ Router: 10.0.0.1 - Type 3
  ⊞ DomainNameServer: 10.0.0.2 - Type 6
  ⊞ End:
```

FIGURE 9-5 The DHCPOFFER message, returned to the client by a server.

EXAM TIP

In many cases, when a computer configured to use DHCP fails to obtain an IP address, it reverts to automatic assignment of a link-local address on the 169.254.0.0/16 network. Windows calls this process Automatic Private IP Addressing (APIPA), but it also goes by other names, such as zero-configuration networking. Although APIPA is not directly associated with DHCP in the Network+ exam objectives, it is important for candidates to understand the relationship between the two technologies.

When the client accepts an IP address offered by a server, it generates a DHCPREQUEST message that contains the name of the selected server in the Server Identifier option and the offered IP address (taken from the yiaddr field of the DHCPOFFER message) in the Requested IP Address option, as shown in Figure 9-6. The client also uses the DHCP Parameter Request List option to request additional parameters from the server.

The client transmits the DHCPREQUEST message as a broadcast because the message not only informs the selected server that the client has accepted its offer, it also informs the other servers that their offers have been declined. The message must have the same value in the secs field and use the same broadcast address as the DHCPDISCOVER messages the client previously transmitted. This is to ensure that the broadcast reaches all the servers that responded with offers (including those on other segments that require the assistance of relay agents).

```
Dhcp: Request, MsgType = REQUEST, TransactionID = 0x1B02DAD1
   OpCode: Request, 1(0x01)
   Hardwaretype: Ethernet
   HardwareAddressLength: 6 (0x6)
   HopCount: 0 (0x0)
   TransactionID: 453171921 (0x1B02DAD1)
   Seconds: 0 (0x0)
 + Flags: 0 (0x0)
   ClientIP: 0.0.0.0
   YourIP: 0.0.0.0
   ServerIP: 0.0.0.0
   RelayAgentIP: 0.0.0.0
 + ClientHardwareAddress: 00-0C-29-5B-29-D2
   ServerHostName:
   BootFileName:
   MagicCookie: 99.130.83.99
 + MessageType: REQUEST - Type 53
 + clientID: (Type 1) - Type 61
 + RequestedIPAddress: 10.0.0.11 - Type 50
 + ServerIdentifier: 10.0.0.2 - Type 54
 + DHCPEOptionsHostName:
 + DHCPEOptionsFullyQualifiedDomainName:
 + DHCPEOptionsVendorClassIdentifier:
 + ParameterRequestList:  - Type 55
 + End:
```

FIGURE 9-6 The DHCPREQUEST message, sent by a client to a server to accept its offered address.

At the time a server generates a DHCPOFFER message, the IP address it offers is not yet exclusively allocated to that client. If addresses are in short supply or if the client takes too long to respond, the server might offer that address to another client in the interim. When the server receives the DHCPREQUEST message saying its offer has been accepted, it generates either a DHCPACK message indicating that the IP address assignment has been completed, as shown in Figure 9-7, or a DHCPNAK message indicating that the offered address is no longer available.

The DHCPACK message contains the options requested by the client in the DHCPREQUEST message and, as with the DHCPOFFER message, can be unicast or broadcast depending on the value of the Broadcast flag in the client's messages.

When the server generates a DHCPACK message, it creates an entry in its database that commits the offered IP address to the client's hardware address. The combination of these two addresses will, from this point until the address is released, function as a unique identifier, called the *lease identification cookie*, for that client. If the server sends a DHCPNAK message to the client, the entire transaction is nullified and the client must begin the whole process again by generating new DHCPDISCOVER messages.

As a final test of its newly assigned address, the client can (but is not required to) use the ARP protocol to make sure that no other system on the network is using the IP address furnished to it by the server. If the address is in use, the client sends a DHCPDECLINE message to the server, nullifying the transaction. If the address is not in use, the address assignment process is completed and the client enters what is known as the *bound state*.

```
Dhcp: Reply, MsgType = ACK, TransactionID = 0x1B02DAD1
  OpCode: Reply, 2(0x02)
  Hardwaretype: Ethernet
  HardwareAddressLength: 6 (0x6)
  HopCount: 0 (0x0)
  TransactionID: 453171921 (0x1B02DAD1)
  Seconds: 0 (0x0)
  Flags: 0 (0x0)
  ClientIP: 0.0.0.0
  YourIP: 10.0.0.11
  ServerIP: 0.0.0.0
  RelayAgentIP: 0.0.0.0
  ClientHardwareAddress: 00-0C-29-5B-29-D2
  ServerHostName:
  BootFileName:
  MagicCookie: 99.130.83.99
  MessageType: ACK - Type 53
  RenewTimeValue: Subnet Mask: 4 day(s),0 hour(s) 0 minute(s) 0 second(s) - Type 58
  RebindingTimeValue: Subnet Mask: 7 day(s),0 hour(s) 0 minute(s) 0 second(s) - Type 59
  IPAddressLeaseTime: Subnet Mask: 8 day(s),0 hour(s) 0 minute(s) 0 second(s) - Type 51
  ServerIdentifier: 10.0.0.2 - Type 54
  SubnetMask: 255.255.255.0 - Type 1
  DomainName: adatum.local - Type 15
  Router: 10.0.0.1 - Type 3
  DomainNameServer: 10.0.0.2 - Type 6
  End:
```

FIGURE 9-7 The DHCPACK message, confirming that the server has bound the offered address to the client.

DHCPINFORM

The addition of a new message type to the revised DHCP standard published in 1997 makes it possible for clients to request TCP/IP configuration parameters without being assigned an IP address. When a server receives a DHCPINFORM message from a client, it generates a DHCPACK message containing the appropriate options for the client without including the lease time options or an IP address in the yiaddr field. The assumption is that the client has already been manually configured with an IP address and does not require regular renewals or any other maintenance beyond the initial parameter assignment.

The most obvious application for the DHCPINFORM message is to configure DHCP servers themselves, which typically cannot use a DHCP-supplied IP address. The server must have a manually configured IP address, but administrators can use DHCPINFORM messages to request values for the other required TCP/IP configuration parameters. This eliminates the need for administrators to configure any of the client parameters manually, apart from the IP address.

Lease Renewal

When a DHCP server uses manual or automatic address allocation to configure a client, no further DHCP communication is needed between the server and the client unless (or until) the client manually releases the address. When dynamic allocation is used, however, the DHCPOFFER messages that the server sends to the client contain options that specify the nature of the address lease agreement. These options include the IP Address Lease Time, the Renewal (T1) Time Value, and the Rebinding (T2) Time Value.

These options contain time values in units of seconds and do not include specific clock times, to account for possible discrepancies between the client and server system clocks. Administrators can specify values for these intervals in the DHCP server configuration. As an example, Microsoft DHCP Server has a default IP Address Lease Time of 691,200 seconds, or eight days. The Renewal (T1) Time Value defaults to 50 percent of the lease time and the Rebinding (T2) Time Value to 87.5 percent of the lease time.

Because the IP Address Lease Time option uses a 4-byte data subfield to specify the number of seconds, the maximum possible absolute value is approximately 136 years. A hexadecimal value of *0xffffffff* (or a binary value of 32 ones) indicates infinity—that is, a lease that never expires.

When a client system with a leased address has entered the bound state, it has no further communications with the server until the system restarts or it reaches the T1 or renewal time. The lease renewal transaction that begins at this time is illustrated in Figure 9-8.

When the client's lease reaches the T1 time, it enters the *renewing* state and begins transmitting DHCPREQUEST messages to the server that assigned its IP address. The messages contain the client's lease identification cookie and are transmitted to the server as unicasts (unlike the DHCPREQUEST messages in the initial lease negotiation, which are broadcasts). If the server receives the message and is capable of renewing the lease, it responds with a DHCPACK-message and the client returns to the bound state with a reset lease time. No further communication is necessary until the next renewal.

If the server cannot renew the lease, it responds with a DHCPNAK message, which terminates the transaction and the lease. The client must then restart the entire lease negotiation process with a new sequence of DHCPDISCOVER broadcasts.

> **NOTE** **RENEWING A LEASE**
>
> This is virtually the same message exchange that occurs each time a DHCP client system reboots, except that the client remains in the bound state. Usually, the server will respond to the DHCPREQUEST message with a DHCPNAK only when the client system has been moved to a different subnet and requires an IP address with a different network identifier. If the server fails to respond at all after repeated retransmissions, the client continues to use the address until the lease reaches the T1 time, at which point it enters the renewing state and begins the lease renewal process.

If the client receives no response to its unicast DHCPREQUEST, it retransmits the message each time half of the interval between the current time and the T2 time has expired. Thus, using the default time values for the Microsoft server, the lease duration is 192 hours (eight days), the T1 time is 96 hours (50 percent of 192), and the T2 time is 168 hours (87.5 percent of 72). The client will send its first DHCPREQUEST message to the server at 96 hours into the lease (the T1 time) and then retransmit at 132 hours (half the time until T2), 150 hours (half the remaining time until T2), 159 hours, and so on until it reaches the T2 time.

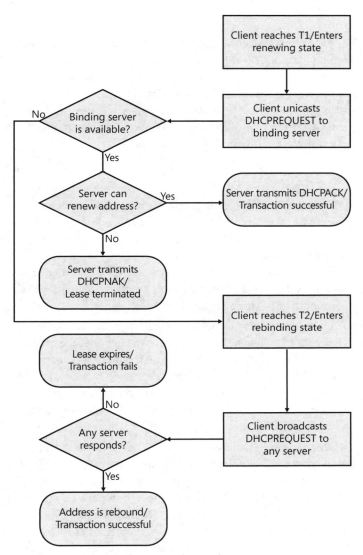

FIGURE 9-8 The DHCP lease renewal procedure.

When the lease time hits the T2 point, the client enters the *rebinding state* and begins transmitting its DHCPREQUEST messages as broadcasts to solicit an IP address assignment from any available server. Once again, the client awaits either a DHCPACK or DHCPNAK reply from a server. If no replies arrive, the client continues retransmitting whenever half of the remaining time in the lease expires. If the lease time does expire with no response from the server, the client releases the IP address and returns to the init state. It cannot send any further TCP/IP transmissions with the exception of DHCPDISCOVER broadcasts.

IP Address Release

While in the bound state, a DHCP client can relinquish its possession of an IP address (whether leased or permanent) by transmitting a unicast DHCPRELEASE message containing the client's lease identification cookie to the server. This returns the client to the unbound state, preventing any further TCP/IP transmissions, except for DHCPDISCOVER broadcasts, and causes the server to place the IP address back into its pool of available addresses. In most cases, an address release like this only occurs when the user of a client workstation explicitly requests it, using a utility such as Ipconfig.exe with the /release option in Windows.

Relay Agents

Because of its reliance on broadcast transmissions—at least from the client side—it would seem that DHCP clients and servers must be located on the same network segment in order to communicate. If this were the case, however, DHCP would not be a practical solution for enterprise networks, because there would have to be a DHCP server on every segment. To resolve this problem, DHCP takes its cue from BOOTP and uses relay agents as intermediaries between clients and servers. In fact, DHCP uses BOOTP relay agents exactly as defined in RFC 1542, "Clarifications and Extensions for the Bootstrap Protocol."

A *DHCP relay agent* (or BOOTP relay agent—the names are interchangeable) is a module located in a computer or router on a particular network segment that enables the other systems on that segment to be serviced by a DHCP server located on a remote segment. The relay agent works by monitoring UDP port 67 for DHCP messages being broadcast by clients on the local network. Normally, a workstation or router would ignore these messages because they do not contain a valid source address but, like the DHCP server, the relay agent is designed to accept a source address of 0.0.0.0.

When the relay agent receives these messages, it inserts its own IP address into the giaddr field of the DHCP message, increments the value of the hops field, and retransmits the packets to a DHCP server located on another segment. Depending on the location of the relay agent, this retransmission can take two forms. For an agent built into a router, the device might be able to broadcast the message by using a different interface than the one over which it received the message. For a relay agent running on a workstation, it is necessary to send the message to the DHCP server on another segment as a unicast.

A message can be passed along by more than one relay agent on the way to the DHCP server. An agent only inserts its IP address into the giaddr field if this field has a value of 0. In addition, the agent must silently discard messages that have a value greater than 16 in the hops field (unless this limit is configurable and has been adjusted by the network administrator). This prevents DHCP messages from cycling endlessly around the network.

When a DHCP server receives messages from a relay agent, it processes them in the normal manner, but transmits them back to the address in the giaddr field, rather than to the client. The relay agent will then use either a broadcast or a unicast (depending on the state of the Broadcast flag) to transmit the reply, unchanged, to the client.

If an entire internetwork is to be serviced by DHCP, every segment must have either a DHCP server or a relay agent on it. Most of the routers on the market today have DHCP/BOOTP relay agent functionality built into them, but for those that don't, the server versions of Windows all include a relay agent service.

DHCPv6

The redevelopment of the Internet Protocol in IP version 6, and particularly the enlargement of the IP address space from 32 to 128 bits, resulted in profound changes in many TCP/IP communications processes, not the least of which was a fundamental reassessment of DHCP's role on the network. In fact, for many network administrators, the question was whether they needed DHCP at all, despite its having been essential with IPv4.

In 2003, the IETF published a revised version of the DHCP standard to accommodate IPv6: RFC 3315, "Dynamic Host Configuration Protocol for IPv6 (DHCPv6)." The basic architecture and essential functions of the service are the same—to dynamically allocate IP addresses and other configuration parameters to network clients—but the message types and formats changed.

DHCPv6 provides a stateful alternative to the IPv6 stateless address autoconfiguration mechanism discussed in Chapter 6, "The Network Layer." The stateless autoconfiguration process enables computers to determine what configuration settings they need and whether they should generate their own link-local addresses or obtain addresses from a DHCPv6 server.

DHCPv6 Message Types

Although they perform many of the same functions as the DHCPv4 message types, the DHCPv6 messages have different names, as follows:

- **1   SOLICIT**   Used by a client system to locate DHCPv6 servers.
- **2   ADVERTISE**   Used by a server in response to a SOLICIT message, to indicate its availability for DHCPv6 service.
- **3   REQUEST**   Used by a client to request an IPv6 address and other TCP/IP configuration parameters from a specific DHCPv6 server.
- **4   CONFIRM**   Used by a client to determine whether an address assigned by a DHCPv6 server is still appropriate for the current link.
- **5   RENEW**   Sent by a client to a specific server to extend the lifetime of its assigned address and update other configuration parameters.
- **6   REBIND**   Sent by a client to any available server after a RENEW failure to extend the lifetime of its assigned address and update other configuration parameters.
- **7   REPLY**   Used by a server in response to a SOLICIT, REQUEST, RENEW, or REBIND message to send an assigned IP address and configuration parameters. Used in response to an INFORMATION-REQUEST message to send configuration parameters. Used in response to a CONFIRM message to confirm or deny the continued viability of an address. Used to acknowledge a RELEASE or DECLINE message.

- **8   RELEASE**   Used by a client to end its use of a particular address.
- **9   DECLINE**   Used by a client to inform a server that an assigned address is already in use on the link.
- **10   RECONFIGURE**   Used by a server to inform a client that it has new or updated configuration parameters to send. The client replies by sending a RENEW or INFORMATION-REQUEST message.
- **11   INFORMATION-REQUEST**   Used by a client to request configuration parameters without an IP address.
- **12   RELAY-FORW**   Used by a relay agent to forward a message from a client or another relay agent to a server or another relay agent. The forwarded message is encapsulated as an option.
- **13   RELAY-REPL**   Used by a server or another relay agent to send a message destined for a client. The message is encapsulated as an option.

The DHCPv6 message format for client/server communications, as shown in Figure 9-9, is much simpler than that of DHCPv4.

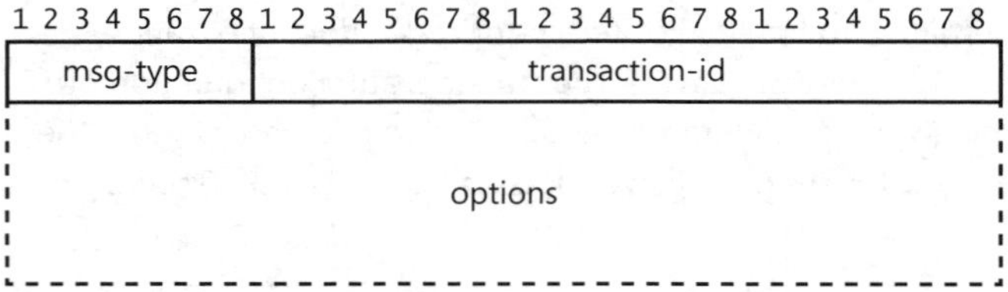

FIGURE 9-9 The DHCPv6 client/server message format

DHCPv6 client/server messages contain only three fields, as follows:

- **msg-type (Message Type), 1 byte**   Contains a code specifying the basic function of the message
- **transaction-id (Transaction Identifier), 3 bytes**   Contains a value that systems use to associate the request and response messages of a single DHCP transaction
- **options (Options), variable**   Contains a series of option fields containing additional information required by the specific message type

Unlike DHCPv4 messages, the DHCPv6 message type is included in a field of its own, instead of as an option, and all of the other information except for a transaction identifier is packaged as various types of options.

Messages involving relay agents—message types 12 and 13—use a different format, as shown in Figure 9-10.

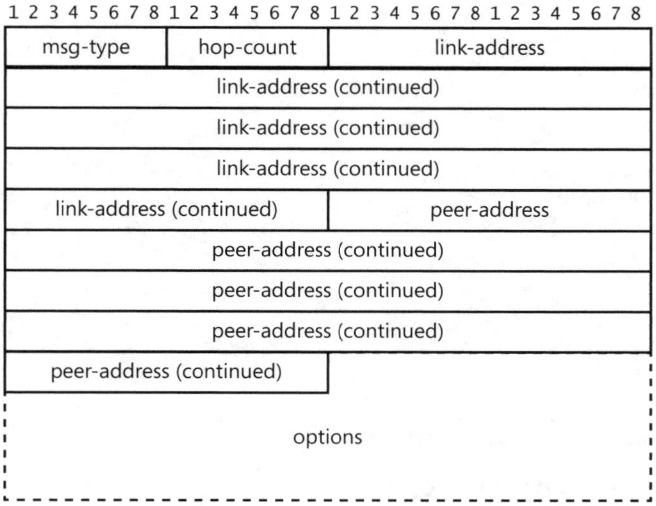

```
1 2 3 4 5 6 7 8 1 2 3 4 5 6 7 8 1 2 3 4 5 6 7 8 1 2 3 4 5 6 7 8
┌──────────────┬──────────────┬──────────────────────────────┐
│   msg-type   │  hop-count   │         link-address         │
├──────────────┴──────────────┴──────────────────────────────┤
│                  link-address (continued)                   │
├─────────────────────────────────────────────────────────────┤
│                  link-address (continued)                   │
├─────────────────────────────────────────────────────────────┤
│                  link-address (continued)                   │
├───────────────────────────────┬─────────────────────────────┤
│    link-address (continued)   │         peer-address        │
├───────────────────────────────┴─────────────────────────────┤
│                  peer-address (continued)                   │
├─────────────────────────────────────────────────────────────┤
│                  peer-address (continued)                   │
├─────────────────────────────────────────────────────────────┤
│                  peer-address (continued)                   │
├───────────────────────────────┐                             │
│    peer-address (continued)    │                            ┊
└────────────────────────────────┘                            ┊
┊                          options                            ┊
┊                                                             ┊
└ ─ ─ ─ ─ ─ ─ ─ ─ ─ ─ ─ ─ ─ ─ ─ ─ ─ ─ ─ ─ ─ ─ ─ ─ ─ ─ ─ ─ ─ ┘
```

FIGURE 9-10 The DHCPv6 relay agent message format.

DHCPv6 messages involving relay agents contain the following fields:

- **msg-type (Message Type), 1 byte**   Contains a code specifying the basic function of the message

- **hop-count (Hop Count), 1 byte**   Specifies the number of relay agents that have forwarded the message

- **link-address (Link Address), 16 bytes**   Contains a global or site-local address that the server uses to identify the client's link

- **peer-address (Peer Address), 16 bytes**   Specifies the address of the client or relay agent from which the relay agent received the message

- **options (Options), variable**   Contains a series of option fields containing additional information required by the specific message type

DHCPv6 Communications

A typical transaction with which a DHCPv6 client obtains an IPv6 address and configuration parameters from a server consists of four messages, transmitted with the User Datagram Protocol (UDP) using port 546 for the client and port 547 for the server.

The client begins the process by generating a SOLICIT message, as shown in Figure 9-11, which it sends to the DHCP servers on the network by using the All_DHCP_Relay_Agents_and_Servers multicast address.

```
⊟ Dhcpv6Client: MessageType = SOLICIT
  ├─ Message: SOLICIT, 1(0x01)
  ├─ TransactionID: 1822855 (0x1BD087)
  ⊞ ElapsedTime:
  ⊟ ClientID:
    ├─ OptionCode: OPTION_CLIENTID 1(0x1)
    ├─ OptionLen: 14 (0xE)
    ⊟ DUIDLLT: link-layer address plus time
      ├─ Type: link-layer address plus time
      ├─ HardWareType: Ethernet
      ├─ Time: 17-Oct-2011 03:13:08
      ⊞ linkAddr: 00-0C-29-5D-EC-17
  ⊞ IA_NA:
  ⊞ ClientFQDN: DomainName:(ᴶSVR2-adatum|local)
  ⊞ DHCPV6EVendorClass:
  ⊟ OptionRequest:
    ├─ OptionCode: OPTION_ORO 6(0x6)
    ├─ OptionLen: 8 (0x8)
    ├─ ReqOptCode: Domain Search List option 24(0x18)
    ├─ ReqOptCode: DNS Recursive Name Server Option 23(0x17)
    ├─ ReqOptCode: OPTION_VENDOR_OPTS 17(0x11)
    └─ ReqOptCode: Fully_Qualified_Domain_Name 39(0x27)
```

FIGURE 9-11 The DHCPv6 SOLICIT message.

DHCPv6 does not rely on broadcast transmissions as DHCPv4 does. The SOLICIT message contains a DHCP Unique Identifier (DUID) option that on a typical Ethernet network contains the client's hardware address and the time the message was generated.

DHCPv6 servers receiving the SOLICIT message respond with an ADVERTISE message, as shown in Figure 9-12, containing an IPv6 address and other appropriate configuration parameters, generated by using the information in the client's DUID.

```
⊟ Dhcpv6Client: MessageType = ADVERTISE
  ├─ Message: ADVERTISE, 2(0x02)
  ├─ TransactionID: 1822855 (0x1BD087)
  ⊟ ServerID:
    ├─ OptionCode: OPTION_SERVERID 2(0x2)
    ├─ OptionLen: 14 (0xE)
    ⊞ DUIDLLT: link-layer address plus time
  ⊟ ClientID:
    ├─ OptionCode: OPTION_CLIENTID 1(0x1)
    ├─ OptionLen: 14 (0xE)
    ⊟ DUIDLLT: link-layer address plus time
      ├─ Type: link-layer address plus time
      ├─ HardWareType: Ethernet
      ├─ Time: 17-Oct-2011 03:13:08
      ⊞ linkAddr: 00-0C-29-5D-EC-17
  ⊟ IA_NA:
    ├─ OptionCode: OPTION_IA_NA 3(0x3)
    ├─ OptionLen: 40 (0x28)
    ├─ IAID: 234884137 (0xE000C29)
    ├─ T1: 345600 (0x54600)
    ├─ T2: 552960 (0x87000)
    ⊞ IAAddress: Ipv6Address:(0x20010db800000000c8ebe05ad42add11)
  ⊞ DomainSearchList:
  ⊞ DNSServers:
```

FIGURE 9-12 The DHCPv6 ADVERTISE message.

The client selects one of the advertised offers and generates a REQUEST message, as shown in Figure 9-13, which it transmits as a multicast to the DHCP servers, to accept the offered settings. The REQUEST message includes a copy of the settings, informing the server which offer it is accepting and at the same time informing any other advertising DHCPv6 servers that the client is not accepting their offers.

```
Dhcpv6Client: MessageType = REQUEST
  Message: REQUEST, 3(0x03)
  TransactionID: 1822855 (0x1BD087)
  ElapsedTime:
  ClientID:
    OptionCode: OPTION_CLIENTID 1(0x1)
    OptionLen: 14 (0xE)
    DUIDLLT: link-layer address plus time
      Type: link-layer address plus time
      HardWareType: Ethernet
      Time: 17-Oct-2011 03:13:08
      linkAddr: 00-0C-29-5D-EC-17
  ServerID:
    OptionCode: OPTION_SERVERID 2(0x2)
    OptionLen: 14 (0xE)
    DUIDLLT: link-layer address plus time
  IA_NA:
    OptionCode: OPTION_IA_NA 3(0x3)
    OptionLen: 40 (0x28)
    IAID: 234884137 (0xE000C29)
    T1: 345600 (0x54600)
    T2: 552960 (0x87000)
    IAAddress: Ipv6Address:(0x20010db800000000c8ebe05ad42add11)
  ClientFQDN: DomainName:(ᴶSVR2-adatum|local)
  DHCPV6EVendorClass:
  OptionRequest:
```

FIGURE 9-13 The DHCPv6 REQUEST message.

On receiving the REQUEST message, the server generates a REPLY message, as shown in Figure 9-14, and sends it back to the client, confirming the acceptance of the address and other settings.

In some cases, DHCPv6 is able to complete a client/server transaction by using only two messages. A client that needs TCP/IP configuration settings but does not need an IPv6 address can generate an INFORMATION-REQUEST message and send it to the servers as a multicast. The server then sends a REPLY message containing the requested settings in response.

There is also a foreshortened address assignment sequence that consists only of a SOLICIT and a REPLY, if both systems agree to it.

EXAM TIP

Most of the DHCP coverage on the Network+ exam is devoted to DHCPv4. One reason for this is that the stateless address autoconfiguration capabilities of IPv6 systems make DHCP less of an essential service on large networks. Another is that the deployment of IPv6 is taking far longer than its designers expected.

```
Dhcpv6Client: MessageType = REPLY
  Message: REPLY, 7(0x07)
  TransactionID: 1822855 (0x1BD087)
  ServerID:
    OptionCode: OPTION_SERVERID 2(0x2)
    OptionLen: 14 (0xE)
    DUIDLLT: link-layer address plus time
  ClientID:
    OptionCode: OPTION_CLIENTID 1(0x1)
    OptionLen: 14 (0xE)
    DUIDLLT: link-layer address plus time
      Type: link-layer address plus time
      HardWareType: Ethernet
      Time: 17-Oct-2011 03:13:08
      linkAddr: 00-0C-29-5D-EC-17
  IA_NA:
    OptionCode: OPTION_IA_NA 3(0x3)
    OptionLen: 40 (0x28)
    IAID: 234884137 (0xE000C29)
    T1: 345600 (0x54600)
    T2: 552960 (0x87000)
    IAAddress: Ipv6Address:(0x20010db800000000c8ebe05ad42add11)
  DomainSearchList:
  DNSServers:
```

FIGURE 9-14 The DHCPv6 REPLY message.

REAL WORLD **DHCP IMPLEMENTATIONS**

In addition to the server operating systems in which you would expect to find DHCP server implementations, there are many other products that provide DHCP services as well. The Windows workstation operating systems, Windows Home and Windows Professional, include a feature called Internet Connection Sharing (ICS) with which a computer can share its Internet connection with other computers on the network. One component of ICS is a simplified form of DHCP called a DHCP Allocator, which provides the other computers on the network with compatible addresses and configuration settings.

Multifunction Internet access devices—often called broadband routers—also usually include DHCP implementations, as do virtualization products that enable you to create a logical network of virtual machines.

DNS

Computers are designed to work with numbers, whereas humans are more comfortable working with words. This fundamental dichotomy is the reason why the Domain Name System came to be. Very simply, the *Domain Name System (DNS)* is a database service that converts computer names to IP addresses and addresses back into names.

Host Tables

In the early days of TCP/IP and the Internet, a need was recognized for a mechanism that would permit users to refer to computers by name, rather than by IP address. The first mechanism for assigning human-friendly names to addresses appeared on UNIX systems and was called a *host table,* which took the form of a file called /etc/hosts. The host table was a simple text file that contained a list of IP addresses and their equivalent host names. The process of adding an entry to this host table was called *name registration*. When users wanted to access resources on other network systems, they could specify a host name in an application, and the system would look up the name in the host table and supply the appropriate address. This process was called *name resolution*.

The host table still exists on all TCP/IP systems today, usually in the form of a file called Hosts somewhere on the local disk drive. If nothing else, the host table contains the following entry, which assigns the host name localhost to the standard IP loopback address.

```
127.0.0.1      localhost
```

Today, the Domain Name System has replaced the host table almost universally, but when TCP/IP systems attempt to resolve a host name into an IP address, it is still possible to configure them to check the Hosts file first before using the DNS. If you have a small network of TCP/IP systems that is not connected to the Internet, you can use host tables on your machines to maintain friendly host names for your computers. The name resolution process will be very fast, because no network communications are necessary, and you will not need a DNS server.

As networks grew, the tasks of maintaining host tables and distributing them to all the computers on the network became increasingly problematic. This was particularly true on the fledgling Internet, which was then called the ARPANET. The task of maintaining the central registry for the ARPANET was at first given to the Network Information Center (NIC) at the Stanford Research Institute (SRI) in Menlo Park, California. The master list was stored in a file called Hosts.txt on a computer with the host name SRI-NIC. Administrators of ARPANET systems would send their modifications in email messages to the NIC, whose administrators would update the Hosts.txt file periodically. To keep their systems updated, administrators used FTP to download the latest Hosts.txt file from SRI-NIC and compile it into new Hosts files for their systems.

This process became increasingly unwieldy as the network grew more rapidly. There were just too many changes to keep up with, and the process was prone to errors caused by accidental typos and duplication of host names.

DNS Objectives

To address the problems resulting from the use of host tables for name registration and resolution, the people responsible for the ARPANET decided to design a completely new mechanism. Their primary objectives at first seemed to be contradictory: to design a mechanism that would enable administrators to assign host names to their own systems without creating duplicate names, and to make that host name information globally available to other administrators without relying on a single access point that could become a traffic bottleneck and a single point of failure. In addition, the mechanism had to be able to support information about systems that used various protocols with different types of addresses, and it had to be adaptable for use by multiple applications.

DNS Standards

The solution was the Domain Name System, the standards for which were published by the IETF in 1983 as RFC 882, "Domain Names: Concepts and Facilities," and RFC 883, "Domain Names: Implementation Specification." These documents were updated in 1987, published as RFC 1034 and RFC 1035, respectively, and ratified as an IETF standard.

Since that time, numerous other RFCs have updated the information in the standard to address current networking issues. Some of these additional documents are proposed standards, and others are experimental.

The DNS, as originally designed, consists of three basic elements:

- A hierarchical namespace that divides the host system database into discrete elements called domains.
- Domain name servers that contain information about the host and subdomains within a given domain.
- Resolvers that generate requests for information from domain name servers.

These elements are discussed in the following sections.

DNS Functions

DNS servers are a ubiquitous part of most TCP/IP networks, even if you aren't aware of it. TCP/IP communications are based solely on IP addresses. Before one system can communicate with another, it must know the other system's IP address. Often, the user supplies to a client application a friendly name (such as a fully qualified domain name, or FQDN) for a desired server. The application must then resolve that server name into an IP address before it can transmit a message to it. If the name resolution mechanism fails to function, no communication with the server is possible.

If you connect to the Internet, you use a DNS server each time you enter a server name or URL into a web browser or other application to resolve the name of the system you specified into an IP address. When a stand-alone computer connects to an Internet Service Provider (ISP), the ISP's server usually supplies the addresses of the DNS servers that the system will use. On a TCP/IP network, administrators configure clients with the addresses of the DNS servers they will use. This can be a manual process performed for each workstation or an automated process that uses DHCP.

In addition to resolving names into addresses, DNS servers can also resolve addresses into names, when necessary. The DNS also plays an essential role in Active Directory Domain Services (AD DS), the Windows directory service.

EXAM TIP

Internet clients must have access to a DNS server to resolve the server names found in URLs. A network that uses Active Directory Domain Services must have a DNS server also, to store information about AD DS domain controllers. Although it is possible for a single DNS server to perform both of these functions, that is often not the case.

Administrators typically place Active Directory resources in the most protected areas of the network, whereas servers requiring constant Internet access are more likely to be on a perimeter network, which is less protected. Candidates for the Network+ exam should be aware of the different roles that a DNS server can play on an enterprise network.

Domain Naming

The Domain Name System achieves the designated objectives by using a hierarchical system, both in the namespace used to name the hosts and in the database that contains the host name information. Before the DNS was developed, administrators assigned simple host names to the computers on their networks. The names sometimes reflected the computer's function or its location, as with "SRI-NIC," but there was no policy in place that required this. At that time, the relatively small number of computers on the network made this a practical solution.

To support the network as it grew larger, the developers of the DNS created a hierarchical namespace that made it possible for individual network administrators to name their systems, identifying the organization that owns the systems and preventing the duplication of names on the Internet.

The DNS namespace is based on domains, which exist in a hierarchical structure not unlike the directory tree in a file system. In the DNS structure, a *domain* is the equivalent of a directory, in that it can contain either subdomains (subdirectories) or hosts (files). The domain hierarchy forms a structure called the DNS tree, as shown in Figure 9-15. Because the DNS delegates the responsibility for specific domains to network administrators all over the Internet, the result is a *distributed database* scattered on systems all over the network.

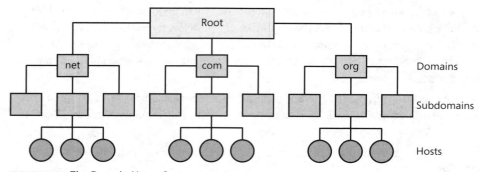

FIGURE 9-15 The Domain Name System tree structure.

To assign unique addresses to computers all over the Internet, IP uses a two-tiered system in which administrators receive the network identifiers that form the first part of the IP addresses and then assign host identifiers to individual computers themselves, to form the second part of the addresses. This distributes the address assignment task among thousands of network administrators all over the world. The DNS namespace functions in the same way: administrators receive domain names and are then responsible for assigning host names to systems within that domain.

The result is that every computer on the Internet is uniquely identifiable by a DNS name that consists of a host name plus the names of all of its parent domains, stretching up to the root of the DNS tree, separated by periods. Each of the names between the periods can be up to 63 characters long, with a total length of 255 characters for a complete DNS name, including the host and all of its parent domains. Domain and host names are not case sensitive and can take any value except the null value (no characters), which represents the root of the DNS tree.

In Figure 9-16, a computer in the *adatum* domain functions as a web server, and the administrator has therefore given it the host name *www*. This administrator is responsible for the *adatum* domain and can therefore assign any host name he wants to systems in that domain. Because *adatum* is a subdomain of *com*, the full DNS name for that web server is *www.adatum.com*. Thus, a DNS name is something like a United States postal address, in which the top-level domain is the equivalent of the state, the second-level domain is the city, and the host name is the street address.

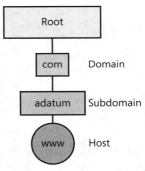

FIGURE 9-16 A DNS name derived from the DNS hierarchy.

Because a complete DNS name traces the domain path all the way up the tree structure to the root, it should theoretically end with a period, indicating the division between the top-level domain and the root. However, this trailing period is nearly always omitted in common use, except occasionally, in cases in which it serves to distinguish an absolute domain name from a relative domain name. An *absolute domain name* (also called a *fully qualified domain name*, or FQDN) does specify the path all the way to the root, whereas a *relative domain name* specifies only the subdomain relative to a specific domain context.

For example, when working on a complex network that uses several levels of subdomains, you might refer to a system that uses a relative domain name of *mail.paris* without a period, because it's understood by your colleagues that you are actually referring to a system with an absolute name of *mail.paris.adatum.com.* (with a period).

It's also important to understand that DNS names have no inherent connection to IP addresses, or any other type of address. Theoretically, the host systems in a particular domain can be located on different networks, thousands of miles apart.

Top-Level Domains

In every DNS name, the first word on the right represents the domain at the highest level in the DNS tree, called a *top-level domain (TLD)*. Top-level domains function as registrars for the domains at the second level. For example, the administrator of *adatum.com* went to the *com* top-level domain and registered the name *adatum*. In return for a fee, that administrator now has exclusive use of the name *adatum.com* and can create any number of hosts or subdomains in that domain. It doesn't matter that thousands of other network administrators have named their web servers *www*, because they all have their own individual domain names. The host name *www* can be duplicated anywhere, as long as the DNS name *www.adatum.com* is unique.

The original DNS namespace called for six generic top-level domains (gTLDs), dedicated to specific purposes, as follows:

- **com**   Commercial organizations
- **edu**   Post-secondary educational institutions
- **gov**   United States government institutions
- **mil**   United States military applications
- **net**   Networking organizations
- **org**   Noncommercial organizations

The *edu*, *gov*, and *mil* domains are reserved for use by certified organizations, but the *com*, *org*, and *net* domains are called *global domains,* because organizations anywhere in the world can register second-level domains within them.

Originally, these top-level domains were managed by a company called Network Solutions, Inc. (NSI, formerly known as InterNIC, the Internet Network Information Center) as a result of a cooperative agreement with the United States government.

In 1998, however, the agreement with the government was changed to permit other organizations to compete with NSI in providing domain registrations. An organization called the Internet Corporation for Assigned Names and Numbers (ICANN) is responsible for the accreditation of domain name registrars. Under this new policy, the procedures and fees for registering names in the *com*, *net*, and *org* domains might vary, but there will be no difference in the functionality of the domain names, nor will duplicate names be permitted.

> **MORE INFO**   **DOMAIN REGISTRARS**
>
> The complete list of registrars that have been accredited by ICANN is available at *http://www.internic.net/regist.html*.

GENERIC TOP-LEVEL DOMAINS

ICANN is also responsible for the ratification of new top-level domains. There have been numerous proposals for the establishment of various new top-level domains; those selected for negotiation of agreements in November 2000 were *aero, biz, coop, info, museum, name,* and *pro.* After a certain amount of discussion, these TLDs have become active, as have some sponsored TLDs, including *asia, cat, jobs, mobi, tel,* and *travel.*

COUNTRY-CODE DOMAINS

In addition to the generic TLDs, there are hundreds of two-letter *country-code top-level domains* (ccTLDs), named for specific countries/regions in their own languages, such as *fr* for France and *de* for Deutschland (Germany). The two-letter codes for countries/regions, territories, and other geographical entities are taken from the ISO 3166 standard, published by the International Organization for Standardization (ISO). Not all of the countries/regions listed in the standard exist in the DNS database, and of those that do, some do not have any domains registered to them.

The Internet Assigned Numbers Authority (IANA) has on record an authoritative trustee for each abbreviation, typically a government organization or official, or someone affiliated with a university. Each domain is permitted to establish its own prices and requirements for registration of subdomains. Some ccTLDs allow open registration to anyone, whereas others maintain citizenship or residence requirements.

> **MORE INFO** COUNTRY-CODE DOMAINS
>
> For a list of the country-code TLDs, as maintained by the IANA, see *http://www.iana.org/domains/root/db.*

Some of the countries/regions that permit open registration of ccTLDs have been more aggressive than others in pursuing registrations of company domains, which has resulted in the fairly common appearance of top-level domains from island countries/regions such as *nu* (Niue), *to* (Tonga), and *cc* (Cocos-Keeling Islands).

There is also a *us* top-level domain that is a viable alternative for organizations unable to obtain a satisfactory name in the *com* domain. The *us* domain is administered by the Information Sciences Institute of the University of Southern California, which registers second-level domains to businesses and individuals, as well as to government agencies, educational institutions, and other organizations. The only restriction is that all *us* domains must conform to a naming hierarchy that uses two-letter state abbreviations at the third level and local city or county names at the fourth level. Thus, an example of a valid domain name would be something like *adatum.chicago.il.us.*

INFRASTRUCTURE DOMAINS

There is one other category of top-level domain: the infrastructure domains, of which there is only one. The IANA manages the *arpa* domain for the use of the IETF, most notably as the host for the reverse name resolution domains, as discussed in "Reverse Name Resolution," later in this chapter.

Second-Level Domains

The registrars of the top-level domains are responsible for registering second-level domain names, in return for a subscription fee. As long as an organization continues to pay the fees for its domain name, it has exclusive rights to that name. The domain registrar maintains records that identify the owner of each second-level domain and specify three contacts within the registrant's organization—an administrative contact, a billing contact, and a technical contact. In addition, the registrar must have the IP addresses of two DNS servers that function as the source for further information about the domain. This is the only information maintained by the top-level domain. The administrators of the registrant's network can create as many hosts and subdomains within the second-level domain as they want without informing the registrars at all.

To host a second-level domain, an organization must have access to two DNS servers. A DNS server is a software program that runs on a computer. DNS server products are available for all of the major network operating systems. The DNS servers do not have to be located on the registrant's network; many companies outsource their Internet server hosting chores and use their service provider's DNS servers.

 The DNS servers identified in the top-level domain's record are the *authority* for the second-level domain. This means that these servers are the ultimate source for information about that domain. When network administrators want to add hosts to their networks or create new subdomains, they do so in their own DNS servers. In addition, whenever an application somewhere on the Internet has to discover the IP address associated with a particular host name, the request eventually ends up at one of the domain's authoritative servers.

 Thus, in its simplest form, the Domain Name System works by referring requests for the address of a particular host name to a top-level domain server, which in turn passes the request to the authoritative server for the second-level domain, which responds with the requested information. This is why the DNS is described as a *distributed database*. The information about the hosts in specific domains is stored on their authoritative servers, which can be located anywhere. There is no single list of all the host names on the entire Internet, which is actually a good thing, because at the time that the DNS was developed, no one would have predicted that the Internet would grow as large as it has.

This distributed nature of the DNS database eliminates the traffic-congestion problem caused by the use of a host table maintained on a single computer. The top-level domain servers handle millions of requests a day, but they are requests only for the DNS servers associated with second-level domains. If the top-level domains had to maintain records for every host in every second-level domain they have registered, the resulting traffic would bring the entire system to a standstill.

Distributing the database in this way also splits the chores of administering the database among thousands of network administrators around the world. Domain name registrants are each responsible for their own area of the namespace and can maintain it as they want, with complete autonomy.

Subdomains

Many of the domains on the Internet stop at two levels, meaning that the second-level domain contains only host systems. However, it is possible for the administrators of a second-level domain to create subdomains that form additional levels. The *us* top-level domain, for example, requires a minimum of three levels: the countries/regions code, the state code, and the local city or county code. There is no limit on the number of levels you can create within a domain, except for those imposed by practicality and the 255-character maximum DNS name length.

In some cases, large organizations use subdomains to subdivide their networks according to geographical or organizational boundaries. A large corporation might create a third-level domain for each city or country in which it has an office, such as *paris.adatum.com* and *newyork.adatum.com*, or for each of several departments, such as *sales.adatum.com* and *it.adatum.com*. The organizational paradigm for each domain is left completely up to its administrators.

The use of subdomains can make it easier to identify hosts on a large network, but many organizations also use them to delegate domain maintenance chores. The DNS servers for a top-level domain contain the addresses for each second-level domain's authoritative servers. In the same way, a second-level domain's servers can refer to authoritative servers for third-level administrators at each site to maintain their own DNS servers.

Zones

To make this delegation possible, DNS servers can break up a domain's namespace into administrative units called *zones*. A domain with only two levels consists of only a single zone, which is synonymous with the domain. A three-level domain, however, can be divided into multiple zones. A zone can be any contiguous branch of a DNS tree and can include domains on multiple levels. For example, in the diagram shown in Figure 9-17, the *paris.adatum.com* domain, including all of its subdomains and hosts, is one zone, represented by its own DNS servers. The rest of the *adatum.com* domain, including *newyork.adatum.com*, *chicago.adatum.com*, and *adatum.com* itself, is another zone. Thus, a zone can be defined as any part of a domain, including its subdomains, that is not designated as part of another zone.

Each zone must be represented by DNS servers that are the authority for that zone. A single DNS server can be authoritative for multiple zones, so you could conceivably create a separate zone for each of the third-level domains in *adatum.com* and still only have two sets of DNS servers.

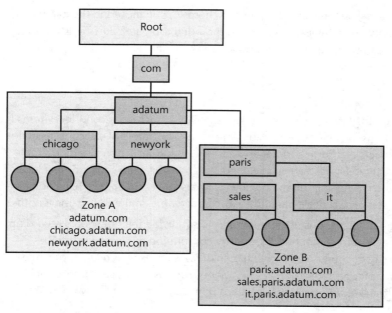

FIGURE 9-17 DNS zones.

Resource Records

DNS servers are essentially database servers that store information about the hosts and subdomains for which they are responsible in *resource records (RRs)*. When you run your own DNS server, you create a resource record for the name of each host that you want the rest of the network to be able to access. There are several different types of resource records used by DNS servers, the most important of which are as follows:

- **SOA (Start of Authority)** Indicates that the server is the best authoritative source for data concerning the zone. Each zone must have an SOA record, and only one SOA record can be in a zone.

- **NS (Name Server)** Identifies a DNS server functioning as an authority for the zone. Each DNS server in the zone (whether primary master or secondary) must be represented by an NS record.

- **A (Address)** Provides a name-to-address mapping that supplies an IP address for a specific DNS name. This record type performs the primary function of the DNS, converting names to addresses.

- **PTR (Pointer)** Provides an address-to-name mapping that supplies a DNS name for a specific address in the *in-addr.arpa* domain. This is the functional opposite of an A record, used for reverse lookups only.

- **CNAME (Canonical Name)** Creates an alias that points to the *canonical* name (that is, the "real" name) of a host identified by an A record. Administrators use CNAME records to provide alternative names by which systems can be identified. For example, your network might have a system with the name *server1.adatum.com*, which you use as a web server. Changing the host name of the computer would confuse your users, but you want to use the traditional name of *www* to identify the web server in your domain. Once you create a CNAME record for the name *www.adatum.com* that points to *server1.adatum.com*, the system is addressable by using either name.

- **MX (Mail Exchanger)** Identifies a system that will direct email traffic sent to an address in the domain to the individual recipient, a mail gateway, or another mail server.

In addition to functioning as the authority for a small section of the DNS namespace, servers process client name resolution requests by either consulting their own resource records or forwarding the requests to another DNS server on the network. The process of forwarding a request is called a *referral,* and this is how all of the DNS servers on the Internet work together to provide a unified information resource for the entire domain namespace.

DNS Messaging

DNS name resolution transactions use User Datagram Protocol (UDP) datagrams on port 53 for servers and an ephemeral port number for clients. Communication between two servers uses port 53 on both machines.

For all of its communications, the Domain Name System uses a single message format that consists of the following five sections:

- **Header** Contains information about the nature of the message

- **Question** Contains the information being requested from the destination server.

- **Answer** Contains resource records supplying the information requested in the Question section

- **Authority** Contains resource records pointing to an authority for the information requested in the Question section

- **Additional** Contains resource records with additional information in response to the Question section.

Every DNS message has a Header section, and the other four sections are included only if they contain data. For example, a query message contains the DNS name to be resolved in the Question section, but the Answer, Authority, and Additional sections aren't needed. When the server receiving the query constructs its reply, it makes some changes to the Header section, leaves the Question section intact, and adds entries to one or more of the remaining three sections. Each section can have multiple entries, so a server can send more than one resource record in a single message.

If the data to be transmitted does not fit in a single UDP datagram, as in the case of zone transfers, the two systems establish a standard TCP connection, also using port 53 on both machines, and transmit the data by using as many segments as needed.

DNS Name Resolution

Although all Internet applications use DNS to resolve host names into IP addresses, this name resolution process is easiest to see when you're using a web browser to access an Internet site. When you type a URL containing an FQDN (such as *www.microsoft.com*) into the browser's Address box and press the Enter key, if you look quickly enough, you might be able to see a message that says something like "Finding Site: www.microsoft.com." Then, a few seconds later, you might see a message that says "Connecting to," followed by an IP address. It is during this interval that the DNS name resolution process occurs.

From the client's perspective, the procedure that occurs during these few seconds consists of the application sending a query message to the designated DNS server that contains the name to be resolved. The server then replies with a message containing the IP address corresponding to that name. Using the supplied address, the application can then transmit a message to the intended destination. It is only when you examine the DNS server's role in the process that you see how complex the procedure really is.

Resolvers

The component in the client system that generates the DNS query is called a *resolver*. In most cases, the resolver is a simple set of library routines in the operating system that generates the queries to be sent to the DNS server, reads the response information from the server's replies, and feeds the response to the application that originally requested it. In addition, a resolver can resend a query if no reply is forthcoming after a given timeout period, and it can process error messages returned by the server, such as failure to resolve a name.

DNS Requests

A client can send a query to any DNS server; it does not have to use the authoritative server for the domain in which it belongs, nor does the server have to be on the local network. Using the DNS server that is closest to the client is best, however, because this minimizes the time needed for messages to travel between the two systems. A client only needs to access one DNS server, but two are usually specified, for fault tolerance purposes.

There are two types of DNS queries: recursive and iterative. When a server receives a *recursive query*, it is responsible for trying to resolve the requested name and for transmitting a reply back to the requester. If the server does not possess the required information itself, it must send its own queries to other DNS servers until it obtains the requested information or an error message stating why the information was unavailable, and must then relay the information back to the requester. The system that generated the recursive query, therefore, receives a reply only from the original server to which it sent the query. The resolvers in client systems nearly always send recursive queries to DNS servers.

When a server receives an *iterative query*, it can either respond with information from its own database or refer the requester to another DNS server. The recipient of the iterative query responds with the best answer it currently possesses, but it is not responsible for searching for the information, as with a recursive query. DNS servers processing a recursive query from a client typically use iterative queries to request information from other servers. It is possible for a DNS server to send a recursive query to another server, thus in effect "passing the buck" and forcing the other server to search for the requested information, but this is considered to be bad form and is rarely done without permission.

Forwarders

One of the scenarios in which DNS servers do send recursive queries to other servers is when a server is configured to function as a *forwarder*. On a network running several DNS servers, you might not want all of the servers to send queries to other DNS servers on the Internet. If the network has a relatively slow connection to the Internet, for example, several servers transmitting repeated queries might use too much of the available bandwidth.

To prevent this, some DNS implementations enable you to configure one server to function as the forwarder for all Internet queries generated by the other servers on the network. Any time that a server has to resolve the DNS name of an Internet system and fails to find the needed information in its cache, it transmits a recursive query to the forwarder, which is then responsible for sending its own iterative queries over the Internet connection. When the forwarder resolves the name, it sends a reply back to the original DNS server, which relays it to the client.

This request-forwarding behavior is a function of the original server only. The forwarder simply receives standard recursive queries from the original server and processes them normally. A server can be configured to use a forwarder in either exclusive or nonexclusive mode. In *exclusive mode,* the server relies completely on the forwarder to resolve the requested name. If the forwarder's resolution attempt fails, then the server relays a failure message back to the client. In *nonexclusive mode,* if the forwarder fails to resolve the name and transmits an error message to the original server, that server makes its own resolution attempt before responding to the client.

Root Name Servers

In most cases, DNS servers that do not possess the information needed to resolve a name requested by a client send their first iterative query to one of the Internet's root name servers. The *root name servers* possess information about all of the top-level domains in the DNS namespace. When you first install a DNS server, the only addresses that it needs to process client requests are those of the root name servers, because these servers can send a request for a name in any domain on its way to the appropriate authority.

The root name servers contain the addresses of the authoritative servers for all of the top-level domains on the Internet. In fact, the root name servers are the authorities for certain top-level domains, but they can also refer queries to the appropriate server for any of the other top-level domains, including the country-code TLDs, which are scattered all over the world. There are currently 13 root name server clusters, and they process millions of requests each day. The servers are scattered widely and are connected to different network trunks, so the chances of all of them being unavailable are minimal. If this were to occur, virtually all DNS name resolution would cease and the Internet would be crippled.

Resolving a Domain Name

With the preceding pieces in place, you are now ready to see how the DNS servers work together to resolve the name of a server on the Internet. The process is as follows:

1. A user on a client system specifies the DNS name of an Internet server in an application such as a web browser. The application generates an application programming interface (API) call to the resolver on the client system, and the resolver creates a DNS recursive query message containing the server name, which it transmits to the DNS server identified in the computer's TCP/IP configuration, as shown in Figure 9-18.

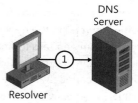

FIGURE 9-18 Name resolution step 1.

2. The client's DNS server, after receiving the query, checks its resource records to see if it is the authoritative source for the zone containing the requested server name. If it is not, which is typical, the DNS server generates an iterative query and submits it to one of the root name servers, as shown in Figure 9-19. The root name server examines the name requested by the client's DNS server and consults its resource records to identify the authoritative servers for the name's top-level domain. The root name server then transmits a reply to the client's DNS server that contains a referral to the top-level domain server addresses.

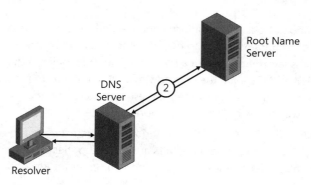

FIGURE 9-19 Name resolution step 2.

3. The client's DNS server, now in possession of the top-level domain server addresses for the requested name, generates a new iterative query and transmits it to a top-level domain server, as shown in Figure 9-20. The top-level domain server examines the second-level domain in the requested name and transmits a referral containing the addresses of authoritative servers for that second-level domain back to the client's DNS server.

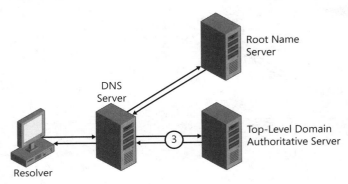

FIGURE 9-20 Name resolution step 3.

4. The client's DNS server generates yet another iterative query and transmits it to a second-level domain server, as shown in Figure 9-21. If the second-level domain server is the authority for the zone containing the requested name, it consults its resource records to determine the IP address of the requested system and transmits that address in a reply message back to the client's DNS server.

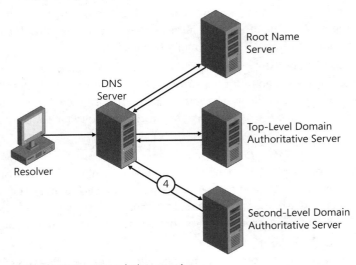

FIGURE 9-21 Name resolution step 4.

5. The client's DNS server receives the reply from the authoritative server and transmits the IP address back to the resolver on the client system, as shown in Figure 9-22. The resolver relays the address to the application, which can then initiate IP communications with the system specified by the user.

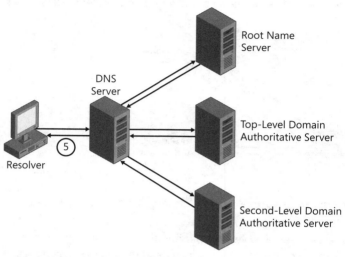

FIGURE 9-22 Name resolution step 5.

Depending on the name the client is trying to resolve, this process can be simpler or considerably more complex than the one shown here. If, for example, the client's DNS server is the authority for the domain in which the requested name is located, no other servers or iterative requests are necessary. On the other hand, if the requested name contains three or more levels of domains, additional iterative queries might be necessary.

This process also assumes a successful completion of the name resolution procedure. If any of the authoritative DNS servers queried returns an error message to the client's DNS server stating, for example, that one of the domains in the name does not exist, then this error message is relayed back to the client and the name resolution process is said to have failed.

DNS Server Caching

The DNS name resolution process might seem long and complex, but in many cases, it isn't necessary for the client's DNS server to send queries to the servers for each domain specified in the requested DNS name. This is because DNS servers are capable of retaining the information they learn about the DNS namespace in the course of their name resolution procedures and storing it in a cache on the local drive.

A DNS server that receives requests from clients, for example, caches the addresses of the requested systems, as well as the addresses for authoritative servers of particular domains. The next time that a client requests the resolution of a previously resolved name, the server can respond immediately with the cached information. In addition, if a client requests another name in one of the same domains, the server can send a query directly to an authoritative server for that domain, and not to a root name server. Thus, users should generally find that names in commonly accessed domains resolve more quickly, because one of the servers along the line has information about the domain in its cache, whereas names in obscure domains take longer, because the entire request/referral process is needed.

EXAM TIP

In DNS terminology, a *caching-only server* is a DNS server that clients use to resolve names, but that is not the authoritative source for any domain.

NEGATIVE CACHING

In addition to storing information that aids in the name resolution process, most modern DNS server implementations are also capable of negative caching. *Negative caching* occurs when a DNS server retains information about names that do not exist in a domain. If, for example, a client sends a query to its DNS server containing a name in which the second-level domain does not exist, the top-level domain server will return a reply containing an error message to that effect. The client's DNS server will then retain the error message information in its cache. The next time a client requests a name in that domain, the DNS server will be able to respond immediately with its own error message, without consulting the top-level domain.

CACHE DATA PERSISTENCE

Caching is a vital element of the DNS architecture, because it reduces the number of requests sent to the root name and top-level domain servers, which, being at the top of the DNS tree, are the most likely to act as a bottleneck for the whole system. However, caches must be purged eventually, and there is a fine line between effective and ineffective caching.

Because DNS servers retain resource records in their caches, it can take hours or even days for changes made in an authoritative server to be propagated around the Internet. During this period, users might receive incorrect information in response to a query. If information is allowed to remain in server caches too long, the changes that administrators make to the data in their DNS servers will take too long to propagate around the Internet. If caches are purged too quickly, then the number of requests sent to the root name and top-level domain servers increases precipitously.

The amount of time that DNS data remains cached on a server is called its *time to live*. Unlike most data caches, the resource record cache's time to live is not specified by the administrator of the server where the cache is stored. Instead, the administrators of each authoritative DNS server specify how long the data for the resource records in their domains or zones should be retained in the servers where it is cached. This enables administrators to specify a time-to-live value based on the volatility of their server data. On a network where changes in IP addresses or the addition of new resource records is frequent, a lower time-to-live value increases the likelihood that clients will receive current data. On a network that rarely changes, you can use a longer time-to-live value and minimize the number of requests sent to the parent servers of your domain or zone.

DNS Load Balancing

In most cases, DNS servers maintain one IP address for each host name. However, there are situations in which more than one IP address is required. In the case of a high-traffic website, for example, one server might not be sufficient to support all of the clients. To allow multiple, identical servers with their own IP addresses to host the same site, however, some mechanism is needed to ensure that client requests are balanced among the machines.

One way of doing this is to control how the authoritative servers for the domain on which the site is located resolve the DNS name of the web server. Some DNS server implementations enable you to create multiple resource records with different IP addresses for the same host name. As the server responds to queries requesting resolution of that name, it uses the resource records in a rotational fashion to supply the IP address of a different machine to each client.

DNS caching tends to defeat the effectiveness of this rotational system, because servers use the cached information about the site, rather than issuing a new query and possibly receiving the address for another system. As a result, it is generally recommended that administrators use a relatively short time-to-live value for the duplicated resource records.

Reverse Name Resolution

The Domain Name System is designed to facilitate the resolution of DNS names into IP addresses, but there are also instances in which IP addresses have to be resolved into DNS names. These instances are relatively rare. In log files, for example, some systems convert IP addresses to DNS names to make the data more readily accessible to human readers. Some systems also use reverse name resolution in the course of authentication procedures.

The structure of the DNS namespace and the method by which it is distributed among various servers is based on the domain name hierarchy. When the entire database is located on one system, as in the case of a host table, searching for a particular address to find out its associated name is no different from searching for a name to find an address. However, locating a particular address in the DNS namespace would seem to require a search of all of the Internet's DNS servers, which is obviously impractical.

To make reverse name resolution possible without requiring a massive search across the entire Internet, the DNS tree includes a special domain that uses the dotted decimal values of IP addresses as domain names. This branch stems from a domain called *in-addr.arpa*, which is located just beneath the root of the DNS tree, as shown in Figure 9-23. Just beneath the *in-addr* domain, there are 256 subdomains named by using the numbers 0 to 255, to represent the possible values of an IP address's first byte. Each of these subdomains contains another 256 subdomains representing the possible values of the second byte. The next level has another 256 domains, each of which can have up to 256 numbered hosts, which represent the third and fourth bytes of the address.

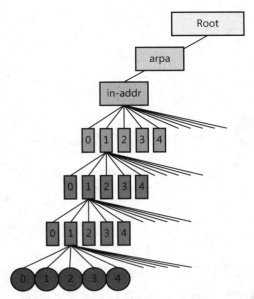

FIGURE 9-23 The *in-addr.arpa* domain hierarchy.

Using the *in-addr.arpa* domain structure, each of the hosts represented by a standard name on a DNS server can also have an equivalent DNS name constructed by using its IP address. Therefore, if a system with the IP address 192.168.214.23 is listed in the DNS server for the *adatum.com* domain with the host name *www*, then there can also be a resource record for that system with the DNS name *23.214.168.192.in-addr.arpa*, meaning that there is a host with the name *23* in a domain called *214.168.192.in-addr.arpa*, as shown in Figure 9-24. This domain structure makes it possible for a system to search for the IP address of a host in a domain (or zone) without having to consult other servers in the DNS tree. In most cases, you can configure a DNS server to automatically create an equivalent resource record in the *in-addr.arpa* domain for every host you add to the standard domain namespace.

The byte values of IP addresses are reversed in the *in-addr.arpa* domain, because in a DNS name, the least significant word comes first, whereas in IP addresses, the least significant byte comes last. In other words, a DNS name is structured with the root of the DNS tree on the right side and the host name on the left. In an IP address, the host identifier is on the right and the network identifier is on the left. It would be possible to create a domain structure by using the IP address bytes in their regular order, but this would complicate the administration process by making it harder to delegate maintenance tasks based on network addresses.

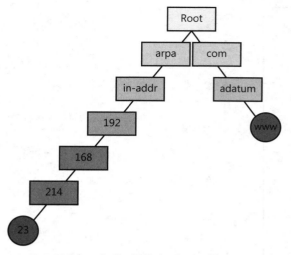

FIGURE 9-24 A host in the DNS database with two resource records.

If, for example, a corporate internetwork consists of three branch offices, each with its own /24 IP address (192.168.1/24, 192.168.2/24, and 192.168.3/24), it is possible to have a different person administer the reverse lookup domain for each site, because the domains would have the following names:

```
1.168.192.in-addr.arpa
2.168.192.in-addr.arpa
3.168.192.in-addr.arpa
```

If the *in-addr.arpa* namespace was constructed by using the byte values for the IP addresses in their traditional order, the third-level domain would be named by using the host identifier (that is, the fourth byte) from the IP address. You might need up to 256 third-level domains to represent these three networks instead of one. Delegating administration chores would be all but impossible, because the *72.in-addr.arpa* domain (for example) could contain a host from all three networks.

DNS Name Registration

As you have already learned, name resolution is the process by which IP address information for a host name is extracted from the DNS database. The process by which host names and their addresses are added to the database is called *name registration*. Name registration refers to the process of creating new resource records on a DNS server, thus making them accessible to all of the other DNS servers on the network.

As it was originally conceived, the name registration process on a DNS server is decidedly low tech. The original DNS standard includes no mechanism by which the server could detect the systems on the network and automatically enter their host names and IP addresses into resource records. In fact, a computer might not even be aware of its host name, because it receives all of its communications using IP addresses and never has to answer to its name.

To register a host in the DNS namespace, an administrator had to manually create a resource record on the server. The method for creating resource records varies depending on the DNS server implementation. Some UNIX-based servers require you to edit a text file, whereas the Microsoft DNS Server uses a graphical interface.

Manual Name Registration

The manual name registration process is basically an adaptation of the host table for use on a DNS server. It is easy to see how, in the early days, administrators were able to implement DNS servers on their network by using their host tables with slight modifications. The most common DNS server software on the Internet, an open-source product called BIND (for Berkeley Internet Name Domain) has used flat text files for its data storage for nearly its entire history. It was only with the release of version 9.4 in 2007 that support for other database formats was added.

The manual name registration process can be problematic on some networks, however. If you have a large number of hosts, manually creating resource records for all of them can be a tedious affair, even with a graphical interface. However, depending on the nature of the network, it might not be necessary to register every system in the DNS. If, for example, you are running a small peer-to-peer network using unregistered IP addresses, you might not need your own DNS server at all, except possibly to process Internet name resolution requests for clients. Windows NT networks and later backward-compatible versions have their own NetBIOS naming system and name resolution mechanisms, and you generally don't need to refer to them by using DNS names.

One exception to this would be if you have a system with a registered IP address that you use as a web server or other type of Internet server. This type of server must be visible to Internet users and, therefore, must have a host name in a registered DNS domain. In many cases, however, the number of systems like this on a network is small, so manually creating the resource records is not much of a problem.

Dynamic Updates

As networks grow larger and more complex, the biggest problem arising from manual name registration stems from the increasing use of DHCP servers to dynamically assign IP addresses to network workstations. The manual configuration of TCP/IP clients is another long-standing network administration chore that has gradually been phased out in favor of an automated solution. However, dynamic assignment of IP addresses means that workstations can have different addresses from one day to the next, and the original DNS standard has no way of keeping up with the changes.

On networks where only a few servers have to be visible to the Internet, it isn't too great an inconvenience to configure them with static IP addresses and use DHCP dynamic alloca-tion for the unregistered systems. However, this situation has changed with the increased prevalence of Active Directory Domain Services (AD DS) on enterprise networks. AD DS relies heavily on DNS to resolve the names of systems on the network and to keep track of the domain controllers that are available for use by client workstations.

To make the use of DNS practical with technologies such as AD DS that require regular updates to resource records, the IETF published RFC 2136, "Dynamic Updates in the Domain Name System." This document defines a new DNS message type, called an *Update*, that systems like domain controllers and DHCP servers can generate and transmit to a DNS server. These Update messages can modify or delete existing resource records or create new ones, based on prerequisites specified by the administrator. For AD DS, the Update message can contain the information for the SVR resource record type, as defined in RFC 2052, "A DNS RR for specifying the location of services (DNS SREV)," which identifies the servers that perform particular functions, such as domain controllers.

NOTE **DNS SERVERS**

Organizations that use AD DS internally and also maintain Internet web servers typically use separate DNS servers for these two applications. The authoritative records for an Internet domain must be accessible to Internet users, but AD DS information is far too sensitive to store on a server that is accessible from the Internet.

Zone Transfers

Most networks that host their own DNS use at least two servers, to provide fault tolerance and to give clients access to a nearby server. To keep the resource records consistent, the DNS standards define a mechanism that replicates the DNS data among the servers, thus enabling administrators to make changes only once.

The standards define two DNS server roles: the primary master and the secondary master. The *primary master* server loads its resource records and other information from the database files on the server's local drive. The *secondary master* server receives its data from another server in a process called a *zone transfer*, which the secondary server performs each time it starts and periodically thereafter. The server from which the secondary server receives its data is called its *master server*, but it need not be the primary master. A secondary server can receive data from the primary master or another secondary server.

DNS servers perform zone transfers for individual zones, and because a single server can be the authority for multiple zones, more than one transfer might be needed to update all of a secondary server's data. In addition, the primary master and secondary roles are also zone specific. A server can be the primary master for one zone and the secondary server for another, although this practice generally should not be necessary and is likely to generate some confusion.

Although secondary servers receive periodic zone transfers from their primary masters, they are also able to load database files from their local drives. When a secondary server receives a zone transfer, it updates the local database files. Each time the secondary server starts up, it loads the most current resource records it has from the database files and then checks this data with the primary master to see whether an update is needed. This prevents the servers from performing unnecessary zone transfers.

NOTE STORING DNS RECORDS

Microsoft DNS Server provides a proprietary option for zone database storage with which the servers can store their data in the AD DS database. This eliminates the need for primary and secondary zones, and for zone transfers, because AD DS has its own far more sophisticated database replication mechanism.

✔ **Quick Check**

1. What is the name of the domain that DNS servers use for reverse name lookups?
2. What is the term used for a DNS server that is deliberately configured to receive recursive queries from other DNS servers?

Quick Check Answers

1. *in-addr.arpa*
2. Forwarder

HTTP

Communication between web servers and their browser clients is largely dependent on an application layer protocol called the *Hypertext Transfer Protocol (HTTP)*. The current version of the HTTP specification, version 1.1, was published by the IETF as RFC 2616 in June 1999. HTTP is a relatively simple protocol that takes advantage of the services provided by the TCP protocol at the transport layer to transfer files from servers to clients. When a client connects to a web server by typing a URL in a browser or clicking a hyperlink, the client generates an HTTP request message and transmits it to the server. This is an application layer process, but before it can happen, the two systems must establish communication at the lower layers.

Unless the user or the hyperlink specifies the IP address of the web server, the first step in establishing the connection between the two systems is to discover the server's address by sending a name resolution request to a DNS server. This address makes it possible for the IP protocol to address traffic to the server. When the client system knows the address, it establishes a TCP connection with the server's port 80, using the standard three-way handshake process defined by that protocol.

MORE INFO TCP

For more information on the TCP three-way handshake, see Chapter 8, "The Transport Layer."

After the two systems have established a TCP connection, the browser and the server can exchange HTTP messages. HTTP consists of only two message types, requests and responses. As with many other application layer protocols, HTTP messages take the form of text commands. In fact, you can connect to a web server with a Telnet client and request a file by feeding an HTTP command directly to the server. The server will reply with the file you requested in its raw ASCII form.

Each HTTP message consists of the following elements:

- **Start line** Contains a request command or a reply status indicator, plus a series of variables

- **Headers (optional)** Contains a series of zero or more fields that have information about the message or the system sending it

- **Empty line** Contains a blank line that identifies the end of the header section

- **Message body (optional)** Contains the payload being transmitted to the other system

HTTP Requests

The start line for all HTTP requests is structured as follows.

```
RequestType RequestURI [HTTPVersion]
```

Version 1.1 of the HTTP standard defines the request messages, which use the following values for the *RequestType* variable:

- **GET** Contains a request for information specified by the *RequestURI* variable. This type of request accounts for the vast majority of request messages.

- **HEAD** Functionally identical to the GET request, except that the reply should contain only a start line and headers; no message body should be included.

- **POST** Requests that the information included in the message body be accepted by the destination system as a new subordinate to the resource specified by the *RequestURI* variable.

- **OPTIONS** Contains a request for information about the communication options available on the request/response chain specified by the *RequestURI* variable.

- **PUT** Requests that the information included in the message body be stored at the destination system in the location specified by the *RequestURI* variable.

- **DELETE** Requests that the destination system delete the resource identified by the *RequestURI* variable.

- **TRACE** Requests that the destination system perform an application layer loopback of the incoming message and return it to the sender.

- **CONNECT** Reserved for use with proxy servers that provide Secure Sockets Layer (SSL) tunneling.

The *RequestURI* variable contains a *Uniform Resource Identifier (URI)*, a text string that uniquely identifies a particular resource on the destination system. In most cases, this variable contains the name of a file on a web server that the client wants the server to send to it, or the name of a directory from which the server should send the default file. The optional *HTTPVersion* variable identifies the version of the HTTP protocol that is supported by the system generating the request.

Thus, when a user types the name of a website into a browser, the request message it generates can contain a start line that appears as follows.

```
GET / HTTP/1.1
```

The GET command requests that the server send a file. The use of the forward slash as the value for the *RequestURI* variable represents the root of the website, so the server will respond by sending the default file located in the server's home directory.

Following the start line, any HTTP message can include a series of headers, which are text strings formatted in the following manner.

```
FieldName: FieldValue
```

The *FieldName* variable identifies the type of information carried in the header, and the *FieldValue* variable contains the information itself. The various headers mostly provide information about the system sending the message and the nature of the request, which the server might or might not use when formatting the reply. The number, choice, and order of the headers included in a message are left to the client implementation.

HTTP Responses

The HTTP responses generated by web servers use many of the same basic elements as the requests. The start line also consists of three elements, as follows.

```
HTTPVersion StatusCode StatusPhrase
```

The *HTTPVersion* variable specifies the standard supported by the server. The *StatusCode* and *StatusPhrase* variables indicate whether or not the request has been processed successfully by the server, and if it hasn't, why not. The code is a three-digit number, and the phrase is a text string.

The code values are defined in the HTTP specification and are used consistently by all web server implementations. The first digit of the code specifies the general nature of the response, and the last two digits give more specific information. The status phrases are defined by the standard as well, but some web server products enable you to modify the text strings in order to supply more or customized information to the client.

For example, most users are familiar with the HTTP 404 code, which is an error message that by default is accompanied by the status phrase "File not found." There are many websites, however, that substitute their own original and often humorous text.

After the start line, a response message can contain a series of headers, just like those in a request, that provide information about the server and the response message.

HTTP Message Exchanges

In the most basic form of HTTP message exchange, the client browser establishes a TCP connection to a server and then transmits an HTTP request message, like that shown in Figure 9-25.

```
Http: Request, GET /
    Command: GET
    URI: /
    ProtocolVersion: HTTP/1.1
    Accept:  text/html, application/xhtml+xml, */*
    Accept-Language:  en-US
    UserAgent:  Mozilla/5.0 (compatible; MSIE 9.0; Windows NT 6.1; WOW64; Trident/5.0)
    Accept-Encoding:  gzip, deflate
    Host:  svrb
    Connection:  Keep-Alive
    HeaderEnd: CRLF
```

FIGURE 9-25 An HTTP request message.

The start line for the message indicates that it is a GET command and that the *RequestURI* value identifies the default file in the website's root directory. In this case, there is no *HTTP-Version* in the request, but it does appear in the Protocol Version field. The Accept header lists the media types acceptable in the response, including the */* value, which enables the client to accept any media type. The Accept-Language and Accept-Encoding headers indicate, respectively, that the response should be in U.S. English and that the gzip and deflate compression formats are acceptable. The User-Agent header identifies the browser used by the client, and the Host header provides the URL supplied by the user in the browser's Address field. The Connection header contains the Keep-Alive value, indicating that the same TCP connection will be used to transmit multiple files.

The server's response to the request, shown in Figure 9-26, specifies that the server is also using HTTP version 1.1, and the StatusCode value of 200 indicates that the request was processed successfully. The Server header identifies the web server software running on the server, and other headers specify the date and time that the request was processed and the media type of the requested file. The Last-Modified header indicates when the requested file was last modified, and the Content Length header provides the total length of the file. The ETag header provides an entity tag for the file; this tag has no function here but could conceivably be used with other headers such as If-Match and If-None-Match for cache checking.

```
⊟ Http: Response, HTTP/1.1, Status: Ok, URL: /
   ─ ProtocolVersion: HTTP/1.1
   ─ StatusCode: 200, Ok
   ─ Reason: OK
 ⊞ ContentType:  text/html
   ─ Last-Modified:  Thu, 26 Jan 2012 19:17:18 GMT
   ─ Accept-Ranges:  bytes
   ─ ETag:  "db6cf21e5fdccc1:0"
   ─ Server:  Microsoft-IIS/7.5
   ─ Date:  Fri, 27 Jan 2012 00:38:40 GMT
   ─ ContentLength:  689
   ─ HeaderEnd: CRLF
 ⊞ payload: HttpContentType =  text/html
```

FIGURE 9-26 An HTTP response message.

When the client has received the initial file, it parses the HTML code inside. In this example, when it encounters an image tag, the browser generates another request message for a file called welcome.png and transmits it to the server, as shown in Figure 9-27.

```
⊟ Http: Request, GET /welcome.png
   ─ Command: GET
 ⊞ URI: /welcome.png
   ─ ProtocolVersion: HTTP/1.1
   ─ Accept:  image/png, image/svg+xml, image/*;q=0.8, */*;q=0.5
   ─ Referer:  http://svrb/
   ─ Accept-Language:  en-US
   ─ UserAgent:  Mozilla/5.0 (compatible; MSIE 9.0; Windows NT 6.1; WOW64; Trident/5.0)
   ─ Accept-Encoding:  gzip, deflate
   ─ Host:  svrb
   ─ Connection:  Keep-Alive
   ─ HeaderEnd: CRLF
```

FIGURE 9-27 An HTTP request for an additional graphic image file.

After the client has requested and the server has transmitted all of the files needed to display the home page for the website, the server begins the process of terminating the TCP connection with the client. When this process is completed, there is no further communication between client and server until the user initiates another request by clicking a hyperlink or typing a URL.

EXAM TIP

Like many application layer protocols, HTTP uses text commands for its messages, rather than the encoded header fields found at the lower layers of the OSI model.

HTTPS

Hypertext Transfer Protocol Secure (HTTPS) is a variant of HTTP that uses the Transport Layer Security (TLS) and Secure Sockets Layer (SSL) security protocols to provide data encryption and server identification services. HTTPS is the accepted standard for secured Internet transactions such as online banking and e-commerce. An HTTPS connection uses the *https://* prefix in its URL and connects by default to port 443, instead of port 80, which is used by HTTP.

> **MORE INFO** **HTTPS**
>
> For more information on HTTPS and the TLS and SSL security protocols, see Chapter 11, "Network Security."

FTP

FTP, the *File Transfer Protocol*, is an application layer TCP/IP protocol that is used by an authenticated client to connect to a server and transfer files to and from its drives. Using FTP is not the same as sharing a drive with another system on the network, nor is it a terminal emulator like Telnet. Access is limited to a few basic file management commands, and the primary function of the protocol is to copy files to a local system, not to access them in place on the server.

Defined by the IETF in RFC 959, FTP has been a common fixture on UNIX systems for many years. All UNIX workstations typically run an FTP server daemon and have an FTP client, and many users rely on the protocol for basic LAN file transfers. FTP is also a staple utility on the Internet, with thousands of public servers available from which users can download files. Although FTP is not as ubiquitous on Windows-based computers as it is on UNIX computers, every Windows operating system with a TCP/IP stack has a text-based FTP client, and web browsers can access FTP servers as well. FTP server capabilities are provided as a part of the Windows Internet Information Services (IIS) package.

Like HTTP, FTP uses the TCP protocol for its transport services and relies on text commands for its user interface. All of the original FTP implementations on UNIX are text based, as is the FTP client included with Windows. However, there are many graphical FTP clients available that automate the generation and transmission of the appropriate text commands to a server.

One of the major differences between FTP and HTTP (as well as most other protocols) is that FTP uses two port numbers in the course of its operations. When an FTP client connects to a server, it uses port 21 to establish a control connection. This connection remains open during the life of the session; the client and server use it to exchange commands and replies. When the client requests a file transfer, the systems establish a second connection on port 20, which they use to transfer the file and which is then terminated immediately afterward.

Most FTP access on the Internet is anonymous, but on LANs, more security is often required. The FTP server in IIS uses local or AD DS user accounts to authenticate client connections, whereas UNIX systems typically use a list of approved user names on the local system for access control.

Although you can protect FTP servers from unauthorized access by using passwords, the FTP messages themselves are utterly unprotected. As with HTTP, the communications exchanged by clients and servers over the FTP control connection take the form of text strings, which they transmit in cleartext. If someone were using a network monitor program to capture packets as they travel over the network, the account names and passwords inside would be easily visible to them.

To address this shortcoming, there are several FTP implementations that add message encryption provided by the TLS, SSL, and Secure Shell (SSH) protocols. These implementations go by various names, such as FTPS and "FTP over SSH." There is also a protocol called SFTP, or Secure File Transfer Protocol, which is not really an FTP variant but a program with similar functionality that uses SSH for file transfers.

FTP Commands

An FTP client consists of a user interface, which can be text based or graphical, and a *user protocol interpreter*. The user protocol interpreter communicates with the *server protocol interpreter* by using text commands that are passed over the control connection, as shown in Figure 9-28. When the commands call for a data transfer, one of the protocol interpreters triggers a *data transfer process,* which communicates with a similar process on the other machine by using the data connection.

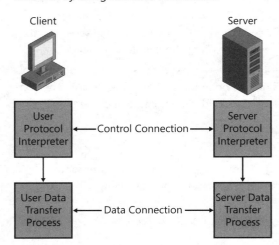

FIGURE 9-28 The protocol interpreters in the FTP client and server exchange control messages.

The commands issued by the user protocol interpreter do not necessarily correspond to the traditional text-based user interface commands. For example, to retrieve a file from a server, the traditional user interface command is GET plus the file name, but after the user protocol interpreter receives this command, it sends a RETR command to the server with the same file name. The user interface can therefore be modified for purposes of language localization or other reasons, but the commands used by the protocol interpreters remain consistent.

An FTP server responds to each command sent by a client with a three-digit reply code and a text string. As with HTTP, all FTP implementations must use the standard reply codes, so that the client can determine its next action, but some products enable you to modify the text that is delivered with the code and displayed to the user.

The first digit of the reply code indicates whether the command was completed successfully, unsuccessfully, or not at all. The second digit of the reply code provides more specific information about the nature of the message.

FTP Messaging

An FTP session begins when a client establishes a connection with a server by using either a GUI or the command line to specify the server's DNS name or IP address. The first order of business is to establish a TCP connection by using the standard three-way handshake. The FTP standard enables clients to operate in two operational modes, which determines which system initiates the TCP connection.

In *active mode*, the client sends its IP address and an ephemeral port number to the server, and the server initiates the connection establishment process. Because clients on networks behind firewalls frequently cannot receive incoming TCP connections, FTP also supports a *passive mode*, in which the client sends a PASV command to the server, and the server sends its IP address and port number to the client, so that the client can initiate the connection.

After the two systems have completed the TCP three-way handshake, the TCP connection becomes the FTP control connection that will remain open for the life of the session. The first FTP message transmitted by the server, announcing and identifying itself, is something like the following.

```
220 Microsoft FTP Service
```

After the client acknowledges the incoming TCP message, it prompts the user for an account name and password and performs the user logon sequence, as follows.

```
USER anonymous
331 Anonymous access allowed, send identity (e-mail name) as password.
PASS mlee@adatum.com
230 User logged in.
```

The client then informs the server of its IP address and the port that it will use for data connections on the client system, as follows.

```
PORT 192,168,2,3,7,233
200 PORT command successful.
```

The values 192, 168, 2, and 3 are the four-decimal byte values of the IP address, and the 7 and 233 are the two bytes of the port number value, which translates as 2025.

> **NOTE PORT VALUES**
>
> By converting these two port bytes to binary form (00000111 11101001) and then converting the whole two-byte value to a decimal, you get 2025.

At this point, the client can send commands to the server requesting file transfers or file system procedures, such as the creation and deletion of directories. One typical client command is to request a listing of the files in the server's default directory, as follows:

```
NLST -l
```

In response to this command, the server informs the client that it is going to open a data connection, because the list is transmitted as an ASCII file.

```
150 Opening ASCII mode data connection.
```

The server then commences the establishment of the second TCP connection, using its own port 20 and the client port 2025 specified earlier in the PORT command. When the systems have established the second connection, the server transmits the file it has created containing the listing for the directory. Depending on the number of files in the directory, the transfer might require the transmission of multiple packets and acknowledgments, after which the server immediately sends the first message in the sequence that terminates the data connection. After closing the data connection, the server reverts to the control connection and finishes the file transfer with the following positive completion reply message.

```
226 Transfer complete.
```

At this point, the client is ready to issue another command, such as a request for a file transfer, which repeats the entire process beginning with the PORT command, or some other function that uses only the control connection. When the client is ready to terminate the session by closing the control connection, it sends a QUIT command, and the server responds with an acknowledgment like the following:

```
221
```

EXAM TIP

FTP is unique among application layer protocols in that it uses two separate ports—TCP ports 20 and 21—for data and command traffic.

TFTP

The *Trivial File Transfer Protocol (TFTP)* is a minimized, low-overhead version of FTP that can transfer files across a network. TFTP uses UDP with port number 69 at the transport layer instead of TCP and does not include FTP's authentication and user interface features. TFTP was originally designed for use on diskless workstations that had to download an executable system file from a network server in order to boot.

A TFTP transaction begins when a client requests a file from a server, after which the server begins sending the file in UDP packets, each containing a 512-byte block of data. The client must return an acknowledgement message for each block before the server can transmit the next one. This packet acknowledgment capability is a feature of TFTP, not UDP. The server's transmission of a block smaller than 512 bytes indicates the end of the file and the termination of the transfer.

EXAM TIP

TFTP was designed for use by workstations with no local storage, and therefore it has a modest memory footprint. The Windows Deployment Server role in Windows Server 2008 R2 enables bare metal workstations with the proper hardware to obtain an IP address from a DHCP server and download a system boot file by using TFTP.

> ✔ **Quick Check**
>
> 1. Some application layer protocols, such as HTTP and FTP, do not use headers with discrete fields when creating their messages. What do they use instead?
> 2. Which two security protocols does HTTPS use to encrypt its messages?
>
> **Quick Check Answers**
>
> 1. Text commands
> 2. SSL and TLS

Telnet

Telnet is a terminal emulation program that provides users with access to a text-based interface on a remote system. Unlike FTP, which is designed for file transfers and has only a limited set of file management commands that can be executed on the server, Telnet enables the remote user to execute programs and configure operating system components. As a result, Telnet and FTP tend to complement each other; together, they are known as the DARPA commands and can provide reasonably comprehensive access to a UNIX or Linux system.

The dependence of Windows on its graphical interface has made Telnet a less popular choice for those administrators. Windows Server 2008 R2 still includes Telnet server and client features, but they are disabled by default. You must install them and enable the server service before you can use them.

Telnet uses the TCP protocol at the transport layer and port 23 by default. Unlike the separate command and data channels in FTP, Telnet mixes commands and data in a single message stream. Telnet actually predates the TCP/IP protocols, having been created for use with mainframe computers in the late 1960s. The standard is one of the earliest RFCs published by the IETF, RFC 15, "Network Subsystem for Time Sharing Hosts."

Like FTP, Telnet was designed at a time when the Internet was a far less dangerous place, and it suffers from a similar lack of security. To access a Telnet server, you must supply a user name and password in the client, which it transmits in cleartext. For this reason, administrators seeking remote command-line access tend to prefer the Secure Shell (SSH) program to Telnet.

Email

Although Internet services such as the web are wildly popular, and recent innovations in communication such as text messaging and instant messaging are a social phenomenon, the service that is the closest to being a ubiquitous business and personal communications tool is email. By combining the immediacy of the telephone with the precision of the written word, no Internet service is more valuable to the business user. Until the mid-1990s, most email systems were self-contained, proprietary solutions designed to provide an organization with internal communications. Then, the rise of the Internet revolutionized the email concept by providing a single, worldwide standard for mail communications that was independent of any single service provider. Today, email addresses are almost as common as telephone numbers, and virtually every network with an Internet connection supplies them to its users.

Email Addressing

An Internet email address consists of a user name and a domain name, separated by an "at" symbol (@), as in *jdoe@adatum.com*. As in the URLs that identify websites and FTP sites, the domain name in an email address (which is everything following the @ symbol) identifies the organization hosting the email services for a particular user. For individual users, the domain is typically that of a commercial service or an ISP; for corporate users, the domain name is usually registered to the organization and is often the same domain used for that organization's websites and other Internet services.

The user name part of an email address (that is, everything before the @ symbol) represents the name of a mailbox that an administrator has created on the mail server servicing the domain. The user name often consists of a combination of names and/or initials identifying an individual user at the organization, but it's also common to have mailboxes for specific roles and functions in the domain. For example, many domains running a website have a *webmaster@adatum.com* mailbox for communications concerning the functionality of the website.

Because Internet email relies on standard domain names to identify mail servers, the DNS is an essential part of the Internet email architecture. As you learned earlier in this chapter, the MX resource record is the one used to identify an email server in a particular domain.

When a mail server receives an outgoing message from an email client, it reads the address of the intended recipient and performs a DNS lookup of the domain name in that address. The server generates a DNS query message requesting the MX resource record for the specified domain, and the DNS server (after performing the standard iterative referral process) replies with the IP address of the email server for the destination domain.

The server with the outgoing message then opens a connection to the destination domain's mail server by using the *Simple Mail Transfer Protocol (SMTP)*. It is the destination mail server that processes the user name part of the email address, by placing the message in the appropriate mailbox, where it waits until the client picks it up.

Email Clients and Servers

Like HTTP and FTP, Internet email is a client/server application. However, in this case, there are several types of servers involved in the email communication process. SMTP servers are responsible for receiving outgoing mail from clients and transmitting the mail messages to their destination servers. The other type of server is the one that maintains the mailboxes, and which the email clients use to retrieve their incoming mail. The two predominant protocols for this type of server are the *Post Office Protocol, version 3 (POP3)* and the *Internet Message Access Protocol (IMAP)*.

EXAM TIP

This is another case where it's important to understand that the term "server" refers to an application, and not necessarily to a separate computer. In many cases, the SMTP and either the POP3 or IMAP server run on the same computer.

Email server products generally fall into two categories: those that are designed solely for Internet email, and those that provide more comprehensive internal email services as well. The former are relatively simple applications that typically provide SMTP support and might or might not include either POP3 or IMAP as well. If not, the administrator will have to purchase and install a POP3 or IMAP server also so that the application's users can access their mail. One of the most common SMTP servers used on the Internet is a free UNIX program called *sendmail*, but there are many other products, both open source and commercial, that run on a variety of computing platforms.

After installing the mail server applications, the administrator creates a mailbox for each user and registers the server's IP address in a DNS MX resource record for the domain. This enables other SMTP servers on the Internet to send mail to the users' mailboxes. Users then configure their clients to access the POP3 or IMAP server to download mail from their mailboxes and send outgoing messages using the SMTP server. ISPs typically use mail servers of this type, because their users are solely interested in Internet email. The server might provide other convenience services for users as well, such as web-based client access, which enables users to access their mailboxes from any web browser.

Many Internet users today rely on web-based mail services, which are designed to hide these details. The servers are there, behind the scenes, but the users don't have to configure a client, and they see nothing but the interface provided in their browsers.

The more comprehensive email servers are products that evolved from internal email systems. Products such as Microsoft Exchange started out as servers that a corporation would install to provide private email service to users within the company, as well as other services such as calendars, personal information managers, and group scheduling.

As Internet email became more prevalent, these products were enhanced to include the standard Internet email connectivity protocols as well. Today, a single product such as Exchange provides a wealth of communications services for private network users. On this type of email product, the mail messages and other personal data are stored permanently on the mail servers, and users run a special client to access their mail. Storing the mail on the server makes it easier for administrators to back it up and enables users to access their mail from any computer.

NOTE EXCHANGE

Email applications such as Exchange are much more expensive than Internet-only mail servers, and administering them is much more complicated.

An email client is any program that can access a user's mailbox on a mail server. Some email client programs are designed strictly for Internet email and can therefore access only SMTP and POP3 or IMAP servers.

Because the Internet email protocols are standardized, users can run any Internet email client with any SMTP/POP3/IMAP servers. Configuring an Internet email client to send and retrieve mail is simply a matter of supplying the program with the IP addresses of an SMTP server (for outgoing mail) and a POP3 or IMAP server (for incoming mail), as well as the name of a mailbox on the POP3/IMAP server and its accompanying password.

The more comprehensive email server products, such as Exchange, require a proprietary client to access all of their features. In the case of Exchange, the client is the Microsoft Outlook program included as part of Microsoft Office.

SMTP

The *Simple Mail Transfer Protocol (SMTP)* is an application layer protocol that was first standardized by the IETF in RFC 821 and updated in RFC 2821. SMTP messages can use any reliable transport protocol, but on the Internet and most private networks, they use TCP with port number 25 at the server.

Like HTTP and FTP messages, SMTP messages are based on text commands. SMTP communications can take place between email clients and servers or between pairs of servers. In each case, the basic communication model is the same. One computer, called the sender-SMTP, initiates communication with the other, the receiver-SMTP, by establishing a TCP connection using the standard three-way handshake.

When the two systems have established a TCP connection, the sender-SMTP computer begins transmitting SMTP commands to the receiver-SMTP, which responds with a reply message and a numeric code for each command it receives. The commands consist of a keyword and an argument field containing other parameters in the form of a text string, followed by a carriage return/line feed (CR/LF).

EXAM TIP

The SMTP standard uses the terms "sender-SMTP" and "receiver-SMTP" to distinguish the sender and the receiver of the SMTP messages from the sender and the receiver of an actual mail message. The two are not necessarily synonymous.

For example, the sender-SMTP system identifies itself to the receiver-SMTP by sending the following command.

```
HELO mailserver
```

The receiver-SMTP system then responds by transmitting its own name back to the sender. Other commands enable servers to identify recipient mailboxes and transmit mail messages.

The receiver-SMTP is required to generate a reply for each of the commands it receives from the sender-SMTP. The sender-SMTP is not permitted to send a new command until it receives a reply to the previous one. This prevents any confusion of requests and replies.

The reply messages generated by the receiver-SMTP consist of a three-digit numeric value plus an explanatory text string, as in the following example.

```
211 System status, or system help reply
```

The number and the text string are essentially redundant; the number is intended for use by automated systems that take action based on the reply, and the text string is intended for humans. The text messages can vary from implementation to implementation, but the reply numbers must remain consistent.

SMTP Transactions

A typical SMTP mail transaction begins (after the TCP connection establishment) with the sender-SMTP transmitting a HELO command, to identify itself to the receiver-SMTP by including its host name as the command argument. If the receiver-SMTP is operational, it responds with a 250 reply.

Next, the sender-SMTP initiates the mail transaction by transmitting a MAIL command. This command contains the mailbox address of the message sender as the argument on the command line. Note that this sender address refers to the person who generated the email message, and not necessarily to the SMTP server currently sending commands.

> **NOTE SMTP**
>
> In a case where the SMTP transaction is between an email client and an SMTP server, the sender of the email message and the sender-SMTP refer to the same computer, but the receiver-SMTP is not the same as the intended receiver (that is, the addressee) of the email message. In the case of two SMTP servers communicating, such as when a local SMTP server forwards the mail messages it has just received from clients to their destination servers, neither the sender-SMTP nor the receiver-SMTP refer to the ultimate sender and receiver of the email message.

If the receiver-SMTP is ready to receive and process a mail message, it returns a 250 response to the MAIL message generated by the sender-SMTP. After receiving a positive response to its MAIL command, the sender-SMTP proceeds by sending at least one RCPT message that contains as its argument the mailbox address of the email message's intended recipient. If there are multiple recipients for the message, the sender-SMTP sends a separate RCPT command for each mailbox address.

The receiver-SMTP, on receiving a RCPT command, checks to see if it has a mailbox for that address, and if so, acknowledges the command with a 250 reply. If the mailbox does not exist, the receiver-SMTP can take one of several actions, such as generating a *251 User Not Local; Will Forward* response and transmitting the message to the proper server, or rejecting the message with a failure response, such as *550 Requested Action Not Taken: Mailbox Unavailable* or *551 User Not Local*. If the sender-SMTP generates multiple RCPT messages, the receiver-SMTP must reply separately to each one before the next can be sent.

The next step in the procedure is the transmission of a DATA command by the sender-SMTP. The DATA command has no argument and is followed simply by a CR/LF. On receiving the DATA command, the receiver-SMTP returns a 354 response and assumes that all of the lines that follow are the text of the email message itself.

The sender-SMTP then transmits the test of the message, one line at a time, ending with a period on a separate line (in other words, a CR/LF.CR/LF sequence). On receipt of this final sequence, the receiver-SMTP responds with a 250 reply and proceeds to process the mail message by storing it in the proper mailbox and clearing its buffers.

MIME

SMTP is designed to carry text messages by using 7-bit ASCII codes and lines no more than 1,000 characters long. This excludes foreign characters and 8-bit binary data from inclusion in email messages. To make it possible to send these types of data in SMTP email, another standard called the *Multipurpose Internet Mail Extension (MIME)* was published in five RFC documents numbered 2045 through 2049. MIME is essentially a method for encoding various types of data for inclusion in an email message.

The typical SMTP email message transmitted after the DATA command begins with a header containing the familiar elements of the message itself, such as the To, From, and Subject fields. MIME adds two additional fields to this initial header, a MIME-Version indicator that specifies which version of MIME the message is using, and a Content-Type field that specifies the format of the MIME-encoded data included in the message. The Content-Type field can specify any one of several predetermined MIME formats, or it can indicate that the message consists of multiple body parts, each of which uses a different format.

For example, the header of a multipart message might appear as follows.

```
MIME-Version: 1.0
From: John Doe <mlee@adatum.com>
To: Tim Jones <timj@contoso.com>
Subject: Network diagrams
Content-Type: multipart/mixed;boundary=gcOp4JqOM2YtO8j34cOp
```

The Content-Type field in this example indicates that the message consists of multiple parts, in different formats. The *boundary* parameter specifies a text string that is used to delimit the parts. The value specified in the boundary parameter can be any text string, just as long as it does not appear in the message text itself. After this header comes the separate parts of the message, each of which begins with the boundary value on a separate line and a Content-Type field that specifies the format for the data in that part of the message, as follows.

```
--gc0p4Jq0M2Yt08j34c0p
Content-Type: image/jpeg
```

The actual message content then appears, in the format specified by the Content-Type value.

The most commonly recognizable elements of MIME are the content types used to describe the nature of the data included as part of an email message. A MIME content type consists of a type and a subtype, separated by a forward slash, as in *image/jpeg*. The type indicates the general type of data, and the subtype indicates a specific format for that data type. The *image* type, for example, has several possible subtypes, including *jpeg* and *gif*, which are both common graphics formats.

Systems interpreting the data use the MIME types to determine how they should handle the data, even if they do not recognize the format. For example, an application receiving data with the *text/richtext* content type might display the content to the user, even if it cannot handle the *richtext* format. Because the basic type is *text*, the application can be reasonably sure that the data will be recognizable to the user. If the application receives a message containing *image/gif* data, however, and is incapable of interpreting the *gif* format, it can be equally sure, because the message part is of the *image* type, that the raw, uninterpreted data would be meaningless to the user, and as a result would not display it in its raw form.

POP3

 The *Post Office Protocol, version 3 (POP3)*, as defined in the RFC 1939 document, is designed to provide mailbox services for client computers that are themselves not capable of performing transactions with SMTP servers. Most of the clients that require a mailbox service are not continuously connected to the Internet and are therefore not capable of receiving messages any time a remote SMTP server wants to send them. A POP3 server is continuously connected and is always available to receive messages for offline users. The server then retains the messages in an electronic mailbox until the user connects to the server and requests them.

POP3 is similar to SMTP in that it relies on the TCP protocol for transport services (using well-known port 110) and communicates with clients using text-based commands and responses. As with SMTP, the client transmits commands to the server, but in POP3, there are only two possible response codes, +OK, indicating the successful completion of the command, and −ERR, indicating that an error has occurred to prevent the command from being executed. In the case of POP3, the server also sends the requested email message data to the client, rather than the client sending outgoing messages to the server as in SMTP.

A POP3 client/server session consists of three distinct states: the *authorization* state, the *transaction* state, and the *update* state. These states are described in the following sections.

The Authorization State

The POP3 session begins with the usual TCP three-way handshake, after which the server transmits a greeting to the client, usually in the form of a +OK reply. At this point, the session enters the authorization state, during which the client must identify itself to the server and perform an authentication process before it can access its mailbox. The POP3 standard defines two possible authentication mechanisms. One of these utilizes the USER and PASS commands, which the client uses to transmit a mailbox name and the password associated with it to the server in cleartext. Another, more secure, mechanism uses the APOP command, which performs an encrypted authentication. Other authentication mechanisms are defined in RFC 1734, "POP3 AUTHentication Command." Although POP3 doesn't require that servers use one of the authentication mechanisms described in these documents, it does require that servers use some type of authentication mechanism.

After the authentication process is complete and the client receives access to its mailbox, the session enters the transaction state.

The Transaction State

When the session has entered the transaction state, the client can begin to transmit to the server the commands with which it retrieves the mail messages waiting in its mailbox. When the server enters the transaction state, it assigns a number to each of the messages in the client's mailbox. The transaction state commands use these numbers to refer to the messages in the mailbox. Some of the commands permitted while the session is in the transaction state are as follows:

- **STAT** Causes the server to transmit a *drop listing* of the mailbox contents to the client. The server responds with a single line containing an +OK reply, followed on the same line by the number of messages in the mailbox and the total size of all the messages, in bytes.

- **LIST** Causes the server to transmit a *scan listing* of the mailbox contents to the client. The server responds with a multiline reply consisting of an +OK on the first line, followed by an additional line for each message in the mailbox containing its message number and its size, in bytes.

- **RETR** Causes the server to transmit a multiline reply containing an +OK, followed by the full contents of the message number specified as a parameter on the RETR command line.

- **DELE** Causes the server to mark the message represented by the message number specified as a parameter on the DELE command line as deleted.

The Update State

When the client has finished retrieving messages from the mailbox and performing other transaction state activities, it transmits the QUIT command to the server, causing the session to transition to the update state. After entering the update state, the server deletes all of the messages that have been marked for deletion and releases its exclusive hold on the client's mailbox. If the server successfully deletes all of the marked messages, it transmits an +OK reply to the client and proceeds to terminate the TCP connection.

IMAP

POP3 is a relatively simple protocol that provides clients with only the most basic mailbox service. In nearly all cases, networks use POP3 servers as a temporary storage medium; email clients download their messages from the POP3 server and delete them from the server immediately afterwards. It is possible to configure a client not to delete the messages after downloading them, but the client must then download them again during the next session. The *Internet Message Access Protocol (IMAP),* version 4 of which is defined in RFC 3501, is a mailbox service that is designed to improve upon POP3's capabilities.

IMAP functions similarly to POP3 in that it uses text-based commands and responses, but the IMAP server provides considerably more functionality than a POP3 server. The biggest difference between IMAP and POP3 is that IMAP is designed to store email messages on the server permanently and provides a wider selection of commands that enable clients to access and manipulate their messages. Storing the mail on the server enables users to easily access their mail from any computer.

Take, for example, an office worker who normally downloads her email messages to her work computer by using a POP3 server. She can check her mail from her home computer if she wants to by accessing the POP3 server from there, but any messages that she downloads to her home computer are normally deleted from the POP3 server, so she will have no record of them on her office computer, where most of her mail is stored. If she uses an IMAP server, she can access all of her mail from either her home or office computer at any time, including all of the messages she has already read at both locations.

To make the storage of clients' email messages on the server practical, IMAP includes several organizational and performance features, including the following:

- Users can create folders in their mailboxes and move their email messages among the folders to create an organized storage hierarchy.
- Users can display in their mailboxes a list of the messages that contains only the header information, and then they can select the messages that they want to download in their entirety.
- Users can search for messages based on the contents of the header fields, the message subject, or the body of the message.

Although IMAP can be a sensible solution for a corporate email system in which users might benefit from its features, it is important to realize that IMAP requires considerably more in the way of network and system resources than POP3. In addition to the disk space required to store mail on the server indefinitely, IMAP also requires more processing power to execute its many commands, and it consumes more network bandwidth, because users remain connected to the server for much longer periods of time. For these reasons, POP3 remains the mailbox server of choice for the largest consumers of these server products: Internet service providers.

Clients connect to an IMAP server by using TCP port 143, by default. A more secure variant, called *IMAP over SSL*, uses TCP port 993. POP3 clients typically connect to the server for only as long as it takes to download the latest messages. An IMAP client can remain connected for the entire time the user is running the program. With IMAP, the email messages typically remain stored on the server. Some client implementations enable users to download messages, but this is intended to be a temporary cache for offline use. The definitive message store remains on the server.

A client connection to the IMAP server consists of four distinct states. After completing the TCP three-way handshake, the connection enters the *not authenticated* state. A mandatory authentication exchange follows, in which the client specifies an authentication method by using the AUTHENTICATE command. The only requirement for the authentication method is that it must not permit the exchange of password information in cleartext.

When the authentication is completed, the connection enters the *authenticated* state, in which the client must select a mailbox to access by using the SELECT command. After the client selects a mailbox, the connection then enters the *selected* state. This is the state that accounts for most of the client's session time, in which the client can view, manage, and manipulate the messages in the mailbox, using commands such as SEARCH, FETCH, STORE, and COPY.

Finally, with its work completed, the client issues the LOGOUT command and enters the *logout* state, in which all access to the mailbox is terminated. The systems can then proceed to terminate the TCP connection.

EXAM TIP

In a typical email client configuration, the program requires the address of a POP3 or IMAP server for incoming Internet mail and an SMTP server for outgoing Internet mail. SMTP is also the protocol that carries traffic between mail servers.

NTP

The *Network Time Protocol (NTP)* is an application layer protocol designed to synchronize the clocks of computers on packet-switching networks with varying degrees of latency. Because transmissions on a packet-switching network are not precisely predictable, there is no way of knowing exactly how long it will take for a packet to travel from its source to its destination. Therefore, any attempt to transmit a time signal over the network with precise accuracy is likely to be futile. NTP is designed to overcome that network latency and enable systems to synchronize their clocks with a great deal of precision.

Computers have varying needs when it comes to clock synchronization. Certain scientific applications might require extreme accuracy, which NTP can provide to within 1 millisecond (ms). For other applications, only a relatively rough level of accuracy is required. On Windows networks, Active Directory Domain Services requires that systems maintain accurate time, so that the Kerberos authentication protocol can function properly and the database replication system can track the occurrence of changes from different sources. However, AD DS does not require anywhere near the 1-ms accuracy that NTP is capable of providing. The Windows Time (W32Time) service included with all Windows versions since 2003 is not a complete implementation of NTP, but it provides sufficient accuracy for its purposes.

NTP, as defined in RFC 5905, "Network Time Protocol Version 4: Protocol and Algorithms Specification," uses UDP with port number 123 to transmit packets containing time stamp messages in one of three formats, as follows:

- **NTP Date Format**   Consists of a 128-bit message that contains 64 bits of seconds information, divided into 32-bit Era Number and Era Offset fields (see Figure 9-29). This provides 2^{64} or 584.5 billion years of resolution. The 64-bit Fraction field provides resolution of up to 0.05 attoseconds. (One attosecond equals 10^{-18} seconds or one quintillionth of a second.)

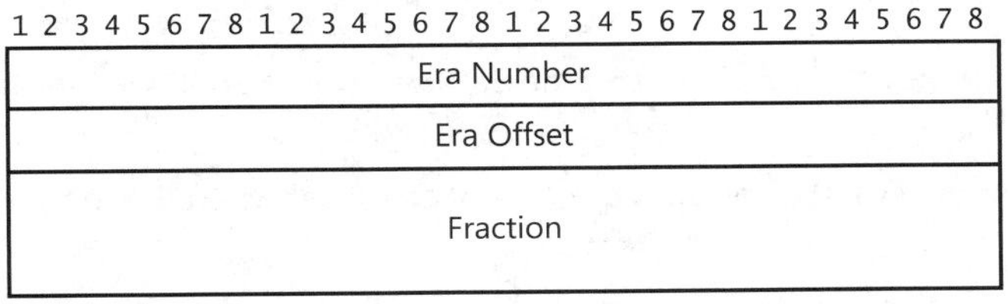

```
1 2 3 4 5 6 7 8 1 2 3 4 5 6 7 8 1 2 3 4 5 6 7 8 1 2 3 4 5 6 7 8
┌─────────────────────────────────────────────────────────────┐
│                         Era Number                            │
├─────────────────────────────────────────────────────────────┤
│                         Era Offset                            │
├─────────────────────────────────────────────────────────────┤
│                                                               │
│                          Fraction                             │
│                                                               │
└─────────────────────────────────────────────────────────────┘
```

FIGURE 9-29 NTP date format.

- **NTP Timestamp Format**   Consists of a 64-bit message that contains a 32-bit Seconds identifier providing 2^{32} or 136.1 years of resolution and a 32-bit Fraction field that can resolve to within 232 picoseconds, as shown in Figure 9-30. (One picosecond equals 10^{-12} seconds or one trillionth of a second.)

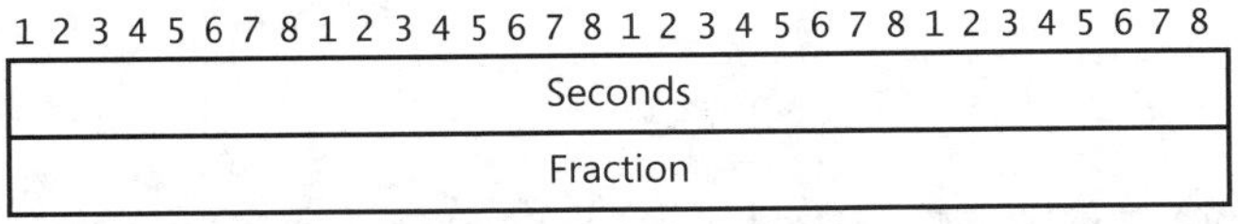

```
1 2 3 4 5 6 7 8 1 2 3 4 5 6 7 8 1 2 3 4 5 6 7 8 1 2 3 4 5 6 7 8
┌─────────────────────────────────────────────────────────────┐
│                          Seconds                              │
├─────────────────────────────────────────────────────────────┤
│                          Fraction                             │
└─────────────────────────────────────────────────────────────┘
```

FIGURE 9-30 NTP Timestamp format.

- **NTP Short Format**   Used in conditions where the larger formats are not justified; consists of a single 32-bit word, divided into a 16-bit Seconds field and a 16-bit fractional second field, as shown in Figure 9-31.

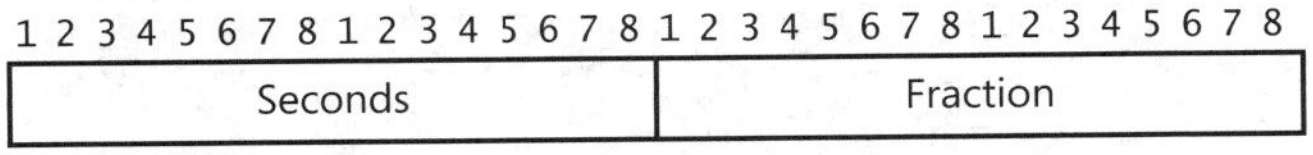

```
1 2 3 4 5 6 7 8 1 2 3 4 5 6 7 8 1 2 3 4 5 6 7 8 1 2 3 4 5 6 7 8
┌──────────────────────────────┬──────────────────────────────┐
│           Seconds            │            Fraction           │
└──────────────────────────────┴──────────────────────────────┘
```

FIGURE 9-31 NTP short format.

NTP time stamps are all based on the number of seconds elapsed since the prime epoch, which is 00:00 hours on January 1, 1900. This Era 0 will run until the year 2036, when the value of the Seconds field wraps and Era 1 begins. Thus, the Era Offset field in the Date Format message will always contain the same value as the Seconds field.

NTP uses a hierarchy of time sources that it designates as primary servers, secondary servers, or clients. A *primary server* is a computer synchronized to a reference clock providing Coordinated Universal Time (UTC), such as an atomic or global positioning system (GPS) time source. A *secondary server* is one that is synchronized to one or more primary servers and provides time signals to other servers and/or clients. A *client* is a system that is synchronized to a primary or secondary server but that does not provide time signals to other systems.

Simply transmitting a single time stamp does not provide the accuracy NTP clients need, however. Because the latency of network communications is unpredictable, NTP compensates for it by calculating the round trip delay time between the client and the server and adjusting accordingly. An NTP transaction actually uses four separate time stamps, as follows:

- **Origin Timestamp (org)**   Specifies the time at the client when the request departed for the server
- **Receive Timestamp (rec)**   Specifies the time at the server when the request arrived from the client
- **Transmit Timestamp (xmt)**   Specifies the time at the server when the response left for the client
- **Destination Timestamp (dst)**   Specifies the time at the client when the reply arrived from the server

This last Destination Timestamp is the one computed at the client by using the variances from the previous three time stamps.

EXAM TIP

The Network+ exam will not require you to know the message formats for the application layer protocols, but you must be familiar with their basic functions and the ports they use.

 Quick Check

1. Which of the email protocols discussed in this chapter does a client program use for outgoing mail?

2. Which of the email protocols discussed in this chapter can a client program use for incoming mail?

Quick Check Answers

1. SMTP

2. IMAP or POP3

Exercise

The answers for this exercise are located in the "Answers" section at the end of this chapter. Now that you are familiar with the functions of various application layer protocols, test your knowledge by filling in the table with the correct functions and port numbers.

Protocol	Function	Port
DHCP		
DNS		
HTTP		
FTP		
TFTP		
Telnet		
SMTP		
POP3		
IMAP		
NTP		

Chapter Summary

- The Dynamic Host Configuration Protocol (DHCP) is a service that network administrators configure with ranges of IP addresses and other settings. Computers and other devices configured to run as DHCP clients contact a DHCP server at boot time, and the server assigns each one a set of appropriate TCP/IP parameters, including a unique IP address.

- A DHCP relay agent is a module located in a computer or router on a particular network segment that enables the other systems on that segment to be serviced by a DHCP server located on a remote segment.

- DHCPv6 provides a stateful alternative to the IPv6 stateless address autoconfiguration mechanism. The stateless autoconfiguration process enables computers to determine what configuration settings they need and whether they should generate their own link-local addresses or obtain addresses from a DHCPv6 server.

- The Domain Name System (DNS) is a database service that converts computer names to IP addresses and addresses back into names.

- DNS servers can break up a domain's namespace into administrative units called zones. A zone can be any contiguous branch of a DNS tree and can include domains on multiple levels.

- DNS servers are essentially database servers that store information about the hosts and subdomains for which they are responsible in resource records (RRs).

- To make reverse name resolution possible without performing a massive search across the entire Internet, the DNS tree includes a special domain that uses the dotted decimal values of IP addresses as domain names. This branch stems from a domain called *in-addr.arpa*, which is located just beneath the root of the DNS tree.

- Communication between web servers and their browser clients is largely dependent on an application layer protocol called the Hypertext Transfer Protocol (HTTP).

- Hypertext Transfer Protocol Secure (HTTPS) is a variant of HTTP that uses the Transport Layer Security (TLS) and Secure Sockets Layer (SSL) security protocols to provide data encryption and server identification services.

- FTP, the File Transfer Protocol, is an application layer TCP/IP protocol that enables an authenticated client to connect to a server and transfer files to and from its drives.

- The Trivial File Transfer Protocol (TFTP) is a minimized, low-overhead version of FTP that can transfer files across a network.

- Telnet is a terminal emulation program that provides users with access to a text-based interface on a remote system.

- The Simple Mail Transfer Protocol (SMTP) is an application layer protocol that carries email messages between servers.

- The Post Office Protocol, version 3 (POP3) provides mailbox services for client computers that are themselves not capable of performing transactions with SMTP servers.

- IMAP functions similarly to POP3 in that it uses text-based commands and responses, but the IMAP server provides considerably more functionality than a POP3 server, including the permanent storage of email messages.

- The Network Time Protocol (NTP) is an application layer protocol designed to synchronize the clocks of computers on packet-switching networks with varying degrees of latency.

Chapter Review

Test your knowledge of the information in Chapter 9 by answering these questions. The answers to these questions, and the explanations of why each answer choice is correct or incorrect, are located in the "Answers" section at the end of this chapter.

1. Which of the following is the term for the component that enables DHCP clients to communicate with DHCP servers on other subnets?

    A. Forwarder

    B. Resolver

    C. Scope

    D. Relay agent

2. Which of the following protocols does a mail server use to transmit messages to the address supplied in an MX resource record?

    A. SMTP

    B. SNMP

    C. IMAP

    D. POP3

3. Which of the following protocols can you use to execute an Ipconfig command on a remote computer running Windows?

    A. HTTP

    B. HTTPS

    C. Telnet

    D. FTP

4. Which of the following resource record types contains the information a DNS server needs to perform reverse name lookups?

    A. A

    B. CNAME

    C. SOA

    D. PTR

Answers

This section contains the answers to the questions for the Exercise and Chapter Review in this chapter.

Exercise

Protocol	Function	Port
DHCP	IP address assignment	UDP 67, 68
DNS	Name resolution	UDP/TCP 53
HTTP	Web publishing	TCP 80
FTP	File transfers	TCP 21, 20
TFTP	Unauthenticated file transfers	UDP 69
Telnet	Terminal emulation	TCP 23
SMTP	Outgoing Internet email messages	TCP 25
POP3	Incoming Internet email downloads	TCP 110
IMAP	Incoming Internet email management	TCP 143
NTP	Clock synchronization	UDP 123

Chapter Review

1. **Correct Answer: D**

    A. **Incorrect:** A forwarder is a DNS server that accepts recursive queries from other servers.

    B. **Incorrect:** A resolver is a DNS client component.

    C. **Incorrect:** A scope is a range of IP addresses that a DHCP server is configured to allocate.

    D. **Correct:** A relay agent is a system that receives DHCP broadcast messages and forwards them to a DHCP server on another subnet.

2. **Correct Answer: A**

   A. **Correct:** The Simple Mail Transfer Protocol uses MX resource records requested from DNS servers to forward mail messages.

   B. **Incorrect:** The Simple Network Management Protocol does not transmit mail messages.

   C. **Incorrect:** Clients use the IMAP protocol to download mail messages. IMAP does not require an MX record address.

   D. **Incorrect:** Clients use the POP3 protocol to download mail messages. POP3 does not require an MX record address.

3. **Correct Answer: C**

   A. **Incorrect:** The HTTP protocol carries web client/server traffic. It does not enable users to execute commands on a remote system.

   B. **Incorrect:** The HTTPS protocol carries encrypted web client/server traffic. It does not enable users to execute commands on a remote system.

   C. **Correct:** The Telnet protocol provides terminal emulation services that enable a user to execute commands on a remote system.

   D. **Incorrect:** The FTP protocol enables a user to execute a limited number of file management commands on a remote system, but the user cannot execute the Ipconfig command.

4. **Correct Answer: D**

   A. **Incorrect:** A resource records contain information for forward name lookups, not reverse name lookups.

   B. **Incorrect:** CNAME resource records contain alias information for A records. They are not used for reverse name lookups.

   C. **Incorrect:** SOA records specify that a server is the authoritative source for a zone. They are not used for reverse name lookups.

   D. **Correct:** PTR records contain the information needed for the server to perform reverse name lookups.

CHAPTER 10

Wide Area Networking

In many ways, the network administrator is the ruler of his or her own empire. Local area network (LAN) equipment is wholly owned by the organization running it, so there is no one outside the company that the administrator has to answer to regarding its operation. Wide area networking (WAN) is a different story, however. Unless your organization has the means to run its own long-distance fiber optic cables or launch its own satellite, WANs require resources provided by an outside telecommunications service provider. WANs are the foreign affairs in the network administrator's portfolio, and a certain amount of diplomacy is needed to set them up and keep them running.

Exam objectives in this chapter:

Objective 3.4: Categorize WAN technology types and properties.

- Types:
  - T1/E1
  - T3/E3
  - DS3
  - OCx
  - SONET
  - SDH
  - DWDM
  - Satellite
  - ISDN
  - Cable
  - DSL
  - Cellular
  - WiMAX
  - LTE
  - HSPA+
  - Fiber
  - Dialup
  - PON
  - Frame relay
  - ATMs
- Properties:
  - Circuit switch
  - Packet switch
  - Speed
  - Transmission media
  - Distance

Objective 5.2: Explain the methods of network access security.

- ACL:
  - MAC filtering
  - IP filtering
  - Port filtering
- Tunneling and encryption:
  - SSL VPN
  - VPN
  - L2TP
  - PPTP
  - IPSec
  - ISAKMP
  - TLS
  - TLS2.0
  - Site-to-site and client-to-site
- Remote access:
  - RAS
  - RDP
  - PPPoE
  - PPP
  - ICA
  - SSH

What Is a WAN?

 A *wide area network (WAN)* is a communications link that spans a relatively long distance and connects two or more computers or LANs together. Most WAN connections are point to point, involving two systems only.

There are three main applications for WANs, as follows:

- To connect a LAN to the Internet
- To connect two LANs at remote locations
- To connect a remote computer to a distant LAN

Virtually all home computer users are familiar with the WAN connection that provides them with access to the Internet, whether it is as modest as a dial-up modem and a standard telephone line or as complicated as a satellite uplink. Companies with offices in different cities or countries typically use private WAN connections to link their individual LANs into one enterprise network. Finally, users who are traveling or working from home use WANs to access resources on the company network.

Each of these applications has different requirements in terms of transmission rates, availability, security, and of course, cost, and there are a variety of WAN solutions available for each one. The following sections examine some of these WAN technologies and their characteristics.

Many WAN technologies are flexible enough to function in more than one type of connection scenario. For example, you can theoretically use modems and telephone lines for any of the three applications listed earlier. However, in terms of actual use, dial-up modems are too slow for LAN-to-LAN connections and too expensive for long-distance remote network connections. They are therefore listed in the area where they see the most use: Internet connections.

The need to rely on an outside service provider for WAN communications can complicate the process of designing, installing, and maintaining a network enormously. LAN technicians are often tinkerers by trade. When problems with the network occur, they have their own procedures for investigating, diagnosing, and resolving them, knowing that the cause is somewhere nearby if they can only find it.

Problems with WAN connections can conceivably be caused by the equipment located at one of the connected sites, but it's far more likely for the trouble to be somewhere in the service provider's network infrastructure. A heavy equipment operator a thousand miles away in Omaha, Nebraska can sever a trunk cable while digging a trench, causing your WAN link to go down. Solar flares on the surface of the sun 93 million miles away can disturb satellite communications, causing your WAN link to go down. In either case, there is nothing that you can do about it except call your service provider and complain.

Telecommunications is a separate networking discipline that is at least as complicated as data networking, if not more so. (If you think that local area networking has a lot of cryptic acronyms, wait till you start studying telecommunications.) A large organization relies at least as much on telecommunications technology as on their data networking technology. If the computer network goes down, people complain loudly; if the phone system goes down, people soon begin to panic.

In many large organizations, the people who manage the telecommunications infrastructure are not the same people who administer the data network. However, the area of WAN communications is where these two disciplines come together. It isn't common to find technical people who are equally adept at data networking and telecommunications; most technicians tend to specialize in one or the other. However, a LAN administrator has to know something about telecommunications if his or her organization has offices at multiple locations that are to be connected by using WANs.

Connecting to the Internet

There are many different WAN technologies that users and administrators can use to connect computers and networks to the Internet, and they provide varying levels of speed, security, and flexibility. The interface that links the WAN to the computer can vary; it can be a serial port, an expansion bus, a universal serial bus (USB) port, or a network interface adapter, but the actual network medium is the WAN service that carries the signals for most of their journey from your network to that of an Internet Service Provider (ISP).

The following sections examine some of the physical layer options that you can use for Internet access connections in the home, the small business, or the enterprise network. Many of the technologies discussed in this chapter have more than one potential application, such as connecting a computer to a private network or connecting two private networks, in addition to connecting a private network to an ISP. The type of WAN connection you choose for a particular installation depends on your networking requirements and your budget.

Public Switched Telephone Network

The *Public Switched Telephone Network (PSTN)* is just a technical name for the standard analog telephone system that has existed in some form since the late nineteenth century, also commonly known as the *Plain Old Telephone Service (POTS)*. This voice-based system, found all over the world, can use asynchronous modems to transmit data between computers at virtually any location. The PSTN service in your home or office probably uses copper-based twisted-pair cable (as do most LANs) and modular RJ11 jacks. RJ11 jacks are similar to the RJ45 (8P8C) jacks used on twisted-pair LANs, except that RJ11 jacks have four electrical contacts (only two of which are needed by the POTS) instead of eight.

The PSTN connection leads to a central office belonging to a telephone service provider, which can route calls from there to any other telephone in the world. Unlike a LAN, which is digital and uses packet switching, the PSTN is an analog, circuit-switched network, as described in Chapter 1, "Networking Basics."

Before computer data can be transmitted over the PSTN, the digital signals generated by a computer must be converted to analog signals that the telephone network can carry. A device called a *modulator/demodulator*, more commonly known as a *modem*, handles this conversion. A modem takes the digital signals fed to it through a serial port, a USB port, or the system bus, converts them to analog signals, and then transmits them over the PSTN, as shown in Figure 10-1. At the other end of the PSTN connection, another modem performs the same process in reverse, converting the analog data back into its digital form and passing it to another computer. The combination of the interfaces to the two computers, the two modems, and the PSTN connection forms the physical layer of the networking stack.

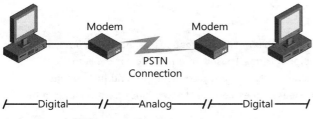

FIGURE 10-1 A PSTN connection between two computers.

The first modems used proprietary protocols for the digital/analog conversions. This meant that users had to use modems from the same manufacturer at each end of the PSTN connection. To standardize modem communications, organizations such as the Comité Consultatif International Télégraphique et Téléphonique (CCITT), now known as the International Telecommunication Union (ITU), began developing specifications for the communication, compression, and error-detection protocols that modems use when generating and interpreting their analog signals.

Today, virtually all the modems on the market support a long list of protocols that have been ratified at various times throughout the history of modem communications. The current industry-standard modem communication protocol is V.92, which defines the 56-kilobytes-per-second (Kbps) data transfer mode that most modem connections use today.

The PSTN was designed for voice transmissions, not data transmissions. As a result, connections are relatively slow, with a maximum speed of only 33.6 Kbps when both communicating devices use analog PSTN connections. A 56-Kbps connection requires that one of the connected devices have a digital connection to the PSTN. The quality of PSTN connections varies widely, depending on the locations of the modems and the state of the cables connecting the modems to their central offices. In some areas, the PSTN cabling is many decades old, and connections suffer as a result. When modems detect errors while transmitting data, they revert to a slower transmission speed. This is one reason that the quality of modem connections can vary from minute to minute.

PSTN/modem connections were, in the past, the primary means for connecting computers to the Internet. However, the emergence of various broadband technologies running at much higher speeds has rendered dial-up connections nearly obsolete. Because the PSTN can connect virtually anyone to anywhere, it is the most flexible WAN connection available. It is possible to use a dial-up connection to connect two LANs together, but the PSTN is too slow to satisfy the needs of most corporate customers. It is also possible for remote users to connect to their home or office networks with the PSTN, but the long-distance charges from any appreciable distance make this an impractical solution.

Integrated Services Digital Network (ISDN)

Although it achieved only modest popularity in the United States in the late 1990s, the *Integrated Services Digital Network (ISDN)* has been around for several decades and has long been a popular solution in Europe, where leased telephone lines are prohibitively expensive. ISDN is a digital communications service that uses the same network infrastructure as the PSTN. It was designed as a complete digital replacement for the analog telephone system, but it had few supporters in the United States until the need for faster Internet connections led people to explore its capabilities.

However, after other high-speed Internet access solutions, such as Digital Subscriber Line (DSL) and cable television (CATV) networks, became available, ISDN was all but forgotten. These other solutions are faster and less costly than ISDN and have eclipsed it in popularity.

ISDN is a dial-up service, like the PSTN, but its connections are digital, so no analog/digital conversions are required. Although ISDN can support specially made telephones, fax machines, and other devices, most ISDN installations in the United States are used only for computer data transmissions.

Because it is a dial-up service, you can use ISDN to connect to different networks. For example, if you have an ISDN connection to the Internet, you can change ISPs simply by dialing a different number. No intervention from the telephone company is required. This is not possible with other high-speed WAN technologies. However, because ISDN needs special equipment, it cannot be used in mobile devices, such as laptop computers, when traveling away from the service location.

ISDN also delivers greater transmission speeds than the PSTN. The ISDN *Basic Rate Interface (BRI)* service consists of two 64-Kbps channels (called *B channels*) that carry the actual user data, plus one 16-Kbps channel (called a *D channel*) that carries only control traffic. Because of these channel names, the BRI service is sometimes called *2B+D*. The B channels can function separately, or the subscriber can choose to combine them into a single 128-Kbps connection.

A higher grade of service, called *Primary Rate Interface (PRI)*, consists of 23 B channels and one 64-Kbps D channel. The total bandwidth is the same as that of a T-1 leased line. PRI is used primarily to terminate a large number of ISDN BRI connections from remote sites into a single site such as a data center or headquarters location. Some organizations also use ISDN as a redundant solution to leased-line connectivity.

ISDN uses the same wiring as the PSTN, but additional equipment is required at the terminal locations. The telephone company provides what is called a *U interface*, which connects to a device called a *Network Terminator 1 (NT-1)*. The NT-1 can provide a four-wire connection, called an *S/T interface*, for up to seven devices, which are collectively called *terminal equipment (TE)*. Digital devices designed for use with ISDN, such as ISDN telephones and fax machines, connect directly to the S/T interface and are called *TE1 devices*. A device that cannot connect directly to the S/T interface is called a *TE2 device*. A TE2 device requires a *terminal adapter*, which connects to the S/T interface and provides a jack for the TE2 device, as shown in Figure 10-2.

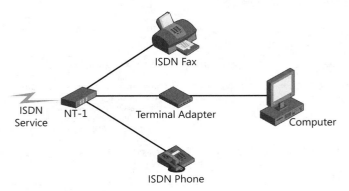

FIGURE 10-2 An ISDN installation.

> **NOTE** **ISDN DISTANCE LIMITATIONS**
>
> Because of the increased speed at which ISDN operates, the length of the connection is limited. The location of the terminal equipment must be within 18,000 feet of the telephone company's nearest central office (or a suitable repeating device).

When you plan to connect multiple devices to the ISDN service, you buy an NT-1 as a separate unit. However, most ISDN installations in the United States use the service solely for Internet access, so there are products that combine an NT-1 and a terminal adapter into a single unit. These combined ISDN solutions can take the form of expansion cards that plug into a bus slot or separate units that connect to the computer's serial port.

ISDN has never been hugely popular in the United States, partly because of its reputation for being expensive and for having installation and reliability problems. In addition, telephone companies began providing various forms of DSL, which proved to be much more popular, because they run at faster speeds, are easier to install, and require less specialized equipment.

However, most of the DSL products marketed to home and small business users are subject to distance limitations. ISDN has a longer range and can use repeaters to extend that range further. Therefore, ISDN can be a viable solution for customers who are a long distance from the nearest telephone company point of presence. Users can also disconnect ISDN links when they are not in use. This allows ISDN customers to avoid paying for bandwidth they are not using and eliminates a potential window through which intruders can access the network.

Digital Subscriber Line (DSL)

Digital Subscriber Line (DSL) is a blanket term for a variety of digital communication services that use standard telephone lines and provide data transfer speeds much faster than the PSTN or even ISDN. Each of the various DSL service types has a different descriptive word or phrase added to its name, which is why some sources use the generic abbreviation *xDSL*. Some of the many DSL services are shown in Table 10-1.

TABLE 10-1 DSL Services and Their Properties

Service	Transmission Rate	Link Length	Applications
High-bit-rate Digital Subscriber Line (HDSL)	Up to 1.544/2.048 Mbps	12,000 feet	Used by large networks as a substitute for T-1 or E-1 leased line connections, LAN and Private Branch Exchange (PBX) interconnections, or frame relay traffic aggregation
Symmetric Digital Subscriber Line (SDSL)	Up to 1.544/2.048 Mbps	10,000 feet	Same as HDSL
Multirate Symmetric DSL (MSDSL)	Up to 2 Mbps	29,000 feet	A variant of SDSL that can use more than one transfer rate, set by the service provider
Asymmetric Digital Subscriber Line (ADSL)	Up to 8 Mbps downstream; up to 1.3 Mbps upstream	18,000 feet	Internet/intranet access, remote LAN access, virtual private networking, video on demand, Voice over IP (VoIP)
ADSL2	Up to 12 Mbps downstream; up to 1.4 Mbps upstream	18,000 feet	Same as ADSL
ADSL2+	Up to 24 Mbps downstream; up to 3.5 Mbps upstream	18,000 feet	Same as ADSL
Rate-Adaptive Digital Subscriber Line (RADSL)	Up to 7 Mbps downstream; up to 1.088 Mbps upstream	18,000 feet	Same as ADSL, except that the transmission speed is dynamically adjusted to accommodate the link length and signal quality
ADSL Lite	Up to 1.5 Mbps downstream; up to 512 Kbps upstream	18,000 feet	Internet/intranet access, remote LAN access, IP telephony, video-conferencing
Very High-Rate Digital Subscriber Line (VDSL)	Up to 51.84 Mbps downstream; up to 16 Mbps upstream	4,500 feet	Multimedia Internet access, high-definition television delivery
Internet Digital Subscriber Line (IDSL)	Up to 144 Kbps	18,000 feet	Internet/intranet access, remote LAN access, IP telephony, video-conferencing

As noted by the transmission rates listed in Table 10-1, many DSL services run at different upstream and downstream speeds. These types of services are described as *asymmetrical*. The different speeds occur because some DSL signals cause greater levels of crosstalk in the data traveling from the customer site to the central office than in the other direction. For end-user Internet access, this asymmetrical behavior is usually not a problem, because web surfing and other common activities generate far more downstream traffic than upstream traffic. However, if you plan to use DSL to connect your own servers to the Internet, make sure that you obtain a service that is symmetrical or that offers sufficient upstream bandwidth for your needs. DSL services are also subject to distance restrictions.

> **NOTE MARKETING ADSL**
>
> From a marketing perspective, the asymmetrical nature of ADSL makes the service more attractive to residential users, who prefer more downstream than upstream bandwidth, and less attractive to businesses, who often require a more symmetrical service. This enables telephone providers to continue selling leased lines to businesses; leased lines are much more expensive than ADSL service.

DSL provides higher transmission rates by using high frequencies that standard telephone services do not use, and by using special signaling schemes. For this reason, in many cases you can use your existing telephone lines for a DSL connection and for voice traffic at the same time. The most common DSL services are HDSL, used by phone companies and large corporations for site-to-site WAN links, and ADSL, which many ISPs use to provide Internet access to end users. DSL is an excellent Internet access solution, and you can also use it to connect a home user to an office LAN, as long as the upstream bandwidth suits your needs.

 An ADSL connection requires an additional piece of hardware called an *ADSL Termination Unit-Remote (ATU-R)*, which is sometimes called a *DSL transceiver* or a *DSL modem*. You will also need a *line splitter* if you will also use the line for voice traffic. A DSL modem does not convert signals between digital and analog formats. (All DSL communications are digital.) The ATU-R connects to your computer by using either a standard Ethernet network interface adapter or a USB port. At the other end of the link at the ISP's site is a more complicated device called a *Digital Subscriber Line Access Multiplexer (DSLAM)*, shown in Figure 10-3.

DSLAM   ADSL   ATU-R   Computer
         Service

FIGURE 10-3 An ADSL connection.

Unlike ISDN connections, DSL connections are direct, permanent links between two sites that remain connected at all times. This means that if you use DSL to connect to the Internet, the telephone company activates the DSL connection between your home or office and the

ISP's site. If you want to change your ISP, the phone company must install a new link. In many cases, however, telephone companies are themselves offering DSL Internet access, which eliminates one party from the chain.

Cable Television (CATV) Networks

All of the remote connection technologies described up to this point rely on cables installed and maintained by telephone companies. However, the cable television (CATV) industry has also been installing a vast network infrastructure throughout most of the United States over the past few decades. In many cases, the long-distance cable network runs use fiber optic cable, but the connections to individual premises—that is, the cable that enters your home or office—is copper-based coaxial. This combination is called a *hybrid fiber coaxial (HFC)* network.

> **NOTE THE LAST MILE**
>
> It is relatively common for telecommunications services to use a different network medium for the connection between the subscriber's premises and the nearest point of presence than they do for their longer distance runs. This run connecting the subscriber to the nearest available switch is often called the *last mile* in telecommunications jargon, although it can often be more or less than a mile.

In recent years, many CATV systems have started taking advantage of their networks to provide Internet access to their customers through the same cable used for the TV service. CATV Internet access can be very fast—sometimes as fast as 50 Mbps downstream—and is typically available at multiple performance levels, with varying prices. CATV networks use broadband transmissions, meaning that the one network medium carries many discrete signals at the same time.

Each TV channel you receive over cable is a separate signal, and all the signals arrive over the cable simultaneously. (If you have two or more TVs in your home, you prove this every day by watching two different programs at the same time using the same CATV connection.) By devoting some of this bandwidth to data transmissions, CATV providers can deliver Internet data at the same time as the television signals. If you already have CATV, installing the Internet service is simply a matter of connecting a splitter to the cable and running it to a device called a *cable modem*, which is connected to an Ethernet network interface adapter in a computer or router, as shown in Figure 10-4.

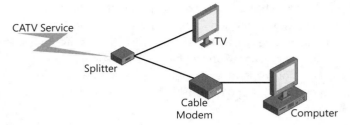

FIGURE 10-4 A CATV connection.

CATV data connections are different from both ISDN and DSL connections because they are not dedicated links. In effect, you are connecting to a metropolitan area network (MAN) run by your cable company. This arrangement has two disadvantages:

- **Bandwidth sharing** With a CATV connection, you are sharing your Internet bandwidth with all the other users in your area. During peak usage periods, you might notice a significant slowdown in your Internet downloads. ISDN and DSL, by contrast, are not shared connections, so the full bandwidth to the service provider's nearest point of presence is available at all times.

- **Security** If you share a drive on your computer without protecting it, someone else on the network might be able to access, modify, or even delete your files. However, you can use a personal firewall product for additional protection.

Like most residential DSL services, CATV data connections are asymmetrical. CATV networks carry signals primarily in one direction, from the provider to the customer. There is a small amount of upstream bandwidth, which some systems use for television products such as pay-per-view ordering. Part of this upstream bandwidth is allocated for Internet traffic. In most cases, the upstream speed of a CATV connection is far less than the downstream speed. This makes the service unsuitable for hosting your own Internet servers, but it is still faster than a PSTN connection.

CATV connections are an inexpensive and fast Internet access solution, but you cannot use them to connect your home computer to your office LAN, unless you use a virtual private network (VPN) connection through the Internet. If you plan to implement VPNs, be sure that the cable modem you use supports them.

Satellite-Based Services

There are still some Internet users who are not located near enough to a telephone provider's point of presence for DSL or ISDN, and who cannot get Internet access through a cable television network. For these users, the only economical high-bandwidth alternative is satellite-based Internet access. As with satellite television, a user of this service must have a satellite dish pointed at one of the geosynchronous communications satellites orbiting the earth.

Unlike early satellite Internet services, which could only download from the satellite and required the user to maintain a dial-up PSTN connection for upstream traffic, today's satellite ISPs provide bidirectional communications. Like DSL and CATV networks, the satellite connection is asymmetric, with a relatively limited amount of upload bandwidth available. Generally speaking, satellite Internet access is more expensive than the other popular alternatives, especially when you factor in the hardware costs, and it is usually not as fast as DSL or CATV, but for some users, it is the only option.

Last Mile Fiber

Telecommunications companies typically use fiber optic cables for long distance runs, because of their resistance to attenuation and electromagnetic interference. However, the so-called last mile—the connection from the nearest switch to the end user's premises—has traditionally been a copper-based medium. Copper cables are relatively inexpensive to install and maintain and have long provided adequate performance and bandwidth within a certain range. However, some of the larger communications companies have launched high-speed broadband services that run fiber optic cables through some or all of the last mile.

Generic names for these services are various, depending on where the fiber optic cable terminates, but they all follow the format *FTTx*, where *x* is the terminus of the fiber optic cable. *Fiber-to the-node (FTTN)* and *Fiber-to-the-curb (FTTC)* refer to services that run fiber to within a few kilometers or less than a kilometer from the subscriber's location, respectively. *Fiber-to-the-premises (FTTP),* sometimes called *Fiber-to-the-home (FTTH),* runs the fiber optic cable all the way to a demarcation point on the outside wall or in the basement of the subscriber's building. *Fiber-to-the-desk (FTTD)* refers to a fiber optic run all the way to a terminal or media converter inside the subscriber's premises.

The performance of a these services depends on the proximity of the fiber optic run to the user's premises. Running the fiber optic cable all the way to the building means that the high-speed services can connect directly to a home or office network running a Gigabit Ethernet or 802.11 wireless LAN. If the fiber terminus is more than 100 meters away, then some sort of interim medium is needed, such as VDSL.

As noted in Chapter 2, "The Physical Layer," fiber optic cable is much more difficult and expensive to install than any of the standard types of copper cable. Deploying fiber in the last mile is an expensive proposition, and one of the methods providers use to control costs is the passive optical network.

A *passive optical network (PON)* is an arrangement in which data from an optical line terminal (OLT) at the provider's central office runs through a single fiber optic cable to a series of optical splitters near the subscribers' premises. The splitters duplicate all of the incoming signals and send them out through separate fiber runs to optical network terminals (ONTs) at the individual users' locations, as shown in Figure 10-5.

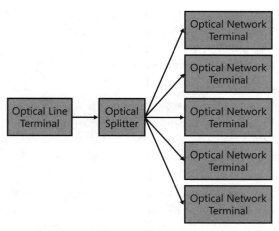

FIGURE 10-5 A passive optical network (PON).

A PON is a lower-cost alternative to an active optical network (AON), because it uses unpowered splitters to duplicate the incoming signals, rather than a complex router that separates the data stream into the packets intended for each subscriber.

Commercial implementations of this technology typically bundle voice, video, and data services into a single package, providing a complete media solution for the subscriber. Internet access is generally available in several tiers, with varying prices. Theoretical speeds can reach as high as 150 Mbps downstream and 25 Mbps upstream.

Cellular Technologies

The WAN technologies discussed in the previous sections are all designed to supply Internet access to homes and places of business, but the fastest growing types of wide area networking are those that deliver the Internet to people's pockets and purses. These are the wireless WAN services, most of them based on cellular communications, that enable smartphones, tablets, and other mobile devices to stay connected wherever they go.

EXAM TIP

Cellular communications is a highly sophisticated area of the telecommunications field, and candidates for the Network+ exam are not expected to be experts in the field. However, they are expected to be familiar with some of the major technologies, including WiMAX and LTE.

There are literally dozens of standards used in cellular communications, which can be roughly categorized as applying to the first (1G), second (2G), third (3G), or fourth (4G) generation of mobile telecommunications. The industry is currently in the midst of a transition from 3G to 4G.

To be characterized as a 3G technology, a standard must conform to specifications published by the International Telecommunications Union (ITU) in a document called "International Mobile Telecommunications-2000 (IMT-2000)." These standards define all types of mobile communications, including voice telephone, not just Internet access.

Some of the most prominent of the 3G standards are as follows:

- **Universal Mobile Telecommunications System (UMTS)** Based on the 2G Groupe Speciale Mobile (GSM) standard, UMTS supports theoretical maximum downstream transfer rates of 42 Mbps. (However, actual realized performance can reach only 7.2 Mbps.) Upgraded several times with other technologies, UMTS is sometimes referred to as 3.5G.

- **Enhanced Data Rates for GSM Evolution (EDGE)** Originally implemented as an enhancement for GSM and referred to as a 2.5G standard, EDGE provides increased data rates (up to 236.8 Kbps) with full backward compatibility and no hardware upgrade requirements.

- **High Speed Packet Access (HSPA)** HSPA supports downstream transfer rates of up to 14 Mbps and often requires only a software upgrade to 3G networks. *Evolved HSPA* (also known as HSPA+), which appeared in 2008 and is now widely implemented, can boost downstream data rates to 84 Mbps, by using multiple-input, multiple-output (MIMO) technology.

To be called 4G, standards must conform to an ITU document called "International Mobile Telecommunications – Advanced (IMT-Advanced)." Two of the most prominent 4G standards are as follows:

- **Worldwide Interoperability for Microwave Access (WiMAX)** Based on the 802.16 standard published by the Institute of Electrical and Electronic Engineers (IEEE), WiMAX is a metropolitan area network (MAN) standard offering transfer rates up to 75 Mbps for mobile devices and ranges up to 50 kilometers. Marketed as a wireless last-mile alternative to DSL and CATV networks, WiMAX is now available in some markets in a variety of devices, including smartphones and external modems.

- **Long Term Evolution (LTE)** LTE is the next iteration of the GSM technology that first appeared in the second generation (2G) and which became HSPA in the third (3G). Although not yet compliant with the ITU standard, LTE is generally considered a 4G technology and supports downstream transmission rates of up to 300 Mbps.

Quick Check

1. **What is the technical name for the standard analog telephone network?**
2. **Which ISDN service is commonly known as 2B+D?**

Quick Check Answers

1. **The Public Switched Telephone Network (PSTN)**
2. **The Basic Rate Interface (BRI)**

Connecting LANs

Compared with local area network connections, WANs are slow and they are expensive. Administrators, accustomed to dealing with LAN transmission speeds measured in hundreds or thousands of megabits per second, suddenly find themselves paying out vast sums of money every month for a connection that runs at a paltry 1.544 Mbps.

All data networking is about bandwidth, the ability to transmit signals between systems at a given rate of speed. On a LAN, when you want to increase the bandwidth available to users, you can upgrade to a faster protocol or add network connection components such as switches or routers. After the initial outlay for the new equipment and its installation, the network has more bandwidth—forever.

In the world of telecommunications, bandwidth costs money, often lots of it. If you want to increase the speed of a WAN link between two networks, you not only have to purchase new equipment, but you probably also have to pay additional fees to your service provider. Depending on the technology you've chosen and your service provider, you might have to pay a fee to have the equipment installed, a fee to set up the new service, and permanent monthly subscriber fees based on the amount of bandwidth you want. Combined, these fees can be substantial, and they're ongoing; you continue to pay as long as you use the service.

The result of this expense is that WAN bandwidth is far more expensive than LAN bandwidth, and in nearly every case, your LANs will run at speeds far exceeding those of your WAN connections, as shown in Figure 10-6.

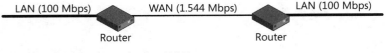

LAN (100 Mbps)
WAN (1.544 Mbps)
LAN (100 Mbps)
Router
Router

FIGURE 10-6 Fast LANs and a slow WAN.

Today, a 10-Mbps Ethernet LAN is old technology, almost obsolete. Most of the new LANs installed today use Gigabit Ethernet, running at 1,000 Mbps, and backbone networks are starting to use 10 Gigabit Ethernet, at 10,000 Mbps. In telecommunications, however, 10 Mbps is a large amount of bandwidth.

The network administrator of a modest business might only be able to dream of having T-1 connections to link to the company's branch offices in other cities. A T-1 is a leased digital telephone line running at 1.544 Mbps. Installing a single T-1 can easily cost thousands of dollars per month, and that does not include the hardware or the installation. However, even the most basic Fast Ethernet LAN that you can build using a hundred dollars worth of hardware from the computer store runs more than 64 times faster than a T-1. This gives you some idea why it's so important to minimize the amount of traffic passing over a WAN link joining two networks. That bandwidth costs real money, and you don't want to waste it transmitting needless broadcast messages or other "junk" traffic.

Leased Lines

A *leased line* is a permanent telephone connection between two locations that provides a predetermined amount of bandwidth at all times. Leased lines can be analog or digital, although most of the leased lines installed today are digital. The most common leased line configuration in the United States is called a *T-1*, which runs at 1.544 Mbps. In Japan, the same type of connection uses the name J-1. The European equivalent of a T-1 is called an E-1, which runs at 2.048 Mbps. Many organizations use T-1 lines to connect their networks to the Internet or to connect remote networks together. For applications requiring more bandwidth, a *T-3* connection runs at 44.736 Mbps, an *E-3* runs at 34.368 Mbps, and a *J-3* runs at 32.064 Mbps. These designations are collectively known as T-carrier, E-carrier, and J-carrier services, respectively.

Leased line services use a framing method called *Digital Signal 1 (DS1)*. A DS1 frame consists of 8-bit channels called Digital Signal 0s (DS0s), plus a framing bit used for synchronization. A T-1 has 24 such channels, as does a J-1; an E-1 has 32 channels. Each DS0 is sampled 8,000 times per second, resulting in discrete 64-Kbps channels. In a T-1, 24 64-Kbps channels with framing bits equals 1.544 Mbps. This transmission technique is called *time division multiplexing.*

> *(24 channels/frame*
> *× 8 bits/channel*
> *+ 1 framing bit/frame)*
> *× 8,000 frames/sec*
> *= 1,544 Kbps or 1.544 Mbps*

Faster connections use successive digital signal levels, the definitions of which vary according to region. The designations, number of channels, and transmission rates for the most commonly used levels of the T-carrier, E-carrier, and J-carrier systems are summarized in Table 10-2.

TABLE 10-2 T-Carrier, E-Carrier, and J-Carrier Configuration Data

	North America	Europe	Japan
DS0	64 Kbps	64 Kbps	64 Kbps
DS1	T-1 24 channels 1.544 Mbps	E-1 32 channels 2.048 Mbps	J-1 24 channels 1.544 Mbps
DS2	T-2 96 channels 6.312 Mbps	E-2 128 channels 8.448 Mbps	J-2 96 channels 6.312 Mbps
DS3	T-3 672 channels 44.736 Mbps	E-3 512 channels 34.368 Mbps	J-3 480 channels 32.064 Mbps
DS4	T-4 4,032 channels 274.176 Mbps	E-4 2,048 channels 139.264 Mbps	J-4 480 channels 97.728 Mbps

A T-carrier connection uses the framing bits, also called synchronization bits, to ensure that both ends of the connection mark the beginning of each frame. This ensures that the data stream in each channel remains separate from the others. This is the only overhead between the two connected points. Because a leased line is a point-to-point connection between two systems only, there is no need for any sort of addressing, as on an Ethernet network. Because the connection is permanent, there is no need for a connection establishment process or a negotiation of protocols, as in a Point-to-Point Protocol connection.

T-carrier services were originally designed for telephony. When a large organization installs its own telephone system, the private branch exchange (PBX) or switchboard is connected to one or more T-1 lines. Each T-1 line is split into the 64-Kbps channels, and each channel can function as one voice telephone line. The PBX allocates the channels to the various users of the telephone system as needed. However, when you use a leased line to connect networks together, you can combine the channels into a single data pipe, or configure them in any combination of voice and data.

You can also install a leased line that uses some, but not all, of the channels in a T-1. This is called a *fractional T-1* service, and you can use it to specify exactly the amount of bandwidth you need.

A T-3 connection is the equivalent of 672 channels of 64 Kbps each, or 28 T-1 lines. This much bandwidth is usually required only by large corporate networks, Internet service providers (ISPs), and other service providers with a need for huge amounts of bandwidth. To install a leased line, you contract with a telephone provider to furnish a link between two specific sites, running at a particular bandwidth. Prices depend on the amount of bandwidth and the distance between the sites, but a T-1 connection can easily cost thousands of dollars per month, plus installation and equipment fees at both ends. At each end of the connection, you must have a device called a *channel service unit/data service unit (CSU/DSU)*, which you connect to your data network by using a router (or a PBX, in the case of a voice network), as shown in Figure 10-7.

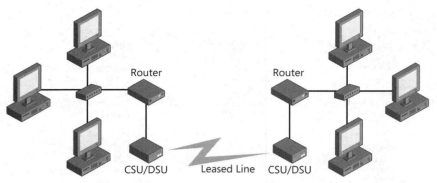

FIGURE 10-7 A leased line connection.

As noted in Chapter 2, the leased line enters the customer's premises and terminates at the CSU/DSU, which functions as the demarcation point, or demarc. A CSU/DSU is actually two devices that are always combined into a single unit that looks something like an external modem. In fact, CSU/DSUs are sometimes called *digital modems*, a term that is incorrect. The CSU part of the device provides the terminus for the digital link and keeps the link alive when no traffic is passing over it. The CSU also provides diagnostic and testing functions. The DSU part of the device translates the signals generated by the LAN equipment into the bipolar digital signals used by the leased line.

> **NOTE** **IDENTIFYING MODEMS**
>
> Any external device providing a connection to a WAN service is commonly called a modem, regardless of the type of modulation/demodulation being performed, if any. References to DSL modems, cable modems, and ISDN modems are common, mainly because all of these devices are little boxes with flashing lights on them. Most professionals aware of the distinction have given up trying to explain the differences.

A leased line contract typically quantifies the quality of service the subscriber will receive by using two criteria: service performance and availability. The performance of the service is based on the percentage of error-free seconds per day, and its availability is computed in terms of the time that the service is functioning at full capacity during a three-month period, also expressed as a percentage. The contract will specify thresholds for these statistics, such as a guarantee of 99.99% error-free seconds per day and 99.96% service availability over the course of a year. If the provider fails to meet the guarantees specified in the contract, the customer receives a financial remuneration in the form of service credits.

Leased lines are a popular WAN solution, particularly for LAN-to-LAN connections, because they supply a consistent, symmetrical amount of bandwidth. However, they do have a significant disadvantage. Because the link is permanently connected, you pay for a specific amount of bandwidth 24 hours a day. If your applications do not run around the clock, you might end up paying premium prices for bandwidth you are not using.

Formerly, the bandwidth of a leased line was set at a particular rate. If your bandwidth needs exceeded the capacity of the line, the only way to augment your connection was to install another line. Today, flexible-rate connections are available from most service providers. You pay for a particular rate and can burst to a higher rate during peak traffic periods, paying extra when you do. Leased line connections can also be upgraded, by changing the CSU clocking at both ends.

As a result, leased lines are excellent solutions for some applications but can be less cost-effective for others.

SONET/SDH

The T-carrier connection standards have been around since all telecommunication was based on copper. However, as fiber optic cables began replacing copper for long distance runs, the various competing telecommunications companies that were the result of the 1984 AT&T divestiture began creating their own proprietary standards for fiber optic communications.

Eventually, these companies began to realize the advantages of having a common standard for fiber optic interoperability, and the result was the *Synchronous Optical Network (SONET)*, as it is called in the United States and Canada, and the *Synchronous Digital Hierarchy (SDH)*, in the rest of the world.

EXAM TIP

Although there are slight differences between the SONET and SDH signaling methods, the two standards describe technologies that are, for all intents and purposes, the same.

SONET is a physical and data-link layer standard that defines a method for building a synchronous telecommunications network based on fiber optic cables. First ratified by the American National Standards Institute (ANSI), SONET was then adapted by the International Telecommunications Union (ITU), which called it the *Synchronous Digital Hierarchy* (SDH). Intended as a replacement for the T-carrier and E-carrier services used in the United States and Europe, SONET provides connections at various *optical carrier (OC)* levels running at different speeds. The idea behind SONET is to create a standardized series of transmission rates and formats, eliminating the problems that can affect connections between different types of carrier networks. The OC levels are listed in Table 10-3.

TABLE 10-3 SONET OC Levels

OC Level	Data Transmission Rate (in Mbps)
OC-1	51.84
OC-3	155.52
OC-6	311.04
OC-9	466.56
OC-12	622.08
OC-18	933.12
OC-24	1244.16
OC-36	1866.24
OC-48	2488.32
OC-96	4976.640
OC-192	9953.280
OC-768	39813.120

In addition to the high speeds available on fiber optic media, these links also use various types of multiplexing to carry multiple signals on a single link. One of these techniques, *wavelength division multiplexing (WDM)*, uses different light wavelengths (which essentially means different colors) to encode different signals.

> **NOTE FREQUENCIES AND WAVELENTHS**
>
> What frequencies are to radio waves, wavelengths are to light. In Chapter 5, "Wireless Networking," you learned about how the radio signals on wireless LANs use frequency division multiplexing to transmit multiple signals at different frequencies, measured in megahertz. On optical networks, wavelength division multiplexing accomplishes the same goal by transmitting multiple signals at different light wavelengths, measured in nanometers. (One nanometer equals one billionth of a meter.)

One WDM variant, called *dense wave division multiplexing (DWDM)*, calls for the use of devices called *erbium-doped fiber amplifiers (EDFAs)*, which are designed to amplify wavelengths in the 1525-nanometer to 1565-nanometer or 1570-nanometer to 1610-nanometer bands without converting them to electrical signals. This is a cheaper and more efficient method of transmitting long-range optical signals than the optical-electrical-optical (OEO) regenerators they replace.

EXAM TIP
The Network+ exam requires candidates to have a general knowledge of technologies such as SONET, but the average network administrator is not likely to have any firsthand experience with them. SONET links form the backbone of the Internet and other global telecommunications networks, but they are not the type of WAN technologies that an organization is likely to install for its private use.

Packet Switching

T-carrier and SONET links are both point-to-point technologies that telecommunications companies have used to create the vast mesh of networks that form the global telecommunications system and the Internet. When you access a website on the Internet, your packets very likely traverse several of these links.

However, the relatively simple frame formats that these technologies use to send signals from one end of a link to the other have nothing to do with the addressing needed to get a request from your browser to a web server in another city. To do that, you must add a packet-switching capability that joins all of these separate links into a mesh. The two packet-switching protocols most commonly used on WAN connections today are frame relay and asynchronous transfer mode (ATM).

Frame Relay

Frame relay is a packet-switching WAN solution that can provide bandwidth similar to that of a leased line, but with greater flexibility. Frame relay services range from 56 Kbps all the way up to T-3 speeds, but the subscriber is not permanently locked into a specific transmission rate, as with a leased line. When you enter into a contract with a frame relay provider, you agree on a specific amount of bandwidth, called the *committed information rate (CIR),* which is the base speed of your link.

However, the frame relay service can provide additional bandwidth (called *bursts*) during your high-traffic periods by borrowing it from other circuits that are not operating at full capacity. In addition to the CIR, you also negotiate a *committed burst information rate (CBIR),* which is the maximum amount of bandwidth that the provider agrees to furnish during burst periods. Your contract specifies the duration of the bursts you are permitted. If you exceed the bandwidth specified in the agreement, you must pay an extra charge.

A frame relay connection is not a permanent link between two points, as is a leased line. Instead, each of the two sites is connected to the service provider's nearest point of presence, usually by using a standard leased line or, formerly, an ISDN connection. The provider's network takes the form of a frame relay cloud, which enables the leased line at one site to be connected to the line at the other site, as shown in Figure 10-8. This connection through the cloud from one point of presence to another is called a *permanent virtual circuit (PVC).*

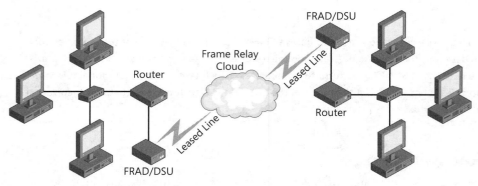

FIGURE 10-8 A frame relay connection.

Because each site uses a local telephone provider for its leased line to the cloud, the cost is generally less than it would be to have a single long-distance leased line connecting the two different sites.

The hardware device that provides the interface between the LAN at each site and the connection to the cloud is called a *frame relay assembler/disassembler (FRAD)*. A FRAD is a network layer device that strips off the LAN's data-link layer protocol header from each packet and repackages it for transmission through the cloud. One of the main advantages of frame relay is that you can use a single connection to a frame relay provider to replace several dedicated leased lines.

For example, if a corporation has five offices located in different cities, it would take 10 dedicated leased lines to connect each office to every other office. By using frame relay, you can create a mesh WAN topology connecting the networks at all five sites by using a single leased line at each location to connect to a common cloud. Because the connections in a frame relay cloud are ephemeral, a single network can simultaneously establish multiple PVCs to different destinations, as shown in Figure 10-9.

In a frame relay arrangement, you pay for only the PVC bandwidth you use (although you must pay for the leased line bandwidth, whether or not you use it). In addition, if you select the right provider, you can use frame relay to connect each of your sites to a local point of presence, reducing the cost of the leased lines.

Other, newer packet-switching solutions, such as Asynchronous Transfer Mode (ATM), have begun to replace frame relay in the marketplace, and many businesses have taken to using broadband Internet services and virtual private network (VPN) connections for relatively low-speed LAN-to-LAN solutions. However, in remote areas not serviced by DSL and CATV networks, a combination of fractional T-1 services and frame relay can be the most economical solution available.

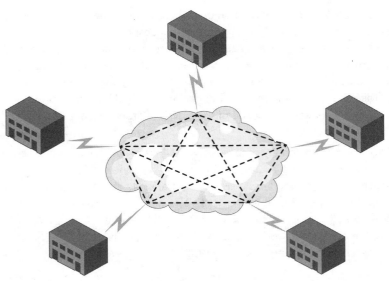

FIGURE 10-9 Five network sites forming a virtual mesh while connected to a single frame relay cloud.

Asynchronous Transfer Mode (ATM)

Asynchronous Transfer Mode (ATM) is a protocol that was originally designed to carry voice, data, and video traffic on both LANs and WANs. Today, ATM is most commonly used in WAN connections. Unlike most data-link layer protocols, ATM uses fixed-length, 53-byte frames (called *cells*) and provides a connection-oriented, full-duplex, point-to-point service between devices. Because the cells are a uniform size, unlike the variable-sized packets used by most networking protocols, ATM can provide a guaranteed, predefined quality of service.

This makes it easier to regulate and meter the bandwidth passing over a connection, because when the data structures are of a predetermined size, network traffic becomes more readily quantifiable, predictable, and manageable. With ATM, it's possible to guarantee that a certain quantity of data will be delivered within a given time. This makes the technology more suitable for a unified voice/data/video network than a nondeterministic protocol such as Ethernet, no matter how fast it runs. In addition, ATM has *quality of service (QoS)* features built into the protocol that enable administrators to reserve a certain amount of bandwidth for a specific application.

There are no broadcast transmissions in ATM, and data is relayed between networks by switches, not routers. ATM speeds range from a 25.6-Mbps service, originally intended for desktop LAN connections, to a 2.46-Gbps service. Physical media range from standard multimode fiber optic and unshielded twisted-pair (UTP) cables on LANs to SONET or T-carrier services for WAN connections.

On an internetwork where ATM is implemented on both the LANs and the WAN connections, cells originating at a workstation can travel all the way to a destination at another site through switches without having to be reencapsulated in a different data-link layer protocol. ATM never gained popularity on the desktop, however, because at the time of its introduction, Fast Ethernet provided better transmission rates and a simpler upgrade procedure. In the same way, Gigabit Ethernet has become the predominant high-speed backbone protocol, largely displacing most ATM backbones. Today, therefore, ATM has largely been relegated to use on WANs.

You can use an ATM packet-switching service for your WAN links in roughly the same way as you would use frame relay, by installing routers at your sites and connecting them to the carrier's points of presence by using leased lines. This process transmits the LAN data to the point of presence first and then repackages it into cells. It's also possible, however, to install an ATM switch at each remote site, either as part of an ATM backbone or as a separate device providing an interface to the carrier's network. In this case, the switch converts the LAN data to ATM cells at each site before transmitting it over the WAN.

 Quick Check

1. What is the term for the path through a frame relay cloud from one point of presence to another?

2. By what name is SONET known outside of North America?

Quick Check Answers

1. A permanent virtual circuit (PVC)

2. Synchronous Digital Hierarchy (SDH)

Remote Access

The third main use for WAN connections is to enable an individual user to access resources on a remote LAN. Many users today spend part of their time telecommuting, or they require access to email and other network resources while traveling or working at home during off hours.

To establish a remote network connection, the computers involved must have the following elements:

- **Physical layer connection**   The computers must be connected by using a WAN technology as a physical medium. In nearly all cases, a remote access solution uses either a direct link to a computer on the target network or an Internet access connection.

- **Common protocols**   The two computers to be connected must use the same protocols at the data-link layer and above. This means that you must configure both computers to use a data-link layer protocol suitable for point-to-point connections.

The computers must also use the same network and transport layer protocols, such as Transmission Control Protocol/Internet Protocol (TCP/IP).

- **Network configuration**   To communicate with a remote network by using TCP/IP, for example, a computer must be assigned an Internet Protocol (IP) address and other configuration parameters appropriate for that network. The remote user can configure the TCP/IP settings if someone familiar with the host network supplies them, but most remote networking solutions enable the network server to assign configuration parameters automatically by using the Dynamic Host Configuration Protocol (DHCP) or some other mechanism.

- **Host and remote software**   Each of the computers to be connected must be running an application appropriate to its role. The remote (or client) computer needs a client program that can use the physical layer medium to establish a connection, such as by instructing a modem to dial a number. The host (or server) computer—sometimes called a *remote access server (RAS)*—must have a program that can respond to a connection request from the remote computer and provide access to the network.

There are three basic methods for accessing a network at a remote location by using a WAN link, as follows:

- Dial-up remote access
- Virtual private networking
- Remote terminal emulation

These methods are discussed in the following sections.

Dial-up Remote Access

The host and client software needed to enable remote workstations to access a network has existed for many years. What has changed is the method by which the two connect. The host software typically runs on a server and listens for incoming connection requests from the clients. Originally, the computers used modems and PSTN connections at the physical layer.

A remote access server can have one modem and telephone line, usually to support remote administrative access, or an array of dozens of modems. Specialized hardware enables a single computer to address an array of modems supporting multiple simultaneous users.

After a client establishes a WAN connection to the remote access server, remote access protocols control the establishment of higher-layer connections and the transmission of data over the WAN link. The operating system and LAN protocols used on remote access clients and servers dictate which remote access protocol your clients can use. In nearly all cases, remote access connections use the Point-to-Point Protocol (PPP) for WAN communications, because PPP includes mechanisms that provide security and support for multiple protocols at the network layer. Older remote access protocols, such as the Serial Line Internet Protocol (SLIP), have fallen into disuse because they do not provide these features.

After the client and server have established a remote access connection, the client can access server resources by using PPP. To enable the client to access resources on the network to which the server is attached, the server functions as a router between the PPP connection and a standard LAN protocol, such as Ethernet. Both PPP and the LAN protocols provide support for TCP/IP at the upper layers. This enables the remote access client to access virtually any type of resource on the server's network, just as if the computer was directly connected to the LAN.

The only perceivable difference to the client is the speed of the connection, which is much slower than a standard LAN connection. The remote access connection can use other physical layer WAN technologies, such as ISDN or a leased line, but the expense of these technologies, and their permanence, makes them unsuitable for many remote access implementations.

Other than the slowness of the connection, the other big disadvantage of dial-up remote access was the cost. Unless the users were all local, the long distance charges for extended dial-up sessions could be extremely expensive.

Virtual Private Networking

After the explosive growth of the Internet in the 1990s, almost every network had an Internet connection, as did almost every home computer user. A *virtual private network (VPN)* is a connection between two computers across an internetwork or the Internet that enables them to communicate in a manner that mimics the properties of a dedicated private network. In most cases, a VPN is functionally similar to a WAN technology, except that the Internet functions as the network medium.

Implementing a VPN

Virtual private networking was developed as a means to provide users with a relatively inexpensive method for connecting to a network at a remote location, as shown in Figure 10-10. VPNs enable users working at home or on the road to connect securely to a remote access server by using the routing infrastructure provided by a public internetwork such as the Internet. From the user's perspective, the VPN is a point-to-point connection between the user's computer and a remote access server. The nature of the intermediate internetwork (also called the *transit internetwork*) is irrelevant because it appears as if the computers are transmitting data over a dedicated private link.

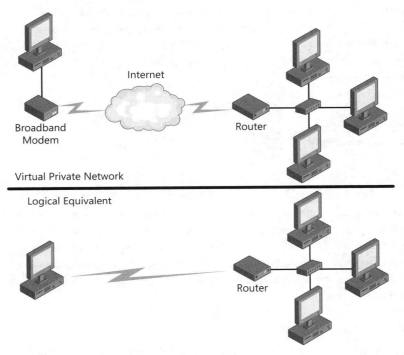

FIGURE 10-10 A virtual private network connection.

A VPN enables both the remote access client and server computers to connect to the Internet by using a local ISP, which keeps telecommunication charges to a minimum. The client then establishes a connection to the server across the Internet, and the server provides routed access to the corporate network. The connection across the transit internetwork appears to the user as a virtual WAN providing private network communication over a public internetwork, hence the term *virtual private network*.

The problem with using the Internet for private network communications in this manner is, of course, security. To allow the client and server to exchange confidential information over a public internetwork such as the Internet, the client and server must have a mechanism for securing the data. The method used by VPNs is called tunneling.

Tunneling Basics

Tunneling, also known as *encapsulation*, is a method for securely transferring a payload across an insecure internetwork infrastructure. The payload might be the frames generated by another protocol, such as PPP, or even a LAN protocol, such as Ethernet. Instead of transmitting the frame as produced by the originating node, the system encapsulates the frame with an additional header generated by a tunneling protocol. The tunneling protocol also encrypts the original frame. This way, even if someone intercepts the packets as they pass over the Internet, the information inside them cannot be read.

The additional header provides routing information so that the encapsulated payload can traverse the intermediate internetwork. The encapsulated packets are then routed between the tunnel endpoints over the transit internetwork, as shown in Figure 10-11. When the encapsulated frames reach the far endpoint, the system de-encapsulates the frames and forwards them to their final destinations.

FIGURE 10-11 A VPN tunnel.

This entire process (the encapsulation and transmission of packets) is what is known as tunneling. The tunnel is the logical path through which the encapsulated packets travel across the transit internetwork. The name is derived from the way that the tunneling protocol creates a secure conduit between two points on the transit internetwork. The original frame produced by the sending computer passes through the tunnel without being accessed or modified in any way, so that the information inside remains intact.

Tunneling Protocols

The most common tunneling protocols used to create VPNs are the Point-to-Point Tunneling Protocol (PPTP) and the Layer 2 Tunneling Protocol (L2TP), as described in the following sections.

POINT-TO-POINT TUNNELING PROTOCOL

The *Point-to-Point Tunneling Protocol (PPTP)* is an extension of PPP that encapsulates PPP frames into IP datagrams for transmission over an IP internetwork such as the Internet. PPTP can also be used in private LAN-to-LAN networking. PPTP uses a TCP connection for tunnel maintenance and uses modified GRE-encapsulated PPP frames for tunneled data. (GRE stands for Generic Routing Encapsulation.) The payloads of the encapsulated PPP frames can be encrypted and compressed.

PPTP tunnels use the same authentication mechanisms as PPP connections and also inherit payload encryption and compression capabilities from PPP. PPP encryption provides confidentiality between the endpoints of the tunnel only. If stronger security or end-to-end security is needed, Internet Protocol Security (IPsec) is the preferred tunneling protocol. Figure 10-12 shows a fully constructed PPTP packet, with the original application data encrypted and encapsulated by PPP, and then the PPP frame encapsulated in turn by the GRE and IP headers. The IP datagram is then packaged for transmission over the transit internetwork, inside another data-link layer frame.

Data-Link Header
IP Header
GRE Header
PPP Header
Encrypted PPP Payload
Data-Link Footer

FIGURE 10-12 A PPTP packet showing the encrypted data being sent, including header and footer information.

NOTE TUNNELING

Tunneling is essentially a violation of the OSI model encapsulation rules you learned in Chapter 1. In a PPTP packet, you have a data-link layer protocol frame encapsulated within a network layer IP datagram (instead of the other way around), and the datagram encapsulated again within another data-link layer protocol.

LAYER 2 TUNNELING PROTOCOL

The *Layer 2 Tunneling Protocol (L2TP)* is a combination of PPTP and Layer 2 Forwarding (L2F), a technology created by Cisco Systems. L2TP is a hybrid of the best features in PPTP and L2F.

L2TP is a network protocol that encapsulates PPP frames to be sent over IP, frame relay, or ATM networks. When utilizing IP as its datagram transport, L2TP can function as a tunneling protocol over the Internet, or it can be used in private LAN-to-LAN networking.

L2TP uses UDP and a series of L2TP messages for tunnel maintenance. L2TP also uses UDP to send L2TP-encapsulated PPP frames as the tunneled data. The payloads of encapsulated PPP frames can be both encrypted and compressed. Windows systems use IPsec to encrypt the data inside L2TP packets instead of PPP encryption. However, it is possible for other implementations of L2TP to use PPP encryption. Figure 10-13 shows an L2TP packet using IPsec authentication and encryption, ready for transmission over a point-to-point WAN connection, such as a dial-up line. The processing steps are numbered in the figure.

Steps 1 through 4 show normal processing prior to IPsec encapsulation. The application information becomes the payload of a PPP frame, which is then encapsulated by L2TP and UDP. Steps 5 through 7 show the IPsec processing, in which the entire UDP datagram is encapsulated and encrypted by IPsec's Encapsulating Security Payload (ESP) protocol. The remaining steps (8 through 10) show the normal encapsulation of the IPsec information in an IP datagram and a data-link layer frame, both of which are necessary to send the packet on the network to its final destination.

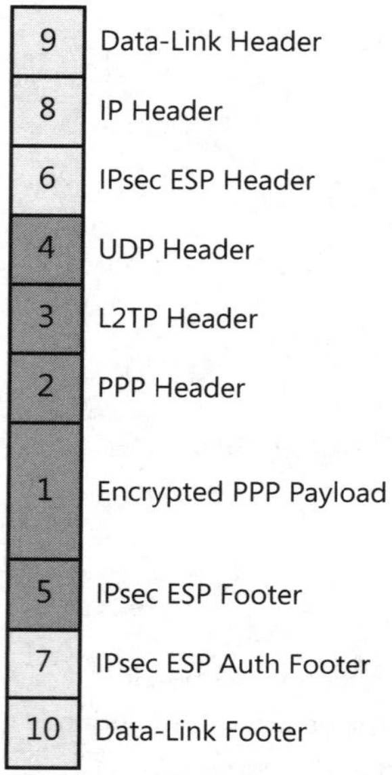

9	Data-Link Header
8	IP Header
6	IPsec ESP Header
4	UDP Header
3	L2TP Header
2	PPP Header
1	Encrypted PPP Payload
5	IPsec ESP Footer
7	IPsec ESP Auth Footer
10	Data-Link Footer

FIGURE 10-13 An L2TP packet showing encrypted data with IPsec authentication, an additional IP header, and data-link header and footer information.

L2TP is similar to PPTP in function. An L2TP tunnel is created between the L2TP client and an L2TP server. The client might already be attached to an IP internetwork (such as a LAN) that can reach the tunnel server, or the client might have to connect to an ISP to establish IP connectivity.

L2TP tunnel authentication uses the same mechanisms as PPP connections. L2TP inherits PPP compression but not encryption. L2TP does not use PPP encryption because it does not meet the security requirements of L2TP. PPP encryption can provide confidentiality but not per-packet authentication, integrity, or replay protection. Instead, L2TP uses data encryption provided by IPsec.

PPTP VS. L2TP

Both PPTP and L2TP use PPP for point-to-point WAN connections, to provide an initial envelope for the data, and then they append additional headers for transport through the transit internetwork. However, there are some differences between PPTP and L2TP:

- PPTP requires that the transit internetwork use IP. L2TP requires only that the tunnel medium provide packet-oriented point-to-point connectivity. L2TP can run over IP (by using UDP), frame relay permanent virtual circuits, or ATM virtual circuits.

- L2TP provides header compression capability. When header compression is enabled, L2TP operates with 4 bytes of overhead, compared to 6 bytes for PPTP.

- L2TP provides tunnel authentication, whereas PPTP does not. However, when either PPTP or L2TP runs over IPsec, it provides tunnel authentication, making Layer 2 tunnel authentication unnecessary.

- PPTP uses PPP encryption, and L2TP does not. The Windows L2TP implementation requires IPsec for encryption.

SSL VPN

Another type of VPN, which does not require any special software on the client side, is called an SSL VPN. SSL VPNs enable a user to connect to a remote site using a standard web browser, with the Secure Sockets Layer (SSL) or Transport Layer Security (TLS) protocol providing encryption services. To establish the connection, a user connects to an SSL VPN gateway at the remote site, completes an authentication process, and is then able to access one or more resources on the remote network.

Using a VPN Concentrator

A VPN concentrator is a hardware device located between the VPN client and server that performs several tasks that enhance the security of the connection, including the following:

- Functions as a tunnel endpoint
- Constructs the tunnel
- Authenticates VPN users
- Encrypts data for tunnel transmission
- Monitors tunnel data transfers

A VPN concentrator is not essential to establish a client/server VPN connection. The client and the server can establish a connection on their own. A concentrator just provides additional functionality.

Remote Terminal Emulation

Although it can use the same WAN technologies as other solutions, remote terminal emulation handles the remote access problem in a different way. The dial-up remote access and VPN solutions enable the client computer to function as a member of the remote network. Any application you launch on the client computer uses the client's processor and memory to run. With terminal emulation, you are taking over a computer on the network and operating it from a remote location. If you execute a program from the client terminal, it actually runs by using the host system's resources.

Terminal emulation has been around since the early days of computing. A program like Telnet enables you to connect to a remote computer and execute commands there. However, graphical user interfaces have complicated the terminal emulation process.

The first graphical terminal emulation program was called WinFrame, designed and marketed by the Citrix Corporation. Citrix created a protocol called *Independent Computing Architecture (ICA)* that defines how a client and server should exchange graphical terminal emulation traffic. ICA essentially defines how the client sends keyboard and mouse input to the server and how the server sends a graphical screen display to the client.

Microsoft also pursued graphical terminal emulation technology, first by licensing it from Citrix, and later by creating their own, which they called Windows Terminal Services. As of the Windows Server 2008 R2 release, the name was changed to Remote Desktop Services. The client program, supplied with all Windows versions, is called Remote Desktop Connection, as shown in Figure 10-14, and the protocol that the two computers use to communicate is the *Remote Desktop Protocol (RDP)*.

Remote terminal connections are based on IP, so they can theoretically use any type of WAN connection, as long as it provides access to the computer the client will control.

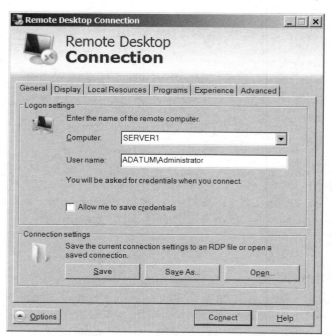

FIGURE 10-14 The Remote Desktop Connection client.

Exercise

The answers for this exercise are located in the "Answers" section at the end of this chapter.

Wingtip Toys has its headquarters in the state capital and has 10 branch offices located throughout the state. Each office has its own LAN, and the company wants to connect them all into a single internetwork by using WAN links. After the WAN links are installed, the company will buy a proprietary tracking software product that allows each of the offices to keep in constant communication with all of the others, simultaneously. The traffic on the internetwork will be very heavy during normal business hours, tapering off to nearly nothing at night. After soliciting the opinions of several different networking consultants, the company has received four proposals, each of which calls for a different WAN technology. The four solutions are as follows:

A. Install a single ISDN connection at each site, enabling users to dial in to the other offices.

B. Install a leased line at each site, connecting it to a frame relay cloud.

C. Install separate leased lines connecting each office to every other office.

D. Connect all of the sites to the Internet service provided by the local CATV company and use VPN connections between the offices.

Based on this information, answer the following questions:

1. Which of these four proposals will successfully enable the users on one LAN to keep in constant touch with all of the other LANs simultaneously? (Choose all answers that are correct.)

2. Which of these four proposals would provide the worst network performance under heavy traffic conditions?

3. Which of the four proposals would provide the best performance at the lowest cost?

Chapter Summary

- A wide area network (WAN) is a communications link that spans a relatively long distance and connects two or more computers or LANs together. Most WAN connections are point-to-point, involving two systems only.

- The Public Switched Telephone Network (PSTN) is just a technical name for the standard, analog telephone system that has existed in some form since the late nineteenth century, also commonly known as the Plain Old Telephone Service (POTS).

- Integrated Services Digital Network (ISDN) is a dial-up service, like the PSTN, but its connections are digital, so no modems are required. Although ISDN can support specially made telephones, fax machines, and other devices, most ISDN installations in the United States are used only for computer data transmissions.

- Digital Subscriber Line (DSL) is a blanket term for a variety of digital communication services that use standard telephone lines and provide data transfer speeds much greater than the PSTN or even ISDN.

- Some of the larger communications companies have launched high-speed broadband services that run fiber optic cables through some or all of the last mile. Generic names for these services are various, depending on where the fiber optic cable terminates, but they all follow the format FTT*x*, where *x* is the terminus of the fiber optic cable.

- A leased line is a permanent telephone connection between two locations that provides a predetermined amount of bandwidth at all times. The most common leased line configuration in the United States is called a T-1, which runs at 1.544 Mbps.

- SONET is a physical and data-link layer standard that defines a method for building a synchronous telecommunications network based on fiber optic cables.

- Frame relay is a packet-switching WAN solution that can provide bandwidth similar to that of a leased line, but with greater flexibility. Frame relay services range from 56 Kbps all the way up to T-3 speeds, but the subscriber is not permanently locked into a specific transmission rate, as with a leased line.

- Asynchronous Transfer Mode (ATM) is a protocol that was originally designed to carry voice, data, and video traffic on both LANs and WANs. Today, ATM is most commonly used in WAN connections.

- There are three basic methods for accessing a network at a remote location by using a WAN link, as follows: dial-up remote access, virtual private networking, and remote terminal emulation.

- Virtual private networking was developed as a means to provide users with a relatively inexpensive method for connecting to a network at a remote location. VPNs enable users working at home or on the road to connect securely to a remote access server by using the routing infrastructure provided by a public internetwork such as the Internet.

Chapter Review

Test your knowledge of the information in Chapter 10 by answering these questions. The answers to these questions, and the explanations of why each answer choice is correct or incorrect, are located in the "Answers" section at the end of this chapter.

1. Which device enables you to use a computer with an ISDN connection?

   A. A terminal adapter

   B. An NT-1

   C. A DSLAM

   D. A U interface

2. What type of cable does a SONET network use at the physical layer?

   A. Unshielded twisted pair

   B. Shielded twisted pair

   C. Coaxial

   D. Fiber optic

3. For which of the following services do you negotiate a CBIR with the provider?

   A. T-1

   B. Frame relay

   C. ATM

   D. PPTP

4. Which DSL type is most commonly used to provide Internet access to residential end users?

   A. ADSL

   B. HDSL

   C. SDSL

   D. VDSL

Answers

This section contains the answers to the questions for the Exercise and Chapter Review in this chapter.

Exercise

1. B, C, and D. Answer B is correct because it is possible to use a single link to a frame relay cloud to connect simultaneously to multiple destinations that are also connected to the cloud. Answer C is correct because this proposal calls for a separate leased line connecting each pair of offices. Answer D is correct because you can create any number of VPN connections to different destinations by using a single Internet connection. Answer A is incorrect because ISDN is a dial-up service that can connect to only one destination at a time.

2. D. Answer D is correct because CATV networks are asymmetrical, with relatively little upstream bandwidth available. For an application like this, the outgoing traffic generated by each office would be much slower than incoming traffic. Answers A and C are incorrect because they provide a continuous amount of bandwidth at all times. Answer B is incorrect because frame relay provides a flexible bandwidth solution that allows for higher speed bursts during heavy traffic periods.

3. B. Answer B is correct because frame relay requires only a single leased line connection at each office and allows the company to contract for the amount of bandwidth it needs at the time it needs it. Answer A is incorrect because a single ISDN connection at each office is not suitable for the application the company wants to run, which requires continuous access to all of the remote networks. Answer C is incorrect because installing a separate leased line between each pair of offices would be very expensive and most of the bandwidth would be wasted. Answer D is incorrect because although the CATV connections are economical, they provide insufficient upstream bandwidth.

Chapter Review

1. **Correct Answer:** A

    A. **Correct:** A terminal adapter enables a TE2 device to connect to the ISDN service.

    B. **Incorrect:** An NT-1 provides the ISDN S/T interface, but an additional terminal adapter is required to connect a computer.

    C. **Incorrect:** A DSLAM is a DSL device, not an ISDN device.

    D. **Incorrect:** The U interface is used by the ISDN service to enter the premises. It does not connect directly to the computer.

2. **Correct Answer:** D

   A. **Incorrect:** SONET is not designed for use with UTP or any other copper cable.

   B. **Incorrect:** SONET is not designed for use with STP or any other copper cable.

   C. **Incorrect:** SONET is not designed for use with coaxial or any other copper cable.

   D. **Correct:** SONET is a standard created for fiber optic cable runs.

3. **Correct Answer:** B

   A. **Incorrect:** A T-1 provides a fixed amount of bandwidth at all times. There is no need for a committed burst information rate, as in frame relay.

   B. **Correct:** A frame relay service contract specifies a committed information rate and a committed burst information rate, which specify how much bandwidth you receive.

   C. **Incorrect:** ATM is a packet-switching solution like frame relay, but it does not require a committed burst information rate.

   D. **Incorrect:** PPTP is a tunneling protocol used for virtual private networking. It is not a WAN solution like frame relay and does not require a committed burst information rate.

4. **Correct Answer:** A

   A. **Correct:** Asymmetric DSL is the type most often supplied to residential Internet customers.

   B. **Incorrect:** High-bit-rate Digital Subscriber Line is used by large companies as a backup for T-1 connections. It is not used for residential Internet customers.

   C. **Incorrect:** Symmetric DSL is used by large companies as a backup for T-1 connections. It is not used for residential Internet customers.

   D. **Incorrect:** Very high-rate DSL is used for multimedia Internet access and high-definition television delivery. It is not used for residential Internet customers.

CHAPTER 11

Network Security

Securing the network has always been one of the administrator's many jobs, but in recent years, it has become a constantly escalating arms race, with attackers and defenders both equipping themselves with ever-more-powerful technology. Security is now a concern in virtually every task an administrator performs. Every new piece of hardware or software offers a potential threat, and keeping up with the latest defensive strategies and tactics is a matter of course. This chapter examines some of the protocols, tools, and concepts that network administrators use in the course of securing a network.

Exam objectives in this chapter:

Objective 5.1: Given a scenario, implement appropriate wireless security measures.

- Encryption protocols:
  - WEP
  - WPA
  - WPA2
  - WPA Enterprise
- MAC address filtering
- Device placement
- Signal strength

Objective 5.2: Explain the methods of network access security.

- ACL:
  - MAC filtering
  - IP filtering
  - Port filtering
- Tunneling and encryption:
  - SSL VPN
  - VPN
  - L2TP
  - PPTP
  - IPsec
  - ISAKMP
  - TLS
  - TLS2.0
  - Site-to-site and client-to-site
- Remote access:
  - RAS
  - RDP
  - PPPoE
  - PPP
  - ICA
  - SSH

Objective 5.3: Explain methods of user authentication.

- PKI
- Kerberos
- AAA (RADIUS, TACACS+)
- Network access control (802.1x, posture assessment)
- CHAP

- MS-CHAP
- EAP
- Two-factor authentication
- Multifactor authentication
- Single sign-on

Objective 5.4: Explain common threats, vulnerabilities, and mitigation techniques.

- Wireless:
  - War driving
  - War chalking
  - WEP cracking
  - WPA cracking
  - Evil twin
  - Rogue access point
- Attacks:
  - DoS
  - DDoS
  - Man in the middle
  - Social engineering
  - Virus
  - Worms
  - Buffer overflow
  - Packet sniffing
  - FTP bounce
  - Smurf

- Mitigation techniques:
  - Training and awareness
  - Patch management
  - Policies and procedures
  - Incident response

Objective 5.5: Given a scenario, install and configure a basic firewall.

- Types:
  - Software and hardware firewalls
- Port security
- Stateful inspection vs. packet filtering

- Firewall rules:
  - Block/allow
  - Implicit deny
  - ACL
- NAT/PAT
- DMZ

Objective 5.6: Categorize different types of network security appliances and methods.

- IDS and IPS:
  - Behavior based
  - Signature based
  - Network based
  - Host based
- Vulnerability scanners:
  - NESSUS
  - NMAP
- Methods:
  - Honeypots
  - Honeynets

REAL WORLD **PHYSICAL SECURITY**

In a field where technology rules and most of the bad guys are human, it is sometimes easy to forget that security begins with the most basic forms of protection. The most elaborate firewall provides no protection against someone picking up your server and walking away with it, nor does it protect against power surges, fires, floods, or other natural disasters. Physical security must be one of the administrator's first principles. A locked data center or server closet, appropriate environmental systems, and regular backups are just as important to a security regimen as firewalls and encryption protocols.

Authentication and Authorization

Authentication is the process of verifying a user's identity, for the purpose of distinguishing legitimate users from uninvited guests. As such, it is one of the most prominent and one of the most visible concepts in security. From driver's licenses to user names and passwords, authentication is a regular part of everyone's daily life. Without authentication, administrators could not control access to network resources. If a network's authentication strategy is not strong enough, viruses, worms, and malicious attackers can gain access to it. Password guessing, password cracking, and man-in-the-middle attacks (in which a third party eavesdrops on a protected communication to gain access to passwords or encryption keys) are all attempts to exploit weaknesses in an authentication strategy. However, an authentication strategy can also be too restrictive, keeping attackers out, but also preventing legitimate users from doing their jobs.

Whether you're withdrawing money from a bank, entering a restricted building, or boarding an airplane, gaining access to a restricted resource requires both authentication and *authorization*. The two processes are closely related, leading many people to confuse them. Before you can board an airplane, you must present both your identification and your ticket. Your identification, typically a driver's license or a passport, enables the airport staff to confirm your identity. This is the authentication part of the boarding process. The airport staff also checks your ticket to make sure that the flight you are boarding is the correct one. This is the authorization process.

On a network, users typically authenticate themselves by typing an account name and a password. The account name identifies the person, and the password provides the computer with some assurance that this person really is who he or she claims to be. After the authentication, the computer has confirmed the user's identity. However, it does not yet know whether the user is allowed to access the resource he or she is requesting.

For example, when an administrator grants one user Read-Only permission to a specific file folder, and another user Read/Write permission to the same folder, the administrator is modifying the authorization, but not the authentication, process. The system authenticates both users in the same way, but the level of access granted to each one is different.

To authorize a user, a computer system typically checks an *access control list (ACL)* that is stored with the resource being protected. An ACL is a list of users, or groups of users, who are permitted to access a resource, as well as the degree of access each user or group is permitted.

Network Authentication Systems

For a network user to be authenticated with reasonable certainty that the individual is who he or she claims to be, the user must provide two pieces of information: some form of identification and some proof of identity. In most cases, users identify themselves with an account name or an email address. The proof of identity can vary, however, depending on the amount of security the network requires.

Proof of identity typically takes one of three forms:

- **Something you know**   Proof of identity usually takes the form of a password. A password is a type of shared secret. The user knows it, as does the authenticating server, which either has the password stored or has some information it can use to validate the password, such as a cryptographic hash.

- **Something you have**   Networks requiring greater security authenticate users by reading information from a smart card or other physical token. A smart card is a credit card–sized device that contains memory in which it stores data, such as a public encryption key. Swiping the card through a reader provides an electronic equivalent of a password.

- **Something you are**   For even greater security, some networks require users to confirm their identities by presenting a physical attribute using biometrics. A biometric system proves a user's identity by scanning a unique body part, such as one or more fingerprints, the retina of the eye, hand geometry, or facial features.

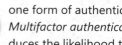

Passwords can be guessed or otherwise compromised, and smart cards can be stolen. A determined intruder can even evade a biometric scan, with sufficient effort. In some cases, one form of authentication alone might not meet an organization's security requirements. *Multifactor authentication* combines two or more of these authentication methods and reduces the likelihood that an intruder would be able to successfully impersonate a user during the authentication process.

The most common example of multifactor authentication is the combination of a smart card with a password. This is a form of two-factor authentication. Typically, smart cards require the user to specify a password to retrieve the key stored on the card. Before you can authenticate to such a system, you must provide a password (something you know) and a smart card (something you have).

> **NOTE** **MULTIPLE FACTORS**
>
> The factors in multifactor authentication refer to different proofs of identity. Requiring a user to supply two passwords would not be multifactor authentication, because if you can penetrate one password, you can penetrate two. A password and a smart card or a password and a fingerprint are both forms of multifactor authentication.

Storing User Credentials

An authentication server must have a way to determine that the credentials supplied by an individual are valid. To do this, the server must store information that it can use to verify the credentials. How and where the server stores this information are important elements of an authentication model.

The method that an authentication server uses to store user credentials determines how difficult it is for attackers to misuse the information. Naturally, it is important that this information remain confidential. Instead of simply storing a list of user passwords on a server, and comparing the password the user provides with the one in the list, it is common practice for the server to store an encrypted or hashed version of the user password. If attackers manage to gain access to the server copy of a user's credentials, they will still need to decrypt the contents before they can use them to impersonate the user.

Understanding Encryption

To protect data that is stored on servers and transmitted over a network, computers use various types of encryption to encode messages and create digital signatures that verify their authenticity. For one computer to encrypt a message and another computer to decrypt it, both must possess a key.

SECRET KEY ENCRYPTION

At the most basic level, encryption is a system in which new characters are substituted for those in the original content, as shown in Figure 11-1. For example, if you create a key specifying that the letter A should be replaced by O, the letter B by F, the letter C by S, and so forth, any message you encode using that key can be decoded by anyone else possessing that key. This is called *secret key encryption*, because you must protect the key from being compromised.

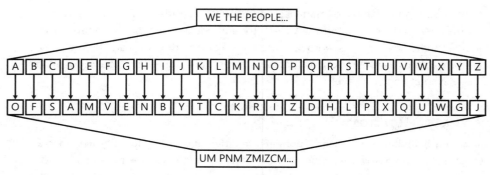

FIGURE 11-1 Secret key encryption.

> **NOTE** **ENCRYPTION CIPHERS**
>
> This type of simple letter substitution code, called a Caesar cipher, is relatively easy for a person to crack, and the work of only a few seconds for a computer. The actual ciphers that computers use to encrypt data (and the mathematical algorithms that implement them) are far more complex and constantly evolving, and the computers perform them on the data in its binary form.

For computer transactions, this type of encryption is useless, because there is no practical and secure way to distribute the secret key to all of the parties involved. After all, if the object is to send an encrypted message to a recipient over the network, it would hardly be appropriate to first send the secret encryption key in an unsecured message. However, there are some applications that use secret key encryption effectively, such as the Kerberos authentication protocol.

PUBLIC KEY ENCRYPTION

For encryption on a data network to be both possible and practical, computers typically use a form of public key encryption. In a *public key infrastructure (PKI)*, every user has two keys, a public key and a private key. As the names imply, the public key is freely available to anyone, whereas the private key is carefully secured and never transmitted over the network. The way the system works is that data encrypted with the public key can only be decrypted with the private key, and conversely, data encrypted with the private key can only be decrypted by using the public key. Data encrypted with a public key cannot be decrypted with that public key, nor can data encrypted with a private key be decrypted by using that private key. It is the protection of the private key that guarantees the security of messages encrypted in this system.

If Alice wants to send Ralph a message, making sure that no one but Ralph can read it, then Alice must obtain Ralph's public key and use it to encrypt the message, as shown in Figure 11-2. Alice can then transmit the message to Ralph over the network, secure in the knowledge that only Ralph possesses the private key needed to decrypt it. Even if an intruder were to intercept the message during transmission, it would still be in its encrypted form, and therefore impenetrable. When Ralph receives the message and decrypts it using his private key, he can reply to it by using Alice's own public key to encrypt his response, which only Alice can decrypt, by using her private key.

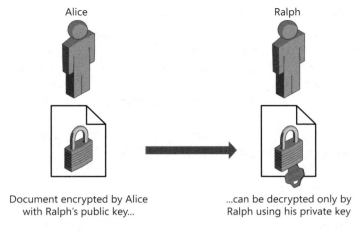

Document encrypted by Alice
with Ralph's public key...

...can be decrypted only by
Ralph using his private key

Therefore, no one can read the document except Ralph

FIGURE 11-2 Document encryption using PKI.

NONREPUDIATION

PKI also works in reverse, to provide a service called nonrepudiation. *Nonrepudiation* is essentially a method for ensuring that the communication you receive from a specific person actually originates from that person. The sender encrypts the data by using his or her private key, and the receiver decrypts it by using the sender's public key, as shown in Figure 11-3. Because no one but the sender has access to the private key, the ability to decrypt it with the public key proves that the sender actually encrypted it. This is sometimes referred to as a *digital signature*.

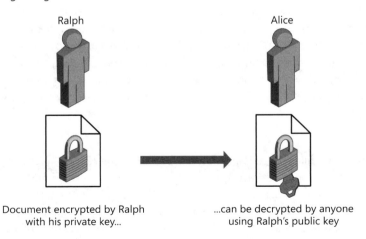

Document encrypted by Ralph
with his private key...

...can be decrypted by anyone
using Ralph's public key

Therefore, the document must have come from Ralph

FIGURE 11-3 Document nonrepudiation using PKI.

Centralized and Decentralized Authentication Models

Determining where to store user credentials requires choosing between centralized and decentralized authentication models. A decentralized authentication model requires each network resource to maintain its own list of users and their credentials. For example, on a Windows peer-to-peer network (that is, one that does not use Active Directory Domain Services), each computer maintains a separate directory of user accounts and passwords. If a user wants to access resources on multiple computers, that user must have a separate account on each one. To change a user's password throughout the network, an administrator must modify the user's account on each computer separately.

Although a decentralized authentication model such as this provides granular control over which users can authenticate to network resources, the decentralized model becomes increasingly difficult to manage as networks grow to more than a handful of systems.

Centralized authentication models provide much simpler management for larger networks, which lowers help desk costs related to account management. In a centralized model, network resources rely on a single system to authenticate users. When users attempting to access a particular network resource supply their credentials in the normal manner, the server hosting the resource relays those credentials to a separate authentication server, which either grants or denies the users access.

Centralized authentication is required to create an environment in which users can access all of their allotted network resources with a single set of credentials, a convenient arrangement known as *single sign-on*. The main drawback of the centralized model is that systems must transmit user credentials over the network, which presents an additional security hazard. Most centralized authentication systems use elaborate forms of encryption to protect this data as it travels over the network.

Most of the operating systems used today are capable of using either a centralized or a decentralized authentication model. Every computer running Windows has a component called the Security Accounts Manager (SAM), which enables it to maintain a list of local users and groups, enabling it to function as a decentralized authentication system. When you log on for the first time to a Windows-based computer, you use a local account, which is authenticated by the SAM running on that computer. The SAM stores users' passwords in a hashed format and locks them to prevent copying while the operating system is running.

DIRECTORY SERVICES

On Windows-based networks, centralized authentication is provided by the Active Directory Domain Services (AD DS) directory service. To use AD DS, you create one or more domains and designate specific servers to function as domain controllers. The domain controllers store the account information for the resources in the domain and are responsible for authenticating all user requests for access to domain resources. Larger networks might use multiple domains, with trusts that enable network resources in one domain to authorize users in another domain. All of the authentication and authorization traffic on an AD DS network uses a specialized protocol called Kerberos.

MORE INFO   KERBEROS

For more information on Kerberos, see the "Authentication Protocols" section later in this chapter.

UNIX and Linux operating systems also maintain individual account databases, and many of them also support some type of centralized authentication. The original standard for this was *Network Information Services (NIS)*, developed by Sun Microsystems, which was designed to function as a Yellow Pages directory for host names, user accounts, and hashed passwords.

NIS was a relatively simple service based on text files, and Sun later released a redesigned program, called NIS+, which provided greater security and a hierarchical directory. Some UNIX and Linux distributions also came to use the Lightweight Directory Access Protocol (LDAP) for centralized authentication.

AAA

Directory services such as AD DS are designed to support local area networks (LANs) on which every user has a permanent account created by an administrator and continuous access to the servers providing authentication and authorization services. There are other situations, however, in which these stipulations do not apply. Remote access environments, for example, have users connecting to a server by using some form of wide area network (WAN) or virtual private network (VPN) link. These users require authentication and authorization also, but they present different challenges.

In the past, these users connected to the servers by using the Point-to-Point Protocol (PPP), which offered a framework providing several authentication options. However, authenticating all of these users was a problem in cases where a constantly changing list of user names and passwords had to be maintained on dozens of servers. This led to the creation of a different kind of centralized service called Authentication, Authorization, and Accounting, or AAA.

MORE INFO   MORE ON PPP

For more information on PPP, see Chapter 4, "The Data-Link Layer."

An AAA server is a computer with the account information needed to grant or deny any user access to the network, as well as the information needed to authorize access to specific resources. Finally, the server includes the capability to maintain accounting information about its activities, such as how often a particular user logs on to the network.

RADIUS

The most common AAA server implementation is called *Remote Authentication Dial In User Service (RADIUS)*. Devised in the early 1990s as a tool for ISPs and other remote access providers, RADIUS is a standard that defines a client/server protocol running on the application layer and using the User Datagram Protocol (UDP) for transport services on ports 1812 and

1813, for authentication and accounting, respectively. Some implementations use ports 1645 and 1646, which are the unofficial ports the service used prior to standardization.

> **NOTE RADIUS STANDARDS**
>
> RADIUS was originally designed by a private company, and only later standardized by the Internet Engineering Task Force (IETF) in RFC 2865, "Remote Authentication Dial In User Service (RADIUS)," and RFC 2866, "RADIUS Accounting."

The RADIUS server provides authentication, authorization, and accounting services to the remote access servers that receive incoming network access requests. The remote access servers contain a RADIUS client, as shown in Figure 11-4, which, after prompting the user for credentials, generates a RADIUS Access-Request message and sends it to the server. The Access-Request message contains one or more attributes, which might specify the user's account name and password, contain a digital certificate, and/or provide other information to help identify the user.

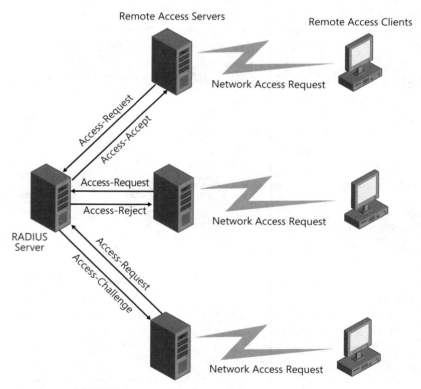

FIGURE 11-4 A RADIUS server and its clients.

The RADIUS server has access to the information needed to verify the user's identity, which it does by using any one of the several remote access authentication protocols described later in this chapter. Some RADIUS servers maintain the user's credentials in an internal flat-file database, whereas others access an external information store, such as an SQL or AD DS database. After processing the user's credentials, the RADIUS server generates a reply and sends it back to the client on the remote access server. The reply message can take one of the following three forms:

- **Access-Accept**   Grants the user access to the network, as requested
- **Access-Challenge**   Requests additional credentials from the user to complete the authentication, such as a smart card, PIN, biometric scan, or secondary password
- **Access-Reject**   Denies the user's requested access to the network

As with other centralized authentication systems, RADIUS simplifies the task of providing updated account information to a large fleet of network access servers. The Windows Server operating systems include a RADIUS implementation, which in Windows Server 2008 is part of the Network Policy and Access Services role. In earlier versions, the software was known as Internet Authentication Server (IAS). There are other implementations for UNIX/Linux, including open source options such as FreeRADIUS.

TACACS+

Terminal Access Controller Access-Control System (TACACS) is another centralized logon solution that enables users that successfully authenticate to one system to access other systems as well. The primary differences between TACACS and RADIUS are that TACACS separates the authentication, authorization, and accounting services into separate processes and uses TCP port 49 for its transport-layer communications, rather than UDP.

Cisco Systems developed the original TACACS into successive standards called extended TACACS (XTACACS) and later TACACS+, which they used to control administrative access to their router and switch products.

Authentication Protocols

Services that perform authentication typically include support for a variety of authentication protocols so that they can service clients with differing capabilities. Whether it is a server on a LAN or a remote access server that does the authenticating, clients can conceivably include older operating system versions or other operating systems altogether.

For example, an ISP providing dial-up access to the Internet these days probably supports clients running operating systems that are 10 or more years old. These earlier systems have fewer authentication options, so the ISP's servers must maintain support for outdated authentication protocols. The same holds true for older LANs, which often have workstations running various older operating system versions.

Windows Authentication Protocols

As with all versions from Windows 2000 up through Windows 7, Windows Server 2008 R2 provides the ability to authenticate a variety of client operating systems. The authentication protocols that these clients use date back to the earliest Windows operating systems and include the following:

- **LAN Manager (LM)** Developed jointly by IBM and Microsoft for use in OS/2 and Windows for Workgroups, Windows 95, Windows 98, and Windows ME, LM is the least secure form of challenge-response authentication because it is susceptible to eavesdropping attacks. Servers that authenticate users with LM authentication must store credentials in an encrypted form called an LMHash.

- **NTLM version 1 (NTMLv1)** A more secure form of challenge-response authentication than LM, NTLMv1 provides authentication services for servers running Windows NT with Service Pack 3 or earlier. NTLMv1 uses 56-bit encryption to secure the authentication data and stores the credentials by using an encrypted form called an NT Hash.

- **NTLM version 2 (NTLMv2)** The most secure form of challenge-response authentication available, NTLMv2 includes a secure channel to protect the authentication process. NTLMv2 uses 128-bit encryption to secure the credentials and provides authentication services for servers running Windows NT with Service Pack 4 or higher, or any Windows system that is not a member of an AD DS domain.

- **Kerberos version 5 protocol** The current default authentication protocol for all AD DS domain systems, the Kerberos protocol is a network authentication service that is designed to be more secure and scalable than NTLM across large, diverse networks.

The differences in the authentication procedures for the NTLM and Kerberos protocols are discussed in the following sections.

NTLMV2 AUTHENTICATION

To support down-level clients, Windows Server 2008 R2 still includes three methods of challenge-response authentication: LM, NTLMv1, and NTLMv2. The authentication process for all of these methods is the same, but they differ in the level of encryption they provide. The following steps demonstrate the flow of events that occur when a client authenticates to a domain controller using any of these three protocols:

1. The client and server negotiate an authentication protocol. This is accomplished through the Negotiate function of the Microsoft Security Support Provider Interface (SSPI).

2. The client sends the user name and domain name to the authenticating server.

3. The authenticating server generates a 16-byte random character string called a nonce.

4. The client encrypts the nonce with a hash of the user password and sends it back to the authenticating server.

5. The authenticating server retrieves the hash of the user password from the security account database.

6. The authenticating server uses the hash value retrieved from the security account database to encrypt the nonce. The value is compared with the value received from the client. If the values match, the client is authenticated.

> **NOTE** **USING LM AND NTLM**
>
> Although the Windows operating systems continue to support LM and NTLM authentications, Microsoft recommends against the use of these protocols, due to the relative weakness of their cryptography.

KERBEROS AUTHENTICATION

The *Kerberos protocol* is an authentication protocol that uses tickets to coordinate the authentication of network clients and servers. Named for the three-headed dog guarding the entrance to Hades in Greek mythology, a Kerberos implementation consists of the following three components:

- **Clients** Users or applications that must be authenticated before they can access network resources
- **Servers** Systems hosting resources that clients need to access
- **Key Distribution Center (KDC)** An authentication server that functions as an intermediary between clients and servers by issuing tickets to clients, which they can use to access server resources

The Kerberos protocol was developed at the Massachusetts Institute of Technology in the early 1980s and is now standardized by the IETF in RFC 1510, "The Kerberos Network Authentication Service (V5)." The Kerberos protocol has been implemented in various UNIX and Linux distributions for years, and it is the default authentication protocol used by the Active Directory Domain Services directory service included in all Windows Server versions from Windows 2000 through Windows 7.

When a client logs on to a network that uses the Kerberos protocol, it sends a request message to the authentication service on a KDC, which already possesses the account name and password associated with that client. The KDC responds by sending a ticket-granting ticket (TGT) to the client, as shown in Figure 11-5. The TGT is encrypted by using a key based on the client's password. When the client receives the TGT, it prompts the user for the password and uses it to decrypt the TGT. Because only that user (presumably) has the password, this process serves as an authentication.

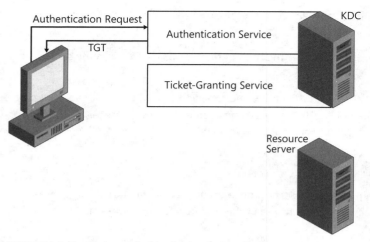

FIGURE 11-5 The Kerberos Authentication Service Exchange.

Now that the client possesses the TGT, it can access network resources by sending a request to a Ticket-Granting Service (TGS), which might or might not be running on the same KDC. The request contains an encrypted copy of the TGT. The TGS, after it has decrypted the TGT and verified the user's status, creates a server ticket and transmits it to the client, as shown in Figure 11-6.

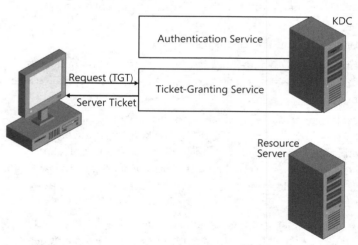

FIGURE 11-6 The Kerberos Ticket-Granting Service Exchange.

The server ticket allows a specific client to access a specific server for a limited length of time. The ticket also includes a session key, which the client and the server can use to encrypt the data transmitted between them, if necessary. The client transmits the server ticket (which was encrypted by the TGS by using a key that the server already possesses) to that server. After the server decrypts the server ticket, the server grants the client access to the requested resource, as shown in Figure 11-7.

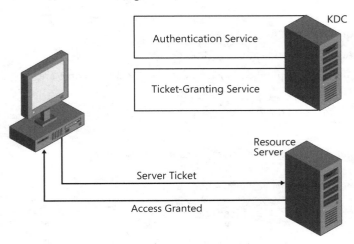

FIGURE 11-7 The Kerberos Server Ticket Exchange.

The client is now authenticated to the network and authorized to access the requested resource. The next exchange between the client and the server will consist of messages specific to the application that requires access to the network resource.

Remote Access Authentication Protocols

Remote access connections, no matter what WAN technology they use at the physical layer, or whether they use a dial-up or virtual private network connection, all use the Point-to-Point Protocol (PPP) at the data-link layer.

PPP controls the authentication process by providing the remote access client and server with the means to negotiate an authentication protocol. During the link establishment phase of the connection process, the computers specify which protocols they can use for authentication, and the two then agree on the securest protocol they have in common. The protocols available to each computer depend on the operating systems they run and the software they have installed.

When choosing a remote access authentication method, administrators must decide whether they want to authenticate users against a RADIUS server, an AD DS domain, or a local user database. Regardless of whether a remote access solution uses RADIUS or another service as its authentication provider, administrators can choose from several authentication methods. Some of the most common authentication options are as follows and are discussed in the following sections.

- Unauthenticated access
- Password Authentication Protocol (PAP)
- Challenge Handshake Authentication Protocol (CHAP)
- Microsoft Challenge Handshake Authentication Protocol (MS-CHAP) version 1 and version 2
- Extensible Authentication Protocol (EAP)
- Preshared key (PSK)

Table 11-1 shows the key features of the various authentication methods.

TABLE 11-1 Key Features of Remote Access Authentication Methods

	PAP	CHAP	MS-CHAP v1	MS-CHAP v2	EAP	PSK
Provides authentication encryption		X	X	X	X	X
Provides data encryption				X	X	X
Provides mutual authentication				X	X	X
Allows changing of passwords during authentication process			X	X		
Requires passwords to be stored with reversible encryption		X	X			
Vulnerable to Replay attacks	X					

UNAUTHENTICATED ACCESS

Many operating systems support unauthenticated access, which means that user credentials, such as a user name and password, are not required. Although leaving a remote access server completely unprotected is, of course, not recommended, there are some situations in which unauthenticated access is useful. Specifically, if you are using a remote access policy to control access by another means, such as callback or caller ID, you might decide that additional authentication is not required.

PAP

Password Authentication Protocol (PAP) uses unencrypted passwords and is the least secure of authentication protocols. Anyone capturing the packets generated during the authentication process can easily read the password inside and use it to gain unauthorized access to the network. The use of PAP is strongly discouraged, especially for VPN connections. Most remote access services disable PAP by default, and administrators should only use it if the remote access client and the remote access server cannot negotiate a more secure form of validation.

CHAP

The *Challenge Handshake Authentication Protocol (CHAP)* is a challenge-response authentication protocol that uses the industry-standard Message Digest 5 (MD5) hashing scheme to encrypt the response—that is, the user's password. This means that anyone capturing the authentication packets will not be able to read the passwords in them. CHAP, however, provides relatively weak protection compared to some of the other authentication protocols. CHAP does not support encryption of the connection data, and the passwords it uses must be stored in a reversibly encrypted format. This means that if users are establishing connections with their standard operating system user accounts, the network administrator must weaken the encryption of those passwords to accommodate CHAP.

Like PAP, CHAP authentication is disabled by default in Windows. CHAP is recommended over PAP, but there are much more capable authentication protocols available. Most networks that use CHAP do so because they have users running operating systems other than Windows that do not support anything else.

MS-CHAP

MS-CHAP is a variation of the CHAP authentication protocol that was designed by Microsoft specifically for its Windows operating systems. There are two versions of MS-CHAP, as follows:

- **MS-CHAP v1**   Version 1 of MS-CHAP is a one-way authentication protocol, meaning that the client computer is authenticated to the server, but the server is not authenticated to the client. MS-CHAP v1 provides both authentication encryption and data encryption, but the encryption is relatively weak because the protocol uses the account password to create the encryption key. The key remains the same as long as the user retains the same password. This provides a potential intruder with more time to crack the encryption, weakening the cryptography. At this time, only older versions of Windows, such as Windows 95 and Windows 98, use MS-CHAP v1.

- **MS-CHAP v2**   Version 2 of MS-CHAP improves on version 1 by adding two-way authentication and increasing the strength of the encryption. Version 2 uses a new encryption key for each connection and for each direction in which data is transmitted. This makes the encryption far more difficult to crack. MS-CHAP v2 is the preferred authentication method for systems that do not use smart cards or public key certificates for authentication. By default, Windows VPN remote access clients use MS-CHAP v2 to authenticate.

EAP

The *Extensible Authentication Protocol (EAP)* is a shell protocol that enables systems to use various types of authentication mechanisms. The primary advantage of EAP is that it enables a computer to use mechanisms other than passwords for authentication, including public key certificates, smart cards, and biometric devices such as fingerprint scanners. Some of the EAP variations supported by Windows are as follows:

- **Protected EAP (PEAP)** The primary application for PEAP is the authentication of wireless users with an account name and password.

- **Message Digest 5 Challenge** Message Digest 5 Challenge (MD5-Challenge) uses the same challenge handshake protocol as PPP-based CHAP, but the challenges and responses are sent as EAP messages. A typical use for MD5-Challenge is to authenticate remote access clients other than those created by Microsoft, such as those running Mac OS X. You can also use MD5-Challenge to test EAP interoperability. EAP with MD5-Challenge does not support encryption of connection data.

- **Smart Card or Other Certificate** This authentication method, also known as EAP-Transport Layer Security (EAP-TLS), enables clients to authenticate by using a smart card or a public key certificate.

It is also possible for third-party applications to add other authentication methods to EAP.

PPPoE

Point-to-Point Protocol over Ethernet (PPPoE) is a TCP/IP standard and is defined in RFC 2516, "A Method for Transmitting PPP Over Ethernet (PPPoE)." PPPoE provides a way to create individual PPP connections between computers on an Ethernet LAN and external services connected to the LAN via a broadband device such as a cable or DSL modem.

Broadband remote network access devices can easily support multiple computers, and Ethernet is the most common protocol used to join the computers to a network and connect them to the broadband device. However, a shared Ethernet LAN does not enable each computer to access remote services that use individual parameters for functions such as access control and billing. The object of PPPoE is to connect multiple computers to a remote network by using an Ethernet LAN and broadband technology, while establishing a separate

PPP connection between each computer and a specified remote service. Each PPP connection has all of the PPP components, such as Link Control Protocol (LCP) negotiation, authentication, and network control protocol configuration.

 Quick Check

1. Which Windows authentication protocol does Active Directory Domain Services use?

2. Which authentication protocol is not recommended because it transmits account names and passwords in clear text?

Quick Check Answers

1. The Kerberos protocol

2. Password Authentication Protocol (PAP)

Tunneling and Encryption Protocols

Applications and operating systems can use security protocol standards to protect data as it is transmitted over a network. These protocols generally use specific types of data encryption and define how the communicating computers exchange the information needed to read each other's encrypted transmissions. Some of these protocols are discussed in the following sections.

> **NOTE   TUNNELING**
>
> Tunneling is a method for securely transferring a payload across an insecure internetwork infrastructure by encapsulating the frame with an additional header generated by a tunneling protocol. For more information, see Chapter 10, "Wide Area Networking."

IPsec

 Internet Protocol Security (IPsec) is the term used to describe a series of draft standards published by the IETF that define a methodology for securing data as it is transmitted over a network. Most of the security protocols that encrypt transmitted data are designed for use on the Internet or for specialized traffic between specific types of clients and servers. Until IPsec was developed, there was no standard to provide comprehensive protection for data as it was transmitted over a LAN.

IPsec protects data by digitally signing and encrypting it before transmission. IPsec encrypts the information in IP datagrams by encapsulating it, so that even if someone was to capture the packets, the information inside would remain uncompromised. Using IPsec can protect a network against a variety of threats, including password penetration, compromise of encryption keys, IP address spoofing, and data modification. An unauthorized user with a network monitor application can still capture packets as they are transmitted over the network, but the user cannot do any of the following:

- Read a packet's contents, because it is encrypted.
- Modify a packet's contents without being detected.
- Successfully spoof a recipient by assuming another user's identity.
- Discover passwords and keys or reuse encrypted packets.

IPsec operates as an extension to the IP protocol at the network layer, so it provides end-to-end encryption, meaning that the source computer encrypts the data, and that data is not decrypted until it reaches its final destination. Intermediate systems, such as routers, treat the encrypted part of the packets purely as payload, so they do not have to perform any decryption; they just forward the encrypted payload as is. The routers do not have to possess the keys needed to decrypt the packets, and they do not have to support the IPsec extensions in any way.

> **NOTE DATA-LINK LAYER ENCRYPTION**
>
> By contrast, encrypting network traffic at the data-link layer would require each router receiving an encrypted packet to decrypt it and then encrypt it again before transmitting it to its next destination. This would add a tremendous amount of processing overhead to each router and would slow down the entire network.

Because IPsec operates at the network layer, it can encrypt any traffic that takes the form of IP datagrams, no matter what kind of information those datagrams contain. To the transport layer protocols encapsulated in the IP datagrams, such as TCP and UDP, and to the applications generating the traffic, IPsec is completely invisible, because the data is encrypted at the network layer, after it leaves the transmitting application and is packaged in the transport layer protocol. Then, at the destination system, IPsec decrypts the traffic before it arrives at the transport layer or the destination application.

> **NOTE IPSEC ACCELERATION**
>
> Encryption is, by nature, a highly processor-intensive task, and implementing IPsec on your network can generate a large amount of additional overhead for the computers that are encrypting and decrypting the traffic. For this reason, there are network interface adapters on the market that offer IPsec acceleration as an additional feature. These products offload the IPsec-specific processing tasks from the system processor to an external processor located on the adapter card.

IPsec Standards

IPsec is based on a series of Requests for Comments (RFCs) that are in the process of being ratified as standards by the IETF. RFC 2411, "IP Security Document Roadmap," explains how the technologies defined in the other documents work together. There are dozens of RFCs concerned with IPsec topics. The most important are as follows:

- **RFC 2401** "Security Architecture for the Internet Protocol"
- **RFC 2402** "IP Authentication Header"
- **RFC 2406** "IP Encapsulating Security Payload (ESP)"
- **RFC 2409** "The Internet Key Exchange (IKE)"
- **RFC 2411** "IP Security Document Roadmap"
- **RFC 3585** "IPsec Configuration Policy Information Model"
- **RFC 3586** "IP Security Policy (IPSP) Requirements"

IPsec Protocols

The IPsec standards define two protocols that provide different types of security for network communications: the *IP Authentication Header (AH)* and the *IP Encapsulating Security Payload (ESP)*. These protocols are discussed in the following sections.

IP AUTHENTICATION HEADER

The IP Authentication Header protocol does not encrypt the data in IP packets, but it does provide the following services:

- **Mutual authentication** Before two computers can communicate by using IPsec, they must authenticate each other to establish a trust relationship. After the computers have authenticated each other, the cryptographic checksum in each packet functions as a digital signature, preventing anyone from spoofing or impersonating one of the computers.

- **Anti-replay** In some cases, intruders can analyze network traffic patterns, determine the functions of certain packets, and use data from captured packets to wage an attack, even when the data in the packets is encrypted. For example, the first few packets that two computers exchange during a secured transaction are likely to be authentication messages. By retransmitting these same packets, still in their encrypted form, attackers can sometimes use them to gain access to secured resources. IPsec prevents packet replays from being effective by assigning a sequence number to each packet. A system using IPsec will not accept a packet that has an incorrect sequence number.

- **Integrity** IPsec uses cryptographic keys to calculate a checksum called a *hash message authentication code (HMAC)* for the data in each packet, and it then transmits that HMAC with the data. If anyone modifies the packet while it is in transit, the HMAC calculated by the receiving computer will be different from the one in the packet. This prevents attackers from modifying the information in a packet or adding information to it.

A system using IPsec can use AH by itself or in combination with ESP. Using AH alone provides basic security services, with relatively low overhead. However, AH by itself does not prevent unauthorized users from reading the contents of captured data packets. Using AH does, however, guarantee that no one has modified the packets en route, and that the packets did actually originate at the system identified by the packet's source IP address.

On a TCP/IP network, a normal packet has a format like that shown in Figure 11-8. A message generated by an application is encapsulated by a transport layer protocol (TCP or UDP), which is in turn encapsulated by IP at the network layer and by a protocol such as Ethernet at the data-link layer.

Ethernet Header	IP Header	Transport Layer Protocol Header	Application Message	Ethernet Trailer

FIGURE 11-8 A typical TCP/IP data packet.

When a computer uses AH to protect its transmissions, the system inserts an AH header into the IP datagram, immediately after the IP header and before the transport layer protocol header, as shown in Figure 11-9.

Ethernet Header	IP Header	IPsec ESP Header	Transport Layer Protocol Header	Application Message	Ethernet Trailer

FIGURE 11-9 The AH header location.

IP ENCAPSULATING SECURITY PAYLOAD

The IP Encapsulating Security Payload (ESP) protocol encrypts the data in an IP datagram, preventing intruders from reading the information in packets they capture from the network. ESP also provides authentication, integrity, and anti-replay services. Unlike AH, which inserts only a header into the IP datagram, ESP inserts a header and a trailer, which surround the datagram's payload, as shown in Figure 11-10.

Ethernet Header	IP Header	IPsec ESP Header	Transport Layer Protocol Header	Application Message	IPsec ESP Trailer	IPsec ESP Authentication	Ethernet Trailer

FIGURE 11-10 The ESP header and trailer locations.

ESP encrypts all the data following the ESP header, up to and including the ESP trailer. Therefore, someone who captures a packet encrypted with ESP can read the contents of the IP header but cannot read any part of the datagram's payload, including the TCP or UDP header.

An IPsec packet can use ESP by itself or in combination with AH. When a packet uses both protocols, the ESP header follows the AH header, as shown in Figure 11-11. Although AH and ESP perform some of the same functions, using both protocols provides the maximum possible security for a data transmission.

Ethernet Header	IPsec AH Header	IPsec ESP Header	IP Header	Transport Layer Protocol Header	Application Message	IPsec ESP Trailer	IPsec ESP Authentication	Ethernet Trailer

FIGURE 11-11 An IP datagram using AH and ESP.

KEY EXCHANGE PROTOCOLS

As with any security solution that provides encrypted communication between two systems, a preliminary negotiation between IPsec systems is necessary, in which the computers authenticate each others' identities, select appropriate encryption algorithms from those they have in common, and exchange the keys they will use to encrypt subsequent transmissions. A collection of these common settings, which the computers will use to execute the various security services associated with IPsec, is called a *security association (SA)*.

The *Internet Security Association and Key Management Protocol (ISAKMP)* provides the means for two systems to create and manage the SAs they will need to complete the preliminary negotiation. It's important to understand that ISAKMP does not actually perform the authentication between the systems, nor does it exchange the keys the systems will need; the protocol only provides the framework within which those events take place. ISAKMP operates independently from any other protocols that complete the preliminary negotiation that sets up the IPsec communications between the two computers.

Other protocols that perform the actual key exchanges include Oakley and Simple Password Exponential Key Exchange (SPEKE) . Another protocol is the *Internet Key Exchange (IKE)* protocol, which incorporates part of Oakley and SPEKE and adds ISAKMP to create a comprehensive, hybrid key exchange solution.

Transport Mode and Tunnel Mode

IPsec can operate in two modes: transport mode and tunnel mode. Transport mode protects communications between computers on a LAN. In transport mode, the two end systems must support IPsec, but intermediate systems, such as routers, do not have to support IPsec. All the discussion of the AH and ESP protocols so far in this chapter applies to transport mode.

Tunnel mode provides security for gateway-to-gateway wide area network (WAN) connections, and particularly virtual private network (VPN) connections, which use the Internet as a communications medium. In tunnel mode, the end systems do not support IPsec; instead, the routers at both ends of the WAN connection use IPsec to secure the data passing over the WAN connection. IPsec, in essence, forms a protected tunnel through an unprotected medium. The internal network traffic between the end systems and the routers uses standard, unprotected TCP/IP communications.

IPsec uses a different packet structure in tunnel mode. In transport mode, IPsec modifies the existing IP datagram by adding its own headers. In tunnel mode, the IPsec implementation creates an entirely new datagram and uses it to encapsulate the existing datagram, as shown in Figure 11-12.

New IP Header	IPsec AH Header	IPsec ESP Header	Original IP Header	Transport Layer Protocol Header	Application Message	IPsec ESP Trailer	IPsec ESP Authentication

FIGURE 11-12 An IPsec tunnel mode packet.

The "inner" IP header is the header from the original datagram, which remains unchanged. The ESP header and trailer surround the original datagram and are themselves preceded by a new, "outer" IP header. This outer header is designed to get the packet only from one router to the other. Although the source IP address and destination IP address of the inner IP header contain the ultimate source and destination of the packet, the outer header contains the IP addresses of the two gateways that form the endpoints of the tunnel.

Tunnel mode communications proceed as follows:

1. Computers on one of the private networks transmit their data by using standard, unprotected IP datagrams.

2. The packets reach the router that provides access to the WAN, and then the router encapsulates them by using IPsec, encrypting and hashing data as needed.

3. The router transmits the protected packets through the secure tunnel to a second router at the other end of the WAN connection.

4. The second router verifies the packets by calculating and comparing integrity check values and decrypts the packets if necessary.

5. The second router repackages the information in the packets into standard, unprotected IP datagrams and transmits them to their destinations on the private network.

EXAM TIP

Although candidates for the Network+ exam are not required to know the packet formats for the IPsec protocols, they should be familiar with the names of the component protocols, the concept of tunneling, and the distinction between IPsec's transport and tunnel modes.

L2TP

As explained earlier in this chapter, tunneling is the process of creating a secure communications conduit through an inherently insecure network. IPsec forms tunnels and encrypts the data passing through them. However, you can also use another protocol, such as the *Layer 2 Tunneling Protocol (L2TP)*, to form the tunnel, while IPsec continues to provide the data encryption service.

As noted in Chapter 10, L2TP is a combination of the Point-to-Point Tunneling Protocol (PPTP) and the Cisco Systems Layer 2 Forwarding (L2F) protocol. L2TP encapsulates PPP frames, such as those used by WAN connections, inside UDP datagrams, as shown in Figure 11-13. It doesn't matter whether the original data being transmitted through the tunnel uses TCP or UDP at the transport layer; each separate datagram is packaged in another UDP datagram before transmission.

IP Header	IPsec ESP Header	UDP Header	L2TP Header	PPP Header	PPP Payload	IPsec ESP Trailer	IPsec ESP Authentication

FIGURE 11-13 L2TP with ESP packet format.

L2TP can encapsulate datagrams to form a tunnel, but it cannot encrypt them. L2TP relies on IPsec's ESP protocol to encrypt and authenticate the UDP datagrams it creates, to protect them from compromise by unauthorized users. Although it is possible to create L2TP tunnels without encryption, this defeats the purpose of creating a VPN connection in the first place, because the data inside the tunnel would not be secured.

IPsec Implementations

All of the current Windows operating systems support IPsec in transport mode, with the server operating systems supporting tunnel mode as well. In the UNIX/Linux world, most of the major operating systems include IPsec support, and there are also several third-party implementations, both commercial and open source, for various distributions. Many routers also support IPsec in tunnel mode for VPNs.

SSL and TLS

Secure Sockets Layer (SSL) is a special-purpose security protocol that protects the data transmitted by servers and their clients. Unlike IPsec, SSL operates at the application layer and can protect only the data generated by the specific applications for which it is implemented. Originally designed by Netscape Communications to protect the HTTP data exchanged by web servers and browsers, SSL began to be used by other applications to protect their traffic as well. For example, email applications using the Simple Mail Transfer Protocol (SMTP) and articles exchanged by newsreaders and servers by using the Network News Transfer Protocol (NNTP) made use of SSL.

SSL protects application layer data in the following three ways:

- **Authentication** Clients and servers can exchange credentials to confirm their identities.
- **Encryption** Data exchanged by clients and servers is encrypted by using public key encryption to prevent the data in intercepted packets from being compromised.
- **Data integrity** Packets are signed with HMAC, which the receiver uses to ensure that the data has not been modified in transit.

Netscape revised the SSL standard several times, culminating in SSL 3.0, which the IETF published as a historic document (RFC 6101) in 2011.

 Transport Layer Security (TLS) is the successor to SSL and is now the standard cryptographic protocol for web communications. Virtually all current web servers and browsers support TLS, as do many other Internet applications. When you access a secured website on the Internet, your browser points to a Uniform Resource Locator (URL) with an *https://* prefix instead of the usual *http://.* The initial exchange between the client and the server then proceeds as follows:

1. The *https://* prefix causes the browser to send its HTTP request to TCP port 443 instead of the standard HTTP port 80. The request also includes a list of the cryptographic standards that the client supports.

2. The server responds to the client's HTTP request by selecting the strongest of the offered cryptographic standards the two have in common and by sending the client its digital certificate and public key.

3. The client contacts the certification authority that issued the server's certificate and confirms the server's authenticity.

4. The client, using the agreed-upon cryptographic cipher, encrypts a randomly selected session number by using the server's public key and transmits it. This is called the session key.

5. The server decrypts the client's session key by using its private key and uses that number to generate keys for the encryption and decryption of all subsequent data transmissions in the session.

In a similar manner, other applications, such as Voice over IP (VoIP) and virtual private networks use TLS for their cryptography.

Unlike the SSL standard, which the IETF only published after its retirement, TLS has been designed and developed by an IETF working group. The current standard is RFC 5246, "The Transport Layer Security (TLS) Protocol Version 1.2."

 EXAM TIP

For the purposes of the Network+ exam, SSL and TLS are essentially the same protocol, with TLS 1.0 being the next upgrade after SSL 3.0. In some instances, TLS versions are notated with a corresponding SSL version number, such as TLS 1.0 (SSL 3.1). Later version releases are TLS 1.1 (SSL 3.2) and TLS 1.2 (SSL 3.3).

Wireless Security Protocols

Wireless networks using the Institute of Electrical and Electronics Engineers (IEEE) 802.11 protocols at the data-link layer are highly susceptible to intrusion. Any person with a wireless-equipped computer can conceivably access the network, simply by wandering into the transmission range of an access point (AP). Encryption of transmissions is therefore imperative on wireless networks, and there are several different protocols available to protect them.

WEP

Wired Equivalent Privacy (WEP) is a wireless security protocol that protects transmitted data by using a *shared secret*, a text string possessed by the AP and the client, as an encryption key. Encrypting the data before it is transmitted helps to prevent unauthorized users from accessing the information in the packets.

To use WEP, administrators must configure all of the devices on the wireless network with the same shared secret. The devices use that one key to encrypt and decrypt all of their transmissions. Any person who gains possession of that key can, at the very least, read the contents of the transmitted packets, and at worst, participate on the network.

Unfortunately, some crafty attackers with experience in cryptography developed methods to discover the shared secret of a WEP network by analyzing captured traffic, even though the packets were encrypted. These attackers quickly exploited the weaknesses they discovered in WEP and spread their key penetration techniques in the form of software tools that they released on the Internet. The combination of free WEP-cracking tools, the ease with which attackers can capture wireless traffic, and the increased popularity of wireless networks led to WEP becoming one of the most frequently cracked network encryption protocols.

> **NOTE WEP WEAKNESS**
>
> The cryptographic weakness of the WEP protocol is based on several factors that make it relatively easy to discover a network's shared key. The first weakness is that the original WEP implementations used a key that was only 40 bits long, because U.S. export restrictions prevented them from being any longer. The shorter the key, the easier it is to crack. The second weakness is that WEP uses a relatively short, 24-bit initialization vector (IV). The IV is a randomized value appended to the shared secret to ensure that the cipher never encrypts two packets with the same key. Unfortunately, the short IV resulted in a reasonable probability of key duplication if an attacker captured a sufficient number of packets.

Apart from its weak cryptography, the other limitation resulting in WEP's vulnerability is that the protocol standard does not define any mechanism for changing the shared secret. On a wireless network with hundreds of hosts, manually changing the shared secret on each device individually is a huge task, and one that is highly prone to error. As a result, WEP networks tend to use the same shared secret for long periods, if not indefinitely. In any cryptographic system, the longer the ciphers use the same key, the more likely it is that an attacker will be able to penetrate it. A WEP installation with an unchanging shared secret gives attackers the cryptographic opportunity they need and all the time they could want to work on infiltrating the network.

If administrators were able to change the shared secret on a regular basis, however, they would prevent an attacker from gathering enough data to crack the key. This would significantly improve WEP's security. There are techniques for dynamically and automatically changing the shared secret to dramatically reduce WEP's weaknesses.

NOTE **STATIC AND DYNAMIC WEP**

A standard WEP implementation that uses an unchanging shared key is sometimes referred to as *static WEP*. When a WEP implementation has a mechanism for automatically changing the shared secret, it is called *dynamic WEP*.

If a wireless network relies on a static shared secret for security, you cannot trust WEP to protect the data transmitted over the network or to prevent unauthorized users from accessing the wireless network. However, if you are forced to use static WEP because you have devices on your network that can support nothing else, there are a few things you can do to improve its security, such as the following:

- Use the highest level of encryption possible: 128-bit or 256-bit. Short keys might be sufficient in some encryption scenarios, but WEP's 40-bit encryption is very vulnerable.

- Locate your access points on a perimeter network to restrict access to internal resources. If users need access to the internal network from a wireless network, they can use a VPN connection.

- Position your APs so that wireless connectivity is limited to locations that you can physically secure, such as the interior of your building.

NOTE **OPEN SYSTEM AND SHARED SECRET AUTHENTICATION**

The WEP standards define two types of authentication: open system and shared secret. *Open system authentication* enables any user to connect to the wireless network without a password, whereas *shared secret authentication* uses a secret key to authenticate users. As illogical as it might sound, open system authentication is actually the more secure of the two. This is because most WEP implementations use the same secret key for both authentication and encryption. An intruder who captures the key during the authentication process might therefore penetrate the data encryption system as well.

802.1X

Early implementations of WEP are not safe for use on today's wireless networks, but it is possible to augment their security by adding 802.1X authentication. 802.1X is a standard developed by the IEEE that defines methods for performing the following tasks:

- Authenticating users connecting to a wireless network
- Authorizing user access to a wireless network
- Dynamically changing WEP encryption keys

802.1X uses the EAP protocol to transmit authentication messages among the client, the wireless access point, and a RADIUS server. As part of the 802.1X authentication process, EAP generates a unique encryption key for each client. The use of RADIUS forces the client to regularly generate a new encryption key, which makes it far more difficult for attackers to gather enough traffic and enough time to penetrate a key. The end result is that a wireless network with older WEP hardware can continue to function while minimizing the vulnerability of the WEP protocol.

The process that a client uses to connect to a network using WEP with RADIUS and 802.1X authentication is considerably more complex than the process of connecting to an unsecured wireless network. The connection process consists of the following steps:

1. When the client computer enters within radio range of the access point, it attempts to connect to the AP's Service Set Identifier (SSID). If the client is configured to use shared network authentication, it authenticates itself to the access point by using the network key. Because the AP is configured to permit only 802.1X-authenticated connections, it issues an authentication challenge to the client. The AP then creates a restricted channel through which the client can communicate only with the RADIUS service.

2. The client examines the RADIUS server's public key certificate to ensure that an attacker is not impersonating the RADIUS server. The client then attempts to authenticate to the RADIUS service, using 802.1X in one of the following ways:

   - If the client and RADIUS service are configured to use Protected EAP (PEAP) authentication, the client establishes a TLS session with the RADIUS service and transmits credentials by using its configured authentication protocol.

   - If the client and RADIUS service are configured to use EAP-TLS authentication, the client authenticates by using public key certificates.

3. The RADIUS service verifies the client's credentials against its directory. If RADIUS can authenticate the client's credentials and the access policy allows the client to connect, RADIUS grants access to the client.

4. The RADIUS service relays the positive access decision to the AP, transmitting the dynamic shared secret to the AP as well. The client and the AP now share common key material that they can use to encrypt and decrypt the traffic that they will exchange.

5. The AP then establishes the client's connection to the internal network, completing the 802.1X authentication process.

In addition to a simple yes or no response to an authentication request, RADIUS can also provide other applicable connection parameters for the user, including a maximum session time. The ability to specify a maximum session time enables the RADIUS service to force the client to reauthenticate on a regular basis. This reauthentication automatically generates a new shared secret, which upgrades static WEP to dynamic WEP.

Each time the shared secret changes, potential attackers must restart the process of cracking the encryption key. If the maximum session time is low enough, it is practically impossible for an attacker to capture enough data to crack the secret key. As a result, dynamic WEP can be adequately secure for many network situations.

WPA

Although WEP with dynamic key changes is secure enough to meet the needs of most organizations, it still has security weaknesses. WEP uses a separate static key for broadcast packets, which an attacker can analyze to build a map of the network's private IP addresses and computer names. In addition, the frequent renewal of WEP keys places an additional burden on the RADIUS service.

To address these weaknesses, the Wi-Fi Alliance developed a new encryption protocol called *Wi-Fi Protected Access (WPA)*. WPA can use the same authentication mechanisms and encryption algorithms as WEP, which enables hardware manufacturers to support WPA within their existing product designs with only a simple firmware modification. However, WPA virtually eliminates WEP's most exploited vulnerability by using a unique encryption key for each packet.

When you enable WPA, you establish a passphrase that is automatically associated with the dynamically generated security settings. This passphrase is stored on the AP and on each of the networked computers. Only wireless devices with the WPA passphrase can join the network and decrypt network transmissions.

There are two encryption options for WPA, as follows:

- Temporal Key Integrity Protocol (TKIP)
- Advanced Encryption System (AES)

TKIP is the encryption algorithm that WEP uses, and many WPA implementations continue to support it. WPA improves upon WEP's implementation of TKIP, however. WPA with TKIP reuses initialization vectors (IVs) less frequently than WEP with TKIP, and as a result reduces the likelihood that an attacker will collect enough traffic to compromise the encryption. Additionally, WPA with TKIP creates a unique encryption key for every frame, whereas WEP can use the same key for weeks or months.

In WPA version 2, known as *WPA2*, the protocol includes support for AES, an encryption algorithm that is more secure than TKIP. The use of WPA2 in combination with RADIUS is known as *WPA2-Enterprise*.

Although it is possible to upgrade the firmware in existing WEP wireless equipment to support WPA, older equipment cannot be upgraded to support AES. As a result, wireless networks with older hardware will probably not be able to use WPA2 encryption unless the organization chooses to upgrade the hardware.

REAL WORLD **SELECTING A WIRELESS ENCRYPTION PROTOCOL**

The biggest problem with implementing encryption on a wireless network is that a device can only use one encryption protocol configuration. Wireless encryption is not like PPP or other protocols, in which systems can negotiate the strongest possible encryption for each connection. An administrator has to choose one encryption standard for the network, and unfortunately, that sometimes means choosing a less effective protocol because there are older devices that need support.

You can have a network with 100 wireless clients, all of which support WPA2, but if there are 10 older computers that can only use WEP, then the administrator must configure all the devices to use WEP, in order to support those 10 computers. The only alternatives are to upgrade the 10 older computers or set up a separate WEP access point for those 10 (which would still be more vulnerable to attack).

Other Wireless Security Techniques

WEP and WPA are the most important wireless networking security technologies. However, there are secondary security mechanisms with which wireless network administrators should also be familiar, including the following:

- Media access control (MAC) address filtering
- Disabling SSID broadcasts
- Device placement

These techniques are discussed in the following sections.

MAC Address Filtering

One common technique that many wireless implementations use to make it more difficult for an unauthorized user to connect to the network is to configure APs to allow network access only to a predefined set of Media Access Control (MAC) addresses. Just as with wired Ethernet, manufacturers assign a unique MAC address (or hardware address) to every wireless network interface adapter.

When an administrator configures an AP to use MAC address filtering, the device ignores any messages from wireless adapters with MAC addresses not on the approved list. Although this does improve security, it has significant drawbacks as far as manageability is concerned. First, administrators must manually maintain the list of MAC addresses on the AP, which can be a difficult task when there are a lot of computers or multiple APs involved. Second, APs typically have limited memory and might not be able to store a large organization's complete list of MAC addresses. Third, if an attacker is knowledgeable and determined enough to circumvent your WEP or WPA encryption, the attacker might also be able to identify and spoof—that is, impersonate—an approved MAC address.

Disabling SSID Broadcasts

APs provide the option of disabling SSID broadcasts, but administrators should not treat this as a security feature. As you learned in Chapter 5, "Wireless Networking," SSID broadcasts enable wireless clients to detect an available wireless network.

Disabling SSID broadcasts can prevent the casual computer user from discovering your network, but it does nothing to prevent a skilled attacker from detecting it. There are free software tools available on the Internet that can quickly identify the SSID of a wireless network that has SSID broadcasts disabled, because 802.11 devices always transmit association/ disassociation messages in unencrypted form, and these contain the network's SSID.

Device Placement

Physical security is difficult to implement for a wireless network, because you cannot protect radio signals with a locked door the way you can cables. Many wireless access points provide sufficient range to allow users located in adjacent offices or even outside the building to connect. This kind of free access can furnish attackers with the time they need to penetrate the security protocols protecting the network. However, there are steps that an administrator can take to minimize the chances of intruders accessing the network from outside.

In addition to distance, the effective range of an access point is based on several unquantifiable factors, including climate conditions, proximity to sources of interference, and composition of walls and other structures. Selecting central locations for your APs within your space is generally recommended, but you also want to make sure that you provide coverage for all the spaces in which your users might need to connect.

The perfect configuration, in which all of your interior space is covered and all of the spaces outside your walls are not, is difficult, if not impossible, to achieve. However, by combining strategic placement of APs with careful selection of antennas and regulation of signal strength, a situation close to this ideal is sometimes possible.

✔ Quick Check

1. The wireless security solution known as WPA2-Enterprise consists of which three protocols?

2. Which IPsec mode connects two intermediate systems—that is, routers?

Quick Check Answers

1. WPA, AES, and RADIUS

2. Tunnel mode

Firewalls

Security is a part of every network administrator's job, whether there is confidential data stored on the network computers or not. Even protecting vital operating system and application files from accidental deletion is a security function. Administrators use various mechanisms to provide security on a network, because different types of protection are needed.

Network administrators routinely use permissions and other mechanisms to control access to network resources. This prevents internal users from accessing restricted resources. However, there is a whole world of potential security hazards outside the private internetwork, and the Internet connection that virtually all networks have today is the door through which these hazards can enter.

A *firewall* is a hardware or software product that protects a network from unauthorized access by outside parties, while letting appropriate traffic through, as shown in Figure 11-14. If your network is connected to the Internet, you must have some sort of firewall to protect it, because intruders can wreak havoc on the network that you have so carefully designed and constructed.

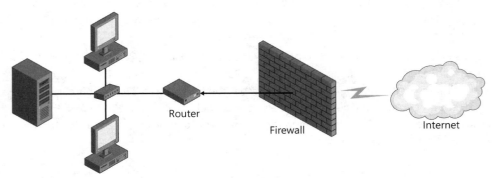

Router   Firewall   Internet

FIGURE 11-14 A firewall blocking unauthorized network traffic.

A firewall is essentially a barrier between two networks that evaluates all incoming or outgoing traffic to determine whether it should be permitted to pass through to the other network. A firewall can take many different forms and can use different criteria to evaluate the network traffic it receives. Some firewalls are dedicated hardware devices, essentially routers with additional software that monitors incoming and outgoing traffic. In other cases, firewalls are software products that run on a standard computer.

In the past, all firewalls were complex, extremely expensive, and used only in professional network installations. These high-end products still exist, but now you can also buy inexpensive firewall software products that protect a small network or an individual computer from unauthorized access through an Internet connection.

Firewalls can use several methods to examine network traffic and detect potential threats. Most firewall products use more than one of these methods and often provide other services as well. For example, one firewall product—a proxy server—not only allows users to access webpages with complete safety, but also can cache frequently used pages for quicker retrieval by other systems. Some of the most common firewall technologies are covered in the following sections.

Packet Filtering

 A *packet filter* is the most basic type of firewall, one in which the system implementing the filter examines each packet as it arrives and decides if it meets the criteria for admission to the network. Packets that do meet the admission criteria are processed by the system in the normal manner; those that do not are silently discarded.

For example, many Internet email servers use the Simple Mail Transfer Protocol (SMTP) for outgoing traffic and the Post Office Protocol 3 (POP3) for incoming traffic. These protocols use the well-known port numbers 25 and 110, respectively. You can configure a firewall with a packet filter that permits only packets destined for port numbers 25 and 110 to pass through, as shown in Figure 11-15. Packets destined for any other port numbers are discarded before they can reach the network and do any damage.

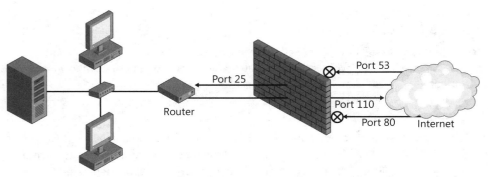

FIGURE 11-15 A firewall filtering out all packets for ports other than 25 and 110.

Creating packet filters is a matter of selecting the specific criteria you want the system to examine and specifying the values that it will allow or deny passage through the filter. Administrators can configure a firewall to filter packets in two basic ways, as follows:

- **Inclusive** The network interface is completely blocked and packet filters specify what traffic can pass through.
- **Exclusive** The network interface is left completely open and packet filters specify what traffic to block.

These two approaches are basic philosophies that pertain to most, if not all, security technologies. An inclusive packet filter implementation (an application of what is sometimes called the *implicit deny* rule) is inherently more secure; however, it can be more difficult to debug because you must make sure that all the traffic that needs to pass through the filters is getting through. Exclusive filtering assumes that the administrator is familiar with all possible threats to the network and knows what filtering criteria the firewall must use to stop them. This is a dangerous presumption.

The criteria most commonly used in packet filtering are as follows:

- **Port numbers**   Filtering by port numbers, also known as *service-dependent filtering,* is the most common type of packet filtering and the most flexible. Because port numbers represent specific applications, you can use them to prevent traffic generated by these applications from reaching a network. For example, to protect a perimeter network containing your company's web servers, you can create filters that allow only traffic using port 80 to enter from the Internet, blocking all other application ports.

MORE INFO   **WELL-KNOWN PORT NUMBERS**

For more information on the well-known port numbers assigned to specific applications and services, see Chapter 8, "The Transport Layer."

- **Protocol identifiers**   The Protocol field in every packet's IP header contains a code that identifies the next protocol that should receive the packet in the networking stack of the destination. In most cases, the code represents a transport layer protocol, such as Transmission Control Protocol (TCP) or User Datagram Protocol (UDP). However, IP datagrams frequently carry Internet Control Message Protocol (ICMP) messages as well. Filtering by using protocol identifiers is not very precise because it blocks or allows all the traffic that uses a particular protocol. However, for certain applications, blocking an entire protocol is necessary, and it is easier than anticipating the specific applications an attacker might use. For example, if you have a network that contains only Internet web and File Transfer Protocol (FTP) servers, you could use protocol filters to limit incoming traffic to TCP packets. Because these servers rely on TCP for their primary functions, you could block all UDP and ICMP traffic, preventing attacks from using any applications that rely on these protocols.

- **IP addresses** IP address filtering lets you limit network access to specific computers. For example, if you have an Internet web server on a LAN with other computers, and you want Internet clients to be able to access only the web server, you can create a filter permitting only those packets addressed to the web server to enter the network from the Internet. You can also use IP address filtering to protect part of a private network. You can create filters that give only certain computers access to the protected LAN, while preventing all others from accessing it.

> **NOTE IP ADDRESS FILTERING LIMITATIONS**
>
> Filtering by using IP addresses is not secure if potential attackers have a way to discover the IP addresses of the computers on your network, such as access to Domain Name System (DNS) records. When an attacker finds out the IP addresses the filter permits to access the network, it is a simple matter to impersonate another computer by using the impersonated computer's IP address. This is called *spoofing*.

- **MAC addresses** Filtering based on MAC addresses (or hardware addresses) provides the same basic functionality as IP address filtering. However, it is more difficult to spoof a hardware address than it is an IP address, so MAC address filters are inherently more secure than IP address filters. MAC address filtering is rarely used on Internet routers or firewalls, but for internal filtering, MAC address filtering is a useful means of restricting access to specific resources.

The four criteria just listed correspond to the application, transport, network, and data-link layers of the Open Systems Interconnection (OSI) reference model, as shown in Figure 11-16. Filters get more specific as you move up in the OSI model. Filtering by port numbers enables you to specify which applications you want to permit through the filter, whereas filtering by IP addresses and hardware addresses enables you to block access by entire computers.

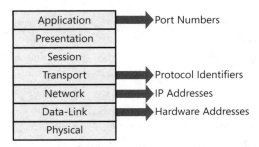

Application	→ Port Numbers
Presentation	
Session	
Transport	→ Protocol Identifiers
Network	→ IP Addresses
Data-Link	→ Hardware Addresses
Physical	

FIGURE 11-16 Packet filtering criteria and OSI model layers.

The real strength of using packet filtering as a security mechanism comes when you combine different types of filters to create a composite solution. For example, you might want to open up the Telnet port (port 23) so administrators can remotely manage the company web servers from home, using the Internet. However, leaving this port open is an invitation for unauthorized Internet users to access your servers. You could add an additional filter that limits port 23 access to only your administrators' IP addresses. This would protect the network without compromising the functionality that the administrators need.

There are two main drawbacks to using packet filtering as a security mechanism:

- Packet filtering requires a detailed understanding of TCP/IP communications and the ways of the criminal mind. Using packet filters to protect your network means participating in an ongoing battle with attackers. Intruders are constantly inventing new techniques to defeat standard packet filter configurations, and you must be ready to modify your filters to counteract these techniques.

- Packet filters can only detect attacks implemented in the packet headers; they do not examine the application data inside the packets. For example, you might configure the packet filters on your firewall to allow all port 80 traffic into the network so that Internet users can access your web server, but at the same time, you could be admitting packets that are designed to attack the web service itself. To examine the application layer data in the packets, you must use a proxy server.

Stateful Packet Inspection

Some packet-filtering firewalls include additional security capabilities, typically in the form of a technique called *stateful packet inspection*. Stateful packet inspection is a generic term for a process in which a router examines incoming packets more carefully than usual.

In a typical packet-filtering firewall, the router is concerned only with the basic criteria listed earlier, such as port and protocol numbers and IP addresses, when it examines packets. A firewall that supports stateful packet inspection examines other network and transport layer header fields as well, looking for patterns that indicate damaging behaviors, such as IP spoofing, SYN floods, and teardrop attacks. SYN floods and teardrop attacks are two forms of DoS attacks in which a target is bombarded with large numbers of packets containing TCP SYN flags or datagrams requiring fragmentation, respectively.

The router also tracks the connections between the systems generating packets by examining the Sequence Number values in the TCP headers. This enables the router to determine the current state of each connection. To gain admittance to the network, packets not only must meet the requirements of the packet filters, but they must also be part of a connection listed in the router's state table.

Because the router must examine each packet more carefully, firewalls that use stateful packet inspection are necessarily slower than simple packet-filtering firewalls. Firewalls with stateful packet inspection are usually also more expensive than firewalls without it.

Though there are some free stateful packet inspection firewalls, such as the Linux Netfilter module, most commercial products are quite costly. However, most commercial products include a graphical configuration interface and better documentation, which makes it easier to set up and maintain the firewall. Different manufacturers implement stateful packet inspection in different ways, so not all routers with this capability offer the same degree of protection.

EXAM TIP

Along with the firewall techniques covered in this section, the Network+ exam objectives also list another basic firewall technique, network address translation (NAT). For more information on NAT, see Chapter 7, "Routing and Switching."

Firewall Implementations

Firewalls typically take two forms, as follows:

- **Hardware firewall**   Also called a network-based firewall or a router firewall, this type of firewall is implemented as part of a router and protects the entire network to which it is connected from intrusions originating on another network.

- **Software firewall**   Also called a host-based firewall or a personal firewall, this type is implemented on a computer and protects only that computer from intrusions originating on the network.

EXAM TIP

With respect to firewalls, the Network+ exam uses the terms "software firewalls" and "hardware firewalls," which can sometimes be misleading. For example, a computer running Windows Server can function as a router, meaning that the Windows Firewall program is technically functioning as a hardware firewall—because it provides protection for an entire network—even though it is implemented as software.

Most routers have packet-filtering capabilities built into them, so you can implement filters at the boundaries between networks. The problem with integrating packet filters into a router is that the filters can introduce a large amount of overhead, slowing down the router's performance. The router must examine each incoming packet, compare it against all of the filters, and then decide whether to admit the packet to the network. If you have a large, complex system of filters, the amount of time needed for the router to process each packet can become a major network performance bottleneck.

When considering the processing overhead of packet filtering, you must decide where that overhead can best be managed. Implementing packet filters on an application server, for example, does not degrade overall network performance as router packet filtering does, but it can degrade the performance of that particular server's functions.

Most operating systems have a firewall with packet-filtering capabilities built into it, but the Windows Server operating systems actually have two. The Routing and Remote Access Service (RRAS) that the operating system uses to function as a router includes a packet-filtering mechanism with which you can create different filters for each network interface on the computer. With RRAS packet filtering, you can apply the following additional capabilities:

- Create filters based on the IP addresses, protocols, and port numbers of a packet's source or destination.
- Create inclusive or exclusive filters.
- Create filters for inbound or outbound traffic.
- Create filters for ICMP messages, specified by the message type and code values.
- Create multiple filters of the same type.

The interface you use to create packet filters in the Routing And Remote Access console is shown in Figure 11-17.

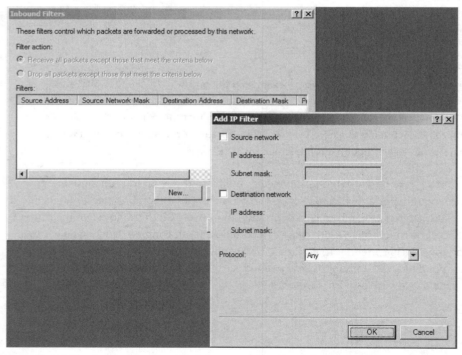

FIGURE 11-17 The Routing And Remote Access console's Inbound Filters and Add IP Filter dialog boxes.

All of the Windows operating systems also include Windows Firewall, which is an automated packet-filtering implementation that can control what network traffic enters and leaves the computer. Windows Firewall has two interfaces, a simpler one that is designed more for the end user, and a more comprehensive interface for administrators.

In the Windows Firewall control panel interface, as shown in Figure 11-18, users can select the programs and features that they want to admit through the firewall. The program then adjusts the packet filters accordingly, so the users do not have to be concerned with port and protocol numbers and other technical details.

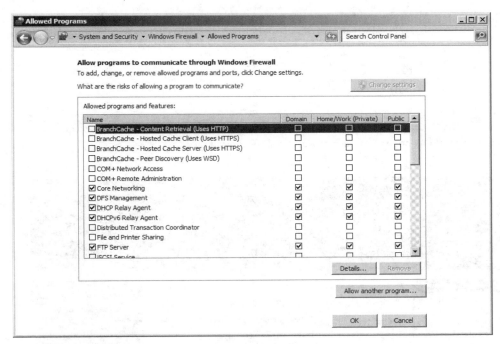

FIGURE 11-18 The Windows Firewall control panel interface.

The other interface is the Windows Firewall with Advanced Security snap-in for Microsoft Management Console (MMC). This snap-in provides a complete list of all the packet filters on the system, as shown in Figure 11-19, and with it you can activate and deactivate them, modify them, or create new filters of your own.

Most UNIX and Linux distributions have packet filtering built into the kernel, although the various operating systems have different tools for managing the filtering rules. For example, Berkeley Software Distribution (BSD) UNIX uses a tool called ipfw, whereas Linux uses iptables. Both of these are command-line tools with extensive sets of arguments and parameters.

Hardware routers have interfaces with similar capabilities to the ones provided by operating systems, but their ease of use can vary from product to product. The broadband routers designed for home and small business users have relatively simple interfaces like that shown in Figure 11-20. More advanced routers provide more comprehensive access and often require more knowledge from the administrator.

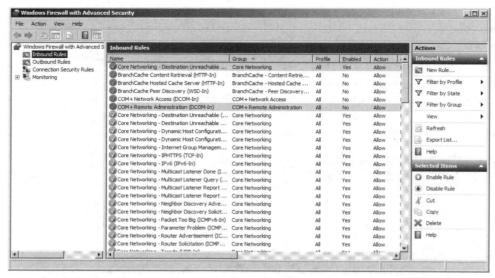

FIGURE 11-19 The Windows Firewall with Advanced Security snap-in.

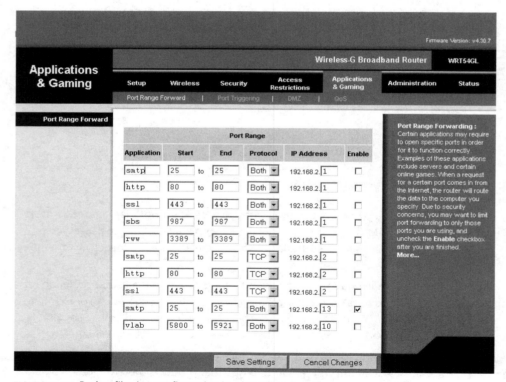

FIGURE 11-20 Packet-filtering configuration in a broadband router.

In addition to routers and operating systems, there are stand-alone firewall products you can run on any computer that also have packet-filtering capabilities. Firewall-based filters have the following two advantages:

- **Better performance** By implementing the routing and filtering functions on different systems, you are less likely to experience degraded network performance.

- **Increased filtering capabilities** Dedicated firewall products are likely to have more advanced packet-filtering capabilities, such as preset filter configurations designed to protect against specific types of attacks.

> *NOTE* **PACKET-FILTERING IMPLEMENTATIONS**
>
> The basic capabilities of most packet-filtering implementations are roughly the same; the differences are in the interface and the configurability of the filters. Two products might have the same packet-filtering capabilities, but one with preset configurations and detailed documentation will be easier to use than one that requires you to design filter configurations yourself and fully understand the TCP/IP communications processes that are affected by the filters you are creating.

Packet filtering is not a perfect security solution. Intruders can still attack a server by using the ports and protocols that the firewall lets through, or find a clever new way to bypass the filters you have in place. The trick to using packet filters effectively is to strike a balance between providing sufficient access to legitimate users and blocking enough traffic to provide protection.

In some cases, the creation of packet filters can be an ongoing battle of wits between the protector and a determined attacker. Every time the attacker finds a way to penetrate the filters, the system administrator modifies them to close the opening that is being exploited. Advanced packet filtering requires a detailed understanding of the TCP/IP protocols and the applications that use them.

Creating a Peripheral Network

Router-based firewalls are an integral part of building a network with concentric layers of security. The outermost layer, the one nearest to the Internet and the dangers it represents, is called a *peripheral network* or a *demilitarized zone (DMZ)*. The peripheral network is where you place the servers that must be accessible from the Internet, such as web, FTP, and SMTP servers, as shown in Figure 11-21. The router connecting this network to the Internet (or to an ISP's network) contains a firewall that you configure to admit the traffic that must reach these servers.

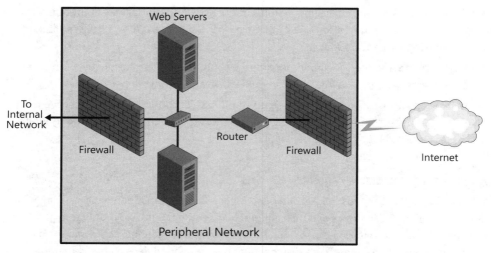

FIGURE 11-21 A peripheral network and the firewall between it and the Internet.

The peripheral network also has another router, which connects it to the innermost network, the one that contains the servers requiring the most protection, such as domain controllers, intranet servers, and file servers hosting confidential files. The firewall on this inner router blocks the traffic that the other firewall admits to the peripheral network. Therefore, users on the Internet can send request messages to the web servers on the peripheral network, but not to the intranet web servers on the inner network.

To create an effective peripheral network, administrators must be aware of the traffic that needs to pass between the outer network and the inner one. For example, if your web server runs an application that requires access to a database, you might want to locate the database server on the more secure inner network. In this case, you must configure the inner firewall to pass the database traffic, but exclude the web server traffic from the Internet.

Other Security Appliances

Firewalls are not the only devices that administrators can use to increase the security of a network. There are a variety of other tools and techniques that help to keep the sides even in the network security arms race. Some of these tools and techniques are discussed in the following sections.

Intrusion Detection Systems

A firewall is a static device, a filter that you configure and that admits or blocks traffic based on the criteria you select. A firewall of this type is not smart, in that the device does not know whether packets contain an attack or not. The firewall simply looks for specific bit patterns in specific areas of incoming packets and reacts accordingly.

An *intrusion detection system (IDS)* is a network protection product, implemented as hardware or software, that operates at a somewhat higher level on the scale of artificial intelligence. An IDS inspects incoming packets or system processes and examines them for evidence of malicious activity. When the IDS finds such evidence, it logs the activity, gathers information about the circumstances, and usually notifies an administrator by email or some other means.

There are two basic types of IDS, as follows:

- **Network-based IDS (NIDS)** A separate device, typically connected to a switch or router at a strategic network interface point, such as a peripheral network. A NIDS accesses network traffic, often by using a technique such as *port mirroring*, and examines the contents of packets, looking for patterns and data types typical of well-known attacks.

- **Host-based IDS (HIDS)** An application or agent running on a computer that analyzes system and application event logs, performs file integrity checks, and monitors registry modifications for evidence of malicious activity.

> ***NOTE* PORT MIRRORING**
> Because switches forward packets to their destinations only, it is not as easy to monitor all of the traffic on a network as it was with a hub. To address this shortcoming, some switches have a feature called *port mirroring*, which takes the form of a special port that runs in *promiscuous mode*. This means that the switch copies all incoming traffic to that port, as well as to the dedicated destination ports. By connecting an IDS or protocol analyzer to this port, an administrator can access all of the network traffic.

In both cases, the IDS includes an interface to a network management program or provides management capabilities of its own. The primary function of the product is to notify specified administrators when the system detects suspicious activity. Some IDS products are stand-alone applications, whereas others are distributed, meaning that they can have multiple information-gathering sensors or agents scattered around the network, all of which report their findings to a central management console.

NIDS products are *signature based*, meaning that they compare the data in the packets they scan to a library of known attack patterns, looking for matches that indicate problems. As new threats are discovered, the manufacturer of the product must update the signature files and release them in the form of updates. An NIDS must be current to be effective.

HIDS products work in a different manner, by tracking system performance patterns and establishing their own baselines. They then continue to monitor performance and note behavior that deviates substantially from those baselines. These types of products are said to be *behavior based*.

An IDS is only capable of detecting anomalous behavior on a network or a host; it can't do anything about the potential attacks it discovers. Other products, called *intrusion prevention systems (IPSes)* can, however. An IPS functions in much the same way as an IDS, except that it is also designed to take specific actions to prevent an attack when it detects one. Among other things, an IPS can discard packets, terminate connections, or create filters on the fly that prevent packets using certain ports or addresses from entering the network.

EXAM TIP

The Network+ exam distinguishes between IDS and IPS types in two ways: by location, using the terms "network-based" and "host-based," and by method, using the terms "behavior-based" and "signature-based." Candidates for the exam should be familiar with all four of these distinctions.

Honeypots

Learning about your adversary is one of the best ways to gain an advantage in any type of conflict. One of the tools that network administrators use to learn about the attacks that threaten them is the *honeypot*, a system designed to function as a lure for attackers.

Although the honeypot contains no actual data of any value, the administrator configures it with the correct applications and settings so that it looks as though it might. After it is in place, the honeypot sits on the network looking attractive to potential intruders.

In this role, the honeypot can be valuable in two ways. First, it functions as a decoy, drawing attacks on itself that could otherwise be directed at the network's actual resources. Second, the honeypot can gather information about the exact nature of the attacks, which can help the administrators bolster the network's defenses.

On a larger scale, administrators might set up several honeypot computers, to create a decoy server farm or workstation LAN, for the same purpose. This configuration is known as a *honeynet*.

Security Threats

Understanding the nature of the threats against a network is an essential part of building an effective strategy against them. The relationship between the attackers and the defenders is a type of arms race, with most of the attackers creating ever-different variations on a few familiar themes. The following sections describe some of the most basic attack concepts.

EXAM TIP

There are literally hundreds of security conditions that are a threat to a network, and administrators must protect against all of them. However, Network+ exam objectives only list a few of the major ones, as described in this section.

Denial of Service

The busier a service is, the longer it takes for customers to get their orders. This axiom applies as easily to networking as it does to retail. When a server is busy processing thousands of incoming requests, performance degrades and all of the clients suffer. A *denial of service (DoS)* attack is an attempt to provoke this very situation by flooding a server or an application with incoming traffic.

In the simplest form of DoS attack, an attacker can use the Ping utility to send an endlessly repeating stream of ICMP messages to a server and bring it to a near halt. This is why the default configuration on many firewalls blocks the ICMP Echo Request messages that Ping generates.

One particularly sneaky form of ICMP-based DoS attack—called a *smurf attack*—involves flooding a network with Ping messages sent to the network's broadcast address. These messages are also spoofed—the source address field contains the IP address of the computer that is the intended victim. This way all of the computers receiving the broadcast will send their responses to the victim, flooding its incoming buffers.

A DoS attack does not have to use ICMP messages, however. All a determined attacker has to do is find an open port on a server, after which it is not difficult to bombard it with some kind of traffic. Some attacks even use the type of traffic the server is designed to accept. For example, an attacker can flood a web server with incoming web requests, excluding the requests generated by legitimate users. In this case, the server administrator can't just close off port 80 in the firewall, because that would exclude all of the incoming traffic. The counter for this type of attack would be to discover where the flood is coming from and block it by its IP address.

A single computer can only transmit so many packets, limiting the potential effectiveness of an individual DoS attack against a large server farm. However, attackers who distribute a type of malware called a trojan can take control of other people's computers without them knowing it. These remote-controlled computers are called *bots* or *zombies*, and the hoard of zombies under one attacker's control is called a *botnet*. The attacker can use the zombies to generate DoS messages from hundreds of systems at once, overwhelming even the most robust application. This is called a *distributed denial of service (DDoS)* attack.

Man in the Middle

A *man in the middle (MITM)* attack is one in which the attacker interposes himself or herself between two individuals who think they are communicating with each other. The attacker receives the messages from each party in the transaction and relays them to the other party, but not without reading them, or even modifying them, first.

The attacker in a man in the middle attack must be able to receive all of the communications generated by both of the other parties to remain a convincing intermediary. While undetected, MITM attackers can use their access to obtain sensitive information, such as passwords and shared keys.

Detection of an MITM attack is sometimes possible through analysis of the latency periods between message transmissions and receipts. The sudden appearance of communication delays between two parties not attributable to other causes can indicate the presence of an intermediary. The best defense against MITM attacks is mutual authentication, such as that performed by PKI systems. In fact, these authentication systems were invented in part to counter this type of attack.

 A variation on the MITM attack, called an *FTP bounce* attack, involves the use of the Port command in the FTP protocol to gain access to ports in another computer that are otherwise blocked. After connecting to an FTP server, the attacker uses the commands within the FTP protocol, but directs them at a different computer. At one time, many FTP implementations could do this, but most developers have since closed this potentially exploitable opening.

Malware

 Malware is a generic term referring to any software that has a malicious intent, whether obvious or obscure. Some types of malware are relatively benign and are intended only to generate business for the distributor, whereas others are deliberate attempts to cause damage with no rational motive. The most common types of malware are as follows:

- **Virus** A type of program that replicates by attaching itself to an executable file or a computer's boot sector and performs a specified action—usually some form of damage—at a prearranged time. Viruses do not spread through a network by themselves; they require a user to run the infected program and load it into memory. Viruses might also replicate themselves through removable media, such as USB flash drives.

- **Worm** A program that replicates itself across a network by taking advantage of weaknesses in computer operating systems. Unlike a virus, a worm can replicate across a network without any user activity. Some worms do nothing more than consume network bandwidth, whereas others can damage files, generate spam email messages, or install a backdoor program, turning the target computer into a zombie.

- **Trojan horse** A nonreplicating program that appears to perform an innocent function but that in reality has another, more malicious, purpose. One common tactic is to insert code into a free game or other application, which turns the computer into a server by opening up specific ports to incoming traffic. This enables an attacker on the Internet to take control of the computer without the owner's knowledge and use it as a zombie for any purpose, including initiating distributed attacks against other targets.

- **Spyware** A hidden program that gathers information about your computer activities and sends it to someone on the Internet. Types of spyware can include *adware*, a relatively harmless program that tracks the Internet sites you visit for the purpose of sending you targeted advertisements, but others are more dangerous, such as those that record your keystrokes and other usage data, to capture your passwords and other sensitive information. Spyware is usually something the user downloads unknowingly, by clicking on a link in an email message or on a webpage.

- **Macro** Macros are application-specific scripts that users can write themselves to automate repetitive tasks. As an application iterates through numerous versions, its developers often strengthen the macro language, sometimes to the point at which it becomes a programming language in its own right. This increased capability enables attackers to exploit the application's macro capabilities and use them to create viruses that replicate and spread through the application.

EXAM TIP

The term "virus" is often inaccurately used as a catchall for various types of malware, including worms, trojan horses, and spyware. The primary characteristic that distinguishes a virus is its ability to replicate itself. The Network+ exam expects candidates to know the differences between the various malware types.

Buffer Overflow

A buffer is an area of computer memory designed to hold incoming data as it is being processed. A *buffer overflow* is a condition in which a program sends too much data to a buffer and it spills over into an area of memory intended for another purpose. The results of a buffer overflow depend on the application and the operating system, but they can include error messages, data corruption, or even a system crash.

Ordinarily the result of a programming error, buffer overflows are sometimes the result of people taking advantage of inherent weaknesses in operating systems or applications and writing code designed to deliberately cause buffer overflows to occur. These attackers can deliver the code to the target system in many different ways, including by viruses, worms, and trojans.

Social Engineering

Sometimes the easiest way for an attacker to obtain sensitive information is simply to ask for it. *Social engineering* is the term used to describe a practice in which a seemingly friendly attacker contacts a user by telephone, mail, or email; pretends to be an official of some sort; and gives some excuse for needing the user's password or other confidential information.

Most people are reasonably helpful by nature, and when someone asks for a favor they can easily perform, they do it. This is particularly true in a corporate environment, where a call from someone you don't know in another department is not unusual. An attacker with a friendly nature and a convincing story can often compel users to give up all sorts of valuable information.

Another, more refined form of this tactic, called *phishing,* consists of sending out an official-looking email message or letter to users that points them to a website containing a form asking for personal information. The email message might appear to be from a bank, a credit card company, or a government agency, and it might contain a request for help or a threat of some inconvenient action if the user does not comply with the instructions provided. The letter and website are, of course, bogus, and the confidential information the users supply goes right to the attacker.

Wireless Threats

As discussed earlier in this chapter, wireless networks have their own specialized security protocols, due to the specialized nature of the threats against them. As with the other threats discussed earlier, the continued development of greater security technologies drives certain people to constantly search for new weaknesses they can exploit.

Some of the most common threats against wireless networks are as follows:

- **War driving** Many wireless LANs today use some form of encryption, but that was not always the case. In the early days of wireless LANs, many people left their networks unprotected, making it possible for unauthorized users to connect to them and access their files or use their Internet connection. War driving is the process of cruising around a neighborhood with a scanner, looking for unprotected wireless networks available for connections.

- **War chalking** A practice associated with war driving in which the people discovering an unprotected network leave a mark on a wall or gatepost indicating its presence, so that future drivers can find it.

- **Cracking** The process of penetrating an encryption protocol by discovering its cryptographic key. An encryption protocol that cannot be cracked has not been invented; it is just a question of how long it will take and how much computing power can be devoted to it. All of the encryption protocols that wireless LANs use—WEP, WPA, and WPA2—are crackable with enough time and effort. The process basically consists of locating a wireless network, using a packet-sniffer program to capture some of its traffic, and then analyzing the contents of the packets to discover the keys used to encrypt them. Wireless network cracking tools are freely available on the Internet, so an attacker does not even have to possess the expertise needed to write them.

> **NOTE** **PACKET SNIFFERS**
>
> A packet sniffer is an application that intercepts and captures packets as they are transmitted over a network. Sniffers are legitimate tools for network administrators, but they are also just as valuable weapons for attackers. For more information, see Chapter 12, "Network Management."

- **Rogue access point** An unauthorized wireless access point connected to a network. This is arguably the greatest possible security hazard for a wireless network administrator, because its perpetrators are often innocents. A user wanting the convenience of wireless laptop access in the office purchases an inexpensive AP and plugs it into the network with no security enabled. This allows anyone in the area to access the wired network without anyone's knowledge.

- **Evil twin** An unauthorized wireless access point deliberately configured to closely mimic an authorized one. Users fooled by the impersonation connect to the access point, which provides the attacker with access to the packets and the data inside them.

Mitigation Techniques

Learning about the threats might be the first step in combatting them, but then the administrator has to devise a strategy for fighting back or preventing them in the first place. Threat mitigation is an ongoing process in which both sides continue to learn. However, there are several standard mitigation techniques that all network administrators should keep in mind, including the following:

- **Training and awareness** In many cases, successful attacks are the result of user error. A person clicks the wrong link, opens the wrong email message, or executes the wrong file, and the door admitting the intruder to the network is opened. Educating users about the potential dangers and what not to do when confronted with them is the best way to protect the network from intrusion.

- **Patch management** Attacks are often possible due to weaknesses in applications or operating systems, which intruders have learned to exploit. Software developers are constantly discovering new weaknesses, and they release updates to close the security holes that result. Keeping all of the computers on the network updated must be an essential part of an administrator's security regimen. In addition, all computers should be equipped with appropriate anti-malware software, which also must be updated on a regular basis.

- **Policies and procedures** For a network to run efficiently, there must be policies in place that govern what administrators and users should and should not do. Published policies can prevent many security breaches before they happen, and proper procedures can enable users to recognize security problems when they happen and take appropriate action.

- **Incident response** Policy should dictate how administrators respond to security-related events, and all threats and attacks should be carefully documented. A history of occurrences can provide evidence of an escalation of tactics, indicating that attackers are targeting the organization specifically.

Exercise

The answers for this exercise are located in the "Answers" section at the end of this chapter.

You are the network administrator at an advertising firm that has, to date, not deployed a Wi-Fi network. Several employees have brought the subject up at meetings, but the owner of the company, fearing security problems, has no intention of deploying a wireless network in the near future, if ever.

This official rejection of the idea has not entirely stopped the adoption of wireless technology, however. Yesterday, you noticed an employee using a laptop to surf the web in the lunchroom, without an Ethernet cable. When you asked the man how he was connecting to the net, he confessed that he had purchased an access point and plugged it into the network port in his office.

You must now explain to the owner why the company needs a wireless network security policy even if he does not want to install a wireless network. Answering the following questions will help you with your preparation.

1. Which of the following risks are posed to your organization by the presence of a rogue wireless network? (Choose all that apply.)

   A. An attacker could use a wireless network card to capture traffic between two wired network hosts.

   B. An attacker could access hosts on your internal network from the lobby of your building with a wireless-enabled laptop.

   C. An attacker could use your Internet connection from the lobby of your building with a wireless device.

   D. An attacker could capture an employee's email credentials as the employee downloads messages across the wireless link.

   E. An attacker with a wireless network card could join your Active Directory Domain Services domain.

2. Which of the following would reduce the risk of a security compromise resulting from a vulnerable rogue wireless network? (Choose all that apply.)

   A. Publishing a wireless network security policy allowing employee-managed access points that have authentication and encryption enabled

   B. Publishing a wireless network security policy forbidding employee-managed access points

   C. Publishing instructions for other employees to access the current employee-managed access point

   D. Deploying an IT-managed access point using open network authentication without encryption

   E. Deploying an IT-managed access point with WPA2 encryption and 802.1X authentication

   F. Educating internal employees about the risks associated with wireless networks

Chapter Summary

- Authentication is the process of verifying a user's identity, for the purpose of distinguishing legitimate users from uninvited guests. As such, it is one of the most prominent and most visible concepts in security.

- Authorization is the process of verifying what access to a protected resource an authenticated user should receive.

- To protect data stored on servers and transmitted over a network, computers use various types of encryption to encode messages and create digital signatures that verify their authenticity.

- Nonrepudiation is a method for ensuring that the communication you receive from a specific person actually originates from that person.

- Centralized authentication models provide much simpler management for larger networks, which lowers help desk costs related to account management.

- The most common AAA server implementation is Remote Authentication Dial In User Service (RADIUS).

- Services that perform authentication typically include support for a variety of authentication protocols so that they can service clients with differing capabilities.

- Remote access connections all use the Point-to-Point Protocol (PPP) at the data-link layer. PPP controls the authentication process by providing the remote access client and server with the means to negotiate an authentication protocol.

- Applications and operating systems can use security protocol standards to protect data as it is transmitted over the network. These protocols generally use specific types of data encryption and define how the communicating computers exchange the information needed to read each other's encrypted transmissions.

- IPsec is the term used to describe a series of draft standards that define a methodology for securing data as it is transmitted over a network.

- Secure Sockets Layer (SSL) is a special-purpose security protocol that protects the data transmitted by servers and their clients. Unlike IPsec, SSL operates at the application layer and can protect only the data generated by the specific applications for which it is implemented.

- Wired Equivalent Privacy (WEP) is a wireless security protocol that protects transmitted data by using a *shared secret*, a text string possessed by the access point and the client, as an encryption key.

- To address the weaknesses of WEP, the Wi-Fi Alliance developed a new encryption protocol called Wi-Fi Protected Access (WPA). Using the same authentication mechanisms and encryption algorithms, WPA virtually eliminates WEP's most exploited vulnerability by implementing a unique encryption key for each packet.

- A firewall is a hardware or software product that protects a network from unauthorized access by outside parties while letting appropriate traffic through.

- A denial of service (DoS) attack is an attempt to degrade the performance of a system by flooding it with incoming traffic.

Chapter Review

Test your knowledge of the information in Chapter 11 by answering these questions. The answers to these questions, and the explanations of why each answer choice is correct or incorrect, are located in the "Answers" section at the end of this chapter.

1. Is checking the birth date on your identification to prove that you are of age to purchase a product an example of authentication or authorization? Explain your answer.

2. Is showing your identification to a cashier to verify that the credit card you are using belongs to you an example of authentication or authorization? Explain your answer.

3. Which of the following protocols should you use to authenticate remote access users with smart cards?

    A. PAP

    B. PEAP

    C. EAP-TLS

    D. CHAP

    E. MS-CHAPv2

4. Which of the following IPsec protocols provides encryption for network communications?

    A. AH

    B. ESP

    C. IKE

    D. EAP

    E. ISAKMP

Answers

This section contains the answers to the questions for the Exercise and Chapter Review in this chapter.

Exercise

1. B, C, and D. Attackers can use a rogue access point that is poorly secured to access your internal network, capture wireless traffic, and use your Internet connection, but they cannot capture wired traffic or gain access to internal resources that require authentication.

2. A, B, E, and F. Deploying an IT-managed access point would be ideal because it would enable employees to take advantage of the benefits of wireless networks while minimizing the risks by allowing IT to configure authentication and encryption. Additionally, educating employees and publishing a security policy reduces the risk that an employee will configure an unprotected access point.

Chapter Review

1. **Correct Answer: Authorization**. In this example, your identity is not being validated—only whether you are old enough to be authorized to complete the purchase.

2. **Correct Answer: Authentication**. In this example, the cashier needs to validate that you are who you claim to be—and your appearance matching the photo and description on your identification card is sufficient proof of that.

3. **Correct Answer: C**

   A. **Incorrect:** PAP only supports password-based authentication.

   B. **Incorrect:** PEAP only supports password-based authentication.

   C. **Correct:** The only remote access authentication protocol that supports the use of smart cards is the Extensible Authentication Protocol with Transport Layer Security (EAP-TLS).

   D. **Incorrect:** CHAP only supports password-based authentication.

   E. **Incorrect:** MS-CHAPv2 only supports password-based authentication.

4. **Correct Answer:** B

    A. **Incorrect:** Authenticated Header (AH) provides integrity checking and other services, but not encryption.

    B. **Correct:** Only Encapsulated Security Protocol (ESP) provides encryption for IPsec communications.

    C. **Incorrect:** The Internet Key Exchange (IKE) protocol provides key exchange services; it does not provide encryption.

    D. **Incorrect:** The Extensible Authentication Protocol (EAP) is a remote access protocol, not an IPsec protocol.

    E. **Incorrect:** The Internet Security Association and Key Management Protocol (ISAKMP) provides the means for systems to create and manage security associations; it does not in itself provide encryption.

CHAPTER 12

Network Management

Network management is a term that encompasses a variety of technologies, techniques, and policies that administrators implement during and after network implementation. In some cases, the ability to manage a network effectively after it is installed is dependent on decisions made prior to and during the installation of the network.

Exam objectives in this chapter:

Objective 1.6: Explain the function of common networking protocols.

- TCP
- FTP
- UDP
- TCP/IP suite
- DHCP
- TFTP
- DNS
- HTTPS
- HTTP
- ARP
- SIP (VoIP)

- RTP (VoIP)
- SSH
- POP3
- NTP
- IMAP4
- Telnet
- SMTP
- SNMP2/3
- ICMP
- IGMP
- TLS

Objective 1.9: Identify virtual network components.

- Virtual switches
- Virtual desktops
- Virtual servers

- Virtual PBX
- Onsite vs. offsite
- Network as a Service (NaaS)

Objective 4.1: Explain the purpose and features of various network appliances.

- Load balancer
- Proxy server

- Content filter
- VPN concentrator

Objective 4.4: Given a scenario, use the appropriate network monitoring resource to analyze traffic.

- SNMP
- SNMPv2
- SNMPv3
- Syslog
- System logs

- History logs
- General logs
- Traffic analysis
- Network sniffer

Objective 4.5: Describe the purpose of configuration management documentation.

- Wire schemes
- Network maps
- Documentation
- Cable management

- Asset management
- Baselines
- Change management

Objective 4.6: Explain different methods and rationales for network performance optimization.

- Methods:
  - QoS
  - Traffic shaping
  - Load balancing
  - High availability
  - Caching engines
  - Fault tolerance
  - CARP

- Reasons:
  - Latency sensitivity
  - High bandwidth applications (VoIP, video applications, unified communications)
  - Uptime

Network Documentation

When maintaining a home or small office network, it is sometimes possible for an administrator to work "on the fly," dealing with issues as they arise, solving problems as they happen, and keeping all of the details about the network in his or her head. When you get beyond a four-node or five-node network, however, this method becomes increasingly unmanageable. You begin to forget some of the details, things slip by that you should have remembered, and you find yourself repeating tasks unnecessarily.

In truth, this network management philosophy is impractical and unprofessional for even the smallest network. Documentation is a critical part of any network management plan, and the time to start thinking about it is well before you install your first network hardware. The planning phase of the network must also be documented, so that the people who have to work on it later know what has been done.

There are many types of documentation that network administrators use and maintain. How and in what form you choose to create these documents is a matter of personal preference and company policy, but the important factor is that everyone involved in the network management and administration processes knows where the documentation is and can access it.

Some of the most important types of network documentation are described in the following sections.

Cable Diagrams

Documentation of your network's cable installation is particularly important, both because much of it is probably hidden from view and because your organization probably had an outside contractor install it. The purpose of having this documentation is so that if something goes wrong with a cable run, or if you want to expand the network, you know where the existing hardware is and don't have to go poking holes in walls and lifting ceilings for nothing.

> **REAL WORLD**   **CABLING DOCUMENTATION**
>
> A company I worked for early in my career had its Ethernet cabling installed by what appeared to be a reputable contractor. The contractor's workers were friendly, appeared on time, did a neat job, and cleaned up after themselves. Some months later, after experiencing chronic network delays and outages that were affecting production, I got a ladder and started examining the cable runs in the drop ceilings, because we were given no documentation by the installers. I found coaxial cables wired in rings, not buses; I found T-connectors (which should only be attached to computers) in the ceiling, attached to each other with barrel connectors; I found unterminated cable ends. In short, my findings made it clear that the installers had no conception of how a coaxial Ethernet network should be installed. Had we asked for and obtained a cable installation diagram before the work began, we might have been able to head off a very expensive problem.

In many cases, the best way to ensure that you have all of the documentation you need is to begin with the five classic questions posed by journalists: who, what, where, when, and how. In the case of a cable installation, ask yourself the following:

- **Who installed it?**   If the cables were installed by an outside contractor, you must have contact information for them and copies of the original contract. Every aspect of the arrangement should be documented; no oral agreements.

- **What was installed?**   Your documentation should include a complete list of all the hardware used in the cable installation, including the bulk cable itself and all connectors, wall plates, patch panels, and other components. Save receipts and invoices attesting to the rating of the cable components. If a contractor agrees to use CAT6 hardware throughout the installation, that contractor should provide documentation to prove that CAT6 was indeed used.

- **Where was it installed?** A wiring schematic or cabling diagram is essential to your document collection. Cable installers must document the exact path of every cable run through walls, floors, and ceilings. The best way to accomplish this is to obtain a copy of the original plan or blueprint for the site and add the cable runs to it. Documents should also record the numbers assigned to each cable end and connector (because that sticky note attached to the patch panel might someday fall off).

- **When was it installed?** For warranty purposes and to track conformance to ever-changing standards, you should record when your cables were installed, especially if you installed different parts of the network at different times.

- **How was it installed?** It is essential to record the decisions made during the cable installation process, such as whether the pinouts conform to the T568A or T568B standard. This enables you to ensure that future cabling work in the network conforms to the same standards.

EXAM TIP

The Network+ exam objectives have used differing terminology for this information throughout the years. The most recent objectives refer to "wire schemes," whereas the N10-004 objectives called them "wiring schematics." Be prepared to see either term on the exam.

Network Diagrams

The terminology is not always consistent, but a network diagram differs from a cable diagram in that its intention is to illustrate the relationships between network components; it is not usually drawn to scale and does not necessarily include architectural elements of the site, such as walls, ducts, and fixtures.

What a network diagram does have is a representation of every device and component on the network and all the connections between them. This means that the diagram includes not only computers, but all of the switches, routers, access points, wide area network (WAN) devices, and other hardware components that make up the network infrastructure, as shown in Figure 12-1.

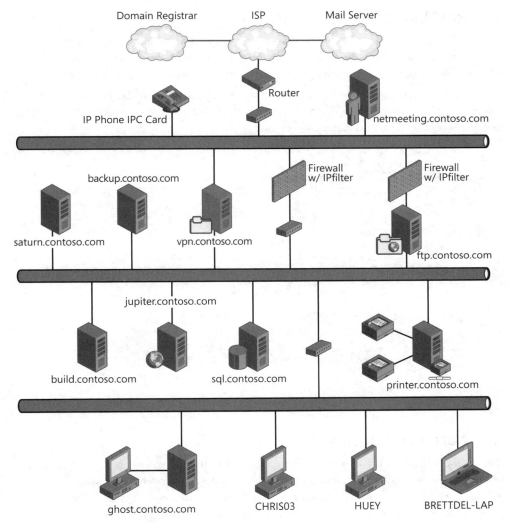

FIGURE 12-1 A network diagram created with Microsoft Visio.

There are numerous software tools you can use to create network diagrams, the most popular of which is probably Microsoft Visio. In most cases, these products use generic icons to represent network hardware components, but there are packages that provide genuine depictions of specific products, enabling you to create a realistic diagram of the racks in your data center, for example.

Network Maps

Network diagrams typically specify only the names assigned to components and depict the connections between them. A network map provides more detail, such as the IP addresses and/or hardware addresses of each component and the speeds at which links operate.

There are several utilities that can automatically create a network map by scanning a network and reading its properties. A map created by the graphical interface for the Nmap utility (covered later in this chapter) is shown in Figure 12-2.

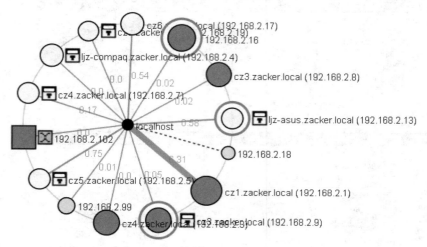

FIGURE 12-2 A network map created with Nmap.

Hardware Configurations

When a new software product is released, and it looks as though you might have to upgrade the hardware in some of your computers to run it, how do you know for sure which computers need the upgrade and which can support it without? There are various tools that can inventory the hardware in your computers, but how many of them can tell you whether a system has memory slots free or room for an expansion card?

The best way to keep track of your computers and their configurations is to document them yourself. Large enterprise networks typically assign their own identification numbers to their computers and other hardware purchases as part of an asset management process that controls the entire life cycle of each device, from recognition of a need to retirement or disposal.

The record for each device should contain all available information about it, including the original documentation for the computer, an inventory of its internal components, and detailed information about its software configuration. This way, anyone seeking to upgrade or troubleshoot the computer can find out what's inside without having to travel to the site and open the case.

The record for each computer should also document any changes that administrators make to it, whether in the hardware or software, so that the information is continually updated.

Change Management

A properly documented network also has written policies regarding how things are supposed to be done. When an administrator troubleshoots a computer, for example, and in doing so replaces a hard drive, there should be more to it than taking the drive out of the box and installing it in the computer. There should be a *change management* policy that leads the administrator through all the ancillary tasks related to the hard drive replacement.

For example, the administrator might have to update the parts inventory to show one less drive in stock; check the warranty status of the failed drive and, if necessary, file a claim; update the computer's record with the serial number and characteristics of the new drive; rebuild the user's local data from backups; and any number of other related tasks.

The same sort of documents should be on file for network-related tasks, including expansions and upgrades, so that the policies used to build the network in the first place are maintained throughout its life cycle.

Baselines

One of the basic principles of network management is to observe and address any changes that might occur in the performance of a system, whether it is a computer or a network. You do this by comparing the system's performance levels at various times. A *baseline* is the starting point for these comparisons.

You can use any tools or any criteria that you want to measure performance. Windows includes a Performance Monitor tool that can display information about hundreds of different system and network performance characteristics, called *counters*, as shown in Figure 12-3. There are also many third-party products.

> **NOTE** **PERFORMANCE MONITOR NAMES**
> Although its functionality has remained largely the same, Performance Monitor has gone by various names in different versions of Windows. In Windows XP, it is called System Monitor. In Windows Vista, the tool is Reliability and Performance Monitor. In Windows 7, it is just Performance Monitor.

In addition to displaying performance data in real time, as shown in the figure, Performance Monitor can also capture data to log files—called *data collector sets*, in some versions—over extended periods of time. To capture an effective baseline, you might want to capture data over the course of several hours, days, or even longer.

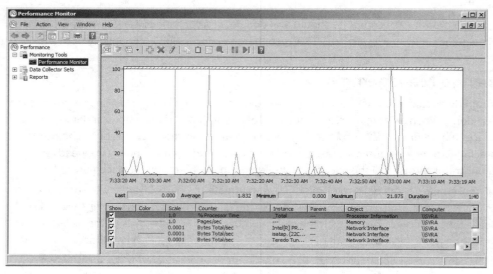

FIGURE 12-3 A Windows Performance Monitor graph.

What is most important is that you document both your exact testing procedure and the initial results of your tests, which will function as your baseline for future comparisons. These documents should become part of the permanent record for the system.

At regular intervals, you should then repeat your tests, using the same tools and the same procedures, and compare the results to your previous ones. If you find major discrepancies between your new results and your earlier ones, you should make an effort to determine why. This basic technique can help you to identify trends in performance that enable you to address problems before they become severe.

EXAM TIP

The Network+ exam does not require candidates to know precisely how to operate Performance Monitor or any other specific data capturing tool. Candidates should, however, understand the concept of the baseline and how it can benefit them as administrators.

Network Monitoring

The activities of a network are, by nature, hidden from view unless you use special tools to observe them. There are a variety of tools that administrators can use to gather information about what is happening on a network and display it for analysis. Some of these tools require an extensive investment in compliant hardware, whereas others require a considerable level of expertise from the operator. Some of the most common network monitoring tools are described in the following sections.

Logs

The most common method for monitoring network activities is by examining logs. A log is simply a chronological list of events that have occurred, generated by a process and sent to a specified destination. Many network components generate log entries, including operating systems, applications, routers, and other devices.

Log entries are a form of one-way message that hardware and software devices are configured to send, either at regular intervals or when specific events occur. No response from the recipient is expected or desired; any action taken as a result of a log entry is left entirely to the consumer.

Logs typically take the form of individual entries saved to text files, many of which can be lengthy and cryptic in nature. That is why there are many tools for interpreting logs, displaying them in a friendlier manner, and culling out the most important information. For the administrator, the most common problem with using logs for network monitoring is that they contain too much information, not too little.

Some of the most commonly used logging tools are described in the following sections.

Syslog

One of the oldest tools for the generation of logs is called syslog. Syslog was developed in the 1980s for use with sendmail, the de facto standard in Simple Mail Transfer Protocol (SMTP) mail servers. Syslog is a protocol designed to send log entries generated by a device or process called a *facility* across an IP network to a message collector, called a syslog server.

Syslog messages begin with two numerical codes. The first code identifies the facility that generated the message, some examples of which are as follows:

- **0** Kernel messages
- **1** User-level messages
- **2** Mail system
- **3** System daemons
- **4** Security/authorization messages
- **5** Messages generated internally by syslog

- **6** Line printer subsystem
- **7** Network news subsystem
- **8** UUCP subsystem
- **9** Clock daemon
- **10** Security/authorization messages
- **11** FTP daemon
- **12** NTP subsystem

The second code uses the following values to specify the severity of the message:

- **0** Emergency: system is unusable
- **1** Alert: action must be taken immediately
- **2** Critical: critical conditions
- **3** Error: error conditions
- **4** Warning: warning conditions
- **5** Notice: normal but significant condition
- **6** Informational: informational messages
- **7** Debug: debug-level messages

Subsequent parts of the syslog message format include a structured data section, which contains information in a format easily parsable by other software entities, and a free-form message section intended to carry more specific information about the event.

Syslog has become ubiquitous on the UNIX and Linux platforms and is common on other operating systems as well, including Windows.

Event Viewer

In UNIX and Linux operating systems, logs are traditionally text files, but the Windows operating systems use a graphical application called Event Viewer to display the log information gathered by the operating system and certain applications running on it.

All computers running Windows maintain the same basic logs. These are essentially *system logs* that display information about operating system events, application activities, and serious system errors. Servers performing certain roles have additional logs, such as those tracking directory service and replication activities.

In Windows Server 2008 and Windows Vista, Microsoft gave the Windows eventing engine its most comprehensive overhaul in many years. Windows Eventing 6.0 includes the following enhancements:

- A new, XML-based log format
- The addition of a Setup log documenting the operating system's installation and configuration history

- New logs for key applications and services, including DFS Replication and the Key Management Service

- Individual logs for Windows components

- Enhanced querying capabilities that simplify the process of locating specific events

- The ability to create subscriptions that enable administrators to collect and store specific types of events from other computers on the network

The primary function of the Windows Eventing engine is to record information about system activities as they occur and package that information in individual units called *events*. When you launch the Event Viewer console, you see the Overview And Summary display shown in Figure 12-4.

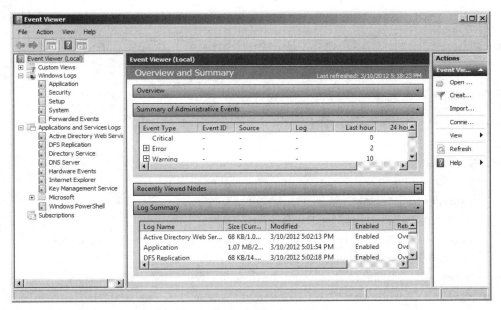

FIGURE 12-4 The Overview And Summary display in the Event Viewer console.

The Summary Of Administrative Events displays the total number of events recorded in the past hour, day, and week, sorted by event type. When you expand an event type, the list is broken down by event ID, as shown in Figure 12-5.

When you double-click one of the event IDs, the console creates a filtered custom view that displays only the events having that ID.

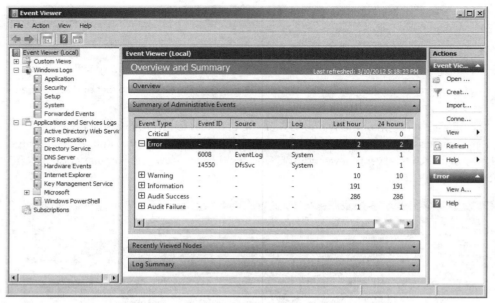

FIGURE 12-5 The event ID breakdown in the Event Viewer console.

VIEWING WINDOWS LOGS

When you expand the Windows Logs folder, you see the following logs:

- **Application**   Contains information about specific programs running on the computer, as determined by the application developer.

- **Security**   Contains information about security-related events, such as failed logons, attempts to access protected resources, and success or failure of audited events.

- **Setup**   Contains information about the operating system installation and setup history.

- **System**   Contains information about events generated by the operating system, such as services and device drivers. For example, a failure of a service to start or a driver to load during system startup is recorded in the System log.

- **Forwarded Events**   Contains events received from other computers on the network via subscriptions.

NOTE **SYSTEM LOG**

The System log is the primary Windows operational log. You should always view this log first when looking for general information about system problems.

Selecting one of the logs causes a list of the events it contains to appear, in reverse chronological order, as shown in Figure 12-6.

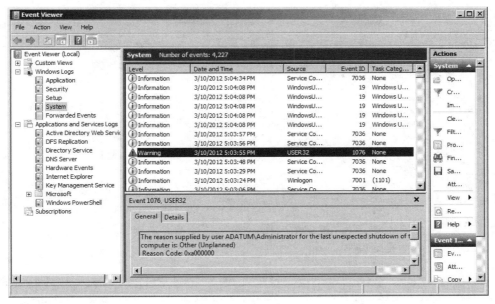

FIGURE 12-6 Contents of a log in the Event Viewer console.

The Windows event logs contain different types of events, which are identified by icons. The four event types are as follows:

- **Information** An event that describes a change in the state of a component or process as part of a normal operation

- **Error** An event that warns of a problem that is not likely to affect the performance of the component or process where the problem occurred, but that could affect the performance of other components or processes on the system

- **Warning** An event that warns of a service degradation or an occurrence that can potentially cause a service degradation in the near future, unless steps are taken to prevent it

- **Critical** An event that warns that an incident resulting in a catastrophic loss of functionality or data in a component or process has occurred

When you select one of the events in the list of events, its properties appear in the preview pane at the bottom of the list. You can also double-click an event to display a separate Event Properties dialog box, as shown in Figure 12-7.

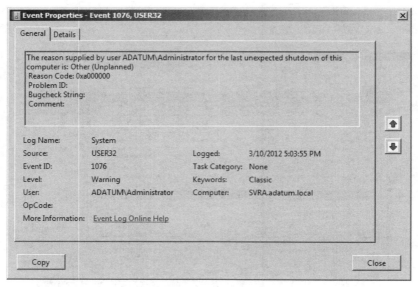

FIGURE 12-7 An Event Properties dialog box.

Because they present events chronologically, all of the Windows logs—and nearly all logs of any type—are *history logs*. However, by using a feature called auditing, you can use the Security log in Windows to maintain a detailed history of specific events, such as when particular users log on and log off.

Auditing is turned off by default, because it has the capability to generate an enormous amount of log information. To activate it, you must configure the appropriate Group Policy settings to specify what types of events you want to audit. Those events then appear in Event Viewer, in the Security log.

VIEWING COMPONENT LOGS

The Event Viewer console contains a great deal of information, and one of the traditional problems for administrators is finding the events they need in a very long list. Windows Eventing 6.0 includes several innovations that can help in this regard.

One of these innovations is the addition of component-specific logs that you can use to examine the events for a particular operating system component or application. Any component that is capable of recording events in the System log or Application log can also record events in a separate log dedicated solely to that component.

The Event Viewer console comes preconfigured with a large collection of component logs. When you expand the Applications And Services Logs folder, you see logs for Windows applications such as Internet Explorer. Then, when you expand the Microsoft and Windows folders, you see a long list of Windows components. Each of these components has its own separate log, called a *channel*.

In most cases, the events in the component logs are nonadministrative, meaning that they are not indicative of problems or errors. The components continue to save their administrative events to the System log or Application log. The events in the component logs are operational, analytic, or debug events, meaning that they are descriptive entries that document the ongoing activities of the component. The component logs are intended more for use in troubleshooting long-term problems and for software developers seeking debugging information.

CREATING CUSTOM VIEWS

Another means of locating and isolating information about specific events is to use custom views. A custom view is essentially a filtered version of a particular log, configured to display only certain events. The Event Viewer console now has a Custom Views folder in which you can create filtered views and save them for later use.

SUBSCRIBING TO EVENTS

The Event Viewer console can provide an enormous amount of information about a computer running Windows, but for an administrator responsible for hundreds of workstations, this can be too much information to handle. You can use the Event Viewer console on one computer to connect to another computer and display its logs, but although this can save network administrators some travel time, it is hardly practical for them to check logs on hundreds of computers on a regular basis.

The Event Viewer console provides a better solution for enterprise network administrators: subscriptions. By using subscriptions, administrators can receive events from other computers (called *sources*) in the Event Viewer console on their own computers (called *collectors*).

Windows Eventing supports two types of subscriptions, as follows:

- **Collector-initiated**   The collector computer retrieves events from the source computer. This type of subscription is intended for smaller networks, because you must configure all of the computers manually.

- **Source-computer–initiated**   The source computer sends events to the collector computer. Designed for larger networks, this type of subscription uses Group Policy settings to configure the source computers.

You create subscriptions in the Event Viewer console, but before you can do so, you must configure both the source and collector to run the appropriate services needed for communication between the computers.

SNMP

When an application or an operating system experiences a problem, it usually generates an error message. You can easily monitor these error messages by reviewing logs, but receiving error messages from other network components, such as routers and switches, can be more difficult.

A stand-alone router doesn't have a screen on which it can display error messages, but it does usually have an administrative interface accessible through a remote connection. However, even with this capability, it is difficult for an administrator who is responsible for dozens or hundreds of devices to monitor them all. In this case, it is possible to arrange for many networking devices to supply administrators with information about their status.

Network management products are designed to provide administrators with a comprehensive view of network systems and processes, by using a distributed architecture based on a specialized management protocol, such as the Simple Network Management Protocol (SNMP) or the Remote Monitoring (RMON) protocol.

 The *Simple Network Monitoring Protocol (SNMP)* is a TCP/IP application layer protocol and query language that specially equipped networking devices use to communicate with a central console. Many of the networking hardware and software products on the market, including routers, switches, network adapters, operating systems, and applications, are equipped with SNMP agents.

> **NOTE MANAGED DEVICES**
>
> The language used by hardware and software manufacturers to identify SNMP-capable devices is not consistent, but whenever you see a network interface adapter, switch, router, access point, or other device that purports to be managed or that claims to have network management capabilities, this means that the device includes an SNMP agent.

An *SNMP agent* is a software module that is responsible for gathering information about a device and delivering it to a computer that has been designated as the network management console. The agents gather specific information about the network devices and store them as managed objects in a *management information base (MIB)*. At regular intervals, the agents transmit their MIBs to the console by using SNMP messages, which are carried inside User Datagram Protocol (UDP) datagrams. The agents use UDP port 161, and the management console uses port 162.

SNMP Versions

The first version of the SNMP standard, which the Internet Engineering Task Force (IETF) published in 1988 as RFC 1065, RFC 1066, and RFC 1067, provides the protocol's basic functionality but is hampered by shortcomings in security. SNMPv1 messages contain no protection other than a community string, which functions as a password, and which the systems transmit in cleartext.

SNMPv2, released in 1993, added some improvements in functionality. One such improvement was a new protocol data unit (PDU) called GetBulkRequest that enables systems to send large amounts of management data in a single message, rather than using multiple GetNextRequest PDUs.

Version 2 also included a new security system that many people criticized as being overly complex. Such was the resistance to this system that an interim version appeared, called SNMPv2c, which consisted of SNMPv2 without the new security system, and with the old version 1 community string instead.

In 2002, the IETF published an SNMP standard with a workable security solution, which became version 3 and was ratified as an Internet standard. SNMPv3 includes all of the standard security services that administrators have come to expect, including authentication, message integrity, and encryption. Many network management products that implement SNMPv3 also include support for the earlier, unprotected versions, such as SNMPv1 and SNMPv2c.

The network management console processes the information that it receives from the agents in SNMP messages and provides the administrator with a composite picture of the network and its processes. The console software can usually create a map of the interconnections between network devices, as well as display detailed log information for each device. When there is a serious problem, an agent can generate a special message called a *trap*, which it transmits immediately to the console, causing it to alert the administrator of a potentially dangerous condition. In many cases, the console software can be configured to send alerts to administrators in a variety of ways, including by email and text messaging.

In addition to their network reporting capabilities, network management products can provide other functions, including the following:

- Software distribution and metering
- Network diagnostics
- Network traffic monitoring
- Report generation

Network management products are available with a wide range of abilities, ranging from relatively modest open-source packages to extremely complex and expensive commercial products.

Deploying a network management system is a complex undertaking. These systems are intended for administrators of large networks who can't possibly monitor all of their network devices individually. To use a product like this effectively, for example, you must be sure that all of the equipment you purchase when designing and building your network supports the network management protocol you intend to use. However, products like these can greatly simplify the tasks of network administrators and can often bring serious problems to their attention before they cause outages.

Protocol Analyzers

A protocol analyzer—sometimes called a *packet sniffer*—is one of the most powerful tools for learning about, understanding, and monitoring network communications. A protocol analyzer captures a sample of the traffic passing over the network, decodes the packets into the language of the individual protocols they contain, and lets you examine them in minute detail. Some protocol analyzers can also compile network traffic statistics, such as the number of packets that are using each protocol and the number of collisions that are occurring on the network.

Using a protocol analyzer to capture and display network traffic is relatively easy, but interpreting the information that the analyzer presents and using it to troubleshoot the network requires a detailed understanding of the protocols running on the network. However, there is no better way to acquire this type of knowledge than to examine the actual data transmitted over a live network.

> **NOTE** **ANALYZER CAUTIONS**
>
> Protocol analyzers are useful tools in the hands of experienced network administrators, but they can also be used for malicious purposes. In addition to displaying the information in the captured packets' protocol headers, the analyzer can also display the data carried inside the packets. This can sometimes include confidential information, such as unencrypted passwords and personal correspondence. Be aware that unsecured communications might be viewable by unintended parties, and avoid their use, if possible.

A protocol analyzer is typically a software product that runs on a computer connected to a network. On an Ethernet network that uses hubs, protocol analyzers work by switching the network interface adapter that they use to access the network into promiscuous mode. When a network interface adapter is in *promiscuous mode*, it reads and processes all the traffic that is transmitted over the network, not just the packets that are addressed to it. This means that the system can examine all of the traffic transmitted on the network from one computer.

On today's networks, however, switches are more common than hubs, and as a result, capturing traffic for the entire network is more difficult. Because switches forward incoming unicast traffic only to its intended recipient, a protocol analyzer connected to a standard switch port only has access to one computer's incoming and outgoing traffic, plus any broadcasts transmitted over the local network segment.

To capture all of the traffic transmitted on the network, you must plug the computer running the protocol analyzer into a switch that supports port mirroring. Switches that support port mirroring have a special port to which they send all incoming traffic.

The most commonly used protocol analyzer is the Microsoft Network Monitor application, mostly because it is available as a free download from the Microsoft website. There are many other protocol analyzer products available for Windows, UNIX, and Linux. The analyzers for Windows are all graphical and provide varying capabilities. For UNIX and Linux, both commercial and open-source protocol analyzers are available, some of which are character based (such as tcpdump), whereas others are graphical. There are also some dedicated hardware products that are essentially special-purpose computers with the analyzer software already installed.

The following sections examine the basic functions of a protocol analyzer, using Network Monitor as an example.

Capturing Traffic

The first step of a protocol analysis is to capture a sample of the network traffic. Network Monitor uses the window shown in Figure 12-8 to control the sampling process.

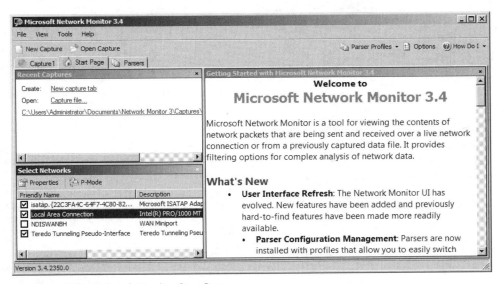

FIGURE 12-8 The Network Monitor Start Page.

After selecting the network interface that you want to use (if there is more than one), you can open a new capture tab and start capturing packets. The program reads the incoming and outgoing packets on the selected network interface and stores them in a buffer for later examination. Depending on your intentions, you can capture a small sample to examine a particular packet type or leave the program running for an extended period to generate an overall picture of the network's traffic pattern.

Protocol analyzers, like log files and performance monitors, can offer a huge amount of information, so the trick to using Network Monitor effectively is zeroing in on what you actually need. When you connect a protocol analyzer to a mirrored port on a busy network, a capture of only a few seconds can yield thousands of packets generated by dozens of systems. Protocol analyzers have filters with which you can select the packets you want to capture by using several criteria, such as the source computer address, the destination computer address, the protocols carried inside the packets, and the information found in the packets. For example, if you are having a problem establishing Hypertext Transfer Protocol (HTTP) connections to your web server, you can use the Capture Settings dialog box, shown in Figure 12-9, to create and apply a filter that captures TCP packets addressed to port 80 only, because that is the port used for HTTP communications.

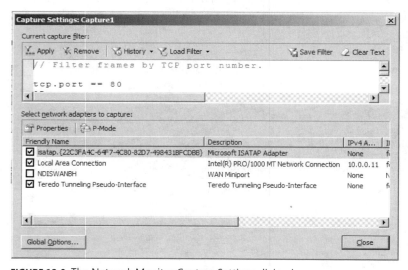

FIGURE 12-9 The Network Monitor Capture Settings dialog box.

You can also use the same interface to create a filter isolating the traffic addressed to your web server. Together, the two filters will limit the packets captured to those addressed to port 80 and destined for your web server.

When you specify capture filters, you get a much smaller traffic sample that contains less of the extraneous information generated by other network processes. For example, if you want to learn how much network traffic is generated by Address Resolution Protocol (ARP) transactions, you can create a filter configuration that captures only ARP traffic for a specific period of time, and then you can work out the number of megabits per hour devoted to ARP from the size of your captured sample. In Network Monitor, the Capture Settings dialog box displays the combination of filters you have chosen and enables you to save capture filter configurations to reuse later.

Displaying Captured Traffic

After you have captured a network traffic sample, a list of packets appears in the Frame Summary pane, as shown in Figure 12-10.

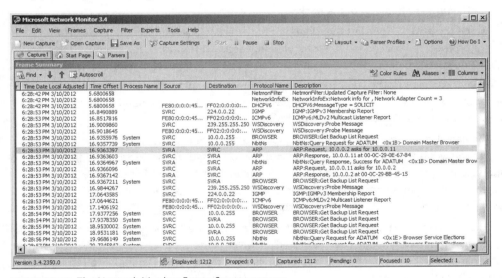

FIGURE 12-10 The Network Monitor Frame Summary pane.

This pane displays a chronological list of the packets in your sample, including the following information:

- **Frame Number**   Shows the number of the frame (or packet) in the sample.
- **Time Date**   Indicates the time and date that the packet was captured.
- **Time Offset**   Indicates the time (in seconds) that the packet was captured, measured from the beginning of the sample.
- **Process Name**   Identifies the process that generated the packet.
- **Source**   Specifies the name or IP address of the network interface in the computer that transmitted the packet.
- **Destination**   Specifies the name or IP address of the network interface in the computer that received the packet.
- **Protocol Name**   Identifies the dominant protocol in the packet. Each packet contains information generated by protocols running at several different layers of the Open Systems Interconnection (OSI) reference model. The protocol specified here indicates the primary function of the packet.
- **Description**   Specifies the function of the packet, using information specific to the protocol referenced in the Protocol field. For an HTTP packet, for example, this field indicates whether the packet contains an HTTP GET Request or a Response message.

From this main display, you can track the progress of transactions between specific pairs of computers on your network. For example, you can see that an exchange of ARP messages between two systems consists of a request and a response.

You can also use the frame summary display to perform a traffic analysis of the network. *Traffic analysis* is a technique for deriving information based on the pattern and frequency of messages transmitted over a network, rather than their contents. For example, a marked increase in the number of incoming packets addressed to a web server is significant in itself, even if you do not know the contents of the packets.

To zero in on a particular message exchange, you can use Network Monitor to apply filters to samples that have already been captured, as well as before the capture begins. The Display Filter pane uses the same interface as that for capture filters. When you apply a display filter, you see only the packets that conform to the parameters you have chosen. The other packets are still there in the captured sample; they are just not being displayed. You can modify the filter at any time to display more or less data.

When you select one of the packets listed in the Frame Summary pane, the frame details and Hex Details panes display the contents of the selected packet, as shown in Figure 12-11.

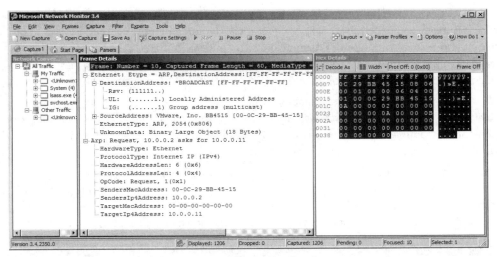

FIGURE 12-11 The Network Monitor Frame Details and Hex Details panes.

The Frame Details pane contains the contents of the selected packet in a fully interpreted, expandable display. The Hex Details pane contains the raw, uninterpreted contents of the packet in hexadecimal and alphanumeric form.

The Frame Details pane is where you can learn the most about the contents of each packet. The analyzer interprets the data in the packet and separates it into the headers for the protocols operating at the OSI model layers. Clicking the plus sign next to a protocol expands it to display the contents of the various header fields.

The Hex Details pane is used primarily to view the application layer data carried as the payload inside a packet. For example, when you look at an HTTP Response packet transmitted by a web server to a browser, you see the HTML code of the webpage the server is sending to the browser.

Port Scanners

A server, by definition, is a software program that stands ready to receive and service requests from clients. For those clients to be able to communicate with the server over a network, the server must open a port and listen for incoming traffic over that port. For example, a web server opens TCP port 80, because that is the well-known port for HTTP traffic, the port that web browsers use to communicate by default.

However, every port left open on a server computer is essentially an unlocked door through which intruders can conceivably enter. A *port scanner* is a software product that displays all of the open ports on a computer or on a network's computers. For network administrators, this is a type of vulnerability scanner that they can use to detect potential security breaches. For the attacker, it can also be a means of finding unprotected entrances into a network.

There are many port scanners available, including Netstat.exe, a relatively rudimentary one provided with all versions of Windows. Arguably the most popular one, however, is Nmap, an open-source, command-line program originally designed for UNIX systems, but that is now available for Windows with command-line and graphical interfaces.

When you initiate a scan with Nmap by supplying it with a network IP address, the program searches the available IP addresses for functioning computers and then runs a series of scripts against each one. The GUI version of the program, called Zenmap, displays the information in a series of screens for each system it finds, as shown in Figure 12-12.

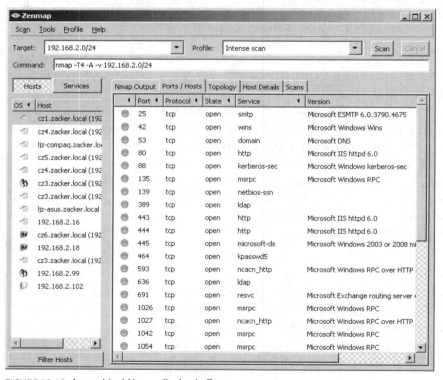

FIGURE 12-12 A graphical Nmap display in Zenmap.

Vulnerability Scanners

A *vulnerability scanner* is a software program that attempts to discover weaknesses in the security of a network and its computers. The differences between protocol analyzers and port scanners and vulnerability scanners can sometimes be subtle. For example, a vulnerability scan typically begins with a port scan, in which the software discovers the computers on the network and locates any open ports they might have.

However, a vulnerability scanner then proceeds to launch a variety of attacks against the open ports, attempting to exploit their vulnerabilities. Although the attacks use the same techniques that actual intruders might use, they are designed not to cause any real damage. However, some products enable you to switch off this safe mode of operation so that you can launch actual attacks against a test platform, to ascertain its vulnerability.

One of the most popular vulnerability scanners is called Nessus, produced by Tenable Network Security. Originally released as open-source software in 1998, Nessus is now a commercial product. Over the years, many additional features have been added, so that in addition to port scanning and a constantly expanding library of exploits, Nessus can now perform the following additional tasks:

- Scan accounts for weak or missing passwords
- Audit antivirus software configurations
- Scan for missing operating system patches and updates
- Check for compliance with system configuration policies
- Locate systems participating in peer-to-peer networks
- Scan for various forms of malware

After completing its scan, Nessus can display a report listing all of the exploits to which computers on the network are vulnerable, as shown in Figure 12-13.

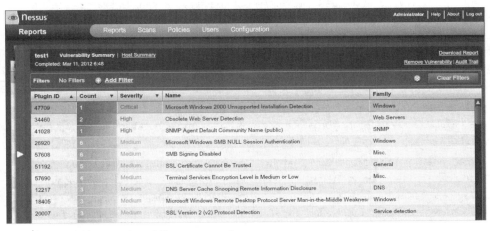

FIGURE 12-13 A Nessus vulnerability scan report.

✔ Quick Check

1. What is the name of the early program created to generate logs for sendmail?

2. What is the term for a tool that actually launches attacks against a resource, to test the strength of its security?

Quick Check Answers

1. Syslog

2. Vulnerability scanner

Virtualization

Virtualization is a relatively recent philosophy in network management. Although virtualization was originally a tool primarily employed for lab testing and pre-production work, administrators are now using virtual components throughout their networks, taking advantage of the flexibility that virtualization provides.

In networking, *virtualization* is a process that adds a layer of abstraction between actual, physical hardware and the system making use of it. A virtual server, for example, is a separate instance of an installed operating system running on a physical computer. However, instead of having the server access the computer's hardware directly, an intervening component called a *hypervisor* creates a virtual machine (VM) environment, and the server operating system runs in that environment.

The hypervisor is responsible for handling all of the hardware calls that the virtual machine makes and passing them along to the correct physical hardware. When you create a virtual machine, you specify what (virtual) hardware should be in it. You can, for example, create three separate virtual hard disk drives on a virtual machine, even if the computer you are using has only one drive. The virtualization software takes disk space from the one physical drive and uses it to create the three separate virtual drives on the virtual machine.

To the operating system running on the virtual machine, there are three drives that behave just as though there were three physical drives. The only difference is that the virtual machine doesn't get the fault tolerance it would from having three physical drives. It is pointless to create a RAID 5 array using the three virtual drives, for example, because there is still only one physical drive.

The advantage of this capability is that the hypervisor can create multiple virtual machines on a single computer, sharing the physical hardware among them. Each virtual machine can then have a separate operating system instance installed on it. The instances appear to the network as separate computers, each with its own hardware, its own addresses, and its own applications. If one virtual machine suffers a software malfunction and crashes, the other virtual machines on the same computer are in most cases unaffected.

To the network administrator, the advantages of virtualizing servers are manifold, including:

- **Isolation**   The more functions a server performs, the more vulnerable it is to intrusion, and the more likely it is for the functions to conflict with each other. With virtual servers, dedicated, separate virtual machines can each run different functions, all on the same physical computer.

- **Power conservation**   Instead of building multiple servers on separate physical computers, you can create multiple virtual machines on one physical computer and save on the electricity needed to power separate devices.

- **Fault tolerance**   Because virtual machines all interface with the same hypervisor, you can easily copy or move a virtual machine from one physical computer to another. This enables administrators to easily maintain offline copies of virtual machines, so that if a physical computer fails, duplicates of its virtual servers are immediately available. Administrators can also maintain copies offsite, for backups in the event of theft or natural disaster.

> **NOTE   NETWORK AS A SERVICE**
>
> Some service providers are in the business of selling access to offsite virtual machines to customers; for a monthly fee, you can create a server at another location that runs any applications you need, just as if you were hosting the VM onsite. Sometimes called *Network as a Service (NaaS)*, this concept is a progenitor of cloud computing.

- **Server consolidation**   You can use virtual machines to combine the workload of several servers onto one physical computer and redistribute the virtual machines as needed. For example, if traffic to your web server suddenly increases, you can remove some of the other virtual machines from the computer on which it is running and allocate more hardware resources to the web server.

- **Testing and evaluation**   Virtual servers enable you to create vast virtual networks that exist entirely on a single computer, for lab testing and software evaluation purposes.

Virtualization Architectures

Virtualization products can use several different architectures to share a computer's hardware resources among several virtual machines. The earlier type of virtualization products, including Windows Virtual PC and Microsoft Virtual Server, require a standard operating system installed on a computer. This becomes the "host" operating system. Then you install the virtualization product, which adds the hypervisor component, sometimes called a *virtual machine monitor (VMM)*. The hypervisor essentially runs alongside the host operating system, as shown in Figure 12-14, and enables you to create as many virtual machines as the computer has hardware to support.

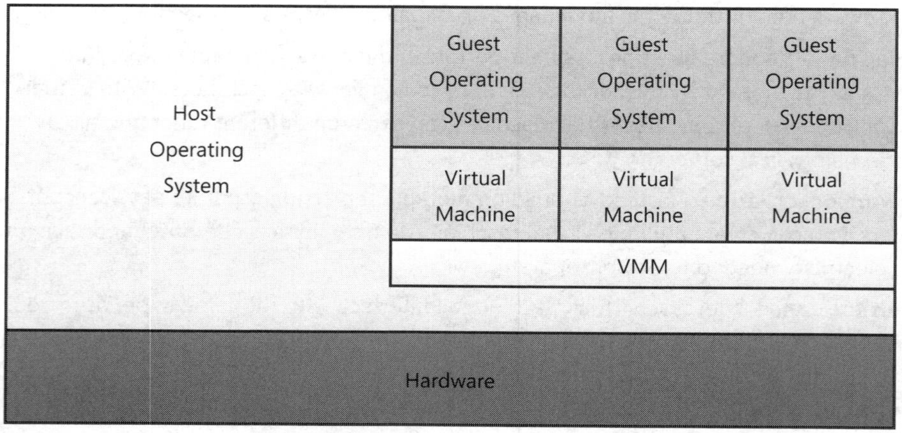

FIGURE 12-14 A hybrid VMM sharing hardware access with a host operating system.

This arrangement, in which the hypervisor runs on top of a host operating system, is called *Type II virtualization*. Using the Type II hypervisor, you create a virtual hardware environment for each virtual machine. You can specify how much memory to allocate to each VM, create virtual disk drives by using space on the computer's physical drives, and provide access to peripheral devices. You then install a "guest" operating system on each virtual machine, just as if you were deploying a new computer. The host operating system then shares access to the computer's processor with the hypervisor, with each taking the clock cycles it needs and passing control of the processor back to the other.

Type II virtualization can provide adequate virtual machine performance, particularly in educational and testing environments, but it does not provide performance equivalent to separate physical computers. Therefore, it is not generally recommended for high-traffic servers in production environments.

The virtualization capability built into Windows Server 2008 R2, called Hyper-V, uses a different type of architecture. Hyper-V uses *Type I virtualization*, in which the hypervisor is an abstraction layer that interacts directly with the computer's physical hardware—that is, without an intervening host operating system. The term "hypervisor" is intended to represent the next level beyond the term supervisor, in regard to responsibility for allocating a computer's processor clock cycles.

The hypervisor creates individual environments called *partitions*, each of which has its own operating system installed and accesses the computer's hardware via the hypervisor. Unlike Type II virtualization, in this case no host operating system shares processor time with the hypervisor. Instead, the hypervisor designates the first partition it creates as the parent partition and all subsequent partitions as child partitions, as shown in Figure 12-15.

The parent partition accesses the system hardware through the hypervisor, just as the child partitions do. The only difference is that the parent runs the virtualization stack, which creates and manages the child partitions. The parent partition is also responsible for the subsystems that directly affect the performance of the computer's physical hardware, such as Plug and

Play, power management, and error handling. These subsystems run in the operating systems on the child partitions as well, but they address only virtual hardware, whereas the parent, or root, partition handles the real thing.

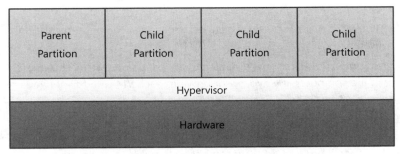

FIGURE 12-15 A Type 1 VMM, with the hypervisor providing all hardware access.

> **NOTE   HYPER-V**
>
> It might not seem as though the Hyper-V role in Windows Server 2008 R2 provides Type I virtualization, because it requires the Windows Server operating system to be installed and running. However, adding the Hyper-V role actually converts the installed instance of Windows Server 2008 R2 into the parent partition and causes the system to load the hypervisor before the operating system.

Desktop Virtualization

Administrators typically use Type I virtualization products, such as Hyper-V, for server virtualization. This type of virtualization can provide the performance levels needed to run high-volume production servers. As mentioned earlier, Type II virtualization provides an excellent platform for education, laboratory testing, and software evaluation. It is also used to enable desktop users to run an instance of another operating system on a single computer, without the complications of dual booting.

In this practice, often called *desktop virtualization*, a user can run applications that are not compatible with his or her primary operating system. For example, there are several products that Mac users can employ to run an instance of Windows so that they can use applications made for the Windows operating system. Other products run on Windows 7 and enable users to install an earlier version of Windows, to run an application that has not been updated.

Windows 7 even includes a feature called Windows XP Mode, which is essentially a fully licensed version of Windows XP that you can install on a computer running Windows 7 with Windows Virtual PC.

Virtual Switching

One of the problems that any server or desktop virtualization solution has to solve is that of network access. A physical computer usually has only one network adapter in it, but if there are multiple VMs running on that computer, each one has its own virtual adapter that needs access to the network. There are several ways that the hypervisor can accomplish this, including the following:

- **Bridging** By creating a bridge from the virtual network adapter in each VM to the physical adapter in the computer, the hypervisor provides each VM with full network access, including its own media access control (MAC) address.

- **Network address translation (NAT)** Some hypervisor products can implement a NAT solution within the hypervisor, creating a separate, private IP network for the VMs. The hypervisor then functions as a NAT router, enabling the VMs to access the physical network through the computer's network adapter.

> **MORE INFO** NETWORK ADDRESS TRANSLATION
>
> For more information on Network Address Translation (NAT), see Chapter 7, "Routing and Switching."

- **Virtual switching** To keep communication within the hypervisor, most virtualization products can create a virtual switch that enables all of the VMs on a computer to communicate with each other, just as if their network adapters were connected to a physical switch. For Type I virtualization solutions, there are also third-party virtual switch products available. These are essentially software switches that provide additional security, management, and wide area networking (WAN) services.

Presentation Virtualization

The term *presentation virtualization* refers to a technology that enables users to access and manipulate a system from a remote location. The Remote Desktop Services (RDS) role in Windows Server 2008 R2 does this by allowing a client program running on another computer to access the operating system on the server. The combination of an RDS server, a Remote Desktop Connection client, and the Remote Desktop Protocol (RDP) enables a user to send keystrokes and mouse movements to the server and receive in return the graphical information needed to create the display.

This enables users at any location to access a Windows desktop running on the server. They can load applications, access network resources, and do nearly anything else that a local user could do from the server console. The user is virtualizing the server's presentation, much in the same way that virtual reality systems enable people to interact with an environment that is not really there.

Application Virtualization

Hyper-V and Remote Desktop Services, in their own individual ways, both virtualize entire operating systems, but it is also possible to virtualize individual applications. When you virtualize an operating system, you create a separate partitioned space with virtual resources that appear just like physical ones to users and applications. You can run as many applications as you need on a single virtual machine, depending on the resources available to it. Virtualizing an application is roughly the same thing, except that you are allocating a set of virtual resources to a single application.

 The RemoteApp capability built into Remote Desktop Services is a form of application virtualization. *RemoteApp* is a Remote Desktop Services feature that enables clients to run server applications within individual windows. The windows are resizable; they have standard system menu and title bar buttons, and they are not constrained by a Remote Desktop Services desktop. In fact, a RemoteApp window is, in most cases, indistinguishable from a window containing a local application.

When a Remote Desktop Services client accesses a RemoteApp application, the server provides a separate operating environment for the application, just as when the client accesses an entire desktop. If the client computer experiences a problem, the application continues to run, because it has its own memory and other hardware resources. The same is true if one of the other Remote Desktop Services sessions on the server experiences a problem. Because the sessions use separate environments, one can fail without affecting the others.

Virtual PBXes

 A *private branch exchange (PBX)* is essentially a telephone exchange—that is, a switchboard—wholly owned and operated by a business or other private entity, rather than by a telephone company. As its core functionality, the PBX routes incoming calls to the proper extensions and provides outgoing callers with automatic access to a line. The original alternative to a PBX for a business was a key system, which required callers to push buttons to select their own lines.

Deciding on the correct telephone solution was always difficult for relatively small businesses, who lacked the knowledgeable staff required to maintain a PBX. This eventually led to the appearance of hosted PBX services—sometimes called *virtual PBXs*—in which a telephone company provided the PBX services to a customer but maintained the actual hardware at their own facility.

 EXAM TIP

The Network+ objectives use the term "virtual PBX," which is actually the trademark of a company providing cloud-based VoIP services. However, the term can actually refer to a software-based telephony solution run on a customer's computer, or to PBX services delivered over the Internet.

Another option is a software-based solution, running on a computer at the customer's site, which provides the same services as a hardware-based PBX.

The recent emphasis on cloud computing has led to the development of several hosted PBX solutions that use Voice over IP (VoIP) to provide services to customers over the Internet. Because of their decentralized nature, the actual company telephones connected by the virtual PBX service can be located anywhere, whereas a traditional PBX was limited to extensions located in the same facility.

Voice Over IP

Voice over IP is a term that describes a method for delivering voice telephony services over an IP network, such as the Internet, rather than the Public Switched Telephone Network (PSTN). Because the Internet is a packet-switching network, the distance between the two callers involved in a VoIP session is irrelevant. With telephony systems using the PSTN, the callers must establish a circuit that remains in place during the entire life of the call. The farther apart the two callers are, the more hardware is needed to create that circuit, and the more expensive it is.

Placing a voice call using VoIP requires some extra steps when compared to a standard PSTN call. The sending system must convert the analog voice signals it receives from the telephone, encode them for transmission, split the data sequence into packets, and then transmit the individual packets in the usual way. The receiving system then performs the same tasks in reverse.

To perform these tasks, VoIP uses several application layer protocols, standards for which the IETF has published as RFCs. These protocols include the Session Initiation Protocol (SIP), which systems use to establish and terminate VoIP sessions, and the Real-time Transport Protocol (RTP), which carries the actual media streams.

Performance Optimization

Network performance is a constant concern for the administrator. When the network slows down, the administrator's phone starts ringing, even when the problem is beyond his or her control. To try to avoid these fluctuations, there are several technologies that administrators can use to optimize network performance. Basically, the objective is to keep the data that users need readily available to them, which administrators can do by concentrating on the following tasks:

- Anticipating needs
- Prioritizing traffic
- Providing redundancy

There are a variety of technologies that address these objectives, some of which are described in the following sections.

Caching Data

Caching is a technique for storing frequently used data in a more available medium, in the anticipation that users will need to access it again. Computers can store data in many different places, and at many different speeds. Accessing data from a server on the Internet is relatively slow. Data stored on a local network server can be accessed faster. A hard drive in the local computer is faster still, and data stored in local memory is fastest of all. Caching is an attempt to anticipate users' needs by storing the most needed data in the fastest practical medium.

Computers and networks have many caching systems. All contemporary PCs have a level-2 memory cache that is faster than the main system memory array, and all hard disk drives have an on-board cache for frequently used data. In TCP/IP networking, the Address Resolution Protocol (ARP) maintains a cache of MAC addresses on every computer, and DNS servers routinely cache names and IP addresses for repeated use.

These are all caching systems that are largely automatic, although administrators can make some minor adjustments to them. For example, specifying a longer DNS cache time for your domain names can yield a marginal improvement in name resolution performance for Internet users accessing your services. However, there are some other caching systems that can provide a performance boost for your network's internal users by storing frequently used Internet data on a local network server.

Proxy Servers

As mentioned in Chapter 6, "The Network Layer," a proxy server is an application layer service that functions as an intermediary for network clients accessing the Internet. Proxy servers protect the clients by preventing direct connections between them and Internet servers, and they also enable administrators to monitor and regulate users' Internet access. Proxy servers can also function as *content filters*, preventing clients from accessing specific content based on a variety of criteria such as domain names, content type, or media type.

One of the other primary functions of a proxy server is to cache the data that clients access from the Internet, storing it on a local server for future use. As the proxy server processes Internet access requests from clients, it checks the cache for each one. If a client attempts to access a website recently accessed by another user, the server will find the data in the cache and use that to satisfy the request. Because the data is coming from a local network server and not from the Internet, performance is much faster, both for that user and for the other users, who will have a shorter wait for their uncached Internet requests.

For networks with multiple proxy servers, there is a way to increase the benefit provided by the caching feature. Protocols such as *Cache Array Routing Protocol (CARP)* enable clients to route requests for specific URLs to the one proxy server containing that cached data. This way, the proxy servers do not maintain duplicate data in their caches, effectively increasing the amount of cached data available to all of the clients on the network.

Cache Servers

There are some products on the market that implement just the web caching capability from the proxy server concept, solely for the purpose of conserving an organization's Internet bandwidth. Some of these products combine a variety of performance optimization capabilities in one package, including load balancing among multiple caches and selective caching of certain traffic types.

EXAM TIP

CompTIA, in the Network+ objectives, refers to the caching server products as *caching engines*. Be familiar with both terms for the exam.

Traffic Control

Networks today often carry more than just programs and document files; they also carry voice and video of various types, as well as other kinds of high-bandwidth traffic. These traffic types can have different priorities to the organization running the network, and some are more latency-sensitive than others, purely by their nature.

For example, a brief delay while downloading a large image file might be moderately annoying, but constant stutters during an important video conference can be positively infuriating and can also make the company look bad to its clients, partners, or stockholders. This is what is meant by "latency-sensitive"; streaming video can tolerate a few lost bits, but after a certain point, they become evident to the user.

Sensitivity is not solely determined by the data type, either. Interruptions during a streaming video are less of a concern when you're watching a music video than when you are making a sales presentation to potential customers.

Another important factor in business networking is the increasing use of VoIP telephony. People are accustomed to a high level of service from the PSTN, and it doesn't take many problems to make a VoIP service unacceptable for business use.

To address these issues, there are several ways that administrators can regulate traffic on a network so that certain types of data receive priority access to the available bandwidth.

Quality of Service

The easiest way to ensure that data types requiring large amounts of bandwidth receive it is to overprovision the network to accommodate the largest conceivable requirements, so that there is never any traffic congestion. This can be an expensive proposition, however.

The other way is to use *Quality of Service (QoS)*, a method for assigning priorities to various types of traffic. Administrators control the types of traffic that receive higher priorities by specifying protocols, ports, IP addresses, users, bit loss rates, or other criteria. The prioritization is achieved in one of the following ways:

- **Integrated services (IntServ)**   A method in which applications communicate with routers to reserve a specific amount of bandwidth. The devices communicate by using a specialized protocol, such as the Resource Reservation Protocol (RSVP).

- **Differentiated services (DiffServ)**   A method that uses bits in the IP header's Type of Service (TOS) to identify the priority to be assigned to the data in the packet.

At the present time, the DiffServ method is proving to be more popular, especially with Internet traffic, because it requires less overhead and less participation from routers.

Traffic Shaping

Traffic shaping is a means of prioritizing packets without prior negotiation between applications and routers and without tagging packets. Implemented in an end system, a router, or a switch, traffic shaping is essentially a system that delays packets, storing them in a temporary buffer, so that others conforming to specified criteria receive priority access to the network.

EXAM TIP

The Network+ objectives have, at various times, used the terms "traffic shaping" and "bandwidth shaping" when referring to the same technologies.

Redundant Services

Redundancy is one of the basic principles of network reliability. By using redundant hardware, redundant data, and redundant services, administrators can provide two vital advantages: fault tolerance and high availability.

Fault Tolerance

Fault tolerance is the ability of a system to continue functioning after a failure of some kind. Network administrators strive for a maximum amount of network *uptime*, because the alternative means ringing phones, lost productivity, and perhaps an unexpected career change.

HARDWARE REDUNDANCY

Servers often have redundant hardware as a hedge against a device failure. Dual power supplies and Redundant Array of Independent Disks (RAID) are common; some organizations even maintain clusters of redundant servers solely for the purpose of fault tolerance.

A cluster is a group of two or more servers bound into a relationship that synchronizes their applications and data. If one of the servers fails, then another immediately takes its place so that the services the cluster provides are always available.

BACKUPS

The most common type of fault tolerance, one that every administrator should have, is a re-cently made backup of all important data. Enterprise networks traditionally use magnetic tape as a backup medium, and many administrators still rely on this technology. With this type of linear medium, the typical practice is to perform periodic full backups of all the data needing protection and, in between full backups, partial backups of any files that have changed.

There are two basic types of partial backups:

- **Incremental**   A backup of all of the files that have changed since the last full or incre-mental backup. To perform a full restore, you must restore the most recent full backup and then each of the subsequent incremental backups, in order.

- **Differential**   A backup of all of the files that have changed since the last full backup. To perform a full restore, you must restore the most recent full backup and then just the single most recent differential backup.

Network backup software products typically implement a job schedule and a media rota-tion scheme that enables the administrator to set up a reliable backup plan that only requires someone to insert the appropriate tape into the drive.

Magnetic tape is an effective backup medium and has its own advantages, but the ever-dropping prices of hard disk storage and the ever-increasing bandwidth of Internet connec-tions has resulted in some new backup strategies.

Hard disk backups are now a practical alternative, due both to the low prices of hard drives and the advent of high-speed external interfaces, enabling administrators to take drives off-site for storage. Another advantage of using hard disks for backups is that they are random access devices. You can create a job that copies only the files that have changed since the last job, and have them simply replace the old versions of the files on the backup disk. You are then left with a full, up-to-date image of the protected data after every job, and no additional incremental or differential backups to restore.

Broadband and other inexpensive, high-speed Internet access services have made the Internet into a viable backup medium. There are now service providers who rent space on well-protected servers, enabling administrators to upload their data instead of backing it up locally. The advantage of this arrangement is that, because the data is stored offsite, it is protected against fire, theft, and disaster.

High Availability

The concept of high availability is similar to that of fault tolerance. In fact, some technologies are capable of providing both. *High availability* is a design principle that calls for a system to achieve a previously determined level of performance and reliability. For example, when a service provider enters into a contract with a client, the provider might agree to include a high availability clause stating that the service must be up and running 99.9 percent of the time over the course of a year. This allows for approximately eight hours of downtime per year; otherwise, the contractor must pay a penalty.

RAID

Technologies such as RAID are as much high availability solutions as they are fault tolerance solutions. A properly configured RAID array ensures that even when a hard disk fails, all of the data stored on the array continues to be available. To maintain that availability, many RAID solutions enable administrators to replace a drive while the unit is running. This is called *hot swapping*.

LOAD BALANCING

Busy servers, whether on the Internet or not, often receive more traffic than a single computer can comfortably handle. When this happens, the only solution is to add another server. A group of servers, all running the same application to provide a single service, is known as a *cluster* or a *server farm*. *Load balancing* is a technique that distributes incoming traffic equally among the multiple servers in the cluster.

When a client accesses a server, it has only one name, and that name must resolve into one IP address. When you add more servers, they obviously must have their own names and addresses, but to the client, they must appear as one. For example, no one could possibly believe that the Microsoft.com website is running on a single server; the traffic would quickly overwhelm an individual machine. So the work is distributed across many servers, all of which answer to Microsoft.com. This is the trick accomplished by a load-balancing solution.

There are several ways to balance a traffic load among servers. The simplest and one of the most common is to use a method called *round robin DNS*. This method is implemented in the DNS server and relies on the name resolution process performed by each client.

In round robin DNS, the server contains multiple resource records for the same server name, each with a different IP address representing one of the computers running the server application. When a client resolves the server name, the DNS server accesses each of the resource records in turn, so that each address theoretically receives the same number of visitors.

There are problems with this technique, mostly due to the caching of DNS information and of server data all over the Internet. Therefore, the traffic received by each server is not exactly balanced with the others, but the solution works adequately in most situations.

There are many more complicated alternatives to the DNS load-balancing approach. Generally speaking, the load balancing is accomplished by a software or hardware component that receives the incoming traffic and selects one of the servers to receive it. Hardware solutions include special switches—actually devices combining switch and router functions—that continually query the servers in the cluster and choose a server to receive each request based on the responses. These go by various names, including multilayer switches, layer 4 switches, and load-balancing switches.

There are also application layer devices called content switches, layer 7 switches, or web switches, among other names. These devices not only perform load balancing, they also can offload some of the processor load from the web servers by performing Secure Socket Layer (SSL) transactions.

Software solutions can take the form of stand-alone programs that monitor incoming traffic and forward requests to the servers in the cluster as needed. Other load-balancing schemes are integrated into comprehensive clustering solutions, such as Failover Clustering in Windows Server 2008 R2. In addition to the fault tolerance provided by having multiple servers replicated and synchronized, these solutions balance incoming traffic among the servers in the cluster.

 Quick Check

1. What is the term used to describe the DNS-based method of load balancing?
2. Which of the two main Quality of Service methods uses tags in the IP header to specify the priority of the data in the packet?

Quick Check Answers

1. Round robin DNS
2. Differentiated services

Exercise

The answers for this exercise are located in the "Answers" section at the end of this chapter.

Download the evaluation version of Nessus from *www.tenable.com*. Install it on your system and use it to scan your computer. When the scan is completed, display the results and answer the following questions.

1. How many vulnerabilities did Nessus find on your computer? How many of those are rated Critical? How many have a High severity rating?

2. Research the vulnerabilities that Nessus located, if you do not understand them. Then describe what actions you must take to eliminate them from your computer.

Chapter Summary

- Documentation is a critical part of any network management plan, and the time to start thinking about it is well before you install your first piece of network hardware.

- Documentation of your network's cable installation is particularly important, both because much of it is probably hidden from view and because your organization probably had an outside contractor install it.

- A network diagram differs from a cable diagram in that its intention is to illustrate the relationships between network components; it is not usually drawn to scale and does not necessarily include architectural elements of the site, such as walls, ducts, and fixtures.

- One of the basic principles of network management is to observe and address any changes that might occur in the performance of a system. You do this by comparing the system's performance levels to a baseline that you have previously established.

- The most common method for monitoring network activities is by examining logs. A log is simply a chronological list of events that have occurred, generated by a process and sent to a specified destination.

- The Simple Network Monitoring Protocol (SNMP) is a TCP/IP application layer protocol and query language that specially equipped networking devices use to communicate with a central console.

- A protocol analyzer captures a sample of the traffic passing over the network, decodes the packets into the language of the individual protocols they contain, and lets you examine them in minute detail.

- Every port left open on a server computer is essentially an unlocked door through which intruders can conceivably enter. A port scanner is a software product that displays all of the open ports on a computer or on a network's computers.

- Virtualization is a process that adds a layer of abstraction between actual, physical hardware and the system making use of it. Instead of having the server access the computer's hardware directly, an intervening component called a hypervisor creates a virtual machine environment, and the server operating system runs in that environment.

- Caching is a technique for storing frequently used data in a more available medium, in anticipation that users will need to access it again.

- Quality of Service (QoS) is a method for assigning priorities to various types of traffic. Administrators control the types of traffic that receive higher priorities by specifying protocols, ports, IP addresses, users, bit loss rates, or other criteria.

- Load balancing is a technique that distributes incoming traffic equally among the multiple servers in a cluster.

Chapter Review

Test your knowledge of the information in Chapter 12 by answering these questions. The answers to these questions, and the explanations of why each answer choice is correct or incorrect, are located in the "Answers" section at the end of this chapter.

1. What is the name of the Windows tool you use to display system logs?

   A. Network Monitor

   B. Performance Monitor

   C. Event Viewer

   D. Syslog

2. Which of the following is a hardware-based load-balancing solution that functions at the application layer of the OSI model?

   A. Content switch

   B. Layer 4 switch

   C. Failover cluster

   D. Server farm

3. Which of the following statements about Type I and Type II virtualization are true?

   A. In Type I virtualization, the hypervisor runs on top of a host operating system.

   B. In Type I virtualization, the hypervisor runs directly on the computer hardware.

   C. In Type II virtualization, the hypervisor runs on top of a host operating system.

   D. In Type II virtualization, the hypervisor runs directly on the computer hardware.

4. Which of the following types of server virtualization provides the best performance for high-traffic servers in production environments?

   A. Type I virtualization

   B. Type II virtualization

   C. Presentation virtualization

   D. Virtual PBX

Answers

This section contains the answers to the questions for the Exercise and Chapter Review in this chapter.

Exercise

1. Answers will vary.

2. Answers will vary.

Chapter Review

1. **Correct Answer:** C

   A. **Incorrect:** Network Monitor is a protocol analyzer; it does not display system logs.

   B. **Incorrect:** Performance Monitor is a tool that displays statistics for specific performance factors; it does not display system logs.

   C. **Correct:** Event Viewer is the application that displays the various Windows system and application logs.

   D. **Incorrect:** Syslog is a tool that was created to generate log files for the sendmail application; it does not display Windows system logs.

2. **Correct Answer:** A

   A. **Correct:** A content switch is an application layer device that provides load balancing and also offloads other tasks from web servers.

   B. **Incorrect:** A layer 4 switch operates at the transport layer, not the application layer.

   C. **Incorrect:** A failover cluster is a collection of computers working together to provide high availability and fault tolerance.

   D. **Incorrect:** A server farm is another name for a cluster of computers; it is not an application layer load-balancing device.

3. **Correct Answers:** B and C

   A. **Incorrect:** In Type I virtualization, the hypervisor does not run on top of a host operating system.

   B. **Correct:** A Type I hypervisor does run directly on the computer hardware.

   C. **Correct:** A Type II hypervisor does run on top of a host operating system.

   D. **Incorrect:** In Type II virtualization, the hypervisor does not run directly on the computer hardware.

4. **Correct Answer:** A

    A. **Correct:** Type I virtualization provides the best performance because the hypervisor runs on the computer with the overhead of a host operating system.

    B. **Incorrect:** Type II virtualization provides poorer performance than Type I because of the need to share processor time with the host operating system.

    C. **Incorrect:** Presentation virtualization is the term used to describe the Remote Desktop Services functionality in Windows. It is not designed for virtualizing servers.

    D. **Incorrect:** A PBX is a telephone switchboard; virtual PBX is not a method for virtualizing servers.

CHAPTER 13

Network Troubleshooting

The process of troubleshooting network problems varies, depending on the size of the organization and the people involved. In medium-sized to large-sized organizations, there is usually a written procedure that determines how technical support calls are registered, addressed, and escalated. In smaller organizations, the process might be much more informal. This chapter describes the tools and procedures commonly used for typical technical support calls. In some cases, the cause of the problem might be simple to identify, such as user error, and the procedures described here illustrate how you can handle even minor problems to everyone's satisfaction. In other cases, the immediate issue itself might seem minor, but it might actually be a sign of a serious problem that affects the whole network.

Exam objectives in this chapter:

Objective 1.8: Given a scenario, implement the following network troubleshooting methodology:

- Identify the problem:
  - Information gathering
  - Identify symptoms
  - Question users
  - Determine if anything has changed
- Establish a theory of probable cause
  - Question the obvious
- Test the theory to determine cause:
  - Once theory is confirmed determine next steps to resolve problem.
  - If theory is not confirmed, re-establish new theory or escalate.
- Establish a plan of action to resolve the problem and identify potential effects
- Implement the solution or escalate as necessary
- Verify full system functionality and if applicable implement preventative measures
- Document findings, actions and outcomes

Objective 2.4: Given a scenario, troubleshoot common wireless problems.

- Interference
- Signal strength
- Configurations
- Incompatibilities
- Incorrect channel

- Latency
- Encryption type
- Bounce
- SSID mismatch
- Incorrect switch placement

Objective 2.5: Given a scenario, troubleshoot common router and switch problems.

- Switching loop
- Bad cables/improper cable types
- Port configuration
- VLAN assignment
- Mismatched MTU/MTU black hole
- Power failure

- Bad/missing routes
- Bad modules (SFPs, GBICs)
- Wrong subnet mask
- Wrong gateway
- Duplicate IP address
- Wrong DNS

Objective 3.6: Given a scenario, troubleshoot common physical connectivity problems.

- Cable problems:
  - Bad connectors
  - Bad wiring
  - Open, short
  - Split cables
  - DB loss
  - TXRX reversed
  - Cable placement
  - EMI/Interference
  - Distance
  - Cross-talk

Objective 4.3: Given a scenario, use appropriate software tools to troubleshoot connectivity issues.

- Protocol analyzer
- Throughput testers
- Connectivity software
- Ping
- Tracert/traceroute
- Dig

- Ipconfig/ifconfig
- Nslookup
- Arp
- Nbtstat
- Netstat
- Route

Troubleshooting Tools

Virtually every operating system with networking capabilities includes support for the TCP/IP protocols. In most cases, the TCP/IP stack includes utilities you can use to gather information about the various protocols and the network. Traditionally, these utilities run from the command line, although there are some graphical versions. In many cases, TCP/IP utilities use the same syntax, even on different operating systems. This section examines some of the most common TCP/IP utilities and their purposes.

The Ping Program

As mentioned several times throughout this book, *Ping* is the most basic of the TCP/IP utilities. Virtually every TCP/IP implementation includes a version of it. On UNIX and Linux systems, the program is called ping, and on Windows-based systems, it is called Ping.exe.

Ping can tell you if the TCP/IP stack of another system on the network is functioning normally and if you have connectivity to it. It can also verify name resolution. The Ping program generates a series of Echo Request messages by using the Internet Control Message Protocol (ICMP), which is encapsulated directly within IP datagrams, and transmits them to the computer whose name or IP address you specify on the command line. The basic syntax of the Ping program is as follows:

`ping target`

The *target* variable contains the IP address or name of a computer on the network. You can use either Domain Name System (DNS) names or Network Basic Input/Output System (NetBIOS) names in Ping commands. Ping resolves the name into an IP address before sending the Echo Request messages, and it then displays the address in its readout. Most Ping implementations also have command-line switches with which you can modify the operational parameters of the program, such as the number of Echo Request messages it generates and the amount of data in each message.

TCP/IP computers respond to any Echo Request messages they receive that are addressed to them by generating Echo Reply messages and transmitting them back to the sender. When the pinging computer receives the Echo Reply messages, it produces a display like the following.

```
Pinging cz1 [192.168.2.10] with 32 bytes of data:

Reply from 192.168.2.10: bytes=32 time<1ms TTL=128
Reply from 192.168.2.10: bytes=32 time<1ms TTL=128
Reply from 192.168.2.10: bytes=32 time<1ms TTL=128
Reply from 192.168.2.10: bytes=32 time<1ms TTL=128

Ping statistics for 192.168.2.10:
Packets: Sent = 4, Received = 4, Lost = 0 (0% loss),
Approximate round trip times in milli-seconds:
Minimum = 0ms, Maximum =  0ms, Average =  0ms
```

In the case of this Ping implementation (from Windows 7), the display shows the IP address of the computer receiving the Echo Requests, the number of bytes of data included with each request, the elapsed time between the transmission of each request and the receipt of each reply, and the value of the Time to Live (TTL) field in the IP header. In this particular example, the target computer was on the same local area network (LAN), so the time measurement is very short—less than 1 millisecond. When you are pinging a computer on the Internet, the interval is likely to be longer.

A successful Ping test such as this one indicates that the target computer's networking hardware is functioning properly, as are the protocols, at least as high as the network layer of the Open Systems Interconnection (OS)I model. If the Ping test fails, there is a problem in one or both of the computers, in the connection between them, or in the name resolution process.

> **NOTE PING TRAFFIC**
>
> One factor that has hampered the usefulness of Ping in recent years is the tendency for firewalls to block ICMP Echo Request messages by default. By using command-line parameters, attackers can easily make Ping bombard a target system with an endless stream of large ICMP packets, as a denial of service attack. Therefore, many administrators use firewalls to prevent those messages from reaching their servers. As a result, a failed Ping test does not always mean that there is a problem.

Traceroute

Traceroute is a variant of the Ping program that displays the path that packets take to their destination. Because of the nature of IP routing, paths through an internetwork can change from minute to minute, and Traceroute displays a list of the routers that are currently for-warding packets to a particular destination. The program is called traceroute on UNIX and Linux systems and Tracert.exe on Windows-based systems.

Traceroute uses ICMP Echo Request and Echo Reply messages just like Ping, but it modi-fies the messages by changing the value of the Time to Live (TTL) field in the IP header. The values in the TTL field prevent packets from getting caught in router loops that keep them circulating endlessly around the network. The computer generating the packet normally sets a relatively high value for the TTL field; on computers running Windows, the default value is 128. Each router that processes the packet reduces the TTL value by one. If the value reaches zero, the last router discards the packet and transmits an ICMP error message back to the original sender.

When you run Traceroute with the name or IP address of a target computer, Traceroute generates its first set of Echo Request messages with TTL values of 1. When the messages arrive at the first router on their path, the router decrements their TTL values to 0, discards the packets, and reports the errors to the sender. The error messages contain the router's address, which Traceroute displays as the first hop in the path to the destination. Traceroute's second set of Echo Request messages use a TTL value of 2, causing the second router on the path to discard the packets and generate error messages. The Echo Request messages in the third set have a TTL value of 3, and so on. Each set of packets travels one hop farther than the previous set before causing a router to return error messages to the source. The list of routers displayed by Traceroute as the path to the destination is the result of these error messages. The following is an example of a Traceroute display.

```
Tracing route to www.fineartschool.co.uk [173.146.1.1] over a maximum of 30 hops:
1    <10 ms     1 ms   <10 ms   192.168.2.99
2    105 ms    92 ms    98 ms   qrv1-67terminal01.cpandl.com [131.107.24.67.3]
3    101 ms   110 ms    98 ms   qrv1.cpandl.com [131.107.67.1]
4    123 ms   109 ms   118 ms   svcr03-7b.cpandl.com [131.107.103.125]
5    123 ms   112 ms   114 ms   clsm02-2.cpandl.com [131.107.88.26]
6    136 ms   130 ms   133 ms   s1-gw19-pen-6-1-0-T3.fabrikam.com [157.54.116.5]
7    143 ms   126 ms   138 ms   s1-bb10-pen-4-3.fabrikam.com [157.54.5.117]
8    146 ms   129 ms   133 ms   s1-bb20-pen-12-0.fabrikam.com [157.54.5.1]
9    131 ms   128 ms   139 ms   s1-bb20-nyc-13-0.fabrikam.com [157.54.18.38]
10   130 ms   134 ms   134 ms   s1-gw9-nyc-8-0.fabrikam.com [157.54.7.94]
11   147 ms   149 ms   152 ms   s1-demon-1-0.fabrikam.com [157.54.173.10]
12   154 ms   146 ms   145 ms   ny2-back-1-ge021.router.fabrikam.com [157.54.173.121]
13   230 ms   225 ms   226 ms   tele-back-1-ge023.router.adatum.co.uk [157.60.173.12]
14   233 ms   220 ms   226 ms   tele-core-3-fxp1.router.adatum.co.uk [157.60.252.56]
15   223 ms   224 ms   224 ms   tele-access-1-14.router.adatum.co.uk [157.60.254.245]
16   236 ms   221 ms   226 ms   tele-service-2-165.router.adatum.co.uk [157.60.36.149]
17   220 ms   224 ms   210 ms   www.fineartschool.co.uk [206.73.118.65]
Trace complete.
```

In this example, Traceroute displays the path between a computer in Pennsylvania and one in the United Kingdom. Each of the hops contains the elapsed times between the transmission and reception of three sets of Echo Request and Echo Reply packets. In this trace, you can clearly see the point at which the packets begin traveling across the Atlantic Ocean. At hop 13, the elapsed times increase from approximately 150 to 230 milliseconds (ms) and stay in that range for the subsequent hops. This additional delay of only 80 ms is the time it takes the packets to travel the thousands of miles across the Atlantic Ocean.

You can use Traceroute to isolate the location of a network communications problem. Ping simply tells you whether or not a problem exists; it can't tell you where. A failure to contact a remote computer could be due to a problem in your workstation, in the remote computer, or in any of the routers in between. Traceroute can tell you how far your packets are going before they run into the problem.

NOTE **TRACEROUTE SHORTCOMINGS**

Because the configuration of the Internet is constantly changing, there is no guarantee that the route displayed by Traceroute is completely accurate. The IP datagrams that execute each step of the Traceroute process might in fact be taking different routes to the same destination, resulting in the display of a composite route between two points that does not actually exist. There is also no way of knowing what the return path is.

Additionally, all routers deprioritize ICMP processes in favor of packet forwarding and other critical router tasks. When a router is busy, it might delay the processing of a Ping or Traceroute packet. The resulting latency numbers will be higher than the delay experienced by actual data packets crossing the network.

Ifconfig and Ipconfig.exe

UNIX and Linux systems have a program called ifconfig (the name is derived from the words *interface configuration*) that you use to configure the properties of network interface adapters and assign TCP/IP configuration parameters to them. Running ifconfig with just the name of an interface displays the current configuration of that interface.

Windows has a version of this program, Ipconfig.exe, which omits most of the configuration capabilities and retains the configuration display. When you run Ipconfig.exe with the /all parameter at the Windows Server 2008 R2 command line, you see a display like the following.

```
Windows IP Configuration
    Host Name . . . . . . . . . . . . : wkstn12
    Primary Dns Suffix  . . . . . . . : adatum.local
    Node Type . . . . . . . . . . . . : Broadcast
    IP Routing Enabled. . . . . . . . : No
    WINS Proxy Enabled. . . . . . . . : No
    DNS Suffix Search List. . . . . . : adatum.local
Ethernet adapter Local Area Connection:
    Connection-specific DNS Suffix  . : adatum.local
    Description . . . . . . . . . . . : Realtek PCIe GBE Family Controller
    Physical Address. . . . . . . . . : 60-EB-69-93-5E-E5
    DHCP Enabled. . . . . . . . . . . : Yes
    Autoconfiguration Enabled . . . . : Yes
    Link-local IPv6 Address . . . . . : fe80::7441:4473:f204:ec1d%10(Preferred)
    IPv4 Address. . . . . . . . . . . : 192.168.2.9(Preferred)
    Subnet Mask . . . . . . . . . . . : 255.255.255.0
    Lease Obtained. . . . . . . . . . : Wednesday, March 14, 2012 8:05:32 AM
    Lease Expires . . . . . . . . . . : Thursday, March 22, 2012 8:05:29 AM
    Default Gateway . . . . . . . . . : 192.168.2.99
    DHCP Server . . . . . . . . . . . : 192.168.2.1
    DHCPv6 IAID . . . . . . . . . . . : 241232745
    DHCPv6 Client DUID. . . . . . . . : 00-01-00-01-14-81-CC-39-60-EB-69-93-5E-E5
    DNS Servers . . . . . . . . . . . : 192.168.2.1
    Primary WINS Server . . . . . . . : 192.168.2.1
    NetBIOS over Tcpip. . . . . . . . : Enabled
```

Ipconfig.exe also has another function associated with the Dynamic Host Configuration Protocol (DHCP): it is the easiest way in Windows to see what IP address and other parameters the DHCP server has assigned to a computer. However, you can also use Ipconfig.exe to manually release IP addresses obtained through DHCP and renew existing leases. By running Ipconfig.exe with the /release and /renew command-line parameters, you can release or renew the IP address assignment of one of the network interfaces in the computer or for all of the interfaces at once.

ARP

As described in Chapter 4, "The Data-Link Layer," the Address Resolution Protocol (ARP) enables a TCP/IP computer to convert IP addresses to the hardware addresses that data-link layer protocols need to transmit frames across local subnets. IP uses ARP to discover the hardware address to which each of its datagrams will be transmitted. To minimize the amount of network traffic ARP generates, the computer stores the resolved hardware addresses in a cache in system memory. The information remains in the cache for a short time (usually between 2 and 10 minutes), in case the computer has additional packets to send to the same address.

UNIX, Linux, and Windows all include a command-line utility that you can use to manipulate the contents of the ARP cache. In UNIX and Linux, this utility is called arp; in Windows, it is called Arp.exe. You can use arp or Arp.exe to add the hardware addresses of computers you contact frequently to the cache, saving time and reducing network traffic during the connection process.

Addresses that you add to the ARP cache manually are static, meaning that they are not deleted after the usual expiration period. The cache is stored in memory only, however, so it is erased when you reboot the computer. If you want to preload the cache whenever you boot your system, you can create a script containing arp or Arp.exe commands and execute it by using an rc file (in UNIX/ Linux) or by placing it in the Startup program group (in Windows).

The arp and Arp.exe utilities use a similar syntax, with many identical command-line arguments. This syntax and some of the most important command-line arguments are as follows.

```
arp [[-a {ipaddress}] [-n ifaddress]] [-s ipaddress hwaddress {ifaddress}]
   [-d ipaddress {ifaddress}]
```

- **-a {ipaddress}**   Displays the contents of the ARP cache. The optional *ipaddress* variable specifies the address of a particular cache entry to be displayed.

- **-n ifaddress**   Displays only the contents of the ARP cache associated with the network interface specified by the *ifaddress* variable.

- **-s ipaddress hwaddress {ifaddress}**   Adds a static entry to the ARP cache. The *ipaddress* variable contains the IP address of the host. The *hwaddress* variable contains the hardware address of the same host. The *ifaddress* variable contains the IP address of the network interface in the local system for which you want to modify the cache.

- **-d *ipaddress* {*ifaddress*}** Deletes the entry in the ARP cache that is associated with the host represented by the *ipaddress* variable. The optional *ifaddress* variable specifies the cache from which the entry should be deleted.

The ARP table of a computer running Windows 7, as displayed by Arp.exe, appears as follows.

```
Interface: 192.168.2.9 --- 0xa
  Internet Address      Physical Address    Type
  192.168.2.1           00-0b-cd-cf-e3-b6   dynamic
  192.168.2.3           00-22-64-34-12-4b   dynamic
  192.168.2.4           00-11-2f-46-c1-46   dynamic
  192.168.2.99          00-1c-10-08-f6-1a   dynamic
  192.168.2.255         ff-ff-ff-ff-ff-ff   static
  224.0.0.22            01-00-5e-00-00-16   static
  224.0.0.251           01-00-5e-00-00-fb   static
  224.0.0.252           01-00-5e-00-00-fc   static
  239.255.255.250       01-00-5e-7f-ff-fa   static
  255.255.255.255       ff-ff-ff-ff-ff-ff   static
```

Netstat

Netstat is a command-line program that displays status information about the current network connections of a computer running TCP/IP and about the traffic generated by the TCP/IP protocols. In UNIX and Linux, the program is called netstat, and in Windows, it is called Netstat.exe. The command-line parameters differ for the various implementations of Netstat, but the information they display is roughly the same.

Using Netstat.exe on a Computer Running Windows

The syntax for Netstat.exe is as follows.

```
netstat [interval] [-a] [-p protocol] [-n] [-e] [-r] [-s]
```

- **interval** Refreshes the display every *interval* seconds until the user aborts the command.

- **-a** Displays the current network connections and the ports that are currently listening for incoming network connections.

- **-p *protocol*** Displays the currently active connections for the protocol specified by the *protocol* variable.

- **-n** When combined with other parameters, causes the program to identify computers using IP addresses instead of names.

- **-e** Displays incoming and outgoing traffic statistics for the network interface. The statistics are broken down into bytes, unicast packets, non-unicast packets, discards, errors, and unknown protocols.

- **-r** Displays the routing table plus the current active connections.
- **-s** Displays detailed network traffic statistics for the IP, ICMP, TCP, and UDP protocols.

Part of the default network connection listing displayed by Netstat.exe -a -n on a computer running Windows 7 appears as follows.

```
Active Connections
  Proto  Local Address          Foreign Address         State

  TCP    0.0.0.0:135            cz12:0                  LISTENING
  TCP    0.0.0.0:445            cz12:0                  LISTENING
  TCP    0.0.0.0:554            cz12:0                  LISTENING
  TCP    0.0.0.0:1025           cz12:0                  LISTENING
  TCP    127.0.0.1:1039         cz12:5354               ESTABLISHED
  TCP    127.0.0.1:1088         cz12:0                  LISTENING
  TCP    127.0.0.1:1138         cz12:27015              ESTABLISHED
  TCP    127.0.0.1:1140         cz12:19872              ESTABLISHED
  TCP    127.0.0.1:5354         cz12:0                  LISTENING
  TCP    192.168.2.9:1141       v-client-4b:https       CLOSE_WAIT
  TCP    [::]:135               cz12:0                  LISTENING
  TCP    [::]:445               cz12:0                  LISTENING
  TCP    [::]:554               cz12:0                  LISTENING
  UDP    0.0.0.0:123            *:*
  UDP    0.0.0.0:500            *:*
  UDP    [fe80::7441:4473:f204:ec1d%10]:1900   *:*
  UDP    [fe80::7441:4473:f204:ec1d%10]:55010  *:*
```

The interface statistics produced by Netstat.exe -e on a computer running Windows 7 look like this.

```
Interface Statistics

                        Received          Sent
Bytes                 2127854975     751579877
Unicast packets          3151802       2833248
Non-unicast packets        64418           995
Discards                       0             0
Errors                         0             0
Unknown protocols             84            65
```

The routing table display produced by Netstat.exe -r appears as follows.

```
===========================================================================
Interface List
 15...00 26 c7 7e 00 e1 ......Microsoft Virtual WiFi Miniport Adapter
 12...00 26 c7 7e 00 e0 ......Intel(R) WiFi Link 1000 BGN
 10...60 eb 69 93 5e e5 ......Realtek PCIe GBE Family Controller
  1...........................Software Loopback Interface 1
===========================================================================
```

```
IPv4 Route Table
===========================================================================
Active Routes:
Network Destination        Netmask          Gateway       Interface  Metric
          0.0.0.0          0.0.0.0     192.168.2.99     192.168.2.9      10
        127.0.0.0        255.0.0.0          On-link       127.0.0.1     306
        127.0.0.1  255.255.255.255          On-link       127.0.0.1     306
  127.255.255.255  255.255.255.255          On-link       127.0.0.1     306
      192.168.2.0    255.255.255.0          On-link     192.168.2.9     266
      192.168.2.9  255.255.255.255          On-link     192.168.2.9     266
    192.168.2.255  255.255.255.255          On-link     192.168.2.9     266
        224.0.0.0        240.0.0.0          On-link       127.0.0.1     306
        224.0.0.0        240.0.0.0          On-link     192.168.2.9     266
  255.255.255.255  255.255.255.255          On-link       127.0.0.1     306
  255.255.255.255  255.255.255.255          On-link     192.168.2.9     266
===========================================================================

IPv6 Route Table
===========================================================================
Active Routes:
 If Metric Network Destination        Gateway
  1    306 ::1/128                     On-link
 10    266 fe80::/64                   On-link
 10    266 fe80::7441:4473:f204:ec1d/128  On-link
  1    306 ff00::/8                    On-link
 10    266 ff00::/8                    On-link
===========================================================================
```

Using Netstat on a Computer Running UNIX or Linux

The command-line parameters for the UNIX/Linux netstat tool are similar to those used in Netstat.exe, but not identical. The UNIX/Linux version has additional parameters. The default netstat display on a UNIX or Linux system is shown in Figure 13-1.

```
[root@localhost /root]# netstat
Active Internet connections (w/o servers)
Proto Recv-Q Send-Q Local Address       Foreign Address       State
Active UNIX domain sockets (w/o servers)
Proto RefCnt Flags     Type      State       I-Node Path
unix  10     [ ]       DGRAM                 980    /dev/log
unix  2      [ ]       DGRAM                 1340
unix  2      [ ]       DGRAM                 1298
unix  2      [ ]       DGRAM                 1264
unix  2      [ ]       DGRAM                 1236
unix  2      [ ]       DGRAM                 1162
unix  2      [ ]       DGRAM                 1128
unix  2      [ ]       DGRAM                 1023
unix  2      [ ]       DGRAM                 992
unix  2      [ ]       STREAM    CONNECTED   490
[root@localhost /root]# _
```

FIGURE 13-1 The default netstat display.

To display the statistics for the system, you run netstat with the -s parameter. The statistics display is shown in Figure 13-2.

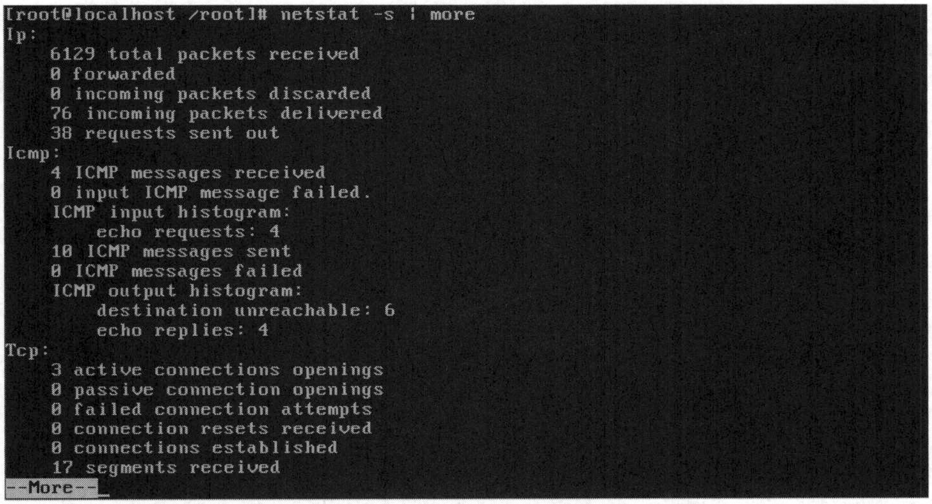

```
[root@localhost /root]# netstat -s | more
Ip:
    6129 total packets received
    0 forwarded
    0 incoming packets discarded
    76 incoming packets delivered
    38 requests sent out
Icmp:
    4 ICMP messages received
    0 input ICMP message failed.
    ICMP input histogram:
        echo requests: 4
    10 ICMP messages sent
    0 ICMP messages failed
    ICMP output histogram:
        destination unreachable: 6
        echo replies: 4
Tcp:
    3 active connections openings
    0 passive connection openings
    0 failed connection attempts
    0 connection resets received
    0 connections established
    17 segments received
--More--
```

FIGURE 13-2 The netstat statistics display.

To display the system's current connections, you run netstat with the -l parameter. The connections display is shown in Figure 13-3.

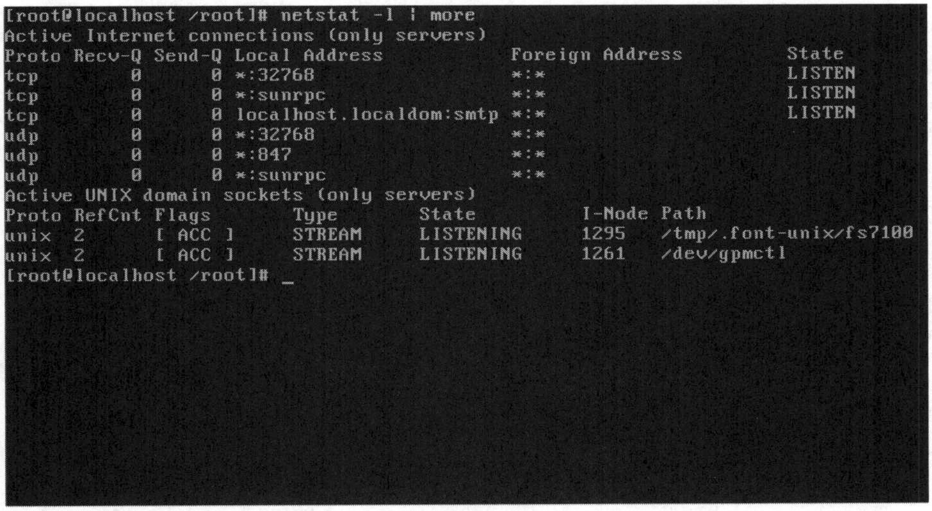

```
[root@localhost /root]# netstat -l | more
Active Internet connections (only servers)
Proto Recv-Q Send-Q Local Address           Foreign Address         State
tcp        0      0 *:32768                 *:*                     LISTEN
tcp        0      0 *:sunrpc                *:*                     LISTEN
tcp        0      0 localhost.localdom:smtp *:*                     LISTEN
udp        0      0 *:32768                 *:*
udp        0      0 *:847                   *:*
udp        0      0 *:sunrpc                *:*
Active UNIX domain sockets (only servers)
Proto RefCnt Flags       Type       State         I-Node Path
unix  2      [ ACC ]     STREAM     LISTENING     1295   /tmp/.font-unix/fs7100
unix  2      [ ACC ]     STREAM     LISTENING     1261   /dev/gpmctl
[root@localhost /root]# _
```

FIGURE 13-3 The netstat connections display.

Nbtstat.exe

Nbtstat.exe is a Windows command-line program that displays information about the Net-BIOS Over TCP/IP (NetBT) connections that Windows uses when communicating with other computers running Windows on a TCP/IP network. The syntax for Nbtstat.exe is as follows.

```
nbtstat [-a name] [-A ipaddress] [-c] [-n] [-r] [-R] [-s] [-S] [-RR]
```

- **-a *name*** Displays the NetBIOS names registered on the computer identified by the *name* variable

- **-A *ipaddress*** Displays the NetBIOS names registered on the computer identified by the *ipaddress* variable

- **-c** Displays the contents of the local computer's NetBIOS name cache

- **-n** Displays the NetBIOS names registered on the local computer

- **-r** Displays the number of NetBIOS names registered and resolved by the local computer, using both broadcasts and Windows Internet Name Service (WINS)

- **-R** Purges the local computer's NetBIOS name cache of all entries and reloads the Lmhosts file

- **-s** Displays a list of the computer's currently active NetBIOS settings (identifying remote computers by name), their current status, and the amount of data transmitted to and received from each system

- **-S** Displays a list of the computer's currently active NetBIOS settings (identifying remote computers by IP address), their current status, and the amount of data transmitted to and received from each system

- **-RR** Sends name release requests to WINS, then starts refresh

EXAM TIP

Unlike most Windows utilities, the command-line parameters for Nbtstat.exe are case-sensitive. When taking the Network+ exam, be alert for questions that differentiate between parameters using uppercase and lowercase.

The NetBIOS cache listing as displayed by Nbtstat.exe -c on a computer running Windows XP appears as follows.

```
Local Area Connection:
Node IpAddress: [192.168.2.11] Scope Id: []
              NetBIOS Remote Cache Name Table

      Name              Type       Host Address    Life [sec]
    ----------------------------------------------------------
    CZ4              <20>  UNIQUE       192.168.2.2       602
    CZ9              <20>  UNIQUE       192.168.2.18      602
    CZ11             <20>  UNIQUE       192.168.2.14      602
    CZ5              <20>  UNIQUE       192.168.2.12      455
    CZ1.ZACKER.LOCA<4C>  UNIQUE       192.168.2.1       172
    CZ10             <20>  UNIQUE       192.168.2.21      602
    CZ1              <20>  UNIQUE       192.168.2.1       602
    COMPAQ-XP        <20>  UNIQUE       192.168.2.27      602
```

The list of NetBIOS names registered by a computer appears as follows.

```
Local Area Connection:
Node IpAddress: [192.168.2.11] Scope Id: []
            NetBIOS Local Name Table

    Name              Type         Status
    ---------------------------------------------
    CZ8          <00>  UNIQUE    Registered
    CZ8          <20>  UNIQUE    Registered
    ZACKER       <00>  GROUP     Registered
    ZACKER       <1E>  GROUP     Registered
```

Nslookup

The *nslookup* (in UNIX) and Nslookup.exe (in Windows) command-line utilities enable you to generate DNS request messages and transmit them to specific DNS servers on the network. The advantage of Nslookup is that you can test the functionality and the quality of the information on a specific DNS server by specifying it on the command line.

The basic command-line syntax of Nslookup is as follows.

```
nslookup DNSname DNSserver
```

- **DNSname**   Specifies the DNS name that you want to resolve
- **DNSserver**   Specifies the DNS name or IP address of the DNS server that you want to query for the name specified in the *DNSname* variable

There are also many additional parameters that you can include on the command line to control the server query process. The output generated by Nslookup.exe in Windows XP looks like the following.

```
C:\Users\craigz.ZACKER>nslookup www.microsoft.com 192.168.2.1
Server:  cz1.zacker.local
Address:  192.168.2.1

Non-authoritative answer:
Name:    lb1.www.ms.akadns.net
Address:  207.46.131.43
Aliases:  www.microsoft.com
          toggle.www.ms.akadns.net
          g.www.ms.akadns.net
```

The Nslookup utility has two operational modes: command-line and interactive. When you run Nslookup with no command-line parameters, the program displays its own prompt from which you can issue commands to specify the default DNS server to query, resolve multiple names, and configure many other aspects of the program's functionality.

Dig

Dig is a name resolution utility that has largely replaced nslookup in most UNIX and Linux distributions, due in part to its extensive list of options and its more detailed output. The basic syntax for dig is as follows.

```
dig @server name type
```

This yields an output like that shown in Figure 13-4.

```
; <<>> DiG 9.7.3 <<>> @192.168.2.1 www.microsoft.com
; (1 server found)
;; global options: +cmd
;; Got answer:
;; ->>HEADER<<- opcode: QUERY, status: NOERROR, id: 28002
;; flags: qr rd ra; QUERY: 1, ANSWER: 4, AUTHORITY: 0, ADDITIONAL: 0

;; QUESTION SECTION:
;www.microsoft.com.              IN      A

;; ANSWER SECTION:
www.microsoft.com.       1066   IN      CNAME   toggle.www.ms.akadns.net.
toggle.www.ms.akadns.net. 60    IN      CNAME   g.www.ms.akadns.net.
g.www.ms.akadns.net.     72     IN      CNAME   lb1.www.ms.akadns.net.
lb1.www.ms.akadns.net.   293    IN      A       207.46.19.254

;; Query time: 25 msec
;; SERVER: 192.168.2.1#53(192.168.2.1)
;; WHEN: Sat Mar 17 15:31:38 2012
;; MSG SIZE  rcvd: 123
```

FIGURE 13-4 Output from the dig program.

Some of the many command-line options for dig are as follows.

```
dig [@server] [-b address] [-f filename] [-k filename] [-m] [-p port#]
  [-t type] [-x address] [-4] [-6] [name] [type]
```

- **@server** Specifies the name or address of the DNS server to be queried.
- **-b address** Specifies the source address to be used in the query.
- **-f filename** Runs the program in batch mode, using the commands in the file identified by the *filename* variable.
- **-k filename** Signs the queries by using transaction signatures found in a key file identified by the *filename* variable.
- **-m** Enables memory usage debugging.
- **-p port#** Specifies the port number to which the program should send queries. The default value is 53.
- **-t type** Specifies the type of query to be performed.
- **-x address** Performs a reverse lookup of the IP address specified by the *address* variable.
- **-4** Performs IPv4 queries only.

- **-6**   Performs IPv6 queries only.
- *name*   Specifies the DNS name to be resolved.
- *type*   Specifies the type of resource records the program should display. The default value is *A*, for host records.

Route

Route.exe, in Windows, and route, in UNIX/Linux, are command-line programs that display and manage the contents of the system's routing table. For syntax and examples, see "Managing Static Routes" in Chapter 7, "Routing and Switching."

EXAM TIP

For the Network+ exam, you should be familiar with the output displays of all the utilities covered in this section.

 Quick Check

1. Which of the tools discussed in this section can you use to locate a faulty router?

2. Which tool has replaced nslookup on many UNIX and Linux distributions?

Quick Check Answers

1. Traceroute

2. Dig

Troubleshooting Methodology

One of the key elements of troubleshooting a network problem is having a plan of action. Many troubleshooting calls are from users who are improperly using software, and these can often be cleared up immediately with some remedial training. When you are faced with what appears to be a real problem, however, you should follow a set troubleshooting procedure, which consists of a series of steps similar to the following:

1. Identify the problem.

2. Establish a theory of probable cause.

3. Test the theory to determine the cause.

4. Establish a plan of action to resolve the problem and identify potential effects.

5. Implement the solution or escalate as necessary.

6. Verify full system functionality and, if applicable, implement preventative measures.

7. Document findings, actions, and outcomes.

Each administrator might use slightly different steps or perform them in a slightly different order, but the overall process should be similar. The following sections examine each of these steps.

Identify the Problem

The first step in troubleshooting a network problem is to determine exactly what is going wrong and to note how the problem affects the network so that you can assign it a priority. In a large network, the network support staff often receives more calls for help than they can handle at one time. Therefore, it is essential to establish a system of priorities that dictates which calls get addressed first.

Establishing Priorities

As in the emergency room of a hospital, the priorities should not necessarily be based on who is first in line. The severity of the problem should determine who gets attention first. However, it is usually not wise to ignore the political reality that senior management problems are addressed before those of the rank and file.

You can use the following guidelines to establish priorities:

- **Shared resources take precedence over individual resources**   A problem with a server or another network component that prevents many users from working must take precedence over one that affects only a single user.

- **Network-wide problems take precedence over workgroup or departmental problems**   A problem with a resource that provides services to the entire network, such as an email server, should take precedence over a problem with a departmental resource, such as a file or print server.

- **Departmental issues should be rated according to the function of the department**   A problem with a resource belonging to a department that is critical to the organization, such as order entry or customer service call centers, should take precedence over a problem with a resource belonging to a department that can better tolerate a period of downtime, such as research and development.

- **System-wide problems take precedence over application problems**   A problem that puts an entire computer out of commission and prevents a user from getting any work done should take precedence over a problem a user is experiencing with a single device or application.

Gathering Information

It is sometimes difficult to determine the exact nature of the problem from the description given by a relatively inexperienced user, but part of the process of narrowing down the cause of a problem involves obtaining accurate information about what has occurred. Users are often vague about what they were doing when they experienced the problem, or even what the indications of the problem were.

For example, in many cases, a user calls the help desk because he or she received an error message, but the user neglects to write down the wording of the message. Training users in the proper procedures for documenting and reporting problems is part of your job as well. It might not be any help now, but it can help the next time a user receives an error.

Begin by asking the user questions like the following:

- What exactly were you doing when the problem occurred?
- Have you had any other problems with your computer lately?
- Was the computer behaving normally just before the problem occurred?
- Has any hardware or software been installed, removed, or reconfigured recently?
- Did you or anyone else do anything to try to resolve the problem?

Identifying the Affected Area

The next step in identifying a network problem is to see whether it can be duplicated. Network problems that can be reproduced are far easier to fix, primarily because you can easily test to see whether a solution was successful. However, many types of network problems are intermittent or might occur for only a short period of time. In these cases, you might have to leave the incident open until the problem occurs again. In some instances, having the user reproduce the problem can lead to the solution. User error is a common cause of problems that might seem to be hardware related or network related.

If you can duplicate a problem, you can set about finding the source of the difficulty. For example, if a user has trouble opening a file in a word-processing application, the difficulty might lie in the file, the application, the user's computer, the file server where the file is stored, or any of the networking components in between. The process of isolating the location of the problem consists of logically and methodically eliminating the elements that are not the cause.

If you can duplicate the problem, you can begin to isolate the cause by reproducing the conditions under which the problem occurred. To do this, use a procedure like the following:

1. Have the user reproduce the problem on the computer repeatedly, to determine whether the user's actions are causing the error.

2. If possible, you should sit at the computer yourself and perform the same task. If the problem does not occur, the cause might lie in how the user is performing a particular task. Watch the user carefully to see if he or she is doing something wrong. It is entirely possible that you and the user are performing the same task in different ways and that the user's method is exposing a problem that yours does not.

3. If the problem recurs when you perform the task, log off from the user's account, log on using an account with administrative privileges, and repeat the task. If the problem does not recur, the user probably does not have the rights or permissions needed to perform the task.

4. If the problem recurs, try to perform the same task on another, similarly equipped computer connected to the same network. If you cannot reproduce the problem on another computer, you know that the cause lies in the user's computer or its connection to the network. If the problem does recur on another computer, then there is a network problem, either in the server that the computer was communicating with or the hardware that connects the two.

If you determine that the problem is in the network and not in the user's computer, the next step is to begin isolating the area of the network that is the source of the problem. For example, if the same problem occurs on a nearby computer, you can begin performing the same task on computers located elsewhere on the network. Again, proceed methodically and document the results. For example, try to reproduce the problem on another computer connected to the same switch, and then on a computer connected to a different switch on the same local area network (LAN). If the problem occurs throughout the LAN, try a computer on a different LAN. Eventually, you should be able to narrow down the source of the problem to a particular component, such as a server, router, switch, or cable.

Establishing What Has Changed

When a computer or other network component that used to work properly now does not, it stands to reason that some change has occurred. When a user reports a problem, it is important to determine how the computing environment changed immediately before the malfunction. Unfortunately, getting this information from the user can often be difficult. The response to the question, "Has anything changed on the computer recently?" is nearly always, "No." Only later will the user remember to mention that a major hardware or software upgrade was performed just before the problem occurred. On a network with properly established maintenance and documentation procedures, you should be able to determine whether the user's computer has been upgraded or modified recently. Official records are the first place to look for information like this.

Major changes, such as the installation of new hardware or software, are obvious possible causes of the problem, but you must be conscious of causes evidenced in more subtle changes as well. For example, an increase in network traffic levels, as disclosed by a protocol analyzer, can contribute to a reduction in network performance.

Occasional problems noticed by several users of the same application, cable segment, or LAN can indicate the existence of a fault in a component of the network. Tracking down the source of a networking problem can often be a form of detective work, and learning to "interrogate" your "suspects" properly can be an important part of the troubleshooting process.

Establish a Theory

When physicians are faced with sick patients, they often use a tool called a differential diagnosis to help them determine what is wrong. A differential diagnosis is an exhaustive list of possible ailments that fit the symptoms. Network troubleshooters can benefit from doing the same thing. After gathering all the information you can, make a list of all the possible problems that fit the circumstances, from the mundane to the extreme.

A user's inability to access a website could be caused by a problem in the user's computer, a problem in the web server, or anywhere in between. When you first begin the troubleshooting process, your differential diagnosis might include everything from an unplugged network cable to solar flares. As you gather more information, you should be able to rule out a lot of the possible causes on your list and work your way down to a manageable few.

The final step of this phase is to select the item from your list that seems to be the most probable cause of the problem. Don't be afraid to question the obvious. To continue the medical metaphor, there's an old doctors' axiom that says, "When you hear hoofbeats, think horses, not zebras." In the context of network troubleshooting, this means that when you look for the probable cause of a problem, start with the obvious cause first.

For example, if a workstation can't communicate with a file server, don't start by checking the routers between the two systems; check the simple things on the workstation first, such as whether the network cable is plugged into the computer. You also must work methodically and document everything so that you don't duplicate your efforts.

Test the Theory

When you have established your theory of the probable cause of the problem, the next step is to test that theory. If you have isolated the problem to a particular piece of equipment, try to determine whether hardware or software is the culprit. If it is a hardware problem, you might replace the unit that is at fault or use an alternative that you know is functioning properly. Communication problems, for example, might force you to start replacing network cables until you find one that is faulty. If the problem is in a server, you might need to replace components, such as hard drives, until the defective component is found. If you determine that the problem is caused by software, try running an application or storing data on a different computer or reinstalling the software on the offending system.

> **NOTE TRIAL AND ERROR**
>
> When testing possible solutions to a problem, be sure to try one solution at a time, and document your actions carefully. Some administrators make the mistake of changing several things at once. The problem might be solved, but you end up not knowing which solution was the effective one.

In some cases, the only way to test your theory involves resolving the problem. For example, if you suspect that a computer's inability to access the network is due to a bad patch cable, the only way to test your theory is to replace the patch cable with one you know is good. If that works, then your theory is confirmed.

In a simple case like this, confirming your theory might actually resolve the problem, but that is not always so. If the problem affects multiple computers, each of which will require modifications, then you might be able to confirm your theory by modifying one, to see if your procedure works.

For example, if multiple users are complaining of slow workstation performance after the installation of a new network application, your theory might be that the computers have insufficient memory. You can test your theory by adding memory to one computer and then seeing if the performance improves. If it does, then your theory is confirmed. However, you will still have to arrange to perform the same modification on all of the other computers experiencing the same problem. In a large enterprise environment, that could represent a large expenditure of time and money.

If your test concludes that your theory is incorrect, then you have to go back to your list of possible causes and decide which of the remaining ones is the next most probable. Then the whole testing process begins again. It is not unusual for a troubleshooter to disprove several theories before arriving at the correct one.

In other cases, you might not be able to actually test your theory, because the solution might have larger repercussions than just fixing the problem. You don't want to take a major network component offline, for example, without considering who will be affected by it. Because other users might need to access to that component, you might have to wait to resolve the problem until a later time, when the network is not in use.

It might even be necessary to bring in outside help, such as a contractor to pull new cables. Arranging for an outside technician can require careful scheduling to avoid having the contractor's work conflict with the activities of the network users. Sometimes you can use an interim solution, such as a substitute component, until your theory can be definitively tested.

Depending on the size of your organization and the chain of command, you might have to escalate the problem by bringing it to someone with greater responsibility than yours, someone who can determine when or if you can safely test your theory.

Establish a Plan of Action

If your theory is proven correct and your solution needs to be implemented on a larger scale, the next step of the process is to create a complete plan of what needs to be done to fully resolve the issue. The plan should include all service interruptions that will be needed and all potential effects on the rest of the network. If the plan includes taking critical network components offline, then it should include the ramifications of that downtime and scheduling recommendations for work during off hours.

It is important, throughout the troubleshooting process, to keep an eye on the big network picture and not become too involved in the problems experienced by one user (or application or LAN). While resolving one problem, you could inadvertently create another that is more severe or that affects more users.

For example, if users on one LAN are experiencing high traffic levels that diminish their workstation performance, you might be able to remedy the problem by connecting some of their computers to a different LAN. However, although this solution might help the users who originally experienced the problem, it might overload another LAN in the process, causing another problem that is more severe than the first one. It might be better to consider a more far-reaching solution instead, such as creating an entirely new LAN and moving some of the affected users over to it.

Implement the Solution

When you have a solution to the problem mapped out and ready, it is time to implement it. If the solution falls within your area of responsibility, you can go ahead and do what is needed. However, if the solution involves other areas, or if special permission is required for the expenditures needed to execute your plan, then this is the time to escalate the issue to someone higher up in your organization's chain of command.

Verify System Functionality

Even if you have already performed small-scale tests to confirm your theory, after your solution is completely implemented, you must test again to confirm its success. To fully test whether the problem is resolved, you should return to the very beginning of the process and repeat the task that originally brought it to light. If the problem no longer occurs, you should test any other functions related to the changes you made, to ensure that fixing one problem has not created another.

At this point, the time you spend documenting the troubleshooting process becomes worthwhile. Repeat the procedures used to duplicate the problem exactly to ensure that the trouble the user originally experienced has been completely eliminated, and not just temporarily masked. If the problem was intermittent to begin with, it might take some time to ascertain whether the solution has been effective. It might be necessary to check with the user several times to make sure that the problem is not recurring.

If the problem ended up being the result of some network condition, or the action of a user administrator, you should consider at this point what must be done to prevent the problem from occurring again. This might involve a change to existing company policy or the creation of a new one.

Document Findings

Although it is presented here as a separate step, the process of documenting all of the actions you perform should begin as soon as the user calls for help. A well-organized network support organization should have a system in place in which each problem call is registered as a trouble ticket that will eventually contain a complete record of the problem and the steps taken to isolate and resolve it.

In many cases, technical support organizations operate using tiers, which are groups of technicians of different skill levels. Calls come in to the first tier, and if the problem is sufficiently complex or the first-tier technician cannot resolve it, the call is escalated to the second tier, which is composed of senior technicians. As long as all who are involved in the process document their activities, there should be no problem when one technician hands off the trouble ticket to another. In addition, keeping careful notes prevents people from duplicating one another's efforts.

The final phase of the troubleshooting process is to explain to the user what happened and why. Of course, the average network user is probably not interested in hearing all the technical details, but it is a good idea to let users know whether their actions caused the problem, exacerbated it, or made it more difficult to resolve. Educating users can lead to a quicker resolution next time or can even prevent a problem from occurring altogether.

EXAM TIP

For the Network+ exam, be sure you are familiar with each of the following steps of the troubleshooting topology:

- Identify the problem:
    - Information gathering
    - Identify symptoms
    - Question users
    - Determine if anything has changed
- Establish a theory of probable cause
    - Question the obvious
- Test the theory to determine cause:
    - Once theory is confirmed determine next steps to resolve problem
    - If theory is not confirmed, re-establish new theory or escalate
- Establish a plan of action to resolve the problem and identify potential effects
- Implement the solution or escalate as necessary
- Verify full system functionality and, if applicable, implement preventative measures
- Document findings, actions, and outcomes

Troubleshooting Connectivity Issues

Connectivity issues on a wired network can conceivably be the result of an improperly configured network adapter or incorrect TCP/IP configuration settings, but with the widespread use of technologies such as Plug and Play and DHCP, these types of problems are becoming less and less frequent. In cases where you cannot trace connectivity problems to the data-link or network layers, you must turn to the physical.

Testing for a physical layer connectivity problem is simple enough: plug a computer that you know is working into the jack of the one that is not. If the good computer fails to connect, then the problem is the network itself, either the cable run or a component at the other end. Plug the other end of the cable run into a port that you know is good and, if it still fails, you know you've got a problem in the cabling.

Chapter 2, "The Physical Layer," describes the tools that administrators use to test cables and the faults that they most commonly find in internal cable runs. The possible faults are numerous: open circuits, short circuits, split pairs, transposed wires, overlength cable runs, bad connectors, excessive interference, and attenuation or decibel loss, for example; but in most cases, the solution is the same: rewire the cable connections at one or both ends of the run. Cable installers should have tested new runs for these issues at the time of the installation, but it is conceivable that cables and connectors could have been moved or damaged since that time.

 EXAM TIP

For the Network+ exam, you should be familiar with the common cable faults listed in this section, and with the nature of the tools used to detect them, including the tone generator and locator, the wire map tester, and the cable certifier.

Troubleshooting Wireless Problems

Wireless LANs have their own unique problems, many of which are mentioned in Chapter 5, "Wireless Networking." The first step in troubleshooting a wireless LAN is to make sure that what you have is actually a wireless problem. If a wired computer experiences the same problem, then you must look at something other than the wireless components.

If the problem occurs only on wireless equipment, then the next step is to consider whether there is any connectivity at all. If the problem is that your wireless devices are not connecting to the network at all, then it's time to look at configuration settings, such as the following:

- **SSID** If you typed the service set identifier (SSID) into a client configuration, make sure that you typed it exactly as it appears in the access point. This is particularly important if you have elected to suppress SSID broadcasting. In addition, if there are other access points in the area that are not broadcasting SSIDs, your systems might be trying to connect to the wrong one. This is called an *SSID mismatch*. You might want to enable SSID broadcasting temporarily so that you can select the correct SSID from a list.

- **Channel** Most wireless LAN devices select the channel used by the access point automatically. If you choose to configure the channel manually, make sure all of your devices are using the same one. If you have multiple access points, configure them to use non-overlapping channels, as described in Chapter 5.

- **Encryption protocol** One of the most common reasons for wireless connection failures is mismatched encryption settings. You can check for this by temporarily turning off all encryption on your access point and your wireless devices. If they connect readily on an open network, then there's a problem with your security configuration. Make sure all of the devices are using the same encryption protocol with the same algorithm. (WPA2-AES and WPA2-TKIP are not the same thing.) If you are working with older devices, you might find that they do not support the latest encryption protocols. If you are running WPA2 on your access point, and you have a computer that only supports WEP, your only options are to reconfigure the access point to use the weaker WEP protocol or replace the network adapter on the computer.

- **Preshared key** If your encryption protocol requires a preshared key, make sure that you've spelled it on your wireless devices just as it appears in your access point.

If your wireless devices are connecting to the access point, but they are connecting at low speeds or experiencing increased latency, it is time to start looking at device placement and possible sources of interference.

- **Signal strength** If the signal a wireless device is receiving is weak, causing reduced connection speeds, the device might just be too far away from the access point. You can resolve this by moving the device or the access point so the two are closer together. You can also purchase a higher-gain antenna for the access point, to boost the signal, or you can simply add additional access points.

- **Interference** If the wireless devices are close enough together to be receiving a strong signal but are not receiving that signal, then you must start looking for sources of interference. Large metal objects, such as refrigerators and HVAC ducts, can block wireless radio signals, as can internal walls, especially if they are made of concrete or cinder block instead of drywall. Because radio signals can bounce off walls and other obstacles, moving access points and other devices a small distance can sometimes yield better connections.

- **Channel selection** Mismatched channels will prevent any connection at all, as noted earlier, but even devices using the same channel can have trouble communicating, if there are other networks in the area using the same one. Because most wireless devices automatically tune to the correct channel for an SSID, you can solve this problem by simply changing the channel on your access point, and all of your other devices will follow.

NOTE **WIRELESS SCANNERS**

There are several applications available that can scan an area for wireless LAN signals and display their strength and the channels they are using. These applications, particularly those for tablets and smartphones, make it easy to survey your network and see how many of your neighbors are using the same channel as yours.

EXAM TIP

The Network+ exam objectives refer to "incorrect switch placement" with respect to wireless troubleshooting. Many wireless access points are actually multifunction devices that include switched ports, but it is not the placement of the switch that is critical; it is the placement of the access point.

Troubleshooting Router and Switch Problems

After they are properly installed and set up, routers and switches don't break very often. Therefore, when you are troubleshooting a network, router and switch issues should be the rare "zebras" that come near the end of your list of possible causes. Problems with routers and switches are most likely the result of incorrect or missing configuration settings, or of some type of hardware or environmental issue.

Some of the router and switch problems you might encounter are described in the following sections.

Hardware Issues

As with any other hardware device, routers and switches are prone to failures caused by the most mundane of issues: power failures. Nearly every experienced administrator has a story about hours spent looking for an obscure technical fault in some piece of equipment or other, only to discover that the cause of the failure was an unplugged power cord.

Experiences like that make checking the incredibly obvious a standard practice that those administrators are not likely to forget in the future. Always make sure that the router or switch is receiving power. The problem with troubleshooting power failures is that routers and switches are sometimes kept in locked server closets or telecommunications rooms, where the power situation is not immediately visible. Intermittent power outages can cause what appear to be mysterious network interruptions, so checking your power source is extremely important.

Also, routers and switches are as susceptible to power spikes as computers, so they should always be equipped with surge protection at the very least, or uninterruptible power supplies (UPSs). Some devices can be equipped with redundant internal power supplies, to prevent service interruptions due to internal failures.

The modular nature of most contemporary business-class routers is another possible source of router errors that are difficult to detect. The proliferation of different fiber optic cable types has led router manufacturers to create replaceable modules, using standards such as Gigabit Interface Converter (GBIC) and Small Form-Factor Pluggable (SFP). These modules plug into a router and make it easy for administrators to connect networks by using various types of cables and connectors.

With any modular architecture such as this, it is possible to purchase a faulty module that fails to function, even while the rest of the router is working. The router should automatically recognize a new module when you power up the router after installing one. Always check the router's interface to make sure that the module has been recognized.

The many different cable and connector combinations available today also make it relatively easy to plug the wrong cable into a router port, whether modular or not. Singlemode and multimode fiber optic cables are not interchangeable, for example, so always make sure that you are using the correct cable, and check that the link lights on the router ports are lit.

Router Configuration Problems

As with any other device on your TCP/IP network, a router must have an IP address and a subnet mask. (In fact, it must have two of them.) Routers don't have keyboards or monitors, so to configure them, you must either connect a terminal by using a serial port or access the router's internal web server with a browser.

Whichever method you choose, you must manually configure the router's network interfaces with TCP/IP configuration settings that are appropriate for the connected networks. The result of incorrect settings, such as an IP address that duplicates one already on the network or an incorrect subnet mask value, is that the misconfigured interface will be unable to communicate with the other systems on the network.

An incorrect default gateway address in the configuration of a router's WAN interface will prevent the router from forwarding outgoing traffic to the WAN provider's network. In the case of a router providing Internet access, an incorrect DNS server address in the WAN interface configuration could prevent clients on the internal network from successfully resolving Internet server names.

Routing Table Problems

Another possible source of router problems is the router's own routing table, particularly if administrators are creating static routes manually. If you connect to the router by using a terminal, you must use a command-line program to create routing table entries. The program is similar to route or Route.exe, with a slightly different, but no less cryptic, syntax.

The slightest typing mistake can result in an incorrect route in the table. Even when you are using a web-based interface, typographical errors are easy to make. Administrators creating multiple routes can also easily skip one, leaving a network unrepresented in the routing table. Convergence problems with dynamic routing protocols that prevent updates from reaching all of the routers on the network can also result in missing routes.

EXAM TIP

For the Network+ exam, be prepared to examine routing table entries and spot those that are improperly configured.

This type of error can be extremely difficult to troubleshoot, because it affects only the traffic going to the destination specified in the incorrect route. The router functions normally except for the traffic going to one network, which ends up being forwarded to the wrong place.

NOTE   DYNAMIC ROUTING

One of the distinct advantages of dynamic routing is that automatically created routing tables are much less prone to errors of this type. Any errors that do appear in a routing table are immediately disseminated to all of the other routers on the network, making the condition they create all the more obvious.

Black Holes

As discussed in Chapter 6, "The Network Layer," the size of the datagrams that IPv4 creates is based on the maximum transmission unit (MTU) of the network to which the system is attached. If, on the path to its destination, a datagram encounters a network with a smaller MTU, the router providing access to that network must split the datagrams into fragments and transmit them separately. This is called an *MTU mismatch*.

Fragmentation is an inherently inefficient process, particularly for the intermediate routers doing the fragmenting. To avoid it, a technique was created called Path MTU Discovery that enables an end system to determine the MTU for an entire route through an internetwork, not just the first hop. This enables the system to create datagrams small enough to travel all the way to their destinations without requiring routers to fragment them.

Path MTU Discovery is simply a series of Internet Control Message Protocol (ICMP) Echo Request messages, the same ones used by the Ping utility. These messages have the Do Not Fragment flag set in the IP header, and they specify a message size equal to the MTU of the end system's network. If the messages do not get through to the destination without being fragmented, the system reduces the message size and tries again. This process is repeated until the system determines the largest packet size that can make it to the destination without being fragmented.

One of the problems with this method is that many routers contain firewalls that block ICMP messages by default. This essentially disables the Path MTU Discovery mechanism and creates what is known as an *MTU black hole*. If your network users experience severe connection problems when accessing the Internet but have no trouble accessing destinations on the local Ethernet network, an MTU black hole is one possible cause. Check the firewall in your Internet access router to see if it is set to block ICMP Echo Request and Echo Reply traffic. Disabling this filter might alleviate the problem.

Switch Configuration Problems

Basic switches, such as those marketed for home users, do not need to be configured; you simply plug them in and they automatically gather the information they need from the incoming packets. However, when you are working with more advanced switches, especially those that provide multilayer functions, such as virtual LANs (VLANs) and routing, configuration is necessary.

Most switches default to an automatic port configuration setting, which causes the switch and the connected device to negotiate common settings for each port. If the settings for the port and the settings in the network adapter of the connected device do not match, the result can be poor throughput or no throughput at all. Depending on which settings are involved, you might or might not see link lights and activity lights on the port.

For the most part, automatic port configuration works well, but if you are dealing with older equipment and are experiencing throughput problems, you might want to consider manually configuring the settings for each port.

The settings you can adjust include the following:

- **Auto versus Manual**   Turns automatic port configuration on or off. If you decide to configure a port manually, you must turn this off.
- **Speed**   When the port and the connected device are configured to run at different speeds (such as 100 megabits per second [Mbps] and 1 gigabit per second [Gbps]), there will be no connection at all, because the two standards use completely different types of signaling.

- **Duplex**   Different duplex settings on the port and the connected device (full duplex versus half duplex) will allow some throughput, but setting them to the same value will greatly increase performance.
- **VLAN**   Illuminated link and activity lights with no communication could be a sign that the port is configured to be in the wrong VLAN. The result is the same as if you plugged a computer with a static IP address on one subnet into a port for another subnet. Normal communication with the VLAN ports on the same switch, but not the ports on another switch, is probably indicative of a problem with the trunking configuration settings that enable communication between switches.

Switching Loops

Another problem common to switches is known as a *switching loop*. The same condition can occur with bridges and is called a bridging loop. A switching loop is a condition that can occur when you have redundant switches on your network to provide multiple paths between destinations. This is often done to introduce a measure of fault tolerance. If one switch fails, packets can take an alternative route through the network.

The problem results when there are multiple connections between two switches. Each switch receives packets from the other switch and forwards them back, creating a loop that circulates packets endlessly. In the case of broadcasts, the switches forward the packets out through all of their ports, causing the number of looping packets to increase exponentially, flooding the network. This is called a *broadcast storm*.

The solution to a switching loop is to leave the redundant switches in place but use a special protocol called the *Spanning Tree Protocol (STP)* on the switches. STP allows only one path for packets through the switching infrastructure, activating others only when a switch fails.

✔ **Quick Check**

1. What is the name for the condition that occurs when the Path MTU Discovery technique fails due to firewalls blocking ICMP messages?
2. How do you prevent broadcast storms from occurring on a network with redundant switches?

Quick Check Answers

1. An MTU black hole.
2. Use the Spanning Tree Protocol.

Network Troubleshooting Scenario: "I Can't Access a Website"

A network user named Alice calls you and reports that she has been trying to access a particular website from her Windows-based computer for several hours and is consistently receiving an error message.

This is a common occurrence for all Internet users, because all Internet resources have occasional and sometimes frequent outages. However, this might also indicate a problem with Alice's computer or with the internal network. Based on the information provided in the scenario, and knowing nothing about Alice's level of expertise, you have no way of knowing whether the problem is caused by user error, a computer configuration problem, a faulty network connection, or a malfunction of the router providing the Internet access. The problem could even be caused by the Internet or the specific website itself—both of which are beyond your sphere of influence.

Incident Administration

The first step for any technical support call is to begin to document the incident. Many help desks use software that technicians can use to document calls and store them in a database. Using help desk software, the technician taking the call can assign a priority to each call; escalate calls to senior technicians, if necessary; list all of the information obtained from the caller; and document the steps taken to solve the problem.

Prioritizing Calls

Because you have only the most rudimentary information about Alice's problem at this point, you cannot accurately assign a priority to this call. If the problem turns out to be with the router or the network itself and a large number of users are affected, it could be very serious, especially if the organization relies on its Internet access for vital business communications. For example, if the organization is a company that sells products over the web and the web servers are located onsite, an Internet connection failure means that the website is down and no orders are coming in. In a case like this, the call might be assigned the highest possible priority. If, on the other hand, revenue-producing work can go on without Internet access, the priority of the call can be somewhat lower. If the problem lies in Alice's computer or in her procedures, the priority of the call can be much lower, unless, of course, Alice is the company president.

Escalating Calls

Many technical support operations separate their technicians into two or more tiers, depending on their expertise and experience. First-tier technicians typically take help desk calls, and if one of these technicians determines that a problem is too serious or complex for him or her to deal with, the technician escalates the call to the second tier. In a well-organized technical support team, the criteria for escalating calls are explicitly documented. For example, problems involving user error and individual workstations might remain in the first tier, whereas network outages and problems affecting multiple users might be immediately escalated. Escalation should also occur when a technician in the first tier makes several earnest attempts to resolve the problem and cannot do so. Of course, political concerns are likely to affect the escalation process, just as in the assignment of priorities. The purpose of this hierarchical arrangement is to prevent the organization's more experienced (and presumably more highly paid) technicians from spending their time fielding calls about elementary problems.

Gathering Information

In this scenario, and in most others as well, the next step in the troubleshooting process is to ask the user about the exact circumstances under which the problem occurred. Until you have more information, it is impossible to assign a priority to the call or determine whether it should be escalated.

Let's say that when you ask Alice to describe what she was doing when the error occurred, she says that she has been trying to open a website in Windows Internet Explorer and after a few seconds received an error message. Because she had always been able to connect to the website before, she tried again several times over the course of an hour but received the same error message every time. Alice did not write down the error message at the time, but she was able to re-create the error by trying again to access the site. The error message was the familiar "This Page Cannot Be Displayed" screen, shown in Figure 13-5, which also says "Cannot Find Server Or DNS Error."

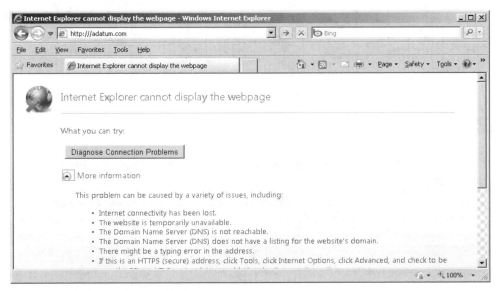

FIGURE 13-5 A common Internet Explorer error message.

This error message is a common one, familiar to every user of Internet Explorer. The error can appear for many reasons: because the web server the browser is trying to contact is down, because the client computer's Internet connection is broken, or because the client's DNS server fails to resolve the DNS name in the requested URL. To determine the cause of the problem, you need to isolate the components that are malfunctioning, which you do by eliminating all of the properly functioning components until you are left with only the problematic ones.

Possible Cause: Internet Router Problem

Difficulty in accessing the Internet is one of the most common problems handled by the help desk in almost any organization with a network that provides routed access to the Internet. For an organization with more than a handful of users, setting up a router that connects to an Internet Service Provider (ISP) is the easiest and most economical way of providing users with Internet access. Depending on the size of the organization and the needs of the users, the router could be a stand-alone unit connected to an ISP by using a leased telephone line, such as a T-1; a computer that connects to the ISP by using a standard broadband connection and that is configured to share that connection with network users; or any one of many solutions falling between these two extremes. A network using a router to connect to the Internet is shown in Figure 13-6.

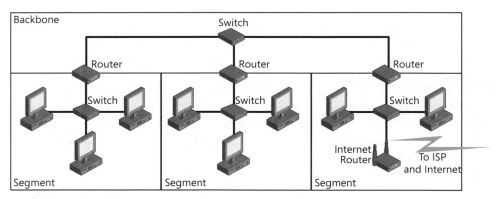

FIGURE 13-6 A shared router connection to an ISP.

Many things can go wrong with this type of routed Internet access solution, including the following:

- **The router's connection to the ISP or the ISP's connection to the Internet is malfunctioning**   A service outage can occur whether the router's connection to the ISP uses a broadband connection, a T-1, or another service such as Integrated Services Digital Network (ISDN). In addition, the ISP providing Internet access is just as likely as your organization is to suffer from network problems. These problems can affect all of the ISP's customers, and there is nothing that you can do about them, except report them to the ISP's own technical support staff.

- **The router device or computer is experiencing a hardware or power failure** If the router connecting the network to the ISP is not functioning, the Internet access requests generated by the client applications running on the users' computers have nowhere to go. When the requested Internet resource does not respond, the client application eventually times out and displays an error message. This condition affects all of the users who access the Internet through that router.

- **There is a problem with the network that prevents access to the router** A broken network cable, a faulty cable connector, or a malfunctioning switch or other network connection device can all prevent a user's Internet access requests from reaching the router, even if the router is functioning properly and is connected to the ISP. The number of users affected by this type of problem depends on the location of the fault and the component that has malfunctioned. For example, if the cable connecting the user's computer to a switch has been severed, only that one computer is affected. If the switch itself is malfunctioning, then all of the computers connected to it are affected. If a central component, such as a backbone cable or switch, is faulty, the problem could extend to a large number of users, or even all of them.

- **The client computer is misconfigured and is not sending Internet access requests to the router** The computer running the web browser or other client application could be experiencing a problem in its networking hardware, its software, or its network configuration. Client configuration problems affect only that client computer and are a common cause of error messages such as the one Alice received.

Generally speaking, a router failure is one of the least likely causes of the problem Alice is experiencing. In addition, if the Internet access router was malfunctioning, you would probably be receiving calls from many different users with the same problem. However, a router problem is one of the easiest causes to check for, and its potential seriousness makes it a high priority. Therefore, it does no harm to eliminate the router as a possible source of the problem as one of the first steps of the troubleshooting process.

The easiest way to test the router is to try to access a website by using a computer that shares the same routed Internet connection as Alice's computer. In Alice's organization, all of the users share a single Internet connection, so you can simply launch a web browser and connect to an Internet website to determine whether the connection and the router are functioning properly. If they are, the source of the problem is likely Alice's procedures, her computer, or her computer's connection to the router.

If your computer also fails to access the Internet, the problem could lie in any one of three areas of the network:

- **In a component that both you and the user use to access the router, such as a switch, a LAN router, or a backbone network** The next step would be to see exactly which of the other users on the network have the same problem. You should then be able to isolate the problem to a particular switch, cable, or other piece of equipment, depending on how widespread the problem is.

- **In the router itself**   To provide the network with Internet access, the router must perform two basic tasks: it must access the Internet itself (through an ISP) and it must forward packets back and forth between the internal network and the ISP's Internet-connected network. If either one of these two functions fails, users cannot access Internet services. If the router is a computer, testing the connection to the ISP is simply a matter of running a web browser on that computer and trying to connect to a website. If that succeeds, check the router configuration to see whether it is communicating with both networks properly and forwarding packets. If the router itself cannot connect to the Internet, the problem might lie in the technology used to connect the router to the ISP.

- **In the connection between the router and the ISP**   All of the wide area network (WAN) technologies used to connect networks to ISPs require hardware at both ends of the connection and a service that provides the communications link between the hardware devices. If the router uses a cable television connection to the ISP, the problem could lie in either one of the two modems involved or in the cable network that provides the connection between them. You can test the modem by replacing it with another that you know works properly. With other technologies, the principles are the same, but testing is likely to be more difficult. It is unlikely that even a large organization has an extra T-1 line sitting around idle.

> *NOTE* **PROXY SERVER CONNECTIONS**
>
> In some cases, network users access websites through a proxy server or another device that functions as an intermediary between the client and the web server. This type of connection introduces another possible source for the problem. However, if you or other users can access the Internet through the same server, you know that it, along with the router and the ISP connection, is functioning properly.

If none of these is the cause of the problem, the difficulty lies in the ISP's network or in the Internet itself. The problem might clear up by itself in a few minutes or hours, but if Internet access is essential to the business, the ISP should be contacted immediately. Dealing with the ISP might be the responsibility of a senior technical support representative, so you might want to escalate the call if the ISP is the problem.

In Alice's case, you determine that the router is functioning normally because you can connect to a website by using your own browser.

Possible Cause: Internet Communication Problem

The next step in narrowing down the cause of Alice's problem is to determine exactly what kinds of network communications are affected. During this procedure, you should methodically test the entire data connection from Alice's computer to the Internet. When a failure occurs, you should trace backward, component by component, until you isolate the source of the problem.

As a help desk technician, you should begin this process while you are still on the telephone with the user. First, ask the user to try connecting to a different website. Using one of the default links supplied with the browser is a good idea because these sites are nearly always in operation and you minimize the possibility of user error. If you must have the user type in a website address, dictate the exact URL to the user, and keep it simple, such as *www.microsoft.com*. If the browser can connect to other websites, you know that the network, the router, and the Internet connection are functioning properly. In this case, the problem can nearly always be traced to either a website that is down or to user error. If the user's web browser cannot connect to any other websites, you should then determine whether any other network communications are possible.

Next, ask the user to open a different client application and try to connect to the Internet. It does not matter which application you select, as long as it connects directly to an Internet server. For example, an email client is a good choice, as long as the user will not connect to a mail server on the local network. As a last resort, you can always have the user launch the File Transfer Protocol (FTP) client from the command line. However, you might have to walk the user carefully through the process of connecting to an FTP server.

If the user cannot access websites with a web browser but can connect to the Internet by using a different client application or even a different web browser, then you know that the problem lies in the browser software running on the user's computer. If the user cannot connect to the Internet by using any client application (and other users can), the next step is to determine which part of the computer's Internet access architecture is failing.

Possible Cause: DNS Failure

One of the most common causes of Internet access problems (and of the error message that Alice received) is the failure of the user's computer to resolve DNS names into the IP addresses that client applications need to communicate with Internet servers. DNS servers are a vital part of any Internet communication that uses a name to refer to an Internet server. IP communications are based solely on IP addresses, not names, so the first thing that a client application does when given the name of a computer, such as *www.microsoft.com*, is to send the name to a DNS server for resolution. When you type the name of a server into your web browser, part of the brief delay that you experience before the webpage starts loading is the time it takes for the client application to generate a DNS Request message containing the server name, send it to a DNS server, and wait for a reply from the DNS server containing the IP addresses associated with the name. Only then can the client transmit its first HTTP message to the web server.

Checking the TCP/IP Client's DNS Configuration

The address of the DNS server that a computer uses to resolve names is supplied as part of the system's TCP/IP client configuration. On a computer running Windows, for example, you can display the DNS server address by executing the ipconfig /all command in a Command Prompt window, as shown in Figure 13-7.

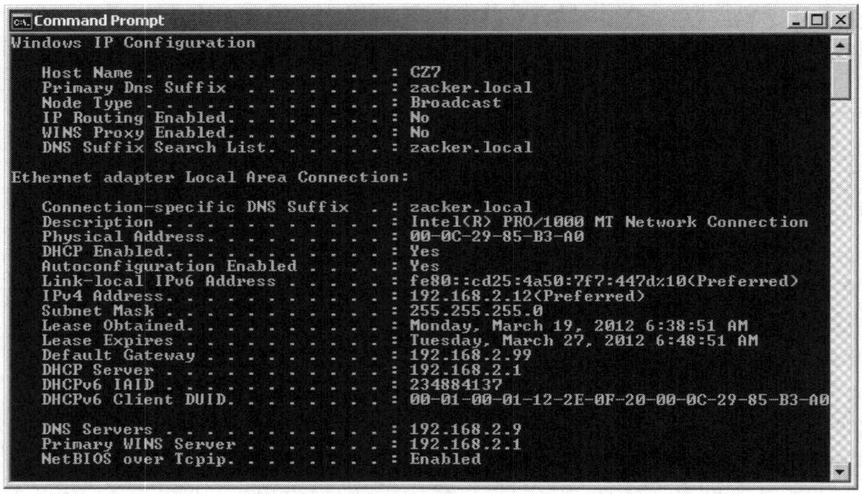

FIGURE 13-7 The output from the ipconfig /all command.

If the addresses of the DNS servers in this display do not point to DNS servers that are up and running, the name resolution process will fail when the user attempts to connect to a web server, resulting in an error message.

The easiest way to test for a DNS name resolution problem is to use an IP address instead of a server name in the web browser's URL field. For example, when the user's browser fails to connect to a web server using its name but other computers can access the Internet, use the Ping program on another computer to resolve the name of the desired server into an IP address, using a command such as the following.

```
ping servername
```

This command first displays the server's name followed by the server's IP address and then displays the results of the attempt to communicate with that server. If the attempt is successful, the program lists each of the replies received from the server. If the Ping command fails to resolve the name (perhaps because the network's DNS servers are not available), you can use the Nslookup command to send a name resolution request to a particular DNS server that you know is operational, on the local network or on the Internet, as demonstrated earlier in this chapter.

> **NOTE PING FAILURES**
>
> A failure of the Ping program to contact a web server does not necessarily indicate a problem. Many web servers today are located behind firewalls that block the ICMP messages that Ping uses, to protect servers from ICMP-based denial-of-service (DoS) attacks. However, Ping should be able to resolve the DNS name, even if the web server is not available.

If the Ping program successfully resolves the name, have the user replace the server name in the browser's URL with the IP address you have discovered. If the browser connects to the server by using an IP address but is unable to do so by using the server name, there is definitely a problem with the DNS name resolution process.

DNS name resolution problems have two major causes: either the computer's TCP/IP client is configured with incorrect DNS server addresses, or the DNS servers themselves are not functioning properly. The easiest way to check the addresses of the DNS servers on the user's computer is to have the user run the ipconfig /all command, as you just did. If the addresses in the ipconfig display are incorrect, you must change them by using the Internet Protocol (TCP/IP) Properties sheet.

> **NOTE   TROUBLESHOOTING IN PERSON**
>
> The user can conceivably perform all of the tests described thus far by following instructions from a help desk technician over the telephone. However, you might want to modify the computer's TCP/IP configuration personally. Depending on the user's location and computing skills and the organization's technical support policies, you might decide to travel to the user's site and personally perform the tests on the computer or use a remote access tool such as Windows Remote Desktop.

If the computer was previously functioning properly, the way in which the DNS server addresses changed might remain a mystery. When users are asked if they have changed anything in their computer's configuration recently, those who have been changing settings they do not understand usually answer, "No." However, if your network uses DHCP servers to configure its TCP/IP clients automatically, you should definitely check the DHCP server configuration to see if it is supplying incorrect addresses to the network clients. If it is, do not manually change the DNS server configuration in the user's computer, but correct the DHCP server's configuration instead. Also, if you are using DHCP, you should check the client DNS settings to make sure the client does not have a manually configured DNS server address when it is supposed to get one from the server. After you have corrected either of these problems, you can repair the user's computer by renewing the DHCP lease with the Ipconfig.exe program.

Checking the DNS Server

If the DNS server addresses in the user's TCP/IP client configuration are correct, the problem might lie in the DNS servers themselves or in the computer's network connection to the DNS servers. The DNS servers that a network uses for Internet name resolution might be supplied by the organization's ISP, or they might be located onsite. If the DNS servers are at fault, multiple users should be experiencing problems.

If the DNS servers belong to the ISP, all you can do is test to see if they are available. If you can contact the DNS servers by using the Ping command with an IP address, you know that they are up and running. However, this does not necessarily mean that they can process DNS

Request messages. Nonetheless, if you can successfully execute a Ping command by using a server name, you have proven that the DNS server can resolve the server's name into its IP address.

If the DNS servers belong to your organization, you can check them more thoroughly. However, this is another area in which the first-tier technician might escalate the call to a senior technician. A Ping test can determine that the DNS server is functioning, but the method for checking the status of the DNS server software itself depends on the operating system and the application software running on the computer. For example, on a computer running Windows Server 2008 R2 and the DNS Server service, you can start by opening the Services console from the Start menu's Administrative Tools program group and checking to see that the DNS Server service is running, as shown in Figure 13-8.

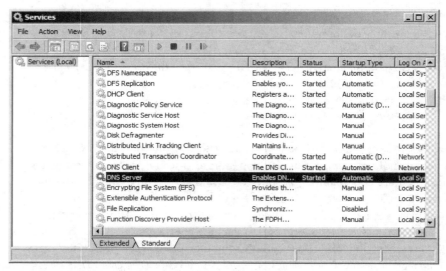

FIGURE 13-8 The Windows Server 2008 R2 Services console.

If the service is not running, you must find out why. The Startup Type field for the DNS Server service should be set to Automatic, indicating that the service loads when the computer starts. If the Startup Type field is set to Manual or Disabled, this is the reason the service is not running. However, before you manually start the service or change the Startup Type setting to Automatic, check with your colleagues to see whether someone has configured it this way for a reason. If the Startup Type is set to Automatic but the service is not running, one of following three things has occurred:

- Someone manually stopped the service.
- The service failed to start.
- The service shut itself down.

Check the computer's Event Viewer console (also accessible from the Administrative Tools group) for log entries that might explain why the service is not running. If the service failed to start during boot time, there should be a log entry indicating the reason. Various types of environmental problems could cause the service to shut down, including a memory shortage or a configuration problem. Troubleshooting issues such as these requires knowledge of the server operating system and the DNS Server software.

If the DNS Server service is running but names are still not being resolved, you need to look at the server software and the DNS communications process in more detail. Examining the DNS server's configuration files is a good place to start. For example, if the server's list containing the names and addresses of the DNS root name servers has somehow been modified or erased, this would prevent names from being resolved, even if everything else is functioning correctly. The DNS server's own network connection and Internet access are also vital to the name resolution process. The server itself might be functioning properly, but if network conditions prevent it from receiving DNS Request messages from the client or if it cannot access the Internet to relay the requests to other DNS servers, the name resolution process stops.

If the DNS server's configuration files show no obvious problems, you might need to use a protocol analyzer to determine whether the DNS server is communicating with the network and the Internet properly. A protocol analyzer is a software program that captures network traffic and displays it for study, as described in Chapter 12, "Network Management." By using the protocol analyzer, you can see the DNS Request packets arriving at the server and the server's own DNS Requests being transmitted to other DNS servers on the Internet, as shown in Figure 13-9.

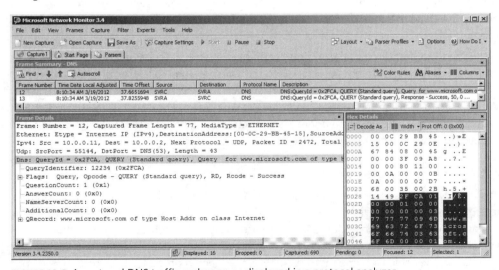

FIGURE 13-9 A captured DNS traffic exchange, as displayed in a protocol analyzer.

To analyze network traffic in this way, you must be familiar with what is known as a *baseline*. In other words, you have to know what the network traffic pattern is supposed to look like before you can determine what's wrong. By analyzing the traffic traveling to and from the server, you might be able to isolate the problem as being in the server's communications with the local network or in its communications with the Internet.

Possible Cause: LAN Communications Problem

If the user's problem is not being caused by an Internet communications problem or a DNS name resolution problem, it is time to start examining the computer's general network communication capabilities. You should begin by having the user try to access resources on the local network. Local network resources can include shared server drives, internal network applications (such as email or database servers), and tools such as Windows Explorer. The best way to start is by having the user try to access nearby resources.

Testing the Local Switch

The first test might be for the user to open Windows Explorer and see whether computers belonging to other nearby users are visible. The assumption here is that other computers nearby are connected to the same network switch as the user experiencing the problem. If there is an internal network communications difficulty, the object is to narrow down where it might be.

You should have information about which computers are connected to specific switches and LANs, preferably in the form of a network map or diagram that shows the cables and connection devices that make up the network. This resource should have been developed during the initial planning stages of the network and should be maintained consistently throughout the network's life. Relying on someone's memory of the network installation makes the technical support process far more difficult, especially when people leave the company or move on to other positions. You should also remember that users probably do not have access to this type of network information and would not know what to do with it if they did.

Windows Explorer displays the computers on the network in terms of domains and workgroups, which probably do not correspond to the switches and LANs that form the network's physical configuration. If you and the user are still working together over the telephone at this point, the user might not understand many of your instructions, so it is important for you to explain carefully what must be done, without introducing unnecessary technical details. In this case, you might consider traveling to the user's site, if that is practical.

Testing the Computer Connection

If the user cannot see other computers connected to the same switch in Windows Explorer, the problem is likely to be in the user's connection to the switch, in the computer hardware or software, or in the user's procedures. In some cases, testing the computer's connection to the switch can be quite easy. If the computer is connected to the switch via a patch cable, you can try replacing the cable with one that you know is functioning properly. If the computer is connected to the switch via an internal cable run, begin by swapping the network cable plugged into the user's computer with a cable from a nearby computer that is working properly. If the user's computer can now access the network, you know that the problem is somewhere in the original cable run, and you can start trying to determine exactly where the problem is.

Begin by swapping out the patch cables at both ends of the connection with replacements that you know are working properly. If the patch cables are not the cause of the problem, you can proceed to test the internal cable run. If you have the proper cable testing equipment, you can test the cable run that way. You can use a multifunction cable tester, a wire map tester, or even an inexpensive multimeter to determine whether the cable is wired properly and signals are getting through.

If there is a break in the cable, the multifunction tester can also tell you where it is in relation to the end you are testing from. If you do not have cable testing equipment, you can plug the patch cables at both ends into a different cable run that you know is working properly. Swapping out equipment wherever possible is one of the most basic and most effective troubleshooting techniques.

Problems with internal cable runs do not happen by themselves. Usually they result when someone working in the spaces where the cables are located accidentally damages one of the cables. In fact, just moving a cable inside a drop ceiling closer to a fluorescent light fixture can be enough to create communication problems on that connection. Therefore, it is strongly recommended that all cables be well secured during installation, even when they are running through relatively inaccessible areas, such as walls and ceilings.

Testing Switch Connections

If the user's computer can see and access other computers connected to the same switch, the next step is to try to access other computers on the same LAN that are connected to different switches. If the user can access computers attached to the same switch but cannot access the other computers on the LAN connected to different switches, the problem might be in the connection between the user's switch and the rest of the network. What you check next depends on the physical configuration of the network. For example, if the user's switch (or hub) is connected to another switch (or hub), that connection might not be functioning properly for several reasons, such as the following:

- **The cable run connecting the two switches is faulty**   As with any network communications problem, the network medium itself could be at fault. If the switches are connected by a patch cable, that cable could have a damaged connector or a kink that caused a break in one or more of the wires. If the switches are connected by an internal cable run, the cable connectors could be wired incorrectly or one of the patch cables could be damaged. Use the cable testing procedures described earlier to check the connection.

- **The connection between the switches does not have a crossover circuit in it**
  In older devices, when you connect one Ethernet switch to another, you must plug one end of the cable into the uplink port on one (and only one) of the switches. This reverses the crossover circuit in the connection, so that the crossovers in the two connected hubs do not cancel each other out. The problem could be that neither end of the cable is plugged into an uplink port or that both ends are plugged into an uplink port. Some switches have a control that you use to specify whether one of the ports functions as an uplink port. If this control is set incorrectly, the result is the same as plugging the cable into the wrong port. Most modern switches configure the crossover circuits automatically, however, so this is no longer a common issue.

- **One or both of the switch ports is damaged**   The switch unit itself might not be functioning properly because of a damaged connector in one of the ports, or for other reasons. Check the link pulse lights (LEDs) for the ports used to connect the two switches together. If both LEDs are not lit when the switches are connected, the two are not communicating properly.

Testing Router Connections

If the user can access computers on other segments of the same LAN, you need to test connections to other LANs. This assumes that the organization's network is really an internetwork that consists of multiple LANs connected by routers or a switched network with multiple VLANs. You can test the computer's connectivity simply by using Ping or Windows Explorer to access computers that are located on other networks. If the user's computer can access hosts in all of the LANs that make up the organization's internetwork, the problem is not one of network connectivity, and you need to look at the computer itself.

If the user's computer can access hosts in some LANs but not others, the problem might be in one of the routers (physical or virtual) that connect the networks together. The difficulty of locating the malfunction depends on how complicated the internetwork configuration is. If the network consists of 30 LANs or VLANs interconnected by dozens of routers with redundant access paths, finding one malfunctioning router can be a complicated process, one that almost certainly has to be attended to by the technicians at the top of the organization's technical support hierarchy.

One method for isolating the router causing the user's problem is to use the Traceroute utility to see exactly where the packets generated by the computer are going. As described earlier in this chapter, Traceroute is a utility that transmits packets to a specified destination and displays a list of the routers that the packets pass through on the way to that destination. When you run Traceroute with the name of the web server the user is trying to reach, the resulting display will indicate exactly how far the packets are going through the local internetwork.

When the packets reach a router that is malfunctioning, Traceroute should stop displaying information. In other words, the last router listed in the Traceroute display should be that of the last properly functioning router in the path to the destination. With knowledge of your network's configuration, you should be able to figure out which router the packets are trying to go to next. This is the router that either is not receiving the packets or is not forwarding them properly, causing the user's communication failure.

For example, suppose that your network consists of multiple LANs containing user computers, all of which are connected to a single backbone LAN, as shown in Figure 13-10.

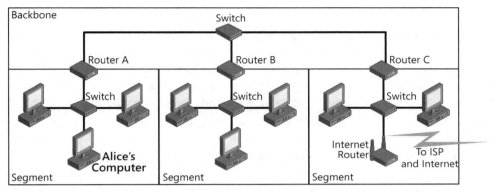

FIGURE 13-10 A single-backbone LAN.

One of the user LANs also contains the router that connects the network to the Internet. Any of the following scenarios could cause the problem that Alice is experiencing. All of these scenarios are likely to cause more than one call to the help desk, however, with the third scenario probably causing a flood of complaints:

- If the router connecting Alice's LAN to the backbone (Router A) fails, Alice's computer would be able to communicate with the computers on her own LAN, but traffic could not reach the backbone or be forwarded to any of the other LANs, including the LAN containing the router that is connected to the Internet. This problem would also affect all of the other computers on Alice's LAN.

- If the router connecting the backbone to the LAN containing the Internet router (Router C) fails, all of the users on the LANs other than the one containing the Internet router would be able to communicate among themselves, but not with users on the Internet router LAN. Also, no one would be able to access the Internet except for the users on the LAN containing the Internet router.

- If the switch on the backbone LAN fails, the result would be the same as in the previous scenario but would also affect all of the traffic between LANs on the entire internetwork. In this case, the internetwork would be reduced to a collection of unconnected LANs, because the backbone would be unavailable to carry traffic between them.

- A cable break on the backbone LAN isolates the LAN served by that cable from the rest of the network, which would make just that one LAN unable to access the Internet or any resources in other LANs, unless, of course, it was the LAN with the Internet router, in which case, it would be the only LAN with Internet access.

Sometimes router failure is a less likely cause of communication problems because of the configuration of the internetwork. The internetwork in this example has only one path between each pair of LANs. To guard against the outages caused by router failures, many internetworks are designed with redundant routers and backbones so that two major failures would have to occur at the same time to cause any of the preceding problem scenarios.

Router failure usually does not result in just one help call. Alice's problem is far more likely to be caused by a procedural error, a configuration error in her computer, or possibly a minor network problem. A router failure would probably result in a general network failure that would cause a large number of simultaneous complaints, which would immediately be brought to the attention of the network's senior support staff and not left to the help desk. When the network administrators are aware of the problem, the role of the first-tier technician is to inform users that they know of the problem and that a fix is forthcoming. There is no need to troubleshoot each call individually when all the calls have the same cause.

Possible Cause: Computer Configuration Problem

If the user's computer cannot access the network in any way and you have determined that neither the network nor the cable connecting the computer to the network is at fault, it is time to look at the computer itself. Although it might seem that it has been a long journey to this point, if a user experiences a problem that prevents any network access, you can omit the switch and router troubleshooting processes described in the previous sections. You might even proceed to this point as soon as you determine that no network communication is possible.

If you determine that the problem is in the computer, the difficulty can exist at almost any level, and it is a good idea to use the Open Systems Interconnection (OSI) reference model to list the various possible causes, as explained in the following sections.

Physical Layer Problems

If you have determined that the cable used to connect the computer to the network is functioning properly, the problem could be in the computer's network interface adapter itself. One common cause of communication problems is a network interface card (NIC) that is loose in its bus slot. If the NIC is not installed firmly into the slot and secured in place with a screw or another device, a tug on the network cable can loosen the card and break the connection between the NIC and the computer. If the NIC is completely disconnected, most operating systems report that the device is not functioning. However, if the NIC is only slightly loosened and not pulled completely out of the slot, the problem could be intermittent and especially difficult to detect. The Device Manager application in Windows can report whether a device is functioning properly, as shown in Figure 13-11.

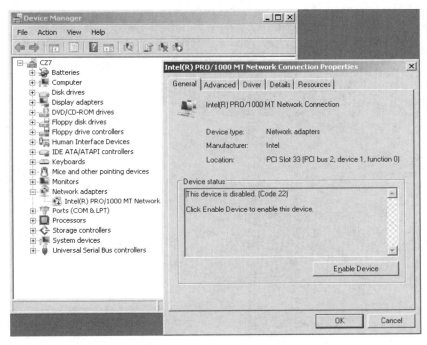

FIGURE 13-11 The Windows Device Manager.

The network interface adapter could also be physically damaged by a power surge, static electricity, or a manufacturing defect. If the adapter's cable connector is damaged, the contacts in the cable plug might not connect properly to the contacts in the adapter's jack. Such problems are difficult to detect, and you usually check the network interface adapter only when you have ruled out all other possible causes of the problem. The solution is nearly always to replace the network interface adapter, but technicians rarely do this until they have checked the configuration of the computer's networking software. If the network interface adapter comes with a diagnostic program, however, and a loopback connector is available, you can test the adapter without having to open up the computer.

Data-Link Layer Problems

Along with the network interface adapter itself, the network interface adapter device driver implements the data-link layer protocol in the computer. The driver must be configured with the same hardware settings as the network interface adapter so that the two can communicate. Incorrect configuration settings can prevent a computer from communicating with the network, but this generally does not occur in a computer that has been functioning properly, unless someone manually changes the configuration settings or a device installation affects them.

When something used to work but now does not, you should ask the user what has changed on the computer. Has the user installed any new hardware or software? Has the user changed any configuration settings? The answer from the user is usually "No," even when it becomes increasingly obvious that something has changed.

In most cases, the hardware settings of both the network interface adapter and the network interface adapter driver are configurable. You generally configure the adapter driver by using an interface provided by the operating system, like that shown in Figure 13-12.

FIGURE 13-12 The Properties sheet for a network interface adapter driver.

Today, most network interface adapters are installed by using Plug and Play (PnP), which automatically configures both the adapter and its driver to use the same settings. The settings chosen are based on an evaluation of the hardware requirements for all of the devices in the computer, so installing a new piece of hardware into the computer can cause PnP to alter the settings of existing devices. Although this is not common, it is possible for PnP to select hardware settings that cause either the adapter or its driver to malfunction. If you determine that some new hardware device has been installed, you might have to disable or remove it to determine whether it is the cause of the network interface adapter's configuration problem. If it is, you might have to manually configure the new device to use it in the computer.

If the network interface adapter configuration or driver parameters have been manually changed (presumably by accident), you should delete the device from the system configuration (again by using Device Manager), restart the computer, and let PnP detect the adapter and reinstall it, reconfiguring both the adapter and the driver in the process.

Network and Transport Layer Problems

Although they span other layers as well, the TCP/IP protocols primarily function at the network and transport layers, and the TCP/IP client configuration is one of the chief causes of network communication problems. Incorrect DNS server addresses can prevent a computer from accessing other computers by name, but other TCP/IP configuration parameters can have an even greater effect on network communications. An incorrect IP address or subnet mask can completely prevent all network communications, and—even worse—an IP address duplicated on a second computer can prevent both computers from accessing the network. Therefore, network communications can be interrupted if the IP address on the user's computer has been changed or if a computer somewhere else on the network has been configured to use the same IP address as the user's computer.

To test for a duplicate IP address, shut down the user's computer and use another workstation to ping the IP address of the user's computer. If you receive a response to the Ping command, another computer is using that same IP address.

An incorrect or missing default gateway parameter can also cause the user's problem. A workstation that is not configured with a correct default gateway address can access the other computers on its own LAN, but it cannot access any of the other LANs on the internetwork. Without a default gateway address, the computer does not know where to send packets that are destined for other networks. This prevents the user's web browser from connecting to any sites on the Internet. In Windows, to modify any of the TCP/IP configuration parameters listed here, use the Internet Protocol (TCP/IP) Properties sheet.

If the network has DHCP servers that configure the network's TCP/IP clients, none of the fields in the workstation's Internet Protocol (TCP/IP) Properties dialog box should have values in them. Manually configured TCP/IP parameters take precedence over those supplied by DHCP. If someone has been "experimenting" by supplying his or her own TCP/IP values, remove them before reactivating the DHCP client.

You also need to know what allocation mode the DHCP servers are using. If they are using automatic allocation, which assigns the IP address to clients permanently, moving the computer to a different subnet requires that you manually release the assigned IP address and renew it so that the DHCP server can assign one from the proper subnet. This is another way for the computer to have an incorrect IP address. If you move computers around on the network frequently, consider using dynamic allocation, which leases addresses to computers for a short period of time and renews them each time the computer starts.

Application Layer Problems

Application layer networking protocols are generally not configurable, but problems at the application level can affect network communications. Virus infections, for example, can affect network communications, and new viruses that can have unpredictable effects on a computer are constantly being invented. If you do not already have antivirus software installed on the computer, you should install it, make sure that the virus signatures are updated, and run a complete system scan, just to be safe.

Applications themselves can be damaged or improperly configured as well, interfering with network communications. For example, if Alice were to modify the configuration of her browser, causing it to access the Internet by dialing out to an ISP instead of using the LAN, she would be unable to access any websites if a modem was not installed or a dial-up account was not properly configured. This problem would be specific to the browser, however, and would be caught when you had Alice try to use another application to access the Internet.

Possible Cause: User Error

User error is one of the most common causes of help desk calls. Listing this possible cause last does not imply that you should go through all of the testing procedures described thus far before addressing the possibility of user error. In fact, you can often quickly determine that the user's equipment and the network are functioning properly and that the problem must be in something the user did. However, in the interests of diplomacy, it is often a good idea to be certain that a procedural error is the problem before you broach the subject with the user. Some people are perfectly willing to admit that they might be at fault, whereas others can be very sensitive about it. Part of your job is to resolve callers' problems without making them feel foolish.

User error can easily be the reason for a failure to access a website, and it can sometimes be difficult to detect when working with the user over the telephone. Many common Internet access problems are caused by entering incorrect URLs into the browser. For this reason, when you are having the user test the system by trying to access other sites, it is best to use existing bookmarks or favorites whenever possible. It might seem as though the user is experiencing a severe Internet connectivity problem, and you might be tempted to perform all sorts of network and hardware tests like those described earlier. Before engaging in such tests, however, make sure that the user is not making a beginner's error such as typing the URL with backslashes instead of forward slashes or inserting three forward slashes after the *http:* prefix instead of two.

In fact, user error is the cause of Alice's problem. She had somehow gotten the impression that three forward slashes were correct and was using them even when you were working with her over the telephone, dictating the URLs of other sites she should try to test her Internet connectivity. You started your dictation with *www*, knowing that typing the *http://* prefix is not necessary in most cases, but Alice added it to each URL on her own, assuming that it had to be there, using three forward slashes instead of two. You could have solved this particular problem almost immediately if you had gone to Alice's location and watched her type the URLs. This is not to say that every call to the help desk should be immediately followed by a trip to the user's location. In many cases, that would be impractical. However, this particular case demonstrates how important the communication between the technician and the user can be.

Many other common procedural errors can interfere with a user's network connectivity, and many of these can be very difficult to catch over the telephone. Sometimes there is no substitute for watching what the user is doing. User logons, for example, are a common source of difficulties. Users often call the help desk because they cannot log on to the network. If a user has been trying to log on repeatedly and is failing every time, you should first check to see if the user has been locked out of the account. Many networks are configured to disable accounts after a certain number of failed logon attempts, in an effort to prevent brute-force attacks by intruders. (A *brute-force attack*, in this case, is an attempt to penetrate an authentication protocol by trying every possible password.)

If the account is not locked, password policies might also be to blame. Users might ignore messages telling them that a periodic password change is required or might attempt to reuse old passwords when policy dictates against it. Two other common occurrences among users on Windows-based computers are trying to log on to the wrong domain or using the wrong account to log on to the local system. The Domain setting in the Logon dialog box might have been changed somehow, which is something that you are not likely to realize without actually watching the user try to log on.

Exercise

The answers for this exercise are located in the "Answers" section at the end of this chapter.

On an internetwork consisting of several user segments connected by a backbone, with an Internet router connected directly to the backbone, specify whether the following network conditions would normally cause Internet access problems for one user only, for all of the users connected to one switch, for all of the users on one LAN, or for the entire internetwork.

1. Both ends of a cable connecting two switches are plugged into uplink ports.

2. The router connecting the network to the ISP is down.

3. The cable connecting a user's computer to the switch is cut.

4. The ISP's connection to the Internet fails.

5. The router connecting a user LAN to the backbone malfunctions.

Chapter Summary

- The ping (in UNIX) and Ping.exe (in Windows) programs generate a series of Echo Request messages using the Internet Control Message Protocol (ICMP) and transmit them to the computer whose name or IP address you specify on the command line.

- Traceroute is a variant of the Ping program that displays the path that packets take to their destination.

- UNIX and Linux systems have a program called ifconfig (the name is derived from the words *interface configuration*) that is used to configure the properties of network interface adapters and assign TCP/IP configuration parameters to them. Windows has a version of this program, Ipconfig.exe, which omits most of the configuration capabilities and retains the configuration display.

- Netstat is a command-line program that displays status information about the current network connections of a computer running TCP/IP and about the traffic generated by the TCP/IP protocols.

- Nbtstat.exe is a Windows command-line program that displays information about the NetBIOS Over TCP/IP (NetBT) connections that Windows uses when communicating with other computers running Windows on a TCP/IP network.

- The nslookup (in UNIX) and Nslookup.exe (in Windows) command-line utilities enable you to generate DNS request messages and transmit them to specific DNS servers on the network.

- Dig is a name-resolution utility that has largely replaced nslookup in most UNIX and Linux distributions, due in part to its extensive list of options and its more detailed output.

- Route.exe (in Windows) and route (in UNIX/Linux) are command-line programs that display and manage the contents of the system's routing table.

- One of the key elements of troubleshooting a network problem is having a plan of action. When you are faced with what appears to be a real problem, you should follow a set troubleshooting procedure.

- In cases where you cannot trace connectivity problems to the data-link or network layers, you must turn to the physical layer.

- The first step in troubleshooting a wireless LAN is to make sure that the problem is actually a wireless problem. If a wired computer experiences the same problem, then you must look at something other than the wireless components.

- Problems with routers and switches are most likely the result of incorrect or missing configuration settings or of some type of hardware or environmental issue.

Chapter Review

Test your knowledge of the information in Chapter 13 by answering these questions. The answers to these questions, and the explanations of why each answer choice is correct or incorrect, are located in the "Answers" section at the end of this chapter.

1. Which TCP/IP utility should you use to most easily identify a malfunctioning router on your internetwork?

    A. Ifconfig

    B. Ping

    C. Traceroute

    D. Netstat

2. Which of the following protocols does the ping program never use to carry its messages?

   A. Ethernet

   B. ICMP

   C. IP

   D. UDP

3. Which of the following commands displays the routing table on the local computer?

   A. Arp -r

   B. Netstat -r

   C. Nbtstat -r

   D. Telnet -r

4. Which command would you use to purge the NetBIOS name cache on the local computer?

   A. Nbtstat -c

   B. Nbtstat -n

   C. Nbtstat -r

   D. Nbtstat -R

Answers

This section contains the answers to the questions for the Exercise and Chapter Review in this chapter.

Exercise

1. All of the users on one switch

2. The entire internetwork

3. One user only

4. The entire internetwork

5. All of the users on one LAN

Chapter Review

1. **Correct Answer:** C

   A. **Incorrect:** Ifconfig is a network configuration utility for UNIX/Linux systems.

   B. **Incorrect:** Ping can test connectivity to another TCP/IP system, but it cannot locate a malfunctioning router.

   C. **Correct:** Traceroute can locate a malfunctioning router by using ICMP Echo Request messages with incrementing TTL values.

   D. **Incorrect:** Netstat displays information about network connections and traffic. It cannot locate a malfunctioning router.

2. **Correct Answer:** D

   A. **Incorrect:** Ping transactions to destinations on the local network are encapsulated within Ethernet frames.

   B. **Incorrect:** All ping transactions use ICMP messages.

   C. **Incorrect:** All ICMP messages are encapsulated within IP datagrams.

   D. **Correct:** ICMP messages are encapsulated directly within IP datagrams; they do not use transport layer protocols such as UDP.

3. **Correct Answer:** B

    A. **Incorrect:** The arp utility is for adding addresses to the arp cache; it cannot display the routing table.

    B. **Correct:** The netstat utility can display the routing table, along with other types of network traffic and port information.

    C. **Incorrect:** The nbtstat utility displays information about Windows NetBT connections; it cannot display the routing table.

    D. **Incorrect:** Telnet is a terminal emulation program; it cannot display the routing table.

4. **Correct Answer:** D

    A. **Incorrect:** Running nbtstat with the -c switch displays the contents of the NetBIOS name cache.

    B. **Incorrect:** Running nbtstat with the -n switch displays the names registered on the computer.

    C. **Incorrect:** Running nbtstat with the -r switch displays the number of NetBIOS names registered and resolved by the computer.

    D. **Correct:** Running nbtstat with the -R switch purges the NetBIOS name cache.

Glossary

1000Base-CX A Gigabit Ethernet specification calling for a special 150-ohm twinaxial cable with two copper cores.

1000Base-LX A Gigabit Ethernet specification supporting long distances using singlemode fiber optic cable.

1000Base-SX A Gigabit Ethernet specification using multimode fiber optic cable and supporting distances shorter than those supported by 100Base-LX.

1000Base-T A Gigabit Ethernet specification that calls for CAT5e or CAT6 cable grades, using all four wire pairs and with a 100-meter maximum segment length.

1000Base-X A collective term for the two Gigabit Ethernet fiber optic configurations, plus a short-run copper alternative.

100Base-T A collective term for the 100Base-T4 and 100Base-TX specifications.

100Base-T4 An alternative Fast Ethernet specification that calls for four wire pairs of CAT3 UTP cable.

100Base-TX The primary Fast Ethernet copper cable specification using two wire pairs on CAT5 cable, with a 100-meter maximum segment length.

100Base-X A collective term for the 100Base-TX and 100Base-FX Fast Ethernet specifications.

10Base-FL A 10-Mbps Ethernet physical layer specification calling for fiber optic cable.

10Gbase-ER A 10 Gigabit Ethernet LAN specification calling for singlemode fiber optic cable and extra-long wavelength signaling.

10Gbase-EW A 10 Gigabit Ethernet WAN specification calling for singlemode fiber optic cable and extra-long wavelength signaling.

10Gbase-LR A 10 Gigabit Ethernet LAN specification calling for singlemode fiber optic cable and long wavelength signaling.

10Gbase-LW A 10 Gigabit Ethernet WAN specification calling for singlemode fiber optic cable and long wavelength signaling.

10Gbase-SR A 10 Gigabit Ethernet LAN specification calling for multimode fiber optic cable and short wavelength signaling.

10Gbase-SW A 10 Gigabit Ethernet WAN specification calling for multimode fiber optic cable and short wavelength signaling.

10Gbase-T A 10 Gigabit Ethernet specification calling for copper-based UTP cables with a 100-meter maximum segment length.

110 block A type of patch panel used for UTP cable connections in telecommunications rooms.

5-4-3 rule An Ethernet policy stating that a network can have as many as five cable segments, connected by four repeaters, of which three of the segments can be mixing segments.

66 block A type of patch panel typically used for telephone cable connections in telecommunications rooms.

8P8C A type of modular connector used for UTP cables in a LAN environment. Similar to and often mistaken for the RJ45 connector.

abstract syntax The native format used by a computer to encode information generated by an application or process.

access control list (ACL) A list of users, or groups of users, who are permitted to access a resource, as well as the degree of access each user or group is permitted.

active mode An FTP operational mode in which the client sends its IP address and an ephemeral port number to the server, and the server initiates the connection establishment process.

ad hoc topology A type of wireless networking topology in which all of the network devices in the BSS are mobile or portable and there is no central access point or base station.

Address Resolution Protocol (ARP) A data-link layer protocol that resolves IP addresses into hardware addresses.

ADSL Termination Unit-Remote (ATU-R) The hardware device located at the client side of an ADSL connection. Also called a *DSL transceiver* or a *DSL modem*. The ATU-R connects to the computer by using either a USB port or a standard Ethernet network interface adapter. *See also* Asymmetrical Digital Subscriber Line (ADSL), Digital Subscriber Line Access Multiplexer (DSLAM).

Asymmetrical Digital Subscriber Line (ADSL) A point-to-point, digital WAN technology that uses standard telephone lines to provide consumers with high-speed Internet access, remote LAN access, and other services. The term "asymmetric" refers to the fact that the service provides a higher transmission rate for downstream than for upstream traffic. Downstream transmission rates can be up to 8.448 Mbps, whereas upstream rates range up to 640 Kbps. *See also* Digital Subscriber Line (DSL).

Asynchronous Transfer Mode (ATM) A network communications technology based on 53-byte cells, designed to carry voice, data, and video traffic over LANs and WANs at speeds ranging from 25.6 Mbps to 2.46 Gbps.

attenuation A type of signal degradation characterized by a signal's weakening in strength the longer it travels on a network medium.

authentication The process of verifying a user's identity, for the purpose of distinguishing legitimate users from uninvited guests.

Authentication Header (AH) One of the protocols used by IPsec to protect data as it is transmitted over the network. AH provides authentication, anti-replay, and data integrity services, but it does not encrypt the data.

authorization The process of verifying the level of access to a protected resource that an authenticated user should receive.

automatic MDI/MDIX configuration (Auto-MDIX) A feature by which Ethernet devices automatically configure the crossover circuits needed to establish network connections.

autonegotiation A mechanism by which Ethernet systems sense the capabilities of the networks to which they are connected and adjust their speed and duplex status accordingly.

autonomous system (AS) The largest and highest-level administrative unit on the Internet.

backbone A network segment that connects multiple other networks together, forming an internetwork.

backoff period An interval that Ethernet systems wait after a collision occurs before retransmitting their data.

baseband network A network that uses a medium that can carry only one signal at a time.

Basic Rate Interface (BRI) An ISDN service that consists of two 64-Kbps B channels plus one 16-Kbps D channel, enabling users to combine the B channels for a single 128-Kbps data pipe or use them separately. Also called *2B+D*, BRI is the primary consumer ISDN service used for Internet access and remote networking. *See also* Integrated Services Digital Network (ISDN), Primary Rate Interface (PRI).

basic service set (BSS) A geographical area within which properly equipped wireless stations can communicate.

basic service set identifier (BSSID) In wireless networking, the 6-byte MAC address of the basic service set. In an ad hoc network, the BSSID is a randomly generated number.

BNC connector A type of bayonet connector used on RG-58 coaxial cables.

Bootstrap Protocol (BOOTP) An IP address assignment protocol, progenitor to DHCP, that can assign addresses but not reclaim them for reassignment.

Border Gateway Protocol (BGP) The exterior gateway routing protocol now in use on the Internet.

bounded media A type of network in which signals are restricted to a specific location. Also known as *wired media*.

bridge A data-link layer device that splits a LAN into two separate collision domains and filters the packets passing between them by using their hardware addresses.

bridge loop A condition that can occur when bridges or switches that have redundant paths through the network begin forwarding traffic in an endless cycle.

broadband network A network that uses a medium that can carry multiple signals simultaneously, by using a technique called multiplexing.

broadband over power lines (BPL) A data transmission technology that is designed to supply homes with Internet access by using the public electric power grid.

broadcast domain The group of computers that will receive a broadcast message transmitted by any one of its members.

broadcast storm A type of switching loop in which broadcast packets are forwarded endlessly around the network.

buffer overflow A condition in which a program sends too much data to a buffer and the data spills over into an area of memory intended for another purpose.

bus topology An arrangement of network connections in which each node is connected to the next one, with both ends terminated to prevent signal reflection.

butt set The standard tool of a telephone network technician, consisting of a one-handed portable telephone with alligator clips for connecting to any accessible line.

cable certifier A handheld cable testing device that compares the actual performance levels of a cable to a set of standardized levels.

cable television (CATV) network A private metropolitan area network (MAN) constructed and owned by a cable television company for the purpose of delivering TV signals to customers in a particular region. Because the network technology they use is compatible with data networking, many CATV companies are now also in the business of providing Internet access to consumers by using the same network that delivers the television service. The downstream transmission rates for a CATV Internet connection far exceed those of standard dial-ups and most other consumer Internet solutions, and the cost is usually very competitive.

Cache Array Routing Protocol (CARP) An application layer protocol that enables clients to route requests for specific URLs to the proxy server containing that cached data.

caching-only server In DNS, a server that clients use to resolve names, but that is not the authoritative source for any domain.

Carrier Sense Multiple Access with Collision Avoidance (CSMA/CA) The media access control mechanism used by 802.11 wireless LANs, a variation of the Carrier Sense Multiple Access with Collision Detection (CSMA/CD) mechanism used by Ethernet.

channel A division within a specified frequency band that enables multiple networks to coexist in the same area by using different parts of the available bandwidth.

channel bonding A technique for combining two 20-MHz 802.11n channels into one 40-MHz channel, increasing the network's data transfer rate.

channel service unit/data service unit (CSU/DSU)
A hardware device that terminates the end of a leased line connection and provides testing and diagnostic capabilities. *See also* leased line.

Classless Inter-Domain Routing (CIDR) A subnetting method that enables administrators to place the division between the network bits and the host bits anywhere in the address, not just between octets. This makes it possible to create networks of various sizes.

client/server networking A computing model in which data processing tasks are distributed between clients—which request, display, and manipulate information—and servers, which supply and store information and resources.

collision In local area networking, a condition in which two computers transmit data at precisely the same time and their signals both occupy the same cable, causing data loss.

collision domain A group of network devices connected in such a way that if two devices transmit at the same time, a collision occurs.

convergence The process of updating the routing tables on all of a network's routers in response to a change in the network (such as the failure or addition of a router).

count-to-infinity problem A condition that occurs when a router detects a failure in the network, modifies the appropriate entry in its routing table accordingly, and then has that entry updated by an advertisement from another router before it can broadcast it in its own advertisements. The routers then proceed to bounce their updates back and forth, increasing the metric for the same entry each time until it reaches infinity (16).

crimper A cable installer's tool for attaching connectors to bulk cables.

crossover cable An unshielded twisted pair cable with the transmit pins in each connector wired to the receive pins in the other connector.

crosstalk A type of signal interference common to UTP cables, caused by signals from one wire bleeding over into another.

cut-through switch A type of switch that begins forwarding an incoming packet as soon as it reads the destination hardware address.

cyclical redundancy check (CRC) An error-detection mechanism in which a computer performs a calculation on a data sample with a specific algorithm and then transmits the data and the results of the calculation to another computer. The receiving computer then performs the same calculation and compares its results to those supplied by the sender. If the results match, the data has been transmitted successfully. If the results do not match, the data has been damaged in transit.

data encapsulation The process by which information generated by an application is packaged for transmission over a network by successive protocols operating at the various layers of the Open Systems Interconnection (OSI) reference model.

datagram A term for the unit of data used by the Internet Protocol (IP) and other network layer protocols.

delayed acknowledgment A TCP packet acknowledgment method in which systems do not have to generate a separate acknowledgment message for every data message they receive.

demarc Short for *demarcation point*, the location where outside services enter a building.

demarc extension In a structured cabling system, the next device on the inside of a building adjacent to a demarc.

denial of service (DoS) A type of security attack that degrades the performance of a system by flooding it with incoming traffic.

dense wave division multiplexing (DWDM) A data transmission technique used on SONET links that calls for the use of devices called *erbium-doped fiber amplifiers (EDFAs)*, which are designed to amplify wavelengths in the 1,525–1,565-nanometer or 1,570–1,610-nanometer bands without converting them to electrical signals. This is a cheaper and more efficient method of transmitting long-range optical signals than the optical-electrical-optical (OEO) regenerators they replace.

DHCP relay agent A software module located in a computer or router on a particular network segment that enables the other systems on that segment to be serviced by a DHCP server located on a remote segment.

dig A name resolution utility that has largely replaced nslookup in most UNIX and Linux distributions.

Digital Signal 1 (DS1) A framing method used on leased lines that consists of 8-bit channels called Digital Signal 0s (DS0s), plus a framing bit used for synchronization.

Digital Subscriber Line (DSL) A type of point-to-point, digital WAN connection that uses standard telephone lines to provide high-speed communications. DSL is available in many different forms, including Asymmetrical Digital Subscriber Line (ADSL) and high-bit-rate Digital Subscriber Line (HDSL). The various DSL technologies differ greatly in their speeds and in the maximum possible distance between the installation site and the telephone company's nearest central office. DSL connections are used for many applications, ranging from LAN and PBX interconnections to consumer Internet access. *See also* Asymmetrical Digital Subscriber Line (ADSL).

Digital Subscriber Line Access Multiplexer (DSLAM) The hardware device located at the server side of an ADSL connection. *See also* ADSL Termination Unit-Remote (ATU-R), Asymmetrical Digital Subscriber Line (ADSL).

direct route A routing table entry for a destination on a local network.

Direct-Sequence Spread Spectrum (DSSS) A type of radio frequency modulation used on 802.11 networks that modulates the signal by using a digital code called a chip, which has a bit rate larger than that of the data signal.

distance vector protocol A routing protocol that uses metrics based on the number of hops to the destination.

distributed denial of service (DDoS) A type of denial of service attack perpetrated by one attacker using remotely controlled computers scattered around the Internet.

distribution system (DS) In wireless networking, an architectural element that connects basic service sets together.

domain An organizational construct used to build a hierarchy not unlike the directory tree in a file system, for the purpose of delegating responsibility for network administration.

Domain Name System (DNS) A database service that converts computer names to IP addresses and addresses back into names.

Dynamic Host Configuration Protocol (DHCP) A service that automatically configures the TCP/IP client computers on a network by assigning them unique Internet Protocol (IP) addresses and other configuration parameters.

dynamic NAT A network address translation technique that translates each unregistered address to one of the available registered addresses.

dynamic routing A method for updating routing tables in which routers use specialized protocols to automatically create routing table entries.

E-1 A dedicated telephone connection, also called a *leased line,* running at 2.048 Mbps. An E-1 is the closest European equivalent to a T-1. *See also* T-1, leased line.

E-3 A dedicated telephone connection, also called a *leased line,* running at 34.368 Mbps. An E-3 is the European equivalent of a T-3. *See also* T-3, leased line.

electromagnetic interference (EMI) A type of radiation that affects the quality of electrical signals traveling over a network medium.

Encapsulating Security Payload (ESP) One of the protocols used by IPsec to protect data as it is transmitted over the network. ESP provides encryption, authentication, anti-replay, and data integrity services.

end system On a TCP/IP network, a computer or other device that is the original sender or ultimate recipient of a transmission.

end-to-end principle A guiding principle of network design stating that it is inherently more efficient to implement application functions in end systems rather than intermediate systems (routers).

Enhanced Interior Gateway Routing Protocol (EIGRP) A hybrid protocol developed in response to the complaints directed at RIP.

ephemeral port number A TCP or UDP port number of 1024 or higher, chosen at random by a TCP/IP client computer during the initiation of a transaction with a server.

Evolved HSPA Also known as HSPA+, a cellular communications standard that appeared in 2008 and is now widely implemented that can boost downstream data rates to 84 Mbps by using multiple-input, multiple-output (MIMO) technology.

extended service set (ESS) In wireless networking, the combination of two or more basic service sets using a common service set identifier and the distribution system that connects them together.

Extensible Authentication Protocol (EAP) A shell protocol that enables systems to use various types of authentication mechanisms.

exterior gateway protocol (EGP) A type of routing protocol that updates the border routers in different autonomous systems.

F connector A type of screw-on connector used on various types of coaxial cable.

fast link pulse (FLP) A variation on the NLP signals used by 10Base-T and 10Base-FL networks that enables Ethernet devices to autonegotiate their speed and duplex status.

fiber optic A type of cable that carries light pulse signals over conductors made of plastic or glass.

Fiber Optic Inter-Repeater Link (FOIRL) An early Ethernet physical layer specification calling for fiber optic cable.

File Transfer Protocol (FTP) An application-layer TCP/IP protocol that enables an authenticated client to connect to a server and transfer files to and from its drives.

firewall A hardware or software product that protects a network from unauthorized access by outside parties while letting appropriate traffic through.

fish tape A tool used by cable installers to pull cables through walls and other closed spaces.

flow control A function of certain data transfer protocols that enables a system receiving data to transmit signals to the sender instructing it to slow down or speed up its transmissions.

FLP burst A 16-bit data packet included within a burst of link pulses.

forwarder A DNS server that is deliberately configured to receive recursive queries from other servers.

frame A unit of data that is constructed, transmitted, and received by data-link layer protocols such as Ethernet.

frame aggregation A data transmission technique that combines the payload data from several frames into one large frame, thus reducing the amount of overhead and increasing the information throughput of the network.

frame relay A WAN technology in which two systems are each connected to a frame relay network called a *cloud,* and a virtual circuit is established between them through the cloud. The advantages of frame relay over a leased line are that the amount of bandwidth provided by the connection is flexible and that one site can be connected to numerous other sites via multiple virtual circuits. *See also* leased line.

Frequency-Hopping Spread Spectrum (FHSS) A type of radio frequency modulation used on 802.11b networks that uses a predetermined code or algorithm to dictate frequency shifts that occur continually, in discrete increments, over a wide band of frequencies.

FTP bounce A type of security attack that involves the use of the Port command in the FTP protocol to gain access to ports in another computer that are otherwise blocked.

FTTx A generic term for various multimedia services that run on fiber optic cable delivered close to the end user's premises.

full-duplex A communication mode in which a device can transmit and receive data simultaneously.

fully qualified domain name (FQDN) A complete DNS name that consists of a host and a domain path all the way up the tree structure to the root.

global unicast address The IPv6 equivalent of a registered IPv4 address, routable worldwide and unique on the Internet.

half-duplex A communication mode in which data can only travel in one direction at a time.

hierarchical star topology An arrangement of network components consisting of two or more switches or hubs connected together and populated by network nodes.

high availability A design principle that calls for a system to achieve a previously determined level of performance and reliability.

high-bit-rate Digital Subscriber Line (HDSL) A point-to-point, digital WAN technology used by telephone companies and other large corporations to transmit data at T-1 speeds.

honeypot A security tool in the form of a system designed to function as a lure for Internet attackers.

hop A unit of measurement used to quantify the length of a route between two computers on an internetwork, as indicated by the number of routers that packets must pass through to reach the destination system.

horizontal cross connect In structured cabling, a term referring to a switch or other device that connects horizontal cable runs together into a network.

host table An early name resolution mechanism for TCP/IP networks that consists of a simple text file containing a list of IP addresses and their equivalent host names.

hub A physical layer device—also known as a multiport repeater—that connects network nodes together by using a star topology.

hybrid topology An arrangement of network components that uses multiple network media with different cabling requirements.

Hypertext Transfer Protocol (HTTP) The application layer protocol largely responsible for web client/server communications.

Hypertext Transfer Protocol Secure (HTTPS) A variant of HTTP that uses the Transport Layer Security (TLS) and Secure Sockets Layer (SSL) security protocols to provide data encryption and server identification services.

hypervisor Sometimes called a virtual machine monitor (VMM), the component in a virtualization product that creates and maintains the virtual machines running on a computer.

IEEE 802.11 The base standard defining the physical layer and media access control sublayer specifications for a wireless LAN protocol.

IEEE 802.11a An amendment to the original 802.11 standard that increases the maximum network transmission rate to 54 Mbps using the 5-GHz band.

IEEE 802.11b An amendment to the original 802.11 standard that increases the maximum network transmission rate to 11 Mbps using the 2.4-GHz band.

IEEE 802.11g An amendment to the original 802.11 standard that increases the maximum network transmission rate to 54 Mbps using the 2.4-GHz band.

IEEE 802.11n An amendment to the original 802.11 standard that defines several new technologies that can theoretically increase the maximum network transmission rate to 600 Mbps using either the 2.4-GHz band or the 5-GHz band.

ifconfig An interface configuration program on UNIX and Linux systems.

impedance mismatch A type of signal distortion caused when signal echoes conflict with the original signals.

Independent Computing Architecture (ICA) A protocol developed by Cyrix Systems that provides communication between thin clients and network servers. *Thin clients* are terminals that exchange keystrokes, mouse actions, and display data with servers that run the user operating system and applications.

indirect route A routing table entry for a destination on a network at least one hop away.

infrastructure topology A type of wireless networking topology in which there is at least one wireless access point that functions as a base station and provides access to wired network resources.

initial sequence number (ISN) A number selected by each computer during the TCP connection establishment process that determines the values the system will use in the Sequence Number field of the TCP header.

Integrated Services Digital Network (ISDN) A dial-up communications service that uses standard telephone lines to provide high-speed digital communications. Originally conceived as a replacement for the existing analog telephone service, it never achieved its anticipated popularity. Today, ISDN is used in the United States primarily as an Internet access technology, although it is more commonly used for WAN connections in Europe and Japan. The two most common ISDN services are the Basic Rate Interface (BRI), which provides two 64-Kbps B channels and one 16-Kbps D (control) channel, and the Primary Rate Interface (PRI), which provides 23 64-Kbps B channels and one 64-Kbps D channel.

interframe gap shrinkage A measurement of the delay between packet transmissions.

interior gateway protocol (IGP) A type of routing protocol that updates the routers within a particular autonomous system.

intermediate distribution frame (IDF) In structured cabling, a telecommunications room that functions as a cabling nexus for a horizontal network.

intermediate system On a TCP/IP network, a router that relays traffic generated by an end system from one network to another.

Intermediate System to Intermediate System (IS-IS) A link state routing protocol, developed at approximately the same time as and very similar to OSPF.

Internet Assigned Numbers Authority (IANA) The organization responsible for assigning unique parameter values for the TCP/IP protocols, including IP address assignments for networks and protocol number assignments.

Internet Control Message Protocol (ICMP) A network layer TCP/IP protocol that carries administrative messages, particularly error messages and informational queries.

Internet Engineering Task Force (IETF) The primary standards-ratification body for the TCP/IP protocol suite and the Internet. The IETF publishes Requests for Comments (RFCs), which are the working documents for what eventually become Internet standards.

Internet Group Management Protocol (IGMP) A protocol used by IP hosts to report their host group memberships to any immediately neighboring multicast routers.

Internet Key Exchange (IKE) A security protocol that provides a method for computers to exchange encryption keys.

Internet Message Access Protocol (IMAP) An application layer protocol for a mailbox service that improves upon POP3's capabilities by providing additional email management capabilities.

Internet Protocol (IP) The primary network layer protocol in the TCP/IP suite. IP is the protocol that is ultimately responsible for end-to-end communications on a TCP/IP internetwork and includes functions such as addressing, routing, and fragmentation.

Internet Protocol Control Protocol (IPCP) A network control protocol designed to support the IP protocol.

Internet Security Association and Key Management Protocol (ISAKMP) A security protocol that provides the means for two systems to create and manage security associations.

intrusion detection system (IDS) A network protection product that inspects incoming packets or system processes and examines them for evidence of malicious activity. When the IDS finds such evidence, it logs the activity, gathers information about the circumstances, and usually notifies an administrator.

intrusion prevention system (IPS) A network protection product, similar to an IDS, except that it is also designed to take specific actions to prevent an attack when it detects one.

IP address A 32-bit address assigned to TCP/IP client computers and other network equipment that uniquely identifies that device on the network.

Ipconfig.exe A Windows command-line program that displays the computer's TCP/IP configuration and provides DHCP control.

IPsec A series of standards that define a methodology for securing data as it is transmitted over a network.

IPv6 A new version of the Internet Protocol (IP) that expands the IP address space from 32 to 128 bits.

Kerberos protocol An authentication protocol that uses tickets to coordinate the authentication of network clients and servers.

keystone connector A type of modular connector that snaps into a keystone wall plate.

late collision A collision that occurs after the last bit of data has left the transmitting system.

latency The delays that occur when a network contains so much traffic that nodes trying to send data experience delays in gaining access to the network medium.

Layer 2 Tunneling Protocol (L2TP) A protocol used to establish virtual private network (VPN) connections across the Internet. *See also* virtual private network (VPN).

layer 3 switching A switching technique that uses virtual routers to connect VLANs together.

leased line A permanent telephone connection between two points that provides a predetermined amount of bandwidth at all times. *See also* T-1, T-3.

link aggregation A technique—also called *bonding*—that enables multiple network interface adapters in a single computer to combine their bandwidth.

link code word (LCW) The fields within an FLP transmission that identify the capabilities of the transmitting device.

Link Control Protocol (LCP) A protocol used by PPP to negotiate communication parameters that two machines have in common.

link-local unicast address The IPv6 equivalent of an Automatic Private IP Addressing (APIPA) address in IPv4. All link-local addresses have the same network identifier: a 10-bit FP of 11111110 10 followed by 54 zeroes.

link state routing A type of routing protocol that works by flooding the network with link state advertisements that contain sequence numbers that indicate the distance from the router to the source.

load balancing A technique that distributes incoming traffic equally among the multiple servers in a cluster.

local area network (LAN) A group of computers or other devices that share a common location and a common medium, such as a particular type of cable.

Long Term Evolution (LTE) A cellular communications standard that is the next iteration of the *Groupe Spécial Mobile* (GSM) technology that first appeared in the second generation (2G) and that became High Speed Packet Access (HSPA) in the third (3G). Although not yet compliant with the International Telecommunications Union (ITU) standard, 3GPP Long Term Evolution (LTE) is generally considered a 4G technology and supports downstream transmission rates of up to 300 Mbps.

loopback plug A cable testing device that plugs into the end of a cable and reflects all signals that reach it back to the source.

main distribution frame (MDF) In structured cabling, a telecommunications room that functions as a cabling nexus for a backbone network.

malware A generic term referring to any software that has a malicious intent, whether obvious or obscure.

man in the middle (MITM) A type of security attack in which the attacker interposes him or herself between two individuals who think they are communicating directly with each other.

maximum transmission unit (MTU) The largest physical packet size that a system can transmit over a network.

media access control (MAC) A method by which computers determine when they can transmit data over a shared network medium.

media converter A physical layer device that connects two networks of the same type but that are using different media, such as two Ethernet LANs using UTP and fiber optic cables.

medium dependent interface (MDI) The connection between a network device, such as a network interface adapter or a switch, and the network medium.

medium dependent interface crossover (MDIX) An uplink port in a hub or switch.

mesh topology An arrangement of network components in which each node is connected to every other node.

mixing segment A length of Ethernet cable with more than two devices connected to it.

modem Short for *modulator/demodulator*, a hardware device that converts the digital signals generated by computers into analog signals suitable for transmission over a telephone line, and back again. A dial-up connection between two computers requires a modem at each end, both of which support the same communication protocols. Modems take the form of internal devices that plug into one of a computer's expansion slots or external devices that connect to one of a computer's serial ports.

Modulation and Coding Schemes (MCSes) A series of indexed combinations of factors used by the 802.11n standard to calculate theoretical data transfer rates.

MTU black hole A condition on a TCP/IP network in which router-based firewalls interfere with the Path MTU Discovery process.

MTU mismatch A condition on a TCP/IP network in which datagrams must be fragmented because they encounter networks with smaller MTUs than that of the network where the datagrams were created.

multicast A network transmission with a destination address that represents a group of computers on the network.

multifactor authentication A combination of two or more authentication methods that reduces the likelihood that an intruder will be able to successfully impersonate a user during the authentication process.

multifunction device A common term for a WAN router with other capabilities, such as switch ports, a wireless access point, and a DHCP server.

multilevel device A network connection device that spans levels 2 and 3 of the OSI model.

multiple channel architecture A technique for deploying multiple wireless access points in the same service set by using non-overlapping channels.

Multiple-Input Multiple-Output (MIMO) A physical layer enhancement that enables wireless devices to multiplex signals over a single channel, by using a technique called Spatial Division Multiplexing (SDM).

multiplexing Any one of several techniques used to transmit multiple signals over a single cable or other network medium simultaneously.

multiport repeater Another term for a hub.

Multipurpose Internet Mail Extension (MIME) A method for encoding various types of data for inclusion in email messages.

multisource agreement (MSA) A type of standard created by manufacturers of networking products, defining a socket used to build interchangeable Gigabit Ethernet physical layer modules.

name resolution A process by which the name of a network device is converted to an IP address.

Nbtstat.exe A Windows command-line program that displays information about the NetBIOS Over TCP/IP (NetBT) connections that Windows uses when communicating with other computers running Windows on a TCP/IP network.

Netstat A command-line program that displays status information about the current network connections of a computer running TCP/IP and about the traffic generated by the TCP/IP protocols.

Network Address Translation (NAT) A firewall technique that enables TCP/IP client computers using unregistered IP addresses to access the Internet.

Network Control Protocols (NCPs) Protocols used by PPP to negotiate connections for each of the network layer protocols they will use during a session.

network interface adapter The hardware implementation of a data-link layer LAN protocol. Usually integrated into computer motherboards, network interface adapters are also available as expansion cards and external USB devices.

network interface card (NIC) Strictly, a network interface adapter provided on an expansion card, but in practice, the term may be used to refer to any network adapter, even if it is built into a motherboard.

Network Terminator 1 (NT-1) The hardware device on the client side of an ISDN installation that provides the straight tip (S/T) interface used to connect equipment to the service, such as ISDN telephones, fax machines, and the terminal adapter that connects to a computer. In some cases, the NT-1 is a separate piece of equipment, but it can also be integrated into a single unit along with a terminal adapter for installations in which only a single computer is to be connected to the service.

Network Time Protocol (NTP) An application layer protocol designed to synchronize the clocks of computers on packet-switching networks with varying degrees of latency.

node A device connected to a LAN.

nominal velocity of propagation (NVP) A measurement of the speed at which signals travel over a network medium.

normal link pulse (NLP) Signals used to verify the integrity of a link between two devices.

Nslookup A command-line utility that generates DNS request messages and transmits them to specific DNS servers on the network.

open circuit A type of wiring error in which one of the wires inside a cable is not connected to the pin at one end.

Open Shortest Path First (OSPF) An interior gateway protocol that provides a link state protocol alternative to RIP.

Open Systems Interconnection (OSI) reference model A theoretical model used for reference and teaching purposes that divides the computer networking functions into seven layers: application, presentation, session, transport, network, data-link, and physical (from top to bottom).

optical time domain reflectometer (OTDR) A fiber optic cable tester that measures a cable's length by transmitting a signal and measuring how long it takes to travel to the other end and back.

organizationally unique identifier (OUI) The first three bytes of a network adapter's hardware address, assigned to the device's manufacturer by the IEEE.

Orthogonal Frequency Division Multiplexing (OFDM) A type of radio frequency modulation used on 802.11 networks that uses multiple carriers running in parallel at low signal rates to provide a data transmission rate that is similar to those of single carrier modulation types.

packet A unit of data that can be transmitted over a data network.

packet filter A basic type of firewall, in which the system implementing the filter examines each packet as it arrives and decides if it meets the criteria for admission to the network.

packet sniffer An application that intercepts and captures packets as they are transmitted over a network.

packet switching A type of network communications in which messages are broken up into discrete units called *packets* and transmitted to the destination.

parallel detection The method by which an Ethernet system capable of autonegotiation reconciles its speed with a system that cannot negotiate.

passive mode An FTP operational mode in which the client sends a PASV command to the server, and the server sends its IP address and port number to the client, so that the client can initiate the connection.

passive optic network (PON) An arrangement in which data from an optical line terminal (OLT) runs through a single fiber optic cable to a series of optical splitters near the subscribers' premises.

Password Authentication Protocol (PAP) An authentication protocol that is seldom used because it uses unencrypted passwords.

peer-to-peer networking A networking system in which each computer can function both as a client and as a server.

peripheral network The outermost layer of a network with concentric layers of security, where the servers that must be accessible from the Internet, such as web, FTP, and SMTP servers, are placed.

phishing A type of security attack that consists of sending out an official-looking email message or letter to users that points them to a bogus website containing a form asking for personal information.

physical layer (PHY) module A 10 Gigabit Ethernet hardware device that contains a transceiver and supports a specific cable and connector.

Ping A command-line tool that specifies whether the TCP/IP stack of another system on the network is functioning normally.

Plain Old Telephone Service (POTS) A common phrase referring to the Public Switched Telephone Network (PSTN), the standard copper-cable telephone network used for analog voice communications around the world.

plenum An air-handling space in a building where network cables are often located, typically the space between a dropped ceiling and the structural ceiling.

point-to-multipoint topology An arrangement of network components in which a single node transmits and multiple nodes receive the data.

Point-to-Point Protocol (PPP) A data-link layer protocol designed for use by WAN connections that consist of only two systems. Because there are only two devices involved, there is no need for the protocol to support complex procedures such as node addressing or media access control.

Point-to-Point Protocol over Ethernet (PPPoE) A TCP/IP standard that provides a way to create individual PPP connections between computers on an Ethernet LAN and external services connected to the LAN by using a broadband device such as a cable or DSL modem.

point-to-point topology An arrangement of network components consisting of two (and only two) nodes connected together.

Point-to-Point Tunneling Protocol (PPTP) A data-link layer protocol used to provide secured communications for virtual private network (VPN) connections. VPNs are private network connections that use the Internet as a network medium. To secure the data as it is transmitted across the Internet, the computers use a process called *tunneling*, in which the entire data-link layer frame generated by an application process is encapsulated within an IP datagram. This arrangement violates the rules of the OSI reference model, but it enables the entire PPP frame generated by the user application to be encrypted inside an IP datagram.

port address translation (PAT) Also known as *masquerading*, this network address method translates all the unregistered IP addresses on a network by using a single registered IP address.

port forwarding A technique in which a NAT router creates a mapping between a specific registered IP address and port number and a specific unregistered address on the private network. This mapping enables traffic that the NAT router would ordinarily block to pass through to its destination.

port mirroring A feature in some switches that takes the form of a port that runs in *promiscuous mode,* meaning that the switch copies all incoming traffic to that port, as well as to the dedicated destination ports.

port scanner A software product that displays all of the open ports on a computer or on a network's computers.

positive acknowledgment with retransmission A description of the packet acknowledgment system that TCP uses, indicating that the destination system acknowledges only the messages that it received correctly.

Post Office Protocol version 3 (POP3) An application layer protocol designed to provide mailbox services for client computers that are themselves not capable of performing transactions with SMTP servers, such as clients that are only intermittently connected.

Primary Rate Interface (PRI) An ISDN service that consists of 23 64-Kbps B channels plus one 64-Kbps D channel, providing an aggregate bandwidth equal to that of a T-1 line. The B channels can be combined into a single data pipe, used individually, or used in any combination. The PRI service is rarely used in the United States but is a popular business service in Europe and Japan. *See also* Integrated Services Digital Network (ISDN).

Private Branch Exchange (PBX) A telephone exchange or switchboard that is wholly owned and operated by a business or other private entity, rather than by a telephone company.

protocol data unit (PDU) A generic term for the data constructions created by the protocols operating at the various layers of the OSI reference model.

protocol stack The multilayered arrangement of communications protocols that provides a data path ranging from the user application to the network medium.

proxy server An application layer firewall technique that enables TCP/IP client systems to access Internet resources without being susceptible to intrusion from outside the network, and with centralized control and management.

pseudo-header A term used to describe a combination of IP header fields that the TCP and UDP protocols include in their checksum calculations.

public key infrastructure (PKI) A system in which every user has two keys, a public key and a private key. Data encrypted with the public key can only be decrypted with the private key, and data encrypted with the private key can only be decrypted by using the public key.

Public Switched Telephone Network (PSTN) The standard copper-cable telephone network used for analog voice communications around the world. Also known as Plain Old Telephone Service (POTS).

punchdown tool A device that cable installers use to connect the wires in a cable to the individual pins of a jack.

quality of service (QoS) A method for assigning priorities to various types of network traffic.

relative domain name A DNS name that specifies only the subdomain relative to a specific domain context.

remote access server (RAS) A host program that can respond to connection requests from remote computers and provide access to a network.

Remote Authentication Dial In User Service (RADIUS) A client/server protocol that provides authentication, authorization, and accounting services usually for remote access servers.

Remote Desktop Protocol (RDP) A protocol created by Microsoft that enables their Remote Desktop Connection client and their Remote Desktop Services server to communicate.

Request for Comments (RFC) A document published by the Internet Engineering Task Force (IETF) that contains information about a topic related to the Internet or to the TCP/IP suite.

resolver The component in a DNS client that generates query messages.

resource record (RR) A type of informational unit in the DNS where host names, IP addresses, and other types of information are stored.

Reverse Address Resolution Protocol (RARP) A protocol in the TCP/IP suite that enables a client to broadcast a system's hardware address and receive an IP address in return from a RARP server.

RG-58 A type of 50-ohm coaxial cable used in early thin Ethernet networks.

RG-59 A type of 75-ohm coaxial cable used for cable television networks.

RG-6 A type of 75-ohm coaxial cable used for cable television networks.

ring topology An arrangement of network components in which signals travel from node to node, eventually ending up back at the source. A ring topology can be physical or logical.

RJ11 A modular four-pin cable connector, typically used for telephone connections.

RJ45 A modular eight-pin cable connector, used for telephone or LAN connections. The term is often used incorrectly when referring to an 8P8C connector.

root name server A DNS server that possesses information about all of the top-level domains in the DNS name space.

router A network layer device that connects two networks together. A router has two network interfaces that selectively relay traffic back and forth between the two networks.

Routing Information Protocol (RIP) A distance vector routing protocol that is one of the most commonly used interior gateway protocols in the TCP/IP suite and on networks around the world.

routing table An internal table maintained by IP routers that contains information about the local and adjacent networks. Routers use their routing tables to determine where to send each packet they receive.

runt A type of packet on an Ethernet network that is shorter than the minimum allowable length, thus interfering with the collision detection mechanism.

scope In DHCP, a range of IP addresses on a particular subnet that a DHCP server uses as a pool for its lease assignments.

secret key encryption A system in which one character is substituted for another, based on a key specifying the letter replacements.

Secure Sockets Layer (SSL) A special-purpose security protocol that protects the data transmitted by servers and clients at the application layer.

security association (SA) A collection of security settings that specifies the keys and algorithms that two systems will use for protected communications.

service-dependent filtering A type of packet filtering that uses port numbers to determine whether packets should be admitted to the network.

service set identifier (SSID) A 32-bit name that identifies a service set and all its members.

shielded twisted pair (STP) A type of network cable containing multiple pairs of wires that are twisted together and shielded and/or screened to minimize crosstalk.

short circuit A type of wiring error in which a pin at one end of the cable is connected to two or more pins at the other end.

silent RIP A situation in which a RIP router processes incoming advertisement messages without advertising its own routing table.

Simple Mail Transfer Protocol (SMTP) An application layer protocol that transfers email messages between servers and from clients to servers.

Simple Network Management Protocol (SNMP) A TCP/IP application layer protocol and query language that specially equipped networking devices use to communicate with a central management console.

single sign-on An environment in which users can access all of their allotted network resources with a single set of credentials.

sliding window A technique used to implement flow control in the TCP transport layer protocol. By acknowledging the number of bytes that have been successfully transmitted and specifying the number of bytes that it is capable of receiving, a computer on the receiving end of a data connection creates a "window" that consists of the bytes the sender is authorized to transmit.

smartjacks A feature of most network interface units. Smartjacks enable the network interface units to perform additional functions such as signal translation, signal regeneration, and remote diagnostics.

smurf attack A type of denial of service attack that involves flooding a network with Ping messages sent to the network's broadcast address. These messages also contain the IP address of the computer that is the intended victim. All of the computers receiving the broadcast, therefore, send their responses to the victim, flooding its in-buffers.

socket On a TCP/IP network, the combination of an Internet Protocol (IP) address and a port number, which together identify a specific application process running on a specific computer.

social engineering A practice in which an attacker with a friendly manner contacts a user by telephone, mail, or email; pretends to be an official of some sort; and gives some excuse for needing the user's password or other confidential information.

Spanning Tree Protocol (STP) A data-link layer protocol that solves the problem of bridge loops by selecting a non-redundant subset of switches and deactivating the others until a fault occurs.

split pair A type of wiring fault in which both ends of a cable are miswired in exactly the same way, scrambling the wire pairs.

spyware A hidden program that gathers information about a user's computer activities and sends it to someone on the Internet.

SSID mismatch A condition on wireless networks where devices are misconfigured to connect to an access point that is not broadcasting its SSID.

stackable hubs Hubs that can be linked together to expand their port density without Ethernet recognizing them as separate devices.

star topology An arrangement of network components in which each node is connected to a central cabling nexus, such as a switch or a hub.

stateful packet inspection (SPI) A generic term for a process in which a router examines incoming packets more carefully than usual.

stateless address autoconfiguration An IPv6 process that automatically assigns a link-local unicast address to each interface in a computer.

static NAT (SNAT) A network address translation technique that translates multiple unregistered IP addresses to an equal number of registered addresses.

static routing A method for updating routing tables in which a network administrator manually creates the table entries.

store-and-forward switch A type of switch that waits until an entire incoming packet arrives before it begins forwarding any data out to the destination.

subnet A group of computers on a TCP/IP network that share a common network identifier.

subnet mask A TCP/IP configuration parameter that specifies which bits of the Internet Protocol (IP) address identify the host and which bits identify the network on which the host resides.

supernet A combination of contiguous networks that all contain a common CIDR prefix. When an organization possesses multiple contiguous networks that can be expressed as a supernet, it becomes possible to list those networks in a routing table using only one entry, instead of many.

switch A data-link layer device that filters packets based on their destination hardware addresses, forwarding incoming packets only to their destinations (if known).

switching loop A condition on a switched network where there are redundant switches providing multiple paths between destinations, and the switches forward packets back and forth to each other in endless loops.

Synchronous Digital Hierarchy (SDH) A physical layer standard that defines a method for building a synchronous telecommunications network based on fiber optic cables. Known as *SONET* in North America.

Synchronous Optical Network (SONET) A physical layer standard that defines a method for building a synchronous telecommunications network based on fiber optic cables. SONET provides connections at various optical carrier (OC) levels running at different speeds, ranging from 51.84 Mbps (OC-1) to 9,953.280 Mbps (OC-192).

T-1 A dedicated telephone connection, also called a *leased line,* running at 1.544 Mbps. A T-1 line consists of 24 64-Kbps channels, which can be used separately, in combinations, or as a single data pipe. Large companies use T-1 lines for both voice and data traffic; smaller companies can lease part of a T-1, which is called a *fractional T-1 service.* Although it uses the telephone network, a T-1 used for data networking does not use a dial-up connection; it is permanently connected to a specific location. *See also* leased line.

T-3 A dedicated telephone connection, also called a *leased line,* running at 44.736 Mbps. *See also* leased line.

telepole A telescoping tool used by cable installers to extend cables through closed spaces, such as dropped ceilings.

Telnet A terminal emulation program that provides users with access to a text-based interface on a remote system.

temperature monitor A device designed to track the environmental conditions in a telecommunications room.

Terminal Access Controller Access-Control System (TACACS) A centralized logon solution that enables users who successfully authenticate to one system to access other systems as well.

terminal adapter A hardware component used to connect a TE2 device to an ISDN connection. The terminal adapter plugs into the straight tip (S/T) interface provided by the NT-1. In some cases, a terminal adapter and an NT-1 are integrated into a single unit, which is specifically designed for installations in which a computer will be the only device using the ISDN connection. *See also* Integrated Services Digital Network (ISDN), Network Terminator 1 (NT-1).

three-way handshake The process that TCP uses to establish a connection between two computers.

time domain reflectometry (TDR) A cable testing technology that measures a cable's length by transmitting a signal and measuring how long it takes to travel to the other end and back.

tone generator and locator A cable testing tool that consists of a device that transmits a signal over a wire or cable and another device that detects the signal.

top-level domain (TLD) A domain located one level below the root domain, which functions as a registrar for domains at the second level.

Traceroute A command-line tool that displays the path that packets take through an internetwork to their destination.

traffic analysis A technique for deriving information based on the pattern and frequency of messages transmitted over a network, rather than their contents.

traffic shaping A means of prioritizing packets without prior negotiation between applications and routers and without tagging packets.

transfer syntax A format used to encode application information for transmission over a network.

Transmission Control Protocol (TCP) A transport layer protocol used to transmit data generated by applications, such as entire files. TCP is a connection-oriented protocol that provides guaranteed delivery service, packet acknowledgment, flow control, and error detection.

transparent bridging The technique by which bridges compile their own address tables from the information in the packets they read.

Transport Layer Security (TLS) A method for encrypting tunneled traffic to protect the privacy of communications.

Trivial File Transfer Protocol (TFTP) A minimized, low-overhead version of FTP that can transfer files across a network without authentication.

Trojan horse A non-replicating program that appears to perform an innocent function, but which in reality has another, more malicious, purpose.

truncated binary exponential backoff In the CSMA/CD MAC mechanism, an algorithm that Ethernet systems use in response to a collision to calculate how long they will wait before retransmitting.

trunking A method for connecting switches that enables the members of a VLAN on one switch to communicate with members of the same VLAN on another switch.

tunneling A technique for transmitting data over a network by encapsulating it within another protocol. For example, Novell NetWare networks at one time supported TCP/IP only by encapsulating IP datagrams within NetWare's native Internetwork Packet Exchange (IPX) protocol. The Point-to-Point Tunneling Protocol (PPTP) also uses tunneling to carry Point-to-Point Protocol (PPP) frames inside IP datagrams.

unbounded media A type of network medium that has no natural restrictions to signal access. Also known as *wireless media*.

unique local unicast addresses The IPv6 equivalent of the 10.0.0.0/8, 172.16.0.0/12, and 192.168.0.0/16 private network addresses in IPv4.

unshielded twisted pair (UTP) A type of network cable containing multiple pairs of wires that are twisted together to minimize crosstalk.

User Datagram Protocol (UDP) A connectionless transport layer protocol used for short transactions, usually consisting of a single request and reply. UDP keeps overhead low by supplying almost none of the services provided by its connection-oriented transport layer counterpart, TCP.

vertical cross connect In structured cabling, a term referring to a switch or other device that connects horizontal cable runs to a backbone network.

virtual LAN *(*VLAN) A network layer technology built into some switches that enables administrators to create logical subnets that exist only in the switches themselves.

virtual private network (VPN) A technique for connecting to a network at a remote location using the Internet as a network medium. A user can dial into a local Internet service provider (ISP) and connect through the Internet to a private network at a distant location, using a protocol such as the Point-to-Point Tunneling Protocol (PPTP) to secure the private traffic.

virtualization A process that adds a layer of abstraction between actual, physical hardware and the system making use of it. The intervening component, called a *hypervisor*, creates a virtual machine environment, and an operating system runs in that environment.

virus A type of program that replicates by attaching itself to an executable file or a computer's boot sector and performs a specified action—usually some form of damage—at a prearranged time.

voltage event recorder A monitoring device that tracks the quality of the power supply in a telecommunications room.

vulnerability scanner A software program that attempts to discover weaknesses in the security of a network and its computers.

war driving The process of cruising around a neighborhood with a scanner, looking for unprotected wireless networks to which to connect.

well-known port TCP/IP port numbers that have been permanently assigned to specific applications and services by the Internet Assigned Numbers Authority (IANA).

wide area network (WAN) A network that spans a large geographical area using long-distance point-to-point connections, rather than shared network media, as with a local area network (LAN). WANs can use a variety of communication technologies for their connections, such as leased telephone lines, dial-up telephone lines, and ISDN or DSL connections. The Internet is the ultimate example of a WAN. *See also* local area network (LAN).

Wi-Fi Protected Access (WPA) A method for encrypting wireless communications that improves upon the privacy provided by WEP.

Wired Equivalent Privacy (WEP) A method for encrypting wireless communications that is standardized and widely deployed, but that suffers from serious well-exploited vulnerabilities.

wireless access point (WAP) A stand-alone wireless device or a wireless-equipped computer that is also connected to a bounded network via a cable, and that provides other wireless devices with access to the wired network resources.

wiremap tester A simple type of cable tester that connects to each of the wires in a cable and detects faults such as opens and shorts.

Worldwide Interoperability for Microwave Access (WiMAX) A metropolitan area network (MAN) standard offering transfer rates up to 75 Mbps for mobile devices and ranges up to 50 kilometers.

worm A program that replicates itself across a network by taking advantage of weaknesses in computer operating systems.

worst case path The route between the two most distant systems on the network, in terms of cable length and number of hubs.

zone An administrative unit used to subdivide DNS domains.

zone transfer A process by which DNS servers replicate their data for fault tolerance and performance purposes.

Index

Symbols

A

N

T

V

W

X

Y

Z

About the Author

CRAIG ZACKER is a writer, editor, and educator whose computing experience began in the days of teletypes and paper tape. After moving from minicomputers to PCs, he worked as a network administrator and desktop support technician while operating a freelance desktop publishing business. After earning a Masters Degree in English and American Literature, Craig supported fleets of Windows workstations and was employed as a technical writer, content provider, and webmaster for the online services group of a large software company. Craig is the author of *Windows Small Business Server 2011 Administrator's Pocket Consultant* and the coauthor of *MCITP Self-Paced Training Kit (Exam 70-686): Windows 7 Desktop Administrator*, as well as having authored and contributed to dozens of other books on operating systems, networking topics, and PC hardware. He has developed educational texts for college courses and online training courses for the web, and he has published articles with top industry publications.